ARTHURIAN STUDIES XXXVIII

A COMPANION TO THE *GAWAIN*-POET

ARTHURIAN STUDIES

ISSN 0261–9814

Previously published volumes in the series
are listed at the back of this book

A COMPANION TO
THE *GAWAIN*-POET

EDITED BY

**Derek Brewer and
Jonathan Gibson**

D. S. BREWER

First published 1997
D. S. Brewer, Cambridge
Reprinted in hardback and paperback 1999

ISBN 0 85991 433 X (hardback)
ISBN 0 85991 529 8 (paperback)

D. S. Brewer is an imprint of Boydell & Brewer Ltd
PO Box 9, Woodbridge, Suffolk IP12 3DF, UK
and of Boydell & Brewer Inc.
PO Box 41026, Rochester, NY 14604–4126, USA

A catalogue record for this book is available
from the British Library

Library of Congress Catalog Card Number: 96–32104

This publication is printed on acid-free paper

Printed in Great Britain by
St Edmundsbury Press Ltd, Bury St Edmunds, Suffolk

Contents

Illustrations

The Manuscript

Acknowledgements

The Editors wish to acknowledge with gratitude the co-operation of the contributors, the sterling work of our in-house editor Caroline Palmer in trying to keep us in order, sorted out and up-to-date, and Dr Raphael Lyne for preparing the indexes. We are also grateful to Professor Ralph Elliott for the use of his photographs, and to Professor Felicity Riddy for her valuable editorial advice at an early stage of the planning of this project.

Conventions and Abbreviations

References are made in author-date form and keyed to the List of Works Cited at the end of the book. The following abbreviations have been used:

EETS   Early English Text Society

ELH   ELH: a Journal of English Literary History

IMEV   Carleton Brown and R. H. Robbins, *The Index of Middle English Verse* (New York, 1943) with R. H. Robbins and J. L. Cutler, *Supplement to the Index of Middle English Verse* (Kentucky, 1965)

MED   H. Kurath, ed. *Middle English Dictionary* Ann Arbor, Mich. 1952–.

OED   Oxford English Dictionary

PMLA   *Publications of the Modern Language Association*

Preface

Our aim in assembling this volume of essays on the *Gawain*-poet has been to provide stimulating introductions to a broad range of topics. We have tried to put together a collection which mixes solid information with original analysis and which provokes the reader to independent investigation and thought. The *Companion* is not intended to usurp the function of any of the excellent annotated editions which have appeared over the years (see List of Editions Cited, below): not every passage is glossed, not every important theme dissected. Nonetheless, we have aimed at a certain completeness. Each essay is focused on a key topic of general importance and can be used by the interested reader – undergraduate, postgraduate or neither – as a starting-point for further reading. The aims of this book, then, differ from those of its distinguished precursor, the collection of 'new perspectives' assembled by Blanch, Miller and Wasserman in 1991, though much of its material will be found complementary.

Contributors were asked independently to write on broadly-defined topics and were given considerable latitude in the manner and form of their approach. Rather than any implicit or explicit party line, then, there are intriguing convergences and divergences of opinion. Because the essays are essentially self-contained, the order in which the chapters appear has no prescriptive status: the reader can begin anywhere and is invited to browse *ad libitum*.

Each essay contains its own principal references to the consolidated general bibliography, to which a separate list of foreign language translations has been appended. No attempt has been made to construct a general bibliography, which would now require a book to itself. There have been several recent full-length guides to secondary material, all of which can be heartily recommended (on all four poems, see Andrew 1979; on *Sir Gawain and the Green Knight* alone, Blanch 1983 and Stainsby 1992). The short bibliographies given in Andrew and Waldron 1978 and Prior 1994 provide useful starting-points.

In the chapters that follow the poems of the Cotton manuscript are analysed from a variety of intersecting perspectives. Perhaps the most important common thread is the belief that, whatever the ontological status of the 'Gawain-poet', joint analysis of *Pearl, Sir Gawain and the Green Knight, Cleanness* and *Patience* is worthwhile and rewarding. If this book sends the reader back to the poems newly alive to their unique complexity and power, this belief will have been vindicated.

Derek Brewer
Jonathan Gibson

Introduction

DEREK BREWER

I

The four poems, *Sir Gawain and the Green Knight* (henceforward *SGGK*), *Patience, Pearl* and *Cleanness* (sometimes called *Purity*), are amongst the great poems in all English literature.

They were written some time toward the end of the fourteenth century, somewhere in the English Midlands, perhaps where North Staffordshire runs close to Derbyshire, and they survive in only one rather unimpressive manuscript with twelve rather poor quality illustrations, now in the British Library, classified (from its origins in the Cotton Library), Cotton Nero A.x. This manuscript of the late fourteenth century was probably written some time soon after the composition of the poems, not by the poet but by a scribe who inevitably made some errors.

We do not know for certain if all the poems were composed by one poet. They have dialect, themes, concepts and attitudes in common, but they are also varied in form, though three are all or mainly in alliterative verse and the fourth, *Pearl*, makes large use of alliteration. It seems unlikely that there were four such remarkably good poets so close together in time, place and attitudes, but there could have been a group of two, or even three, as it were a 'school' of poets, closely associated in traditional forms. So far no totally reliable objective tests have been devised to separate or unite the poems, or (if by one man) to determine their order of composition. (The probability of a woman author, though not absolutely beyond the limits of conjecture, is exceedingly small.) The establishment of reliable attribution and date would undoubtedly enhance our understanding, as the establishment of a chronology did for the understanding of Shakespeare in the nineteenth century. Meanwhile most critics and scholars who have studied the poems closely have felt that they are all by one person, though there are some learned dissentients. For practical purposes in this book we assume, if not without some slight reserve, a single author, whom we call 'the *Gawain*-poet', though some scholars have preferred to call him 'the *Pearl*-poet'.

We therefore have no personal name for our poet (or, less likely) poets. Nor do we know whether he were clerical or lay, and if lay, married or single. In *Pearl* he represents himself as a father mourning a dead two-year-old child, and in *Patience* as poor, but both of these might be consonant with his being either clerical or lay. He must have been educated, obviously, and of a certain social standing. He is a courtly poet of some kind of court. Perhaps these very uncertainties about him that we experience reflect ambiguities in his own experience which contributed to the rich paradoxes and internal tensions of the poetry.

The society in and for which he wrote is also uncertain. Opinions about it range from supposing it to consist mainly of provincial minor gentry to the more noble fringes of the king's court, bearing in mind Richard II's associations with Cheshire, which borders on the north-west of Staffordshire. These and many other interesting questions are explored further by distinguished experts in the pages that follow.

The manuscript first attracted scholarly attention with the edition of *SGGK* by Sir Frederick Madden in 1839. Eventually the other poems were edited in the nineteenth century but they attracted little further interest. Even following the edition of *SGGK* by Tolkien and Gordon in 1925, and the appearance of the poem on the English syllabus of the University of Oxford, only philological attention, admirable in itself, was paid to it. When I first read the poem as an undergraduate in 1946 I could still buy the 1936 reprint of Tolkien and Gordon's edition. There was not a single critical article available (happy days?). Tolkien himself lectured on the poem to a small group of devotees, confining himself entirely to textual cruces (often forgetting to tell us which line he was discussing), and doing obscure (to me) battle with some mysterious entity, prophetically as it may now seem, called something like 'Gollancz'.[1]

The first person to discuss the poem as poetic, having artistic symbolic power, was John Speirs (1949), in no less a journal than *Scrutiny* (of which I in Oxford had barely heard). Those days are past, and all their aching joys. Some pioneering books and articles appeared in the 1950s (Savage 1956): critical studies began to blossom in the 1960s (for example, Benson 1965; Burrow 1965; Spearing 1970; essay collections by Blanch 1966; Howard and Zacher 1968). Since then the stream of discussion has become a river.

It would be fascinating to trace the changes in critical response and opinion. On the whole the enthusiasm of earlier studies has to some extent yielded to the cynicism and disillusionment of the more recent literary climate. Yet the poems have a certain obstinacy of assertion which prevents them being totally submerged by purely modern assumptions, while modern

---

1 Even I eventually discovered that the reference was to the admirably ingenious Early English Text Society edition by Sir Israel Gollancz, no relation to Gollum (Gollancz 1940).

attitudes have revealed greater complexities and deeper concerns in the poetry than were perceived before.

Yet it may be useful as an introduction to a book intended both for scholars and students to emphasise in an old-fashioned way what all the present contributors take for granted, the worth of the poems read at a simple literal level, accepting them in the first place as far as possible on the poet's own terms, an historical rather than 'historicist' reading. The terms are those familiar to social anthropologists who study pre-industrial societies. These societies, fourteenth-century England among them, despite many differences have similar general characteristics. They are small agrarian-based societies, hierarchical, accepting inequalities, conservative, authoritarian and patriarchal; with primitive technology, low productivity and no obvious means of improving it. They live in a world of struggle and extremes, never far from famine, surrounded by death, where feast and fast, enemy and friend, death and laughter, are closely bound together (Camporesi 1989, 29–30, 43). Such societies, though deeply enmeshed in material circumstances over which they have little or no control – the weather, the success of crops, disease and death – respond with a sense of mystery to a universe which contains forces beyond their knowledge and control, which they must co-operate with and accept, or hope to propitiate, or manage by non-material means like prayer. Only occasionally, as in feasts, can they arise above that natural world of which they are ineluctably a part, yet they sense a spiritual reality working behind and through nature. This situation can still be observed, for example in many parts of Africa and India. (Medievalists do well to travel in the Third World where they can study societies analogous to European medieval society at first hand.)

These traditional societies are so to say soaked in religion. Granted major differences between various great religions of the world they yet have more in common with each other in worldview than they have with post-industrial, post-Christian modern Western societies to which most (not all, we hope) readers of this book will belong, whatever their individual beliefs or attempts at belief. Many if not most products of modern societies will be atheists, and even if not will normally think it pointless to pray for rain or thank God for a good harvest. Yet such prayers are habitual to a pre-industrial society. They can be found in the Church of England Book of Common Prayer, which though more or less finalised as late as 1662 has deep medieval roots and offers an excellent entry to the mentality of medieval Christendom. Prayers For Rain; For fair Weather; In the time of Dearth and Famine; In the time of War and Tumults; In the time of any common Plague or Sickness, all following the Litany with its comprehensive set of requests, give a very fair cross-section of the concerns of a traditional agrarian community, such as is represented by the *Gawain*-poet.

Religion in these communities is both more and less materialistic, more and less spiritual, than such fragments of a religious view as remain in post-industrial society. Atheism is inconceivable, God is near: Gawain rides with 'no man but God' (696); Jonah has a continuous argument with God; God writes mysteriously on palace walls; imperiously summons men to a banquet. God is very materialistic. Yet he calls men to deny the flesh, deny natural lusts. God as a spirit is taken as it were more casually, yet ultimate reality is felt to be spiritual, transcendental. Heaven truly exists as a spiritual realm, yet is made of solid gem-stones, and gem-stones in this world are rich in spiritual and also health-giving virtues.

All is gathered together, or thought to be gathered together, in a unity. The material, moral, spiritual elements of life are intimately twined together. As Gellner puts it (1994, 140) the circle of truth, hierarchy, social merit, social reality (he might have added physical and moral reality) is complete. Or we may here rather note how well the symbol of the pentangle, adding its numerological unities to the physical, moral, spiritual qualities, represents the apparently unified worldview natural to the kind of society we are discussing, which is by no means naive, unintellectual, or coarse, despite its fundamentally archaic, holistic quality.

Since experience shows that unity is hard to obtain, that one kind of good may be incompatible with another kind of good (courtesy with chastity in some circumstances, for example), there are always tensions. Evil appears which breaks unity, and has to be accounted for. Much of the interest in the poems of the *Gawain*-poet arises from the considerations of the tensions inherent in any worldview. It is very hard, perhaps impossible, to keep the pentangle absolutely intact in this world.

The *Gawain*-poet was an exact contemporary with Chaucer, Langland, Gower. He is as English as they are. But his work, apart from what is shared as a common basis, called by Burrow 'Ricardian' (Burrow 1971), is in temper and interest, not to say style and dialect, very different (an argument for a different audience).

In southern and eastern England at this time there were other elements arising, more distinctions. The growth of a money economy, the Ockhamist division of faith and reason, the Lollard impeachments of traditional piety in the name of a newly radical Christianity, are variously reflected in Chaucer and Langland, but not in the *Gawain*-poet. He remains of a more traditional cast of mind. Compare, as a small but typical example, his treatment of the ancient arming-*topos* in *SGGK* with Chaucer's flippant treatment of the same *topos* in *Sir Thopas*. This is not to say that the *Gawain*-poet is static or backward-looking in any pejorative sense. He feels his themes strongly, he tests them and his characters vigorously, and there is a certain modern vein in his work, even in religion as Watson suggests below. In *SGGK* as Pearsall shows (below) he extends the notion of honour in an 'honour-driven' society; he maintains a certain ambiguity of judgment; he can be fierce, but mercy and pity are shown; he has a sardonic humour; in *Pearl* he questions the notions of hierarchy and narrow paternalism which he attributes to himself as the mourning father, with remarkable self-consciousness. Such elements are not to be exaggerated but they illustrate the originality of his evocation of traditional values.

How 'English' is the *Gawain*-poet? His language, obviously, is English, within a tradition different from that of Chaucer, Langland and Gower, all of them more southern, but not therefore more nor less English. Our poet is firmly tied to the North Midlands in language. Because his English is different from that of his great contemporaries, and because the main stream of standard English continued after his time away from the north, in the direction of Chaucer's and Langland's, he may seem provincial. Chaucer, to judge from *The Reeve's Tale*, found northern dialect comical, and so perhaps did Londoners generally. Puttenham, in his *The Arte of English Poesie* (1589), writing a couple of centuries later, strongly advises against the use of 'northern' speech as spoken even by noble men and gentlemen, 'though no man can deny but that theirs is the purer English Saxon at this day, yet it is not so Courtly nor so currant as our Southerne English is, no more is the far Westerne man's speach' (145). Puttenham opts for the language of the court and shires up to sixty miles from London. How far this was generally felt in the fourteenth century beyond the rather *avant-garde* Chaucer's circle is hard to know. Local dialects are not regarded with contempt today in many parts of Europe; they may not have been in fourteenth-century England. To paraphrase Tolkien's characterisation of the regional language of the *Ancrene Wisse*, a work admittedly written in the early thirteenth century (Tolkien 1929), the *Gawain*-poet's language, polished, elaborate, well-stored with elegant French words, enriched with Old Norse words, sturdily English, is just as much the language of an English gentleman as is Chaucer's. It may retain some stylistic traits that Chaucer thought oldfashioned, such as the non-ironic use of *hende*, but to be a trifle oldfashioned is not necessarily to be socially or educationally inferior.

The poet is deeply set in the tradition of alliterative verse, which descending, however indirectly, from Old English poetry was soundly English. The poet is part of the hidden continuity, or revival, or rediscovery, for verse, of the alliterative rhythms so entrenched in English speech at all periods. In the fourteenth century alliterative verse was particularly associated, as some of the poets themselves noted, and as Chaucer witnesses in reverse, with the northern and western parts of the country. In this respect the *Gawain*-poet is historically more English than Chaucer and Gower, but again we should note his use of iambic metrical forms and numerological structures associated with European verse, and on the other hand the association of Langland's alliterative poetry, and that of *St Erkenwald*, with non-provincial London.

The *Gawain*-poet has different sets of differences from and similarities with different contemporaries. Like Langland he writes in alliterative verse, is deeply devout, has a sardonic humour, is not interested in romantic ('courtly') love. Unlike Langland, he is very courtly. Like Chaucer he is courtly, but in a different style. He is not ironic, or flippant, and does not tell secular comic tales, but he is more attracted to courtly festivity than is Chaucer, who is dismissive, not to say *blasé*, about feasts, and who mocks Arthurianism. Chaucer knew the alliterative style, and lightly touches on it, significantly, for battle-scenes (*The Legend of Good Women*, 635–6; *The Knight's Tale*, *Canterbury Tales* I 2605–13). Chaucer's Parson, being a 'Southren man', can not '*geeste, rum, ram, ruf, by lettre*' (*Canterbury Tales* X 2603–13) which sounds mocking, and perhaps represents Chaucer himself, though the Parson adds that he holds rhyme but little better (which the Chaucer of the *Retractations* might also have agreed with). Chaucer uses more modern French sources than does the *Gawain*-poet, partly because Chaucer holds with 'the newe jet' of love-poetry, but each poet is heavily dependent on French.

One could pursue these differences and similarities between the three or four poets a good deal farther, but enough have been considered to make us wary of generalisations, even if they all come within the 'Ricardian' period (Burrow 1971). The closer they are looked at, the greater seems the difference between their poetic temperaments and the interests of their implied audiences, within the general cultural similarity referred to earlier. Chaucer and Langland were writing for readers geographically very close, different as they were in interests, and it must be that the linguistic difference of the *Gawain*-poet, implying geographical distance, and his different tone and content, also imply a different readership or audience.

It is sometimes argued that each poet knew the work of the others. Of course they shared the same general cultural background; of course it is a physical possibility that they passed each other in the street. But Chaucer and Langland would have found the *Gawain*-poet's dialect difficult. The total ignorance of Chaucer and his friends of the Cheshire knight Sir Robert Grosvenor until the latter claimed the Scrope arms, as witnessed in the Scrope-Grosvenor case (below, 71–5), shows no acquaintance at the King's court with Cheshire society, or the kind of group in whose dialect the *Gawain*-poet wrote. The grounds for supposing that Chaucer knew the work of the others is slight; there are absolutely no signs that the *Gawain*-poet knew the work of any of them.

There is no good reason to consider any of these great poets as more essentially English than the others, nor to regard the *Gawain*-poet as more cut off from general European influences. On the one side the *Gawain*-poet writes in an older English tradition than do Chaucer or Gower; on the other one could make a case for *Pearl* being more truly in the new exquisitely-wrought International Gothic Style, with its numerological base, its concatenation, mixture of rhyme and alliteration, emphasis on precious things, on the pearl, and on the supremacy of the image of the Blessed Virgin, than anything Chaucer wrote. From this point of view the wonderfully elaborate Goldenes Rössel now at Altötting in Southern Germany but probably made in Paris, with at its peak the Virgin, at its base a silver knight in full armour on horseback, the whole encrusted with pearls, is a splendid icon of the devotional, chivalric, courtly tone of *SGGK* and *Pearl*. It lacks the poet's robustness, the feel for the harsh northern winter landscape, as it lacks the harshness of the Flood, or of Jonah's adventures, but these surround the poet's inherent delicacy of devotion and social perception.

No visual image can sum up the variety and the paradoxes of these poems. They are not very much like any other poems, though they show us a good part of what it was to be English in sentiment, rooted and grounded in English middle ground, proud of 'British' ancestry, and its history of 'bliss and blunder' in this island, aware of European origins and culture. Some of these characteristics the *Gawain*-poet shares with earlier alliterative poems. But all this creates an imaginative literary image. We are not recreating the image of an actual living man, since we have, probably fortunately, no knowledge of him. Literature is different from life. To judge from recent evidence the actual lives of poets are usually far from exemplary.

However that may be, his poetic tradition, English as it might be, was soon lost (Brewer 1983, 177–80, 209–11) except in so far as it merged later with the mainstream.

II

In making a general appreciation of the *Gawain*-poet's work, we note that all four poems, whether or not by one single poet, have the same general pattern.[2] In each some passionate selfish desire is met and controlled. The poet has a taste for drastic, extreme situations: the Flood; prophesying in a hostile land; poignant meeting with the beloved dead to learn a hard lesson about death; keeping one's word at the apparent cost of death. They are ultimate tests of the spirit. In the end the spirit wins a qualified victory.

In *Patience*, selfishness takes the form of resentment against poverty; in *Cleanness*, of illicit sexuality; in *Pearl*, of fruitless mourning; in *SGGK* (most complex and least personal) it is a combination of sexual desire, worldly self-regard, fear of death. In each case the protagonist has to do what he does not want to do. So Jonah in *Patience* does not want to go to hostile Nineveh to preach an unpopular message, which is what God wants him to do: so the poet at the beginning of *Pearl* cannot reconcile himself to the loss of his daughter, and in a deep sense does not want to; he wants his daughter, and without her he wants to go on wanting her: so Gawain does not want to keep his promise. In *Cleanness* there is no outstanding protagonist, the poem differing in this as in other ways from the other three, but the character nearest to a protagonist, Lot, again has to act to some extent against his natural desire.

---

2 The following few pages are partly taken, with cuts and alterations, from Brewer 1967. For an introductory account of the *Gawain*-poet see Brewer 1983, 155–80.

What one naturally wants is to be rich, to be idle, to give in to one's own feelings, to feel sorry for oneself, to be lecherous, to save one's skin, to go with the crowd. And the poet feels this very strongly. But he feels even more strongly that to follow one's immediate personal selfish desires leads into unreality. Paradoxically, the deepest reality of the world runs against our immediate wishes. To put it more bluntly, in terms which the story of Gawain makes plain, if we follow our immediate responses we destroy ourselves. The *Gawain*-poet admits that much of reality goes against the grain, but he is also passionately convinced of the ultimate beauty and joy of reality: in moral terms he is in love with virtue, 'in her shape how lovely'. So selfish rebellious desire is not merely repressed, and a grim asceticism is not substituted as the proper norm of conduct. The poet has no ideal of negation. Rather, against self-regard is a yet more powerful, a more beautiful ideal, that is centred on the brilliant image of the court, and which may perhaps best be thought of as 'courtesy' itself, in an extended, ideal, but not unreal, sense. Between the poles of self-regard and courtesy the poet's passionate thought flows in a brilliant arc: the tension between them is the source of the splendour of his poetry.

The tension, a form of self-contradiction, may be illuminated in part by the modern critical interest, deriving especially from the work of Lacan (as mediated for example by the work of Brennan 1989 and MacCannell 1986), in the internal self-contradictions, the paradoxes, inherent in some powerful poetry.[3] Such interest will find a fertile field in the work of the *Gawain*-poet. This is not surprising in so Christian a poet. Historical Christianity is founded on paradox, starting with the Incarnation. The whole Bible is fertile, to its advantage, in inconsistency, self-contradiction and paradox. St Paul is rich in them (see especially 2 Corinthians VI, Romans V, Galatians V). Perhaps 'contradiction', especially 'self-contradiction', and paradox, are due to take the place of the New Criticism's 'irony' as the defining characteristic of poetry. At least they are in part well-suited to our poet, who is always conscious of tensions, of being pulled in two different directions.

This is not to deny that our poet, like the Bible and most literature, is 'phallogocentric' – how could he be anything else? That is to say that his cultural outlook, for good historical reasons apart from intrinsic merit, was heavily biased in favour of the male outlook and verbal expression, and of the desire for a central ordering and unity of experience. The desirability of these qualities has been challenged by Lacan and his followers, if I understand them, not without reason even if denying reason. But for example if there is patriarchy in *SGGK* and *Pearl* there is also a questioning of patriarchy. In both there is a feminisation of the subject. In *Pearl* is the paradox of hierarchy that is equality. The uncertainty of closure in both these poems and

---

[3]   I am indebted to Dr Sarah Kay of Girton College for Lacanian references. She is not responsible for any incomprehension I may show.

the profound ambiguity of *SGGK* deserve recognition. The unnamed seductive Lady, and her formidable aunt, embody, as I have argued elsewhere (Brewer 1980) a powerfully ambiguous female principle. The Green Knight in his baffling greenness and ultimate disappearance may even be said to represent, in a Lacanian – or Pickwickian – sense a non-significance in the Symbolic order (MacCannell 1986, 125). The power of the image is its emptiness, for the reader to fill with meaning if he or she wishes. Again, in all the poems unity, which Lacan wishes to remove, is shown as broken, though the desire to repair it is felt.

If in this conflict of contrarieties the ultimate victory goes to the side that is positive, life-affirming, hopeful, and if the interest of the poems arises in part from the conquest of adverse circumstances, it is clear that the poet must conceive of much of life as ineluctably harsh. The roughness of experience is given climatic and symbolic (as well as realistic) expression in such an episode as the terrifying storm which Jonah endures; but indeed his whole mission is painful, with the storm, his swallowing by and regurgitation from the whale, and various suffering from both men and elements in Nineveh. The episodes in *Cleanness* are full of suffering, not always deserved – friends in the Flood 'embrace each other and dree their doleful destiny and die together', 'love looks to love and takes his leave to end all at once, and part for ever'. In *Pearl* the father's loss is poignant, and the vision of the dead girl offers no easy comfortable consolation; the father must live sorrowful and alone. Gawain has a stern destiny, and must travel through bitter weather over rough country to meet it, as well as avoiding temptations to pleasure.

The harshness of experience is partly met by the simplest and most widespread of reality-principles. In this life you must take the rough with the smooth, and put a good face upon it, as in that admirable proverb attributed in the twelfth century to Alfred: 'Tell your sorrows to your saddle-bow, and ride singing forth'.

It is a world that calls for pity, such as God in *Patience* expresses for the weak and innocent, the little children, women and dumb beasts who should not be destroyed because of the wickedness of men (501–19). The poet concludes this poem rather strikingly, exhorting himself to be patient 'in payne and in joye',

> For he þat is to rakel to renden his cloþez
> Mot eft sitte with more vnsounde to sewe hem togeder. (525–7)

As Anderson remarks, it is a 'homely generalisation'. It sounds like a proverb and the sententious style, the emphatic utterance of recognisable home-truths, is characteristic of the poet's style and his society. In fact the poet has taken the Biblical expression for sorrow, 'Rend thy clothes' (2 Chronicles: 34, 27) and with perhaps an association with the sententious 'A time to rend and a time to sew' (Ecclesiastes: 3, 7), has evoked a characteristically sardonic domestic reversal, a touch of dry humour at his own expense.

In *Pearl* the glorified daughter tells her father, 'who needs shall thole, be not so thro' (334), that is, in Biblical phrase, don't kick against the pricks; it is no good sorrowing for ever (351–2). You must take the 'sad winter' with 'the sweetness of summer' as it is put in *Cleanness* (525) and as it is more subtly and expansively conveyed in the lovely lines on the passing of the seasons in *SGGK* (500–31).

The poet continually goes beyond an admirable unsentimental stoicism. There is a frequent subtle humour, often dramatically conveyed in speech. Jonah's testiness in some of his conversations with the Almighty is an example. There is a wry amusement at fatherly obtuseness or irritation in *Pearl*, and the poet represents himself as a father making the naive supposition, quite missing the true point, being at once too proud and too fatherly-depressive, that his little daughter might be made a countess in heaven – but a queen, that is much too high (489–93). In *Cleanness*, where the poet permits himself a freedom of abrasive narrative comment which is not found in the other poems, he sarcastically remarks that Belshazzar's *lemmans* (concubines) had to be called *ladies* at the feast (1370); and that Chaldean clerks knew no more of the writing on the wall that 'if they had looked at the leather of my left boot' (1581). Gawain's sly pretence at remaining asleep when the lady slinks in at his bedroom door, and many of the passages between him and his would-be seductress, are delightful high comedy. Comedy and seriousness can lie very close together in medieval literature, as in Shakespeare, without damaging each other.

The spirit of affirmation and enjoyment comes out particularly well in the zest with which rough weather is portrayed, yet with a touch of pity for those who suffer, whether human or not. The winter landscape of *SGGK*, so vividly evoked – with the first description ever of a waterfall, that Romantic image, in English literature (2173) – earlier also includes a note of the unhappy birds

þat pitosly þer piped for pyne of þe colde.   (747)

Anyone who has walked the Derbyshire hills in winter, especially when the snow 'snitters down full snart', will respond to such marvellous descriptions. They are also very unusual. Northern European poets, living in a climate less than genial for much of the year, usually prefer, as Chaucer does, the prettier flowers and meadows of the warm South for imaginative wandering.

The landscapes are not the only richly descriptive passages. The poet has a zest for technical details of all kinds. The most celebrated passage is the description of the breaking of the deer in *SGGK*, a fine passage of what one might almost call the poetry of technology, a type of poetry rarely attempted since. The sea-faring passages in *Patience* are equally precise and vivid – and not so difficult. Another aspect of the poet's interest in technical detail, this time in an intellectual, not concrete, realm of experience, is the theological discussion in *Pearl* on the doctrine of salvation by grace. In none of these is it likely that he used language excessively technical for his expected audience, but he shows himself informed and interested in a wide variety of subjects and, equally important, in the relevance of the subject to the particular poem. His descriptions are not digressions; they are integral to the form, though the form is not the Coleridgean and nineteenth-century 'organic form'. Perhaps I may be permitted to call it 'Gothic'. It relies on amplification, is decorative, relying on well-established themes that are part of the general inheritance, not always closely related to the linear development of the narrative.

The poet's enjoyment in describing the violence and hostility of nature, and the technical details of man's thought and activity, is found at an even higher degree in his love of splendour. *Patience* has least of this: it would be inappropriate in a poem in which the poet is encouraging himself to bear poverty without complaint. Splendour bursts out in *Cleanness*, paradoxically enough, in the descriptions of Belshazzar's feast, which is an example of that wanton uncleanness (because of the sacrilegious use of the vessels from the Temple) which the poet condemns. The holy vessels themselves are described with characteristic verve and splendour, and the whole feast is portrayed with the same sort of relish that the poet brings to a storm. He has his touches of sarcastic humour, as in the comment on ladies that are no ladies and the puzzled Chaldean clerks already mentioned, and he calls Belshazzar a 'dotel' and his barons 'boasters on bench'; but he loves the glorious display of courtly splendour. It is not the magnificence he disapproves of, but the ill-use made of the holy vessels. As to courts, they are for him the natural image on earth of the heavenly kingdom. At the beginning of *Cleanness* God is a king in his court. Heaven is God's court, God is a 'hende [courteous] lord' (1172), as he is in *Patience* (398), and to attain heaven is to be 'known in his court' (1053). The natural climax of such a vision, where splendour is unlimited, is *Pearl*. Heaven is a whole noble country of gleaming rocks, crystal cliffs, bright woods with silver leaves that trill like bells, gravel of precious pearls of orient, fresh fruits, birds of flaming colours and enchanting music. Above all rises the vision of the New Jerusalem made as in Revelation of precious stones, where God himself is sun and moon and lamp-light, and where the poet sees, in the procession of virgins, all crowned a king or queen, his own 'little queen' full of mirth. Not even Milton can match this marvellous evocation of high ideal brilliance, of materialistic spirituality, so characteristic of the poet, which is yet filled with the warm human love of the enraptured observer. How characteristic of the poet that such mystic rapture is achieved only at the moment of its loss, and we are immediately made abruptly conscious of the lowly earth, where our bodies must struggle for life, and eventually be buried.

Yet the visionary splendour remains in an earthly record, and once again, in *SGGK*, the apogee of earthly splendour is envisaged in courtly festival. Indeed, the poet never portrays a court, either on this earth or as a figure of heaven, which is not in festival. In *SGGK* there are two courts. One is Arthur's. The other is Bertilak's, who is really the Green Knight; though Gawain does not know his other shape when he stays at Bertilak's court on his way to meet the Green Knight and take the beheading blow from him. So powerful is the image of the court with the poet that both Arthur's and Bertilak's courts show the same splendid and admirable way of life. Indeed, Bertilak's court, since it is presented more extensively, is shown more fully as admirable. At Arthur's court the Christmas and New Year's feast is in every way delightful, the knights are the bravest and best, the ladies the most beautiful and best of the whole world, and they are all young. Arthur is even boyish ('childgered') in his enthusiasm.

There are critics who find this enthusiasm for Arthur's court ironical on the poet's part, and suspect that the poet is being critical, though I do not recollect that the equally boyish horse-play of the middle-aged Bertilak is ever condemned. Perhaps we should ask ourselves if there is not a vein of seventeenth-century Puritanical condemnation of ceremony, a utilitarian condemnation of the 'aestheticisation' of social life, in such criticism. The proto-Puritan Langland, if I may be forgiven the phrase, might have condemned the Christmas feasting, music and games, but it seems unlikely that the *Gawain*-poet did. (See 'Feasts' below). And any modern reader who enjoys a party and a good dinner, while there are poor in his own country, and many millions starving in the world at large, is in much the same position as the *Gawain*-poet, and the student-age men and women of Arthur's court.

Although Bertilak's court houses Morgan la Faye, deadly enemy to Arthur, Guinivere and to her own nephew Gawain (since she has devised a plot to kill him) Bertilak's court is said to be glad to learn even better manners from Gawain (908–27). Bertilak's own pleasure and the honour he says he feels in housing Gawain (1031–6) may perhaps be regarded with suspicion, but unless all his large household is in the secret of Bertilak's Jekyll-and-Hyde personality, which seems unlikely, we should probably take their pleasure and their own good conduct at face-value. This raises other interesting questions about the nature of the story in *SGGK*. No poet more enjoys, or better performs, the descriptions of feasts and courtly pastimes than the *Gawain*-poet, and no court in literature, one may venture to guess, is better conducted than Bertilak's. Moreover, it is a fully Christian courtliness. Our ideas of Christianity, or at any rate of medieval Christianity, may find it hard to accept that the splendour of courtly life could co-exist with a sincere Christian belief: but if we deny such co-existence we deny the evidence of history, and the plain words of the *Gawain*-poet. At Bertilak's court everyone goes to Mass as the first act of each day. They eat fish on fast days. It may not be very spiritual, but the court is fully Christian in the historical reality of Christianity.

This certainly makes for ambiguity in the presentation of Bertilak/Green Knight. There is also more ambiguity in *SGGK* in the presentation of Gawain, as many critics notice who claim that Gawain has failed. Even Arthur for such critics is presented ambiguously. This is not the place to argue that point, but we notice the openness of the final departure of the Green Knight still in his greenness, not turned back into his *alter ego*, going 'wherever he wished' (2478). We cannot follow him out of the story into his 'real' shape as we can Stevenson's Jekyll-and-Hyde. He is not that kind of character. Nor can we easily accept at face-value his account of why he came to Arthur's court in the first place, in order to frighten Guinivere to death by seeing his head chopped off. As he had failed what was the point of Gawain a year later coming to his solitary test? The truth is that the story is about Gawain, and everything is seen through his eyes.[4] That does not lessen the ambiguity but changes it somewhat. Ambiguity does not imply uncertainty: rather that the poet is here playing with us (see further on this and related matters Ganim 1983, 55–78). The other poems have less occasion to do so.

The acceptance of the rough with the smooth, humour, love of splendour and virtue, are characteristic of positive acceptance in the poet's view of life. The greatest crime, he says, in *Cleanness*, in what must be one of his most typical remarks, is 'scorn of oneself' 'heyng of seluen' (579); the special reference is presumably to sodomy, but the form of generalisation is significant. The poet is not an ascetic. The same poem includes a fine passage in praise of the physical joys of love and marriage (697 ff.).

In fact, the most characteristic attitude of the *Gawain*-poet is praise. The most ancient type of poetry was praise-poetry. This in itself is striking in an age when satire and complaint were so strong in Chaucer and Langland. Enough, too, has been said of the poet's estimation of the harshness of life to suggest that his praise is not merely a sentimental complacency. *Patience* and *Cleanness* are usually rightly called homilies; and *Cleanness*, with its reference to the Fall of the Angels, the Flood, the destruction of Sodom, and the fate of Belshazzar, cannot be accused of turning a blind eye either to literary images of evil, or to what these images tell us about real life. Yet both these poems are quite as much laudations, justifications of God's ways to men, as condemnations of vice. There is nothing in *Cleanness* of the dreary and sometimes nauseous advocacy of virginity found in some other medieval writings. The poet certainly says that the sins of the flesh are the worst (thereby differing from most medieval and most modern thought), but there is nothing neurotic in his condemnation of uncleanness. His aim is to 'commend cleanness', just as, in *Patience*, he sets out to praise (since he has no choice) Poverty (47), and works through to the conclusion in his last line that 'Patience is a noble point'. In *Pearl*, beginning with praise of his Pearl and sorrow for its loss, he ends glad in the sorrowful dungeon of this world that Pearl is pleasing to God, who makes of all of us both his homely labourers and his precious pearls.

---

[4] I thought I had solved these problems in Brewer 1976, further developed in Brewer 1980, but some critics disagree, and I refrain here from pressing the case. I merely note that comments such as that in Putter 1995, 141, misunderstand and grossly misrepresent my argument.

The only basis for an understanding of *SGGK* is to realise that the poem, whatever else it is, is in praise of 'good Gawain', 'hende Gawain', as he is so often called. The poem is perhaps more complex than the others, but here too the end is praise and reconciliation, with laughter in addition. That there is laughter, and that other knights take enthusiastically to the baldrick which Gawain wears as a penance to remind him of his one weakness, has sometimes been taken as an index both of Gawain's failure and the triviality, incomprehension and generally deplorable nature of Arthur's court. The truth is that what for some outstanding men is failure, represents for the rest of us a standard to which we can rarely hope to attain, but with which we like to associate ourselves.

In attempting to describe the general quality of these delightful poems I have been tracing the positive affirmations to be set against the representation of the grim and negative and disagreeable aspects of experience. As we move from concrete description to love of splendour, to praise, so we move to more complicated attitudes, deeply enmeshed in the culture of the time, which show an interplay of the positive and negative elements whose tension makes for great poetry. The poems are about moral states and personal relationships. They are about the human individual opposite another person. Jonah is having an argument with God through most of *Patience*. God is the King who can be obeyed or disobeyed in *Cleanness*. The poet-father is instructed by, or arguing with, his glorified daughter, throughout *Pearl*. In *SGGK* the network which holds all together is the network of personal obligations and relationships of which Gawain is the centre; his loyalty to Arthur, to his plighted word, and so to the Green Knight; his obligations to his host in the castle, to his host's wife as she is that, and more equivocally, as she is, or ought to be, a lady. These relationships are, of course, sometimes hostile. Thus, when men are disloyal to God, who is thought of as their feudal lord, to whom they have an absolute obligation, he is angry with them. These oppositions and reversals are fruitful of some paradoxical relationships and situations in the poems. Jonah, fleeing God's command to go to Nineveh, is terrified by the storm, swallowed by a whale (with a superb description of the whale's nasty stomach) and spewed up on the shore of the very land he had refused to go to. In *Pearl* a father, paradoxically, has to be instructed by his daughter – he might say with Prospero, 'What, my foot my tutor?' And the answer is 'Yes, indeed'. The paradox is part of the general pattern of an alternating flow within relationships. Again, the anger of God is terrible. But when the anger of God in *Patience* is appeased, it is greatly to Jonah's annoyance, embarrassment, and peevish complaint. In *Cleanness* Christ is known as king of nature by his 'cleanness' (1087), and God's court is 'clean'. If Christ is 'clean' he is 'courteous', 'by nobility of his nurture', and repudiates filth, yet those who were dirty called on that 'courteous one' and claimed his grace, and 'he healed them with courteous speech' (1098). In *Pearl* 'the grace of God is great enough' to accomplish with ungrudging generosity the supreme paradox of equality within hierarchy and hierarchy without inequality; that is, everyone of the blessed is a king or a queen, yet Christ and Mary his mother are still supreme; everyone is at the service of the others, yet none is inferior. In *SGGK* the personal relationship between Gawain and the lady is a paradoxical reversal of the expected situation, since it is the lady who woos the courteous Gawain.

In this respect we need to recall the complex structures of honour in the 'honour-driven' society represented, or created, by the poet.[5] Honour is the esteem in which one is held, according to severe criteria, by society. It therefore involves relations with others, traditionally the most powerful aspect of honour. It also creates internal obligations to maintain one's own self-esteem. Self-esteem depends to some extent on the esteem in which the self believes himself, or herself, to be held by others, but in its finest form the internalised form of honour, in the form of conscience, is utterly independent, or self-dependent, as Gawain is, without an audience. The French word *honour*, and the older English word, *worship*, echo through the poems. For men honour has to be worked for, and involves powerful obligations. When the honour-society is also hierarchical obligations to superiors are re-inforced. Guests who refuse the king's invitation dishonour him and must pay the penalty. Children should honour their father and mother, as the Fifth Commandment says. Gawain has obligations in honour to King Arthur, to his host Bertilak and in consequence to their wives. Internally he has obligations to himself, to keep his promise, to his own disadvantage, even when it seems that no one else in the world would know that he had not done so, as the guide suggests (2118–25). The internal obligations merge into conscience, a sense of guilt, even, Pearsall suggests below, embarrassment.

The social and mental structures of honour are of great importance but cannot be pursued further here. It must be enough to note that the *Gawain*-poet in his various poems and in various ways progresses towards a kind of internalisation of values, though represented in a way different from the modern. For him, internal factors may be represented by external agents, including his concept of God. Relationships *between* persons are related to relationships as it were *within* the individual person. The relationship between Gawain and the lady, for example, is conditioned by the play of forces *within* Gawain. The lady is not significant here as an independent personality in her own right, for we never see into her mind, any more than we see into Bertilak's. They are not rounded characters. We never see them on their own together. What kind of a conversation could husband and wife have had with

---

5   There is a substantial body of work devoted to honour, mostly by social anthropologists (for example, Pitt-Rivers 1966), and until recently neglected by literary critics and historians. See however Barber 1957; Brewer 1968, 1982; Burrow 1984; Miller 1993; Stewart 1994 with valuable bibliography; Putter 1995, 149–87. The concepts of honour are widespread in earlier societies, from Iceland to Japan, China to Peru.

Morgan la Faye, as they plan to seduce Gawain so that his head may be cut off, and thus also to cuckold Bertilak, cuckoldry being the greatest dishonour, especially when the husband agrees? The question is outside the range of the poem, as it would be in a folktale. The moral battle-field of the poem is located exclusively in Gawain's mind, into which alone we are allowed to look. Within Gawain's mind there is a relationship between, on the one side, his natural lust, his natural fear, and even, on one occasion, his natural anger against the lady's flirtatiousness (1657 ff.), and on the other, his obligations to his own chastity, to his own plighted word, his own courtesy, all aspects of his own honour. His relationship to the lady is controlled by his management of these internal relationships. Similarly, God's relationship to men in the other poems is controlled by the relationship 'within' God, between his righteous anger on the one side, and his mercy and grace on the other. These internal relationships may be summed up, in all their variety, as the conflict, within a person, of 'natural' impulse against self-control. The poet has developed a highly internalised concept of honour.

Self-control bespeaks the self-conscious, inner-directed individual, with his own internal standards to be met independent of external demands – Gawain is the obvious example, both with the lady, and when the guide says to him, 'Why don't you just slip off? No one will know you never met the Green Knight' (2118–25). God is also in much the same position: he is his own law. Though we must call such self-control *inner*-directed, it is nevertheless exercised continually in the poems in relation to *other people*; as Gawain's integrity drives him to the encounter he fears will be fatal; as God's mercy is shown to the people of Nineveh; and as the blessed in heaven, all kings and queens, yet worship Mary Queen of Courtesy. In self-control there must be self-denial: yet self-control also results in the pouring out of mercy and grace, and in deeds undertaken for others' sakes. In the pattern of personal relationships we have yet another example of the interrelation of opposed yet associated elements, though of greater complexity: in this case it is an example of the relationship between the individual and the group.

In the relationship between the individual and the group honour is Christianised and Christian virtue is the controlling force, in regard both to the individual's attempt to maintain a high personal standard of integrity, and in the obligation of the individual to behave with active goodness towards others. Jonah has to make himself carry God's warning to Nineveh: Lot has to protect his guests from his evil neighbours: the blessed in heaven achieve the same end, both as glorified in themselves, and as rejoicing in the glory of others. Gawain must be true to his word though it seems to mean death, and fulfil all his social obligations to the lady although she tries to seduce him.

Gawain's virtue, as the pentangle shows, is not a single quality. In *SGGK* it comprises bravery with tact, good manners and not least chastity. This last is not a virtue with any resonance in the modern world, but in the logic of the story chastity is the magic that equalises Gawain with the Green Knight's magic ability to survive decapitation. (In modern terms chastity is perhaps best expressed as the 'passive heroism' subtly expounded by Jill Mann (1994).) Such is certainly the underlying structure of the story. If he had been seduced it would have meant that in every sense he had lost his head. It should also be remembered that chastity is a main theme in *Cleanness*. Most modern critics prefer to emphasise Gawain's *trawthe* – signifying more than modern *truth*, and implying a profound integrity.

The poet has yet another virtuous key concept: courtesy. The word is significantly used in all the poems, though least in *Patience* and *Cleanness*. In *Patience* Jonah actually accuses God of courtesy, when reproaching God for his mildness towards Nineveh, and courtesy suggests patience. In *Cleanness* Lot's moderate and placatory words to the mob are called courtesy, and courtesy in the poem is identified with cleanness both literal and metaphorical. In *Pearl* the paradoxical loving relationships of hierarchy and equality, and God's own grace, are called courtesy. In *SGGK* courtesy is partly the expression of noble manners and speech, brilliantly analysed in Spearing's classic analysis of Gawain's request to Arthur for permission to take on the adventure of the Beheading Game (Spearing 1964). Courtesy develops from this into the highest moral and spiritual quality, more explicitly developed by the poet than the concept of honour (Brewer 1966). In *Pearl* it is the equivalent of divine Grace.

III

All works of art are inherently symbolic, as is witnessed by the way succeeding generations validly see more than is immediately expressed in their literal meaning. The purpose of the preceding pages has been partly to emphasise the poetic pleasure and interest of the text and partly to assert what seems to me to be the primary historical meaning of the poems in terms of its own assumptions, which were also part of my own cultural conditioning. These assumptions have often been not merely attacked in the late twentieth century, as they have been before, but virtually demolished. The doctrine of chastity, for example, has become almost incomprehensible to recent generations in the West. Chivalry has been decried as licensed brutality: chivalric romance a plot by the upper class to keep the workers down, and so forth. The fabric of modern life is relativist and fragmented. The intrinsic truth of modern values, doctrines and assumptions is not in question here, but rather its applicability to early literature which rests, by contrast, on absolutist and holistic assumptions.

Some modern views and modern critical scholarship can be fruitfully applied in various ways to earlier literature, as the later pages of this volume illustrate. Amongst them is the very concept of historical and cultural relativity. Other societies have different scales of values etc. which it repays us to understand and sympathise with, and sometimes to translate into our own values.

Symbolism is of more general import than sign or allegory. Such intentional allegory as there is in the *Gawain*-poet's poems is discussed by Martin (below), but a case has been made for an underlying pattern or drive, of which the poet himself may not have been fully conscious, which accounts for superficial inconsistencies, lack of logical causality, in *SGGK*, as already noted. An example of a somewhat similar kind in *Patience* is convincingly urged by Diekstra (1994), where certain medieval allegorical readings of the story of Jonah are supported by reference to modern psychoanalysis. Such interpretations need close reference to the literal manifest text before their latent power can be agreed; if the latent and manifest levels reveal a similar truth at different levels their truth and power are increased.

More objectively quantifiable, though not always obvious, are numerological structures in literature. There can be no doubt that these exist, and were consciously intended in some texts, although awareness of numerology is remote from most modern literary response (Curtius 1953, 501–14). Composition ordered by repetition of significant numbers has a long history in Greek, Latin and Judaic thought. For medieval literature its basis was in the Bible and the Fathers, especially St Augustine (MacQueen 1985). In medieval English literature the incontrovertible thoroughgoing example is *Pearl*, with 101 stanzas, linked in groups of 5 with one exception of a group of 6, 12 lines in a stanza and thus a total of 1,212 lines. Furthermore $12 \times 12 = 144$, and the figure of 144,000 is important as being the number of the Brides of the Lamb mentioned in Revelation 14. (Revelation is itself richly numerological.)

SGGK has 101 stanzas, like *Pearl*, and it may be significant, as Arthur (1987) notes (22), that the description of the pentangle on Gawain's shield, with its emphasis on the number 5, is exactly 50 lines long (619–69). The number 5 is a Boethian 'circular' or 'spherical' number, which however often it multiplies itself always ends in 5, thus asserting its 'fiveness' (Davis 1993; Martin, below). The number was frequently used in devotional literature, 'The five joys of the Virgin' etc. (Green 1962). The whole question is discussed more fully by Duggan (below, 238).

As Curtius, MacQueen, Fowler, Duggan and others illustrate, an emotional, imaginative and intellectual life inhered in numbers. Poets used them up to the Renaissance (Fleming 1981; Hieatt 1968; Fowler 1970). We modern readers need here, as elsewhere, to educate our sensibilities.

Less precise, but undoubtedly operative, at a subconscious level, are folkloric numbers, which no doubt are at the root of the more conscious and elaborate numerology of learned clerks. Olrik, in a seminal article, called attention to the 'rule of three', the rule of 'two in a scene'. In general the European folktale fondness for numbers three and seven may easily be noted. They are deep in our minds still (Olrik 1965). The folkloric 'three' is particularly effective in *SGGK* (Burrow 1965).

In general, study of the folktale can help the understanding of medieval literature, especially medieval romance. The closeness of romance to folktale has in the past been regarded as a matter for reproach – see the summaries of romances in Hartung and Severs 1967, I, *passim*. But the way folktales operate, in their representative, often symbolic, functions, in the clarification of a clear though often not logical line of narrative, in the use of stereotyped but not thereby less effective characterisation, in the relatedness of one tale to another and the retellings of variants, and in several other respects, all help us to understand the way medieval literature affected its original audience or readership, and may now interest the modern reader. The Old and New Testaments themselves are both in content and method closely similar to folktale (Brewer 1979b). This is far from impugning their religious value – rather the opposite. (It is no good trying to read the Bible like a novel, even a non-naturalistic modern novel.) But that is not the question here. The *Gawain*-poet's (or poets') affinity with the Parable of the Wedding Feast, the extraordinary story of Jonah (an unusual exemplar of Patience, usually illustrated by Job's less adventurous life), the Flood, testify in the most obvious way to his feeling for the folkloric elements of Biblical story. He shows it too in his feeling for the mystery at the heart of things, for the underlying power in the universe, ambiguous in its exercise. The basic story of *SGGK* also has much in common with folktale despite its courtliness and literary polish. Something of this folktale feeling comes out in a purely secular way in his presentation of the Green Knight. Those critics who saw him as a vegetation-god, etc. were no doubt mistaken, but they were surely right in responding to his power and ambiguity. He too, like many figures in folktale and medieval romance, is inadequately accounted for in terms of normal material cause-and-effect. It may be that if, as has been suggested, the Green Chapel is an ancient funeral barrow, a burial mound (Brewer 1948; denied by Elliott below 113), the Green Knight, a deeply threatening figure to those who have not the magic life-giving charm of chastity, is a local folk reminiscence of beings who are frequent in Old Norse literature, supernatural mound-dwellers, representatives of death (Simek 1993 s.v. 'burial-mound', '*draugr*').[6] The presumed area of the poet's origin has plenty of barrows and underwent plentiful Norse influence. England lost almost all its genuinely ancient folk-lore in the Industrial Revolution but that had not happened in the fourteenth century. As usual with our poet the analogies and connections are close and suggestive but not conclusive and he retains his ambiguous originality. The

---

6 There are many barrow-wights (as Tolkien has taught us to call them), i.e. mound-dwellers, in the Old Norse sagas, and particularly in the less literary genres of Icelandic folktales and legends. It is said that most Icelanders, like many Irish people, can point to an 'inhabited' burial mound in their district. See also Chadwick 1946, 50–65 and 106–27. I am much indebted to Dr Andy Orchard of Emmanuel College, Cambridge, for information about Norse material.

Green Knight represents in one sense death, since death is the one thing you can be sure of finding if you go out to look for it, as the Green Knight tells Gawain (455; Zimmer 1956). The poet may owe a suggestion for this to Old Norse folklore. There was also in Northern folklore a cult of the axe (Simek 1993 s.v. 'Axes cult of'). The Green Knight's 'Danish axe' which he carries when he appears from the cliff beside the Green Chapel (2223) has a precedent in the medley of arms carried by a group of soldiers in *Cligès* (Gregory and Luttrell 1993) by Chrétien de Troyes, and in Guy of Warwick, but it is a most unusual weapon for a knight, and 'Danish' may have caught the poet's eye (Oakeshott 1964, 34–46). Its predecessor of the previous year is kept on the wall in Arthur's hall as a reminder, almost as a symbolic cultic object.

The poet's mind is one that is clearly receptive of mystery, whether from folktale or religion (not easily distinguished from each other). In religion he moves easily between almost mystical vision to careful rational exposition, both seen in *Pearl*, which is also an exposition of dream-vision, another traditional source with deep Biblical as well as secular roots. Similarly, he ranges from Arthurian adventure, though with an original twist, based via French romance on ultimately Irish folktale (Brewer 1992) to Biblically based moralisation. Again, he unifies originally oral delivery, the twos and threes of folktale, with a highly literate style – for numerology despite its roots, is the quintessence of literacy, counting lines written on a page.

The poet unifies these multiple sources of his inspiration. It seems fair to say that he reveals in the structure of his stories, especially that of *SGGK*, a mythopoeic creativity, but he combines with that the finest, most elaborate, self-conscious verbal artistry. It seems amazing either that one man should sustain such a range, or that there should be more than one man, in one small town, village or lord's retinue, at the same time, so close in temperament, who possessed such genius.

Supposing him to have been one man his poems raise some interesting problems for modern criticism, particularly for devices and desires dear to the heart of that most literate of critical techniques, the New Criticism, with its fundamental concept of the ubiquity of irony as the essence of poetry, and the consequent necessity of inventing the Narrator in order to detach the poet from responsibility for the face-value of what he has written. These problems are effectively discussed by Spearing below and need no further comment here, but there is one 'special point' that has its own human interest: the degree of personal involvement on the part of the poet in *Pearl*. If we assume that he is writing as a proxy for a mourning father, we shall read and feel the poem differently, and respond differently, from a reading which assumes that, like Boccaccio in writing his Latin poem *Olympia*, the poet is genuinely mourning his own dead child. Of course we shall never know the actual truth in a provable way. But we can say quite clearly that the poet *means* us to take the poem directly and genuinely. In the same way we may take as genuine his references to his own poverty in *Patience*. Sincerity is not enough to make a good poem, but there is no reason why a good poem should not be heartfelt by the poet, whether joyful or sad. If we took Wordsworth's sonnet 'Surprised by joy' to be a kind of ventriloquism we would read it differently. As it happens, we know it is not, and it is on the same subject, the death of a beloved daughter. It would be pointless to take *Pearl* in any other way.

The *Gawain*-poet expresses through his poems a great variety of interest and a powerful, complex poetic personality. It is so rich that we may have here the product of more than one poet and further discriminations may be possible between the poems and their various qualities. That is only one of many routes of imaginative exploration, not all touched on here, open to future readers.

1

Theories of Authorship

MALCOLM ANDREW

Common Authorship

The dominant theory regarding the authorship of *Pearl, Cleanness, Patience,* and *Sir Gawain and the Green Knight* (henceforward *SGGK*) is, of course, that they were composed by a single anonymous poet – who is generally termed 'the *Gawain*-Poet', or, rather less commonly, 'the *Pearl*-Poet'. It has been normal to assume that this poet was a man and that he lived in the North-West Midlands.[1] These assumptions have been shared by a great majority of scholars writing on the four poems – those content to focus exclusively on the poems themselves, those interested also in reconstructing the circumstances of their composition, and those who attempt to identify the poet. The theories of this last group are considered separately below, in the section headed 'hypothetical identifications'.

The essential evidence for common authorship of the four poems derives from their survival in a unique manuscript (see Edwards below). The case is strengthened by various additional facts: that the manuscript contains no other work and is unique as a collection of alliterative poems, and that it was written by a single scribe in a consistent dialect. Beyond this, the case depends on the detection and evaluation of shared characteristics among the poems. These characteristics have included correspondences of vocabulary and stylistic features, the thoughtful and inventive use of verse forms and narrative framing, a propensity for balance and symmetry in the shaping of narrative, the highly skilled handling of viewpoint and perspective, a penchant for original and often startling imagery, and the recurrence of key images and themes.[2] While evidence of this kind tends to be inconclusive, it has proved highly persuasive. Scholarly awareness and perception of such characteristics does, of course, evolve during the period from the mid-nineteenth to the late twentieth century. In particular, scholars become increasingly

---

1 The narrative voices in all of the poems, particularly *Pearl*, show signs of male identity; on the North-West Midlands, see Duggan below, 240–2.

2 For examples of the case for common authorship, argued cogently on grounds such as these, see Brewer 1967; Spearing 1970, 32–40; Vantuono 1971; Hieatt 1976.

aware that parallels in vocabulary and phrasing are unreliable indicators of common authorship, as appreciation of the formulaic nature of alliterative verse develops. With this broad proviso, however, it is possible to generalise about the characteristics specified above. Taken together with the evidence from the manuscript, they lead both Sir Frederic Madden and Richard Morris, the first two editors, to believe that the poems were written by a single poet. The issue for Madden, Morris, and their immediate successors is somewhat complicated, both by the attribution of various other works to the *Gawain*-Poet and by several (uniformly unconvincing) attempts to identify him. It may, nonetheless, be observed that, during the century following the publication of Madden's edition, all of those who edit the poems and most of those who write about them subscribe to the theory of common authorship. By the early years of the twentieth century, it had become customary for editors to consider the topic at some length in their introductions. The views expressed by Israel Gollancz, in the preface to his edition of *Patience* (1913), are typical. He states:

> It is now generally accepted, in respect of the four poems, that all the evidences of dialect, vocabulary, art, feeling, and thought, conclusively point to identity of authorship; but nothing definite has yet been discovered as to the author. (Unnumbered page)

Such views receive the endorsement of J.P. Oakden in his massive and influential two-volume study, *Alliterative Poetry in Middle English* (1930, 1935).

Though the great majority of editors and commentators in the late nineteenth and early twentieth centuries would have accepted, with Gollancz, that nothing definite is known about the poet, the temptation to speculate about his life proves irresistible. It is regularly assumed that, by establishing the provenance of the manuscript, scholars effectively identified the general area in which the *Gawain*-Poet lived and worked. Offering a relatively uncommon qualification to such views, E.V. Gordon argues, in the introduction to his edition of *Pearl* (1953), that, while the dialect of the manuscript indicates 'the poet's place of upbringing, it is not necessary to assume that he was actually living there when he wrote' (xliii). This argument is taken a step further by Morton W. Bloomfield in his well-known article on *SGGK* (1960), where he contends:

> In the minds of some investigators, the location of the dialect seems to be reliable evidence for locating the castle where the *Gawain*-poet wrote his poem or where Bercilak held court. This does not seem to me to be very soundly based. Why a poet should have to put the scene of his poem and be himself located in the area of the dialect he uses in writing is not at all evident (10).

These remain, however, minority views. Most commentators continue to assume that the poet would have lived within the broad area indicated by the dialect of the manuscript;[3] many, associating this with the combination of aristocratic tenor and deep learning in his work, speculate that he could have been a member of a noble household in the region. Such arguments can be used to support the identification of a potentially appropriate household, as when Oakden (1930) suggests that the poet could have been a retainer of John of Gaunt, living in Clitheroe Castle (257–61). They are, of course, regularly employed in attempts to identify the poet as a specific individual (see below).

The urge to speculate about the poet's life also generates openly and admittedly hypothetical biographies. Towards the end of the nineteenth century, such biographies appear in Bernhard ten Brink's *Early English Literature* (1877/83) and in the introduction to Israel Gollancz's first edition of *Pearl* (1891). These biographies, and their successors, tend to place particular emphasis on *Pearl*, since it (supposedly) reveals more than the other poems about the personal life of the poet – above all, that he was the father of a girl who died in infancy, and whose death was a bitter blow to him. Similar speculations continue to appear in the work of twentieth-century editors and commentators, though, with increasing awareness of the essential fictiveness of narrative poetry, they become more qualified and circumspect. Nonetheless, it remains possible, in the mid twentieth century, for a respectable and cautious scholar to speculate as follows about the poet's life:

> He may have been a chaplain in an aristocratic household: that he once had a daughter is no decisive argument against this, for he may, for instance, have been ordained later in life. (Gordon 1953, xlii)[4]

The hypothetical biography of the poet was also taken, among earlier scholars, to have a bearing on speculations as to the order in which the poems were written. Both ten Brink and Gollancz imagine a similar progression: from *SGGK*, a composition of the poet's carefree youth, to *Pearl*, which records the great tragedy of his middle years, to *Patience* and *Cleanness*, works of his sad and reflective old age. It rapidly becomes apparent that such conjecture is unduly literal-minded. By the turn of the century, scholars are arguing, on grounds of relative literary quality and assurance, that a more likely sequence would be *Patience* and *Cleanness* (in either order), followed by *Pearl* and then *SGGK* (e.g. Osgood 1906, xlix). More recent editors and commentators have not deviated significantly from this view, though they have tended to become increasingly cautious and circumspect on the topic (e.g. Anderson 1969, 5).

Such circumspection has, on the whole, not been reflected in attitudes to the theory of common authorship. It is clear that most editors and critics working on the four poems during the period since c.1950 have continued to

---

[3] For contrasts between the dialect of the scribe and the dialect of the poet see Duggan below, 240–2.
[4] For a view sympathetic to the autobiographical reading, see Brewer above, 20–1.

believe that they were written by a single poet. The reasons for this conviction are still those summarised above – though with an increasing emphasis on aspects of narrative technique, as methods of literary analysis have shifted and developed. Commentators have regularly invoked an argument propounded by Dorothy Everett (1955):

> It seems easier to assume a common author than to suppose that two or more men writing in the same locality and the same period, and certainly closely associated with one another, possessed this rare and, one would think, inimitable quality (68).

Similar views are expressed by various influential scholars (e.g. Anderson 1969, 4; Spearing 1970, 37; Pearsall 1977, 170). Endorsement of the theory is, however, not unanimous. John W. Clark argues against it in a series of articles (1949–51) which analyse differences in vocabulary and usage among the four poems. Morton W. Bloomfield, in his magisterial essay on *SGGK* (1960), states that he 'still consider[s] the case not proved' (9). Scepticism is also expressed by David Lawton (1982b), who detects a tendency to wishful thinking in the supporters of the common authorship theory, and maintains that their argument is 'generally . . . cast in intuitive terms or in frank appeals to critical convenience' (9). There have been several attempts to prove or disprove the case by means of (supposedly) objective authorship tests, but these have, as yet, proved inconclusive. (They are considered in a separate section below.) Meanwhile, it would be fair to state that a substantial majority of commentators would share the view expressed by D.J. Williams (1970b):

> There is no proof that these four poems were written by one man, but the feeling that they were dies hard among most readers of them, including myself (143).

St Erkenwald

At first glance, there is no obvious reason why the *Gawain*-Poet should sometimes have been credited with the composition of *St Erkenwald*. This is an alliterative poem of 352 lines, the unique text of which survives in a late fifteenth-century paper manuscript, British Library MS Harley 2250 (ff. 72v–75v). Scholars have generally dated its composition to the late fourteenth century; its most recent editor specifies the probable period 1385–1410 (Peterson 1977b, 14–15). While the dialect of the text is broadly similar to that of *Pearl*, *Cleanness*, *Patience*, and *SGGK* (Oakden 1930, 87–9), *St Erkenwald* is emphatically a London poem, written in praise of the capital's patron saint.

The attribution of *St Erkenwald* to the *Gawain*-Poet dates back to the late nineteenth century.[5] Many of the attributions of alliterative poems to

---

5   The history of this theory is summarised by Peterson 1977, 15.

particular authors (named or anonymous) made during this period later proved unreliable, as appreciation of the formulaic nature of alliterative verse developed. The four poems of the Cotton manuscript and *St Erkenwald* were attributed, by various scholars, to authors including Huchoun of the Awle Ryale and Ralph Strode: such theories are considered separately below, in the section entitled 'Hypothetical identifications'. The attribution of *St Erkenwald* to the *Gawain*-Poet does, however, outlive these flimsy theories, and is endorsed by the first two editors of the poem, Sir Israel Gollancz (1922) and Henry L. Savage (1926). Both argue the case on the basis of shared stylistic features, vocabulary, phrasing, themes, and outlook. The attribution is, nonetheless, described as 'very dubious' by J.R.R. Tolkien and E.V. Gordon, in the introduction to their contemporaneous (1925) – and very distinguished – edition of *SGGK* (xviii). Though it is regarded more sympathetically in J.P. Oakden's influential survey of alliterative poetry (1930, 1935), his views are sometimes misrepresented by later scholars. A careful reading of Oakden's work suggests a slight but significant shift of opinion between his first volume and his second. In the former (1930), he deems the case 'probable' (255). In the latter (1935), he concludes:

> The close similarity between [*St Erkenwald*] and the works of the *Gawain* poet can only be explained either by a theory of common authorship or as due to a conscious imitation by a sympathetic disciple. The parallels in phraseology are *not* sufficient to enable us to decide definitely in favour of either of these two theories (93).[6]

During the period since c.1950, the theory has lost ground rapidly. It is reviewed in a scholarly and judicious article by Larry D. Benson (1965a), who finds the case unconvincing and concludes emphatically that *St Erkenwald* was not written by the *Gawain*-Poet. His argument proves highly influential. The two subsequent editors of *St Erkenwald*, Ruth Morse (1975) and Clifford Peterson (1977), are by no means committed to the theory – Morse regarding it as improbable and Peterson, though sympathetic to it, as no more than possible. Coincidentally, the scholars who produced the standard individual editions of the four poems between 1953 and 1977 are unanimous in discounting the theory that the *Gawain*-Poet wrote *St Erkenwald* (Gordon 1953; Anderson 1969, 1977; Davis 1967). Though some works designed for a non-specialist readership continue to describe it as probable, this reflects an 'assimilation lag'[7] in scholarship rather than any serious commitment to the theory. Writing a general account of alliterative poetry in 1970, D. J. Williams refers to it as a thing of the past (1970b, 129).

The theory does, in fact, gain a further brief lease of life in a curiously

---

6 It is, therefore, curious that both Benson (1965, 393) and Peterson (1977, 16) should state that Oakden 'remained convinced' by the attribution.

7 The phrase is borrowed from Garbáty 1962, 605–11.

tangential manner. The attempt to identify the *Gawain*-Poet as Hugh or John Massey – which begins rather obscurely in 1956, but gains some prominence during the 1970s – involves evidence from *Pearl*, *SGGK*, and *St Erkenwald*. It therefore implies endorsement of the notion that *St Erkenwald* was among the poet's works. The Massey hypothesis (which is considered more fully below) seems virtually discredited by the end of the 1970s. In 1982, an authoritative commentator again consigns the theory that the *Gawain*-Poet wrote *St Erkenwald* to the past – David Lawton stating that it 'was once ascribed to the "*Gawain*-poet" ' (1982b, 11). This time, the appropriateness of the past tense is likely to prove permanent.

Hypothetical Identifications

The urge to find a name for the *Gawain*-Poet has proved a strong one, and various hypothetical identifications have been proposed. The earliest of these hypotheses would identify the poet with 'Huchoun of the Awle Ryale', a Scottish writer credited by Andrew Wyntoun in his early fifteenth-century *Orygynale Cronykil* with the authorship of 'the Awntyre off Gawane'. This attribution is accepted – with regard to all four poems – by the first editor of *SGGK*, Sir Frederic Madden (1839, 301–4). It is firmly rejected by Richard Morris, the first editor of *Pearl*, *Cleanness*, and *Patience* (1869), on the ground that the dialect of the manuscript indicates a poet writing not in Scotland but in the North-West Midlands (see above). Nonetheless, the case is advanced with conviction by George Neilson (1900, 1902). He identifies Huchoun with 'Sir Hew of Eglintoun', commemorated in Dunbar's 'Lament for the Makaris', associating his name with the inscription 'Hugo de' in the manuscript (f. 91r). The Huchoun theory is questioned by several scholars and finally discredited by Henry Noble MacCracken (1910). Meanwhile, another hypothesis had been propounded. In his first edition of *Pearl* (1891), Israel Gollancz takes up a suggestion made by the German scholar C. Horstmann, arguing that the author of the four poems may be identified as Ralph Strode (l–lii).[8] The basis for this theory is the following citation from the fifteenth-century catalogue of the library of Merton College, Oxford:

> Radulphus Strode, nobilis poeta fuit et versificavit librum elegiacum vocatum Phantasma Radulphi.

The *Phantasma Radulphi* is identified as *Pearl*, and its author as the 'philosophical Strode' to whom (among others) Chaucer dedicated *Troilus and Criseyde* (5.1857). Challenging this hypothesis, J.T.T. Brown (1897) points out the lack of evidence to suggest that Strode was a poet. He argues that there are signs

---

[8]   The attribution is also made by Gollancz in his entry on Strode in the *Dictionary of National Biography* (1885–1900).

of some confusion, among Renaissance antiquarians, between the biographies of Ralph Strode and of David Rate, confessor to King James I of Scotland and a celebrated poet. While Brown does not attempt to contend that Rate was the author of the four poems, his article could be taken to raise this as a possibility. Be that as it may, no support for such a notion is forthcoming.

When J.P. Oakden writes in 1930 that 'fanciful theories concerning the author' of the four poems 'are no longer fashionable' (1), he is apparently referring to those discussed above. He does, in fact, go on to report quite sympathetically (259–60) a more recent hypothesis which might be considered almost equally fanciful: that of Oscar Cargill and Margaret Schlauch (1928). In their article, '*The Pearl* and Its Jeweler', they 'propose . . . not only to call the maiden by her name, but also to suggest a name for the author of this masterly elegy and of *Sir Gawain and the Green Knight*' (105). They contend that '*The Pearl* is an elegy written on the death of Margaret, granddaughter of Edward III, not by her father', John Hastings, Earl of Pembroke, 'but by some one closely connected with her father and the court and (possibly as guardian) with the little girl herself' (108). Speculating that this person might have been one of the secular clerks of the Pembroke household, they name five such individuals to whom John Hastings showed particular favour. They then proceed to narrow this group down to just two – John Donne and John Prat – on the grounds that the former was associated with John of Gaunt and the latter was described as 'the King's Minstrel' (117–23). A few years later (1932), Coolidge Otis Chapman proposes that the four poems could have been written by John of Erghome, an Augustinian friar from York and author of the Latin verse *Prophecy of John of Bridlington* (c.1370). This proposal is based mainly on supposed similarities between the reading and outlook of the *Gawain*-Poet and of Erghome, and on the fact that the *Prophecy* was dedicated to Humphrey de Bohun.[9] Neither of these theories gains any significant support, though that of Cargill and Schlauch is briefly revived by Thomas A. Reisner (1973), who suggests that 'powdered' in *Pearl* (line 44) could allude to the coat of arms of the Prat family.

Since the 1950s, speculation as to the identity of the *Gawain*-Poet has been dominated by a series of hypotheses regarding signatures, acrostics, and cryptograms involving the names Hugh and John Massey.[10] The first of these is propounded by Ormerod Greenwood (1956) in the introduction to his verse translation of *SGGK* (6–12). He links the family name 'Masse', inscribed in the manuscript of *St Erkenwald* (which he assumes to have been written by the *Gawain*-Poet), with the inscription 'Hugo de' in the Cotton MS (f. 91r), to

---

[9]   A patron of alliterative poetry, based in the West Midlands, and mentioned specifically in Hulbert 1931, cited by Chapman.

[10]   In various forms and spellings, including: Hugo de Masse, Hugo de Masci, I. Masci, I. Macy, John Massy, and John Massi.

arrive at the name Hugo de Masse.[11] Greenwood bases the remainder of his argument on numerological evidence, pointing out that the value of 'Hugo de Masci' in the medieval alphabet is 101, which matches the number of stanzas in *Pearl* (and *SGGK*), and that 'Margery Masci' (the putative name of the maiden in *Pearl*) has twelve letters, and may therefore be related to the use of twelve in the poem, both structural and symbolic. He detects a pattern of puns on 'Hugo de' and 'Masci' in the text. The Masseys are identified as a family from Cheshire – a region which corresponds with the dialect of the manuscript.

Some time later, this theory is developed in a composite article by Barbara Nolan and David Farley-Hills (1971). While the former detects an anagram of 'I. Masci' and a possible acrostic reading 'paye Masci' in the text of *Pearl*, and therefore suggests that the poet's name was John rather than Hugh, the latter observes that Hoccleve refers in a short poem, addressed to John of Lancaster (son of Henry IV), to one 'maister Massy' as a skilled rhetorician and judge of poetry. In two short articles published in 1974, Clifford Peterson first detects an 'anagrammatic signature' reading 'I. d. Masse', in the text of *St Erkenwald*, and then attempts to identify Hoccleve's 'maister Massy' as John Massey of Cotton in Cheshire. The next contribution to the debate is another composite article, by Thorlac Turville-Petre and Edward Wilson (1975). While the former contends that 'maister Massy' is William Massy, 'Receiver-general and General Attorney to John of Lancaster' (130), and that Hoccleve's motive for addressing him is the prosaic one of begging, the latter provides a learned and cogent rejection of the anagrams and cryptograms detected by Nolan and Peterson. Turville-Petre's assertion is challenged by Farley-Hills (1975) and by Peterson – in yet another composite article, with Wilson (1977). It is striking that, by this time, Peterson has accepted Wilson's argument against cryptograms. Meanwhile, two more commentators contribute to the debate. William Vantuono (1975) detects the inscriptions 'I macy' in the scrollwork on f. 62v and 'macy' at the bottom of f. 114r, suggesting that these could represent the name of an illuminator or of the poet, and that, in the latter case, his proposed identification would be John Massy of Sale in Cheshire. Katherine L. Adam (1976) maintains that the 'extra' stanza of *Pearl* (stanza 76) contains an acrostic of 'John Massi' (901–05), and briefly mentions another in *SGGK* (1746–49). Reviewing the theory as a whole in the introduction to his edition of *St Erkenwald* (1977), Peterson does not accept the existence of the signatures detected by Vantuono, and rejects the suggestions of Adam on the basis of the argument earlier propounded by Wilson (19–23, 57–58). He concludes that 'no hidden signatures have been demonstrated in either *Pearl* or *St. Erkenwald*' (57). The final contribution to this debate – at least for the present – is an article by Erik Kooper on John

---

[11] On the manuscript of *St Erkenwald*, see Peterson 1977, 9–10. For a fuller summary of Greenwood's thesis, see Nolan and Farley-Hills 1971, 295–6.

Massey as the 'encoded author' of *SGGK* (1982). He stresses the importance of the number of stanzas in the poem, detecting 'a signature, a cryptogram, and an acrostic' (158) in the fifth stanza, and also a possible signature in *Patience*.

One last hypothetical identification must be recorded, even though it was proposed only in passing. Michael J. Bennett (1979) provides an interesting and scholarly argument to the effect that the cultural milieu for the work of the *Gawain*-Poet was the court of Richard II, which had strong connections with the North-West, especially Cheshire.[12] Discussing evidence of literary interests among the aristocracy and gentry of this region, he mentions that Humphrey Newton, whose apparent familiarity with *SGGK* in the early sixteenth century was noted by Rossell Hope Robbins (1943), had an ancestor, Richard Newton, who wrote some occasional verse at the end of the fourteenth century. Bennett quotes the relevant lines, and, while admitting that they are 'crude and unpolished', claims to discern in them 'definite stylistic affinities' with *SGGK*, and goes on to assert that Richard Newton might be regarded as 'a major poet of the alliterative school, or perhaps even as the anonymous *Gawain*-poet himself' (67–8).[13] This notion is firmly rejected by Derek Pearsall (1982) – who stresses, however, the value of Bennett's study as a whole. Pearsall also offers a broad judgement of the theories reviewed above, contending:

> These attributions are based on such naive and improbable assumptions concerning what constitutes evidence as to bring the study of attribution into disrepute (52).

Authorship Tests

The desire to establish whether or not *Pearl*, *Cleanness*, *Patience*, and *SGGK* were actually written by a single poet has generated a series of attempts to devise and apply objective tests of authorship. Though the nature of such tests has changed in recent years with the development of computing, the efforts of earlier scholars remain significant. During the late nineteenth and early twentieth centuries, attributions were based largely on comparative study of vocabulary, alliteration, phraseology, and stylistic mannerisms (Menner 1920, xiii–xix). This approach can be seen to culminate in the massive two-part survey of J.P. Oakden (1930, 1935). In his first volume (1930), which concentrates on dialect and metre, Oakden expresses appreciation for the work of his predecessors, qualified by the proviso that 'a still surer test is the metrical one' (73). His own metrical test, reported in Appendix 1 (251–3) involves statistics for the frequency of various features, including alliterative

---

12 Cf. Bennett 1983 and below in this volume.
13 The theory is not repeated in Bennett's later work.

types, extended half-lines, vocalic alliteration, alliterative groups, and violations of natural stress for the sake of alliteration. The result of this is to confirm
the common authorship of the three poems written entirely or predominantly
in the alliterative long line – *Cleanness, Patience,* and *SGGK.* In his second
volume (1935), Oakden surveys and tabulates the use of alliterative phrases
in a wide range of Middle English texts. With regard to the four poems of the
Cotton MS, he concludes that 'the author . . . was [relatively] restrained in his
use of stock phrases, and did not employ a given phrase repeatedly' (264).
Oakden is, manifestly, conscious throughout that differences in form and
style between *Pearl* on the one hand and *Cleanness, Patience,* and *SGGK* on the
other make the interpretation of much comparative data difficult. He also
acknowledges the more general difficulty of attempting to decide whether
stylistic affinity indicates common authorship or imitation. Subsequent
scholars have become increasingly aware not only of this problem, but also
of the significance of shared formulae, as understanding of the nature of
alliterative verse has developed. Even so, Oakden's authority on this subject
remains far from negligible.

Several decades pass before the next substantial attempt at an authorship
test, that of Göran Kjellmer (1975). His method is to establish norms for the
texts (the four poems and *St Erkenwald*) as a group, and then to observe and
record deviations from these norms. He measures seven linguistic dimensions – lexical frequency, clause length, sentence length, clause linkage types,
subordinator types, passive forms, and alliteration. The result of this test is
to identify *Pearl* as the deviant text, even when *Winner and Waster* is added
to the group or *St Erkenwald* is omitted. In Kjellmer's view, 'everything goes
to indicate that "the *Pearl* poet" did not write *Pearl*' (98). His findings are
questioned by R. Derolez (1981), on the grounds that the methods used for
establishing the norm are open to challenge and that the deviations from the
norm reflect the obvious differences in style and structure between *Pearl* and
the other poems.[14] The next contribution to the topic is that of William
McColly and Dennis Weier (1983), who offer a statistical analysis of the
frequency of function words in the four poems and *St Erkenwald.* They
conclude that *Pearl* and *SGGK* were probably written by different poets, but
that the common authorship of *Cleanness, Patience,* and *St Erkenwald* is more
likely. A few years later (1987), McColly casts doubt on the reliability of the
method used in this article, reporting that it would indicate substantial and
apparently significant differences between the first and the second half of
Cleanness (divided 'randomly' between lines 1144 and 1145). Finally, R.A.
Cooper and Derek Pearsall (1988) offer an authorship study, the essential
premise of which is 'the basic traditional assumption that there are certain
unconscious features of expression that characterize the style of the individual

---

[14] These would include the (relatively) shorter lines, metrical structure, rhyme scheme, use
of alliteration, and first-person narration in *Pearl.*

writer, and that these are susceptible to quantitative analysis' (372). They omit the text of *Pearl* and the 'bob-and-wheel' lines of *SGGK* from consideration on metrical grounds, and analyse the remaining corpus of lines attributed to the poet in comparison with three 'control' poems written in the alliterative long line.[15] The analysis deals with the distribution of alliterative syllables, the relationship between alliteration and syntax, and the frequency of function-words. Cooper and Pearsall argue that the demonstrated 'clustering and overlapping of so many metrical and stylistic characteristics in the three *Gawain* poems cannot readily be explained except in terms of common authorship' (354).

The results of these studies are, plainly, inconclusive. One recurring feature – also apparent in earlier studies – is the difficulty of comparing *Pearl* with the other three poems, given its distinctiveness in terms both of style and form. The prospect of a fully convincing authorship test, which could firmly establish whether or not all four poems were written by the same poet, would still seem remote.

---

[15] These are the *Morte Arthure*, the *Parliament of the Three Ages*, and the *Siege of Jerusalem*.

2

Poetic Identity

A. C. SPEARING

Was the Gawain-*Poet a Poet?*

Looking back on my book, *The Gawain-Poet: A Critical Study* (Spearing 1970), after a quarter of a century, I am surprised at the innocence with which I was able to employ the word 'poet' to refer to the hypothetical author of the four poems in MS Cotton Nero A.x. 'The *Gawain*-poet' and 'the *Pearl*-poet' were terms in wide currency then as now, and in them I suppose the word 'poet' was intended to convey two things – that the four compositions had a single author, and that their quality was such that he could properly be called a poet, not a mere versifier. I remain convinced of the truth of both assertions (and I take it for granted throughout the present chapter); what now seems surprising is my lack of concern for the *historical* significance of the term 'poet', for when these poems were being written the application of this term to a writer in the vernacular carried a specific charge of meaning. Kevin Brownlee notes that the earliest French use of the word *poète* for a vernacular writer was apparently by Deschamps in the 1370s, writing of Machaut in a poem upon the latter's death, as 'Noble poete et faiseur renommé' (Brownlee 1984, 7).[1] In English the earliest comparable uses may be Chaucer's somewhat later praise of Dante as 'the grete poete of Ytaille' (*Monk's Tale* VII 2460) and 'the wise poete of Florence' (*Wife of Bath's Tale* III 1125), and of Petrarch as 'the lauriat poete' (*Clerk's Prologue* IV 31).[2]

What did it mean in the fourteenth century to call a vernacular writer a poet? More work remains to be done on this question, but from investigations by Brownlee and others the following seems to emerge. 'Poet' was a term of

---

[1] Brownlee was apparently unaware of the valuable earlier studies by Tatlock (1921) and Olson (1979). Olson notes the dangers of 'the unacknowledged carryover of modern ideas of "poet" and "literature" into a period which did not categorize discourse as we do' (286). See also Schmidt 1987a, Appendix, 'Poet, Maker, Translator, Versifier'; and Patterson 1989 on the distinction between 'the humanist "poete," who claimed a transhistorical prospect' and 'the courtly "maker" ' who 'offered a ritualistic rehearsal . . . of familiar tropes of socially valuable modes of speaking and feeling' (119).

[2] Chaucer is cited from Benson 1987. In the last case the work by Petrarch under discussion was in Latin, not Italian.

high praise, implying the vernacular writer's status as a modern classic, the producer of learned compositions of intrinsic value and lasting beauty, comparable with such ancient masters of *poesye* as 'Virgile, Ovide, Omer, Lucan, and Stace' (*Troilus and Criseyde* V 1790–2). More specifically, the emerging figure of the vernacular poet expresses a consciousness of poetic vocation: he presents himself as a writer, for whom poetic composition is a goal in itself, a secular goal so important as to risk competing with religious values. And this consciousness frequently extends beyond individual compositions and individual genres to include a sense of the poetic oeuvre as a unified achievement attached to a name that will last.

In a prologue to the complete collection of his own works, Machaut relates how Love provides him with *matere* for his writing, *grande sustance* out of which he can make poems (Brownlee 1984, 17). His goal, then, is not the experience of love but the poems that can be made from it, and composing those poems is the defining activity of the poet's existence. 'The lover . . . becomes an instrument of himself as poet, and his love-life becomes a series of occasions to write poetry' (Wimsatt 1991, 85). Similarly, in *The Parliament of Fowls*, Africanus promises Chaucer that the forthcoming vision will provide him not with a taste of love, 'For thow of love hast lost thy tast, I gesse' (160), but with 'matere of to wryte' (168); the outcome will be the very poem we are reading. And in *The House of Fame* we get a comic glimpse of writing as an obsessional vocation that draws its victim away from social life into a painful solitude:

> thou wolt make
> A-nyght ful ofte thyn hed to ake
> In thy studye, so thou writest! (631–3)

In a secular context, poetic composition may be unproblematic as a goal in life, but the same cannot be true in a religious context. In a famous passage in *Piers Plowman*, Langland represents himself as rebuked by Ymaginatif precisely for spending his time writing poetry and adding to the number of existing books rather than concentrating on religious duties:

> And thow medlest thee with makynges – and myghtest go seye
>   thi Sauter,
> And bidde for hem that yyveth thee breed; for ther are bokes
>   ynowe . . . (B XII 16–17)[3]

'Meddling with makings' is a disparaging description of poetic activity, but the life this phrase evokes *is* that of a poet -- the poet whose life-work the successive versions of *Piers Plowman* seem to have been. One way in which the concept of 'life-work' can be realized is for the poet to create or oversee the creation of a manuscript that collects his productions in various genres

---

3 Langland is cited from Schmidt 1978.

as a unified and coherent body of work, as an oeuvre . . . The poet no longer simply composes verses, songs, or dits, but, in addition, concerns himself with the transcription of his various works – with their codicological existence.[4]

Petrarch did this with his Italian lyrics, carefully organizing his *Rime sparse* into a single sequence; Machaut followed suit, and so, later, did Froissart, Christine de Pizan and Charles d'Orléans, each in such a way that 'the sequence of texts defines a particular poetic personality and the development of his career' (Huot 1987, 211). No evidence remains for any such activity by Chaucer, the most 'advanced' fourteenth-century writer in English, despite the concern expressed in his poem to 'Adam Scriveyn' for the production of exact manuscript copies of his works. But another way in which awareness of an oeuvre can be created is through a poet's listing of his own poems, and Chaucer does this three times over, in the Prologue to *The Legend of Good Women*, in the *Man of Law's Prologue* (where we get another self-mocking glimpse of the poet as compulsive writer), and in the *Retractions*. Chaucer's *Retractions* and Langland's encounter with Ymaginatif can stand side by side as places where the very critique of poetic vocation from a religious standpoint testifies to that vocation's power. Finally, to be a poet is to name oneself as such, whether directly or riddlingly in one's own writings or in authorized rubrics as the writings are 'published'. In English especially most earlier vernacular writers are anonymous, whereas the 'poets' of the late fourteenth century name themselves as 'Geffrey' or 'Longe Wille' or 'John Gower' and may be more explicitly named by scribes.[5]

If these examples give some sense of what it meant for a fourteenth-century vernacular writer to be a poet, where does 'the *Gawain*-poet' stand in relation to them? That question provides a useful entry to my concern with his self-presentation in writing, but I must say at once that I see no simple answer to it. The *Gawain*-poet's situation is somewhat paradoxical. The very existence of MS Cotton Nero A.x is a striking phenomenon, for there is no comparable collection of major poems by a single poet writing in English before the fifteenth century. The fact that it contains illustrations makes it even more unusual, because it is 'one of the earliest [English] literary manuscripts to be illustrated' (Lee 1977, 18; cf. Edwards below). This surely looks like a manuscript designed to present a 'unified and coherent body of work' produced by a single master – four poems, in three different genres

---

4 Brownlee 1984, 15. The extent of Machaut's control over the production of manuscripts of his collected works is questioned by Kibler and Wimsatt 1987: 'our research calls into question the contention that he carefully oversaw the production of manuscripts of his collected works, as well as the notion that he held a concept of himself as a "poet" in anything like the modern sense of the term' (43). For a valuable sketch of the late-medieval poetic sequence and its 'bookness', see Burrow 1988a.

5 Of the substantial body of discussion of authorial self-naming, see especially Middleton 1990 and De Looze 1991.

and three variant forms of alliterative verse, forming a single oeuvre. Yet
whose body of work is it? There is no general prologue; there are no
identifying rubrics. Still, it might be only by chance that the poet remains
unnamed (perhaps the manuscript is a copy of a more informative original);
or it might even be that those scholars are right who believe that a name such
as Massy is anagrammatically encrypted in one or more of the poems. But,
even if either of these explanations should be true, what most distinguishes
this codex from collections by other fourteenth-century 'poets' such as
Petrarch and Machaut is the complete absence from the contents of any
authorial self-presentation *as writer*.

In *Sir Gawain and the Green Knight* it may not be surprising to find apparent
indications of oral delivery, for these (whether real or fictive) are typical of
Middle English romances. The poet presents himself as telling his story in an
I-you relationship to listeners whose attentiveness, tastes and knowledge he
must take into account in shaping his narrative:

> Now wyl I of hor seruise say yow no more,
> For vch wy3e may wel wit no wont þat þer were . . . (130–1)[6]

> And hit lyfte vp the y3e-lyddez and loked ful brode
> And meled þus much with his muthe as 3e may now here . . .
>
> (447–8)

> And quy þe pentangel apendez to þat prynce noble
> I am in tent yow to telle, þof tary hyt me schulde . . . (623–4)

> And 3e wyl a whyle be stylle,
> I schal telle yow how þay wro3t. (1996–7)

As is also common with romances, a written source is mentioned as authority
for the story, told 'As hit it is breued in þe best boke of romaunce . . . Þe Brutus
bokez þerof beres wyttenesse' (2521–3). Yet the poet never claims to have *read*
this source, indicating instead that he has *heard* it as the supposed audience
will now hear his own retelling:

> If 3e wyl lysten þis laye bot on littel quile,
> I schal telle hit as-tit, as I in toune herde,
>   with tonge,
>   As hit is stad and stoken
>   In stori stif and stronge . . . (30–4)[7]

---

6 *Sir Gawain and the Green Knight* is quoted from Tolkien and Gordon 1967.
7 See the valuable discussion of this passage by Kowalik 1992, 41–3; but her emphasis on
   textuality in the poet's work needs to be complemented by recognition of its recurrent
   denials and occlusions of its own writtenness. The poet's systematic omission of all claims
   to have produced a written text makes the interpretation of lines 33–6 as referring to 'The
   form in which it is (here) set down and fixed' (Andrew and Waldron 1978, 208) seem
   unlikely, and confirms the preferability of Tolkien and Gordon 1967's punctuation.

There are other references to the source as heard rather than read; hearsay is the authority for such statements as that the English call the pentangle the endless knot (630); and so determined is the poet to negate the textuality of his source and thus deny himself any direct association with writing that he even refers to it with the seemingly self-contradictory expression 'Þe bok as I herde say' (690).

In *Patience* and *Cleanness* the role of source is filled not by the 'Brutus bokez' but by the age's supreme book, the Bible. The poet figures as expositor of Scripture and preacher of accepted doctrine, but still always as one speaking to listeners. Thus in *Patience* he closes a kind of prologue, a first-person passage in which his grasp of the need for patience is related to his own experience of life, by appealing to an audience potentially as restless as that of romance:

> Wyl ȝe tary a lyttel tyne and tent me a whyle,
> I schal wysse yow þerwyth as holy wryt telles. (59–60)[8]

Even the writtenness of 'holy wryt' is imagined as transmitted through speech:

> I herde on a halyday, at a hyȝe masse,
> How Mathew melede þat his Mayster His meyny con teche.
> > (9–10)

He *heard* what Matthew *spoke* concerning Christ's teaching – teaching which was itself orally delivered in the Sermon on the Mount. Similarly in *Cleanness* the poet begins from the Beatitudes as words spoken by Christ and repeated in the liturgy, their textuality conspicuously occluded:

> Me mynez on one amonge oþer, as Maþew recordez,
> Þat þus of clannesse vnclosez a ful cler speche. (25–6)

The parable of the Great Feast, too, is presented not as a written text but as words that 'Maþew melez in his masse' (*Cleanness* 51). We might hypothesize a poet of determined orthodoxy, anxious to avoid any Lollard fetishization of God's written word as separable from the living practice of the Church;[9] but if so, this is only part of a more general denial of textuality.

That denial is all the more unexpected in so clerkly a poet, a book-lover who describes someone purified by absolution as 'polysed als playn as parchmen schauen' and compares God's destruction of the Cities of the Plain

---

8 *Cleanness, Patience* and *Pearl* are quoted from Andrew and Waldron 1978.
9 Aers, however, rightly notes (1993, 73) the 'silent marginalization' of the Church in *Pearl*'s treatment of loss and mourning.

to 'leuez of þe boke þat lepes in twynne' (*Cleanness* 1134, 966). Nor was his reading confined to religious books; indeed, it included the secular work in which Brownlee (1984, 13) finds the first emergence of the 'new notion of poetic identity' that was later to be developed by Machaut and Chaucer, Jean de Meun's *Roman de la Rose*.[10] Yet in the main bodies of *Patience* and *Cleanness* he appears intermittently but consistently not as a writer but as one speaking to hearers, in phrases such as 'as 3e may wyt hereafter' (*Cleanness* 1319), 'I haf yow þro schewed' (*Cleanness* 1805) and 'as I er sayde' (*Patience* 28). My argument is not that these poems and *Sir Gawain and the Green Knight* were really designed for oral delivery (they may or may not have been), still less that the manuscript contains written transcriptions of orally composed material; my point is that the way the poet presents himself in writing is as a listener to speech and a speaker to listeners, never as a writer.[11]

The absence of the poet as writer is most striking in *Pearl*. This is the only first-person narrative in the manuscript, it stands in the tradition of Marguerite poems inaugurated by the *poète* Machaut, and it belongs to both of the genres, dream-poem and elegy, in which poetic self-consciousness is most likely to emerge.[12] Yet here no such self-consciousness is expressed. In the initial waking section, 'I' appears in an allegory of mourning as a jeweller regretting the loss of a pearl. In the dream, 'I' finds the pearl and the heavenly world where she now lives, seeing, he repeatedly insists, exactly what St John saw in the Apocalypse. One recent scholar has noted that

> The apocalypse is a completely literary form, a message disseminated through a book: 'What thou seest, write in a book' (Apocalypse 1:11) is the watchword ... The scribal character of apocalypses, then, contributes to a strong self-consciousness of literary activity ...
>
> (Kerby-Fulton 1990, 81)

In *Pearl* just this is absent. John's role as 'visionary scribe' (Nolan 1977, 55) is acknowledged only once – 'As John hym wrytez 3et more I sy3e' (1033) – and there is no acknowledgment of the further act of writing by which the poem becomes a confirmatory supplement to the text created by John. Nothing is said of the difficulty of writing down such a dazzling sight; there is no prayer,

---

10 Jean de Meun is referred to in *Cleanness* 1057 and material is also borrowed from the *Roman* in *Pearl* 749–52.

11 Kevin Gustafson points out to me that in many Middle English devotional texts and translations speech is associated with vernacular appropriation of Latin texts, and orality may itself be a trope for vernacular authorship. The bearing of this on the *Gawain*-poet's self-presentation deserves further consideration.

12 For the dream-poem, see Spearing 1976, where I also note that in *Pearl* 'the Dreamer never appears in the role of poet' (119); for the elegy, see Sacks 1985 on 'the unusual degree of self-consciousness regarding the actual performance of the work at hand' (2). For the Marguerite tradition, see Wimsatt 1991, 97–101.

as in *The House of Fame*, for help 'to endite and ryme' (520) 'So sely an avisyon' (513); the emphasis is on the inadequacy of the senses, not the inadequacy of the pen, though it is once stated that the delight aroused by the Lamb's approach would be 'To much . . . of for to melle' (1118). Overwhelmed by longing, 'I' inadvertently brings the dream to an abrupt end and reflects on its lessons. This is the point at which, if anywhere, we might expect him to acknowledge his role as writer and the dream's function as the source of material for poetic composition, 'matere of to wryte'. An obvious parallel would be Chaucer's *Book of the Duchess*, which ends with the poet roused from his dream, finding in his hand the book that had stimulated it, and thinking,

> Thys ys so queynt a sweven
> That I wol, be processe of tyme,
> Fonde to put this sweven in ryme,
> As I kan best, and that anoon. (1330–3)

But in *Pearl* there is no such moment that brings us to recognize an identity between dream and poem.

If any poetic self-consciousness is to be found in *Pearl*, it is of a more oblique kind. Of the four poems, this displays the most ostentatiously elaborate verbal artistry; it is also a poem *about* artistry of a different but equally elaborate kind, that of the jeweller. The lost pearl is refound in a brilliantly adorned heavenly setting, where she has been transformed from a fading rose to 'a perle of prys' (272), and a rich accumulation of metaphors merges her beauty and value into that of paradise and of Christ himself, 'þat gay Juelle' (1124). It is tempting to read the jeweller as a figure of the poet, and to see the two fused, as Brownlee writes of the 'lover-protagonist and poet-narrator' in the final sequence of Jean de Meun's *Roman de la Rose*,

> *by means of poetry*, for the entire sequence is recounted in terms of metaphor and symbol, in such a way as to valorize the language of metaphor and symbol (i.e., poetic discourse) which does not require any separable gloss in order to be completed. (Brownlee 1984, 13; Brownlee's italics)

In *Pearl*, though, 'the language of metaphor and symbol' is attributed not to the poet but to the transcendent realm of his vision. The poem's 'I' may be a jeweller, but its central focus of value, the pearl, is a symbol of what is already perfect in itself. The jeweller's art does not create the pearl: the dreamer recognizes, when he asks the pearl-maiden, 'Quo formed þe þy fayre fygure?' (747), that her beauty has no natural origin, not even Pygmalion's almost magical artistry; and the terms expressing this recognition, perhaps significantly, are borrowed from Jean de Meun, for whom Pygmalion is a figure of the lover-poet creating the object of his own idolatry. The jeweller's art does not even transform the pearl as it might do a diamond, revealing a brilliance beyond that of its natural state; as a medieval Latin love-lyric about a lady called Margarita puts it, 'this precious Pearl has value of herself, not polished by a craftsman's hand'.[13] At best the jeweller can provide a setting, comparable to the *cofer* (259), *forser* (263) or *kyste* (271) of which the maiden speaks as enclosing her – terms that seem to evoke a coffin as much as a jewel-box. Our wish to find in poetry a reflexive and self-referential art needs to be resisted, if we are not to distort the poet's self-understanding, which in *Pearl* involves the conspicuous omission of any claim to be regarded as a poet.

'The greatest gift Machaut offers Chaucer is the notion of a poet writing poetry about the writing of poetry by a poet' (Calin 1994, 294); but this is precisely what is lacking in *Pearl* and the other Cotton Nero poems. The *Gawain*-poet differs markedly from the new vernacular poets of his age in the absence of any expression of poetic vocation, an absence extending to complete repression of his role as writer and reluctance even to refer to his sources as written texts. How then does he present himself in his poems? Here again he differs from poets such as Chaucer and Machaut. Chaucer's poetic 'I' varies somewhat from one poem to another, and latterly he experiments with impersonation of distinct fictional narrators. But in the many writings where 'I' is in some sense Geoffrey Chaucer – the four dream-poems, the *Troilus*, the *Canterbury Tales* frame-narrative, many of the shorter pieces – the various 'I's form a series marked by family resemblance, and strongly influenced by the 'I' of Machaut's first-person writings, that 'inept, blundering narrator who is also an inept, blundering lover' (Calin 1994, 227). The Chaucerian 'I', though by no means perfectly self-consistent, strongly tends to be modest, self-deprecating, lacking in worldly experience, studious yet slow to learn, and so on. In the Cotton Nero poems no such continuity can be found. There the 'I' of narration is generically determined: in *Sir Gawain and the Green Knight* the 'I' is a storyteller absorbed in his story, in *Cleanness* and *Patience* he is an expositor, in *Pearl* he is both a storyteller and the experiental focus of his story.

The 'I' of the Gawain-Poet

Here it will be helpful to pause to clarify the concept of this 'I' of narration. Why not call him 'the narrator'? – a familiar figure in discussions of medieval writing, and one given clear definition by modern narratological studies. Gérard Genette quotes the first-person opening of Proust's *A la recherche du temps perdu* and observes that

> obviously, such a sentence . . . can be interpreted only with respect to the person who utters it and the situation in which he utters it. *I* is identifiable only with reference to that person . . . (Genette 1980, 212)

---

[13] Cited by Nolan 1977, 158, n. 5, from Dronke 1968, II. 386.

What is striking here is the application of the word 'person' to the narrator, plainly implying that this agent is envisaged as possessing the ontological consistency attributed to human individuals in real life. Later, discussing the choice whether or not 'to have the story told by one of its "characters" ', Genette apologizes for using the term *personnages* (characters), which connotes 'the "humanness" of the narrative agent', even though that role might be assigned to an animal or even an inanimate object (244 and n. 74); but his assumption is evidently that even if the narrator were a donkey or a guinea, it would be treated as possessing the consistency of a 'person'. Similar assumptions underlie other theoretical studies. Gerald Prince defines 'narrator' as 'The one who narrates, as inscribed in the text', and the status of that 'one' as the textual equivalent to a person is made clear by the added remark that

> A narrator may be more or less overt, knowledgeable, ubiquitous, self-conscious, and reliable, and s/he may be situated at a greater or lesser distance from the situation and events narrated . . . (Prince 1988, 65)

Mieke Bal offers a definition seemingly more remote from these humanizing assumptions – 'that agent which utters the linguistic signs which constitute the text' – but even she goes on to make deductions about specific narrative situations in terms betraying the expectation that such agents will possess the attributes of human beings:

> It may be that Ottilie has told the narrator this anecdote. If that is so, it will, no doubt, be indicated somewhere in the text. If not, it seems self-evident to presuppose that the narrator/character-witness was present at the scene. (Bal 1985, 120, 125)

A film theorist, liberated from anthropomorphizing assumptions by the impersonal nature of the medium with which he deals, may be able to recognize that for narratology 'the locations of enunciation itself – enunciation being, supposedly, purely textual – are nevertheless perceived as persons of some kind' (Metz 1991, 747); but it is rare to find narratologists making use in practice of the distinction recently drawn by Monika Fludernik between 'the ontology of a personal teller figure' and 'his or her function as a mouthpiece of the narrating process' (1993, 441).

Modern narratological studies almost invariably take as their norm narratives written from the eighteenth century onwards, and to such narratives the concept of 'the narrator' as a consistent, locatable person is almost invariably appropriate. In these cases, narratological analysis can properly begin from narratorial epistemology: in principle, the question how 'the narrator' knows what s/he tells us will always have an answer. With medieval narratives, no such expectations apply. In medieval culture, stories simply exist (somewhat as jokes exist in our culture), in an autonomous realm dependent on no knowledge on the part of their tellers except knowledge of stories themselves. This is true even where 'the narrator' seems to be strongly characterized as something more than 'a mouthpiece of the narrating process'. A familiar example is Chaucer's *General Prologue*. Here we encounter a relatively consistent narrating 'I' belonging to the family of Chaucerian 'I's mentioned above, yet there is no answer to many possible questions about the sources of this narratorial agent's knowledge. How does he know what battles the Knight has fought in, or how the Prioress responds to trapped mice, or how the Guildsmen's wives feel about their husbands' chances of becoming aldermen? Doubtless we could invent fictional answers to such questions (though it might be hard to explain how he can both know that the Merchant is in debt and know that no-one knows it), but this would be to misunderstand the nature of this type of narrative discourse. In it 'the narrator' is not a self-consistent fictional person with a consciousness of the kind attributable to real persons, but a series of local effects of narration itself. If that is true of the figure commonly referred to as 'Chaucer the pilgrim', it is surely still truer of the nameless and shifting 'I' of the poems in the *Gawain*-manuscript.

This is perhaps most easily seen in *Sir Gawain and the Green Knight*, where the narrative is recurrently personalized without our ever being incited to identify 'the narrator' as a particular person.[14] This personalization is at its most explicit in the literal use of first- and second-person expressions of the kind indicated previously, foregrounding processes of telling, judgment and response in which we are invited to participate: 'I attle to schawe' (27), 'þat may ʒe wel trawe' (70), 'I deme hit not al for doute' (246), 'Wyt ʒe wel, hit watz worth wele ful hoge' (1820), and similar locutions, available in principle to be adopted by any reciter and any listeners. At one extreme, the effect of such personalization is to merge the spheres of the fiction and of its delivery and reception. The narrator enters the story-space to admonish the hero –

> Now þenk wel, Sir Gawan,
> For woþe þat þou ne wonde
> Þis auenture for to frayn
> Þat þou hatz tan on honde (487–90)

---

[14] This sentence was written before the publication of Blanch and Wasserman 1995, the final chapter of which asserts that the *Gawain* narrator *is* a particular person – a fallible storyteller whose ' "facts" are not always correct' and whose unreliability is shown, for example, in the excessive length of his allegorization of the pentangle (136). For these critics, as for many others, the fallible narrator has the great advantage of enabling them to absolve the poet of responsibility for any parts of the narrative that do not appeal to them. For a more sustained argument against the assumption that the 'I' of medieval narrative corresponds to a consistent fictional person, see my forthcoming article, 'A Ricardian "I": The Narrator of *Troilus and Criseyde*'.

– or he implies the coexistence of hero and listeners in a silence that makes storytelling possible:

> Let hym lyӡe þere stille,
> He hatz nere þat he soӡt;
> And ӡe wyl a whyle be stylle
> I schal telle yow how þay wroӡt. (1993–6)

But the poet need not always go this far, for, given sufficient references to 'I' and 'you', including 'ethic datives' as in 'He metez me þis godmon inmyddez þe flore' (1932), we become sensitized to the way that many other features of the general rhetoric of narration *imply* the presence of a storyteller and listeners. This is surely true of impersonal constructions that narrowly avoid the use of 'I': 'Hit were to tore for to telle of þe tenþe dole' (719) or 'A mensk lady on molde mon may hir calle' (964) or 'Such a sowme he þer slowe . . ., to deme were wonder' (1321–2). And a multitude of devices offer possible alternatives to what happened, thus suggesting the operation of narratorial choice. *Oppositio* is one such device – 'Haylsed he neuer one, bot heӡe he ouer loked' (223) or 'And he baldly hym bydez, he bayst neuer þe helder' (376) – and others are less readily definable figures involving comparison between two successive events – 'If he hem stowned vpon fyrst, stiller were þanne/ Alle þe heredmen in halle' (301–2) – or between what could have happened and what did:

> Hade hit dryuen adoun as dreӡ as he atled,
> Þer hade ben ded of his dynt þat doӡty watz euer. (2263–4)

Indeed, there is a sense in which all deictics (expressions in which *Sir Gawain and the Green Knight* is enormously rich) imply some degree of personalization of the narrative. We can observe this from the beginning in the contrast between the almost complete impersonality of the first stanza, where even *Bretayn* is treated as one nation among others, and the immediacy of the second, produced not only by the introduction of the first person ('I wot . . . I haf herde telle . . . I attle to schawe . . . I schal telle hit as-tit . . . ') but by other forms of deixis ('Ande quen þis Bretayn watz bigged bi þis burn rych . . . on þis folde . . . of alle that *here* bult . . .'). Deixis predominates in the next stanza too – 'Þis kyng . . . þo rich breþer . . . þise gentyle kniӡtez . . . þis fayre folk . . .' – and virtually throughout the poem thereafter. Seeing the matter in these terms makes it clear, I believe, that what is involved is not the characterization of an individual narrator whose distinctive point of view we must recognize and interpret, as if he were the 'I' of *A la recherche du temps perdu* or of *Doktor Faustus*; it is a pervasive heightening of the general characteristics of the narrating process in Middle English romance – dramatic immediacy, emotional identification, wholehearted commitment to a fictive reality shared by story and audience.

Something comparable is true, given the difference of genre, in the two Scriptural poems. Here the explicit first person, relatively infrequent, seems to have two main functions. First, there is the 'I' of the framework into which the poems' Scriptural stories are fitted – three stories in *Cleanness*, one in *Patience*. This 'I' is so presented as to claim the authority to interpret Scripture. In *Cleanness* his authority derives from study:

> I haue herkened and herde of mony hyȝe clerkez,
> And als in resounez of ryȝt red hit myseluen,
> Þat þat ilk proper Prynce þat paradys weldez
> Is displesed at vch a poynt þat plyes to scaþe;
> Bot neuer ȝet in no boke breued I herde
> Þat euer He wrek so wyþerly on werk þat He made . . .
> As for fylþe of þe flesch þat foles han vsed. (193–202)

By such means, he has gained understanding and authority to interpret God's meanings; and thus he is able to select, and to shape into a poem, Scriptural narratives that demonstrate God's hatred of impurity:

> Þus vpon þrynne wyses I haf yow þro schewed
> Þat vnclannes tocleues in corage dere
> Of þat wynnelych Lorde þat wonyes in heuen. (1805–7)

In *Cleanness* the role of this 'I' is focused more sharply as an analogy emerges between him and Daniel. Daniel is the central figure of the last Scriptural story, and he announces himself to Belshazzar as being (like the poet) an expositor of a threefold narrative, a divine message

> merked in þrynne,
> Þat þretes þe of þyn vnþryfte vpon þre wyse.
> Now expowne þe þis speche spedly I þenk . . . (1727–9)

In *Patience* there is less emphasis on study (though here too the 'I' of the framework has listened carefully to God's word in the Bible), and correspondingly more emphasis on what he has learned about the poem's theme from his experience of life:

> Ȝif me be dyȝt a destyné due to haue,
> What dowes me þe dedayn, oþer dispit make?
> Oþer ȝif my lege lorde lyst on lyue me to bidde
> Oþer to ryde oþer to renne to Rome in his ernde,
> What grayþed me þe grychchyng bot grame more seche? (49–53)

If the 'I' of the framework in *Cleanness* bears some similarity to Daniel as a clear-sighted expositor, that of *Patience* is more like Jonah, who has to learn from experience how little choice he has about preaching God's word. Paradoxically, it is in these two poems with their declared dependence on Scripture that we come closest to a sense of specifically poetic consciousness, for in them Scripture itself is seen as conveying meaning through *forme* (literary design) as well as through content. *Cleanness* begins by stating that if someone knew how to praise purity aptly,

> Fayre *formez* myȝt he fynde in forþering his speche,
> And in the contraré kark and combraunce huge, (3–4)

while in *Patience* the shaping of the Beatitudes to begin with poverty and end with patience is seen as conveying an affinity between these two qualities,

> For in þe tyxte þere þyse two arn in teme layde,
> Hit arn fettled in on *forme*, þe forme and þe laste. (37–8)[15]

Within the Scriptural narratives the functions of the explicit first and second persons are similar to those in *Sir Gawain and the Green Knight*. The reality and immediacy of events are confirmed by first-person commentary, ranging from speculation to sarcasm: Lot ordered his wife to serve no salt to his angel guests, 'Bot ȝet I wene þat þe wyf hit wroth to dyspyt' (*Cleanness* 821), and when Belshazzar summoned enchanters to interpret the writing on the wall they understood as much 'As þay had loked in þe leþer of my lyft bote' (*Cleanness* 1581). And we are interpellated as listeners to whom the storyteller owes as much deference as if he were the reciter of a romance: 'ȝif ȝe wolde tyȝt me a tom telle hit I wolde . . .' (*Cleanness* 1153). Here as in *Sir Gawain and the Green Knight*, even in the absence of explicit references to 'I' and 'you', other forms of deixis have the effect of personalizing the narrative without producing consistent impersonation of a specific narrator; more important, both Scriptural poems are governed by a rhetoric whose effect is to make narrative expository. Lengthy analysis would be necessary to provide full support for this statement, but a single example may offer some clarification. The conclusion of the final Scriptural story in *Cleanness* is a greatly amplified version of the closing verses of Daniel 5:

> . . . et praedicatum est de eo quod haberet potestatem tertius in regno suo.
> Eadem nocte interfectus est Baltassar rex Chaldaeus.
> Et Darius Medus successit in regnum annos natus sexagintaduos.

This simple narrative is expanded into over fifty lines of Middle English verse (*Cleanness* 1745–96), from which I offer two illustrative extracts:

> þys watz cryed and knawen in cort als fast,
> And alle þe folk þerof fayn þat folȝed hym tylle.
> Bot howso Danyel watz dyȝt, þat day ouerȝede;

---

15 See Benson 1965b, 166, on this passage as an indication of the poet's awareness of 'the semantic function of form'.

Ny₃t ne₃ed ry₃t now with nyes fol mony,
For da₃ed neuer anoþer day, þat ilk derk after,
Er dalt were þat ilk dome þat Danyel deuysed . . .   (1751–6)

Baltazar to his bedd with blisse watz caryed;
Reche þe rest as hym lyst: he ros neuer þerafter.
For his foes in þe felde in flokkes ful grete,
Þat longe hade layted þat lede his londes to strye,
Now ar þay sodenly assembled at þe self tyme . . .   (1765–9)

When I wrote about *Cleanness* and *Patience* in *The Gawain-Poet: A Critical Study* (Spearing 1970), I was especially interested in the poet's imaginative realization of his Vulgate sources – the addition of concrete detail and the evocation of time and space occupied and defined by that detail. Examples from the lines quoted would include the mention of Belshazzar's bed, the imagining of subordinates to carry him there and to take pleasure in Daniel's promotion, and the sensory evocation of nightfall (more details of which are given in other lines not quoted). What most strikes me now is rather the reprocessing of linear narrative as logical exposition, by an implied 'I' possessing the authority, personal and/or institutional, to explain purpose as well as sequence. The poet converts the relatively simple syntax of Old Testament narrative into hypotactic forms, full of subordinate clauses, and the structure of subordination implies his ability to grasp God's purpose in the syntax of the 'fair poem' that is sacred history (Augustine 1945, Bk XI ch. XVIII (II.327)). He makes frequent use of explanatory conjunctions such as *for* (1755, 1767) and *bot* (1753). (In both Scriptural poems *for* is a favourite conjunction, often prominently placed, as here, as the first word of a line; *forþi*, supplying consequence as *for* supplies cause, is another favourite.) Deictics such as *now* (1754, 1769) imply narratorial presence in the midst of events. Emphatic demonstratives such as *þat ilk* (1755, 1756) and *þe self* (1769) indicate firm grasp of the connections among the components of the narrative. Perhaps most strikingly, locutions such as 'Bot howso Danyel watz dy₃t' (1753) and 'Reche þe rest as hym lyst' (1766) imply simultaneously God's irresistible control over events, regardless of the wishes and concerns of the stories' human actors, and the poet's ability to recognize that control and his authority to expound it. The overall effect, here and in *Patience*, is of what I have called 'expository narrative', personalized but without impersonation: 'I' is not the label of a fictive person but the effect of a narrative genre.

I come finally to the first person of *Pearl*; and here there will surely be resistance to any suggestion that the 'I' should not be imagined as a fictive person. I do not deny that *Pearl* tells a story about a person referred to as 'I' (and by the pearl-maiden as 'thou') – a story conveyed with deliberate obliquity, but as to whose interpretation there is general agreement. A man's beloved daughter died in infancy; bitterly mourning her loss, he had a vision in which he encountered her once more, transfigured and now capable of informing him of fundamental truths about grace and salvation. At his request, she allowed him to see her at a distance as a Bride of the Lamb in the New Jerusalem; unable to resist attempting to join her, he brought the vision to a premature end, but subsequently recognized that he must accept 'þat Pryncez paye' (1176) and commit her to God with a father's blessing. The protagonist of this sequence of events is as solid a person as Gawain or Jonah (it would not be hard to imagine a third-person version of his story), but we cannot disregard the effect caused by the telling of his story by as well as about 'I'. This is a respect in which *Pearl* differs from the illuminated Apocalypse manuscripts to which it has profitably been compared (e.g. Nolan 1977; Whitaker 1981), for there St John watches and participates but cannot be the subject of a narrative *énonciation*. Like other medieval dream-poems, *Pearl* is couched in the first person and the past tense. One consequence is that 'I' represents simultaneously the 'I' of narration in the textual present and the person to whom the events happened in the extra-textual past; and yet the story concerns a transformative experience undergone by that person, bringing him new understanding of his past and thus (we may suppose) enabling him to write as he does in the present. If we are to find ontological consistency in the poem's 'I', it seems necessary to read it in terms of a pervasive irony. Every past-tense statement of what 'I' saw, thought, felt, did, will have to represent ignorance seen through the aperture of a subsequent enlightenment, and the appropriate mode of reading will involve a sense of superiority over that 'I', who foolishly mourned, felt foolish surprise at finding his pearl not really lost but a queen in heaven, foolishly imagined it possible to rejoin her, and so on.

This has been the normal way of reading *Pearl*. In my book (Spearing 1970) I called the poem's 'I' 'ridiculously inept', 'hopelessly literal-minded', 'amusingly undignified'; others have criticized him as 'thoughtless', 'confused', 'naïve', 'prideful', 'obtuse', 'irritable', 'cantankerous', 'querulous', 'slow-witted'. My sense that something is wrong with this way of reading is more a matter of intuition than of cognition. The poem is one of exceptional emotional and moral intensity, and for this very reason I feel a certain discomfort in the easy triumph it seems to offer over this person called 'I' (generally referred to by critics as 'the narrator'). Other dream-poems appear to offer a similar triumph, but perhaps arouse less discomfort because their moral and spiritual claims are less exalted. In Chaucer's *Book of the Duchess*, the Chaucerian 'I', as our only possible informant about the content of his dream, is put in the position of knowing things that he then appears not to know. We have to learn from him, because there is no-one else from whom we can learn it, that the cause of the black knight's grief, revealed in words he overhears him speaking, is that

> my lady bryght,
> Which I have loved with al my myght,
> Is fro me ded and ys agoon. (477–9)

Yet from then until near the end of the dream, 'I' does not know this; and this ignorance of what he has himself told us is generally interpreted as revealing his astonishing naïveté, or alternatively his astonishing tactfulness in pretending not to have overheard the knight's confession.

I suggest that such interpretations are mistaken, and that this apparent coexistence of knowledge with ignorance is a consequence of the double function of the first person, as the protagonist of past events constituting the narrative *énoncé* and as a textual effect of the narrative *énonciation* by which these events are revealed to us. I further suggest that something similar is even more likely to be true of *Pearl*, where, as we have seen, the 'I' of the *énonciation* is never realized as its writer, and where, moreover, he is never given a fictive existence of any kind in the present. In *The Book of the Duchess* the 'I' who read and dreamt and the 'I' who writes eventually coincide in the textual present; in *Pearl* that never happens. Moreover, in *Pearl* the ultimate truth towards which the poem points, the divine *mysterys* (1194) that the protagonist realizes he has missed, is one that neither we nor the poet can fully grasp. Perhaps in *Pearl*, at least, that is why the *Gawain*-poet is so reluctant to claim for himself the dignity of being a poet. It is in falling short that *Pearl* comes nearest to expressing what cannot be expressed in human language; and that is another reason for questioning interpretations that contrast the errors of 'the narrator' with correct understandings supposedly available to the poet and his readers. No correct understanding is possible except for those beyond death who, like the pearl-maiden, 'þur3outly hauen cnawyng' (859); in the realm we share with the poet, it is only the shape of error that reveals the boundaries of truth.

For me, the consequence of seeing *Pearl* in the terms outlined here is to permit the recognition of a single understanding as unequivocally and unironically present at every moment in the story told, and thus to remove the discomfort of feeling myself encouraged to triumph over the past inadequacies and misunderstandings of 'the narrator'. The poem's protagonist is represented as fully capable throughout of criticizing his own imperfections, recognizing that before his vision

> Þa3 kynde of Kryst me comfort kenned,
> My wreched wylle in wo ay wra3te, (55–6)

that during it his powers cannot match what it has to offer –

> I stod as stylle as dased quayle
> For ferly of þat frech fygure (1085–6)

– and that after it he has missed the possibility of a deeper understanding of God's *mysterys*. 'Any inclination to judge is forestalled because he judges himself.' (Davenport 1978, 10). We do not need to construct a 'narrator' as the ground on which to feel morally superior to this intensely self-critical protagonist, and if we can resist the temptation to do so we shall gain a more valuable experience as readers. I think it possible that we shall also achieve an experience closer to that of *Pearl*'s medieval readers, for whom the distorting concept of 'the narrator' did not yet exist.[16]

---

16 For reading earlier drafts of this chapter and helping me to improve it, I am grateful to Kevin Gustafson, Barbara Nolan, Lisa Samuels, and Elizabeth Spearing.

3

Gender and Sexual Transgression

JANE GILBERT

In this essay, anthropologically inspired methods are applied to the study of gender and sexuality in three of the Cotton Nero poems: *Cleanness*, *Pearl* and *Sir Gawain and the Green Knight* (*Gawain*). The argument is that all three poems use the same basic idea of what constitutes 'transgressive' and (as a corollary) 'proper' gender and sexuality; this essay sets out to study both that basic schema and the varying uses made of it in the different texts (so far as I can determine, *Patience* does not fall into the same pattern). This, then, is an investigation of 'gender' in a very broad sense: as a system of classification of sexual relations. The principal focus will be on the male characters; nevertheless, a debt is owed by anyone writing on gender and sexuality in the *Gawain*-poet's works to those who have focused more on the female characters: Stanbury 1993 on *Pearl*; Fisher 1989; Heng 1991, 1992; Kamps 1989 on *Gawain*. (I have not been able to consult Dinshaw 1994.)

Cleanness

Cleanness contains a clear depiction of gender and sexual transgression, and an equally clear condemnation of that transgression. Two main sexual sins are described in the poem. The first is committed by those who live immediately before the Flood:

> Þer watz no law to hem layd bot loke to kynde,
> And kepe to hit, and alle hit cors clanly fulfylle.
> And þenne founden þay fylþe in fleschlych dedez,
> And controeued agayn kynde contraré werkez,
> And vsed hem vnþryftyly vchon on oþer,
> And als with oþer, wylsfully, upon a wrange wyse:
> So ferly fowled her flesch þat þe fende loked
> How þe deȝter of the douþe wern derelych fayre,
> And fallen in felaȝschyp with hem on folken wyse,
> And engendered on hem jeauntez with her japez ille. (263–72[1])

---

[1] References to both *Cleanness* and *Pearl* are taken from Andrew and Waldron 1987.

Apart from the vague description of the first part of this quotation, the most obvious sexual act is the fornication of humans with devils. These unnatural acts cause God to wipe out almost the entire human race. A second sort of sexual act which offends God is specified later in the poem: it is the homosexuality of the men of Sodom. To quote God himself,

> 'Þay han lerned a lyst þat lykez me ille,
> Þat þay han founden in her flesch of fautez þe werst:
> Vch male matz his mach a man as hymseluen,
> And fylter folyly in fere on femmalez wyse.' (693–96)

The poet emphasizes that he is not putting forward a general condemnation of sexuality by having God eulogize the joys of 'natural' sexuality, the *kynde crafte* (697–710). Disapproval is directed exclusively towards the sexual modes designated as differing from this 'natural' and 'clean' version.

Spearing (1987, 181–82) sums up what the two main instances of 'unclean' sexuality in *Cleanness* have in common:

> The offences of mankind that provoke the Flood are defined precisely as offences against the universal system of categories that depend on separation and appropriateness – the integrity of the human species as against other species, and the integrity of the basic binary classification that assigns appropriate roles to the two sexes. As Mary Douglas puts it, 'Holiness means keeping distinct the categories of creation' (p. 53). When sexual intercourse takes place within the same sex, or between one race and another (in this case between human females and the fallen angels), these categories begin to blur, and the whole system is threatened.

Transgressive sexual desire in *Cleanness* is that which adopts an object forbidden because it falls into what, in the ordered taxonomy of the universe, is defined as an impermissible category. Ideal and unclean sexuality, then, are defined categorially.

If we adopt the terms which anthropology uses to categorize human sexuality, the two 'unclean' cases in *Cleanness* can be seen to be complementary. They correspond to two forms, endogamy and exogamy, which in anthropological discourse are more commonly framed in exclusively heterosexual terms.[2] In the majority of societies, the universe of people is divided into three categories, which determine sexual availability. Firstly, there is the category which is 'too similar', or 'too close' to the subject. In anthropological literature, this is usually discussed as incest, with the subject and the object

---

2 Furthermore, these terms are generally used for kinship structures: that is, they are not about who can sleep with whom, but about who can form an alliance by marriage with whom. In the case of medieval Christianity, however, sex outside marriage being strictly prohibited, permissible sexual relations and kinship structures can be treated as broadly the same thing.

belonging to the same basic kingroup; but the category of the 'too similar' could equally well be applied to gender, thus disqualifying homosexuality. In the second place, there are those people with whom sexual relations are permitted. These people are defined by a certain kind of distance from the subject: for example, a particular degree of kin – or sexual difference. These people, however, also share a degree of similarity or closeness to the subject; and this distinguishes them from the third category of people, those who are 'too different', or 'too distant' from the subject. These people are considered to belong to a different order of being altogether: the boundary which separates them from the subject is sacrosanct. Both the mating of human with devil and that of man (in the sense of 'male human') with man in *Cleanness* represent couplings which are unacceptable according to these criteria: the former because subjects mate across categories that are considered too different from each other, the latter because mating takes place within a single category, between those considered too similar. I shall call the former type of sexual relation 'extreme exogamy', and the latter, 'extreme endogamy'.[3]

What defines these categories, though? Do the definitions of 'too-similar' and 'too distant' remain the same, in every text, in every culture? Clearly, the answer is no. The form taken in *Cleanness* by overly endogamous relationships makes them relatively easy for us nowadays to see as transgressive; the God of *Cleanness*'s condemnation of homosexuality as 'unnatural' represents an attitude still available and, indeed, deeply entrenched within our culture. Scholarship has shown, however, that there is nothing 'natural' about the ways in which different cultures construct the categories which underlie the regulation of sexuality (in an anthropological context, see Moore 1988; in a historical context, Foucault 1981). The notion of 'natural' sexuality is a powerful political device, which functions to place certain, ideologically highly charged ideas outside the bounds of discourse: to make them, that is, almost impossible to question (Foucault 1981). As such, what is meant by sexual 'nature' varies according to the particular culture using it. Furthermore, it is an inconsistent category even within a 'single' culture: in the Middle Ages, 'natural' sexuality was invoked both to support and to condemn homosexuality (Boswell 1980, 145–56, 303–32). Other categories which similarly use the terminology of the 'natural' also vary between cultures. For example, it is known that the degrees of kinship within which the Church has permitted marriage have shifted hugely over time (a major change was made at the Fourth Lateran Council in 1215: see Brundage 1987, 356): hence, the definition of incest, a sexual transgression which depends on categories of kinship, has varied. Just because the version of acceptable sexuality put

---

3 I should emphasize that the object of analysis here is not homosexuality but homophobia. That is, I am not suggesting that the representation of homosexual desire as desire for someone extremely (or overly) similar to oneself is in any sense an adequate or accurate one; in *Cleanness* at least, it simultaneously is produced by and justifies anti-gay prejudice.

forward in *Cleanness* appears to accord largely with that which conservative brands of present-day Western culture designate as 'natural', then, is no reason to accept it without analysis; on the contrary, it is a very good reason for analyzing it with some care.

While extreme endogamy is easy for modern readers to spot in *Cleanness*, things are rather different when it comes to the poem's definition of overly exogamous relationships. No very strong feeling of transgression is attached today to the idea of humans mating with angels or with devils. Nevertheless, as Spearing makes clear in the passage quoted above, another form of extreme exogamy is miscegenation, or sexual intercourse between people of different races; the act carried the death penalty in many medieval societies (Brundage 1987, 461–62, 518), and the political issue is still very much alive today (for instance in issues of 'ethnic cleansing'). In the case of the *Gawain*-poet's works, it is important to appreciate the power attached to such overly exogamous relationships. Indeed, while there is a formal distinction between extreme exogamy and endogamy, in effect the two modes are associated, even identified. Lévi-Strauss noted the same association in some of the cultures he studied: 'incest [. . .] even combines in some countries with its direct opposite [son antithèse], inter-racial sexual relations, an extreme form of exogamy, as the two most powerful inducements to horror and collective vengeance' (1969, 10). Throughout, this combination has been associated with Sodom: recent critical work has shown how the sexual category called 'sodomy' cannot simply be taken to mean (male) homosexuality, but merges inextricably ideas of homosexuality and of foreignness (Goldberg 1994, 1–22; see also the other essays in this volume. Patton 1994 contains an especially pertinent application to representations of Aids). The association of extreme endogamy with extreme exogamy is found in *Cleanness* in exemplary form with the presentation of the sin of Sodom, in which confusion of gender is combined with confusion of ontological category. The description of the angels shows two beautiful creatures of indeterminate status:

> [Loth] sy3e þer swey in asent swete men tweyne;
> Bolde burnez wer þay boþe with berdles chynnez,
> Ryol rollande fax to raw sylk lyke,
> Of ble as þe brere-flour whereso þe bare scheweed.
> Ful clene watz þe countenaunce of her cler y3en;
> Wlonk whit watz her wede and wel hit hem semed.
> Of alle feturez ful fyn and fautlez boþe;
> Watz non aucly in ouþer, for aungels hit wern,
> And þat þe 3ep vnder3ede þat in þe 3ate syttez.   (788–96)

According to God (692–96, quoted above), the sin of the men of Sodom is to take other men and treat them as if they were women. The angels are beardless and beautiful, with silken hair, fair complexions and clear eyes: these details are standard in portraits of romance heroes, but also in those of romance heroines (Colby 1965, 25–72; esp. 68–69). In many such romances, characters described like this cross-dress: youths successfully disguise themselves as girls, and vice versa.[4] Although designated in the poem as both unnatural and unholy, then, the men of Sodom's reading of the angels as 'feminine' falls well within the guidelines produced by medieval literature.

This 'unclean' interpretation of the portraits is countered by a 'proper' one. As Lot recognizes, the beings' beauty actually indicates their otherworldly status: they are not humans at all, but angels. As such, of course, they are no less sexually taboo than human males would be. The sin of Sodom is thus double, at once overly endogamous and overly exogamous. Lot, trying to save both the angels and the men of Sodom from the imminent breaking of this double sexual taboo, offers his daughters in place of the angels. As Spearing (1987, 182) points out, these daughters function as representatives of heterosexuality, the legitimate alternative to the overly endogamous relations of homosexuality. The girls also, however, represent a correction to overly exogamous desire, since they, as humans, belong to the same order of being as the men. In *Cleanness*, Sodom is a site at which extreme endogamy and extreme exogamy are one; and this pairing of the two modes of sexual transgression will reappear with significance in *Pearl* and *Gawain*.

Sexuality, the cultural reading of the direction which sexual desire takes and the mode it adopts, cannot be separated conceptually from gender (Rubin 1991). When the poem claims that the men of Sodom's sin is to treat men as if they were women, this interpretation in some sense allows for no true 'homosexuality' at all. The sin is presented as a form of heterosexuality, with a person considered to be masculine having intercourse with a person considered to be feminine.[5] The discrepancy between God's view and that of the men of Sodom here turns on the interpretation of the proper relationship between two terms which modern theory calls 'sex' and 'gender'. 'Sex' is considered to be a quality of the body, and is defined by genital anatomy: by

---

4   Examples of boys being mistaken for or disguising themselves as girls are *Floire et Blancheflor* and *Floris et Liriope*; there is also the fabliau *Trubert*. Girls disguise themselves as youths in, among others, *Aucassin et Nicolette* and *Le Roman de Silence*.

5   Boswell (1980, 23–26, 156–58) notes that this construction of male homosexuality (which, historically, is by no means the only one) occurs in cultures which combine anti-gay prejudice with misogyny: since femininity is considered absolutely inferior to masculinity, it is degrading for a man to do anything 'feminine'. Boswell argues that 'the anxieties [of many Church fathers] about homosexual acts were largely responses to violations of gender expectations rather than the outgrowth of a systematic approach to sexual morality' (1980, 157–58): a reading supported by the virtual absence of condemnation of female homosexuality in these writings. Boswell includes a translation of the twelfth-century Latin debate between Ganymede and Helen (a text which survives in translations in a variety of languages), in which it is interesting that Helen, the proponent of heterosexuality and anti-gay prejudice, describes the objects of male homosexual desire as effeminate, while Ganymede, exemplary object of that desire, argues strongly that he does not, nor wants to resemble a woman (1980, 381–89; e.g., ll. 185–92).

that which determines which of the two possible roles in biological sexual reproduction the person can take. 'Gender' is the name given to the complex of roles which the person can play in society, culture and sexuality. Distinguishing these two concepts allows for what Butler (1990, 6) calls 'a radical discontinuity between sexed bodies and culturally constructed genders': since 'if gender is the cultural meanings that the sexed body assumes, then a gender cannot be said to follow from a sex in any one way'. In modern terms, then, the God of *Cleanness*, who sees the objects of sodomitic desire as properly masculine, supports a continuum between sex and gender; the men of Sodom, who see these objects as legitimately feminine, promote discontinuity between sex and gender. In God's eyes, the 'feminine' man, object of desire in Sodom, is a monster of perversity.[6] *Cleanness* makes it clear that God is to be believed: that, as the omniscient creator of all things, his judgement on the categories involved is correct. The only benchmarks of improper gender and unclean sexuality are failure to perceive these *clane* classifications (Glenn 1983–84; Johnson 1984, 120, remarks that 'the *Glossa Ordinaria*, quoting Isidore, says that Sodom means blindness'), or dissent from them. There are no perverse desires in *Cleanness*, then; there are only perverse interpretations.

Through the figure of God, *Cleanness* operates a powerfully authorized enforcement of a particular brand of sexuality, and a corresponding condemnation of other versions, represented here by the dual sin which is extreme endogamy and exogamy. For the rest of my analysis, I shall continue to use the definitions of normative and transgressive sexuality outlined in *Cleanness* as a touchstone, in order to demonstrate how the other two poems create a more complex and nuanced picture while nevertheless retaining the same basic model.

Pearl

In *Cleanness*, the privileged form of sexuality – that associated with God – is all-human heterosexuality. To it are opposed any desires defined by God as overly endogamous and exogamous: these are designated transgressive. As a literary homily, *Cleanness* is wedded to the idea of compulsory heterosexuality, in a way which is quite foreign to the courtly and mystical

---

6 Butler (1990, 7) has recently challenged the sex/gender distinction: 'gender is not to culture as sex is to nature; gender is also the discursive/cultural means by which "sexed nature" or "a natural sex" is produced and established as "prediscursive", prior to culture, a politically neutral surface *on which* culture acts' (Butler's italics). She discusses (1990, 106–11) recent work on chromosomes, supposedly the ultimate determinants of 'natural' sex, and shows how strenuously scientists have attempted to tidy up the empirical evidence by forcing it into a binary gender classification which, in fact, radically misrepresents it. In *Cleanness*, God's endorsement lends even stronger ideological support to the categories designated as 'natural'.

discourses used by both *Pearl* and *Gawain*. In the heavenly context depicted by *Pearl*, the distinction between 'ideal' and 'transgressive' desire is erased: all-human heterosexuality is shown to be as inappropriate as are extreme endogamy and exogamy. Having discredited all these forms of sexuality, the poem ultimately provides a new form of ideal desire: one which breaks down altogether the preceding distinctions.

As is universally recognized, the Dreamer's desire for the pearl he has lost, and for the Maiden who represents it for much of the poem, is phrased in terms borrowed for the most part from the courtly love lyric; its expression is erotic. As a form of desire, it partakes of both endogamous and exogamous extremities. On the one hand, the Dreamer's desire for the Maiden is apparently incestuous: as he himself says, 'Ho watȝ me nerre þen aunte or nece' (233). Critics usually start from the assumption that the Maiden represents a real-life dead baby daughter; her presence thus needs no explanation. It would be more helpful, however, to ask why the poet makes the object of sexual desire in this poem a daughter. This girl is obviously far too close kin to the Dreamer for her to be a licit object of desire. The same questioning can be extended to the issue of the Maiden's age. Again, critics have generally asked why a two-year-old should be represented as grown up (the usual answer is that she represents a version of the *puella senex* topos; see, for instance, Levine 1977) but one can equally well ask why a baby should be there at all. The child's age works to strengthen the impression of transgressive and inappropriate sexuality: sexual desire for a child only two years old was no less taboo in the Middle Ages than it would be now. The Dreamer's love thus combines sexual and paternal affection.

His language continues this ambiguity. When the pearl itself is first introduced, it is described in womanly terms:

> Perle plesaunte, to prynces paye
> To clanly clos in golde so clere:
> Oute of oryent, I hardyly saye,
> Ne proued I neuer her precios pere.
> So rounde, so reken in vche araye,
> So smal, so smoþe her sydez were. (1–6)

The emphasis here on smallness, which is so typical of portraits of courtly ladies (Colby 1965, 65), will later be seen to express the small size of the baby girl. Roundness and smoothness similarly occupy a semantic space which combines childishness with femininity. Feminist critics have long (Greer 1971) complained that women are infantilized in Western culture – that the features which are considered to constitute their sexual attractiveness are in many cases those of the child: small size, slight figure, large eyes, smooth skin, lack of body hair. In *Pearl*, this combination works powerfully to emphasize the idea of incest with a very young daughter, and thus to render the desire the Dreamer expresses disturbing.

On the other hand, the Dreamer's desire for the Maiden is also presented as overly exogamous. She herself points out the distance between them, objectified by the river which separates their respective banks. He may not come over the river to her, because he is still alive. Furthermore, he will never be allowed to take part in the procession of the virgins following and adoring the Lamb: these are special souls, quite different from those of people who have died in adult life, and who are not 'saf by ry3t'. The Dreamer is in every way ontologically too different from the Maiden for his desire for her to be legitimate.

The Dreamer's desire for the Maiden is thus doubly disqualified by the poem: like the desire of the men of Sodom for the angelic youths, it is at once too endogamous and too exogamous. In *Pearl*, however, this desire is not contrasted to all-human heterosexuality. On the contrary, the forms designated in *Cleanness* as 'normative' and 'transgressive' respectively are here collapsed into each other: the Dreamer expresses his transgressive wishes in the dominant medieval discourse of heterosexual human desire – that of *fin'amors*, or courtly love. *Fin'amors* appears in *Pearl* with two power configurations, both entirely conventional; and they are discredited together, as a matching pair. The poem opens with an image of a male subject controlling a female object. The Dreamer describes himself, the lover, as the Jeweller; the woman he loves is denied any subjectivity by being reduced to a piece of jewellery, an object made by him. More even than a figure of her death, this image renders her inanimate, as if she had never truly been alive. There is no question of her operating independently of the Jeweller. The relation between the lover-maker and the beloved-made recalls Pygmalion, whose story is told at length in the *Roman de la Rose* (the direct echoes of the *Rose* in *Pearl* have often been documented; see, for example, Gordon 1953; Pilch 1964; Vantuono 1984). The power-relations at this point represent one strand of the courtly tradition: that in which the male is dominant. They are also those which give the father authority over his child. This expression of courtly sexual desire is thus associated in the poem with the Dreamer's incestuous desire for his baby daughter: in other words, with the overly endogamous version of his desire.

In the vision, by contrast, the Maiden is granted the dominant subjectivity. Critics have noted the extent to which the Dreamer sees her as the power-source in the world of the vision: for instance, after she has told him that God will be the judge who decides whether or not he will be allowed to cross the stream, he accuses her of condemning him to remain on the other side (Gross 1991, 84):

> 'Þur3 drwry deth boz vch man dreue,
> Er ouer þys dam hym Dry3tyn deme.'
>
> 'Demez þou me,' quoþ I, 'my swete,
> To dol agayn? Þenne I dowyne.'   (323–26)

In the vision, she is said to be beyond the power of earthly makers such as

Pygmalion (745–55). The Maiden is now a *domna*, a stock figure of courtly lyric, the lady of higher social rank and stronger will than the poet-lover, and who is accorded masculine gender (Kay 1990, 84–131). Being more powerful and active than the Dreamer, she occupies the 'masculine' position, while he plays the 'feminine' role of passivity and submission. This gender-reversal is an entirely standard part of *fin'amors*; and in *Pearl*, it does not substantially change the nature of the Dreamer's desire for the Maiden. At most, it may confirm the perversity of that desire: the 'feminine' man may attract disapproval here, as in *Cleanness*. The etiology of the Dreamer's feminization is, however, quite different from that in Sodom: there, men were feminized by becoming objects of homosexual desire, while here, a man is feminized by the subjective experience of heterosexual desire. Barthes (1979, 14) phrased the principle: 'a man is feminized not because he is inverted but because he is in love'. *Fin'amors* with this gender configuration is associated with the Dreamer's desire for the Maiden as heavenly queen, and therefore as a creature who belongs to a different category of being: that is, it is identified with the overly exogamous side of his desire.

Instead of all-human heterosexuality being opposed to extreme endogamy and exogamy as in *Cleanness*, then, in *Pearl* it is divided into two forms, each of which is identified with one of the openly transgressive modes. The inversion which *Pearl* operates on *Cleanness* is radical. It is not just that, in directing this sort of desire towards the Maiden, the Dreamer shows the same failure of perception as the men of Sodom manifested with regard to the angels. The sexual mode which in *Cleanness* occupied the ideal ground is itself discredited.

There is, nevertheless, a representation of ideal sexuality in *Pearl*: it is the desire directed towards the Lamb at the end of the poem, and which unites Maiden and Dreamer. It is noticeable that this desire is presented as ambiguous: it oscillates between 'normative' and 'transgressive' forms. On the one hand, it is represented as a marriage, an image which recalls institutional heterosexuality and gender hierarchy. On the other, the creature at its centre is the Lamb: at once a heavenly creature and an animal, above and below the human, and therefore doubly exogamous. With the vision of the New Jerusalem, *Pearl* moves into mysticism: a genre in which normative, bridal and conjugal imagery is commonly combined with polymorphous sexuality and fluid gender. This combination becomes ideal – so long as the object of desire is Christ. Lochrie (1991, esp. 38–47) shows how the desire for redemption in late medieval mysticism is expressed as an erotic focus on the fissured and fragmented body of Christ, and particularly on the bleeding wound in his side (an addition made by the *Pearl*-poet to the Apocalypse texts that formed his main source: Field 1986, 11–14). This wound, as Bynum (1982; 1991, 151–79) demonstrates, was considered to add to Christ's body an element of feminine gender: it is, therefore, the precise site of this ambiguous bigendering or crossgendering which becomes the locus of redemption. It is important to realize that the elevation of 'unclean' sexuality and gender-configurations in mysticism does not mean that they cease to be considered transgressive; rather, it is that impurity becomes the royal road to holiness. Lochrie sums up this paradoxical mechanism succinctly: mysticism 'introduces fissures as tokens of perfection and defilement as its means' (1991, 41). Mystical glorying in transgression and impurity, sexual and otherwise, is found over and over in medieval writings. (According to Kristeva (1982, esp. 90–132), its principal theorist, this glorying in what she calls 'abjection' is a distinguishing characteristic of Christianity as opposed to Judaism, a distinction perhaps relevant to the contrast between *Cleanness* and *Pearl*). The Dreamer's much-derided attempt to cross the river can be seen in the light of Lochrie's description of the mystic's actions: 'through excess of desire, the transgression which leads to knowledge and union is produced, but it requires defilement and risks culture' (1991, 41). In this context, although his act may remain a failure, it is not just a failure. His refusal to respect the boundary which separates him from the Maiden, far from being a result of perverse misinterpretation (analogous to the sin of Sodom), becomes a sign of his salvation. He takes the risk that every mystic takes. His immersion in the river testifies to that desire for fusion with the divine which characterizes visionaries such as Julian of Norwich. Similarly, his desire for his child-bride, precisely because of its transgressive nature, becomes the symbol of his desire for the sacred (on child-brides in mysticism, see Bynum 1991, 151, 165). Those things normatively considered to be transgressive remain so: but this transgression, in leading the visionary beyond the confines of the world below, becomes the means and the sign of transcendence, and therefore of access to the divine.

In both *Pearl* and *Cleanness*, the divine view of gender and sexuality must prevail. The models themselves are, however, quite different. Whereas *Cleanness* takes seriously the obligations of the literary homily genre to enforce compulsory heterosexuality through a discourse of the 'natural', *Pearl* cleaves to mysticism, and thus portrays the divine order as one of fluid, ambiguous gender and undecidable sexuality. It is an order which would be anathema to *Cleanness*.

Sir Gawain and the Green Knight

In *Gawain*, the basic framework worked out in *Cleanness* is complicated by a new sort of sexual transgression, one absent from the other two poems. The presence of adultery alters the value of the other terms in the sexual taxonomy.

When the Green Knight reveals Morgan le Faye's plot to Gawain, the hero reacts violently:

> 'Corsed worth cowarddyse and couetyse boþe!
> In yow is vylany and vyse þat vertue disstryez. [. . .]

For care of þy knokke cowardyse me taȝt
To acorde me with couetyse, my kynde to forsake,
Þat is larges and lewté þat longez to knyȝtez.'

(2375–76, 2379–81)

This self-accusation, and particularly the allegation of covetousness, has puzzled critics. It is at least possible, however, that Gawain is here arraigning himself for a sexual sin. The second of the three meanings given in the *MED* for *coveitise* is 'strong sexual desire; concupiscence, lust'.[7] It may be a surprise to learn that the hero thinks that he has committed such a transgression when, in a poem pervaded with sexuality, he has tried so hard to keep himself pure. Where and how has the transgression occurred? The framework established in *Cleanness* provides one way of approaching this question in *Gawain*.

In *Cleanness*'s terms, the most obvious example of a transgressive sexual act occurs when Gawain kisses Bertilak:

He metez me þis godmon inmyddez þe flore,
And al with gomen he hym gret, and goudly he sayde,
'I schal fylle vpon fyrst oure forwardez nouþe,
Þat we spedly han spoken, þer spared watz no drynk.'
Þen acoles he þe knyȝt and kysses hym þryes,
As sauerly and sadly as he hem sette couþe. (1932–37)

In kissing Bertilak, Gawain mimics the Lady, reproducing the style of her kisses to him. This scene thus shows precisely the same definition of male homosexuality as was found in *Cleanness*: it involves a change of gender, in which an anatomical man is regendered as sexually feminine. Gawain's kisses are, then, extremely endogamous; in *Cleanness*, they would be transgressive.

A key to the value of this extreme endogamy in *Gawain* is found in the paired sexual form which inevitably accompanies it. Extreme exogamy is less evident in this than in the other two poems. Here, it consists in Gawain's relation to the Virgin Mary. The Virgin, a being of an altogether different order from Gawain, plays the part of his courtly lady. It is her image that he bears on the inside of his shield, where the sight of her revives his courage, should it flag (648–50): a role conventionally given to the knight's secular lady (Hanning describes this as the 'chivalry topos' (1977, esp. 54–60)). It is said that Gawain is the Virgin's own knight (1769). She is invoked to protect him from the Lady's blandishments: the potential sexual relationship with the

---

7 Two interesting examples are given from the earlier version of the Wyclifite Bible, c.1384. Eph 4.19: 'Thei bitoken hem wilf to vnchastite, in to worchinge of al vnclennesse in coueityse [L. *avaritiam*]'. Dan 13.8: 'Susanne . . . walkide in the gardyne . . . And the eldre men . . . brennyden in the coueitise [L. *concupiscentiam*] of hir eius'. Johnson (1984, 120) further notes Augustine's argument that 'what appears as simple lust may be more complex and have avarice as its primary impetus.'

Lady and the more abstract one with the Virgin are thus put forward as
alternatives. In every way, the Virgin replaces the flesh and blood lady who
is the typical romance knight's inspiration; the relationship with her is
carefully constructed as a parallel to the usual sexual love. The Virgin belongs,
however, to a different ontological order, and Gawain's 'sexual' relationship
with her therefore echoes the transgressively exogamous desire of the *Pearl*
Dreamer for the Maiden, or of the men of Sodom for the angels.[8]

Gawain's acts, then, fit clearly into the structure of transgressive sexual
relationships as they are delineated in *Cleanness*. There is in this poem,
however, a complicating factor present in neither of the others: all-human
heterosexuality, insofar as it is available to Gawain, is identified with adultery,
itself a sexual sin. The 'normative' form of sexuality is thus rendered illicit.[9]

The Lady of Hautdesert represents the principal focus of human heterosexuality in the poem. It is her beauty that inspires in Gawain the only
explicitly erotic feelings he is given in the poem. He responds to her on their
first meeting; but on her final visit to his bedside, this desire comes near to
overwhelming his resistance:

> He se3 her so glorious and gayly atyred,
> So fautles of hir fetures and of so fyne hewes,
> Wi3t wallande joye warmed his hert. (1760–62)

The only object which the poem offers Gawain that is consistent with the
normative form of all-human heterosexual desire makes such desire adulterous.[10] In his efforts to evade this adultery, the most ingenious strategies are
his 'transgressive' sexual acts. His attachment to the Virgin Mary is set up as
a protection against adultery. Indeed, it is the knight's last bastion of defence:

> Gret perile bitwene hem stod,
> Nif Maré of hir kny3t mynne. (1768–69)

In Gawain's moment of greatest danger, Mary is invoked to prevent his
seduction. Gawain's courtly relation to the Virgin is thus part of his armour
against adultery. The same is true of his relation with Bertilak. The feminine
style Gawain adopts when kissing the lord has a significance beyond mere
mockery. In his mimicry of the Lady, Gawain is not just playing any woman,

---

8   This is not, of course, to argue that courtly desires addressed to the Virgin are invariably
    transgressive in medieval literature. On the contrary, they are often ideal.
9   There was in *Cleanness* a suggestion that not all forms of all-human heterosexuality were
    licit: in his speech to Abraham, God qualifies the 'kynde crafte', stating that its pleasures
    must be enjoyed within marriage and in secret. These opinions, like many of the *Gawain*-
    poet's ideas about proper and improper sexuality, owe much to Augustine. For
    Augustine's opinion that marriage 'made something good out of the evil of sex', and for
    his strictures about privacy, see Brundage 1987, 89, 81, respectively.
10 Critics have argued that the aim of the poem itself is to contain the sexuality of its other
    women, Gwenore and Morgan la Faye: Fisher 1989; Kamps 1989.

he is playing this woman: he is actually masquerading as the Lady. By thus taking on her persona, Gawain is enabled to redirect her adulterous kisses towards their proper owner, her husband. Gawain's extreme endogamy, like his extreme exogamy, is thus performed with the aim of avoiding the sin of adultery. Paradoxically, he employs these supposedly transgressive forms as a means of enforcing marital fidelity, an idealized version of all-human heterosexuality.

The paradox is less striking from Gawain's own point of view, since he himself sees no transgression in extreme endogamy and exogamy. Apart from their correction of the Lady's desire, Gawain's extremely endogamous kisses also have a further significance: in his own person, Gawain kisses Bertilak to express his preference for the lord over the Lady. Although he chooses an erotic format, the preference Gawain here intends to express is not, I would argue, a homosexual one. It is, rather, 'homosocial': a term which designates 'social bonds between persons of the same sex' (Sedgwick 1985, 1).[11] In Gawain's case, he wishes to show Bertilak that he feels greater allegiance to such homosocial bonds than to heterosexual ones; in practice, that his sexual desire for the Lady will not cause him to commit adultery, because another man – her husband – would be harmed thereby. In the process of establishing this inter-male solidarity, Gawain ironically shows a disregard for gender, feminizing himself by his mimicry of the Lady. The emphasis for Gawain here, then, is less on the distinction between the 'homo' and the 'hetero' – less on gender – than on the opposition between the 'social' and the 'sexual'. He does not see his kisses to Bertilak as representing any sort of sexuality, much less a transgressive one. This can only work because nothing of his feelings for Bertilak appears to Gawain to constitute sexual desire. The only sexual transgression Gawain recognizes – adultery – falls within the realm of all-human heterosexuality, because this is the only form of 'sexuality' that he recognizes as such.[12] Not only does Gawain acknowledge no transgression in extreme endogamy and exogamy: he believes that, precisely because of

11 Sedgwick emphasizes that the expression in erotic terms of affection between men may not 'mean' genital homosexual desire, but may rather constitute a declaration of homosocial bonding in a way considered to be elegant and sophisticated. Such expressions may therefore coexist with violent anti-gay prejudice. Sedgwick's exemplary reading (1985, 28–48) of Shakespeare's Sonnets shows how these early modern English texts combine an insistence on the value of institutionalized heterosexuality (the exhortations to the Friend to marry) with the homoerotic expression of affection and desire between men; an affection which may or may not include genital sexual activity, but, on the Poet's part at least, certainly expresses greater allegiance to the Friend than to the Dark Lady.

12 I am not here disagreeing with Heng (1991, 1992), who argues that the *luf-talkyng* between hero and Lady itself constitutes a seduction. The poem is pervaded with eroticism: but Gawain himself has an extremely reductive definition of sexuality, which leads him to discount the vast majority of the desires circulating in the text. Sedgwick comments on the variability even within a single culture of 'what *counts* as sexuality' (1985, 2). For an incisive commentary on modern constructions and their politics, see Weeks 1985, 3–14.

their absolute opposition to all-human heterosexuality, practising these forms will protect him from adultery, and therefore from sexual sin.

Gawain, then, keeps his *cortaysye clane* by refusing altogether to take part in heterosexuality. He supports it for others: there is never any suggestion that Bertilak should give up his would-be unfaithful wife. This form of sexuality, then, retains its normative status. Gawain tries to regulate human heterosexuality: to make it conform to the highest state of which it is capable. At the same time, he himself aspires to the spiritually still higher state of celibacy: which is signified by extreme endogamy and exogamy, since for Gawain these relations are non-sexual, and indeed represent the abjuration of sexual activity altogether. Gawain pursues an ideal of asexual chivalry, similar to that found in the *Queste del Saint Graal* and Malory's *Sankgreal*. There is in *Gawain*, then, an inversion of the order of *Cleanness* not dissimilar to that with which *Pearl* ends up: all-human heterosexuality is felt to be inappropriate to the protagonist's situation, while the ideal and the sacred are aligned with extremely endogamous and exogamous forms. The situation is, nevertheless, quite different: whereas in *Pearl*, the overly endogamous and exogamous modes retained their value of transgression even as they became sacred, in *Gawain*, the hero sees no sexuality, and therefore no transgression in these modes.

It would appear, then, that extreme endogamy and exogamy are not the sexual sins of which Gawain accuses himself at the Green Chapel. On the contrary, he adopts these forms precisely as protection against the only sexual transgression he recognizes, which is adultery. And yet it seems that they fail to safeguard his chastity. The sin of which Gawain ultimately arraigns himself is an all-human, heterosexual one:

> 'And comaundez me to þat cortays, your comlych fere,
> Boþe þat on and þat oþer, myn honoured ladyez,
> Þat þus hor knyȝt wyth hor kest han koyntly bigyled.
> Bot hit is no ferly thaȝ a fole madde,
> And þurȝ wyles of wymmen be wonen to sorȝe,
> For so watz Adam in erde with one bigyled,
> And Salamon with fele sere, and Samson eftsonez –
> Dalyda dalt hym hys wyrde – and Dauyth þerafter
> Watz blended with Barsabe, þat much bale þoled.
> Now þese were wrathed wyth her wyles, hit were a wynne huge
> To luf hom wel, and leue hem not, a leude þat couþe.
> For þes wer forne þe freest, þat folȝed alle þe sele
> Excellently of alle þyse oþer, vnder heuenryche þat mused;
> And alle þay were biwyled
> With wymmen þat þay vsed.
> Þaȝ I be now bigyled,
> Me þink me burde be excused'.   (2411–28)

Gawain's error, like those of the paragons he lists, has lain in the *use* of women: the term denotes sexual intercourse (see e.g. *Cleanness*, 267, quoted above). He sees his relation with the Lady as no different from that of David with Bathsheba, or of Samson with Delilah. It appears that all his precautions have been useless. His careful avoidance of sleeping with, or even admitting to, desire for the Lady gains him nothing. His devotion, expressed as extreme exogamy, to the Virgin Mary does not preserve him. Similarly, his preference for Bertilak over the Lady, a preference manifested as extreme endogamy, fails to guarantee his purity.

Where and when, though, has the sin taken place? The Green Knight claims (and Gawain accepts) that his failure centrally involves the last day of the exchange of winnings contract. Certainly, there is evidence here to support Gawain's own theory that he has been seduced by the Lady. His concealment of the girdle from Bertilak can be read as an adulterous act. The fact that, as the Green Knight says, he does not conceal it for *wowyng* (2367), as a sign of his own lust for the Lady, is important; nevertheless, Gawain's are not the only intentions in question. Because he has taken it upon himself to correct the Lady's adulterous sexuality in his own person by returning to her husband the kisses wrongly alienated, he should obviously do the same with the green girdle which he believes she gave him as a love-token (a name it retains in the rest of the poem: e.g. 1874, 2033, 2438). By concealing a gift that, in his eyes, is a sign of her adulterous passion, he is effectively aiding and abetting her supposed infidelity.

Is this, then, Gawain's sexual sin? It is striking that, in his vituperative diatribe, there is no mention of adultery, and that not all the examples of fallen men cited are adulterers. Gawain seems to see his failure as due, not specifically to adultery, but generally to a masculine brand of all-human heterosexuality. More noticeable still, although it is cited as the cause of sin, this sexuality also becomes the source of pardon: Gawain's similarity to the heroes of concupiscence is given as a reason for him to be excused. A single cause is identified by the knight for his downfall: women. According to his diatribe, it is not so much masculine sexuality which is at fault, as the female sex. Although this is its strongest formulation in the poem, this attitude can be seen to underlie the hero's behaviour earlier in the poem, particularly in the bedroom scenes. Gawain's typical strategy in evading the Lady's adulterous propositions is to ascribe all the desire in the situation to her:

> 'Bot to take þe toruayle to myself to trwluf expoun,
> And towche þe temez of tyxt and talez of armez
> To yow þat, I wot wel, weldez more sly3t
> Of þat art, bi þe half, or a hundreth of seche
> As I am, oþer euer schal, in erde þer I leue,
> Hit were a folé felefolde, my fre, by my trawþe.' (1540–45)

The aggressive implication is that what is in question here is not theoretical knowledge of the art of love, but actual experience of desire: Gawain is effectively ascribing to the Lady far more sexual desire than he himself feels. He thus echoes the common medieval view of women as creatures of excessive sexual desire.[13] In this context, the Lady's forward sexuality in the bedroom scenes, while at one level it genders her as masculine, is simultaneously the sign of excessive femininity (Heng 1992 argues for the same gender combination; for other 'wooing women' in romances, see Weiss 1991). In his misogynistic diatribe, then, Gawain reaffirms views which he has evidently held throughout the poem: that women are deceptive, and that their effect on the men they seduce is invariably morally, spiritually and practically detrimental. The hero sees sexuality as the source and root of all sin, and women as the source and root of all sexuality. Extreme endogamy and exogamy thus appear asexual to the hero because they represent a mode of desire untainted by feminine sexuality. Bertilak as a man and the Virgin Mary as a woman devoid of sexuality are, for Gawain, the ideal objects of desire. The opposition between extreme endogamy and exogamy on the one hand and all-human heterosexuality on the other means that these two figures jointly represent the abjuration of relations with sexual women. Hence, to cleave to them is to avoid sin. And yet, at the end of the poem this scheme has not worked. Gawain has apparently sinned, somehow, somewhere. He himself can only perceive this sin as a sexual relationship – which, in his definition, means an all-human, heterosexual relationship. Sin, for Gawain, is exclusively the result of contact with a sexual woman, and the inevitable consequence of such contact: 'to luf hom wel and leve hem not' is, as he says, not a feasible option.

Gawain himself, then, never sees that there might have been any problem with his adoption of extremely endogamous and exogamous modes: that they might have spilled over into sexual sin. Nevertheless, there is a reading in which his extreme endogamy, at least, contributes to his sin. On the last day of the exchange of winnings, it is noticeable that Gawain exerts himself to make the delivery of the kisses particularly seductive (1932–37, quoted above). On this last day, the kisses become a blind, intended to distract Bertilak from seeking for any further gifts. In his misogynistic diatribe, Gawain describes deceit as the result of sexual relations; from this point of view, he himself 'seduces' the lord with his final set of kisses. The kisses that Gawain delivers up to Bertilak, kisses that he believes to be pure because extremely endogamous, thus become the symbols of his own deception of the lord.

When he conceals the girdle, Gawain conspires in the betrayal of the lord; when he kisses him, he himself deceives him. Previous to this act, *Gawain*

---

[13] It is, nevertheless, clear that Gawain does feel desire for the Lady: the 'wi3t wallande joye' described at 1762. Ferrante (1975, 2) describes the mechanism in action here perfectly: 'Woman, as the most obvious object of male concupiscence, is made to represent lust and thus is held responsible for it; the object of temptation becomes the cause.'

inverts *Cleanness*'s values in such a way that normative sexuality, identified with adultery, becomes transgressive, while extreme endogamy and exogamy become the marks of an ideal (a)sexuality. Due to Gawain's behaviour in the last exchange, however, this new hierarchy is no longer tenable: the forms of ideal sexuality cease to be separable from those of sexual transgression. It appears that the hero's belief in the wholesale asexuality – the *clannes* – of extremely endogamous and exogamous forms is not only reductive but inaccurate; Gawain ignores the existence of polymorphous sexuality at his peril. *Gawain* thus endorses the powerful, apparently inevitable association of extreme endogamy and exogamy with transgression found in the other two poems. There are links with genre here: romances, although they enjoy gender and sexual play, typically end up enforcing heterosexuality as an ideal. It may be that the Lady's definition of chivalry as properly rooted in all-human heterosexual desire (1512–27) is the one the audience is supposed to accept as 'correct': such sexuality, after all, does not have to be adulterous, whatever Gawain thinks.

In three of the Cotton Nero poems, then, sexual transgression and inappropriate gender are important themes, causing major concern both to the characters and to the poet. The definition of transgression can in each case be analysed in terms of the categories of 'too-similar' and 'too-different', with their correlative designation of forms of sexuality as extremely endogamous or exogamous; these two forms of transgressive sexuality are generally associated. Despite these basic similarities, however, the value given to any one sexual act or gender configuration, varies across the three poems. *Cleanness* is relatively straightforward in its espousal of normative, all-human heterosexuality and the sex-gender continuum. *Pearl* is more complex, relying on a paradox by which sexual and gender transgression ultimately become the mark of the sacred. *Gawain*, more convoluted still, leaves us in doubt about which of two interpretations we are to consider superior. The hero can be seen as a paragon of (a)sexual virtue, whose perceptions are mistaken only when he believes himself to have sinned; alternatively, the romance can be read as a ringing endorsement of all-human heterosexuality, in which Gawain's paranoid gynophobia causes him to conflate this perfectly acceptable, indeed ideal sexual form with the undoubted sin which is adultery.

4

The Historical Background

MICHAEL J. BENNETT

A scene in the mid-1380s. Geoffrey Chaucer found himself in Friday Street, to the west of St Paul's, in London. It was a busy street, whose inns and lodging-houses were much favoured by out-of-town nobles and their retinues. Chaucer noticed the arms on a shield hanging outside an inn, and thought they indicated the presence in London of Sir Richard Scrope, a Yorkshire knight, but a man of note in the realm at large. To Chaucer's surprise, the shield belonged not to Scrope but to a Cheshire knight, Sir Robert Grosvenor. Chaucer had never heard of him, or of his claim to bear the Scrope arms, until that time, and he testified to this effect in October 1386 in the court of chivalry. Nonetheless Grosvenor was a man of some standing. He had served in a number of royal expeditions, and in 1389 he was appointed sheriff of Cheshire. While the evidence in the court of chivalry was presented in French, Grosvenor may not have been entirely at home in the language, and the substance of the final award was presented to him in his 'mother tongue' (*Calendar of Close Rolls 1389–1392*, 392). Grosvenor almost certainly sought Scrope's pardon in the dialect of the *Gawain*-poet.

To present the historical background to *Sir Gawain and the Green Knight* and associated poems implies a quest, however vain in the ultimate sense, for the anonymous poet himself. Narrowing the focus to manageable proportions involves making assumptions. The dating is most problematic. The works may have been written as early as the 1360s or as late as the manuscript itself, around 1400. Still, it is a fair assumption that the *Gawain*-poet was alive in the middle of this period, say the mid-1370s to mid-1380s. Happily, there is a firm consensus that the dialect of both the scribe and the author of the poems of MS Cotton Nero A.x is north-west Midlands, the dialect region centring very much on Cheshire. It is not only the dialect that localises the poem. The quest for the Green Chapel brings Sir Gawain into Cheshire from Wales, and then across the county to the forested ridges that form its eastern boundary. The *Gawain*-poet knows this countryside well. In his description he uses dialect words which have left their mark on the local toponymy. It is in this district that Sir Gawain finds not only the Green Chapel, a strange crevice in the rock, but also the castle of Sir Bertilak de Hautdesert.

Sir Robert Grosvenor is an appropriate reference-point in an investigation
of the world of the *Gawain*-poet. They were almost certainly contemporaries
and compatriots. Grosvenor's manor-house at Hulme lay only a few miles to
the north of the area pin-pointed by dialectologists, and very much on the
road between Chester and the uplands associated with the Green Chapel.
Indeed Grosvenor was one of the hereditary foresters of Delamere,[1] a forest
which Sir Gawain might be imagined traversing in the final stages of his
quest. More significant in respect of Grosvenor's value as reference-point is
his pivotal position in county life at this time. If the *Gawain*-poet was a local
man active in the late fourteenth century, Grosvenor would assuredly have
known him. In any event the evidence presented on Grosvenor's behalf in
the heraldic dispute helps elucidate the world of manor-house and monastery in late fourteenth-century Cheshire. It also points to a wider world of
military service, careerism and courtly connection which is hard to ignore in
any assessment of the social and cultural context of the finest works of the
alliterative revival in the north-west Midlands.

I

The north-west Midlands form a fairly identifiable region.[2] Comprising
Cheshire, south Lancashire, and adjacent parts of Staffordshire and Derbyshire, it was a region of relatively late settlement. The Romans had built forts
at Chester and Manchester, cut roads across the Pennines to York, valued the
salt-springs of Cheshire and the lead-mines of the Peak District. Likewise the
Angles had settled in the more fertile valleys, and brought the heavy soils
under the plough. Still, at the time of Domesday Book the region was
relatively poor, of dispersed settlement, and with large areas still under forest
jurisdiction, if not actual forest cover. Low population density and economic
marginality are attested by a distinct lack of institutional development. Apart
from the city of Chester, there were no urban centres of any real significance.
The point can be made most forcefully in respect of ecclesiastical geography.
Chester itself was a city without a cathedral and a bishop, but quite a number
of the second-order towns, like Nantwich, Macclesfield and Liverpool, lacked
even a parish church. The region boasted some of the largest parishes in the
country, and indeed some of the remotest chapelries. Monasteries were
likewise few and far between. The only Benedictine house of old foundation
was St Werburgh's in Chester. The new orders made some headway in the
twelfth and early thirteenth centuries, but the early histories of Dieulacres (in
north-west Staffordshire) and Whalley (in south Lancashire) were very

---

[1] It is noteworthy that a later version of the story of *Sir Gawain and the Green Knight* has King
Arthur holding court at 'Flatting castle' in Delamere forest in Cheshire (Hales and
Furnivall 1868, II, 61).
[2] The following discussion is more fully documented in Bennett 1983.

chequered. Edward I clearly felt he was filling a gap when he founded Vale Royal in 1277. The last Benedictine house established in pre-Reformation England was Upholland Priory founded by Sir Robert Holland in 1318.

At the time of the Domesday Book and for two hundred years thereafter, Cheshire and environs were a frontier zone, economically, politically and culturally. It took the demographic and economic expansion of the thirteenth century and Edward I's conquest of Wales to begin the process of transforming and more fully assimilating the region with the rest of lowland England. Even so its distinctiveness within the larger realm continued. The region continued to have a reputation, as befitted a frontier, for turbulence. Raiding across the Welsh border, alongside a life-style which blended pastoral farming and forest clearance with the more settled agricultural pursuits, made the region one where military accomplishments were prized and habits of violence tolerated. To compound the tendency, the region was looked to as a recruiting-ground in the conquest and settlement of Wales, in the Irish colony and, later, in the Hundred Years War. The impact of the Black Death and the economic crisis of the late fourteenth century further constrained the region's cultural development. The monasteries were hit especially hard. Edward I's grand scheme would have given Vale Royal the largest conventual church in England, but it was never fully realised. In the century after the Black Death it was continuously in debt or under caretaker management.

The distinctive character of the region was accentuated by other factors, not least the pattern of feudal geography. The earldom of Chester had palatinate status. Originating as a marcher lordship, whose lords had been granted or usurped quasi-regal powers, it had passed to the crown, and was held either by the king himself or his eldest son. Though somewhat isolated and administratively separate from the rest of the realm, Cheshire ceased to be wholly a backwater in the fourteenth century, but its connections with the royal household, in the short term at least, sharpened rather than dulled its sense of identity. The pattern was replicated, in more modest form, in Lancashire. The lords of Lancaster in the fourteenth century were princes of the blood, and Edward III accorded Lancashire the status of a palatinate in 1351, confirmed in favour of his son John of Gaunt in 1377. In practice during the last years of Richard II's reign, and formally after the accession of Henry of Lancaster in 1399, the whole region constituted a bastion of royal power.

It was a fact of some significance, too, that the lords of Chester and Lancaster were not resident in the region. Their overarching territorial power, which in the case of the lords of Lancaster extended to include the barony of Halton in Cheshire and the lordship of High Peak in Derbyshire, left little head room for the development of a resident nobility. Apart from a few minor baronial families in adjacent areas of Staffordshire and Shropshire, like the Audleys and the Stranges, and apart from the noble lineages who held lordships in the Welsh marches, the north-west Midlands was wholly lacking an aristocratic presence. In terms of landholding within the region, there was a further retreat of aristocratic influence in the late fourteenth century. Non-resident nobles increasingly sold off their property interests in the region to local men who were better-placed to realise their value. The Stanleys of Lathom were the chief beneficiaries of this trend, laying the foundations for their growing hegemony and for their elevation to the peerage in 1455, when the region acquired for the first time a resident noble lineage.

In the meantime knightly and gentry oligarchies dominated the life of the region. In his heraldic dispute with Sir Richard Scrope, Sir Robert Grosvenor was wholly out-classed by his Yorkshire rival in the witnesses he was able to muster. In an impressive show of solidarity in the north-west Midlands, gentlemen and clerics from both sides of the Mersey testified on Grosvenor's behalf, but there was not a single nobleman willing to speak for him in any of the sessions held across the kingdom. Still, the depositions made by men of the region furnish useful insights into local gentry culture. Physical evidence regarding the Grosvenors' use of the disputed arms was not wholly lacking. There were the arms on a cross on the grave of Grosvenor's father at Nether Peover, the coat-armour of his grandfather, who died 'before the great pestilence', hanging over his tomb at Great Budworth church, and the arms painted on an altar-piece in Grey Friars, Chester, where his great-grandfather was buried. There were depictions in stone or glass at St Werburgh's abbey, Combermere abbey, Vale Royal abbey, Norton priory, and other churches and chapels. Still, the only secular buildings where the arms were said to be depicted were the hall and the chambers of Sir Thomas Dutton's seat at Dutton, and the halls of William Praers of Baddiley and John Donne of Utkinton (Nicolas 1832). Interestingly, there is no mention at all of written records, books of hours, heraldic texts or literary works. The impression is that the local gentry culture was predominantly visual and oral, and lacking in solidity and depth.

What appears in profuse detail is the record of service of the Cheshire and Lancashire gentry in the wars of the fourteenth century, and the whole episode is testimony to the importance of soldiering abroad in the region's emerging self-awareness. Sir Robert Grosvenor was very much representative of the local gentry class in his military record. In his youth he had accompanied his father-in-law Sir John Danyers in Edward III's last expedition to France in 1359–60. In the late 1360s he served under Sir James Audley, a lieutenant of the Black Prince, in the remarkable chevauchée which cut through northern France, and crossed the Loire to join the defence of Guyenne. In 1372 he mustered at Sandwich for Edward III's last expedition to France, and in 1385 served in Richard II's invasion of Scotland. Even so, Grosvenor cannot be regarded as a career-soldier. Among the men who testified on his behalf was Sir Hugh Calveley, then living in well-earned retirement in his native Cheshire. This doyen of chivalry began his career in France in the 1340s, and was merely the most celebrated and successful of many local knights and archers who pursued the profession of arms. Soldiers of his generation established their careers in the French wars prior to 1360, served in the 'free companies' in wars in Italy and Spain in the 1360s and 1370s, and continued on as commanders and garrison-captains through to the late 1380s. While a number appear largely to have severed their ties with the region, the majority retained their links with home, recruiting local men in times of war and, if they were fortunate, buying up land in times of peace.

The clerks who testified on Grosvenor's behalf were for the most part men of local consequence, but it must not be thought that the north-west Midlands was at this time noted only for its brawn. A group of clerks from the region had established successful careers at Westminster as early as the 1340s. John Winwick was keeper of the privy seal and acting chancellor of the realm in 1360. Thomas Thelwall was another notable chancery clerk who served for a time as chancellor of the duke of Lancaster. At the time of the Scrope-Grosvenor dispute local clerks were well-positioned in both the royal administration and the church. John Macclesfield was a clerk in the privy seal office. A secretary to Richard II, he was appointed keeper of the wardrobe in 1398. In the late 1380s likewise Thomas Langley, a native of Prestwich near Manchester, was secretary to John of Gaunt, while Robert Hallum, who hailed from near Warrington, was registrar of the archbishop of Canterbury. Langley subsequently became bishop of Durham and served as chancellor to three Lancastrian kings, while Hallum served as chancellor of the university of Oxford and became bishop of Salisbury.

The factors behind the relatively sudden rise of local men to national prominence are manifold. The earliest clerks to establish themselves at Westminster were Lancashire men who had gained experience in the administrative machine of the earls of Lancaster. Once established in office, they took on their kinsmen and compatriots as apprentices, and showed an early interest in the provision of more formal educational opportunities. John Winwick sought to endow a college at Oxford, and younger members of his connection were graduates. By 1400 many local clerks were finding their way to university, and some, like Hallum, achieved high academic distinction. Soldiering, though, clearly acted as a lead sector in the opening up of wider opportunities. The connections between war and business are all too evident. Soldiers needed merchants to advance funds, supply equipment, and launder booty, and it is perhaps not surprising to find kinsmen of notable local captains established in trade in London. Thomas Knolles, mayor of London, was a kinsman of Sir Robert Knolles, and Christopher Tildesley, Richard II's goldsmith, was a scion of a Lancashire family with strong martial traditions. Military commanders likewise needed men with notarial, financial and legal skills. Some notable clerks, like Thomas Langley and Thomas Stanley, may have begun their careers in this fashion. Some soldiers must themselves have been educated as well as resourceful, like Sir David Cradock, a retainer of the Black Prince and later mayor of Bordeaux, or John Norbury, a retainer of Henry of Bolingbroke and later treasurer of the royal household. A few, like

Sir Richard Cradock, courtier, connoisseur of chivalry and ambassador, were clearly men of real cultivation.

The success of local men in the wider realm often led to the purchase of land elsewhere, and formed the basis of Cheshire's reputation in Tudor times as the 'seed-plot of gentility'. In the mean time, though, it had a perceptible impact on regional life. Towards the end of the fourteenth century there are signs of increasing prosperity and some strengthening of the fabric of cultural life among sections of county society. Though most of the manor-houses long remained timber-framed, there is record of a number of halls being rebuilt in stone. William Stanley of Storeton, bailiff of the forest of Wirral until its disafforestation, was using the profits of office to build Storeton hall in stone in the 1370s. In the 1390s Henry Sutton, abbot of St Werburgh's, secured licences to crenellate his manor-houses at Ince and Sutton. In many cases there are clear links between architectural enrichment and the fruits of careerism. A group of churches in south Cheshire seems to have been extended and embellished in the 1380s, apparently from the profits of war. Sir Hugh Calveley's collegiate church at Bunbury is the best documented example. In the 1390s John Macclesfield, Richard II's secretary and privy seal clerk, was building his town-house or castle in stone in Macclesfield. Around the same time Sir John Stanley, a cadet of the Stanleys of Storeton line and a successful career-soldier, set about building the Tower at Liverpool.

II

The land depicted by the *Gawain*-poet in describing his hero's arrival in the Wirral and his journey across Cheshire to seek in the foothills of the Pennines his tryst with the Green Knight is far from the realities of the late fourteenth century. It was no wilderness inhabited by monsters, and while the description of the countryside around the Green Chapel fits the scenery of the Pennine uplands and the Peak District very well, the general point remains that it is essentially an imagined landscape of romance and adventure. While relatively remote and sparsely settled by comparison with the rest of England, it was nevertheless a land of human habitation, studded with villages and manor-houses. At the time of the Black Death forest jurisdiction continued to prevail over half the county, and there may have been some fear that wilderness would re-establish itself. Yet forest clearance continued, and indeed in 1376 Wirral was disafforested. Of course, it may well be that in the imagination of the rest of England it was a pretty wild and rugged place (as indeed it can appear even today to the solitary walker over the hills in winter time), an image intensified by the region's reputation for lawlessness. If so, though, it would seem to be a wry self-reference from a poet and an audience who knew the stereotypes current in the rest of the country.

All the same, the region scarcely seems an auspicious milieu for a strong literary culture. Men of learning were thin on the ground,[3] and there is no clear evidence of any school functioning at this time. A few monasteries represented the only real institutional supports for higher culture. There were no nobles resident in Cheshire or south Lancashire, and while a number of minor lords were based on the fringes of the region they were not of the stature to dispense patronage on any scale. What there were, of course, were scores of manor-houses, some of which doubtless provided centres for the cultural life of their neighbourhoods. What is clear, though, is that the region was undergoing a significant transformation in the late fourteenth century. Soldiering and other forms of careerism were bringing more opportunities and wealth to the region, and at the same time drawing it more into the national mainstream. The paradox is that the conditions for cultural production in the region became more favourable at the time when its regional culture was most under threat. Sir Robert Grosvenor's entanglement with the court of chivalry is symbolic: the local community of honour was being integrated in, and subordinated to, a national one.

The chronology of the 'alliterative revival' cannot be established with any precision. The assumption is that it began in the south-west Midlands, and that it reached its full flowering in the late fourteenth century. In tracing the origins of the alliterative revival in the west Midlands generally, Derek Pearsall (1981) has presented a persuasive case for religious houses as key centres for the transmission and transformation of a regionally based, literary culture. While Cheshire monasteries were not as well-endowed as their counterparts in the south-west Midlands, their libraries would have included the main Latin works used as sources by the alliterative poets. After all, Ranulph Higden, the author of *Polychronicon*, a universal history in Latin, was a monk at St Werburgh's, Chester in the middle decades of the fourteenth century. In any case the north-west Midlands may have been the beneficiary of traditions preserved and developed to the south. There appears to have been a slow retreat northwards of the alliterative long line in the later middle ages, which, though in recession, could stage remarkable revivals, as in late fifteenth-century Scotland.

Needless to say, the major poets did not work in cloistered seclusion. A real strength of the alliterative long line was its capacity to render into formal-sounding English the secular romances traditionally presented to aristocratic audiences in French. What Pearsall regards as especially significant were the links between monasteries and noble lineages, as, for example, between Bordesley abbey and the Beauchamps, earls of Warwick. With respect to Cheshire in the late fourteenth century, of course, the connections were more between monasteries and gentry families, as, perhaps, between Vale Royal

---

3 The poll-tax returns of 1379 indicate that there were, at the most, four graduates resident in Cheshire and south Lancashire at this time (Bennett 1973, 8–9).

and the Grosvenors.[4] Still, the bulk of the work of the alliterative revival fits well enough a pattern of gentry patronage. In this reading, the masters of alliterative verse pursued their calling not in castles but in the manor-houses of knightly families, like the Grosvenors of Hulme, the Stanleys of Storeton, the Mascys of Tatton, and, across the border in Derbyshire, the Vernons of Haddon. Turville-Petre has argued that the audience may well have been even less socially exclusive. He points to the nature of the surviving manuscripts, mostly modest compendia emanating from the households of provincial gentry. With regard to the poems, which imply audiences of lords and ladies, it is argued that such imagined audiences are after all part of the fiction: 'if in reality they are gouty bailiffs . . . it is not the duty of the poet to remind them of it' (Turville-Petre 1977, 38).

It is likely enough that the audience of even the finest works of the alliterative revival included people who were not lords and ladies. Indeed there were many armigerous families in Cheshire and Lancashire who in terms of wealth and culture would scarcely be regarded as 'gentle' at all in other parts of the realm. Still, it is salutary to note just how little textual evidence there is for an association between the alliterative revival and a backwoods manor-house culture. About the only poem that testifies to literary activity in the household of a Cheshire gentleman prior to 1400 is some doggerel by Richard Newton (Bennett 1979, 69). Obviously written for merriment, it testifies at least to some awareness of the literary traditions of the time. The statement of the author of the *Destruction of Troy* that it was written at the request of a knight suggests a local manor-house, but until the historical identity of John Clerk of Whalley, the name encoded in the text, can be ascertained, it cannot be assumed that it was wholly a local production. While a number of alliterative poems survive in anthologies of local gentlemen, it is striking that they are compilations of the mid-fifteenth century or later, and even then they are often produced by households with careerist connections, like, for example, the Booths of Dunham Massey. The documented support for alliterative poetry by the local gentry, is in any case scarcely reassuring in terms of quality of the work. The romances relating to Sir Gawain which were happily anthologised by the gentry in Tudor times pale by comparison with *Sir Gawain and the Green Knight*, and it is tempting to infer a decline in the refinement of the audience as well as the capacity of the poet.

Conversely, some of the most ambitious alliterative poems in the north-west Midlands dialect survive in manuscripts with no clear connection with the gentry of the region. The manuscript containing the works of the *Gawain-*

---

[4] One poet from the north-west Midlands who seems to fit the pattern is John Audelay, a chaplain of Lord Strange of Knockin but resident in Haughmond abbey, Shropshire (c.1422). What is interesting, though, is that Audelay had retired to Haughmond after a career in the service of Lord Strange, who was generally based in the Home Counties, and specifically after his involvement with his lord in a notorious act of sacrilege in the parish church of St Dunstan's in the East, London (Bennett 1973).

poet is a case in point, especially since it is earlier than the gentry anthologies and unique in that it includes only alliterative verse, indicating a closeness to the poet himself. Perhaps, as G. Mathew (1968, 116–17) hypothesised, it is a rough copy from a presentation manuscript. At the same time works like *Winner and Waster* and *The Parlement of Thre Ages* survive only in the anthologies produced in other parts of the country, suggesting that appreciation of them was not limited to the region in whose dialect they were written (Lawton 1982b). Given that the horizons of so many men from the north-west Midlands extended far beyond their native heath, it seems a little perverse to be focusing too narrowly on the backwoods gentry, men barely distinguishable in life-style from the 'gouty bailiffs' who ran their estates and wore their livery.

The links between literary activity and increasing mobility are all too evident. Richard Newton, the crude versifier, served in France as an archer, and may in later life have been a member of Richard II's bodyguard: the patron of the *Destruction of Troy* may well have been a prominent local captain. Evidence of experience of the French wars can be inferred in two alliterative poems, albeit from the north Midlands rather than from the north-west Midlands. Thus the anonymous author of the alliterative *Morte Arthure* appears to have had firsthand experience of war and to have reflected deeply on the experience (Barnie 1974, 147–50). His description of the muster and embarkation of Arthur's army at Sandwich brings to mind Edward III's proposed expedition of 1372 which involved Grosvenor and his friends. *The Lament for Sir John Berkeley*, recently brought to light by Turville-Petre, is even more evocative of this world. It concerns a Leicestershire knight, Sir John Berkeley of Wymondham, who took part in a campaign in Brittany, but died on the way home in 1375. Written shortly afterwards by a disconsolate retainer, it is an elegy which praises his magnanimity and generosity, presenting a lively picture of Berkeley's household at Wymondham, where there was always meat and mirth, the dalliance of damsels, and the reading of romance (Turville-Petre 1982, 332–9).

Few works of the alliterative revival are provincial in their outlook. A number of the poems in the north-west Midlands dialect appear to address the concerns of a world opening up through social mobility and careerism. *Winner and Waster* and *The Parlement of Three Ages*, probably written in the decade or so after the Black Death, communicate a sense of traditional values under threat, and a sense of generational change associated with young people leaving the 'west'. *St Erkenwald* refers to 'London, in England', in a curiously distant manner, somewhat at odds with the growing experience of local people with the capital, and indeed the poem, though written in the Cheshire dialect, is set firmly in the metropolis. It is the story of an early bishop of London, the city's patron saint, whose feast-day was fully established in the 1380s. Likewise a number of the alliterative works not only seem to reflect, in their vivid descriptions of combat, fortifications and armour, the military interests of the gentry, but also, in their language and themes, prompt the sort of reflection on war and the chivalric code appropriate to men with real campaign experience. The alliterative *Morte Arthure* was written not so much to provide 'gouty bailiffs' with a taste of martial adventure but to prompt a knightly audience to give thought to the folly as well as the glory of war. *Sir Gawain and the Green Knight* likewise seems concerned to test, in subtle ways, the values of knighthood, not least a knighthood that cares too much for the comforts of court (Scattergood 1981). The whole corpus of MS Cotton Nero A.x represents a sustained engagement with 'courtesy' (Brewer 1966; Nicholls 1985).

Given the themes and concerns of some of the works it is not impossible that they were written outside the north-west Midlands, for an expatriate audience. Social mobility in the later middle ages was not simply a matter of individuals pursuing their fortunes, but of regionally-based networks grouped around the successful careerists and linked, often enough, to some of the greatest patrons in the land. Cheshire and Lancashire soldiers formed the most obvious expatriate group. While the region had no resident noblemen, it certainly had men who lived nobly. Successful soldiers-of-fortune like Calveley and Knolles lived in princely style in France, holding court at various times in castles in Brittany and Guyenne. Their retinues were typically made up of men from their native region, and indeed the Cheshire brogue must have been common in the camps and garrison-towns in Brittany and Guyenne.[5] Likewise with other trades and professions, it is a matter of successful individuals representing much larger networks. Local men who established themselves in trade in London appear to have been closely connected.[6] The local clerks who attained prominence in the Lancastrian and the royal administrations were unashamedly clannish. Even a true churchman like Bishop Hallum of Salisbury staffed his household and colonised the cathedral chapter with clerks from the archdeaconry of Chester.

This wider frame of reference inevitably raises new possibilities with respect to the social and cultural contexts of the finest works of the alliterative revival. It is especially important to acknowledge the manner in which the ambitions and achievements of men from the region broadened and strengthened local links with great magnates and the court, creating niches more aristocratic and courtly than were available in the dialect region itself. In part it was simply a matter of the value of the region as a recruiting-ground in the Hundred Years War. Noblemen valued whatever links they had with local

---

5   Thus in November 1365 Sir Thomas Wettenhall, seneschal of the Rouergue, Sir David Cradock, his lieutenant, and James Mascy, castellan of Millau, entertained Sir Hugh Calveley and his company who passed through Millau en route to Castile: all men from Cheshire (Morgan 1987, 135).

6   Note the group of London merchants, including Hugh Liverpool, mercer, who hailed from the Liverpool area (Bennett 1983, 126, 125n). *Pace* Strohm (1992, 16), 'Hochon' of Liverpool was probably of burgess stock, and was admitted into the mercers' guild by the mid-1390s.

knights and squires who could recruit at short notice companies of proficient archers. Some magnates, like the earls of Salisbury and Arundel, held marcher lordships abutting Cheshire, while others forged connections through office-holding. Even after the scaling-down of the war-effort in the late 1380s, however, there was scarcely a single nobleman of any stature who did not have at least one knight or squire from the region on their pay-roll. Above all, of course, there were the royal lords of Chester and Lancaster. John of Gaunt, duke of Lancaster drew into his service many local men both from Lancashire itself and from his lordships in Cheshire, Staffordshire and Derbyshire. By the same token Edward, the Black Prince, who was earl of Chester until his death in 1376, acted like a magnate in building up his retinue in Cheshire. Between 1377 and 1399, of course, the earldom of Chester was held directly by Richard II. In the late 1380s the young king embarked upon a policy of building up the palatinate as a royalist power-base. It was a policy that was to have a major impact on the lives of many compatriots and contemporaries of the *Gawain*-poet.

III

Traditionally scholars have assumed a courtly context for *Sir Gawain and the Green Knight* and *Pearl*, albeit in the north-west Midlands itself. The two poems are of an entirely different order and tone from most of the works of the alliterative revival. It is not merely a matter of their great technical accomplishment and literary aspiration. It is that the works reveal both a close knowledge of the aristocratic culture of the time, and a deep immersion in the worlds of chivalry and courtesy. The poet is an insider, a courtier's courtier, adding complexity and refinement to issues of faith and honour, and points of ethics and etiquette. Moreover he assumes a courtly audience. In his descriptions of aristocratic and courtly life, he does not seek to impress or presume to educate the people for whom he wrote. Indeed in his account of Gawain's quest he adopts, to a surprising degree, the view-point of the royal court rather than the baronial household. *Pearl* is a work of even greater refinement, a work for reflection and discussion in the chamber rather than the hall. *Sir Gawain and the Green Knight*, too, would have prompted a mixed audience to debate 'in a half-serious mood of chamber casuistry' the nature and degree of Gawain's fault (Burrow 1971, 120). Still, the overwhelming impression is that the latter was a poem to be recited in the great hall for the entertainment and edification of the entire court at a Christmas feast.

J.R. Hulbert's thesis (1931) that the alliterative revival was a magnate-fostered regional riposte to a court-sponsored, metropolitan culture is no longer tenable. Still, the notion that the *Gawain*-poet was attached to a provincial noble household, perhaps like that of Sir Bertilak, remains attractive to a number of critics. There is the well-attested association between

William of Palerne, an early alliterative romance in the dialect of the south-west Midlands, with Humphrey Bohun, earl of Hereford. If the author of this indifferent work enjoyed aristocratic sponsorship, in however an indirect form, it would indeed be odd to deny the possibility with respect to the *Gawain*-poet. This line of thinking led H.L. Savage (1956) to an elaborate theory regarding Enguerrand de Coucy, duke of Bedford, the celebrated French lord whose marriage to Isabella, daughter of Edward III, led to brief but distinguished career in England. In presenting Coucy as a possible patron of *Sir Gawain and the Green Knight*, Savage made a great deal of his holding lands in north Lancashire, his status as a Garter knight, and his role in the founding of the new Order of the Star. While there is no evidence that Coucy ever visited Lancashire or recruited local men into his household, the theory cannot be dismissed entirely. Similar and better arguments, though, could be presented on behalf of most members of the nobility, and indeed of the royal family itself in the late fourteenth century.

A great deal depends on the presumed date of *Sir Gawain and the Green Knight*. A recent assessment of the costume, armour and architecture of the poem makes a date as early as the middle of the fourteenth century seem feasible (Cooke 1989), though perhaps only if the *Gawain*-poet moved in the most fashionable circles. Needless to say, the north-west Midlands in the 1360s was far more insular than it was in the 1380s. Even in the earlier period, though, there were clerks and knights in the retinues of most noblemen, especially the royal lords of Chester and Lancaster. A glance at the sons of Sir Robert Holland (d.1328), lieutenant of Thomas earl of Lancaster, might be instructive. Robert (d.1373), the eldest son, inherited his lands and his claim to the peerage, but his younger brothers, Thomas and Otes, achieved greater distinction, being founder-members of the Order of the Garter. Thomas (d.1360) made the most remarkable match of the age, marrying Joan of Kent, granddaughter of Edward I and future wife of the Black Prince (Holland 1917). While the Holland brothers may have been born in Lancashire, none of them lived there. Still, Robert retained the ancestral Lancashire lands, and Thomas's sons, half-brothers of Richard II, continued to acknowledge a 'cousinage' in the region.

A surprising number of local men can be found in and around the court of Edward III. From the late 1360s, however, the focus shifts very much to the latter's sons, Edward of Woodstock, 'the Black Prince' and earl of Chester, and John of Gaunt, duke of Lancaster. Both princes recruited extensively in the region. After the Black Prince's death in 1376, a number of Cheshire men continued in the service of his widow, Joan of Kent, and indeed of his son, Richard II. But it is the household of John of Gaunt that has seemed to Elizabeth Salter and others the most plausible setting for 'courtly' literature in the north-west Midlands dialect (Salter 1966–7, 1983). He lived in grand, princely style, and his large retinue always included knights and clerks from the region. Yet it should not be assumed that as duke of Lancaster he held court in or especially identified with Lancashire. He was a European prince who spent years on end out of the country. He was a great magnate, heavily involved in affairs of state, with territorial interests stretching from south Wales to north-east England. His main residences were in London, Hertford and Leicester, and visits to Lancashire were rare and brief. His castles in the Midlands gave him some accessibility to men from the north-west. Tutbury Castle, on the border between Staffordshire and Derbyshire, is a natural focus of interest, not least because of traditions regarding a 'court of minstrelsy' and Christmas festivities. Gaunt, though, never spent a Christmas at Tutbury. The closest he came to the north-west Midlands in the festive season was Leicester castle, where he kept Christmas in 1380 and 1385, and in 1397 and 1398 (Goodman 1992).

During the 1380s new players begin to emerge as possible patrons. Richard II was resentful of John of Gaunt's power, and the size of the Lancastrian retinue in the Scottish expedition of 1385 prompted him to look to the military resources of his own palatinate of Chester. The growth of aristocratic opposition to the court likewise underlined the need for an independent power-base. Robert de Vere, duke of Ireland, the king's favourite, led the way in forging links with local soldiers, notably Sir Thomas Molyneux and Sir John Stanley. The king himself spent a fortnight in Cheshire in July 1387, and over the summer De Vere ensconsed himself in Chester Castle. The latter lived in some style, giving the region for a while the feeling of a real court. His fine furniture and tapestries at Chester were inventoried in 1388 (Clarke 1937, 118–19). More notoriously, he set up in his household Agnes Lancecrona, a Bohemian lady-in-waiting of Queen Anne, who had been abducted from Berkhamstead by William Stanley 'of Wirral'. Finally, in November 1387 De Vere and Molyneux led an army from Cheshire against the king's baronial opponents, most notably the duke of Gloucester and the earls of Arundel and Warwick. The Cheshire men were put to flight at Radcot Bridge, De Vere fled overseas, and a fearful retribution was exacted from the court party in the 'Merciless' Parliament of 1388.

The region was now thrown back on its own resources. The king and his court were in eclipse, and in no position to nourish the loyalties of Cheshire. John of Gaunt was overseas, prosecuting his claim to the crown of Castile, and from Spain came reports of heavy casualties among the local men in his company. The costs of Cheshire's involvement in the Radcot Bridge campaign may have been considerable. A decade later Richard II sent 3,000 marks to Chester by way of compensation. In the mean time unprecedented demands for taxation were laid upon the palatinate, and in 1391 there was active resistance to the collection of a subsidy of 1,000 marks. In 1392 Sir Robert Grosvenor stood before the lords in parliament to hear the failure of his appeal against the verdict of the court of chivalry, which had imposed on him ruinous costs and damages of 500 marks. Insisting that 'the highest and most sovereign thing that a knight ought to guard in defence of his estate are his troth and his arms', and that in both of them Grosvenor had impeached him, Scrope required him to make an abject confession and throw himself on his mercy (*Calendar of Close Rolls 1389–1392*, 390–2). To add to the gloom in the region, it was felt that the peace negotiations with France were robbing local soldiers of their livelihood. In 1393 there was a rising in Cheshire against the king's uncles who, it was felt, were responsible for government policy.

Richard II had resumed the reins of power in 1389, but was understandably reluctant to provoke further confrontation. Still, he was able to retain Sir John Stanley, who was well-placed to resurrect the old connection. As justiciar of Ireland from 1389–91, he was at the hub of a network of Cheshire and Lancashire soldiers. In 1393 he was sent from the king's side to negotiate with the rebels, and in the following year he was active in the recruitment of local men to serve in the king's first expedition to Ireland. There were other Cheshire men in the royal service whose careers somewhat transcended factional alignment. Sir Richard Cradock was a knight of the chamber, whose connections with his native shire were probably relatively slight. John Macclesfield, who was to invest the profits of office in his home-town, was a royal clerk of long standing. However, the presence of such men in the king's entourage in the 'golden age' of the Ricardian court is worth noting. Cradock can be found on embassies, transporting the king's jewels, officiating in the court of chivalry. When Froissart presented his love-poems to the king in 1395, it was Cradock who took them for safe-keeping (Johnes 1842, II. 577). Macclesfield, who served for a time as Richard's secretary, was a senior colleague of the poet Thomas Hoccleve in the privy seal office, and owned a collection of biblical and historical works.

The king himself may have given countenance, if not active encouragement, to the production of courtly verse by men from the region. Richard II's role as patron of literature has of late been played down, partly in response to rather naive assumptions about the court and its place in literary history. What is neglected in this line of thinking is the role of the royal court as a general stimulus to cultural activity. The king's visit to Cheshire in 1387, the larger involvement which it symbolised, and the continuing prominence of a number of local men in the royal service into the 1390s, offer possible contexts for the composition of verse which, though in provincial dialect and metre, seems redolent of the royal court. Stylistically *Pearl* would not be out of place in the international gothic culture associated with the court of Richard II from the mid-1380s. The rich description, the allegorical form, and the intricate structure of the *Pearl* correspond to what is known of the king's personal taste, which was for exquisite objects, jewels, and especially, it seems, pearls. Thematically, the poem can perhaps be linked with Queen Anne's death in 1394 and the *consolatio* Richard found in marriage to the eight-year-old French princess, a marriage which was to bring peace, Christian unity and the recovery of Jerusalem (Bowers 1995). The vision is clearly articulated in Philippe de Mézières's *Letter to Richard II*, itself replete with jewel imagery, and is given visual form in the Wilton Diptych (Gordon 1993, 59–60).

Sir Gawain and the Green Knight may likewise be considered, without incongruity, in this setting. The poet's descriptions of court life and chivalric display may not be from personal experience, but, given the presence of Cheshire men at court, it is not unreasonable to suppose that the *Gawain*-poet was a participant-observer. The Smithfield tournament of 1390, when the king first displayed his new white hart badge, and when twenty ladies led the twenty knights of the king's team to the lists by means of golden chains, must have been especially memorable (Lindenbaum 1990, 4). While events of this kind were staged in Edward III's reign, *Sir Gawain and the Green Knight* is more evocative of the court of Richard II than of his grandfather. It was Richard's companions who were branded as knights of Venus rather than Bellona, the bedchamber rather than the battlefield (Riley 1864, 156). Like the world of *Sir Gawain and the Green Knight*, Richard's court was a post-heroic world in which knights, if not a prey to temptation, were in danger of going to seed. The knightly code, once so simple, now seemed infinitely more complex. Of course, there is a more earthy side to *Sir Gawain and the Green Knight*. The challenge of 'nature' to 'nurture' in the poem gives some credence to the idea of a vigorous regionally-based aristocratic court in some sort of opposition to an effete, royal court. This ambivalence, though, can be found in the character of Richard II himself. He has been too readily dismissed as a listless aesthete. At times Richard was extraordinarily energetic, campaigning vigorously in Scotland and Ireland, and willing to commit himself to arduous travel, even in winter. The Westminster chronicle and other sources document a passion for hunting. His favourite companion in the 1390s was his cousin, the duke of Albemarle, another great hunter, who later translated Gaston Phoebus's *Livre de Chasse*, adding to his source English customs relating to great royal hunts (Orme 1992, 136–8).

While Richard II spent most of the early 1390s in palaces and hunting-lodges in the Thames valley, there were signs of growing disaffection with London and the Home Counties. In 1391–2 a major dispute with London led to the movement of government offices to York, submission by the city-fathers at Nottingham, and a triumphal re-entry into London. At the same time there are striking initiatives which attest an interest in the wider realm. The king's expedition to Ireland in 1394–5 is testimony to this new out-reach, and perhaps marked the beginning of a new phase of royalist assertion. On his return, negotiations for his second marriage required his presence in the south, and involved visits to Calais, but he revisited York and spent time at Nottingham. Finally, in the summer of 1397 he ordered the arrest of Gloucester, Arundel and Warwick, and immediately set about raising a large force in Cheshire to support the royalist coup. In the Westminster Parliament the three senior Appellants were condemned as traitors, and the palatinate of Chester was raised to the dignity of a principality. He then left the capital, and spent most of the rest of his reign in the Midlands. He celebrated Christmas and New Year at Lichfield, met parliament at Shrewsbury, visited his new principality, and then embarked on a long tour of the West Midlands. He returned to Cheshire in August, and headed back southwards to Coventry to preside over the judicial duel between Henry of Bolingbroke and Thomas Mowbray, the dukes of Hereford and Norfolk. At the end of the year he followed a similar course, keeping the festive season at Lichfield and visiting his principality in the New Year. Finally he returned south to organise his expedition to Ireland. When he returned to Chester in August 1399 it was as Bolingbroke's prisoner.

The regionalism of Richard II's politics in his last years is very striking. In part it was a negative response to the experiences of the late 1380s, a reaction against London and the rebellious south-east. He claimed not to be safe in the southern half of his kingdom, and recruited a retinue of loyal Cheshire men to protect him. There may have been a positive side as well, an embracing of his kingdom's larger British identity, incorporating both its Anglo-Saxon and its Celtic past. The king's apparent interest in the older regional centres and their cults is striking. In his last years he visited most of the cathedral towns and larger monasteries in the western half of the kingdom, including places with Arthurian associations like Bath, Chester and Cardiff. Since he had visited each of their shrines, it was probably at his instigation that the feast days of St David, St Chad and St Winifred – three 'provincial' saints – were added to the national calendar early in 1398. When the Kenilworth chronicler criticised the king for allowing his guardsmen to address him familiarly in their 'mother tongue', he testified to the fact that the Cheshire dialect was heard in the royal chamber. The lines attributed to them include a reference to the king's local favourite, Peter Legh of Lyme (Clarke 1937, 98):

> Dycun, slep sicur[l]y quile we wake, and dreed nought quile we lyve sestow: ffor zif thow haddest weddet Perkyn douzter of Lye thow mun well halde a love day with any man in Chester schire in ffaith.

From 1397 Richard II retained local men on a massive scale (Davies 1971; Gillespie 1975). He granted annuities to some seventy odd knights and gentlemen from Cheshire, and quite a number more from Lancashire. He retained a bodyguard of several hundred Cheshire archers, and he had at call a much larger force of some two thousand men. It was not an especially selective exercise. Many of the archers were rough-and-ready soldiers, though a fair number were younger sons of gentry families. The knights and squires who received the livery of the white hart, though, were representative of the upper echelons of county society. It is thus possible both to take at face value the hostile comments of contemporary chroniclers that the archers were thugs bent on rapine, and to argue that the king's Cheshire retainers cannot but have included patrons of alliterative verse. All the local families whose names have been associated with the works of MS Cotton Nero A.x figure in the retinue. Members of the Mascy clan, whose surname has been discerned in word-play in *Pearl*, were very much to the fore (Nolan and Farley-Hills 1971; Peterson 1974b, 1977). Richard Vernon, lord of Haddon Hall in the Peak District, was another annuitant. Finally Sir John Stanley, often cited as a possible patron (Mathew 1968, 166; Wilson 1979), was controller of the wardrobe, and probably responsible for the organisation of the retinue.

In his last years Richard had Cheshire men in constant attendance, but it is the times that he spent with them in the north-west Midlands that command most attention. They were the times when the court came to the region, and when courtly poetry in the local dialect must have been the order of the day. Richard found Lichfield a congenial base: the gateway to the north-west Midlands, it was reasonably accessible to the rest of the kingdom. The grand proportions of the bishop's palace made it the perfect backdrop to the display of his regality. His sojourns at Lichfield included the Christmas and New Year of 1397–8 and 1398–9. It was a high honour: the king made a great deal of the entire season.[7] The festivities were magnificent by any standards. The chroniclers refer to daily tournaments and the huge quantities of food consumed (Stow 1977, 151), while financial records document expenditure on lavish gifts and silverware. The guests-of-honour were the papal legate and the son-in-law of the Byzantine Emperor Manuel II, but the Cheshire knights and squires of the livery of the white hart were there in strength. Another attraction of Lichfield was that it gave access to Cannock Chase, and the king must certainly have hunted from the bishop's lodge at Beaudesert. It was situated in high country, hard by an old iron age fortress, a few miles north of Lichfield. The name and the site are evocative of Hautdesert.

There are other links between court life in the late 1390s and *Sir Gawain and Green Knight*. It is odd to find, first of all, the king in locations associated with the poem. After a visit to Cheshire early in 1398, he returned to his principality twice over the summer. He was based several times at Holt Castle, which he developed as his main treasure-house. From this castle on the Dee, he travelled westwards as far as Flint and eastwards as far as Macclesfield, on the edge of the Peak District. He and his party knew, then, both the cross-over from Wales into Wirral, and the forests and fast-flowing streams of the Peak District. At Macclesfield he was entertained by Peter Legh of Lyme and John Macclesfield, his clerk, and served trout caught in a Pennine stream. A visit to Flint probably involved a pilgrimage to the Holy Well of St Winifred, whose cult was at this stage being actively promoted. The Anglo-Saxon virgin and martyr, of course, had been decapitated, and her head miraculously restored.

There was another story about an amputated head newly in circulation. In the autumn parliament of 1397, the earl of Arundel, the most implacable of

---

[7] He celebrated his birthday on the day of the Epiphany, and held in special devotion the cults of the nativity of John the Baptist, the Three Kings and the Holy Innocents.

the king's opponents, had been condemned to death, led through London by the Cheshire archers, and beheaded on Tower Hill. But after the blow had been struck, the headless trunk raised itself to its feet, remaining erect for a few eerie moments. His burial place in the Carmelite convent in London rapidly became a place of popular veneration, and popular report was that his head and body had been miraculously reconstituted. According to Walsingham, the king suffered nightmares on this account, posting Cheshire guardsmen around his chamber, and sent a group of noblemen to exhume Arundel's body. It was discovered that the body and head were attached, but by the stitching of the friars. It may be that the king's mind was somewhat eased, but the story of a headless adversary who might live to fight another day was not unfamiliar to the king and his company. Memories of this episode must have been especially fresh when the court was lodged at Arundel's castle at Holt, another name suggestive of Hautdesert.[8]

After the close of parliament in October 1397, and as stories of Arundel's head began to circulate, the king had withdrawn from the capital to Wood-stock, preparatory to his move to the Midlands. On All Saints Day there arrived in England one of Europe's most famous knights on an errand every bit as ominous as that on which Sir Gawain set out. It was Ramon de Perelhos, a Catalan nobleman and crusader, intent on visiting St Patrick's Purgatory in Ireland. The king entertained Perelhos at Woodstock, and provided him with an escort to Chester and letters of commendation for Ireland. Like Sir Gawain, he set out to traverse the kingdom of 'Logres' in November. At each stage he was warned of the great dangers of the Purgatory. In Ireland he was enter-tained at Christmas time by a lord as hearty and wild as the Green Knight himself, 'King' O'Neil. The Purgatory itself was a grotto cut into the rock on an island, where Perelhos had to contend alone with the evil spirits. The Catalan pilgrim crossed back to 'Oliet' (Holyhead) in the new year, meeting up with the king and his court at Lilleshall Abbey, near Shrewsbury, and doubtless enthralling the company with tales of his adventures (Jeanroy and Vignaux 1903).

Another famous knight, mindful over the winter of 1397–8 of ominous undertakings and appointments, was Henry of Bolingbroke. His involve-ment in the coup of 1397 had placed him in a dilemma, brought to a head by a conversation in December with the duke of Norfolk. On the advice of his father, John of Gaunt, he presented an appeal of treason against Mowbray at the Shrewsbury parliament in February. Throughout the winter, spring and summer he can be traced riding back and forth across the country, perhaps fitting in a pilgrimage to Bridlington, and ever conscious of the forthcoming duel with Mowbray. Eventually a date was set for Coventry, and the two protagonists were splendidly armed in the latest style. The duel was halted

---

[8] For Jean Creton (1824) it was a castle 'que hoult en appelloit, Sur une roche moult hault assis estoit' (123n).

at the crucial moment, and the two men sent into exile. Within a year Bolingbroke was to return and eventually lay claim to the throne. In the mean time the troubles had helped speed the death of his father. Soon after the affair had been brought to the king's notice, Lancaster made his final will, providing for tapers to be burnt around his body, ten in memory of the ten commandments, seven each for the works of charity and the deadly sins, five each for the wounds of Christ and the senses misspent, and three in honour of the Trinity (Armitage-Smith 1904, 421). Though active throughout 1398, he retired for Christmas to his castle at Leicester a sick man, and died early in the new year.

Some thirty miles to the west Richard II held his last great Christmas feast at Lichfield. Gaunt's death and the moves taken to bar Bolingbroke from his patrimony set in train the unravelling of the regime. According to Froissart, there were ominous signs at the Garter feast at Windsor. The king fielded a team of knights dressed in green against all comers, but the event was not well-supported (Johnes 1842, II. 681). Since there were vacant stalls in the Order of the Garter it would be interesting to know if new candidates, perhaps including Sir John Stanley, were proposed.[9] The king's expedition to Ireland in May was a magnificent affair, well-attended by the remnants of the peerage, but little of substance had been achieved when news came of Bolingbroke's landing. The king returned to south Wales and under cover of night made his mad dash across country in a failed bid to reach Chester before the rebels. The route of the king and his companions, and indeed the rest of the bodyguard as they straggled home, must have been close to that sketched out for Sir Gawain: through unknown country until Anglesey and the coastline of north Wales came into view. Eventually Richard agreed to terms at Conwy, but by the time he crossed the Dee back into Cheshire it was all too evident that he was Bolingbroke's prisoner.

There were few who had kept their 'trothe' with Richard II. For Jean Creton and the French author of *Traison et Mort* it was a shabby tale of betrayal. Even the nobles closest to the king and the leaders of the Cheshire retinue made their submission. The only casualty was Peter Legh of Lyme who was executed at Chester. Richard was led back to London, and pressured into a sort of abdication. Henry of Lancaster now laid claim to the throne. It is not quite the end of the series of tantalising parallels in detail or mood with *Sir Gawain and the Green Knight*. The Ricardian lords organised a new Christmas game. Under the cover of the Christmas festivities they planned to gain entry into Henry IV's court on Twelfth Night and murder him and his sons. A rising at Chester was organised: and indeed the rebels succeeded in capturing the castle and recovering Peter Legh's head. The main conspiracy failed, however, sealing the fate of Richard II. The wheel of fortune had moved full circle

---

[9] Stanley was elected in 1405, the first Knight of the Garter based in Cheshire or south Lancashire.

in the short year between Christmas 1398 and Christmas 1399. There was much thought as to who had kept their oaths and bargains, much reflection on 'trawthe' and 'traison'. 'Honi soit qui y mal pense.'

IV

Sir Gawain and the Green Knight is by no means a tract for the times. Its allusions to contemporary events, if they exist at all, are slight and glancing, and no more than suggestive. If it was written in the late 1390s, though, it is hard to ignore the historical context. If the poet and his audience were men from Cheshire or its environs, they must, willy-nilly, have been caught up in the Ricardian drama. It may well be the case, of course, that the works of the *Gawain*-poet were written earlier. Even so, the events of the late 1390s remain interesting, if not relevant. The *Gawain*-poet and the people for whom he wrote lived on after the poem's composition. If they were still alive in the 1390s, the odds are that they would have had some involvement with the retinue or household of Richard II. The likelihood must be that at least on some occasion during the king's time in the north-west Midlands, the opportunity was taken to present to the court the finest poetry of the region, and *Sir Gawain and the Green Knight* was given an airing.

The connection between the finest alliterative verse of the north-west Midlands and the fortunes of Cheshire men at the royal court may provide some explanation of the sudden drying up of the springs of patronage and creativity. The survival of the finest works in a single manuscript, after all, makes it probable that the extant works represent only a sub-set of the *Gawain*-poet's *oeuvre*. It seems reasonable to assume, after all, that there would have been some local works, not necessarily by the master himself, more explicitly favourable to Richard II. In any case there is the larger problem of how it was that the great flowering of alliterative verse in the region in the late fourteenth century withered in the fifteenth century. Alliterative traditions were kept alive to some degree among the local gentry, but the pattern of decline may be an argument against the notion that the *Gawain*-poet needs no other milieu than the manor-house. Still, it is perhaps possible to learn somewhat of the 'golden age' from what came after. Alliterative poetry continued to enjoy high patronage in fifteenth-century Scotland, and it is interesting to note that the memory was preserved there of an earlier master by the name of Huchon of the Awle Royale, Hugh of the royal household (Amours 1906, 18–27). In a later and cruder version of *Sir Gawain and the Green Knight*, the adventure ends, as does the original, with Gawain's return to Arthur's court and the establishment of a new chivalric order. In the later version, the order is specifically identified as the Order of the Bath, popularly assumed to have been founded by Henry IV in 1399 (Hales and Furnivall 1868, II. 77).

5

Christianity for Courtly Subjects:
Reflections on the Gawain-Poet

DAVID AERS

> We give a much more unlimited approval to their idea that the life of
> the wise man must be social. For how could the city of God . . . either
> take a beginning or be developed, or attain its proper destiny, if the life
> of the saints were not a social life? (Augustine 1950, XIX.5, p. 680)

These reflections on the *Gawain*-poet set out from a poem by one of his
contemporaries. *Piers Plowman* interweaves an individual quest for salvation
('tel me þis ilke, How I may saue my soule', I. 83–84)[1] with a sustained critical
exploration of English institutions and communities after the Black Death
(Aers 1980, chapters 1–3; Simpson 1991; Justice 1994). Langland's treatment
of penance, a major preoccupation, exemplifies the ways in which interiority
and spirituality are formed within determinate institutions and social networks. These, in the poet's view, are shaped by market values. Law itself is
commodified and the poet's satire comes from and contributes to an increasingly widespread conviction that there was a general crisis of both order and
legitimacy (Kaeuper 1988, chapters 2–4; Harding 1984). But the church itself,
at all levels, so *Piers Plowman* maintains, had become assimilated to current
market relations and the secular powers these sustained (for example, Pr
81–86, XV. 80–145, 539–67; Scase 1989). The sacrament of penance, without
which the eucharist should not be received (as Conscience notes, XIX.
385–90), is explored as a crucial example of this process. Its critical, reforming
force abandoned, it can work to naturalize and internalize current social
relations and goals which Langland saw as major obstructions on the journey
to God (for example, III. 32–63, XIX. 383–409). Against this, the poet draws
on a tradition which saw penance as 'a public act' demanding a transformation of both inner and outer forms of life (Bossy 1985, 47–48). This is why
restitution becomes a decisive demand in the poem (Frank 1957, 100–9; Stokes

---

1 References to *Piers Plowman* throughout this chapter are to the B version edited by Kane
and Donaldson (1988); where the C version is referred to, the edition is Derek Pearsall's
(1978).

1984). It is inextricably bound up with a traditional conception of justice which itself unites inner and outer, individual and collective, private and public, contingent particular and divine teleology. No transformation of self can be achieved in isolation from changes in social practices (V. 270–71). Restoration of justice in the soul entails a transformation of relations in the community, and the demands of this transformation may certainly be radical (for example, XV. 80–145, 539–67). Similarly, resistance to reforming justice in social relations proves to be an overwhelming impediment to interior trans-formations (as in XIX–XX). This Christian-Aristotelian vision is then driven by Langland to confront (and not only once) the possibility that contempo-rary communities, including the church, are such that practical reason be-comes lost and no-one knows what constitutes just action, what one owes to one's neighbors. The penitent Haukyn is left weeping but still without a clear sense of how to live justly in his world (XIV. 323–35) while by the end of the work we encounter a culture actually rejecting *Spiritus Iusticie*, the 'chief seed þat Piers sew', the virtue without which none will find salvation (XIX. 405–6; Simpson 1991, 242–43). The register within which Langland represents this is not without interest to readers of the *Gawain*-poet and his courtly language of piety. Peace resists the kind of penitential practice that the poem has repeatedly depicted as indicative of the church's assimilation by the existing structures of profit and power. But Peace is overruled and, significantly enough, by *hende speche* (XX. 348–54). The culture of Christian discourse here is courtly as the confessor speaks 'curteisly' and impresses Conscience who empowers him to take over the sacrament of penance. The forms of courtesy are integrated with 'pryvee paiment', echoing the earlier exchange between Mede and her confessor (III. 32–63). This combination certainly consoles Christians. But it also induces the final catastrophe of the poem, showing itself to be the fantasy and illusion of a demented optimism (XX. 355–79). Conscience now confronts the effects of his actions and abandons the church to seek for the sources of salvation outside the ark. Although the ark desig-nated itself as that outside of which there could be no salvation, it is shown here to have become an impediment to the activity of grace, an institution now shaped by Antichrist's forces (XX. 51–386).

Langland's struggles to see how Christian-Aristotelian traditions of jus-tice, and penance, could withstand certain corrosive forces in his culture, including, finally, its 'hende speche', can help us focus on strategies through which the *Gawain*-poet addressed this culture. *Piers Plowman* can also encour-age appreciation of some of the consequences of the *Gawain*-poet's strategies. Although this chapter concentrates on *Sir Gawain and the Green Knight*, many of the issues raised and conclusions reached seem to me, perhaps surpris-ingly, relevant to the other poems in Cotton Nero A.x.

Some influential studies have read *Sir Gawain and the Green Knight* as a poem sharply focused on aspects of the culture approached in this chapter through Langland's troubled meditations. Al Shoaf, for example, maintains that the poet sought to reconcile 'the old values of chivalry and feudalism' with 'the abstract market forces' of 'commercialism in the fourteenth century' (Shoaf 1984, 3). The poem shows that all humans live 'in a web of relations largely commercial' (47) and that all 'value' is the product of 'human subjectivity' (32). Sir Gawain must learn that he, like all humans, is 'subject to a pricing', 'enmeshed in the market' and 'a commodity' (37–39). At Hautdesert he engages in 'business transaction' with Sir Bertilak and becomes 'enmeshed in commerce' (61). Jill Mann too argues that the poem explores 'the fundamental realities of mercantile life' from within 'the tradition of Aristotelian commentary' and fuses 'knightly and mercantile values' (Mann 1986, 313, 294, 314), while Stephanie Trigg relates its examination of exchange and value to 'political instability' in late fourteenth-century England (Trigg 1991, 265–66).

Is the poet concerned to examine and revise received Christian-Aristotelian teaching in the face of contemporary 'commerce' and 'mercantile life'? We should recall that in this tradition exchanges for profit, as St Thomas Aquinas argued, are justly censured since they are devoted to the acquisition of gain which knows no boundaries and tends to infinity ('deservit cupiditati lucri, quae terminum nescit, sed in infinitum tendit', Aquinas 1894: II–II. 77.4, resp.). St Thomas allies this judgement with a qualification that was certainly to have an important life in the Middle Ages: the lack of a virtuous end in gain ('lucrum') does not mean that in itself gain is necessarily vicious. This being so, 'lucrum' can be ordered to a good end. What does he have in mind? In transactions that are aimed at moderate 'lucrum' to support a household, to support the poor ('indigentibus') or to serve the common welfare ('propter publican utilitatem'), 'lucrum' becomes a just wage for labour rather than an end, a goal (II–II. 77.44, resp.). This is certainly the framework within which Langland strives to analyze the problems he encounters in his culture, and we can see a deployment of St Thomas's qualification to the condemnation of commercial pursuits in *Piers Plowman* (VII. 22–39). Yet Langland's work should help us grasp just how this is definitely not the ethical and political terrain on which the *Gawain*-poet's attention is fixed, either in *Sir Gawain and the Green Knight* or anywhere else, even in the parable of the disconcerted labourers in *Pearl*, a text that could certainly have encouraged engagement with the Statute of Laborers and conflicts over the just price of labour and commodities (Aers 1988, chapter 1). Markets, market values and a profound involvement of English ruling elites both in the profits generated through market transactions and in the profits of war, including the investment in mercenaries, none of this was at all novel in the period after the Black Death (Miller and Hatcher 1978, 173–97; Hewitt 1966; Allmand 1988, 73–76, 102–11, 120–35). What was novel was the consequences of the demographic collapse, combined from the 1370s with lower prices of food, consequences that involved a shift in the balance of forces between classes to which the Statute of Laborers and the great Rising of 1381 were responses (Hatcher 1994). Yet

Sir Gawain and the Green Knight carefully brackets all these areas of ruling class experience, both traditional and novel. No fourteenth-century aristocrat, no prince, could be as removed from the economic dimensions of noble identity as Sir Gawain or Sir Bertilak, none as removed from the conflicts catalyzed by effects of the Black Death. While Sir Gawain's military skills turn out to be of little interest to the poet, it should be noted that the other weapons of his class, political, legal and economic, weapons as essential to its identity, are rendered invisible. The poem carefully occludes all contemporary conflicts over the extraction and distribution of 'lucrum'.

How then should we read the vocabulary of exchanges, of 'chaffer', 'chevisaunce', 'prys' and 'pay', one to which scholars such as Taylor, Shoaf and Mann have drawn attention? Any reading should at least take note of what we have already observed: namely, that this vocabulary belongs, in this poem, to a discourse from which the realities of fourteenth-century commodity production and exchange have been purged, a discourse *without* production and *without* the producers who were proving forceful opponents to gentry and courtly elites in the years around 1381. In this context, something that could certainly have been purchased as a commodity in contemporary markets, something like a jewelled girdle, venison, fish or a kiss, ceases, in fact, to belong to what Mann (1986) calls 'the fundamental realities of mercantile life'. They are, instead, located in courtly worlds where exchanges (of clothing, food, kisses or blows) are exchanges of gifts, not, carefully and precisely not exchanges of commodities in fourteenth-century commerce. As Britton Harwood has observed, drawing on the work of Marcel Mauss and Pierre Bourdieu, the poet's model is an 'economy of the gift' (Harwood 1991, 438–88; also Davenport 1978, 162–64). This economy had rules which mediated fierce competition for power and status, an economy that remained part, though only part, of the culture and self-identity of those Mervyn James (1978) describes as 'honourmen'. So when the poet's extensive descriptions of the immense luxury of Arthur's court include a reference to the fact that the royal tapestries were embroidered with the best jewels that money could buy (74–80),[2] there is no concern to focus on this reference as a topic for reflection. Indeed, making this a topic for reflection, in the poet's culture, would mean an engagement with problems around the just price, the sale of labour power and contemporary law, problems faced in *Piers Plowman* (III, VI–VII and C III. 290–405). Unlike Langland, the *Gawain*-poet simply sets aside what Mann calls 'the world of the market' (Mann 1986, 297: cf. Harwood 1991, 486).

If the poet's relations to his culture are such as I have outlined, what becomes of the church and its administration of the sacraments? Especially what becomes of the one so central to *Piers Plowman*, the one which, in the words of Jean Gerson, 'gives life back to the dead', the sacrament of penance?

---

2   For the *Gawain*-poet's works I use Andrew and Waldron (1987).

(Brown 1987, 56). The church, like the communities of Camelot and Hautde-sert, is extracted from its place in the networks of contemporary markets, networks that so fascinated Chaucer and appalled Langland. It becomes a church totally assimilated to the poem's version of courtly existence. There are no signs of any gaps between the secular elites and the church's ministers, no tensions between elite forms of life (including the readiness to kill in sport, as at lines 96–99) and the church's teachings or liturgy. Nor are there any signs of criticism being directed against the poem's priests, whether the bishop feasting at Arthur's high table in a place of honour (109–15) or at chaplains so fully integrated to the life of courtly abundance and display, one that is a feature of the chapel itself (917, 928–74; see Nicholls 1985). At both Camelot and Hautdesert Christianity is thoroughly assimilated to the celebration of forms of life aspired to by contemporary gentry and nobles. The pentangle itself, far from being an emblem of unworldly transcendentalism, enshrines exclusively upper class virtues ('fraunchyse', 'cortaysye') and draws the term 'clannes' into the same domain, as John Burrow has shown (Burrow 1965, 47–48: see *Sir Gawain and the Green Knight*, 607–14, 651–55). In this form of Christianity the five wounds of Christ and the figure of the Virgin Mary sacralize the values of the secular nobility in the poet's own culture. The wounds of Christ and the image of Mary are placed on the very symbol of class power, privilege and violence – the warrior's shield. Indeed, Gawain is said to draw his knightly fierceness and courage in battle from the image of the Virgin Mary (644–50). Sir Robert Knolles, Sir Hugh Calveley, John of Gaunt or Henry V, like most late medieval knights, would have identified with this version of the church and Christianity (Keen 1984; Coss 1993, chapters 3–6). True enough, by the end of the poem the girdle supersedes the pentangle as Gawain's emblem. But this, as we shall see, involves no trans-formation of the church or of the Christianity to which the poem's elites subscribe, elites that continue to include Gawain.

Before discussing the poem's ending, however, I wish to consider the sacrament of penance in this text. The first scene of confession is an emphati-cally orthodox one between Gawain and a priest which culminates in the knight's absolution (1876–84). The account of this episode seems one of the most unequivocal pieces of writing in the poem. We are told that Gawain sought out a priest in the chapel to hear his confession, confessed himself completely, shewing all his misdeeds, begged for mercy and begged for absolution. The priest absolves him, an absolution carefully and strikingly recounted by the poet:

> And he asoyled hym surely and sette hym so clene
> As dome3day schulde haf ben di3t on þe morn. (1883–84)

These words emphasize that the priest accepts the confession as a good one, an adequately complete one carried out with due contrition. They also show the poet stressing the *efficacy* of the church's sacrament. Gawain seems far more secure in the face of death and the last judgement than Langland's penitents in Passus five, Haukyn in Passus fourteen or Will in Passus twenty. Yet this scene has generated a substantial literature, a veritable encyclopedia of scholastic teaching on confession and penance (Burrow 1965, 104–10; Barron 1980, 87 ff. and 121–29; Morgan 1991, 133–42).

There are good reasons for this. First, there is the fact that Gawain did not give the gift of the girdle to Bertilak, thus breaking the agreement made in a game he was playing with his host. This has made many critics doubt that the poet could have meant what he wrote, – namely, that Gawain's confession is complete, a sound one, and that he received valid absolution. Second, there is Gawain's later mortified reaction when the Green Knight draws attention to his retention of the girdle (2331–438). The last thing Gawain seems to have here is the feeling of being 'clene', although this was what the priest had pronounced him the day before, when he had clearly determined to keep the girdle (Burrow 1965, 110). It is certainly tempting to join in this inquiry, to begin one's own *summa de casibus conscientiae*: for example, to observe that as major an authority as Jean Gerson insisted that penitents need not confess venial sins and warned confessors against fostering a destructive scrupulousness (Brown 1987, 63–64, 68–72); or to speculate about whether an undetected offence in a game must be taken to a confessor. However, it seems to me that these temptations should be resisted. As Wendy Clein argues, the poet himself refuses 'to indicate that there is anything sinful in Gawain's intention to conceal the girdle from the host' (Clein 1987, 114). The confession is presented as valid and the priest's absolution as being in accord with the church's teachings on the saving powers of this sacrament.

If there is a question here, it runs as follows: could a canonically sound confession and absolution be both licit and spiritually quite worthless, irrelevant? And if so, is Gawain's an example of this, one symptomatic of a massive gap between orthodox claims about the sacrament of penance and spiritual realities? Could it be that the fusion of 'chivalric' and 'Christian' values (Burrow 1965, 105) has consequences less than helpful on the journey to the creature's end? Could such a fusion have transformed the sacrament of penance into a therapeutic social form devoid of sacramental power, devoid too of the ability to encourage the kind of inward journey described by Piers (V. 592–629)? It is certainly striking that Gawain's confession opens out no inner spaces of the kind we have seen emerging in his time at Hautdesert (Aers 1988, 162–66). As for the sacraments, they were *said* to incorporate Christians into the body of Christ, extending Christ's merits to his members so that Christians could live in Christ and Christ live in Christians (for example, Aquinas 1894, III. 19.4, III. 60–64). They were necessary to human salvation (III. 61. 1. resp.), the expression and constitution of 'a life of love between Christians and God' (Davies 1993, 357). Yet what happens *immediately* after Gawain's confession is not designed to suggest that his attention, his heart has been directed in ways such as this:

And syþen he mace hym as mery among þi fre ladyes,
With comlych caroles and alle kynnes joye   (1885–86)

Such behaviour is certainly appropriate to a great nobleman and is not, of course, incompatible with a love directed by sacramental grace towards Christ. Nevertheless, the poet has given us a striking sequence whose juxtapositions offer a powerful image of the way this church and its sacrament of penance is immersed in, even subordinate to, courtly forms of life and its erotic games.

The questions posed above, concerning not whether Gawain's confession was sound or unsound but addressing the spiritual efficacy of the church's sacrament, cannot simply be dismissed as historically impossible, as anachronistic. Far from it, a radical attack on the church's claims for its sacrament of penance was part both of Waldensianism and of Wyclifism, forms of Christianity that radically undermined traditional legitimations of the church's power, authority and wealth (Leff 1967, II. 452–85, especially 457, 463, 479; Cameron 1984, 86–92; Hudson 1988, 294–301). Could the *Gawain*-poet's relations to his culture include some elusive convergences with such critical views on the late medieval church and its sacramental powers? Before my own answer to this question emerges the second confessional scene needs to be recalled.

There Gawain confronts a knight who seems to have powers of surveillance that a penitent would ascribe to God. What Gawain had experienced as private, secret space turns out to have been subject to another's gaze.[3] This, as John Burrow observed, leads into a passage 'especially rich in penitential matter', one that 'follows closely the actual order of the confessional' (Burrow 1965, 127; see *Sir Gawain and the Green Knight*, 2341–93). Burrow demonstrated how the dialogue between the Green Knight and Gawain elicits 'confessional self-analysis', a request for penance, 'an act of restitution' and a concluding 'absolution' (Burrow 1965, 128–32). Other scholars have elaborated and qualified Burrow's reading, even identifying the Green Knight with Christ, the judge who is merciful and strong (Harwood 1991, 491; compare Morgan 1991, 152–61; Clein 1987, 122–24; Spearing 1970, 219–29, 1987, 201–6). But what is especially intriguing about Burrow's analysis, in the present context, is its conclusion. He decides that although the exchange between the Green Knight and Gawain follows conventional penitential forms and has a penitential effect far greater than the one enacted with the priest, it is 'not a "real" confession' (132). How does Burrow know this? He knows it because 'Bercilack, being a layman, has no power of absolution' (132). All we have, finally, is a 'pretend secular confession' which, 'theologically speaking' cannot remedy 'the inadequacies of a sacramental one' (133; see similarly, Davenport

---

[3]   A different set of preoccupations around the 'gaze' in this poem are explored in Stanbury 1991b, chapter 5.

1978, 174). Two points need making here. The first is that it was certainly orthodox teaching that in an emergency 'if no priest is available, one can gain God's forgiveness if one desires it and confesses one's crime to one's [lay] companion [secundum tamen Augustinum tanta est virtus confessionis quod si deest copia sacerdotis, meretur tamen ex voluntate veniam a Deo qui crimen confitetur socio]' (*Fasciculus Morum*, ed. Wenzel, 1989, 466–67). Perhaps Gawain's situation is one that would legitimize and sacralize confession to his companion. The second point takes a very different direction. Even if one concedes that it was traditional to allow confession to a layman in the absence of a priest, the challenge of Wyclifite ideas and practices in later fourteenth-century England gave such strands of orthodoxy a very different resonance. For example, the Lollard preacher William Thorpe, defending his radical views on confession against Archbishop Arundel, invokes just the tradition noted by the author of *Fasciculus Morum* (Hudson 1993, 83, lines 1919–22). For a Wyclifite this was a logical step on the path to the doctrine that absolution can only be licit if it is declarative of God's prior and quite independent forgiveness (82), a doctrine incorporated in a cluster of beliefs profoundly subversive of the Roman church.

Furthermore one might recall that in the four decades before Arundel's *Constitutions* (1409) it was possible for those belonging to the elite to have, and show, sympathy with positions that challenged the church's power and authority, as the 'Lollard' knights testify (McFarlane 1972). In these contexts, it becomes plausible for someone to suggest that the *Gawain*-poet might have entertained some perspectives that could be unfolded in directions incompatible with Catholic orthodoxy. Perhaps a ruling class layman could fulfill a priestly role far more effectively than the official minister of the church. It is the layman, not the priest, after all, who is shown to stimulate self-scrutiny and acknowledgment of moral vulnerability (2433–36). The distance between such perspectives and those of Sir John Clanvowe's treatise *The Two Ways* (Scattergood 1975), or even more determinedly Wyclifite ones, need not be great. Yet although the distance might not be great, the poet chose not to travel it. Whatever the critical potential some of his poem's perspectives could have held for some late fourteenth-century readers brooding about the church, its alignments with the wealthy, its pastoral activities and its administration of penance, the poet himself chose not to actualize them. His modes of writing leave us in considerable doubt even as to what would constitute satisfaction, the third part of penance, that which pertains especially to justice, 'the virtue which gives to each his own' ('satisfactio stat cum illa virtute cardinali que dicitur justicia', *Fasciculus Morum* (Wenzel 1989), 496–97). What does Gawain actually owe, and in what form, to his aunt ('Morgne þe goddes')[4] . . . to the lady . . . to his court . . . to his church . . . to Christ? How does the return to

---

[4] On Morgne la Faye and her powerful but repressed role, see Aers 1988, 170–73; Heng 1991; Scala 1994.

Camelot deal with this? For the court there are no problems. The 'broþerhede' has survived the tests instigated by Morgne la Fay, tests challenging the virtues appropriate to a community of Christian 'honourmen'. Joyfully it assimilates its courageous and chaste representative together with his story and new emblem. The court's traditions and forms of life are adequately vindicated, a vindication to which neither Bishop Bawdewyn nor Gawain offer objections (2913–21). Nor, contrary to the views of some modern scholars, does the poet (contrast Benson 1992, 37). And how could he, with any cogency? For he himself offers not the slightest hints of alternative forms of life for the chivalric classes to pursue, not the slightest hints of forms of Christianity outside the court church. There are, it seems, no alternatives. Not even for Gawain. However pronounced his public display of 'schame' as he tells his story (2501–5), its moral, psychological and theological dimensions are undecidable (Spearing 1970, 236, 1987, 203–7; Clein 1987, 125–38; Stanbury 1991b, 109–13; for tellingly *antithetical* determinations compare Harwood 1991 and Benson 1992). Whatever it may seem, it too is readily assimilated by the knight's community, an assimilation perfectly congruent with Gawain's prior decision to continue with the chivalric life and the pursuit of 'prowes of armes' (2433–38). Whoever added the motto of Edward III's order of the garter after the poem's ending ('Hony soyt qui mal y pence') responded appropriately to these aspects, assimilating Gawain's 'schame' to the values and language of a contemporary royal court.

This ending tells us much about the poem's relations to contemporary culture, its ethical and political orientations. The poet is suggesting that whether knights display the psychological, moral and introspective tendencies represented by Gawain or the apparently different ones represented by Arthur and the rest of the 'broþerhede', whether the sacrament of penance is spiritually powerful or not, whether a priest or a nobleman may stimulate a more contrite disposition, whether the church is more or less thoroughly incorporated in the elites' worlds, even whether there are large domains of indeterminacy and undecidability or not, none of this is of much consequence since nothing much will change anyway. Nor is this a matter for lamentation or complaint. That too would have little consequence, as Gawain's own lamentations illustrate so nicely. True enough, the lamentations in his case involve taking a new emblem but, as we have just seen, that turns out to have no consequences for knightly forms of life, including Gawain's. The poet suggests that while there are potentially tricky conflicts within the elites' codes, and while there are some potentially threatening family relationships from a darker past, one need not worry about these very much, because even if one does, the worrying will change nothing, nor could it. There are no alternatives and none are necessary. The existent codes of honourmen, with their virtually Christless Christianity, are good enough for this world. And they are unequivocally sanctioned by the one church, by Bishop Bawdewyn and his clergy. How then, asking Langland's question again, may I 'saue my soule' (I. 83)? Certainly you don't need to worry about the world in which most people lived, about the forms of justice in existing communities or about current debates on the role of the church. You should respect the general values of 'honourmen' but don't feel bad about being a lot more pragmatic and a lot less perfectionist than Gawain (550–65, 2505–30). Do, however, follow Gawain in maintaining a certain sexual discipline. Indeed, the poet links the possibility of adultery with an ensuing exchange between the two knights which would now go beyond their nightly kissing to an act exposing them to the homophobic and annihilating rage of God against the people of Sodom, people whose acts so fascinated this poet (*Cleanness*, 693–96, 947–1056; see Dinshaw 1994, 206, 216–19).

I do not think that the other poems in Cotton Nero A.x substantially change the picture emerging from my discussion of *Sir Gawain and the Green Knight* and the forms of Christianity it sustains. In the terms of *Cleanness*, what must individuals and communities do to 'loke on oure Lorde with a leue chere' (23–26)? The answer is reiterated throughout the poem: avoid 'fylþe', for 'fylþe' disgusts God and when he is disgusted he becomes massively destructive, mad ('wod', 204). What then is 'fylþe'? It is constituted as those sexual acts categorized as 'agayn kynde' (265–72, 671–1048), acts outside the heterosexual 'play of paramorez' God personally established (689–708).[5] It also includes open contempt of God, such as Baltazar's (1393–548, 1766–804). If this is 'vnclannes' what is 'clannes' (1805–10)? The poem's notions of 'ryȝtwys' action (294) are extremely sparse but consideration of Christ should give us the fullest answer available. Christ becomes a representative of a thoroughly courtly Christianity, a divine Sir Gawain. The radically inclusive prophet of the Gospels whose rejection of received categories of clean and unclean was a profound affront to his orthodox adversaries, becomes one whose 'hende' touch shunned 'ordure' and could cut and carve food with the cleanness which made even knives of Toulouse redundant (1101–8). Rather than the poor Christ of St Francis and *Piers Plowman* (XI. 185–94, 232–42), or the teacher of love and kindness in the figure of the Samaritan (XVII. 50–356) or the radical teacher of Lollardy, we encounter a Christ made in the image of a courtly Christianity, one who would have been at home in Camelot or the courts of late medieval England. Penance itself is abstracted from all concern with justice and the political orders which facilitate or obstruct this virtue (1113–48), while the eucharist is assimilated to a discourse which has nothing to say about its role in cultivating union between fellow creatures in Christian communities (5–16: compare Aquinas 1894, III.73 and III.79), and nothing, carefully nothing, to say about the contemporary body of Christ (Beckwith 1992; Rubin 1991). Despite the divine terrorism directed against those the poet constitutes as 'perverse' (Spearing 1987, chapter 7: cf.

---

5   On such constitutions see Dollimore 1991, 27–28 and chapters 8–17. On *Cleanness* here see Frantzen 1996.

Dollimore 1991), the actual content of the virtuous life has become as thin and depoliticized as any that flows from a Kantian categorical imperative. This, it seems to me, is one of the most powerful effects of the *Gawain*-poet's revisions of Christian tradition, revisions made in response to the same cultural forces that *Piers Plowman* addressed. No wonder, then, that at the end of *Pearl*, despite the dreamer's intransigent rejections of his sanctified instructor's teachings, and despite her emphasis on the role of grace, the poet insists, without irony, that 'Hit is ful eþe to be god Krystyin' (1202). Courtly and 'gentle' readers, as long as they confined themselves to approved heterosexual acts, could find great comfort in their poet, 'Pelagius redivivus'.

6

The Materials of Culture

The Roaches

Landscape and Geography

RALPH ELLIOTT

When Gawain sets out from Camelot in early November on his 'anious uyage' (535), he journeys at first through the nondescript regions of romance familiar from other tales of Arthurian adventure 'bi frythez and dounez' (695), where hostile creatures confront him. He fights with wolves and dragons, bears and boars, giants and *wodwos*, strange denizens of forests and high fells.

But unlike the accustomed spring or summer landscapes, Gawain's is a cold, inhospitable, wintry one, where snow and sleet, naked rocks and freezing streams prove more perilous than any living antagonists. Admittedly, travelling in November in medieval times was generally confined to important missions and accompanied by considerable hardship (Stokes and Scattergood 1984, 78), but in departing from the familiar landscapes of Arthurian romance, the poet deliberately added a fresh dimension to his narrative. For at a certain point the landscape of wintry hazards in 'contrayez straunge' (713), with its waterfalls heavy with icicles and its birds piping piteously for pain of the cold, changes as the features of Gawain's journey become 'individualised and sharply focussed' (Boitani 1982, 63), and the formulae of conventional *descriptio loci* are replaced by closely observed topographical details described in words drawn from the poet's own north-west Midland dialect.

From the moment Gawain enters 'bi a mounte' into the deep forest of lines 740ff., the reader, or listener, can visualize the scene with surprising clarity: the deep valley with its tangle of oaks, hazel, and hawthorn, lined by hills on either side, and 'ro3e raged mosse rayled aywhere' (745). The word *raged*, glossed 'ragged, shaggy' by Tolkien and Gordon, is in fact a dialect word meaning 'covered with rime, hoarfrosted', a highly evocative word in the wintry context. And underfoot is the marshy terrain of 'misy and myre' (749), where *misy* is another striking dialect word, unique in Middle English. What Sarah Stanbury has perceptively called the poet's 'consistent adoption of a visual poetic as a pervasive mode of thought' (Stanbury 1991b, 127) is considerably enhanced by his choice of rare topographical words which add what we may call local authenticity to the scenes he describes. Stanbury does not mention this aspect, but its significance should not be underrated.

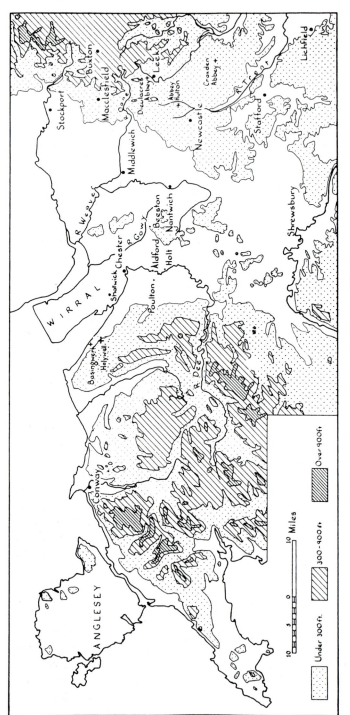

The *Gawain* Country (shows N. Wales and the Wirral)

The poet's attention to details, his highlighting of significant features, his acts of 'poynting', to use a term employed by both Chaucer and by the *Gawain*-poet in line 1009 (cf. Burrow 1971, 69ff.), serve important narrative purposes. They direct attention to the symbolic import of the scenes described: the entanglement of the forest mirrors Gawain's ensnarement in the beheading compact and anticipates the amorous temptations that lie ahead; the miry terrain suggests insecurity, moral frailty, 'vntrawþe'. Moreover, the poet's pinpointing of closely visualized features of landscape, particularly with the aid of local words like *misy* and others yet to be mentioned, also serves to alert his audience to specific locales, actual places familiar to himself and, we may assume, to his audience also.

It is worth noting that only one stanza of more generalized description of mountains and streams, of hostile encounters and freezing nights, separates Gawain's entry into the *forest* of line 741, a word describing an area subject to special jurisdiction, set aside for the preservation and hunting of game, from his earlier arrival in the clearly identified region of North Wales and Wirral. The latter had been a *forest*, but is now called a *wyldrenesse*. The poet uses the word *forest* only once more, appropriately when referring to the locale of the deer hunt (1149).

The landscape descriptions that follow the knight's journey through the wintry, hoar-frosted forest display the same attention to detail, the same 'poynting', already noted. The sudden appearance of Bertilak's castle provides ample illustration. Our concern here is not with the architectural details of Castle Hautdesert, but with its location in a topographical setting embracing the forest of the three hunting scenes and the Green Chapel itself, the focal point of the whole adventure.

There is something ambiguous about the topography of Bertilak's castle, as if the poet were hinting at its dual role in the narrative. Unless he is choosing words for mere alliterative convenience, which is not his usual style, we may well be justified in attaching deeper significance to his choice of particular descriptive words. The castle is set in an open space within the forest ('abof a launde', 765, 'pyched on a prayere', 768), on rising ground ('on a lawe', 765) – a haven welcoming the weary traveller in answer to his prayer. At the same time it is 'loken vnder boȝez' (765), closed in by the boughs of massive trees, suggesting concealment and possible danger (cf. Cockcroft 1978, 465). That the poet is happily punning on the *prayere* of 759 and the *prayere* of 768 is another indication of the rich texture of his vocabulary.

The forest surrounding Hautdesert, the hills and valleys, bogs, and tangled brush, streams and rocky outcrops, all contribute distinctive scenes to each of the three hunts. The parallelism between Bertilak's sport in the open country and his wife's sport in Gawain's close bedroom has often been commented upon; in the present context it is the remarkable congruence between the animals hunted – deer, boar, and fox – and the territory of each hunt that adds further moment to the poet's consummate artistry

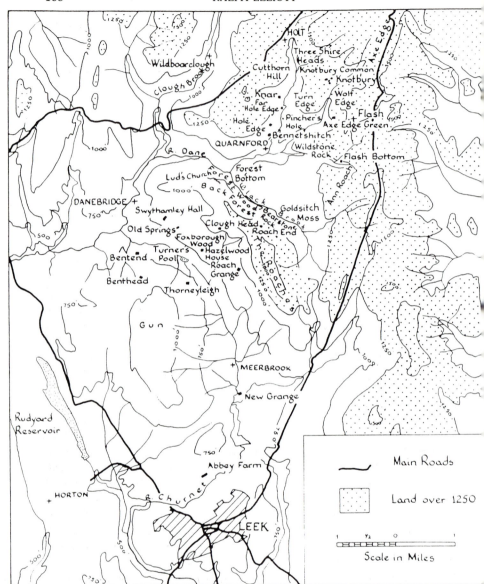

The *Gawain* Country (shows parts of Cheshire, Staffs and Derbyshire)

in combining close visual observation of landscape with, in this case, the realism as well as the symbolism of the chase.

The deer hunt of the first day is impressionistic rather than sharply focused. Here it is the movement of entire herds that is sketched, while the landscapes of largely nondescript *bonkkez* and *klyffes* alternate with equally nondescript *holtez* and *heþe* and 'depe sladez' (1159). It is the ear rather than the eye that is being targeted by rapid motion and striking sound effects, bugles blowing, hounds baying, horns and shouts echoing as if 'klyffes haden brusten' (1166). Yet it is worth noting that the poet's repeated use of the definite article seems to indicate specific features, while the pointedly demonstrative 'þat forest' of line 1149 is a reminder that all this action is taking place in the demesne of Hautdesert.

On the second day the hunt opens beneath an escarpment, the *rocherez* of line 1427, an unusual word repeated at the start of the fox hunt (1698), possibly the same landmark as those bursting 'klyffes'. The landscape of the boar hunt is sharply visualized. Individual landmarks are pinpointed: 'þe rogh rocher' (1432), 'þe knarre' (1434), 'þe knot' (1434), 'þe boerne' (1570). Unusual topographical words appear: *kerre, flosche, knarre, knot, rasse*. That all these words figure on the map of what was most likely the poet's own home ground reinforces the impression that he was drawing on familiar scenes in the creation of his narrative.

The third day's hunting terrain brilliantly mirrors the fox's darting and dodging, turning and twisting as he is glimpsed but for a moment in the brush, along a hedge, leaping across a thicket of thorns (*spenne*, 1709), creeping stealthily along the edge of marshy scrub (*strothe*, 1710), until confronted by three hunters in a narrow passage through the undergrowth (*þrich*, 1713), before heading back 'to þe wod' (1718). The words *spenne, strothe*, and *þrich* are also part of the poet's distinctive vocabulary, here employed to multiply the obstacles facing the fox trying to elude his pursuers in terrain such as is here described. For a discussion of these and other topographical words in the poem see Elliott 1984.

The hunting scenes in *Sir Gawain and the Green Knight* (henceforward *Gawain*) illustrate admirably what has been called the poet's 'technique of moving repeatedly from the general to the particular . . . in his descriptions of space' (Stanbury 1991b, 3). Of the other poems in the Cotton manuscript it is *Pearl* which is closest to *Gawain* in employing this technique of landscape description, aptly described as cinematographic (Renoir 1958, 127). The transition from the closely visualized *erber* in the opening of *Pearl* to the magnificent scenery of the dream landscape has its parallels in the hunting passages in *Gawain*, with their shifting focus from sweeping terrain to a single conspicuous 'rogh rocher vnrydely . . . fallen' (1432), or 'a hole . . . of a rasse bi a rokk þer rennez þe boerne' (1569–70), or 'a littel dich' (1709).

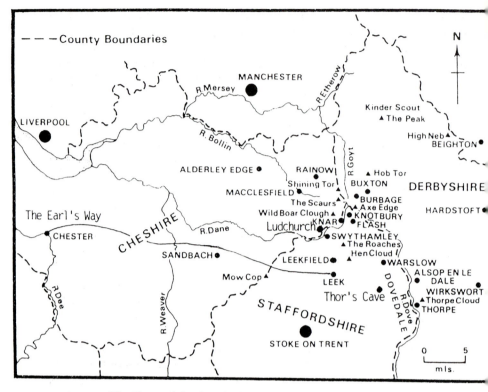

The Heart of the *Gawain* Country (shows area near Leek)

In *Pearl* the poet's journey leads from the narrow enclosure of his aromatic *erber* (38) into a dream world of spectacular colours where trees have blue trunks, their leaves shimmering silver. But the landscape, however surreal, is still composed of familiar topographical features called by familiar names, the same, often unusual, words as in *Gawain*. But whereas in *Gawain* it is places that are specifically mentioned, in *Pearl* it is the season, 'in Auguste in a hyȝ seysoun' (39), which Derek Brewer has convincingly identified with the Feast of the Assumption of the Blessed Virgin Mary on 15 August, an appropriate day to commemorate a child's entering into the blessed state of becoming a Bride of Christ (Brewer 1983, 166). And is it, one may wonder, a mere coincidence that in August 1380 John of Gaunt, patron of poets, Chaucer among them, the leading nobleman of his day with vast possessions in the north-west Midlands, chose the Feast of the Assumption of the Virgin as the day for the annual gathering of his minstrels at his Staffordshire castle of Tutbury?

The poet's dream takes him into a landscape of *klyfeȝ, rokkeȝ, downeȝ,* towards a forest and a river filled with precious stones gleaming like stars 'in wynter ny3t' (116) when country folk, *stroþe-men* (literally 'dwellers in marshy land growing with brushwood', cf. *Gawain* 1710), are asleep. The poet's brief vision of a bright starry winter's night in a landscape of hills and water and woodland is a memorable counterpoint to Gawain's trudging through the frozen forest leading to Hautdesert.

The complex metrical structure of *Pearl* tends to favour topographical formulae and enumeration more in the manner of traditional *descriptio loci* rather than the specific focusing which characterizes the landscapes in *Gawain*. Hence such lines in *Pearl* as 'And rawe3 and rande3 and rych reuere3' (105) or 'Of wod and water and wlonk playne3' (122), and formulae like 'of doun and dale3' (121), 'by slente oþer slade' (141), 'by stok oþer ston' (380). The effect of this technique is to underline the sheer exuberance of the *adubbement*, the overpowering splendour of the landscape traversed by the poet in his dream pilgrimage, and of the heavenly city, 'þat schyrrer þen sunne wyth schafte3 schon' (982). It is worth noting that the *Pearl* dreamer *blusched*, 'gazed' (980) at the celestial 'burghe' on its hill, much as Gawain *blusched* at castle Hautdesert suddenly appearing before his eyes. The word is a favourite with the *Gawain*-poet; it occurs in all four poems in the manuscript, reinforcing his, or his characters', particular habit of close visual observation.

In *Cleanness* and *Patience* landscapes are less central to the action than in *Gawain* or *Pearl*. Yet, when opportunity offers, as in the description of the Flood (*Cleanness* 361 ff.), the temptation to describe the waters as engulfing 'hy3e hylle3', 'mountayne3 on mor', and all the wild beasts of the woodlands, is not resisted. The result is a striking transformation of an English landscape into the setting of a familiar biblical story, graphically visualized until Noah's Ark finally 'on a rasse of a rok hit rest at þe laste' (*Cleanness* 446).

Even in *Patience*, least topographical of the four poems, there is a moment when the poet's eye discerns features in the sea recalling familiar scenes in a recognizable landscape. Thus he focuses on the whale as

> he swenge3 and swayues to þe se boþem,
> Bi mony rokke3 ful ro3e and rydelande strondes,
>
> (*Patience* 253–4)

closely paralleling the hunters in *Gawain* who 'sweyed togeder' (1429) before the boar 'swenged out þere' (1439) in a landscape studded with rocks and marshes. Even while depicting the depth of the ocean, the poet's art draws strikingly on his vision of familiar England landscapes.

Not two miles from castle Hautdesert lies the goal of Gawain's quest, the Green Chapel, 'in spenne', as Bertilak puts it (1074), a tag which connotes something of the wild, thorny scenery awaiting Gawain. This is no building, however, but a place so weird that Derek Brewer expressed convincingly

In Ludchurch

what others too have felt when reading the poem: 'Whatever it is, the poet is not making up something out of his head. There is just that mixture of vagueness and detailed description which is to be expected when a man describes something which he expects his audience easily to recognize' (Brewer 1948, 13).

Following the Guide's directions in lines 2144–48, Gawain descends into a valley, where his bewilderment is nicely portrayed as he surveys a scene of natural wilderness with high banks above, a cascading stream at the bottom of 'þe brem valay' (2145), and reaching skyward a group of 'ruʒe knokled knarrez with knorned stonez' (2166), an unexpected landmark which provides not only a memorable line of alliterative sonority but a topographical detail which does indeed look very much like something the poet was not making up out of his head.

What Gawain eventually discovers is no Chapel Perilous of romance but an uncanny natural phenomenon carved into the hillside on his left, half cave, half crevice, hollow inside with tufts of grass (glodes) clinging precariously to its steep rocky sides. This has frequently been taken to be a barrow, an ancient burial mound, not inappropriately called a 'chapel', although it is not easy to visualize a barrow with 'a hole on þe ende and on ayþer syde' (2180). Admittedly, the Green Chapel, whatever it is, is amply endowed by the poet with supernatural, if not funerary, associations as a desolate and baneful oratory, a cursed, disastrous church, a place fit for a 'borelych burne' like the Green Knight or indeed the devil himself. But it is important to remember that both the word berʒ (2172) and the word lawe (2175) are normally used in Middle English toponymy to denote simply a hill. The poet's 'balʒe berʒ' is a rounded hill (Smith 1956, I 18), while he had previously used lawe to describe the elevated position of Bertilak's castle. While lawe figures in Middle English, not least in alliterative poetry, with the general meaning of 'hill', berʒ is quite rare except in place-names. Both words, however, must be regarded as largely bereft of whatever funerary associations they may have carried in Old English.

It is not inappropriate to call Gawain 'in many ways a fourteenth-century detective fiction' (Stanbury 1991b, 109), and not the least of Gawain's problems was finding his way to the Green Chapel and then recognizing it in the 'olde caue, or a creuisse of an olde cragge' (2182–83) confronting him. The poet, as Brewer surmised, clearly knew such a place and how to find it, and such a place does actually exist.

Like any good writer of detective fiction the Gawain-poet is careful to drop a clue now and then to help the reader or listener towards solving whatever mystery is enshrined in his narrative.

It is not unusual for medieval poets to mention actual place-names, but it is unusual to trace an Arthurian knight's journey along a well-defined route through North Wales, across the estuary of the Dee into Wirral, and then

Inside Ludchurch

follow him into hilly country until he eventually reaches a remote castle appropriately called 'High Wilderness', with a very peculiar 'chapel' nearby, which is described in such circumstantial detail that it is almost as good as a photograph.

The inclusion of real place-names was clearly important to the poet, as was his mentioning personal names. It is worthy of note that the only major character in *Gawain* who remains unnamed is Bertilak's wife. Hers is primarily a symbolic role as the beautiful temptress of Hautdesert. To resist her advances is as much a challenge for Gawain as finding his way from Camelot to the Green Chapel.

The 'realistic' geography of *Gawain* may well have been intended by the poet to direct his audience's attention towards the locale of that mysterious half cave, half crevice where the final encounter takes place. This is even more probable if this weird chapel happens to have close links with other places in the vicinity with which the poet and his audience may have been associated. Several times the use of the definite article suggests familiarity with the 'real' places mentioned *en route*. The Knight reaches 'þe Norþe Walez' (697), leaves 'þe iles of Anglesay' (698) on his left, fares across 'þe fordez by þe forlondez' (699) at 'þe Holy Hede' (700), until he enters 'þe wyldrenesse of Wyrale' (701). Thereafter, as we noted earlier, the geography again assumes a 'romantic' colouring, but the route leads unmistakably into hilly country, the landscape of Hautdesert and its surrounding hunting terrain of forest, marshland, and mysterious Green Chapel.

Where exactly Gawain crossed the Dee into Wirral the poet does not say, but two places merit special attention. One is Aldford, the 'old ford' where Watling Street crossed the river south of Chester, whose significance is mentioned below; the other is close to Holywell, which is about a mile inland on the Welsh side of the estuary. The latter may well be the poet's 'Holy Hede', for it was here, according to tradition, that Prince Caradoc, failing to seduce St Winefride, struck off the saint's head. The spot became the most famous healing well in the British Isles and a popular place of pilgrimage. To make Gawain pass this very place on the way to his own expected decapitation adds a touch of irony to the poem not uncharacteristic of the *Gawain*-poet.

The poet's word *forlondez*, best explained as deriving from Old Norse *forlendi* 'land between sea and hills', aptly describes the low-lying coastal strip between the Clwdian Range and the tidal estuary of the Dee where Holywell is situated. Three hundred years after Gawain another intrepid traveller, Celia Fiennes, crossed the Dee after leaving Holywell, describing in her diary the shifting fords (*fordez*) created by tide and quicksand.

That Wirral was indeed a *wyldrenesse* in the late fourteenth century is amply attested by contemporary records of lawlessness and local rebellions (Bennett 1983, 93–5, 208–9). The poet was clearly as familiar with local Cheshire conditions, where

wonde þer bot lyte
þat auþer God oþer gome wyth goud hert louied,   (701–2)

as with its geography.

After crossing the Dee, Gawain probably followed the Earl's Way, or Earlsway, a well-established medieval route whose name was first recorded about the year 1200 (Palliser 1976, 80). This led from Chester in an easterly direction straight towards the nearest hill country, the moorlands beyond Leek, where north Staffordshire borders on Cheshire and Derbyshire, where the poet's dialect has been authoritatively located (McIntosh 1963, 5; McLaughlin 1963, 14), where the poet's unusual topographical terms appear in local place-names like Knar, Knotbury, Flash, and where several caves vie for the distinction of having inspired the Green Chapel. The poet probably knew these.

One of these is Thor's Cave, some six miles west of Leek, the 'Capital of the Moorlands', above the river Manifold. Less than a mile to the north is another cave, at Wetton Mill in the same valley, which boasts several holes and resembles the Green Chapel in some respects, as has been well argued (Kaske 1970, 111–21). Neither of these caves is a barrow, although some prehistoric artifacts have been found in Thor's Cave, whose earlier name appears to have been Thurse Cave, the giant's cave. It is probable that the poet was familiar with the Manifold valley including the underground passage of the river in this region of the Pennine limestone country for several miles, only to reappear further down with rushing water. The phenomenon is the likely model for the phrases 'goteȝ of golf' in *Pearl* 608 and 'goteȝ of þy guferes' in *Patience* 310, both vividly describing currents of water gushing forth from deep cavities.

However, there is another spot which bears an even stronger resemblance to the Green Chapel, I believe, than either of the two caves in the Manifold valley. Although it is of course conceivable that the poet drew on more than one real locale in the creation of his Green Chapel, several of the features of this third site are sufficiently arresting to think that he was primarily thinking of one specific place. This is Ludchurch or Lud's Church, a natural cleft in the side of a rounded hill above the river Dane on the Staffordshire-Cheshire border, truly half cave, half crevice, as the poet says, overlooked by a group of oddly twisted *knarrez* whose appearance earned them the name Castle Cliff Rocks, and rich in local legends and traditions involving Lollardry (cf. Davies 1961, 19), truly 'a chapel of meschaunce' (2195).

Ludchurch is a stupendous cleft of some 100 yards in length, from 30 to 40 feet in depth, and with a breadth ranging from six to ten feet. Its walls are vertical and overhanging, with tufts of grass clinging to them. Entrance is through a cavelike opening in the hillside, and at either end there are holes leading into the earth, partly explored by adventurous potholers. It is indeed a very odd 'church'. The name Lud's Church was known to the seventeenth-century Staffordshire historian Robert Plot; perhaps it was originally the 'Lollards' Church'. Of particular interest is that in the time of the *Gawain*-poet it formed part of the possessions of the Cistercian abbey of Dieulacres, which was originally founded at Poulton (its 'holy head'), near Aldford, the previously mentioned ancient fording place on the Dee a few miles upstream from Chester, before being moved into the Staffordshire moorlands near Leek to escape the depredations of the neighbouring Welshmen.

When *Gawain* was composed the monks of Dieulacres, who were incidentally keen hunters and indeed poachers in neighbouring royal forests, were maintaining regular contact with their possessions in Chester and across the Dee, presumably following much the same route as Gawain's likely course.

One of their possessions was a grange in the forest about five miles north of the abbey, at a place called Swythamley Park, overlooked by a lengthy escarpment called The Roaches (recalling the poet's *rocherez*), where the earls of Chester once owned a hunting lodge on an eminence recorded as Knight's Low ('on a lawe'). This was never a castle like Hautdesert, but its location *just two miles from Ludchurch* suggests yet again that the *Gawain*-poet's realistic geography was firmly rooted in the familiar landscapes of this corner of the north-west Midlands of England.

Castles

MICHAEL THOMPSON

At the time the *Gawain* poems were written castles had had three hundred years of history in this country, and the derelict or ruinous castle was already a common feature of the landscape. The innumerable earthen motte-and-baileys of the Norman period had lost their wooden superstructures and had either been converted to stone or abandoned. The twelfth century, particularly the first half, was the great period of castle-building and most of the castles of the poet's time had their origin then, surviving by continuous maintenance and use, additions and alterations. There had been a very notable change in the form of the castle at the end of the twelfth century when instead of a keep or *donjon* or great tower reliance was placed on an enclosing curtain wall, fortified with towers placed along its length, which protected the domestic buildings inside dominated by the huge hall (Thompson 1991, ch. 6). *Sir Gawain and the Green Knight* (*Gawain*) makes no reference to a keep in Bertilak's castle, and its absence from the long description (765ff.) must surely mean that this was intentional.

There was a no less important change in castle design, in the whole concept indeed, in the mid-fourteenth century. The Crown, hitherto the main castle-builder, stopped erecting castles after the 1360s, although the second half of the fourteenth century saw the construction of a number of new-style castles in which display and appearance were as important as defence (Thompson 1991, ch. 10). Regular geometrical, normally of rectangular shape, symmetrical frontages with towers at equal intervals, smoothly dressed and squared stone in even courses, much more elaborate domestic buildings with large windows, broad lake-like moats, elegant gatehouses with recesses for draw-bridge and slots for chain arms (unlike the earlier see-saw bridge), are picture-book features with which we are familiar. The most distinctive features of these late castles which so altered their appearance were machicolations, and as they fascinated the poet but may be quite unfamiliar to the reader it is worth devoting a little attention to them.

When a defender stood on the wall walk of a castle he could not see the base of the wall without leaning out and exposing himself to fire. This was overcome by constructing a cantilevered wooden platform, the *hourds*,

Figure 1. Viollet le Duc's figure illustrating the operation of
machicolations (*bautels*).

projecting in front of the wall so that through apertures in it he could see
the wall base and drop missiles. Line 1190 in *Cleanness* refers to this at the
siege of Jerusalem: 'In bigge brutage of borde bulde on þe walles (*Brutage,
bretasche, hourds*).[1] Transmuted into a permanent stone part of the wall the
hourds became *machicolations* (a term not used in English until the eighteenth century): Viollet le Duc's drawing (fig. 1) shows how they were
formed on stone corbels linked by little arches (the poet's term) or lintels
to support the parapetted gallery, from which a figure has dropped a mis-
sile, 'E' in the figure.

Derived from the eastern Mediterranean, machicolations were little used
in the thirteenth century, as for example in Edward I's castles in Wales, and
as late as the 1340s were hardly used at Maxstoke castle in Warwickshire

---

1   References to the poems are to Vantuono 1984.

(Thompson 1991, 170). They took off, so to speak, when their decorative value was grasped (in France at first), and the classic examples built by the earls of Warwick at Warwick Castle, Guy's and Caesar's towers (Thompson 1988, 75–8) can only be a few years earlier than *Gawain*. In the former case they are set at the top of the tower and in the latter set well below to give a 'crown' appearance (a French speciality). They continued in use long after they had lost all functional purpose and were revived in the eighteenth and nineteenth centuries. The poet's interest in them certainly implies a date after about 1360.

How did the poet describe them without using the French word? In the manuscript non-initial 'u' and 'n' are indistinguishable so if we alter *bantel* and *enbanen* in the printed text to *bautel* and *enbauen* we have what is probably a dialect variation for ME *boutel* (Mod. English bowtell) and ME *embouen*. An analogy is *enbrauden*, used by the poet for ME *embrouden* (embroider). Both words have the same root, OE *boga*, arch, and so we can render them 'little arch' (a diminutive) and the verb 'arch over'. Lines 1458–9 in *Cleanness* illustrate the meaning, referring to the Jewish goblets produced at Belshazzar's feast:

> Couered cowpes foul clene as casteles arayed
> Enbaued vnder batelment wyth bautelles quoynt.

This may be rendered as 'Cups with lids finely shaped as castles/Arched over under the battlements with neat little arches'. A glance at figure 2 shows what is meant. Line 992 of *Pearl*:

> Wyth bautelez twelue on basyng boun

would mean 'With twelve little arches set firm on corbels', referring to lengths of machicolations on the walls of New Jerusalem. The vertical and diagonal lines on its walls shown on folio 42b may crudely represent this. Gates are the weakest point and the gate at Bodiam Castle, Sussex, shows their use in the late fourteenth century (fig. 3). At Hautdesert castle

> Enbaued under þe abataylment, in þe best lawe   (790)

may read as 'arched over under the battlement in the best style'.

Turning now to castles in the poems the three words *mote* (i.e. moat, not motte), *burghe* and *castel* are used apparently indifferently to designate them. We are left in no doubt that their main function was for living in:

> Haf ȝe no woneȝ in castel-walle
> Ne maner þer ȝe may mete and won   (*Pearl*, 917–18)

In fact castles play no part in the story in *Pearl*, *Cleanness* and *Patience*, but a castle is central to the whole story of *Gawain*.

Figure 2. Caesar's Tower, Warwick Castle, showing
French-style machicolations (*bautels*)

Is Bertilak's castle inspired by a real one? The present writer is not the first
to have suggested that the poet was influenced by Beeston Castle, Cheshire
(Thompson 1989). We last hear of Gawain's journey from Camelot when he
reached the Wirral, and the Cheshire dialect is that in which the poem is
written (Tolkien and Gordon 1967, xiii–xiv; cf. Duggan below, 240–2). From
the top of its rock Beeston castle dominates the Cheshire plain and was no
doubt familiar to the poet and his readers (fig. 4). Its bleak isolation accords
well with the name *Hautdesert* of Bertilak's castle, while its rocky locality
recalls the barren ground traversed by Gawain on his way to the Green
Chapel. A negative point in favour is the absence of a keep since further north
a great tower was almost *de rigueur*.

Beeston castle had royal associations and so social prestige: Edward the
Black Prince in 1354 had enclosed a large wooded area at Peckforton, half a

Figure 3. Gatehouse of Bodiam Castle, Sussex, c.1390, with *bautels*
(photo A.E. Thompson)

mile to the south of the castle, as a deer park, although he had to remove a
length of fence to let some deer out in 1357 because there was insufficient
pasture for so many (*Register* 1930–33, III. 147, 273). The barrier on the edge
of a deer park consisted of a ditch on the inside and a fence on a bank outside
to prevent the deer leaping over it. A traveller (like Gawain) coming from the
south would see on his left the Black Prince's fence and the castle on its hill
through the trees and surely the following lines (764–70) by the poet must
refer to this:

> Er he watz war in þe wod of a won in a mote
> Abof a launde, on a lawe, loken under boȝez
> Of mony borelych bole aboute bi þe diches
> A castel þe comlokest þat euer knyȝt aȝte
> Pyched on a prayere, a park al aboute,

Figure 4. Aerial view of Beeston Castle, Cheshire, perhaps the inspiration
for the castle of Hautdesert (Cambridge University Collection of
Air Photographs: copyright reserved)

With a pyked palas pyned ful þik
Þat vmbeteȝe mony tre mo þen two myle

The deer park would of course play a great part in Bertilak's hunting expeditions.

Beeston Castle is an uncompromising early thirteenth-century structure albeit still in active use when the poem was written (Colvin 1963, II. 559–60) but the poet sought to introduce late fourteenth-century features when he came to close quarters as his own tastes and those of his readers would certainly have required. When therefore Gawain stood at the castle gate waiting for the porter to obtain authority to lower the bridge the castle he saw looked late fourteenth-century. It is worth briefly running over the details in lines 786 to 817.

Other vernacular poems refer to a *double dich* (786) which seems to mean not two moats but one that required a double throw or cast when digging to clear the spoil: if you could throw from the shovel ten feet then in order to dig a moat forty feet wide the soil had to be thrown twice either side to empty the ditch. Ashlar, finely dressed stone (789) and machicolation (790) need no comment. The gatehouse was flanked by two towers with the bridge between and beyond a portcullis and gate leading to a narrow passage, wide enough for a cart (three metres) with a porter's lodge on one side. Extending on either side from the gatehouse was the curtain wall, its wall walk behind the parapet on top and interrupted at intervals by projecting towers (*garytez*, 791) that overlooked its face. Although gunports had already come into use in the south the 'mony luflych loupe' (792) were long slits with a short cross slit and 'oellet' at the bottom for sighting. These would be at three levels facing three directions in the towers, and in the merlons on the curtain, the upward divisions of the crenellated parapet, and were designed for use with long or cross-bows.

Barbican (793) could be a pair of parallel walls projecting in front of the gate to confine an enemy's attack but in the fourteenth century it often meant a fortified outer enclosure or bailey, of which there is a very good example visible in the aerial view of Beeston castle (fig. 4). The great roof of 'þat halle ful hyȝe' (794) would have been visible and all sorts of pinnacles, points and crockets of which the chalk-white chimneys are the most interesting (798). In the late fourteenth century it was a favourite practice to place ornaments, sometimes human figures, on top of the battlements which could of course be painted, gilded or whitewashed. The poet described the picture as like the cut-out of paper for a table decoration. This is a period when people admired the beauty of a castle rather than its defensive qualities.

The contrast between the outside and the inside of a castle was quite remarkable since the inner face of the curtain was lined with domestic buildings creating the impression of a country house. Here Gawain, who would have entered on horseback, dismounted and his horse was led away.

As the modern reader may be unfamiliar with a domestic plan of this period (they are surprisingly uniform) a slight excursus is necessary. There was no such thing as a compact house: since Saxon times the dominating feature was the great hall open to the roof where the whole household ate their two meals of the day (Thompson 1995). This had a service or lower end and an upper end adjoining the lord's quarters. At the lower end there were three doors in the gable wall, a central one leading to an external kitchen flanked by doors into the pantry and buttery, for bread and drink. The entry to the hall was at the lower end in the long wall usually (not in a castle of course) faced by another door creating a through passage separated from the main body of the hall by a screen. At the upper end the floor was slightly raised (the dais) and there was a special bow window, the oriel, lighting the place where the high table stood.

Large windows gave light from the courtyard side of the hall (usually deliberately designed to face south) and there were possibly smaller ones facing the moat. The former could be traceried as in a church and there might be pairs of facing stone seats within the embrasures, the only fixed furniture within the building. Traditionally windows were closed by internal shutters but by this date and at this social level glazing is most likely, and more or less essential in the oriel. The tables set longitudinally for the household and transversely at the high end for the lord and chief officers and guests were demountable on trestles and set up for each meal. When the tables were stacked all was free for other functions such as use for court sessions. Seating was on benches except at the high table where there were chairs set with their backs to the gable wall and probably beneath an awning or canopy projecting from it. At night lighting was by 'waxen torches' (1650) and these with the light from the central fire must have created a lurid, flickering effect. The floor would be mortared and strewn with reed or straw that could be periodically replaced. The lower part of the wall might be wainscotted with hangings higher up.

About two-thirds of the way along the floor towards the upper end was the rectangular stone hearth, the smoke from the fire of which made a high roof essential; the huge timber roof, blackened by smoke, was one of the most impressive features of the hall. To modern eyes it is the central hearth that is so difficult to come to terms with:

> þer fayre fyre vpon flet fersly brenned   (832)

Externally the roof was likely to have been stone tiled and to have carried a large structure, the louver, fitted with slats to allow the smoke to escape while keeping the rain out. It was crowned by a weather vane and being a source of considerable pride was probably decorated heraldically.

Two-storeyed transverse wings flanked the hall at either end and the main chapel was usually just beyond that at the upper end. Gawain was entirely

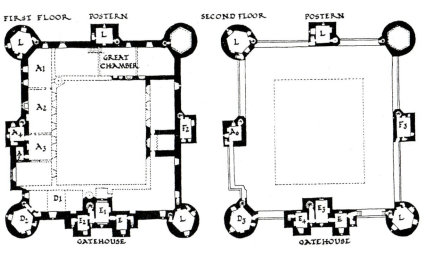

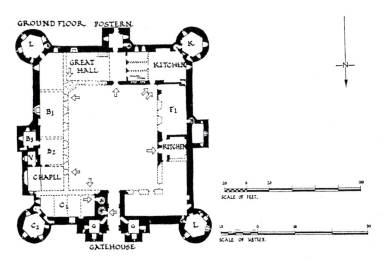

Figure 5. Plans at three levels of Bodiam Castle (P. Faulkner;
Royal Archaeological Institute)

concerned with the upper end and the service end of the hall is never
mentioned in the poem. By the late fourteenth century the rooms were
numerous and lodging ranges of college style with separate 'sets' had already
appeared in castles in the south of the country (Windsor and Amberley).
Figure 5 shows plans of the different levels at Bodiam Castle, Sussex, on the
south coast dated by licence to crenellate of 1386. In the poem the hall is
always called *halle* or French *sale*, but the use of the undifferentiated term

'chamber' for every other room means that one can only guess as to where it was situated.

After being shown his room Gawain washed and repaired to a chamber where he sat in:

> A cheyer byfore þe chemne, þer charcole brenned.   (875)

A chair was a rare article of furniture and its use conferred a mark of dignity. As in the hall a table had to be set up on trestles for his food:

> Sone watz telded vp a tapit on trestez ful fayre.   (884)

A remarkable feature is the difference in the form of heating between hall and chambers. The latter had fireplaces (875, 1667), a hood or canopy with a flue in the wall thickness to the chimney above. A wall fireplace did not become normal in the hall until the next century.

There is no reference to a parlour, the name that in the late fourteenth century had already been conferred on the ground floor room adjoining the upper end of the hall. The well-known passage by Langland that condemned the lord for withdrawing from the hall in order to eat in the parlour (Skeat 1869, 148) need not be repeated here. Cheshire was no doubt a remote area but the lack of reference to a parlour, just where we would expect Gawain to be entertained, suggests the poem was written not later than 1400. The plan of Haddon Hall in figure 6 shows a fourteenth-century lay-out with later alterations so that the central hearth in the hall has been transferred to the wall in the fifteenth century, and the parlour, although probably in this position from the fourteenth century, has been altered, particularly by the addition of a bow window.

A castle normally had a main chapel and several smaller ones and private oratories so:

> Chaplaynez to þe chapeles chosen þe gate   (930)

At least two masses a day would be normal as well as before and after a journey or special undertaking. In this case the service gave Gawain an opportunity to see the whole household, particularly the female part of it.

There is no way of saying where Gawain's bedroom would be situated, in a lodging range or even in a tower. Luxuriously furnished, it was also probably equipped with a fireplace and latrine in a wall recess. Most people slept on a palette with palliasse and a bed is clearly a mark of status. Gawain's bed had a curtain that could be drawn round it but no tester or canopy on top; the former was common from the twelfth century and the latter not usual until the next century. The bed may have had, as in the illumination, a raised back, and Gawain probably slept naked as he seems to be shown to do in the illumination. This was normal.

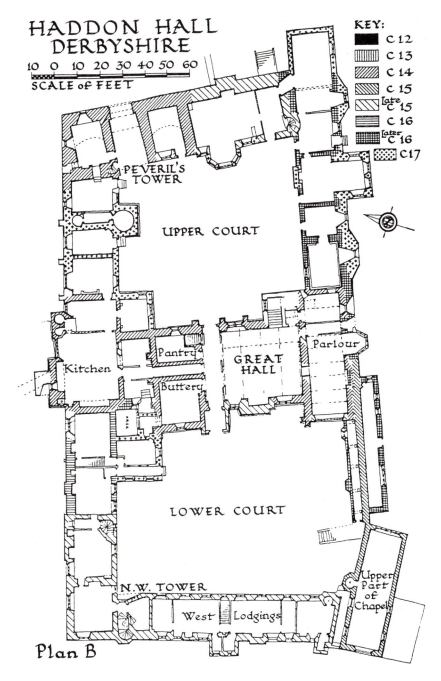

Figure 6. Ground-floor plan of Haddon Hall (P. Faulkner;
Royal Archaeological Institute)

The poet gives no information about the rest of the courtyard and one cannot usefully pretend to describe it. However, the kitchen, because of the smoke from its great fireplaces and the ovens for baking bread, would have been conspicuous and the source of what must have been the pervasive odour of burnt wood inside a castle.

Camelot is described as a castle (*bur3*) in line 259 and its hall was clearly of standard medieval pattern. The dramatic episode of a meal being interrupted by a rider on horseback entering and riding up the hall recalls the arrival of the King's Champion in Westminster hall during the Coronation feast (seen for the last time at George IV's coronation in 1820). It was a familiar device to heighten drama, especially if a poem was being read out in the hall. It was quite feasible in an English hall on the ground floor but not so on the first floor, entered by steps at right angles as in a French hall.

Feasts

DEREK BREWER

Feasts are a normal part of human life everywhere, except in cases of total poverty. They mark occasions which are not infrequent but are more special than the course of ordinary everyday affairs. They involve the most immediate necessities, food, drink and society, but for that very reason are highly symbolic, carrying a great charge of religious, social, personal, political, psychological implications. Of their very nature their celebration in life and art is interconnected. They may also be closely related to their opposite, the fast. Fast and feast may be part of a larger cycle of life (Bynum 1988; Henisch 1976).

At their extremes, as incredibly wasteful extravagance occurred in the medieval period as with modern pop-stars. But there were psychological, social and political compulsions as well as ostentation, adding to the sense of belonging to an élite and the delight in luxury. There are also some counter-elements to be recognised and contained – notably consciousness of the existence of the poor, the ever-present possibility of famine.

Royal feasts were extraordinarily lavish. To give examples: at Christmas 1251 Henry III caused to be consumed 430 red deer, 200 fallow deer, 200 roe deer, 200 wild swine, 1300 hares, 358 swabs (it is not clear what these were), 115 cranes and thousands of other beasts and birds (Rackham 1989, 52). Edward I gave a tremendous feast at Westminster on Whitsunday, 22 May 1305 in honour of the knighting of Edward of Carnarvon, with which the king associated some 300 other knights to all of whom he promised free robes and a great banquet. Again the amounts are staggering. For meat, 400 oxen, 800 sheep, 400 pigs and 40 boars were called for. In addition a torrent of fish and fowl, thousands of eggs, tons of wheat, floods of wine were required. A huge crowd of families, friends, retainers and hangers-on, beside the usual number of courtiers, would have had to be fed (Bullock-Davies 1978, xvii, xxxix). This was an unusually grand occasion with political motivation as the spur, but feasts of almost equal size were regularly held at the Christian festivals of the year. The noun 'feast' is earliest recorded in English to denote a religious festival, c.1290 (*MED*), though secular uses of the verb are virtually contemporary (c.1300). At this period the secular and religious aspects of life are often not separated.

The installation of Archbishop Neville at York in 1467 illustrates the point. The higher clergy rivalled the higher nobility. Part of the food included 300 quarters of wheat, 300 barrels of ale, 100 barrels of wine, 104 oxen, 6 wild bulls, 1,000 sheep, 304 calves, 304 *porkes*, 400 swans, 2,000 geese, 10,000 capons, 2,000 pigs (which seem to be different from the *porkes* or hogs), 104 peacocks, 13,500 birds, and vast quantities more of pasties, game, fish, even seals, jelly, hot and cold custards, spices, sugared delicacies, wafers. There were six thousand guests, and the feast must have lasted several days. The precision and the roundness of numbers may encourage some scepticism, even allowing for the well known clerical efficiency of these households, but there is no reason to doubt the orders of magnitude.

As a last English example nearer the date of the *Gawain*-poet we may note the chronicler Thomas Walsingham's reference to the coronation feast of Richard II. The banquet was held in the Great Hall at Westminster. The crowd was so vast and close-packed that it required the exertions of the Duke of Lancaster, as Seneschal of England, and a number of assistants, all on horseback, to force a way for the servants to bring the food. Walsingham says that the reader would not believe the details of the size and splendour of the feast and the crowd, and gives only one example. In order to display the magnificence of the kingdom, he says (a significant remark), a marble column was erected in the middle of the palace, on the top of which was erected a great golden eagle, from under whose feet four jets spouted different kinds of wine throughout the day, and 'not even the poorest men were forbidden to drink' – another significant remark (Riley 1864, I. 338).

Chronicles and archives refer to a myriad other feasts, in detail or in passing. There was enormous elaboration, as Cosman liberally illustrates by word and picture, including recipes. Bakhtin has vividly suggested how the consumption of food is itself a highly symbolic act, ingesting the world (Cosman 1976; Bakhtin 1968). A feast might well be a conscious political as well as social act by those who gave it, while those who were invited paid with their subservience for welcome luxury of food and drink, a break in routine, for recreation, play, singing, dancing, entertainment, and the sense of being an élite, or on the fringes of it. For host and guest it was an act of triumph by culture over nature, an establishment of power, control, civilisation, hierarchy, social bonds.

The clearest and best documented examples of the elaborate organisation of a feast come from the Continent. A very elaborate feast with a long dramatic episode was given in Paris in 1378 (Loomis 1958). Perhaps the most striking example, though a little late for our poet, was the great feast given by Philip the Good of Burgundy at his chateau in Lille, 17 February 1454. Its object was to launch a crusade and incite knights to make a vow to join in. Because the vow was made on a live pheasant it became known as the Feast of the Pheasant (Lafortune-Martel 1984).

The feast contained some elaborate intermissions – the famous *entremets*, the symbolically significant decorations and entertainments, invented by the French, which were introduced, broadly speaking, between the various courses, or indeed, as in the present case, seem eventually to have been produced simultaneously with the food and drink. The elaboration of this feast may be measured by the fact that it did not finish until 4 a.m., having probably started in the early evening.

Twenty four *entremets* were put on the tables or nearby, and a member of the court said in a letter later that he believed nothing so sublime and splendid had ever been done before. Among the *entremets* made either of pastry or actual wood and paper, painted and gilded, and including actual people, were a holy church, including a lady sitting on the church personifying it; a ship; fountains; a statue of St Andrew; the chateau of Lusignan with its famous fairy, half-woman, half-serpent, Melusine; an Indian forest with wild beasts; and a stupendous pie under whose crust was concealed an orchestra of 28 musicians, who played alternately with the church bells. There was also a procession through the hall of animals, monsters, and allegorical personages. Three scenes were played from the life of Jason. These were perhaps the sort of thing our poet calls 'interludes' (*Sir Gawain and the Green Knight* (henceforward *SGGK*), 472). The banquet took its name from the central *entremets*. An official carried in a live pheasant and formally asked the duke and his company to make 'useful' vows on the noble bird.

Although the actual number of guests seems to have been no more than 24 there were great numbers of spectators. The Feast of the Pheasant makes particularly clear what underlay so many feasts: an intellectual and imaginative structure which moved the whole affair into the realms of play, often specifically elementary drama, and symbolic social significance, yet play and drama in the service of a specific politico-religious purpose. Belshazzar's feast in *Cleanness* is precisely of this kind. (See also 'Feasts' in Brewer 1992.)

It is not surprising that a good deal of thought went into the holding of actual feasts, and that there was both rationalisation and instruction.

The thirteenth-century encyclopaedist, Bartholomaeus Anglicus, as translated by John Trevisa, comments that

> Meat and drinke is ordeined and conuenient to dinners and to feasts, for at fests, first meat is prepared and made in a redinesse, guests be called togethers, formes, and stooles be set in ye hal, and tables, clothes and towells bee ordeined, disposed and made readye. Guests be set with the Lorde in the chiefe place of the boord and they sit not downe at the boord before the guests wash their handes . . .

Children and servants, knives, spoons, bread and drink, etc., etc., with music, are all duly organised, then comes the conclusion with fruit and spices, washing, grace, more drink 'for gladnesse and comfort' etc., then men take their leave (Batman 1582, Lib. VI, chap. 23).

Chapter 24 continues with a history of the development of feasts, and gives the thirteen qualities of the feast, dinner or supper. They include convenient time and place, 'the heart and glad cheere of him that maketh the feast', variety of food and drink, courtesy and honesty of servants, friendship and company of guests, mirth of song and music, plenty of light of candles, special deliciousness of food, 'long during of the supper' following hard work, not having to pay, and finally sweet sleep afterwards.

Besides the somewhat obvious but not negligible generalisations about the pleasures of commensality drawn by Bartholomaeus from the learned tradition, we may note two at a rather higher level. First, the feast is a break in routine, a break from work – it is exceptional. Second, the emphasis is on the achievement of orderliness in celebration; material and social orderliness and hierarchy.

All these long-standing concepts, valuably traced by Nicholls (1985), were turned into practical instruction in vernacular handbooks in the fourteenth and fifteenth centuries, with a reference to which we may conclude our survey of what feasts actually were like. The fullest such handbook is the early fifteenth-century *Book of Nurture* by John Russell, comprising 1,250 lines which vary from 12 to 15 syllables each. In one manuscript the work is ascribed to John Russell, one-time servant with Duke Humphrey, who died in 1447. Probably not all the text is by Russell, who may have re-written an earlier work and had his own contribution added to by the scribe. The value of Russell's work lies in its plain matter-of-factness, its fullness, and its representativeness. Russell gives a huge amount of detail which fills in the picture so far sketched. One is impressed by the minuteness of instruction and the immense elaboration of the whole concept and practice of feasts. We are led through the duties of the numerous servants, going down to how to fold the cloth when laying the table. Ability to name the various foods and drinks is insisted on. How to behave properly (e.g. do not pick your nose), how to carve, what the difference is between fish and flesh, are carefully laid down. There are a considerable number of menus, and much is made of the variety of components of each several course. Instructions on how to look after the lord when he takes a bath are included, with other instructions for a chamberlain. Amongst the menus are included a form of *entremets*, which Russell calls a *sotelte*. These seem to be elaborate table decorations, moralising emblems, for example a series of devices, which must have been small models, of the Four Ages of Man, or the Four Seasons. These are nothing like so elaborate as the living and sometimes speaking *tableaux* of the greatest French royal feasts, but they are an equally clear indication of the way a feast was shot through with symbolic imagery. The *Gawain*-poet refers in *SGGK* to such things indirectly when he remarks on the beauty of the white towers and pinnacles of the castle that seemed cut out of paper (802), and describes them directly in Belshazzar's feast (*Cleanness* 1407–12).

The verses which Russell composes, or reports, for these *soteltes* form a natural bridge to the descriptions of feasts, where both the actual nature of the feast and its joyous festivity, with further significance, are naturally made even clearer. Twelfth-century Arthurian romances naturally offer a rich field (Ruck 1991, 44–8).

The serious as well as joyful purposes implicit in the feast are revealed as we might expect in the *Gawain*-poet, especially in *Cleanness*. After the evocation of God as an imperious king, and a condemnation of priests who are defiled, the poet moves into a description of the parable of the Wedding Feast, based on both Matthew (22: 1–14) and Luke (14: 16–24). There are interesting differences between these two Biblical accounts. Matthew has a king give the feast, and destroy those who ill-treated his servants. The guest without a wedding garment is cast into outer darkness. Luke prefaces his account with the Dominical injunction not to give feasts to your friends and rich neighbours lest they repay you with other feasts, and thus, by implication, you lose merit (or advantage). Rather give a feast to the poor, the maimed, the lame and the blind (14: 12–14). This goes directly against the usual practices and aims of feasts in medieval society and the *Gawain*-poet ignores it, unlike Langland. Luke's feast is given only by 'a certain man' who is less drastic in punishing those whose refusals of his invitation have became almost proverbial for their domestic ingenuity. The *Gawain*-poet, as he says (51), follows mainly Matthew, using that portion of the gospel read in the Mass.

The king's feast at the beginning of *Cleanness* is fully in accord with fourteenth-century notions, and neither the poet nor the Gospel writers are troubled by the problem of how a man compelled to come unexpectedly to a feast can be blamed for not having the appropriate clothes. Since others could be properly dressed, we assume that he could have been, but it is an unimportant detail in the light of the general purpose of the story. There is in all accounts a curious blend of realism and of folktale arbitrariness and hyperbole. The passage amply illustrates how important the feast is to the giver, who needs to give, and needs his guests for the sake of his own honour and to exercise his own power. We note too that as part of the social structure of gifts it is an insult by a lower-rank person to refuse an invitation from a higher, though by acceptance he confirms his own lower status and his obligation towards the king. At the same time the guest is also honoured by the invitation.

In this instance the poet regards the feast with all its plenty of bulls and boars, poultry, partridges, swans, cranes, as entirely good. He accepts the parable's lesson that the poor and needy are worthy to be honoured, though only after those of higher estate have been invited and have rudely refused. Finally, it must be remembered that for all the local realism the story of the feast is told as an image of heaven, and in all cases the story line is at least partly driven by its illustrative or exemplary purpose, which may even create illogicalities on the literal level, as with the man in dirty clothes.

Other feasts illustrate the general theme of *Cleanness*, like that modest feast given by Abraham to the angels, much enjoyed by them (829–30), but more elaborate is another feast given by a king, at once very similar and very different, which concludes *Cleanness*. It is a negative illustration of the theme of 'cleanness'. The King Belshazzar defiles the holy Jewish vessels looted from the temple in Jerusalem by using them for his secular feast. (On the importance and symbolic significance of the vessels, see Morse 1978.)

The poet presents the feast with sarcastic gusto and rich realism. Kings and lords are obliged to come to do reverence to the king, listen to his revelry, look at his concubines and call them ladies. They and he are alone on the dais (not unknown in actual feasts). Knights and barons crowd in, trumpets play, food is carried in on silver dishes, there are little houses built of paper, carved on top, tipped with gold, crowning the dishes. The dishes are carved with elaborate figures of animals and birds, with precious blue enamelling, and one whole large device is carried into the hall by men on horseback. The poet relishes the glory while condemning the perverted behaviour. Belshazzar orders in the holy vessels which he has looted from the Temple, sacrilegiously drinks from them, and gets more and more wildly drunk till God is sickened. He sends first warning, then disaster. Feasting is not bad in itself but is condemned when turned to evil purpose (*Cleanness*, 1357–60).

The splendid but interrupted feast is used again by the *Gawain*-poet in *SGGK*. Here the feast seems good, but it is used, as traditionally in Arthurian romance, as an invitation to an 'adventure', in this case the apparent though deferred death-threat represented by the Green Knight. The festival is a glorious fifteen-day celebration, and the poet emphasises the youthfulness of the court and of Arthur himself as *sumquat childgered* 'somewhat boyish' (86) (which some critics interpret unfavourably). That these are the very early days of Arthur's court is significant of the tone the poet takes and the type of story he wants to tell, with a young fresh Gawain, famous indeed, but without the later history of adventures and *amours* of many a story. Some critics have seen in the sprightliness of the court an implicit condemnation. Burrow however points out that the poet conforms 'to the tradition of its genre in favouring the young and the new', including the New Year, and this fair folk in their first age. Youth may not have everything its own way, but this courtly high-spirited youthful festival is presented in its own cheerful terms (Burrow 1984, 173–5). The compulsion to come, the exercise of power, are subordinated to legitimate joy and merry making. Decorum is not violated – except by the Green Knight. Exciting trumpet-music plays in the food, as music does still sometimes 'play in' the guests at formal dinners. The seating at High Table is strictly hierarchical, with the king at the centre, and the most honourable guest, Bishop Baldwin, on his right, the queen as his consort on his left. Gawain, the sister's son, the heir-apparent, next in honour, sits on her left, and his younger brother Agravain, another nephew, on Gawain's left again. Yvain, known in other English romances, like Baldwin himself, sits on Baldwin's right.

As in most formal feasts the other side of the table is unoccupied so that food may be served. The other guests of lower status sit at tables endwise to High Table which is on the dais across the hall at the further end, though as was customary they are served in pairs. To emphasise the carefree plenty in a society whose base-line is real hunger, all are served double helpings, and both beer and wine (106–29). Arthur stands politely chatting in front of High Table (the word *hende*, 'polite', not being devalued in the poet's idiolect) while all wait for something interesting to happen. Apart from the delay it is a scene and a protocol that might be followed today at a grand dinner of the Lord Mayor of London or in a Cambridge or Oxford college hall. Haddon Hall in Derbyshire offers just such a setting. The Round Table has become a traditional name, remote from its Arthurian origin.

The fifteen days of Arthur's feast is the traditional Arthurian and romance period, as editors note. 'Fifteen' is a 'magic' number from long back, found in Middle English religious formulas as well as in the period of feasts. (French of course still refers to a *quinzaine* as what English persists in calling a for(teen)night, fourteen being also a highly significant and related number.) At certain periods the feast of Christmas began on the feast-day known as *O Sapientia* (from the first words of the Antiphon – the alternate singing in the religious office of scriptural sentences – which is set for the 16th, or in some non-English calendars, the 17th December (see Cross 1958)). It may be worth noting that fifteen days from 17th December brings us to New Year's Day, the day of Arthur's great and presumably concluding feast of the festival. Formulaic and apparently thus empty as the traditional length of the Christmas festival in Arthur's court therefore may appear, it may nevertheless fit the author's interest in numerological patterns.

A similar hall setting, with the emphasis this time on Christmas games, is the scene of the Christmas feast at Bertilak's castle. As the games seem to have been quite boisterous the tables, which would have been boards on trestles, would have been removed after the meal. By contrast with Arthur's festival, the feast at Bertilak's castle apparently lasts only four days – Christmas Day; St Stephen's Day, 26th December; St John's Day, the 27th; Childermas (Holy Innocents' Day) the 28th (though the scribe has missed out the line, supplied as 1022a by Gollancz 1940 and Silverstein 1984). The syntax is slightly confusing here and there may be more scribal error, but it is certainly on this last day, the 28th, that though there was drink and dancing, the guests depart 'on the gray morn' (1024). The hunting episodes, and the temptations offered by the Lady, take place during daylight on the 29th, 30th, 31st, December, and the entertainments, those hearty party-games, and the bargains made, take place in the evening, still not very late, for it would have been dark by 4 p.m. and the hunters safely home.

But there is also a feast that is no feast in Bertilak's castle. Gawain arrives, presumably about the middle of the day, for there is still plenty of light, on the day we call Christmas Eve. The day before a major ecclesiastical feast like Christmas Day was in theory kept as a fast, being part of the traditional vigil before the feast. This does not bother Arthur's court as far as we are told, but it explains why the splendid private dinner with lots of wine given to Gawain in his own room on his arrival at the castle is politely, but in a sense accurately described by his attendants as a 'penance' (897). This is because it is composed entirely of fish, regarded as a penitential food. But it is superbly and variously cooked, and Gawain with equal politeness and accuracy, though with less devotion, describes it as a feast. Quite subtle nuances of courtly decorum, ancient conventions of hospitality, high standards of etiquette, and rather equivocal religious practice, are involved here. Serious-minded people like Langland would condemn such equivocation, of which monks themselves, let alone secular nobility, were sometimes accused. Opinions may differ, but it would seem to me that in this case, as with other aspects of the courtly life and feast, the poet by no means condemns either the rather nominal penance that Gawain endures, or the fact that the wine went a little to his head. What else should good wine do after such an arduous journey? Wine was not forbidden in the Bible or elsewhere. Gawain is thus fortified and cheered for the Mass he then attends and his consequent meeting with the ladies, all conducted with perfect propriety. The poet has no more of a problem with such comforts than do Trollope's wealthy clergy when they have a good dinner with wine during Lent. There is a whole religious mentality expressed here, which whatever we may think of it now is not hypocritical.

Even the boisterousness of Bertilak's party-games, or the doubtless pleasant stir of the dancing, giving of New Year gifts, and perhaps kissing-games of Arthur's court, are all well-ordered. *Per contra*, it has been argued by Bakhtin (1968, 88) that feasts offered the occasion for disorder, for 'carnivalesque' subversiveness, that is, for popular 'creative' hostility to the 'official culture'. 'Carnivalesque' has become a favourite modern critical adjective, but it only slightly fits the medieval English scene. It is clear that at many feasts, as in that quoted above from Walsingham, there was a great deal of pushing and shoving in an overcrowded hall. In such crowds, in the volatile and violent state that characterised medieval society, there is always the possibility of riotous behaviour. It is further clear that such behaviour is highly unwelcome, and that any release it may afford is destructive and joyless. With our poet, and with the many feasts recorded in medieval history and literature, the prime aim was orderly official festivity. Even such consciously parodic festivals and celebrations as that of the 'boy bishop' were ritualistic and were hierarchically structured and controlled. There were riots, rebellions and subversive outbreaks in plenty in medieval England, and it is of course part of Bakhtin's argument that they were officially deplored and repressed, but there is no evidence that they were jolly. Perhaps they (dis)ordered these things better in France. In England they were quite understandably characterised by a savage bitterness. The notion of joyous subversiveness seems more typical of modern critical thought than of medieval practice.

Nevertheless Bakhtin's insight is of value in considering the *Gawain*-poet's

works. The sense of liberation created by carnival may be suggested by the
Green Knight's intrusion on Arthur's feast in *SGGK*. Orderly the feast may
be, in the poet's imagination, and in the Arthurian tradition generally, but it
is a necessary preliminary to its own interruption, in a word, to disorder. It
is an invitation to 'adventure'. Although poised to begin, it cannot be pro-
ceeded with until it is interrupted. The period of waiting is a fine example of
what the anthropologist Victor Turner regards as a 'liminal' situation, betwixt
and between (Turner 1969). As such it has both liberating potentiality and
danger, which are realised at the entrance of the Green Knight. His advent is
indeed an *entremets*, and Arthur calls it such, an example of the playing of
enterludes that well become Christmas (472). The Green Knight's unceremo-
nious rudeness and the challenge of the Beheading Game may thus perhaps
be regarded as 'carnivalesque'. They are hostile, but they release new energy
in the hero. The element of play, of fantasy, and our tacit understanding of
romance, encourage our enjoyment and expectation of a happy outcome. The
'carnivalesque', itself a liminal situation, is subversive, accepted, and refresh-
ing. There is nothing 'popular', in the sense restricted to low-class people,
about the Green Knight. He does not represent the oppressed peasantry any
more than he represents nineteenth-century fantasies of vegetation gods and
the survival of pagan religions. As he himself insists, he stays well within the
courtly rules. At the dénouement a year later, his manner is gracious, even
paternal, when he congratulates Gawain on having done, on the whole, very
well indeed, with only a slight and natural shortcoming.

If the feast at the beginning of the poem is an invitation to adventure, the
feast nearly a year later, at Bertilak's castle, is fun and games for the guests,
and an exercise in festive power for the host, who in manner is not unlike the
imperious host at the beginning of *Cleanness*. Furthermore, there is no feast
to mark the end of Gawain's adventure. It would have been as otiose as that
account of Gawain's adventures on the way home which the poet declines to
relate. His poetic economy and tact are superb. A feast often marks the end
of an Arthurian adventure, as for example in Malory's 'Tale of Sir Gareth',
but the poet avoids so firm and simple a closure here, leaving us with an
ambiguity well reflected in the variety of critics' judgments on how well
Gawain has done.

One might argue that Belshazzar's feast is in a way subversive, even wildly
'carnivalesque', in that it is a blasphemous defiance of God, and therefore
subversive. But it is also, from Belshazzar's point of view, part of his own
'official culture'. Here the lesser official culture confronts the greater. It is
straightforward rebellion, rather than carnival where there must be some
element of play. The result is an overwhelming victory for the official culture
of God, for which both the Bible and the poet are enthusiastic spokesmen.

The darker background of a society which was always in danger of famine,
and which pressed cruelly on its poorer members, gives the feast by contrast

a brighter light and makes even more understandable festive joy. The Biblical notes have already been marked. The *Gawain*-poet himself obliquely refers to the darker background when he devotes a whole poem (*Patience*) to the virtue of patience and connects it with the endurance of his own poverty. But his solution, characteristic of his own conformist temper, and of an agrarian economy of low productivity where indeed 'ye have the poor with you always' (Mark 14: 7), is to bear suffering patiently. Langland, who probably knew poverty more intimately and certainly felt for the poor more strongly, describes feasts but, in line with Luke (14: 12–14), calls vigorously on his readers not to give feasts to kin or rich men, but to the sorrowful, crooked and poor (*Piers Plowman*, B XI, 189–97). It is a moving passage. A little further on Langland is scathing about a good dinner at court, where Conscience and Clergy and Patience and the poet himself are given food inferior to that at High Table – a common custom not only in the Middle Ages. He is sarcastic about the fine food consumed by one who not four days before was preaching at St Paul's (B XIII, 22–67). He concludes the Passus by advising rich men at their feasts to have a learned man as storyteller to cheer them with the story of Good Friday, and a blind man or a bedridden woman for a jester, rather than the usual minstrels (B XIII, 436–59). Though he preaches reversal, a real subversiveness, a world-upside-down very different from the usual hedonistic version, Langland cannot get away from the concept of the feast. In this he echoes the preaching of the Gospels and of many medieval preachers who constantly called attention to the plight of the poor (however bishops might behave – and some did indeed give their broken meats to the poor). The influential twelfth-century *Policraticus* by John of Salisbury contains in Chapter VII of Book VIII an extended condemnation of feasts (Pike 1972). The devotional tradition also paid due attention to the fast, the complement, ordained by the Church, to the feast. But the only fast the *Gawain*-poet notes is the splendid fish supper Gawain first receives when he arrives at Bertilak's castle, where the food may be technically that of the fast, but the concept is rather that of polite self-depreciation.

In summary, and in larger context, in our Christian Western tradition there has always been a certain duality of attitude towards feasts. Thus feasting and fasting have both been presented as ideals (Bynum 1988). Sometimes feast and fast are hostile contrasts, sometimes, and more often, complementary opposites. Feasting and fasting are both plentifully recorded in Old and New Testaments and equally commended. Jesus went to many dinner parties apparently with pleasure and the miracle of the marriage feast at Cana exemplifies his approval. The Last Supper, which we continuously commemorate in the Eucharist, is a kind of feast. As the church developed historically it evolved many festivals which included feasts. But Jesus also fasted forty days in the desert, commemorated by the period of Lent. Perhaps all religions worthy of the name have fasts and feasts. But in Western Europe the feast also has an existence independent of religion. A confusion developed so that a religious festival was often called a feast, by natural association. To celebrate a saint or even the Saviour, you have a feast. Also as is well known, the Church deliberately took over previous pagan feasts and festivals, as at Christmas and Easter. Yet while Christianity may use feasts, as it must use all natural human activity, its ultimate message must transcend even the symbolism it uses. In consequence in our historical development the feast has to be regarded as a natural, even secular element, which Christianity may use to express joy and commitment, but which in our culture is so to speak free-standing, essentially secular. The feast is natural, human and good but no more central to Christianity than is the fast. In this respect Europe seems to differ from what the anthropologists report of some African societies. There the feast is central to the religion in some tribes (Goody 1982).

Another general point arises here. In contrast with African societies, the feast in Europe seems always to be an expression of hierarchy, and consequently, of order in society. Order implies the risk of disorder. We again find duality, but here unified. In Europe the feast is the expression of a certain social dynamism, whereby tensions and even conflict are both built in and contained. The feast is therefore also an event which contains some internal contradictions.

Quite noticeable in the *Gawain*-poet is that he does not include the king's distribution of gifts as part of the feasts which catch his imagination, though they were often an important element in actual life. But even in actual life in the later Middle Ages gift-giving seems to have become dissociated from feasts. We see a progressive 'aestheticisation' of courtly life, such as Lee Patterson has noticed in Chaucer (Patterson 1991, 197–230), though we may not agree that this is a self-destructive process. Courtly activity is beautified and becomes less utilitarian, more ceremonious, more poetic, gratuitous and purely human.

Yet the exercise of power, particularly clear in the Parable of the Wedding Feast at the beginning of *Cleanness*, more or less explicit with Belshazzar, implicit with Arthur and Bertilak, must always be recognised as an important element in the giving of the feast.

One aspect of this power relationship was the feast as conspicuous wasteful consumption, the 'potlatch', which demonstrates the power and resources of the giver of the feast even while diminishing them (Mauss 1954). No great lord could afford socially not to entertain lavishly even if he could not literally afford it. Even Charlemagne had this problem. Einhard records that Charlemagne's officials were worried by the expense of his entertainment of foreign guests. Charlemagne replied that the advantage to his prestige more than compensated for the nuisance of their presence (Henisch 1976). Power and utility may paradoxically best be achieved by apparently non-utilitarian means.

Feasts are by no means, however, only cold-hearted calculations for obtaining power and influence. Sometimes they are, but they could not be used cynically if they did not have a more natural, spontaneous and agreeable significance. There are many obvious good things about feasts – the pleasures of eating, talking, meeting old and making new friends. There may be sexual stimulation and opportunity. Order brings comfort and security. Moreover there is the pleasure of being chosen, of being an élite. Unworthy people are not allowed, or are thrown out, as the parable of the Wedding Feast illustrates. The feast confers social self-esteem, as well as physical well-being, on an élite. Social order and unity imply moral order and unity. We need and passionately desire the harmony of order and unity. The gratuitousness of the feast is itself a blessing. The feast is a temporary visit to 'Heaven'. Moreover it may lead to new events, new people, surprising developments. Even if a Green Knight is unlikely to ride into our hall, a new beginning is made, new friends found, new ideas, new energies, new projects are born. There is a triumphant element that gathers up the past and projects into the future.

Moreover it is notable that in real life, as in medieval poems, the presence of ladies was one of the delights of the feast. Only in the original primitive twelfth-century Arthurian fantasy of the Round Table, designed to prevent quarrels over precedence, were there no seats for ladies.

The feast is a triumph of society over nature (Clein 1987). The hall is a manmade victory over nature, created by building, by excluding the elements and consuming the products of nature, animal and vegetable. When held at night the warmth of fire and the brightness of torch and candle are more triumphs over nature. We keep out evil. Yet nature when subdued is also good, if only to support ourselves.

The feast is a positive assertion. As such the *Gawain*-poet's appreciation of it, even when he condemns the perversion of the feast, or wryly notes the negative aspects of what he is celebrating, is characteristic of his generally positive attitude.

Note

For an admirable general survey of feasts in courtly life see Bumke 1991, 178–230, with extensive bibliography. His range of reference is limited, however, almost entirely to the twelfth and thirteenth centuries, and to Continental, mainly German, sources. English literature is not mentioned, nor much English historical evidence. Some of the present note is based on Brewer 1991, which includes more reference to Chaucer, omitted here, and less to Langland.

Jewels in Pearl[1]

FELICITY RIDDY

I

When Richard II was preparing to leave on his Irish campaign in 1399 he was concerned about who would look after his queen, the ten-year-old French princess Isabella. He sought the advice of her chamberlain, Sir Philip de la Vache, her doctor, Master Pol, and her confessor as to whether his cousin, Lady Mary de Coucy, was a suitable person to put in charge of the child in his absence.[2] After some shuffling of feet, the three men allowed themselves to be pressed into saying that, in their opinions, Lady de Coucy would not do. The confessor said she was not sensible ('saige') enough, while Sir Philip suggested that her reputation was not good enough ('elle ne me semble pas assez honnourable'). Master Pol was more explicit: he said that she lived in greater estate than the queen herself, with eighteen horses and more. 'She keeps two or three goldsmiths, and six or eight embroiderers, and two or three dressmakers, and two or three furriers, as many as you or the queen. And she has also built a chapel which cost fourteen hundred nobles' (Williams 1846, 25–6). On hearing this, Richard paid Lady de Coucy's outstanding bills and sent her back to France. Lady Mortimer, the recently widowed countess of March, took her place.

Lady de Coucy's expenditure on luxuries seems to have offended these sober gentlemen, not simply because of its extravagance but because it ran

---

[1] I gave an earlier version of this article, entitled 'Apocalypse Then', as my inaugural lecture at the University of York on May 23, 1994, and I am grateful to my colleagues Richard Marks and Amanda Lillie for their advice and guidance. The lecture was dedicated, as this is, jointly to my granddaughter, Isabel Riddy, and to Jill Rickers, who wrote an outstanding York MA thesis in 1992 on the Apocalypse imagery of the Great East Window of York Minster while in the early stages of the illness from which she died in 1995.

[2] She was born in France in 1366. Her mother was Edward III's daughter, Isabella, and her father was a French nobleman, Enguerrand, Sire de Coucy. Edward III created him duke of Bedford, but on Richard II's accession in 1377 he resigned his English honours and committed himself to the French cause. His wife and younger daughter returned to England, but his elder daughter Mary remained with him in France. She came to England in 1397 as a member of the household of Isabella of France.

counter to their notions of degree. She was spending on a royal scale; although of royal blood on her mother's side, she was only a duchess.[3] Master Pol apparently did not think it inappropriate for the king and queen to employ so many goldsmiths, embroiderers, dressmakers and furriers, but a duchess who did the same thing was clearly rather scandalous.[4] *Pearl*, of course, records a similar, scandalized sense of the difference between a countess and a queen: the dreamer can accept that in heaven his daughter might have become the first, but finds it hard to believe that she can have become the second. In Edward III's reign an attempt had been made to regulate spending on jewels and clothing in order to clarify social difference and prevent people getting above themselves. The sumptuary laws of 1363, which were aimed at consolidating hierarchy and degree, laid down, for example, that no-one below the rank of a knight with an income of over one hundred pounds, or below a merchant or artisan with an income of over five hundred pounds, was allowed to wear jewellery of gold set with precious stones.[5] Although this legislation was repealed a year later, nevertheless it provides a context for interpreting the way in which the Pearl-maiden's appearance is represented. She has, the dreamer notes with a fine late-fourteenth-century eye for social caste, an expression solemn enough for a duke or an earl (211). She is dressed in a 'bleaunt' (163) of shimmering white 'biys' (197), which was a luxury cloth worn by people of high status,[6] edged with the most beautiful pearls the dreamer has ever seen. The white kirtle she wears underneath it has a double trimming of pearls, while on her head is a pinnacled crown adorned with pearls in the shape of exquisite flowers (208). Her crown could have come straight from the inventory of Queen Isabella's jewels, which includes many items given to her as presents on her arrival in England in 1397: the crown of gold with eight fleurons ('couronne d'or a huit flerons') which the duke of Gloucester gave her, her cap with large pearls made in the style of roses ('chapeau de grosses perles fait a maniere de roses'), and the headdress of pearls set in the style of trefoils and large pearls ('coiffe de perles assise a maniere de triffle et de grosses perles') which was a present from the king.[7]

The maiden is, of course, not only dressed in clothing fashionably adorned with pearls (Kunz and Stevenson 1908), but is represented as a pearl herself. A recent study of the poem by an influential critic remarks that the opening stanza 'presents a narrator identified as a mourner, his language one of

---

3 She married Henri, duke of Bar in 1393.

4 The criticisms of Lady de Coucy's lack of 'saigesse' may, of course, also have been a coded message to the king about the folly of courtly luxury in general.

5 See *Statutes of the Realm* (London, 1810–28), i, 380–1:37 Edw. III, c. 8–14.

6 That 'biys' is a luxury cloth is clear from the citations in *MED*, 'bis', n.(1).

7 The inventory was compiled on behalf of the king of France in order to ensure that the jewels were returned when the widowed Isabella was sent back to France after Richard II's death. It is printed in Williams 1846, 108–13.

intimate feelings. As a host of critics have demonstrated, this language is the conventional language of the courtly poetry of love evolved over the preceding two centuries.' (Aers 1993, 57). To read the narrating voice only as that of a mourner in the opening stanzas overlooks the fact that it is simultaneously identified as a jeweller's; in fact, the language of the jeweller's craft and trade precedes that of the courtly lover. The pearl which is identified in the first line as 'plesaunte to prynces paye', worthy of being set 'in golde so clere' (2), is linked in the third with exotic trade goods ('Oute of Oryent'),[8] and is next an object of the narrator's keen professional appraisal: 'Ne proued I neuer her precios pere' (4), 'Quere-so-euer I jugged gemme3 gaye/I sette hyr sengeley in synglere' (7–8).[9] Only when this has been established does the language of courtly longing supervene. The dreamer is identified as a jeweller not only implicitly in the first stanza, but explicitly at lines 252, 264, 265, 276, 288 and 289. The maiden is a 'juele' (23, 249, 253), and a 'gemme' (289). Later she twice uses the word 'juelle' herself of the Lamb – 'My lombe, my lorde, my dere juelle' (795, and 1124) – and the dreamer uses it of the procession in the Holy City at 929.

These metaphors go along with the extraordinary emphasis placed on precious stones and metals throughout the poem. The glittering landscape of the dream – its 'crystal klyffe3' (74), the trees with their leaves like 'bornyst syluer' (77), the gravel of 'precious perle3 of oryente' (82), the river-bed that gleams with 'emerad, saffer, oþer gemme gente' (118) – owes something to the paradisal garden of the *Roman de la Rose*, and thus to secular literary traditions of aristocratic opulence. On the other hand, the description of Jerusalem, 'so nwe and ryally dy3t' (987), in lines 985–1040, is derived directly from the Book of Revelation where it is the final stage of St John's vision, at the end of time. The New Jerusalem is shown to him as a city built entirely out of gold and layer upon layer of twelve different kinds of precious stones, with gates of pearl. Throughout the Middle Ages the Book of Revelation was used as a source of information about jewels, which were believed to have magical and healing powers or 'virtues' (see Power 1922). The whiteness of the pearl, for example, was held to signify virginity, its smallness represented humility, and its power 'is said to be against the shedding of blood, against the suffering of the heart and for the strengthening of the spirit'.[10] This

---

8 In the Middle Ages there was an extensive trade in precious stones from the East. This trade came through the Mediterranean, which was a source of high-quality pearls. Marian Campbell observes that by the twelfth century the native ' "Scotch pearls" . . . were cheaper than the oriental', so the latter were more highly prized. (Campbell 1991, 116). According to John Cherry, 'Rubies came from India and Ceylon; sapphires from Ceylon, Arabia and Persia. Emeralds came from Egypt and turquoises from Persia or Tibet, and amethysts from Germany or Russia' (1992, 22).

9 All quotations are from Gordon 1953.

10 'Virtus autem hujus lapidis dicitur esse contra sanguinis effusionem, contra cordis passionem et ad spiritus confortationem', from the life of Saint Margaret, in Jacobus de Voragine, *Legenda Aurea* (Graesse 1890, 400).

symbolic system is used explicitly in *Cleanness* (1117–32), where the precious-ness of the pearl is said not to derive from its monetary value, but because it is a signifier of purity. Information about the significations of jewels was assembled in encyclopaedias, as well as in the specialised handbooks known as lapidaries, written in Latin and in the vernaculars, which discuss the properties of the precious stones from which the Heavenly City in Revelation is constructed.[11]

The Book of Revelation, like the *Roman de la Rose*, was in many ways a high-status text in the later Middle Ages. In the second half of the thirteenth century and for much of the fourteenth it had a particular vogue in England as devotional reading in sumptuous manuscripts. These Anglo-Norman Apocalypses were luxury objects commissioned by aristocratic clerical and lay patrons, female and male. They contain complex cycles of illumination, often with over a hundred pictures accompanying a text.[12] In the fourteenth century these cycles, established in manuscripts, were transferred into monu-mental forms, moving from small-scale, intimate images in books designed for domestic meditation, to large-scale images on buildings in a variety of art forms.[13] The Apocalypse was woven, for example, in the cycle of huge life-size tapestries commissioned in 1379 at Angers for the chapel of Louis, duke of Anjou, and was painted on the walls of the chapel at Karlstein Palace in Prague, whose patron was the father of Richard II's first wife. In England it was used on the roof-bosses of the Norwich Cathedral cloister, begun by 1346; on the walls and ceiling of the chapel at Berkeley Castle by the 1390s;[14] on the great East Window in York Minster, commissioned in 1405; on the walls of the chapter house at Westminster Abbey, probably painted in the first decade of the fifteenth century. No single impulse lies behind these monu-mental Apocalypse cycles, but it is hard not to see them as in some sense – given the kinds of buildings they are in and the kinds of people who commissioned them – statements of a final hierarchy and order which is sanctified by their visionary biblical source. *Pearl* brings together the personal scale of the Apocalypse manuscripts and the high didacticism of these monumental representations of Revelation. All of them take for granted, and indeed can be said to issue out of, Revelation's paradoxical justification of wealth and opulence in the Heavenly City – paradoxical because the book also contains a strain of denunciatory satire directed against merchants and

---

[11] For English examples, see Evans and Serjeantson 1933.

[12] There is an extensive literature on medieval English Apocalypses, including James 1931; Henderson 1968; de Winter 1983; Emmerson and Lewis 1985. See also Morgan 1988. The relation between *Pearl* and English Apocalypse manuscripts is dealt with in Whitaker 1981.

[13] This had begun to happen in the thirteenth century: in the Apocalypse window in Bourges Cathedral; in carvings on the west portal of the cathedral at Rheims; in frescoes painted by Cimabue in the high church at Assisi.

[14] These do not survive, and are only known from a contemporary reference (Perry 1925, cxxiv–vi).

materialism. Although *Pearl* questions the value of 'tresor', it does so from within, rather than outside, the luxury system of which both it and the Apocalypses are a part.

II

In Middle English, 'juel' meant not only a precious stone but also, more commonly, a highly wrought art-object.[15] This meaning is clear from *Cleanness*: when Nabuzardan presents to Nabuchadnezzar the 'juelrye' (1309) he has looted from the temple of Solomon, it includes the 'chef chaundeler' (1272), the golden 'condelstik and the crown als' (1275), the 'goblotes garnyst of sylver' (1277), basins, dishes and beautiful plates, vials and vessels 'of vertuous stones' (1280). It is these 'jeules out of Jerusalem' (1441) which Belshazzar is later to defile at his feast. The gold basins, ewers, cups, beakers, bowls, goblets and vials that are brought forth on that occasion are described with the lavish detail of an inventory. Their extravagant realism – lids shaped like castles, embossed, engraved and inlaid with leaves, fruit, birds and animals and set with precious stones (1456–84) – is not biblical but late fourteenth-century International Gothic.[16] *Pearl*, with its extraordinary technical elaboration and its complex verbal interplay, is itself a jewel in this sense. The idea that an utterance might be a jewel is suggested within the poem itself, when the dreamer says of the maiden's speech: 'And jueles wern hyr gentyl sawez' (278). The poem uses both alliteration and end rhyme, and the stanzas are linked by concatenation. A linking word or syllable runs through a group of six stanzas before it is changed, and there are twenty groups. The last line of the poem links up with the first. Nothing of this formal dexterity had been achieved before in any surviving Middle English poem. Lyricists had certainly experimented with very complex short forms, but this is on a sustained and massive scale. As a jewel, the poem locates itself among other highly-wrought, prestigious art-objects, religious and secular, of the late fourteenth century: the elaborate reliquaries, caskets, crowns, brooches and

---

15 See *MED*, 'jeuel' n. 1(a) and (c). Elaborate artifice is characteristic of the jewels of the period. For example, a late fourteenth-century jewel in the form of an M, now owned by New College, Oxford, is described in the college's *Liber Albus* as 'this costly and sumptuous jewel [Jocale] all in silver and gilt bearing the glorious likeness of the very Mother of the Lord and the likeness of the Archangel Gabriel with a crystal vase set in the middle, *wonderfully crafted*, from whose opening may be seen to arise a lily all of silver' (New College Archive 9654, fol. 15, quoted in Alexander and Binski 1987, 483, with photograph. The translation from Latin is by John Cherry. My italics).

16 Around 1360 Petrarch, in his *De Remediis*, ch. 4, denounces the contemporary fashion for decorating goldsmiths' work 'with entire forests and their inhabitants, all kinds of trees, beasts, birds, human faces and whatever else the eye can see, the ear hear and the mind invent'; quoted by Krautheimer 1982, 61.

cups that were the products of the jeweller's craft.[17] The figure of the maiden, with her 'bornyste quyte' (220) clothing adorned with pearls and her elaborate crown, seems to emanate from the aristocratic taste for white enamelling *en ronde bosse* which is such a striking new feature of the *de luxe* works of art of the end of the fourteenth century.[18] Probably the most famous surviving example is the spectacular 'Goldenes Rössel' (Little Gold Horse), now in Altötting, a reliquary given by Isabel of Bavaria to her husband Charles VI in 1404, and probably made in Paris. It was set with ninety-seven pearls, twenty-three balas rubies and twenty-one sapphires. The image of the Virgin in the upper part, made of gold and covered with white enamelling apart from her golden hair, has six pearls surrounding a ruby on her breast. In the lower part is the gold horse with white enamelling *en ronde bosse* from which the piece takes its name.[19] There are references to work of this kind in the French royal inventories from before the 1380s, and a surviving English example from the 1390s is the Dunstable Swan, a livery badge in the form of a swan of white enamelled gold.[20]

The poem about jewels which is itself a jewel thus associates poetry in the English language for the first time with prestige art; *Pearl* associates itself with the international aristocratic luxury system – including fine food and wines, expensive horses, costly fabrics, tapestries and art works of various kinds – that is the matrix for one kind of high culture in the late Middle Ages.[21] Master Pol's denunciation of Lady de Coucy, which brings together her horses, her jewels, her clothes, and her architectural patronage (she had spent fourteen hundred marks on building a chapel), can be seen as a critique of her role in that culture, and possibly of that culture itself. The matrix for another kind

17 Examples of the kind of work I have in mind are: the King John cup now in King's Lynn, made around 1340, possibly in England, of silver-gilt with translucent enamel depicting courtly figures; the Royal Gold Cup of the Kings of France and England, with enamelled scenes from the life of St Agnes, made in Paris about 1380, now in London; the gold crown, set with rubies, sapphires, pearls and diamonds, now in Munich, which may have been made in London in the 1390s and was sent to Bavaria in 1402 with Henry IV's daughter Blanche on her marriage to Ludwig III; the reliquary of the Order of Saint-Esprit, of gold enamelled *en ronde bosse* (see n. 18), set with rubies, pearls and sapphires, possibly made in London around 1410 for Henry IV's wife, Joan of Navarre, and now in Paris. For descriptions and illustrations of medieval jewellery and jewel-making, see Lightbown 1978, 1992; Hinton 1982; Delahaye 1989.

18 Enamelling *en ronde bosse* is a method of applying enamel to the surface of a three-dimensional figure made of gold or silver. The surface is roughened to allow the enamel to adhere to it. The technique developed in the second half of the fourteenth century. See Gauthier 1972. In the Wilton Diptych, probably of around 1395–9, Richard II's badge of the white hart seems to be *en ronde bosse*.

19 See Lightbown 1978, 67. There is a photograph of this piece in Cherry 1992, 51.

20 The Dunstable Swan is in the British Museum; see Cherry 1969, 38–53. A photograph of it is in Alexander and Binski 1987, 488.

21 For an accessible account of aristocratic expenditure on luxury goods in the fourteenth century, see Dyer 1989, chapters 2 and 3.

of high culture in the late fourteenth century is the literary internationalism that Chaucer uses. *Troilus and Criseyde*, which was written in the 1380s and thus is possibly more or less contemporaneous with *Pearl*, makes a bid to place English poetry in a grand European tradition at the conjuncture of different kinds of old and new writing in Latin, French and – most dazzlingly – Italian. That is, for Chaucer the court poet, at that stage of his career in the 1380s, literary internationalism is the route by which the English vernacular can move into glamorous new areas and do glamorous new things. *Pearl*, I am suggesting, goes not for the glamour of European literature but for the glamour of European luxury.

The high culture sustained by the luxury system is the product of exchange between craftsmen, merchants and aristocrats: between the court and the city. The narrating voice of *Pearl*, shifting between jeweller and courtly lover, is an acknowledgement of this. The jeweller provides a social identity very different from those adopted by Chaucer and Langland. The speaker in Chaucer's dream visions is a bookish failed lover who reads himself to sleep; in *Piers Plowman* the speaker is a dissatisfied vagrant, half hermit, half layabout, who falls asleep wherever he happens to be. Both of these are marginal figures, without precise social location, positioned half-outside the systems of thought or structures of feeling with which their poems engage. A jeweller is in some ways different. The word is first recorded in English in the early fourteenth century,[22] and is used of one who works with or trades in gems and precious stones. Jewellers were urban, because they depended on the wealthy clientèle which a large centre of trade could supply. They were allied to goldsmiths; in fact, in the fourteenth century goldsmiths are quite frequently described as jewellers as well. The goldsmiths' guilds, in London and in other large towns, were part of the urban patriciate (Reddaway and Walker 1976), and their customers were mostly wealthy aristocrats and churchmen. Lady de Coucy is alleged to have maintained two or three goldsmiths, while John of Gaunt's register shows that he bought from goldsmiths in London and Paris, which was the centre of the trade. The dreamer as jeweller is thus not himself an aristocrat; the jeweller practises a closely-regulated craft, dedicated to the highly-skilled production of and trade in luxury objects. The merchant of the parable of the pearl of great price

---

[22] See *MED*, 'jeueler' n. Marian Campbell cites the occurrence in the London subsidy roll of 1319 of 'Alice la Jueler'. She comments that 'The medieval understanding of the term *jeweller* is problematic, for it seems to mean variously a retailer of goldsmiths' work (including jewellery), a retailer of gemstones, an appraiser of gemstones, and only sometimes the craftsman who worked or set the stones' (Campbell 1991, 151 and n.). In the A-text of *Piers Plowman*, cited in *MED*, Mede is characterized as 'a Iuweler,/ A Mayden of goode' (Passus II. 87). This use of 'Iuweler' is translated by *MED* as 'one who owns or loves jewels', but probably means 'one who deals in jewels', given the criticism of Mede for giving lavish bribes, which I discuss below. *Pearl* 252 is cited as the only other parallel for *MED*'s suggested meaning, but there is no need to read the latter example in a transferred sense.

translates quite naturally in *Pearl* into a 'jueler' (730 and 734) – a trader in precious stones – who takes the enormous financial risk of giving for the pearl 'all hys god' (734). *Pearl* is positioned at the meeting-point between aristocratic and urban values which sanction acquisitiveness: the desire to own beautiful things, the taste to recognise and commission them, the leisure to enjoy them, the money to buy them, the skill, training and capital to make them. The poem reminds us that the court is not separate from the merchant or the artificer: and in the Book of Revelation the place of gold and jewels is not a court but a city.

Jewels in the Middle Ages were indicators of aristocratic taste, standing and wealth; they were not merely aesthetic but functional. Jewels were also – and had long been – a form of currency, both literal and symbolic. When, for example, Richard II borrowed £2,000 from the City of London in 1380, he deposited as security a collection of jewels, headed by a 'coronet . . . set with balasses [rubies], emeralds, sapphires, diamonds, and large pearls' which he asked to borrow back two years later for his wedding, leaving instead a gold headpiece decorated with pearls and precious stones, like the maiden's 'coroun of grete tresore' (237; Riley 1868, 443–4). So the coronet is both a valuable portable item which can be pawned, and a symbol of majesty. The jewels with which it is set are the most highly prized in the medieval hierarchy of precious stones: sapphires, according to the thirteenth-century encyclopaedist, Bartholomaeus Anglicus, are 'most apt to fyngres of kynges' (Seymour *et al.* 1975, 205), while a fifteenth-century lapidary says that 'the gentel rubie . . . hathe vertu above all other precios stones' and that it is of such lordship that 'when he that cometh bereth it amonge other men, all they schul do him honor and grace' (Evans and Serjeantson 1933, 110). The combination of pearls, sapphires and rubies, set in silver and gold, is frequently found in princely collections of goldsmiths' work of the fourteenth and fifteenth centuries (Stratford 1993, 209, 211, 324, etc.).

Nevertheless, as valuable portable goods and symbols of status, jewels are also currency of a slightly different kind: they are objects of exchange, part of the elaborate system of gift-giving and receiving through which networks of power, reciprocity and obligation were maintained. John of Gaunt's accounts for 1382, for example (Lodge and Somerville 1937, I. 231–3), reveal his payments to goldsmiths for the ostentatious luxury goods – drinking bowls, rings, tablets, brooches – made of gold, engraved, enamelled, set with precious stones, which he had distributed at the previous New Year to the king and queen and to members of his circle (including 'Philippe Chaucy', the poet's wife, who was the sister of John of Gaunt's mistress, Katherine Swynford). Medieval jewels and plate are paradoxically mobile and fluid; they are passed from person to person, melted down into coin, formed and reformed, travelling along the networks of social obligation that existed not only within the aristocracy but between the aristocracy, the church and the urban patriciate as well. It is because of their plasticity and malleability that very little has survived from the huge amounts of secular goldsmiths' work which we know from inventories and wills to have existed in the late Middle Ages.[23]

Pearl can be seen as part of the same system of exchange as these jewels. It is not necessarily a directly personal or autobiographical poem, though critics often write as if it were. In fact there is a common, unexamined assumption that medieval English poets wrote for themselves.[24] If it were true, it would mean that writing poems was the only one of the comparable crafts in which this was the case. Painters, sculptors, musicians, the artists and craftspeople whose collaborative skills are brought together in the making of illuminated manuscripts and tapestries, all of these worked to commission in the fourteenth century. There are many manuscript illuminations in which authors are shown presenting copies of their books to patrons. What we see in these donor pictures is only one half of the system of reciprocity that they in fact record. They are visual reminders of the obligations of largesse that is to come, or a record of largesse already received. In trying to imagine an occasion for the composition of *Pearl* then, we might think of an obit for a dead child – a commemorative mass performed each year on the day of her death.[25] The person who commissioned *Pearl* may have been someone retained by, or

---

[23] See, for example, in addition to the inventory of Queen Isabella's jewels already referred to, Stratford 1993; Myers 1959–60.

[24] The model for the poet who writes for himself comes from Italy, which had a very different literary and artistic culture from that of England in the fourteenth century. Boccaccio, who was possibly a generation older than the author of *Pearl*, drew on Dante and Petrarch, as well as on classical poets, in cultivating the idea of poetry as a vocation rather than the craft or trade for which I am arguing. In his *Genealogia deorum gentilium* Boccaccio says: 'Whatever the vocation of others, mine, as experience from my mother's womb has shown, is clearly the study of poetry'. The epitaph he composed for himself ends: 'His father was Bocchaccius, his homeland Certaldo, his pursuit was nourishing poetry' (Massera 1987, ix–x, xxi). Boccaccio's *Olympia*, which may have provided the author of *Pearl* with a model, is autobiographical in a way I am suggesting *Pearl* may not be: it is a Latin elegy for the poet's five-year-old daughter, Violante, cast in the form of dialogue between the dead Olympia and her father Sylvius, an old shepherd. It is one of a series of eclogues on public and personal subjects – classicizing pastoral poems on the Virgilian model – written over many years and completed before 1367–8, the date of the autograph manuscript. In *Olympia* the dead child consoles her father for his loss and tells him about the joys of heaven; it was probably not composed before the late 1350s, some years after Violante's death. See Massera 1987, 154–73.

[25] After the Peasants' Rising in June, 1381, John of Gaunt did not go back to London until November of that year, when a formal reconciliation took place between him and the mayor and aldermen; see Goodman 1992, 91. Two silver bowls must have been presented to him on that occasion, since the 1382 register shows him paying to have the queen's coat of arms engraved in the bottom of two silver bowls which he had recently been given by the citizens of London, and which he gave in turn to the queen on her coronation (the coronation from which Richard II had got the crown out of hock); see Lodge and Somerville 1937, I. 232. The reason for Gaunt's entry into the city in November 1381 was ostensibly to attend a mass for the soul of his first wife, Duchess Blanche, who had died twelve years earlier. The mayor and aldermen accompanied him to St Paul's and escorted him out of the city again afterwards. It is conceivable that Chaucer wrote *The Book of the Duchess* for such an occasion. Thus we have coming together a ritual commemoration of the dead, a

obliged to, or desirous of favours from, or wanting to be reconciled with, or in any one of the variety of gift-giving and receiving relationships with one of the aristocrats who held lands in the Cheshire/Staffordshire region and whose households were constantly on the move around their manors and between these, London and the royal court. Perhaps we are looking for an aristocrat who had lost a child called Margery or Margaret, since the Latin 'margarita' means 'pearl'.[26]

This comes perilously close to arguing that the dead little girl is merely an object of exchange among men, and that the poem is simply a precursor of the exchange that would have taken place had the real child lived to marry. But what I am talking about in this process of cultural exchange is not merely the commodification of art, whether it is a jewelled cup or a jewelled poem, though it is that, of course. During the Peasants' Rising, when the rebels who ransacked the Savoy destroyed John of Gaunt's treasure – grinding up his rings and jewellery in mortars, as they are reported to have done by one chronicler, rather than looting them[27] – they must have had a sense of these not merely as material currency, but as objects of 'virtue', alive with power and lordship, as in my earlier quotation about the ruby: 'when he that cometh bereth it amonge other men, all they schul do him honor and grace'. A poem may also be an object of 'virtue' and not only a commodity.

III

The 'virtue' of *Pearl* lies in its rhetorical power to persuade the reader of the spirituality of its attitudes to wealth and status, for which jewels are a metonym. I have been arguing that the poem is the creation of the luxury system which the maiden endorses and sanctifies; similarly, in *Cleanness* there is no acknowledged contradiction between the excessive opulence of Solomon's treasure and its signification as a symbol of undefiled holiness. In *Pearl* one source of the child's authority over her father is social: she is represented as a queen in the court of heaven, and heaven itself – the jewelled landscape, the jewelled city – is associated with the prestige and power of aristocratic luxury. The religious feeling that sustains *Pearl* is not unlike that

---

ceremonial gift-giving, and élite politics, which perhaps provides a model for a context for *Pearl*.

[26] The suggestion that the name of the dead child may have been Margery or Marguerite was first made by Gollancz (1891, xliii).

[27] Walsingham reports of the mob who sacked the Savoy that 'In order that the whole community of the realm should know that they were not motivated by avarice, they made a proclamation that no one should retain for his own use any object found there under penalty of execution. Instead they broke the gold and silver vessels . . . into pieces with their axes and threw them into the Thames or the sewers; . . . they ground up rings and other jewels inlaid with precious stones in small mortars, so that they could never be used again.' (Dobson 1983, 169–70).

which characterizes another exquisite, high-status, late fourteenth-century work of art, the Wilton Diptych. This altar-piece of the late 1390s is, like *Pearl*, a visionary work which brings together the courts of earth and heaven in an atmosphere of refined personal piety and aristocratic opulence.[28] Although issues of status in *Pearl* are a source of debate, as I have already pointed out – the father cannot believe that the dead child is a queen on her first day – nevertheless luxury is not subjected to the hostile criticism available in other contemporary religious and political discourses. In *Wynnere and Wastoure*, for example, the debate – which is not resolved – is focused directly on luxury, which Winner castigates. Unlike in *Pearl* and the Wilton Diptych where she is queen of heaven, Winner uses the Virgin, with her 'wedes . . . pore' (420) as an example of poverty and as a rebuke to Waster's 'pompe and pride' (422).[29] The description of 'Mede the mayde' in Passus II of the B-text of *Piers Plowman* might almost have been written directly against the *Pearl*-maiden and the values of which she is a product. Mede drips with jewels – rubies, diamonds, two kinds of sapphires – and in Passus III she distributes to the men of Westminster 'Coupes of clene gold and coppes of silver, / Ringes with rubyes and richesses manye, / The leeste man of her meynee a moton of gold' (22–5), in return for their promise to smooth the way for her to marry as she pleases. The whole of this Passus is an indictment of contemporary gift-exchange, which is represented merely as a form of corruption. As Conscience warns the King: 'In trust of hire tresor she teneth ful manye' (124) and 'By Jesus! with her jeweles youre justice she shendeth . . .' (155).[30] For Langland luxury goods cannot be spiritualised into symbols of heavenly power, but remain resolutely material and political. The position *Piers Plowman* adopts

---

[28] The Wilton Diptych, which is in the National Gallery, London, was probably commissioned by Richard II in the late 1390s; see Gordon 1993 for recent discussion, bibliography and illustrations. Like *Pearl*, the Wilton Diptych exploits some of the meanings given in late fourteenth-century culture to the innocence of youth – in this case, the innocence of young boys. One wing depicts Richard as a fashionably-dressed young boy kneeling in front of his patron saints, Edmund, Edward the Confessor and John the Baptist, while on the other the infant Christ leans towards Richard from the arms of his mother, flanked by eleven elegant angels who wear Richard's livery badge of the white hart. Note that the pearl which the maiden wears on her breast also turns out to be a livery badge. The procession of virgins in the New Jerusalem all wear the same clothes as the maiden, and each has on her breast 'þe blysful perle wyth gret delyt' (1104). At 1108 the narrator comments that 'alle in sute her liuréȝ wasse'; they are all represented as, in late fourteenth-century terms, retainers of the Lamb. I am grateful to Helen Barr for pointing this out to me.

[29] Trigg 1990. Trigg dates the poem 1352–c.1370. Lois Roney has recently argued that both Winner and Waster represent bad examples of economic practice: 'one produces but does not consume, the other consumes but does not produce' (Roney 1994, 1092). Winner's moralistic castigation of Waster's luxury is, in Roney's view, itself economically short-sighted.

[30] Quotations are from Schmidt 1987b.

towards 'Mede' may help us to understand the attitude of Richard II's advisers towards the ostentatious spending of Lady de Coucy.

Nevertheless, the materiality of treasure is a problem in *Pearl* too, though here because of its transience. Jewellers do not own jewels, or at least not permanently: jewels pass through their hands. In this sense the relation between jeweller and jewel brilliantly catches the temporariness of the relation between parent and dead child, as well as the latter's preciousness. The representation of the dead child as a pearl at the very beginning of the poem thus sets up a language that is used throughout to address ideas of human preciousness, value and loss. Early in his exchange with her the dreamer asks: 'What serueʒ tresor, bot gareʒ men grete/When he hit schal efte wyth teneʒ tyne?' (331–2). We might expect the answer to this question to be a version of that provided by Holy Church to the dreamer in Passus II of *Piers Plowman*: 'Whan alle tresors arn tried, Truthe is the beste' (134). We might expect the treasure that is not lost to be Christ, and the various transformations of the pearl image to come together in the image of the Lamb as 'gay juelle' (1124), surrounded by the virgins, the elders and legions of angels. But *Pearl* does not end with this vision of achieved union but in separation, as the dreamer wakes from his dream: 'Þerfore my ioye watʒ sone toriuen/And I kaste of kytheʒ þat lasteʒ aye' (1197–8). The poignant transience of dreams is not unlike the dreamer's sense of the poignant transience of 'tresor'. While the poem confronts and attempts to contain mutability and to provide consolation in the face of death, at the same time the voice of religious authority is undermined because the maiden – as a dream – participates in that transience, and the poem re-enacts her father's loss. If we return briefly to the fourteenth-century luxury system, to all those glittering objects which seem to be so permanent, and which are used in the poem as symbols of eternity in contrast with the transitoriness and mutability of the world, we can see that jewels themselves are ambivalent. I have already suggested that they are paradoxically mobile and fluid, constantly melted down and reshaped, or – as with John of Gaunt's jewels – even ground into powder. The Italian sculptor Ghiberti tells the story of a fourteenth-century goldsmith, Gusmin of Cologne, who was employed by Louis, duke of Anjou, the patron of the Angers Apocalypse tapestries. When the duke had Gusmin's beautiful works of art melted down in order to finance his 'public needs', Gusmin was so broken-hearted that he gave up his craft and went into a hermitage.[31] The narrating voice in *Pearl* is that of a mourner, bereft at his loss, but his grief is expressed not only in the language of courtly love. The persona of the jeweller also

---

[31] Ghiberti, *I Commentarii*, bk II, ch. 17. Gusmin has not been identified, but he must have been in the service of the duke of Anjou between 1360 and 1380; the duke's 'public needs' were the conquest of Naples. See Krautheimer 1982, 62–3. For the full text of Ghiberti's account of Trecento art in his *Commentarii*, see Courtauld Institute n.d., translated from von Schlosser 1912.

allows for other kinds of broken-heartedness, of which the story of Gusmin reminds us: the merchant's grief for the loss of the jewel he had only temporarily owned, and the craftsman's grief for the destruction of the jewel which he, as jeweller/father, had made.

The Hunts in Sir Gawain and the Green Knight

ANNE ROONEY

> The game causeth ofte a man to eschewe þe vij deedly synnes . . . for
> whan a man is ydul and recheless . . . it is a thyng which draweth men
> to ymaginacioun of fleishly lust and plaisire, for suche men han no lust,
> but alway for to abyde in oon place, and thenketh in pryde or in auarice
> eiþer in wrethe, oiþer in slawthe or in gloteny or in lechery or in envie.
> (Edward Plantagenet, 2nd Duke of York, *The Master of Game* (Baillie-
> Grohman and Baillie-Grohman 1904, 4–5))

That the hunt keeps men from sin is a common conceit in Middle English
literature. Although probably a protestation against the condemnation the
church often heaped upon hunters, the belief held wide currency. Tolerance
of the hunt rested on the assumption that it was the lesser of several evils the
resting knight may choose to indulge in. When knights and nobles were not
out doing knightly deeds, they were better occupied in hunting than in many
of the other things they might get up to, so in its rightful place and amongst
the right people, hunting could be declared laudable. On the other hand

> It is, after all, well-established in chivalric romance that knights who stay
> in bed, like Erec and Yvain, and spend their time inside in the company
> of ladies are asking for trouble. (Barnes 1993, 132)

Yet are we to criticise Gawain for resting in his bed instead of hunting? Almost
certainly he is drawn to imagining fleshly lust and pleasure, but does he really
come unstuck through sloth (Scattergood 1981)? It seems harsh to accuse him
of this. He has passed many dangers and hardships on his way to Bertilak's
castle, and has been assured that he can complete his mission easily on the
last day of the year. If we put ourselves in Gawain's shoes for a moment, it is
easy to see the appeal of Bertilak's proffered leisure. He has been travelling
through the cold and the wet, then spends a pleasant Christmas in a hospitable castle. In a few days, he expects to have his head cut off. He can get up
early in the morning and ride around in the frost trying to kill things, or stay
snuggled up in a warm bed and get up when he feels like it. The preferred
choice is not necessarily the morally (or even socially) better choice, but it is

understandable. We sympathise with Gawain as he accedes to the desire for
a peaceful lie-in. But perhaps the question is pointless. Setting aside natural
human inclination, Bertilak has *offered* that he spends time at ease; he has *not*
offered to take Gawain hunting. It would be discourteous to reject what has
been offered and ask to join in Bertilak's sport uninvited. We can't blame
Gawain for staying in the castle, even if to do so is to invite trouble – he is
offered no alternative.

The hunt and seduction scenes in the third fitt seem at first to represent
something of a hiatus in the action of the poem. The hunts in particular, since
Gawain himself does not feature in them, may appear to be a distraction, even
a holiday from the main purpose of the narrative. As such, the interlinked
scenes have attracted a lot of critical attention. For the most part, this has
centred on Gawain's behaviour in the bed-chamber, which is not our purpose
here. However, the bedroom scenes cannot be taken out of context. The
Gawain-poet does expend considerable energy and narrative effort on the
hunt scenes and we must ask why. They undoubtedly have intrinsic interest,
particularly for a medieval audience familiar with the finer details of the
procedures they describe, and we must not forget that the *Gawain*-poet is
prone to extensive treatment of details of courtly paraphernalia and behaviour for their own enjoyment. But the treatment of the hunts is so considerably extended that we are invited to look for a more concrete purpose in their
placing in the narrative.

Much of what has been written about the hunts in *Sir Gawain and the Green
Knight* (*Sir Gawain*) has focused on a supposed parallel of pursuit – Bertilak
hunts animals while his wife hunts Gawain – and has drawn on the French
tradition of the love-hunt. This theory has been expounded at length by
Marcelle Thiébaux in *The Stag of Love* (1974). In fact, the love-hunt as a motif
held remarkably little appeal for Middle English writers, and the parallel is
of interest in only the broadest sense. Thiébaux has to substitute a hunt for
the hart for the deer-drive of the poem to make the point she wants to make
about the hunt instructing Gawain (his increased self-knowledge comes
rather from the bedroom scenes than from the hunts, though). She finds
interesting uses of vocabulary that suggest hunting activity in the bedroom
scenes – 'cache', 'fonge' and so on – to demonstrate Gawain's role as hunted
prey. However, none of the critics who cite the love-hunt as a model for the
hunts in the poem manages any particular sophisticated or extended reading
on the basis of it. That there are parallel and contrasting pursuits taking place
appears to be an idea the poet has recognised and signalled rather casually,
but not explored or developed at any great length and it cannot offer us any
particularly interesting insights into the poem.

Other role models for the hunter have included the hunting devil and the
hunting Green Man (Speirs 1949; Levy 1965). Neither figure is common in
the courtly literature of medieval England. The hunting devil turns up in
devotional and moral works, but usually with emphasis on trapping rather

than the noble hunt. Without a wholesale association of Bertilak/
Knight with the devil, this reading of the hunt scenes adds li
understanding of *Sir Gawain*.

An early, indeed pioneering, proponent of a symbolic link be
hunts and bedroom scenes was H.L. Savage, who found characteri
animals hunted paralleled in Gawain's behaviour. Thus on the first day he is
timid like the deer, on the second day bold like the boar and on the final day
wily like the fox (Savage 1956). Peter McClure (1973) finds the animals
demonstrating traits that Gawain must quell in himself if he is to succeed in
avoiding the danger of the seductions. Other critics have found sins symbolised by the different animals, and sins which Gawain is tempted to commit
in the parallel bedroom scenes (Ingham and Barkley 1979; Morgan 1987;
Gallant 1970; Longo 1967; Levy 1965). Interpretations of this type may
attribute to Bertilak the role of either God or the devil.

The diversity of these symbolic readings of the hunts should alert us to
their shaky foundations. If the *Gawain*-poet intended any single, clear symbolic meaning, he has desperately muddled the issue; it is more likely that
he didn't intend any of these as the main purpose of the hunting scenes. We
should look carefully at the poet's choice of hunts to help elucidate his
purpose, in incorporating them into his narrative and developing them at
such length. A symbolic meaning would be easier to develop if he could
include a hunt for the hart, the most noble of game and the most thoroughly
developed symbolically in the literary heritage of Europe. However, Bertilak's hunters specifically do *not* hunt the hart, which is out of season. On the
first day, they engage in a deer drive. This is described at length in the early
fifteenth-century hunting treatise *The Master of Game* in a form remarkably
similar to that it takes in the poem. Female and immature deer are flushed
out of the woods and driven towards the waiting hunters who attack them
with arrows and with their hounds. A large number of deer are killed, and at
the end of the day are ritually cut up ('broken') following well-established
procedures. There are relatively few treatments of the deer-drive in Middle
English literature, but one notable one is in another alliterative poem, *The
Awntyrs off Arthure*, and again it features Gawain. We shall return to this poem
and the tradition to which it belongs (Hanna 1974).

On the second day, Bertilak and his men hunt a single wild boar. This was
a formidable adversary, and the advice of the hunting manuals was that it
should not be tackled on foot with a sword, as Bertilak does, but from
horseback or with a boar-spear. In departing from actual practice, the *Gawain*-
poet is following an established tradition of heroic depiction; great heroes
from Classical literature to medieval romance traditionally kill a ferocious
boar with a sword, thus amplifying the bravery and heroism of their deed.
In other respects, this hunt again follows the pattern described in the hunting
manuals for hunting and cutting up the boar. We can conclude that the
Gawain-poet chose to follow the literary heroic model rather than real-life

practice because he wanted to endow Bertilak with the heroism associated with single-handed slaughter of the boar with a sword.

On the final day, Bertilak kills only a fox. He shows his disdain for the creature when presenting his winnings to Gawain, and this is quite in keeping with the low regard in which the fox was held as an object of the chase. The Middle English hunting manuals give very little space to the fox, and it was probably trapped as vermin more frequently than hunted. It was regarded as ignoble prey for a gentleman, and there appears to have been little ritual or formal procedure attendant upon its pursuit. Why this sudden departure? It may be to throw the bedroom scene into relief, or perhaps to change tack and suggest that this time there is a parallel between the behaviour of the hunter's prey and Gawain. The fox in the field swerves aside to try to avoid its fate. We may see Gawain deviating from his path of denial to take the girdle in the hope that it will save him from his anticipated fate. The symbolism cannot be taken very far. The poem does not condemn Gawain whole-heartedly for his fault and he is hardly reduced in our eyes to the status of the wily and ignoble fox. Marcelle Thiébaux (1970) has suggested a link with Henry of Lancaster's *Livre de Seyntz Medicines* in which the fox pelt is a symbol of sin which should be outwardly displayed, as Gawain later chooses to display the green girdle. However, the *Livre* is concerned with stopping up fox holes to trap the fox, and not with the courtly hunt. It is difficult to find any meaningful parallel to the fox-hunt, either within *Sir Gawain* or in other works.

If we look at the pattern of interlaced hunts and bedroom scenes from the viewpoint of a medieval audience, we may identify a couple of motifs common in contemporary literature which fit the action of *Sir Gawain*. One is from verse romance, and the other from the alliterative tradition to which *The Awntyrs* belongs, two forms of literature with which the *Gawain*-poet has explicitly linked his poem in its early lines.[1]

On a first hearing, without knowing the outcome of the poem, a medieval listener may well have recognised a familiar motif from verse romance in which the hero is seduced by an absent hunter's wife or daughter.[2] In the English seduction motif, sexual activity is always initiated by the woman – perhaps a projection of optimism on the part of male authors as much as a reflection of real life. In *Amis and Amiloun*, Belisaunt twice attempts to seduce Amis while her father is out hunting and threatens to accuse him of rape when he rejects her advances; on the second occasion he gives in (Leach 1937, ll. 493–636). In *Generydes*, his step-mother tries to seduce Generydes while his father is out hunting. When he refuses her, she tears her clothes and tells the steward that Generydes attacked her (Wright 1878, ll. 477–515). These are

---

1   On whether alliterative poetry can be grouped together as a body, see Lawton 1983.
2   On hunting motifs in Middle English verse romance, see Rooney 1993, chapter 3.

instances of the well-known motif of Joseph and Potiphar's wife (Genesis xxx). The Lady hints at this possibility, too:

> 3e ar stif innoghe to constrayne wyth strenkþe, 3if yow lykez,
> 3if any were so vilanous þat yow devaye wolde. (*Sir Gawain*,
> cited from Tolkien and Gordon 1967, 1496–7)

In *King Horn*, Horn and Rimenhild meet while her father is out hunting. Fikenhild betrays them to the king and Horn is exiled (McKnight 1901, ll. 683 ff.). In Malory's *Morte Darthur*, Aggravayne persuades Arthur to go hunting so that Guinevere and Lancelot will meet in his absence and evidence of their affair can be discovered (Vinaver 1990, III. 1163). In *The Avowing of Arthur*, Arthur tests Bowdewynne's vow never to be jealous of his wife by hiding a knight in his wife's bedroom while Bowdewynne goes hunting, revealing his presence on Bowdewynne's return (Brookhouse 1968).

The emphasis in all these instances is on opportunity rather than pursuit, and *Sir Gawain* is alone in giving any prolonged development to the activity of the hunter which could encourage a comparison of the hunt and the seduction. It also, of course, gives prolonged treatment of the seduction. The three bedroom scenes concentrate on Gawain's discomfiture, his preoccupation with maintaining his courtesy and his self-respect, and an endearing confusion as he tries to retain the lady's good opinion at the same time as negotiating his way around her desires. The scenes are characterised by a warm humour that increases our affection for Gawain. We do not sense the real danger in them, though some of us may share his concern for his soul being imperilled by any rash action. Instead, whether or not as modern readers we recognise a familiar motif with an uncertain outcome, we and the medieval audience alike seize upon the new interest of the seduction and enjoy it for its own sake. We may wonder whether Gawain will succumb or, assured that he will not, relish his display of love-talking in attempting to extract himself as gracefully as possible from a difficult situation.

As an episode in courtly romance, the coupling of a seduction attempt and a hunt is sufficiently familiar for an audience to greet the new departure with interest and await its outcome. However, the hunts fit into another literary tradition which we are less likely to be aware of but which may have been more accessible to a medieval listener, particularly on second and subsequent hearings. There are several alliterative poems which feature hunting episodes, more or less extended, in which the hunt stands as an emblem of secular courtly life and indulgence. This is set in contrast to some figure or episode reminiscent of man's mortality – a *memento mori* made all the more poignant by its juxtaposition with the pinnacle of worldly enjoyment embodied in the hunting scene.[3]

---

[3] On the use of this motif in Middle English literature, see Rooney 1993, chapter 4.

In the *Awntyrs off Arthure*, Gawain and Guinevere are isolated after a deer-drive and confronted by the ghost of Guinevere's mother who offers a dire warning against pride and lechery. In *The Parlement of the Thre Ages*, a poacher falls asleep after killing a stag and dreams of Youth, Middle Age and Old Age (Offord 1959). The final figure proclaims his despair in the face of impending death and denies the value of beauty, wealth and worldly pleasure. *De tribus regibus mortuis* shows three kings engaged on a boar-hunt confronted by three animated corpses who bemoan the fate they suffer after death as a result of their dedication to pleasure during life.[4] In 'Somer Soneday' the narrator wanders away from a hunt and sees a vision of Fortune's Wheel on which he witnesses great men fallen low and dying (Turville-Petre 1989, 140–7). 'The Lament for Sir John Berkeley' gives a brief hunting narrative as an introduction to a meditation on the death of the nobleman (Turville-Petre 1982). Moving away from the alliterative tradition, Chaucer's *Book of the Duchess* juxtaposes a hunt with the misery of the bereaved Black Knight. There are several lyrics, too, which employ this juxtaposition of hunt and *memento mori*. In each of these poems, the hunt stands as an emblem of worldly pleasure or secular enjoyment which contrasts with the miserable inevitability of death. Where there is a moral message, it is clear: the pleasures of the courtly life distract men from a proper concern with virtue and their coming fate. *The Book of the Duchess* is not explicitly moralistic in its tone, but uses the hunt as a counterpoint to the knight's despair; it represents the courtly life from which he is temporarily excluded by his grief (but to which he may choose to return). In *Sir Gawain*, not only the splendid hunt but the action in the bedroom exemplify the courtly life which stands in stark contrast with the grim appointment at the Green Chapel; John Burrow has commented on the Lady's similarity to Dame Life in the alliterative *Death and Life* (Burrow 1965, 99). The bedroom scenes present another facet of worldly enjoyment – one explicitly concerned with lechery, which is usually a focus of the condemnation of earthly pleasure that the *memento mori* invokes.

In *Sir Gawain*, Gawain is not about to be surprised as he is in the *Awntyrs off Arthure* by a meeting that will make him mindful of his mortality – he is already fully preoccupied with it and anticipates it in the form of his appointment at the Green Chapel. For the audience, the Pride of Life is embodied in Bertilak's hunting and the Lady's love-talking and the expected figure of mortality is the Green Knight. We may be aware that Gawain is unlikely really to be beheaded, but can still expect a warning and stark reminder of death to compare with the message of Guinevere's mother, the three dead kings or Old Age. Consideration of man's mortality is more skilfully internalised in

---

4   *De tribus regibus mortuis* is printed as poem 54 in *The Poems of John Audelay* (Whiting 1931), 213–23. It is unlikely that Audelay actually wrote the poem, but it is a well-known motif. Cf. Tristram 1976, 162–7.

Sir Gawain than in the other alliterative treatments of this theme. We see symptoms of Gawain's preoccupation with what he imagines is his fate even as he tries to sidestep the Lady's advances. His sleep is restless, he thinks ahead to his appointment and he is perhaps more concerned with avoiding immorality than he would be if death were not apparently imminent. In this poem, the realisation of man's mortality is skilfully moved into the main character's psyche rather than just played out in the narrative action, but even so the juxtaposition of familiar Pride of Life images with the reminder of life's transience at the Green Chapel has powerful resonances.

In a poem like *Sir Gawain*, in which the surprise of the ending can strike us on only the first reading or hearing, the poet needs to cater for two different types of audience. Oral poetry, like drama, radio, television or any other performance art, is essentially a serial medium; the listener cannot turn back, except in his or her memory, to an earlier point to compare or gather recollections. Time spent pondering earlier parts of the performance has its cost, too, as the performance continues and we may miss what is going on while we think back. However, on a second occasion, the audience does not need to pay such strict attention to plot development and can watch more closely the development of themes and characterisation. When we know the outcome of Gawain's test, we can look out for additional nuances of meaning in the action of the narrative. The first time an audience heard *Sir Gawain* they may well have identified the common motif of a woman seducing a man while her husband is out hunting. In the heroic boar-hunt, they may have seen the implication of Bertilak as a traditional hero of romance. By the time they got to the fox-hunt, which may confound their expectations, it is already time to turn back to the main action of the poem and consider again Gawain's appointment at the Green Chapel. On a second hearing, perhaps, the importance of the hunt as a metaphor for worldly pleasure, common in contemporary alliterative poetry, may strike a more resonant chord. The experiences of Gawain at Bertilak's castle are now known to be linked with his confrontation with mortality in the form of his impending meeting with the Green Knight. The poem is a rich and complex interplay of different poetic traditions and themes and we need not find it necessary to identify a single, unswerving purpose in the inclusion of the hunt scenes. Instead, we can see the *Gawain*-poet fusing elements from different narrative traditions, particularly from the verse romance and alliterative forms with which he explicitly links his poem, for it is indeed a 'stori stif and stronge, With lel letteres loken' (34–5).

Armour I

MICHAEL LACY

Introduction

The last decades of the fourteenth century lie at the threshold of what Claude Blair called 'The Great Period' of European armour in his authoritative work on the subject (1958). Mail armour, composed of interlinking rings of iron or steel, had been the predominant form of armour in western Europe since the fall of the Roman Empire, but its reign was coming to an end. From the middle of the thirteenth century, mail was increasingly supplemented with hardened leather, or plates made from iron or low-grade steel, and by the fifteenth century the steel-making ability of medieval metallurgists allowed the ar-mourers to create the intricate and elaborate plate armours that reduced mail to a largely secondary role.

The fourteenth century was thus a very experimental time for the armour-ers of western Europe; the slow development from mail to plate armour was entering its final phases, and as the quality of steel and skill of the armourers grew, the armours became increasingly complex and innovative as a balance was sought between the warrior's needs for defence and flexibility. Studying this important transitional stage of defensive costume is difficult, not only because of the relative complexity of the armours, but also because so few armours from this period have survived to the present day. Researchers are largely limited to iconographical sources, such as manuscript illuminations, funerary monuments and paintings, or documentary evidence in the form of wills, accounts and literary references. Each source, by itself, has inherent limitations; in the case of iconography, the technical ability of the artist and symbolic conventions can cause confusion, and with documentation, the terminology is often vague, and the descriptions uninformative.

The Cotton manuscript of *Sir Gawain and the Green Knight* (*Gawain*) is a rare example of a work that includes both written and iconographic description of the same armour, and thus provides a valuable opportunity to compare the medieval terminology of armour to its artistic representation. In addition to this valuable conjunction of sources, the armour depicted in *Gawain* happens to be of a very similar type to an exceedingly rare and well preserved armour from Chartres Cathedral. This armour, made for the young

Charles VI when he was Dauphin, was deposited in the great cathedral sometime around 1383 (Blair 1958, 63–5, 76, 171), and has survived more or less complete to the present day; the remaining armour consists of a visored bascinet helmet (complete with mail aventail), a coat armour, a right arm and leg harness,[1] and a pair of gauntlets. By comparing the armour described and illustrated in *Gawain* with the Chartres armour, and with other late four-teenth-century documentary and iconographical sources, we can obtain a clear picture of the armour the author of the poem was trying to describe to us, and place it in its proper historical context.

Analysis

Gawain is depicted in armour in two of the four illustrations of the poem: folios 129b and 130. Both are rather crudely executed, and have suffered the effects of ageing, particularly in the case of 129b which is very indistinct in some areas. The first of the two, folio 129b, shows Gawain on horseback, armed with a lance, confronting the Green Knight, who is holding his fearsome axe. The last illustration depicts Gawain on his return to Arthur's court; he is shown kneeling before the king and queen, his left hand grasping the monarch's right in greeting, with his right hand resting on his knee. Both illustrations appear to show Gawain in the same armour. In the text, Gawain's armour is described in detail in two major scenes, both of which recount his arming before setting out on his adventures; lines 566–91 and 605–8 describe the knight arming and setting forth from Arthur's Hall, and lines 2011–24 recount his arming at Hautdesert before his final encounter with the Green Knight.

The two illustrations in the manuscript which depict Gawain in armour show him dressed in a fashion that is very typical of the last twenty years of the fourteenth century, and which is remarkably similar (if not in some cases identical) to the armour worn by many of the hundreds of soldiers depicted in another late fourteenth-century manuscript, the *Grandes Chroniques de France*,[2] also at the British Library. The distinguishing features of the late fourteenth-century armour depicted in both of these works are the bascinet helmet, with its characteristic mail aventail, the padded coat armour, the 'hourglass' gauntlets, and the fully developed steel leg harness.

The **bascinet helmet** (described in *Gawain* simply as a 'helme', 605–7, 2317)

---

[1] The word 'harness' is often used to describe a complete suit of armour that is composed of many individual pieces. In a more limited form, the word is used to describe a complete element of a suit of armour, usually for the arm or leg, that is itself composed of many individual pieces. For example, an associated sabaton (foot armour), greave (lower leg armour), polyn (knee armour) and cuisse (thigh armour) will for the sake of brevity often be called a 'leg harness.'

[2] 'Grandes Chroniques de France ou de Saint Denis', British Library MS Royal 20 C. VII.

was the most popular type of helm for the knightly class in the fourteenth century.[3] The helm itself was pointed at the top, and came down low at the back and sides to cover the back of the head and the cheeks. Towards the end of the fourteenth century, the point had become quite pronounced, and had been moved toward the back, giving the rear of the helm an almost vertical profile (the nearly crescent-shaped helm shown in *Gawain* is almost certainly an artistic exaggeration). To protect the vulnerable neck, a small cape of mail, called an aventail ('auentayle', 608), was suspended from a leather band, affixed to the helm by means of small staples, called vervelles. On richer helms, the leather band was often covered with a protective band of metal, which was sometimes highly decorated (Blair 1958, 67, B,C); in the *Gawain* illustrations, it is coloured gold, probably representing gilt lateen, a common form of decoration at that time. With the aventail secured in place, only the face was exposed; in some cases, a visor was attached to the helm[4] (as shown in many of the figures from the *Grandes Chroniques*) to provide complete, if claustrophobic, protection. The bascinet from the Chartres armour is such a helm, mounted with an acutely pointed visor that has come to be known as a *Hounskull* (Blair 1958, 70).

The bascinet helmet is a development of the *cervelle*, a small skullcap that was often worn under the great helm in the late thirteenth and early fourteenth century (Blair 1958, 47). Although not mentioned in *Gawain*, the great helm was a standard part of the knight's equipment at this period;[5] it was, however , becoming obsolete for field use, and was to be relegated to the tourney field in the fifteenth century.

Both *Gawain* and numerous folios in the *Grandes Chroniques* depict the **coat armour** ('cote-armure', 586), a padded coat that is very often shown worn over the torso armour and arms in the closing decades of the fourteenth century.[6] The coat armour preserved at Chartres is just such an armour, and is in excellent condition; like the one depicted in *Gawain*, it is of red cloth and

---

3   In the Inventory of Thomas, Duke of Gloucester taken in 1397, of the 17 headpieces listed, 12 are bascinets, 2 are kettlehats, and 3 are described as helms for the joust of peace. See Dillon and Hope 1897.

4   Bascinet helms without visors like Gawain's are not at all uncommon in late fourteenth-century art and documentation; apparently, some warriors preferred to sacrifice the greater protection of the visor for improved visibility and ventilation. The great majority of English effigies and funerary monuments that show bascinets do not depict them with visors, or any means of attaching them (see Dillon and Hope 1897, 283).

5   A great helm is part of the achievements of the Black Prince, hung above his tomb in Canterbury Cathedral.

6   It is interesting to note that while the coat armour is extremely common in manuscript illustrations from the late fourteenth century, it is very rarely depicted in tomb effigies of the same period. Perhaps the depiction of the bulky and rather plain coat armour was not considered as impressive as the armour which lay beneath, which would provide a better display of the deceased's wealth. Edward, the Black Prince, is depicted in Canterbury in the sleeveless and tight fitting jupon, while the coat armour was hung with his achievements.

is made in the form of a long coat, fashionably narrow at the waist and padded at the chest, and terminates at mid-thigh length with gentle scalloping. The sleeves are very large and full, as they would have to have been to allow room for the arm harness beneath (just visible below the right gauntlet in *Gawain* folio 129b, and below the left in folio 130).[7] Another famous coat armour is that of Edward, the Black Prince, which was preserved at Canterbury Cathedral. This coat armour differs from the Chartres coat in that it is covered with a heraldic blazon, while the Chartres coat is of crimson silk damask with a woven pattern of birds and foliage. The Black Prince's coat armour also has short sleeves, although recent research has suggested that they may have once been longer (Arnold 1993).

The **gauntlets** ('glouez of plate', 583) are of the broad cuffed 'hourglass' form (somewhat exaggerated in the illustrations), common in the later fourteenth century, and seen in great numbers in the *Grandes Chroniques*. In the *Gawain* illustrations, they are coloured gold, which probably again represents gilt lateen.[8] These types of gauntlets are usually composed of a close fitting plate covering the back and sides of the palm, with a broad cuff, giving the gauntlets their 'hourglass' form; the fingers would have been protected by small scales or plates sewn onto a leather glove that was attached to the inside of the main plate.

The **leg harness** depicted in both *Gawain* and the *Grandes Chroniques* is the fully developed plate leg armour, which was in use from about the 1370s (Blair 1958, 63). The harness is composed of the sabatons ('sabatounz', 574) for the protection of the feet, the greaves ('greuez', 575) to protect the lower leg, the polyns ('polaynez', 576–7) for the knees and the cuisses ('quyssewes', 578–9) which cover the thigh. Together, these four elements provided almost total protection for the legs; a complete set of armour of this kind for the right leg is also preserved at Chartres Cathedral. In the manuscript illustrations, the polyns are shown in gold, again representing the gilt lateen decoration as seen on the gauntlets and aventail.

In addition to the main features of late fourteenth-century armour that are visible in the two illustrations, the text also mentions several other pieces of equipment that one would expect to find on a knight of this period; the arming doublet, bracers, couters, a coat of mail and a coat of plates, which would have all been hidden from view by the coat armour.[9] These items are

---

7   The *Gawain* artist was probably attempting to portray a coat armour with long, not three-quarter length sleeves; the exposed vambrace in folio 130 is most likely an attempt to show the foreshortening effect caused by Gawain's reaching arm – note that his right arm is fully covered by its sleeve.

8   Blair 1958, 66; also, the 'Inventory of Thomas, Duke of Gloucester' which lists 'iiij peir gantz de plates dout ij garnisez de laton enorrez . . .' (Dillon and Hope 1897, 306).

9   One piece of defensive equipment that would not have been obscured by the coat armour, but which is nevertheless not depicted in the illustrations, is the shield. It is mentioned in lines 619 and 2318, and while its blazon of the gold pentangle upon a red field is described

revealed to us by their appearance in the two arming sequences described in the poem. As the armour of the late fourteenth century was fairly complex, so too was the arming process; this is described in detail in lines 566–91 (the arming at Camelot) and in 2011–24 (the arming at Hautdesert). Armour was put on in layers, starting with a padded garment called an **arming doublet** (described in *Gawain* as a 'dublet of a dere tars', 571). An arming doublet was a quilted garment made in the fashion of a civilian doublet and worn under the armour to prevent chafing and to help protect the wearer from the concussion of blows. Padded garments have been used throughout the period that armour was worn, and have been known by a variety of names (gambeson, aketon, pourpoint, etc.); the word 'dublet' occurs in a military context in documents from the fourteenth to the sixteenth century (Blair 1958, 77–8; Meyrick 1821). The 'crafty capados' in line 572 may refer to an arming cap, a quilted headpiece worn under the helmet (Blair 1958, 78), but such caps are not usually mentioned as being lined with fur ('blaunner', 573).

As the armour all overlaps downward, the next step in the arming process was to put on the sabatons, and work upwards; the greaves, polyns and cuisses were fastened (574–9), the **mail shirt** ('bryne', 'bruny', 580–1, 2012, 2018) was put on over the arming doublet (580–1), followed by the arm harness consisting of **bracers** for the forearms (and possibly upper arms as well), **couters** ('cowters', 582–3) for the elbows and then the gauntlets (584). The coat armour was then put on, covering the arms and torso (583–4), and finally, the helmet (605–7).

It was usual for knights at this period to wear additional armour over the mail (but usually under the coat armour) in the form of a **coat of plates** (often called at this time a 'pair of plate' or simply 'plates'), or a brigandine, these being two different but closely related armours made in the form of a fabric or leather vest lined with metal plates.[10] It is interesting to note that while Gawain does not arm himself with such a garment when setting out from Camelot, he does avail himself of the use of his 'platez' and 'paunce'[11] (2017) when arming at Hautdesert. Perhaps the knight considers the protection of his mail and coat armour sufficient for the hazards of the road, while he chooses full battle-armour for the inevitable conflict with the Green Knight?

at length in 620–65, no real description of the shield itself is given (although 2318 does hint that the shield was hung upon Gawain's back by a strap, usually referred to as a *guige* (Blair 1958, 181)). One can presume that the shield was of the ubiquitous 'heater' shape, common in the late fourteenth century. It is curious, considering the many lines devoted to the shield and its device, that it was not depicted in the accompanying illustrations.

10 The Inventory of Thomas, Duke of Gloucester has 4 'peir briganters' and 6 'peir plates' listed within (Dillon and Hope 1897, 306).

11 A paunce was a reinforcing piece worn over the lower abdomen, later called a plackart (Blair 1958, 80). Three 'pauncers' of steel are also listed in the inventory of the goods of Thomas, Duke of Gloucester (Dillon and Hope 1897, 305).

1. Detail of BL Cotton Nero A.x fol. 130 showing Gawain kneeling before Arthur. The acute point of the bascinet and flare of the gauntlet cuffs are artistic exaggerations, but other than that, he is shown in armour that is very typical of the last two decades of the fourteenth century.

2. Miniature from *Grandes Chroniques de France* (fol. 136), showing a knight armed in full plate legs, coat armour, 'hourglass' gauntlets, and bascinet helmet with aventail and visor.

3. Coat armour of Charles VI of France, from Chartres Cathedral. It is made of white linen, covered with red silk damask, and is stuffed with wool, c.1383.

4. Visored bascinet helmet from Chartres Cathedral, a very fine example of late fourteenth-century armour. The aventail is original, but has been mounted for display without the leather band that would have originally held it fast to the helm. Good examples of this type of helm can also be found at the Tower of London and the Wallace Collection.

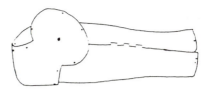

6. Arm harness, composing a couter and a hinged vambrace, from Chartres Cathedral.

7. Right hand gauntlet from Chartres Cathedral (missing the digits). This is an example of the typical 'hourglass' form, common in the late fourteenth century. They were once decorated with gilt bronze or lateen. Several gauntlets of this type are displayed in the Royal Armouries at the Tower of London.

5. Leg harness of Charles VI of France, from Chartres Cathedral.

All drawings by author.
1: After British Library MS Cotton Nero A.x, Art.3, f. 130.
2: After British Library MS Royal 20 C. VII, f. 136.
3–7: After Chartres Cathedral/Royal Armouries Photo Library.

The first arming sequence in *Gawain* is of particular interest because it faithfully describes every stage of the arming sequence in the correct order; when one compares the arming at Camelot (566–91) to the arming sequence described in a mid fifteenth-century treatise on arms (Dillon 1900), the similarites are immediately seen:

> How a man schall be armyd at his ese when he schal fighte on foote.
> He schal have noo schirte up on him but a dowbelet of ffustean lynyd
> with satene cutte full of hoolis.

The manuscript then goes on to describe the arming doublet in greater detail before returning to the arming sequence:

ffirste ye must sette on Sabatones and tye hem up on the shoo . . . And
then griffus & then quisses & þe the [sic] breche of mayle[12] . . . And the
brest And þe vambras And þererebras And then glovys . . . And then his
basinet

Thus the arming sequence in the poem is not simply a literary account of
the fine armour Gawain is equipped with; it is an accurate account of the
process in which it was put on.

Conclusion

Gawain's war gear, as described both in the body of the poem and in the two
accompanying illustrations, is perfectly consistent with what is known about
the armour in the last two decades of the fourteenth century. Both text and
illustrations agree on the distinguishing features of late fourteenth-century
armour; the bascinet helm with aventail, the coat armour, the gauntlets and
the full plate leg harness. In addition, the text describes those parts of the
armour that would have been hidden from view, but which we would expect
to find on a knight of this period, namely the arming doublet, the coat of mail,
bracers and couters, and the coat of plates. As befits a hero of Arthur's hall,
Gawain's armour is described at every turn as being richly decorated and of
the finest workmanship, with gilt lateen gauntlets, helm decoration, couters
and polyns, whose 'lest lachet oþer loupe lemed of golde' – armour worthy
of a prince or king to the poet's contemporaries. The detailed descriptions in
the text, not only of the armour itself, but of the correct arming procedure,
give strong evidence that the author of the poem was indeed very familiar
with the arms and armour of his age, as was asserted by Tolkien and Gordon.
   The strong corroboration between text and illustration on the subject of
armour may hint that the artist too was fairly knowledgeable about armour;
although it has been pointed out that the text and the illustrations do not
concur on a number of points (even major ones, such as the colour of the
Green Knight's face and beard; Tolkien and Gordon 1967, xiii; cf. Edwards,
below, 210, 213), there is little disparity between the two on the subject of
Gawain's armour. Gawain is depicted almost exactly as he is described in the
poem; the tall helm (correctly identified as a bascinet by the artist, not by its
name in the text where it is referred to simply as a 'helme', but by its
association with the 'auentayle', and perhaps by the bascinet's popularity in
the artist's contemporary period), the red coat armour (red being the colour
of the field of Gawain's heraldic device, as described in the poem – line 619),

---

12 By the mid fifteenth century, the steel breastplate had made the mail shirt largely redundant, and it was often replaced by a 'breech of mail', a skirt that was tied onto the bottom
of the arming doublet, to cover the hips and upper thigh. See illustration accompanying
the above Ordinance, reproduced in Edge and Paddock 1988, 118.

and the full steel leg and arm harness. Only relatively minor details, such as the embroidered band above his aventail, his sword and spurs, are absent in the illustrations.

Gawain thus stands not only as one of the finest works of medieval English literature; it is also an important documentary source for the study of late fourteenth-century English armour, and illuminates an important episode in the development of European armour as a whole.

Armour II: The Arming Topos as Literature

DEREK BREWER

The correspondence of the description of the arming of Gawain, 566 ff, to the actualities of late fourteenth-century armour (except for the blazon on his shield) has been clearly demonstrated. It is the earliest precise description of English medieval armour that we have, and when compared with the brilliance of the Black Prince's contemporary armour preserved at Canterbury Cathedral may not seem too extravagant even in the richness of its decoration. It witnesses to the poet's genius for concrete descriptive detail. It is also part of the taste for informative instruction noted by Shepherd as characteristic of the cast of mind of traditional English alliterative poetry (Shepherd 1970). Some critics see further symbolic or even allegorical significance in Gawain's armour (Watson 1987).

Besides reflecting the material world the arming also has its place in the narrative development, since Gawain must be armed to undertake his dangerous adventure. Yet the elaboration of the arming may seem excessive for the development of the story, of what may be called the horizontal dimension, even granted our pleasure in realistic description. The reason for the expansion of the description of arming has more to do with other dimensions, as it were vertical, which intersect the narrative line. They establish connections and resonances with other literary works and with cultural knowledge and assumptions. Such intersections are characteristic of the way all 'commonplaces' or *topoi* work in traditional literature from ancient epic to the seventeenth century (Brewer 1984, 68–73).

The formal arming of the hero, usually at a crucial moment in the development of the story, is an example of such a *topos*. It probably dates in ultimate origin from the misty past of the Babylonian epic *Gilgamesh* but first emerges as a literary form, as far as records go, in the *Iliad*. From there it runs to early twentieth-century Yugoslav folk-epic, though in most European literature it fades out during the sixteenth century or earlier (Brewer 1979a).

There are four extended passages of arming in the *Iliad*, in each case concerning a different hero (III, 328–38; XI, 15–46; XVI, 130–44; XIX, 367–91). Each passage begins with the same three formulaic lines and continues, though with minor variations, the same pattern, naming in order greaves, corslet, sword, shield, helmet, spear. It is a literary ritual which probably corresponds with an actual ritual, before a hero sets out on a desperate venture. It is not fully realistic, in that an actual warrior, even of Homer's date, would have had a number of extra pieces of protective armour which are not mentioned.

There are traces of the *topos* in the Old Testament (I Samuel 17: 38–9; Isaiah 59: 17); but St Paul in particular makes use of it, adapted to the metaphor of spiritual warfare, Ephesians 6: 13–17, in a passage that used to be familiar as the lesson for the first Sunday in Lent.

Virgil employs the *topos* in relation to Turnus (*Aeneid* XII: 87–96). It occurs in *Beowulf* (1446–64), in the ancient Irish epic, *Táin Bó Cúalnge*, and later Irish works, but occurs most obviously and frequently in medieval French romances (Ruck 1991, 130–1). The clearest examples, which our poet may well have known, occur in Chrétien de Troyes' *Eric et Enide* (691–726; 2624–64; quoted in translation, Brewer 1992 with other examples). In the latter case Erec stands on a splendid carpet, as Gawain does (568–9), emphasising the formality and importance of the occasion. The order and items of arming are as usual. Chrétien does not bother with realistic detail such as the 'sabatounz', and other essential but less poetical items of 'goodly gear'. In French romance at times someone, often a lady, helps arm the knight.

In the Arthurian tradition the *topos* begins about 1135 with Geoffrey of Monmouth's *Historia Regum Britanniae* IX: 2, lines 104–11 (Hammer 1951, quoted Brewer 1984, 230–1). This is indebted to Virgil's arming of Turnus, but Geoffrey gives Welsh names to shield, sword and spear, an archaic device which also suggests his knowledge of other examples of the arming *topos* widespread in an oral as well as literate tradition in Welsh. It seems that Geoffrey also found the detail of the inspiring image of the Blessed Virgin on the inside of Arthur's shield in Nennius, who gave the first 'historical' account of Arthur, *Historia Brittonum*, ch. 56.

The arming *topos* re-enters the English language after *Beowulf* through Layamon's *Brut*, early thirteenth-century, itself an adaptation of Wace's French adaptation of Geoffrey's *Historia*. Layamon romanticises the *topos* and keeps the image of the Virgin on Arthur's shield. This is also referred to, on the authority of Geoffrey, by the biblical commentator Holcot and in a fifteenth-century sermon (Green 1962; Vantuono 1984, 274–5), but appears in no other description of a formal arming, even of Arthur, apart from its occurrence in *Sir Gawain and the Green Knight* (*SGGK*).

In the alliterative tradition in the fourteenth century a good example of formal arming occurs in *The Morte Arthure*, 900–19. In these later examples the formal arming is described only of the hero of the poem, usually before his most significant battle. It is therefore appropriately placed in *SGGK* before Gawain sets off on his ominous journey. The second occasion of Gawain's arming, on leaving Bertilak's castle (2011–20), is not formal and omits all except a few practical details. It is part of the line of narrative and lacks the resonances of the earlier passage with its ritualistic heroic overtones.

The traditional and conventional – which is to say the imaginative and emotive – importance of the arming of Gawain is the more marked in that the specific adventure on which he is embarked, to endure a beheading without defending himself, does not require armour. But what is a knight without armour? It represents his readiness to meet all contingencies, his bravery, and his essential function within the whole culture. The first arming passage in *SGGK* is the finest example of the formal *topos* known to me. Not only is it fully realistic but it is deepened by its elaborate moral implications. The most significant of these is the blazon of the pentangle on Gawain's shield. This is unique. Blazon of any kind is rarely mentioned in formal arming, and the pentangle never apart from here.

Blazon

From the twelfth century onwards knights developed increasingly elaborate insignia on their shields, at first for the purposes merely of recognition, but soon to make more complex statements about identity, heredity, ideals, worth. The art or science of heraldry was developed by the specialist knowledge of heralds so that, in Gage's words, the vocabulary of blazon becomes a vocabulary of value (Gage 1993, 82). In it were expressed the chivalric ideals. Although in origin the language of heraldry was simply the current vernacular French it rapidly developed its own technical jargon partly by the use of fossilised French terms, partly by stylisation of the formal description of 'arms' (meaning the blazon on the shield, not 'weapons' or 'armour'). The language of blazon often ran counter to ordinary colour language (Gage 1993, 81). For an account by two modern heralds, see Bedingfeld and Gwynn-Jones 1993. From around 1500 heraldry became even more elaborate and fanciful, as its military use disappeared.

In early French Arthurian romance the blazon on shields, where it is noticed at all, is principally used as a means of identification. It does not seem to be 'moralised'. All the Arthurian knights eventually had a blazon, sometimes several, usually of a fairly simple, mainly geometrical kind, attributed to them. In ordinary life the development of more elaborate arms involved emblematic animals, very extensive punning on names or localities, and more colours. Several blazons are attributed to Gawain in the romances but it seems that by the end of the fourteenth century in France the most usual blazon for the French Gauvain was the two-headed eagle (Pastoureau 1983; 1982, 302). This is susceptible of varying symbolic interpretations, but obviously the eagle represents a noble fighting spirit.

In his use of the pentangle as Gawain's blazon the *Gawain*-poet displays his usual witty mixture of tradition and innovation.

It was becoming customary at the end of the fourteenth century to invent new blazons for Arthurian knights, and as already remarked, there was a general tendency to 'moralise' blazons. But the pentangle is in general very rare, and in Arthurian literature unique to *SGGK* as a blazon. (Silverstein has a full note in his valuable edition of *SGGK* (1984).) In heraldry a five-pointed star, known as a mullet, is relatively common, but not found on its own except once in a graffito on a church wall shown on the breast of a knight (Pritchard 1967, 53). The mullet lacks the internal structure of lines and fives that makes the pentangle so significant. What is called a pentagram by Pritchard is said to be very common as a graffito on medieval English parish church walls. It was often known as 'Solomon's seal'. In England, rather more mundanely, it also seems often to have been used as a mason's mark (Pritchard 1967, 88). Pritchard does not comment on the only pentangle she illustrates, from Shillington in Bedfordshire (Pritchard 1967, 14). This is in close conjunction, indeed overlapping, with the figure of a bearded man in a bascinet with aventail, unquestionably of the fourteenth century. It is tempting to think that the pentangle suggests the knight's chivalrous virtues. At Horseheath in Cambridgeshire is a graffito of a man wearing a crown, with a 'mullet' or 'pentagram' on his breast. The sole charge on the shield in the west window of the church is a mullet, and it is the shield of the fourteenth-century Earl of Oxford, Aubrey de Vere (53).

The relative commonness of pentangles justifies the *Gawain*-poet's comment that the English call the figure 'the endless knot' (*SGGK* 629–30), and suggests something of the widespread hints that may have prompted his unique use of it (though it was also often used on seals (Silverstein 1984, 130)). For the poet's use of the pentangle is certainly original. It is also to be remarked that he does not use heraldic language, except perhaps for *goulez* 'red', the background colour, technically called the 'field'. The pentangle is the 'Ordinary', which is normally geometrical (Bedingfeld and Gwynn-Jones 1993, 43–4). No example is given elsewhere of a pentangle as an Ordinary. Gawain's pentangle is of the most precious and significant metal, gold, and there is no further charge or elaboration, as the poet now takes his own direction for explaining the moral significance of the pentangle. Gold signifies obedience and faith in the *Tractatus de Armis* written in England in the late fourteenth century by John de Bado Aureo (Bedingfeld and Gwynn-Jones 1993, 52).

The centrality to the poem of the description of the pentangle, with its extraordinary wealth of cultural resonances, devotional, numerological, hierarchical, moral, theological, has been well demonstrated by several scholars, for example Morgan (1991), and Davis (1993 and below). The description of the pentangle may well be described as the core of the assumptions implicit and explicit in the poem, which the story and style exemplify. Green (1962) regards it as ambivalent and questionable, but that interpretation seems to go against the dominant meaning of the text if we assume that the poet is writing in good faith, and Green himself agrees that the device signifies Christian moral perfection.

The rich inter-connections of the pentangle extend beyond the literal 'surface' of the poem and its linear conduct. Being a long static exposition, it is, as already noted, a 'vertical' intersection of the linear narrative, with relationships beyond the narrative to historical, moral, social, concepts and meanings. It is used as a signal of those further meanings, which are diffused throughout the whole poem. For this reason it is not necessary for the poet to invoke the pentangle explicitly in reference to Gawain's shield on the only other occasions when the shield and its blazon might be mentioned, when Gawain re-arms himself without formality for the final stage of his journey to the Green Chapel to keep his promise to receive the return blow from the Green Knight. Nor need the pentangle, any more than the picture of the Virgin on the shield, be specifically invoked in contrast with the green girdle, so much less potent, indeed so trivial. It may be noted that it was illegal to carry any form of magic charm in a tournament. The green girdle is a false charm, whose only ultimate value for Gawain is as a memento (but cf. below, 326–8).

The formal arming is thus an enhancement of the hero's status, seriousness of purpose, his position in an ancient line of heroic honourable warriors governed by an unquestioned ethic of bravery and adventure, to which are now joined specifically Christian, or Christianised, virtues of courtesy and chastity dear to the poet's heart and variously praised in all his poems. Although the arming is a marker of the hero, and of the onset of the main action, the description is not in itself part of the story-line, of the sequence of cause and effect. Once it has done its work of enhancement and glorification, both material and moral, it need play no further part in the advancement of the narrative sequence of events.

The tradition of the formal arming was coming to an end at the close of the fourteenth century, as chivalric material and literary culture changed. Chaucer mocks it in *Sir Thopas*. Its use marks our poet's conservatism combined as usual with a rich development of tradition, and his great difference from Chaucer's frequently ironic, *avant-garde* attitudes.

There are no significant later examples of the arming *topos* in English (leaving aside fifteenth-century manuscript copies of poems composed earlier). Malory will have no truck with it. There is perhaps a faint echo in Shakespeare's *Antony and Cleopatra*, and parody in Pope's *Rape of the Lock* deriving from Pope's knowledge of the classics. Fortunately, the *Gawain*-poet so strengthens it that its elaboration, realism and moral force have an immediate effect. But it is even more appreciated when its long history as a regular feature of epic and romance is known, with its connotations of splendour and bravery, fulfilling and exceeding the reader's expectations.

The Colour Green

DEREK BREWER

One specific point, the greenness of the Green Gome, or Knight, has been used as the key to so many general interpretations of *Sir Gawain and the Green Knight* (*SGGK*) that an historical investigation of the significance attributed to the colour green should establish firm rather than inadvertently anachronistic associations on which criticism should be based. It will also contribute to another relevant topic, neglected until recently, the cultural history of colour.

In *SGGK grene* is used forty-four times of the *gome* or *knyȝt* in green and his appurtenances (it alliterates both with *gome*, and with the *gold* with which he is liberally sprinkled). 'Green' is used five times of the lady's girdle, twice of grass, once of spring, once of the green holly. (One instance, 157, is doubtful.) By contrast it is used only four times in *Cleanness* (twice of vegetation), twice in *Patience* of vegetation only, twice in *Pearl* of precious stones only. The predominance in *SGGK*, and in that poem the emphasis on the Green Knight, amply justifies critical interest.

The crux of the matter, the real strangeness, the deep ambiguity, lies in the greenness of the Green Knight's complexion, for complexion, skin-colour, must be meant by the reference to his 'hwe', 'Set in his semblaunt sene' (147–8). The court might indeed feel wonder, though later in the poem there is little emphasis on his bright green face.

What does the greenness of the Green Knight mean? Earlier criticism used it, following an enthusiastic essay by John Speirs, itself developing hints from Jessie Weston and E.K. Chambers, as an opportunity for seeing the Green Knight as an emanation of a vegetation-god, a life-giving spirit, despite his clear, if genial, enmity to Gawain and Arthur's court (Speirs 1949).

The ambiguity inherent in the whole of *SGGK* gave some justification for this interpretation, though we should beware of those whose hostility to us is cloaked in a cheerful apparent absence of personal animosity. Essentially the conception of the vegetation-god was a projection of that wider cult of 'nature' and neo-paganism common in English literary circles in the earlier part of the twentieth century, as seen in D.H. Lawrence, E.M. Forster, Kenneth Graham (in the chapter on 'The Piper at the Gates of Dawn' in *The Wind in the Willows*), A.E. Waite, and many others. It was often combined with a taste for the occult, for discovering ancient myths and mysteries driven under-ground by the oppressive rationality of medieval Christianity, as in Jessie Weston, for whom all surviving Arthurian story was but the pathetic detritus of much greater pagan works now lost. Another example is J.G. Frazer's immensely influential *The Golden Bough* (1890–1915). (Cf. Cooper in this volume.) The contemporary political 'green' movement is not unconnected with it.

All this anthropology is now outdated and in part merited the attack by C.S. Lewis on 'The Anthropological Approach' (Lewis 1962). Modern social anthropology is a quite different matter. The so-called Green Man – the architectural feature of a face peering through leaves, widespread in ancient, and medieval building – called 'the foliate head' has no relation to the Green Knight (Basford 1978). The Wild Man, furry, inarticulate, living in woods, carrying a club, is a 'woodwose', one of Gawain's enemies on his 'anious vyage' (721), widely imagined in medieval Europe, but with nothing to do with the Green Knight (Bernheimer 1952).

We return to the Green Knight. The greenness of his skin is the bizarre feature, unique to this poet. Green clothing and accoutrements are common-place. The only other instance in medieval record or literature of persons with green skin so far known turns out to be irrelevant, and needs only brief discussion, though it again shows how modern prepossessions may be inadvertently foisted on to medieval evidence.

The Essex chronicler Ralph of Coggeshall has a story, found also in the Yorkshire chronicler William of Newburgh, in each case relating to the late twelfth century. Two small children were discovered near Woolpit in Suffolk, emerging during the harvest from a cave in the district. They were distraught, spoke incomprehensibly, and were green in colour. At first they would eat nothing, but eventually accepted beans. A local knight, Sir Richard de Calne, took them in. They were baptised, eventually took to a more varied diet, learnt the language, and lost their original colour. The boy soon died, but the girl grew up, married, lived in King's Lynn, and had a family. Neither chronicler mentions the supernatural, or fairies, in their connection, though even the generally sceptical William of Newburgh, who scorned Geoffrey of Monmouth's Arthurian history, has elsewhere some other first-class stories of wonders. The likely core of the matter is that these very small children, herding or following flocks, strayed from their forest village, spoke little, and (in modern terms) did not know their own home address. They were prob-ably suffering from chlorosis, a deficiency disease which gives the skin a greenish tint, hence the term 'green sickness'. With a better diet it disappears. The children were kindly looked after by Sir Richard and the girl at least survived. That the children might have come from fairyland is a speculation projected on to the original accounts by modern scholars (Stevenson 1875; Dickins 1934; Briggs 1976).

There are no other characters in medieval European literature that I am aware of, apart from these unfortunate children, who have green complexions. If there were it would mean that they were ill. All the more striking is the vivid green complexion of our Green Gome who is clearly in the best of rude health.

We turn to a consideration of how the colour green and what it symbolised were thought of in medieval culture. In a famous passage Huizinga (1955) comments on the symbolic significance attributed to colours in the Middle Ages. The message is repeated by Pastoureau (1990) who claims that all *décor* in the medieval period was functional, ideological, social, symbolic; expression of hierarchy, associations, correspondences and oppositions; and that colour was cognitive and taxonomic (51). Huizinga remarks that the symbolic significance attributed to blue and green was 'so marked and particular as to make them almost unfit for usual dress' (272–4). This last is plainly untrue as far as ordinary literary description and manuscript illumination are concerned. Blues and greens are liberally distributed with no systematic moral approval or opprobrium. In his pioneering study Ott (1899, 136–8) shows the predominantly favourable view of green in French literature to 1400, despite the references to sourness, immaturity, avarice and jealousy that also occur.

Huizinga supports his arguments with quotations from Deschamps and others, and these adverse comments on the colour green as indicative particularly of inconstancy in love may be added to from Chaucer, e.g. *The Squire's Tale* (*Canterbury Tales* V. 646, cited from Benson 1987), or in the poem dubiously attributed to him, 'Against Women Inconstant', with its refrain 'In stede of blew thus may ye were al grene'. There is nothing in these medieval accounts, unfavourable to the colour as they are, to suggest the supernatural. Nor are they at all consistent with the widespread use of and comment on green to be noted below.

According to Katharine Briggs green is a fairy colour and for this reason is so unlucky that many Scotswomen refuse to wear green at all. On the other hand she also finds that 'red runs green very close'. The choice of colours for Scotswomen's dress is clearly limited (Briggs 1976, 108). Briggs remarks that fairies are called 'greencoaties' in Lincolnshire, where the inhabitants think it unlucky to mention the word 'fairy', and 'greenies' is the name given to fairies in Lincolnshire. There they are dressed in green coats with red caps, but Briggs considers this latter dress to be the product of Jacobean literary influence. While this may encourage modern fantasies about the magical or supernatural associations with the colour green, it cannot make it seem very life-enhancing, and Briggs quotes no medieval evidence at all, apart from the green children of Woolpit already referred to.

There is just one medieval reference known to me that supports the superstition that green is an unlucky colour. The fourteenth-century Florentine writer of comic anecdotes, Franco Sacchetti, at the end of one story reflects on the differences between men's natures – one will not do this, another likes something strange, etc. He remarks amongst other examples of superstitious men that 'there are others who will not dress themselves in green, which is the prettiest colour there is' (Brewer 1996, 84).

This has nothing to do with inconstancy in love, or with the supernatural, except in so far as superstitious fear may reflect a sense of supernatural hostile power. It is possible, in the light of the eighteenth- and nineteenth-century examples, that such a superstition, not otherwise recorded, existed in the more northerly parts of the English Midlands in the fourteenth century as it obviously did in Italy, and that it sounded a note of dread of bad luck in the Green Knight's extreme greenness. Even in this example, however, Sacchetti's own scorn for the superstition shows that it had limited distribution and was offset for many by the beauty of the colour green. We end up with the usual ambivalence. *OED* and *MED* give a number of quotations with a variety of unfavourable connotations for 'green', including the obvious and still current meanings of sourness and immaturity.

None of this seems likely to make the Green Knight's complexion endear him to us. It encourages unfavourable interpretations. But as with so much medieval systematisation there are so many alternatives, ambiguities, if not downright internal contradictions, that all generalisation must be qualified.

The favourable or neutral connotations of 'green' in medieval English far outnumber the unfavourable. Green was generally felt to be an agreeable colour, associated with the spring of the year, pleasant to the eyes. That is why, in Chaucer's *Friar's Tale*, as D.W. Robertson long ago pointed out, 'the Devil wears green' (Robertson 1954). It is the Devil's hypocritical device to mislead people about his wicked intentions. Huntsmen in general wear green because it is a pleasant colour and deceives their prey, hiding the huntsmen's evil intent. As much, by a paradoxical twist, could almost be said of the Green Knight, except that he barely hides his evil intent.

That green is an attractive but not magical colour is amply attested by medieval encyclopaedists such as Bartholomaeus Anglicus. In his book XIX *De Coloribus* he devotes a chapter to the colour green. He comments on its pleasantness, but also some unfavourable aspects (Batman 1582). The lapidarists, commenting on the valuable properties of precious stones, also speak well of green. Thus the longest of English lapidaries, the Peterborough Lapidary, which gathers up the comments of the encyclopaedists and other Latin and Anglo-Norman writers, records of smaragdus that it has the name above all precious stones of green colours and comforts the eyes and increases riches (Evans and Serjeantson 1933, 103). Furthermore the emerald, according to the Douce Lapidary, also surpasses 'all the greennesses of greenhead', and signifies the greatest greenhead of him that is the great greenhead of the Trinity, and in Apocalypse signifies the faith of the four Evangelists (Evans and Serjeantson 1933, 26).

What is more, despite condemnation, green seems to be the favourite colour of dress for medieval heroines (Brewer 1982, 163, n. 10). To take one further example from Chaucer, Alceste, a truly faithful wife if ever there was one, and represented as Queen to the God of Love, wears a dress 'in real [i.e. royal] habit grene' (*Legend of Good Women*, Pro.F214, G146). The god himself is clothed in silk embroidered with green sprays. That Alceste is dressed in green and crowned with a coronet of white pearls is repeated (Pro.F242, G174), together with a list of her womanly virtues, and again repeated (F303, G229). It is the whiteness of the pearls which particularly express her loyalty, but there is no doubt about her green dress; and her whole *ensemble* of course evokes the 'daisy', perhaps rather, in modern terms, the 'marguerite'. Huizinga's citations are few and partial and his theory almost completely wrong.

In the English and Scottish ballads fairies sometimes wear green, but that could be because it was a common colour. The version of the group of ballads about Thomas the Rhymer from Mrs Brown, c.1800, gives the Fairy Queen a skirt of grass-green silk, and Thomas acquires a pair of shoes of velvet green in his seven-year sojourn. Scott retains these in his slightly later version. In Scott's *The Pirate* (1822) a character refers to fairies as having green coats and a pair of wings (Chapter XX). In the ballad 'Tam Lin', 'Janet has kilted her green kirtle / A little above her knee' but whatever the lovers' adventures they are earthly creatures and Janet is soon 'As green as glas' because she is pregnant. In another version Tam Lin is covered by a green mantle to protect him from the fairies (Child 1882, I. 317–29, 335–8). The conclusion must be that in so far as green became associated with fairies the belief arose in the late eighteenth century in the northern parts of England and in Scotland. It is an element of literary Romanticism which spreads through other layers of society. A conclusive piece of evidence of its late association with fairies is provided by the mid-fifteenth-century version of Thomas the Rhymer which Child prints from the Thornton Manuscript. Here there is no mention of green, except one incidental topographical reference to a 'green plain'.

To take another aspect of the use of green in the medieval period, it was the colour most frequently used in the twelfth century to paint the helm (Pastoureau 1982, 45–6) and a helm 'as green as glass' is recorded in an English manuscript of about 1500 (*MED*, s.v.a.). No special significance seems to be attached to this. In Arthurian romance, including Malory, many knights wear green armour. If it was mail it could be painted; if plate, strips of coloured material were stuck to it. According to Ruck (1991) armour in twelfth-century French Arthurian romance might be black, blue, green, red (the most popular) or white, which last might mean unpainted, or painted white, or polished (130). The cloth surcoat over the armour was variously coloured, with red being again the most popular. Gawain's own surcoat is red, as, incidentally, is the Lady's dress when she first meets Gawain, 952 (unless it is her complexion – the favoured rosiness – which is referred to as red, as is certainly the case, mixed with white, later (1205)). Red was the most valuable dye (Gage 1993, 80).

Of course the Lady's girdle is green, and must have made a fine contrast against Gawain's red surcoat when he wore it going to the Green Chapel, for despite its being a secret gift he does not conceal it. The Green Knight says the girdle is his own, and that his own wife wove it (2358–9). Gawain's only fault is in not restoring it to the Green Knight as part of the Exchange of Winnings (2354–7). In his mortification Gawain restores it, ungraciously enough (2377), and is then openly given the gold-hemmed girdle, by the Green Knight, 'For hit is grene as my goune' (2396), as a memento and token of the 'chaunce of þe Grene Chapel' (2399). Its greenness has no significance in itself, apparently, though later Gawain chooses to impose moral significance on his wearing of it, and later still the knights of the Round Table impose a quite different significance upon their wearing of it, purely as a memento associating themselves with the nobility of Gawain. Arbitrary personal significations attached to originally neutral objects are entirely human and natural.

In heraldry in the later medieval period there was an increasing attempt to systematise and moralise blazon, and then colours became associated with astrology and the calendar. It is a splendid example of how men in the medieval period attempted to create a wholeness in their interlaced experiences of the universe, linking the material with the moral, the spiritual, the cosmological. An important anonymous French treatise perhaps of the fourteenth century in the Bibliothèque Mazarine demonstrates an early heraldic effort of this kind (Gage 1993, 83–4). Even here there is ambiguity and self-contradiction, or rather, the constant possibility of interpreting the same symbol or colour either *in bono* or *in malo*. The lion may symbolise either Christ or the Devil. (It may be noted that ambiguity of signs is a constant aspect of human life. When driving a car, the flash of a headlight may warn of a police-car ahead and you'd better slow down, or it may acknowledge a courtesy, or it may say that you are a damned dangerous fool to overtake in that way against oncoming traffic.)

In heraldry red was the favourite colour. Green was relatively rare in early shields of arms perhaps for the simple reason, it has been suggested, that it did not show up well against the natural colours of the countryside (Bedingfeld and Gwynn-Jones 1993, 56). A curious development, indicative of the fluidity of concepts, was the change of the meaning of *sinople* from 'red' to 'green' in the fourteenth century. Perhaps green was becoming more popular, or simply commoner.

The effort to moralise heraldry attributed many significances to the colour green. A useful summary is provided in *Le Blason des couleurs en armes, livrees et devises*, written about 1450 by one known as the Sicilian, or Sicily, Herald to Alphonse V, king of Aragon (Cocheris 1860).

For Sicile, green signifies the virtues of joy; beauty; shame; the emerald; youth; the planet Venus; strength; Thursday; the season of spring. It is worn by joyous and determined young people, commonly on garters and girdles 'and in the month of May you will see no other colour worn than green'. A particularly brilliant example of ladies (though not gentlemen) wearing green dresses is the picture for May in that wonderfully illuminated manuscript *Les Très Riches Heures du Duc de Berry* (Longman and Cazelles 1969). It is appropriate for the young, young married people, also parrots (Cocheris 1860, 46–7). The second part of the treatise repeats and amplifies these characteristics, adding to 'green' for example, the significance of 'readiness to fight' (Cocheris 1860, 83–4). The value of the treatise is that it is highly derivative, using the Bible and the Church Fathers, repeating the mish-mash of pseudo-correspondences that represents the tradition. But according to Gage (1993) the significances are quite different from those of the treatise in the Bibliothèque Mazarine referred to above.

Green is said to be rare in English blazon, and indeed in Europe, from the thirteenth to the fifteenth centuries (Pastoureau 1982, 138–9). Nevertheless, a Green Count, Amadeus, Count of Savoy (1334–83) was well known, and always dressed from the age of fourteen completely in green. There were close connections between Savoy and England in the second half of the fourteenth century (d'Arderne 1959). A Green Squire, Simon Newton, with associations with Lichfield in the English Midlands has also been tracked down (Highfield 1953). There is no reason to associate either of these men with *SGGK*.

The Green Knight carries, besides his formidable axe, coloured green, whose significance needs no laborious explanation, a holly branch – holly which is greenest when groves are bare (206–7). Andrew and Waldron (1978) note that a branch in the hand was a sign of peace. They note also the typical ambivalence of having it match the fearsome axe. A fifteenth-century carole asserts the 'mastery' of holly over ivy, and the jolliness of holly's merry men as against the maidens of ivy left out in the cold to weep and wring their hands (Greene 1977, no. 136). Another celebrates holly with 'alleluia' (Greene 1977, no. 137). But in the caroles only ivy is associated with Christmas (Nowell), and its greenness emphasised (Greene 1977, nos. 138, 139, 39.1). Ivy is personified as feminine, as against holly's masculinity (discussed with folkloric origins by Greene 1977, cxxii–vii). Nevertheless, the association of both with Christmas seems clear. The symbolic femininity of ivy, despite its superior greenness, and the rather undramatic appearance a strand of ivy would make in the Green Knight's hand, make holly the inevitable choice of greenery for him to carry. Its prickliness also fits in with his aggressive masculinity, and its greenness in winter with his vitality and power of survival.

A brief glance may be taken at what people actually wore. This may be most directly done by the reader looking at the many manuscript illuminations of the period either in libraries or in the excellent volumes of reproductions now available. Further comment is given by the costume-historian Stella Newton (Newton 1980).

In the middle of the fourteenth century in France and England elaborate court records were kept of clothing and its costs and decoration. A great variety of colours and costumes were in use for both sexes. Green seems as much favoured as white, blue, red, violet, purple, black. This variety may be seen in the dress of Chaucer's Canterbury pilgrims. Clothing was frequently parti-coloured and theatrically vivid, though moralists and some chroniclers and Chaucer's Parson in his *Tale* condemned it on grounds both of cost and modesty.

Why then did the *Gawain*-poet choose green? It was not inherent in the plot of the Beheading Game which is the nucleus of the story, nor necessary for the ostensible purpose of frightening Guinivere to death. All colours had a variety of potential symbolism and some ambiguity. The visitant is obviously supernatural, hostile and in some ways associated with death, but with a certain geniality. Black was an obvious option. But black had associations with the church, with mourning, penitence, shame (Harvey 1995, 43–4). These associations are dismal rather than threatening. Some liveliness might have been derived from the fact that devils in miracle-plays usually wore black, but they lacked dignity and were even occasionally ridiculous. Black was not yet the colour of power. The poet's final stroke of genius in making his visitant strange is to attribute the dominant colour of his clothing to his complexion. A man of black skin would have been a curiosity but 'Aethiopians' were known. They were not unnatural.

Speculation may range over the other available colours. A red-faced man in red might have been too commonplace. A blue-faced man, despite the frequency of blue dresses, seems somehow ridiculous. Neither white nor yellow seem, in comparison with green, to have the same ambivalent mixture of the pleasant and familiar, the natural, with strangeness, that with wisdom after the event we can now praise in *SGGK*.

The dress of the Green Knight is very smart and courtly, with its pure white ermine as lining, its tightness round his admirably athletic flat belly and slim waist, showing off his broad shoulders, and lavishly adorned with gold. According to Newton it would have been fashionable c.1365–70, but unusual in shape by 1380 (Newton 1980, 64). It is a wonderful example of power-dressing without armour. As Gawain's armour seems to have been fully up-to-date we can perhaps assume that the Green Knight's costume is also at the height of fashion.

Finally we call to witness the use of colours in the manuscript, a poor but remarkably unusual product when compared with many of the manuscripts of Chaucer and Gower, or even the more generally workaday manuscripts of *Piers Plowman*. It is described elsewhere (see Edwards below). The illustrations are coloured drawings of crude workmanship, possibly by an amateur. (Lee (1977) speculates that draughtsman and colourist may have been different.) Assuming one artist, he did not know traditional iconographical patterns, and like many book illustrators did not attempt to follow the text closely, though he did choose salient events in the texts to illustrate. So he shows Noah's Ark to illustrate the Flood episode in *Cleanness* (f. 60r, Pl. 5), but he shows it neither as described in the text nor as traditionally and elaborately depicted (for example in the early fourteenth-century so-called 'Queen Mary's Psalter' (Warner 1912, 10–12)). He shows the Ark as a rather crowded small rowing boat, clinker-built. Nor does he show any acquaintance with the tradition of splendid illustration in the many manuscripts of the Apocalypse (for an example *Cloisters Apocalypse*, 1971). The artist's vision of the New Jerusalem from *Pearl* (f. 42, Pl. 4) is pathetically inadequate.

His colours are fairly strong though coarse, comprising red, blue, green, yellow, brown. In the illustration of Noah's Ark the woman is in blue, one man in green, another in red. The first illustration of the Dreamer in *Pearl* (f. 41, Pl. 1) bears no similarity to portrayals of St John the Divine at the beginning of his vision of the Apocalypse. Despite the poet's description of a jewelled landscape the trees are green, the river dark green with spots of white and red, the ground yellow. The Dreamer is in red with at his neck the strange floating hood, or cloak, or emanation of his spirit, coloured blue.

There are four illustrations of *SGGK*. The first (f. 94v, Pl. 9) is a double, before and after the beheading, showing a bearded Gawain twice, in red. The Green Knight and his horse are green all over, but his face is pale, his hair is yellow, and red blood spurts from neck and head. Arthur in the upper portion wears blue and Guinivere green. The man to the left of the Queen holding a sword is perhaps Agravayn, who has been moved up as Gawain has been shifted over to Arthur's right, and wears pink.

The next illustration (f. 129, Pl. 10) shows Gawain in bed with bare shoulders and the Lady tickling his bearded chin – an episode the poet has neglected to tell us about. Gawain's bedclothes are green with the folds shown in darker green, on a red base. The Lady is in a high necked white dress with spots of blue and red, similar to that worn by the Pearl, and totally different from the *décolleté* described in the text. She has a 'tressour' over her yellow hair. The curtain is dark blue.

The next illustration (f. 129v, Pl. 11) is the scene at the Green Chapel. Almost the whole page seems to have been smeared with green, but the Green Knight, in his short green gown and green hose, has a pale face and yellow hair, with a green axe. Gawain has a pointed darkish helmet, no visor, a red surcoat, a red spear, dark leg-armour, no baldric and no shield. The harness of the horse is red. A dark blob bottom right is presumably the cave with apparently a vase of stiff red and white flowers on top, a mysterious motif which is repeated six more times in the picture. There is no snow unless the small white blobs round the Green Knight are meant to suggest it.

The last picture (f. 130, Pl. 12) is of Gawain's return to the court. In a frame Arthur is shown top left in a blue gown, Guinivere in green, and a courtier to her left wearing red and carrying a sword. All have yellow hair. Gawain (presumably) is shown half crouching centre front, much smaller and beardless, his face partly hidden by his dark blue aventail, his surcoat red, his leg armour dark blue, but his knee pieces yellow. Arthur holds out his right hand to Gawain and holds a yellow object which looks like the haft of a partly drawn sword, since it has a patch of faint blue beneath suggesting a blade. Again there is no sign of the baldric. What the artist thinks he is showing is hard to say.

It is clear that neither the colour green nor any other colour had a special significance for the artist. He is careless in his reading of the text and can in no sense be regarded as a valid interpreter of the text.

Gage in his impressive examination of colour and culture comes to the conclusion that symbols in the medieval period were readily invented and were very fluid. In particular, 'colour was an imaginative embellishment' (Gage 1993, 87). That is surely true of the poet's literally brilliant invention of *enker grene* for the colour of the complexion of Gawain's challenger. The power of the greenness lies partly in the unusual adjective, of Norse derivation, *enker*, 'vivid'. There is nothing sickly or undernourished about the greenness of the Green Knight. Its significance lies in the wide range of possible meanings of 'green', both good and bad, its very commonness as a colour in the world, and by contrast its uniqueness as a colour of skin, its bizarreness, and the very openness, or perhaps non-existence, of its implications in this case. Not surprisingly, at the end of the poem, the 'kny3t in þe enker grene' is described as going 'Whiderwarde-soeuer he wolde' (2476–7), an open-ended dismissal of an enigmatic agent, the stimulus to action but not the central character in the story. There is no 'realistic' base or background for such characters in romance and wonder-tale. Their testing function completed, they depart 'whithersoever they wish'. As such the very greenness of the Green Knight allows him to be absorbed into some natural world, yet points also to a sense of its ultimate mystery, its forces beyond our knowledge, though not, if we carry ourselves well, out of our control.

The moral of this excursus on the significance of green in *SGGK* and other medieval English literature is that explicit historical evidence (i.e. actual use) contemporary comment (e.g. encyclopaedists, etc.), where available, must complement equally important imaginative personal response. Knowledge and imagination extend each other's powers. The pentangle is symbolic because the poet tells us so. As for green, who knows?

Some Names

DEREK BREWER

Names are important in themselves, and as illustrating the range and type of the writer's mind, though some medieval scribes could get unfamiliar names wildly wrong, as for example in Chaucer's wide range of names. The *Gawain*-poet's range of names is less striking, with one notable instance, but it illustrates something of the range of his interests and reading, and on the whole the scribe seems to have been reliable. There are no serious mistakes. The poet uses 69 names in *Sir Gawain and the Green Knight* (*SGGK*), 25 in *Pearl*, 54 in *Cleanness*, 24 in *Patience*, not counting the variant forms. Most are Biblical except in *SGGK* where almost all are Arthurian, or pertain to the well-known 'history' of Britain. In *Cleanness* occur references to *Clopygnel* and the *Rose* (1057) referring to Jean de Meun's *Le Roman de la Rose*. There follows a description of the Dead Sea based on *Mandeville's Travels* but no names are taken from Mandeville. In *Cleanness*, *Porros*, and *Perce* (Persia) are derived from the Alexander romances (Anderson 1977). Some other names, e.g. *Arystotel* (*Pearl* 75), and *Ynde* (India) (*Cleanness* 1231, 1272) are common knowledge, but reveal *Cleanness* as geographically the most wide-ranging of the poems.

Patience also has its exoticism. The names of the heathen gods invoked by Jonah's crew, not in the Bible, are *Vernagu* (165), a giant from the Charlemagne romances, like the deity *Mergot* (167), in a cluster with *Diana*, known in the vernacular at least since Layamon, but also known through French and Latin accounts, like the semi-classical *Aquiloun* and *Ewrus* (133) the northerly and eastern winds, though their names may have come via the Bible (Anderson 1977, s.v.), and *Neptune* (166), though here Anderson points out that the manuscript reading *Nepturne* suggests the scribe's confusion with *Saturn*. All these names in *Patience* are the poet's addition to the Biblical account, though he shows nothing like the classical Latin knowledge of Chaucer and Gower. *Ragnel*, historically once a pagan king, then a god, finally a devil, is casually invoked when a sailor kicks Jonah awake (188) and the poet's knowledge, as Anderson notes, probably comes from contemporary miracle plays.

Pearl's references to *Aristotle* and *Pygmalion* (749–52) probably again show the poet's knowledge of *Le Roman de la Rose* in Gordon's view (Gordon 1953), rather than remoter Latin sources. The comparison of the Virgin to the *Fenyx of Arraby*, though not commonplace, is well-known in devotional literature, and is shared with Chaucer (*Book of the Duchess*, 982–3; cited from Benson 1987). It too may have been suggested by *Le Roman de la Rose*.

It is an interesting speculation whether 'pearl' in *Pearl* is meant also to signify a personal name. The personal name 'Pearl' is not recorded as such in Middle English but its Latin form *margarita*, well-known from the Biblical parable of 'the pearl of great price', gives rise to the English female names *Margaret, Margery*, in various spellings frequently found in medieval England from c.1000 onwards (*OED*, Withycombe 1977). *Margaret* was the name of one of the most popular maiden-martyr saints, whose story was well-known in medieval England in the vernacular. It is also a name for the daisy, as well as for the precious stone so popular in the fourteenth century. A child named *Margaret* or *Margery* might have been the actual historical subject for as rich a load of association, symbol and allegory as Beatrice, an undoubted historical figure, was for Dante.

The Biblical names in the poems derive from forms normal for the times, *Nabugodonozar* being a customary variant derived from the Greek of the *Nebuchadnezzar* favoured later. A scribal curiosity pointed out by Anderson (1977, *Cleanness* 1226n) is that the scribe always writes the name as if it were French, *Nabugo de Nozar*, and perhaps the poet himself was under the impression that *Nabugo* (1226, 1233) was a complete first name, since its use appears to fit the line metrically (see below 231).

The Arthurian names are all familiar in the texts known to the poet (see for example Lacy 1991). Arthur and Gawain, it may be argued, are presented rather in the serious spirit of the earlier English alliterative poems in the metrical tradition of the *Gawain*-poet than in the more variable spirit of the French tradition, except in the opinion of critics who see a deeply comic or derisive tone in *SGGK*. Lancelot has no English roots and is ignored by our poet. The ultimate, possibly Celtic, origins of the names Arthur and Gawain cannot have been known to the *Gawain*-poet. By his time they were fully naturalised in the copious and complex Arthurian stories in both French and English, as in many other European languages. There is one apparent exception, *Bertilak*. Earlier editors favoured the form *Bercilak*, still preferred by some. It is well known that *c* and *t* are difficult to distinguish in late Gothic script. Anderson points out in relation to the Biblical name *Zedethyas* (1169) that *t* and *th* regularly alternate as spellings with *c*, *ch*, in Latin and French.

The name *Bertilak* must derive from French romance. A character called Bertholai appears for example in *Lancelot do Lac*, which may precede the so-called Vulgate *Lancelot*, though both are of the early thirteenth century. Bertholai appears as an old knight who substitutes the false Guinivere for the true Queen out of hostility to Arthur and love of the surpassingly beautiful false Guinivere. What is interesting for our purposes is that in two of the French versions his name appears as 'bertelac' (Kennedy 1980, 585.21). When the plot is discovered both the lady and the knight confess and are burnt. The story in various versions appears in accounts of Merlin, and ultimately in the sole English version recorded in the unique manuscript, Cambridge University Library Ff. 111 11, *Merlin* (Wheatley 1899). Although this manuscript is of the mid-fifteenth century it has most interesting versions of the name. On its first occurrence f.113 (II. 322) he appears as 'Bertelaux the traitour'. His story is promised for later telling and indeed appears at some length on ff. 163v–167r (ed. cit., 467–70). Here the name appears very clearly written successively as 'Bertelak' (four times), 'Bertelak the rede' (i.e. 'red'), 'Bertelak the reade', 'Bertelak le Rous', 'Bertelays', 'Bertelais le Rous'. This makes clear that the form in *SGGK* must be Bertilak, not Bercilak. Although we never learn why he should be called 'the red' we learn a little more about the kind of character that is associated with the name. By this time, when the story has been so often retold, he is indeed an originally noble and vigorous knight, but he is a murderer as well as the lover of the false Guinivere. The full account need not be given here. Eventually he is banished and rejoins the false Guinivere, herself now discovered and also banished to an abbey in a 'wild place', where he meditates revenge. The manuscript is unfinished so we do not learn his end from it. Our poet presumably picked up the name from some fourteenth-century Arthurian version in French or English (most likely French), where he found the themes of hostility to Guinivere and association with a decidedly shady lady of great beauty.

The place-name *Hautdesert* (*SGGK* 2445) is also of course derived from French. A survey of the place-names in *SGGK* shows that most are derived from Arthurian 'history', for example, *Bretayn, Camylot, Logres,* familiar in romance. Gawain begins his journey here in the land of romance. The specific detail of *Northe Walez, Anglesay, Holy Hede, Wyrale* (697–701) of Gawain's journey is unusual in Arthurian romance, but these English names (not of course Welsh) whatever they tell us about the poet's game-playing are not in themselves remarkable, though they denote real places. As to *Hautdesert* we seem to be back in the land of romance, but that may not quite be so.

In medieval England a small number of castles and a few other places were given French names. Of these only *Beaudesert* resembles the name of Bertilak's place of origin, and occurs in only two instances, one in Staffordshire, not too far from *Gawain*-country, and the other in Warwickshire (Mawer and Stenton 1924, 199). Neither however would seem to have anything that may be referred to *SGGK* (see above 87).

Desert has nothing to do with sand but means wild, uncultivated country. *Haut* meaning 'high', together with *desert* suggest the wild hilly country and moorland where Bertilak's castle is situated. As a place-name *Hautdesert* is not in fact quite unique. It has not so far been noted that there is an analogous *Autepeek* first recorded as such in 1330. It is called *Haute Peek* in 1375, 1380, about the time that the *Gawain*-poet was writing. This is the area now known as High Peak, a name first recorded in English in 1490 (Cameron 1959, 1), lying due east of the Wirral and directly in Gawain's way. The landscape is as described in *SGGK*. The area was more extensive then, and could well have included the place where the poet came from. It was scattered with castles often now ruined or disappeared, and many tumuli or barrows. The poet may well be making a partly-concealed reference to his own native district. Such a reference, playful and half-hidden, would be very like him.

Another aspect of names is the act of naming, or revealing one's personal name, a frequent motif in Arthurian literature. The concealment yet possible disclosure of the dead girl's name in *Pearl* may be a resonance we shall never appreciate. Equally mysterious, though in a very different way, is Bertilak's revelation of his own name, after the testing of Gawain at the Green Chapel. This is a fine rhetorical device. How could Gawain not have heard his host's name during his stay in his castle? An irrelevant question, which the speed and cunning of the narrative prevents us from asking, at least while we are reading. In folktale, romance, perhaps all narrative, ignorance of a name, refusal to reveal it, or the timing of the disclosure of a person's name, is always significant. To be able to name a person gives a certain power over him or her, while at the same time, to be known by your name gives you a certain status. Names have a powerful relation to identity and self-awareness.

In Arthurian romance different kinds of power are asserted by either refusing to give one's name, or by asserting it. The revelation of one's own name expresses self-confidence, and may be either a challenge or a gesture of friendship. When the Green Knight first enters Arthur's hall he refuses to tell his name; he is aggressive and insolent. When he tells his own name at the winding up of the story, he is friendly, reveals his own secrets (almost a 'confession' to match Gawain's alleged 'confession' to him), and by such revelation achieves a kind of closure.

It is only a kind of conclusion. Questions remain unanswered. The name itself is strange, with no known story or family or associations attached to it. And we do not know who is the 'true' Bertilak, whether he of the green complexion, or the hearty ruddy lord of the castle. Should we indeed think of a single 'true' Bertilak, since when he gives his name he is in his green form, though he asserts his identity as the husband who encouraged his wife to seduce Gawain and thus cuckold himself? (Gawain's chastity has protected not only his own life but his host's honour, for cuckoldry was universally considered, with cowardice, the greatest masculine dishonour.) Ambiguity remains the final note.

We come to the ladies' names. Of the two only 'Morgne la Faye' (2446), 'Morgne þe goddes' (2452) is named. She is well known in Arthurian romance as Arthur's half-sister and enemy. Her well-known enmity to and estrangement from Arthur, together with the late discovery of her identity, make it plausible that Gawain should not recognise his aunt. Furthermore, the poem, for all the wide knowledge of Arthurian romance that is implicit in it, is curiously self-contained as an Arthurian narrative. All this, together with the supernatural powers hinted at in the references to her, and found elsewhere in Arthurian romance, make his ignorance easy to accept. Her presence, together with the revelations of Bertilak, cast a retrospective mysterious magic over the castle itself.

Finally we come to Bertilak's wife, never referred to except as 'the lady'. The absence of a name, or of the slightest hint of a name, is highly significant. A curious instance of our human need for names, and their importance, is the frequency with which students, and even some recent critics, refer to her as 'Lady Bertilak'. To do so is a solecism as absurd as if one were to refer to Guinivere as 'Queen Arthur'. It also involves a misjudgment of the tone of the poem and of the Lady's place in the story. She is indeed Bertilak's wife, but that the Lady is never given a name is a reflection of her function as an instrument (like the false Guinivere herself in the earlier story) in the machinations of Bertilak/Green Knight and 'Morgne þe goddes' rather than a person of independent identity and character. The lack of a name, like the fact that Bertilak is himself never named (nor apparently does Gawain enquire his host's name, throughout Gawain's stay in Bertilak's castle), until Bertilak names himself in the final revelations, is a further index of the token nature of ordinary characterisation of him and his wife, as required by and appropriate to their functions in the folk-tale-like romance story.

7

The Manuscript: British Library MS Cotton Nero A.x

A. S. G. EDWARDS

British Library MS Cotton Nero A.x is a rather unprepossessing manuscript. It is quite small in size (4¾ x 6¾ inches), its smallness emphasized by the fact that it was apparently cropped at some point in its binding history. As it is now constituted[1] it comprises only ninety vellum leaves, consisting of seven gatherings of twelve leaves (each with a catchword), preceded by a single bifolium and concluded by a gathering of four leaves. The manuscript has been regularly ruled for thirty-six lines to a full page. The text area is ruled and bounded in plummet and measures approximately 3¾ x 5¾ inches.

This is the only surviving Middle English manuscript collection consisting solely of alliterative poems. The four poems appear in the manuscript in the following order: *Pearl* (fols 41–59ᵛ), *Cleanness* (fols 61–86), *Patience* (fols 87–94) and *Sir Gawain and the Green Knight* (*Sir Gawain*) (fols 95–128ᵛ). They were all written by a single scribe, writing in what has been characterised as 'a very individualistic small, sharp, angular character' (Wright 1960, 15). This scribe apparently copied the manuscript as a single construct, rather than as a series of discrete units: there is no correlation between the various texts and quire boundaries. His transcription seems to have been generally careful, although it is not possible to establish how many of the manifest errors made in the course of copying were introduced by him or existed in his exemplar. There are a number of indications of erasure and correction, some possibly by another, perhaps later hand (for details see Gollancz 1923, 12–39).

The dialect of the scribe has been quite precisely localized to a part of Cheshire (McIntosh, Samuels and Benskin 1986, III, s.v. 'Cheshire', 36–54 passim). While the scribal dialect does not, of course, necessarily reveal the place of actual writing, it does seem consistent with possible topographical allusions in *Sir Gawain* (cf. Elliott above 113; Duggan below 240–2). Otherwise there are no clear indications of the early ownership of the manuscript. The

---

[1] The manuscript was not re-foliated when unrelated materials, with which it had been bound in the seventeenth century, were removed in 1964. There is an early sequence of numbering in ink from 37 to 126. However, the modern pencil foliation, which is followed here, runs from 41 to 130. Hence, fol. 41 is actually the first leaf of the manuscript.

name 'Hugo de' is written in the upper margin of the recto of the first leaf of *Sir Gawain* (fol. 95). And it has been claimed that the name 'J. Macy' appears in the marginal decoration on fols 62^v and 114 (Vantuono 1975; 1981). Even before this 'discovery' (which to some eyes at least, my own included, does not appear to be a name), the Masseys had been the subject of extensive speculation in connection with the manuscript (Peterson 1974b; Nolan and Farley-Hills 1971; Peterson and Wilson 1977). Forms of the name have been discerned in anagrams in *Pearl* and in *St Erkenwald*, a poem which survives uniquely in another manuscript, British Library MS Harley 2250, which has sometimes been claimed as part of the canon of the poet who is held to have written all the poems in the Cotton manuscript.

Leaving aside such speculations, the history of the Cotton manuscript is unknown before the early seventeenth century. The important researches of Edward Wilson (1979) do provide some grounds for believing that the Cotton manuscript may have been owned by, and, indeed, written for the Stanley family of Staffordshire and Cheshire, a family that had an evident interest in vernacular literature (they owned an important manuscript of Chaucer's poems) and whose family crest includes a holly tree (cf. *Sir Gawain* 206–7). However, the earliest specific reference to it occurs in a list of manuscripts made before 1614 by a Yorkshire book collector, Henry Savile of Banke, where it is described as 'An owld booke in English verse beginninge Perle plesant to Princes pay in 4°. Limned' (Watson 1969, 68 [274]). By 1621 it had passed into the hands of the great antiquary, Sir Robert Cotton. In that year it was recorded in his library catalogue, described as 'Gesta Arthuri regis et aliorum versu anglico' ('deeds of King Arthur and other matters in English verse').[2]

Parallels in language have been noted between *Sir Gawain* and a poem by another northern poet, Humfrey Newton, in the fifteenth century (Robbins 1943). And the appearance of a version of the *Gawain*-narrative, *The Grene Knight*, in the mid-seventeenth-century Percy Folio manuscript (British Library Add. MS 27879, 203–10), suggests a continued circulation for this poem (cf. Rogers, below). But we have no way of knowing for certain whether this circulation depends at all on the surviving Cotton manuscript, or rather on some other copy or version of the poem now lost.

Cotton Nero A.x is not a holograph and it is clearly separated by some interval from the original transcription of the poems it contains. The inscription at the end of *Sir Gawain*: 'HONY SOYT QUI MAL PENCE' (fol. 124^v), the motto of the Order of the Garter founded by Edward III in about 1348, provides the earliest possible date for the transcription of the manuscript itself.[3] On paleographical grounds the manuscript can be dated to the second

---

[2] British Library MS Harley 6018 ('Catalogus Librorum Manuscriptorum in Bibliotheca Roberti Cottoni 1621'), fol. 112^v.

[3] It is not, however, certain that the inscription was copied at the same time as the text or by the same scribe.

half of the fourteenth century (Doyle 1982, 92; Wright 1960, 15 suggests the last quarter of the century). There have been attempts to push the transcription forward a little into the early fifteenth century, largely on the basis of the illustrations, particularly of styles of clothing which include details which are not recorded before this later date (on the dating see Doyle 1982; Horrall 1986). But since the illustrations were added later to the manuscript (see below) they offer little assistance in dating the transcription of the poems themselves. The hand of the scribe has not been identified in other manuscripts and there is no clue as to his identity or the motives that led to his transcription.

We have no way of determining how many stages of copying precede the manuscript. There are a quite large number of smaller, manifest scribal errors, more than four hundred at a recent count,[4] many involving obvious mechanical transcriptional failures – dittography, minim error, and eyeskip, for instance. Many of these can be confidently emended to recover the original reading. Other textual anomalies may be the consequences of a more extensive transmissional history and the attendant opportunities of corruption. There seems to be evidence of some confusion in the text in *Patience* where editors often differ considerably in their sense of the ordering and positioning of lines 510–15; some are even uncertain whether they belong in the poem. Lines 901–12 of *Pearl* are also problematic since this stanza disrupts the otherwise invariable pattern of five-stanza groupings. Several editors have argued for the removal of either this stanza or one of the others within this group. In addition, there are points where lines have been lost in the course of transmission. The rhyme scheme establishes that there is clearly one line, 472, missing in *Pearl*. And in *Sir Gawain*, one day, December 28, is lost from the chronology of lines 1021ff, perhaps as the consequence of a line having been omitted between lines 1022–23 at some stage in the course of copying. Other anomalies in the received texts do exist which seem to have resisted either comment or resolution. One anomaly in *Sir Gawain* is the fact that the hero implicates both Bertilak's wife and Morgan le Fay in the plot against him: 'Boþe þat on and þat oþer, myn honoured ladyez' (2412) some lines before Bertilak has revealed the latter's role (2456–66).

The question of the transmission of the texts in the manuscript is related to another issue: whether the poems it contains have been copied together since their original composition, or whether they were brought together at some later point in their textual history. Oakden suggests that each of the four poems was originally copied separately and postulates several stages of intervening copying for each of them before their appearance together in Cotton Nero A.x (Oakden 1935, II. 261–63). The issue has an obvious importance for the assumption of common authorship upon which most

---

[4] I have taken this very rough figure from the textual notes in Andrew and Waldron 1978.

modern scholarship operates, an assumption that becomes less secure if these poems were only collocated together at a relatively late point in their textual histories.

We cannot resolve these textual and attributional problems. But it is sensible to be aware of them and to be conscious of the fact that modern forms of presentation for the poems in this manuscript as the works of 'the *Pearl*-poet' or 'the *Gawain*-poet' are not necessarily based on evidence that is as secure as we would wish it to be. There are other ways in which the forms in which we encounter these poems in modern editions are misleading, ways which may impinge on matters of literary interpretation.

To begin with the most obvious: we read these poems as edited texts, texts, that is, that are the outcome of a large number of editorial decisions that affect both general and particular aspects of the presentation of these works. To begin with, all punctuation, most capitalization and some word division in the poems is supplied by editors, who generally seek to follow modern usage in such matters. But this does not mean that treatment of them is uniform between editions. At times, even such seemingly straightforward matters as punctuation can become problematic. For example, there is considerable difference in punctuation between editions of the opening lines of *Sir Gawain*, given the disagreement or uncertainty of editors as to the identity of the 'tulk' referred to in line 3, who could be either Aeneas or Antenor (see Burrow 1988b). And other passages in the same poem can be plausibly repunctuated to convey different sense. Capitalization can also vary. The various pronominal forms of address to God in *Cleanness*, for example, are not consistently capitalized. The 'grene kny3t' in *Sir Gawain* (for example, 390, 417) is in some editions the 'Grene Kny3t'. The 'grene chapel' (451) can be the 'Grene Chapel' and 'nw3eres morn' (453) 'Nw 3eres morn'. This last example makes clear that even such questions as where (or whether) word division should occur can be open to editorial debate; thus an editor of *Pearl* must decide whether the text should read in line 382 'marere3' or 'mare re3,' and an editor of *Cleanness* whether to read 'for ferde' or 'forferde' in line 386. Even transcription can pose interpretive problems. The name of the Green Knight in *Sir Gawain* has been variously rendered by editors as 'Bernlak', 'Bercilak' and 'Bertilak.' Such decisions are a normal part of the editorial process; but it is wise to be conscious that the texts we read have been mediated even in such small but significant ways by editorial intervention.

There are other aspects of the manuscript of which we also need to be conscious as we study the poems it contains in modern editions. For example, none of the poems has any title in the manuscript. This is not a point of any great significance; but *Cleanness*, for example, is sometimes titled *Purity* by modern editors (see, for example, the edition by Menner 1920); and *Sir Gawain* has been titled *Sir Gawain and the Grene Gome* (Jones 1972; see p. 8 for the reasons). Also, the presentation of the verse forms at times is very different in some modern editions because of no general agreement as to the scribe's intention. *Patience* and *Cleanness* are printed by some editors in quatrains (Gollancz 1913, 1921; Anderson 1969), following the argument of Kaluza (1892), and in accordance with the apparent scribal notation in the manuscript, even though not all of the poem as it appears there is actually in quatrains. Other editors print the poem as blank verse (Andrew and Waldron 1978). And in *Sir Gawain* the 'short' line of the 'bob' is not written by the scribe directly above the 'wheel,' the concluding cross-rhymed quatrain of each stanza, but in the outer margin, on occasions some lines above the wheel. This is regularized by modern editors. Only the twelve-line stanza form of *Pearl* has posed no interpretive problems in representing the metrical form as presented in the manuscript.

Editions also vary markedly in their treatment of the decorated initials in the poems. There are forty-eight such initials ranging in size from two to fifteen lines, all in blue with red penwork. There are twenty-one in *Pearl* (lines 1, 61, 121, 181, 241, 301, 361, 421, 481, 541, 601, 661, 721, 781, 841, 913, 961, 973, 1033, 1093, 1153), thirteen in *Cleanness* (lines 1, 125, 193, 249, 345, 485, 557, 601, 689, 781, 893, 1157, 1357), five in *Patience* (lines 1, 61, 245, 305, 409) and nine in *Sir Gawain* (lines 1, 491, 619, 763, 1126, 1421, 1893, 1998, 2259). Each poem begins with a large initial, fifteen lines in *Pearl*, the first poem in the manuscript, and eight lines for each of others. Initials of this size are not otherwise employed. The majority of the others are three-line ones. Most of these occur in *Pearl* (nineteen) and in *Cleanness* (ten). *Sir Gawain* contains two six-line initials (lines 1126, 1998), and *Cleanness* one five-line (line 1157); there are three four-line initials, one each in *Pearl* (line 61), *Cleanness* (line 557) and *Sir Gawain* (line 491).

The nature and frequency of these initials have, at times, been held to be of some interpretive significance. They have been generally regarded as constituting forms of internal division, marking off sections of each poem, and possibly reflecting more complex significations. For example, their function in *Cleanness* has been seen as connected to 'the tripartite organization of the poem as a whole' (Spendal 1976), while Donna Crawford, in a subtle and important study, has seen them as exemplifying the poem's 'geometrical art' because of the various ratios that are revealed through the intervals between them (Crawford 1993).

Modern editions do not always reflect the internal divisions of each of the poems as indicated by the initials. Those in *Sir Gawain* have been the subject of particular debate. Some scholars have argued that the traditional four-fitt division of the poem, introduced in the first edition of the poem by Sir Frederic Madden in 1839 and retained by all subsequent editors, is misleading. It has been pointed out that there are nine large initials in the manuscript and that their positioning may have structural significance since they all 'occur at points in the plan of the narrative which mark recognizable stages in the progress of the story' (Hill 1946, 71). This insight has been refined a little by Tuttleton (1966) and more extensively by Blenkuer (1977), who sees them as related to various structural patterns of triads. Somewhat more closely rooted in the manuscript itself are the arguments of Michael Robertson (1982) who posits an intended division of the poem by the initials into groups of eleven stanzas, a division that reflects various structural and symbolic significances. There seems to be a growing sense that these initials possess some significance for the structure and hence the interpretation of the poems, even if there is not yet a consensus as to what that significance is.

Some of the arguments about the interpretation of the significance of the large initials and, to a lesser degree, the lineation of the poems, are related to the recurrent preoccupation with number symbolism in the manuscript. Such arguments have been applied most frequently to *Sir Gawain* (for references see Käsmann 1974). There have also been demonstrations of the presence of number symbolism in *Pearl* (Kean 1965) and in *Patience* (Gilligan 1989). The numerical patterns that have been discerned sometimes fail to take account of some aspects of the presentation of these poems in the manuscript. They often depend upon the actual lineation of the poems. Here again, there are some differences between manuscript presentation and the edited texts. For example, as I have noted, the 'bobs' in *Sir Gawain* are never written as separate lines, a fact that not all advocates of number symbolism in the poem are disposed to discuss, and which may, in itself, raise some interesting implications (see Bachman 1980).

Another very striking aspect of the manuscript not always fully reflected in modern editions is the presence of illustrations. There are twelve pictures in all: four appear on the bifolium before the beginning of *Pearl* (fols 41–42^v), two between *Cleanness* and *Patience* (fols 60^{r-v}), two before *Patience* (fols 82^{r-v}) and four for *Sir Gawain*, one before the beginning of the poem (fol. 94^v), and three at the end (fols 129^{r-v}, 130). Before any discussion of their significance the subjects of each one will be briefly summarized:

Pearl

[1] fol. 41: The dreamer, clad in a red gown[5] with a blue collar, lies asleep in an 'erber grene' (38) beside a stream. Here the water is painted a very dark olive-green; in [2]–[4] it is blue.

[2] fol. 41^v: The dreamer stands by the stream.

[3] fol. 42: The dreamer stands by the stream; on the other side is the figure of the Pearl-maiden, clad in white, with a yellow crown.

[4] fol. 42^v: As in [3] dreamer and Pearl-maiden are on opposite banks of the stream. The maiden is now set between two structures, one a battlement, the other seemingly a church.

---

5   The gown is the same colour in [3]; but in [2] and [4] it is different shade of red, almost crimson.

1. BL MS Cotton Nero A.x, fol. 41: *Pearl*: the dreamer asleep.
By permission of the British Library.

2. BL MS Cotton Nero A.x, fol. 41ᵛ: *Pearl*: the dreamer by the stream.
By permission of the British Library.

3. BL MS Cotton Nero A.x, fol. 42: *Pearl*: the dreamer and the Pearl-maiden.
By permission of the British Library.

4. BL MS Cotton Nero A.x, fol. 42ᵛ: *Pearl*: the dreamer and the Pearl-maiden
    again. By permission of the British Library.

Cleanness

[5] fol. 60: (cf. lines 403–45). Seven figures appear in Noah's Ark, which is painted orange-brown. To the left of the mast are two figures, a woman in a blue robe and white headdress and a bearded man in an olive-green robe. To the right of the mast are five figures. Closest to the mast is a figure in a crimson/purple robe; next to him is an oarsman in an olive-green robe. In the water are two fish, the larger swallowing a third.

[6] fol. 60ᵛ: (cf. lines 1529–676): Daniel is at Belshazzar's feast. Two crowned figures, a man in a blue robe and a woman in a red one, are at a table. In the foreground is a kneeling figure, at whom the man is pointing; he is wearing a robe of varying shades of olive-green, with some portions in red and the bottom of the robe in purple. To the left, a hand holding a pen has just written the words 'mane . techal . phares' in a scroll.

Patience

[7] fol. 86: Two figures are in an orange-brown boat. The one on the left is wearing a reddish/purple robe and holding an oar while the one to the right, in a red robe, casts a third into the sea: 'Of þat schended schyp men schowued hym sone . . . þe fol ʒet haldande his fete, þe fysche hym tyd hentes; Withouten towche of any tothe he tult in his þrote' (247, 251–2).

[8] fol. 86ᵛ: To both the extreme left and right are buildings linked by battlements. Next to the building on the left is the most prominent figure, Jonah, exhorting the other three kneeling figures. The most prominent of these figures is a woman in a green robe. Below her are two figures: on the left is a bearded man in a blue robe; on the right is a bearded man in a red robe and blue cowl.

Sir Gawain

[9] fol. 94ᵛ: Four figures are standing behind a table; the one on the extreme left, in a red robe, is holding an axe. Next to him is a crowned king, in a blue robe, and another man in a red robe, both with drawn swords. Between them is a crowned queen in green. In the foreground is a mounted, olive-green, headless figure, holding his head in his right hand, with blood coming from both head and neck. Facing him is a bareheaded figure in a red jerkin and blue tights, holding a large axe.

[10] fol. 129: A male figure lies supine in a red bed, covered by a blanket of varying shades of olive-green; his face is being touched by a woman standing before him in a high-necked robe of green and red dots wearing a yellow headdress. Behind her is a blue curtain supported by a yellow rail.

5. BL MS Cotton Nero A.x, fol. 60: *Cleanness*: Noah's Ark.
By permission of the British Library.

6. BL MS Cotton Nero A.x, fol. 60ᵛ: *Cleanness*: Daniel at Belshazzar's feast.
By permission of the British Library.

[11] fol. 129^v: (This illustration is painted largely in various shades of olive-green, and is the least discernible.) In the upper part of the picture a figure in dark olive-green stands holding a large axe; below him, in the foreground is a mounted knight in armour. The upper body part of the armour is red. At the bottom right is a large black cavity, presumably the 'oritore' (2190) of the Green Knight.

[12] fol. 130: Three standing figures appear, the one to the left a crowned king in a blue robe, the middle one a crowned queen in an olive-green robe; on the right is a figure in a red robe holding a sword. Before them kneels a figure in armour, the body part of which is red, the rest blue. They are all surrounded by a blue arch with blue pillars.

In several respects, such pictures are rather unusual in Middle English verse manuscripts of this period. First is in the actual number of pictures, more than survive in any other Middle English romance manuscript. Indeed, only two other surviving Middle English manuscripts of verse romances contain illustrations on any scale. One, which antedates Cotton Nero A.x, is the famous Auchinleck manuscript (National Library of Scotland Advocates MS 19.2.1), a very large collection of romances and other verse texts, probably produced in London in the 1330s or 1340s. Although only six miniatures now survive it probably once included more than thirty (for discussion see Pearsall and Cunningham 1977, xv). The second is interesting because it provides the only parallel involving alliterative romance. This is the 'Alexander and Dindimus Fragment' in Bodleian Library Bodley 264, part II (fols 209–15^v), a manuscript executed c.1400. This is exceptionally elaborate, containing nine column miniatures, to five leaves of plain text. (For some comparison of the illustrations in Cotton and Bodley see Doyle 1983, 166–7.) Both the Auchinleck and Bodley manuscripts differ significantly from Cotton Nero A.x. These are large compilations, very elaborately prepared and seemingly the result of careful organization of the work of scribes and artists into close sequences of activity. As is explained below, this was not the case with the Cotton manuscript.

The Cotton manuscript is also unusual in that the illustration draws directly and closely on the subjects of the narrative. This relationship is not always so pronounced in the other near-contemporary Middle English illustrated verse texts I have noted. The 'Alexander and Dindimus' fragment provides the closest parallel. Like it, the illustrations in the Cotton manuscript provide careful reflections of events within each of the narratives. There are admittedly some anomalies: the most notable is the illustration of Noah's Ark for *Cleanness* on fol. 60. The text specifies that there were 'aȝtsum in þat ark' (411). But the illustration only includes seven figures. Moreover, the poem asserts that the Ark is 'withouten mast . . . oþer hande-helme hasped on roþer' (417, 419). This is a specification not included in the Biblical account.

7. BL MS Cotton Nero A.x, fol. 86: *Patience*: Jonah being cast into the sea.
By permission of the British Library.

8. BL MS Cotton Nero A.x, fol. 86ᵛ: *Patience*: Jonah at Bablyon.
By permission of the British Library.

It is also contradicted by the illustration which shows someone steering the boat with an oar. In other illustrations details are gratuitously added of no narrative significance: [2] and [3] show a fish swimming in the stream, presumably to 'authenticate' it. [9], the first illustration in *Sir Gawain*, is a little puzzling in that two figures among those in Arthur's court appear holding large axes. The one in the foreground is clearly Gawain at the moment after the decapitation of the Green Knight. The other, on the dais, seems to resemble Gawain and may represent him at a point before the decapitation. If so, it is an atypical attempt by the artist to combine two different moments in the narrative within a single scene. But in the poem Gawain never holds the Green Knight's axe while he is on the dais.

These inconsistencies between text and illustration suggest that the artist did not have a close knowledge of the poems he was illustrating. He may have been working within guidelines provided to him by the owner of the manuscript.[6] These instructions were probably given some time after the poems were copied into the manuscript. As the late Sarah Horrall noted, the first folio of *Pearl*, the first text in the manuscript, 'looks dark and rubbed, as if it had lain for a time as an unprotected outer quire' (Horrall 1986, 191) while the preceding bifolium containing the illustrations for the poem is unmarked, suggesting an interval between transcription and illustration. Codicological evidence tends to support this view. The four illustrations for *Pearl* appear on a bifolium that is codicologically distinct and anomalous in terms of the manuscript's collation. It could easily have have been added at some later time. Three of the four *Sir Gawain* illustrations appear on blank leaves at the end of the final gathering (fols 129^{r-v}, 130), leaves which naturally lent themselves to an illustrative afterthought. The construction of the manuscript seems to have been originally designed to allow a blank leaf or a blank verso between each of the poems so that each begins on a new recto. With one exception the other illustrations occur as full page ones on those pages or leaves which separate individual poems. The exception is fol. 86, where the final eleven lines of *Cleanness* run over on to the recto of an otherwise blank leaf. Here the first of the *Patience* illustrations appears anomalously as a half-page one. This suggests a lack of co-ordination between scribe and artist that supports the view that the two activities took place at different points in time if not in place.The other leaves, containing full page illustrations, are fols 60 (between *Pearl* and *Cleanness*), 86 (between *Cleanness* and *Patience*) and 94^v (between *Patience* and *Sir Gawain*). That these leaves were left blank for some period after the copying of the manuscript is demonstrated by the traces of offset from fol. 86 on fol. 85^v and of fol. 95 on 94^v. Hence these leaves were placed on top of each other while the ink was still damp, indicating that they

---

6 I owe this suggestion to Dr Kathleen Scott; I am greatly indebted to Dr Scott for permitting me to read a draft of her entry on the Cotton manuscript for her forthcoming book on later Gothic illumination in England and for discussing her work with me.

9. BL MS Cotton Nero A.x, fol. 94ᵛ: *Sir Gawain and the Green Knight*:
The Green Knight at Arthur's court. By permission of
the British Library.

10. BL MS Cotton Nero A.x, fol. 129: *Sir Gawain and the Green Knight*:
Gawain and Bertilak's wife. By permission of the British Library.

11. BL MS Cotton Nero A.x, fol. 129ᵛ: *Sir Gawain and the Green Knight*:
Gawain at the Green Chapel. By permission of the British Library.

12. BL MS Cotton Nero A.x, fol. 130: *Sir Gawain and the Green Knight*:
Gawain's return to Arthur's court. By permission of the British Library.

had not yet been painted. That illustrations were not intended for all the pages that now contain them is further confirmed by the fact that some of the original blank leaves or pages had been ruled and bounded.[7] There would have been no point in ruling them if illustration was planned. In addition, the inscription within [6] is written by someone other than the main scribe, which seems to suggest that he was not available at the time of the manuscript's decoration.

This evident hiatus between copying and decoration must have resulted from a change in ownership and/or a subsequent more ambitious vision for the manuscript by an early owner. Given the evidence for northern provenance for the manuscript, it seem reasonable to assume that the artist was also provincial. His provinciality has often been equated with a lack of artistic achievement. W.W. Greg, in a review of the Gollancz facsimile, is particularly dismissive: 'it is perhaps not surprising that the 'artist' who drew these queer pictures should have been unable to refrain from rendering his work yet less attractive through the use of his child's paintbox' (Greg 1924, 227–8). His view is emphatically restated by R.S. and Laura H. Loomis:

> The nadir of English illustrative art is found in the caricatures which accompany the unique MS of *Gawain and the Green Knight* . . . It is ironic that one of the most exquisite and technically the most finished of medieval English poems should be illustrated by infantile daubs. (Loomis and Loomis 1938, 138)

More recently, Jennifer A. Lee has attempted to discriminate between the activities of the artist who drew the pictures and the actual painter, characterizing only the latter as 'an amateur' (Lee 1977, 19). But this hypothesis is not demonstrable and hence does not materially help in responding sympathetically to the paintings. The most recent research has found stylistic parallels for these illustrations and even found another that may be the work of the same artist.[8] It is, however, remotely possible that there could be more than one painter involved on the basis of apparent variations in palette between some of the illustrations, such as the different colours of red used in [1] and [3] when compared to that in [2] and [4], or the painting of water olive-green in [1] but blue in [2]–[4].

Without doubt there are aspects of the illustrations that suggest a limited technique, particularly in the lack of perspective and the curious elongation of the human form in some pictures (for example, [6]–[8]). Such limitations must be set against the complexity of devising illustrations directly from narrative possibly without stylistic models. (There does not seem to have been any attempt to seek such models, even though there were developed

---

7 Fols 60[r–v] and 130[v] have been ruled and bounded. On the other hand, fols 86[v] and 94[v] have not.

8 The evidence is set out in Dr Scott's forthcoming account of the manuscript's illustration.

medieval traditions of Old Testament Bible illustration that could be relevant to *Jonah* and *Cleanness* and the English traditions of Apocalypse illustration have been suggested as sources for *Pearl*.) While some of the pictures contain obscurities or inconsistencies, they all show conscientious attempts to reflect the texts and significant moments within them. In such respects the achievement of the artist(s) is creditable. It is also unusual in its quite careful series of responses to vernacular poetic texts.

The illustrations are one of a series of aspects of the Cotton manuscript that cannot be finally resolved. Just as the identity of the artist or the motives that led to the execution of his paintings are obscure, so is much else about the manuscript. What person(s) was (were) responsible for commissioning it? What were his/her motives? Where were copies of these poems found? Were they found together? If not, what are the implications of the decision to join them in a manuscript? What was the subsequent early history and circulation of the Cotton manuscript? Our inability to answer these questions with any degree of certainty does not, of course, diminish our appreciation of the poems it contains. But our awareness of the form in which they are preserved may make us properly conscious that such unanswerable questions lie behind the fortuitous survival of the solitary witness to these extraordinary works.[9]

9 For comments on drafts of this chapter I am much indebted to Dr Scott and Professors Elizabeth Archibald and Derek Pearsall.

8

Meter, Stanza, Vocabulary, Dialect

H. N. DUGGAN

The four poems preserved in MS Cotton Nero A.x provide some of the most intriguing problems for students of Middle English philology. Only Chaucer and Langland among late fourteenth-century English poets wrote poetry of similar imaginative and moral power, and since their recuperation in the last century scholars have devoted vast efforts to determining their authorship and provenance, to describing their metrical and stylistic features, and to explicating their complex thematics. Because we lack an authorial text of any of these poems, attempts to describe the language and style of the *Gawain*-poet must begin, even now after generations of scholarly analysis, with reminders of what we do not know. Without a compelling test for common authorship, every statement about *the* language of *the* poet should be accompanied by a qualification: we may have a linguistically homogenous manuscript in which dialect translation has obliterated two (or three or even four) originally different sets of linguistic, metrical, and stylistic features.[1] That is unlikely, but skepticism is in order.[2]

As the editors of the *Linguistic Atlas of Late Middle English* (McIntosh, Samuels and Benskin 1986; hereafter *LALME*) have demonstrated, Middle English scribes frequently engaged in dialect translation, copying their exemplars not letter for letter but fluently translating from one dialect into their own (McIntosh 1963, 1973; Benskin and Laing 1981). A single copying might

---

[1] For the argument that some or all of the four poems in Cotton Nero A.x are by different poets, see Clark 1949, 1950ab, 1951; Kjellmer 1975; and Tajima 1978. The case for common authorship is treated as 'not proved' by Bloomfield (1961) and skeptically by Lawton (1982b, 9; 1994, 152). For not wholly successful attempts to prove common authorship, see Vantuono 1971; Derolez 1981; McColly and Weir 1983; McColly 1987; Cooper and Pearsall 1988. See Andrew above, 23–33, for a detailed discussion.

[2] The computer promises to make more thorough and sophisticated attribution tests possible. I am presently working with Professor Eric Eliason on a statistically based study of lexical, metrical, and syntactic features of alliterative verse which have, thus far, tended to show *Patience* and *Cleanness* clustering more closely together than any other of the unrhymed poems in the tradition and with *Gawain* grouped more tightly with them than with any other poems. However, we are in very preliminary stages of investigation, and it is too early to conclude that these three poems are the work of a single poet.

well erase most orthographic features of the original dialect. For poems in unrhymed alliterative verse, a series of such dialect translations could erase most features of the poet's spelling and morphology. We may see a clear instance of this phenomenon in the Ashmolean manuscript of *The Wars of Alexander*, where the scribe, writing in County Durham perhaps as much as three quarters of a century after the composition of the poem, so thoroughly translated his original into his own dialect that W.W. Skeat took it to have been composed 'in a pure Northumbrian dialect, in some county lying between the Humber and the Tweed' (xx). Instead, the original was composed well to the south and west of Durham, perhaps near Merseyside (Duggan and Turville-Petre 1989, xxv–xliii). The existence of a second manuscript and the closeness of the poetic translation to the Latin source provide the bases for comparative analysis that permit us to distinguish the immediate scribal forms from those of the poet (Duggan and Turville-Petre 1989, xvii–xxiv, xliii–li).

Many sources of information are denied us. In those fortunate instances when we know the name or birthplace of the poet (e.g., Chaucer's *Canterbury Tales* or Langland's *Piers Plowman*) scholars may recover features of the original dialect by studying other works in the poet's natal dialect. For texts surviving in a number of copies, studying relict forms common to many or all the extant witnesses may offer evidence of provenance (Samuels 1988, 201–3; Benskin 1991). In a corpus like most Middle English alliterative poetry in which nearly all poems are anonymous or where we know nothing of the named author, it is primarily analysis of the author's *usus scribendi* in regard to rhyme and alliteration that enables us to distinguish authorial dialects from scribal. Comparison of the manuscript forms with the rhyme evidence in *Pearl*, with alliterative practice in *Patience* and *Cleanness*, with rhyme and alliteration in *Sir Gawain and the Green Knight* (*Gawain*), and with the rhythmic structures of all four poems provides our best evidence for distinguishing the poet's language from that of the scribe.[3]

Until very recently to attempt to use metrical evidence for such purposes would have been *ignotum per ignotius*. However, recent discoveries about the fourteenth-century alliterative long line have made it possible to determine with confidence several aspects of phonological and morphological structure that were formerly matters of conjecture. We are fortunate, as well, that the *Gawain*-poet wrote not only in the unrhymed alliterative long line but in a foot-counted rhymed metrical form as well. We now know that though *Pearl* exhibits a high density of ornamental alliteration, it is an alliterative poem in only trivial senses of the term. Composed in a flexible iambic tetrameter, its metrical structures have much to tell us about differences between the poet's and the scribe's linguistic usages. Moreover, the rhyming bobs and wheels of

---

3 None of the various attempts to find a name for the poet encrypted in the poems or margins of the manuscript is convincing.

the *Gawain*-stanza often provide useful corroboration of evidence supplied by *Pearl*.

The unrhymed alliterative long line in Middle English consists of two *verses* or *half-lines* divided by a *caesura*. The first of these is called variously the *a-verse* or *on-verse*, the second the *b-verse* or *off-verse*. Each verse may have two or (in the case of the a-verse) three *lifts* and one to four *dips*. A *lift*, also called a *stave*, is occupied by a single metrically prominent syllable, a *dip* by one to several unstressed syllables. Following A.V.C. Schmidt (1984), I distinguish a *full stave*, a metrically prominent syllable accompanied by alliteration, from a *blank stave* in which there is metrical prominence and no alliteration. Schmidt's further refinement of this notion, the *mute stave*, in which metrically significant alliteration falls on an unstressed syllable, is not a stave at all in the sense that it carries no metrical stress. However, it is a structural feature of at least one poet's alliterative line (Langland's), and some small inconsistency in terminology is preferable to needless proliferation of terms. Though the manuscripts of other poems from time to time offer apparent instances of mute staves, these are in every case inauthentic, the product of scribal error (Duggan 1987a). The terms *lift* and *dip* are conventional and do not refer to raised or lowered pitch, though changes in pitch constitute one of the several means by which metrical and linguistic stress is achieved. In almost all discussions of metrics the word *stress* covers a variety of different means by which English speakers give emphasis to one or more syllables in a phrase. Stress is less an acoustic phenomenon than a psychological one, a perceptual cue created not only by relative volume but also at various times by duration, pitch, (dis)juncture, and in poetry by metrical expectation. In general, word stress is subordinate to phrasal stress, and phrasal stress in alliterative poetry, as in normal speech, tends to fall on the tonic syllable of semantically important words.[4]

Metrists have traditionally described the rhythms of Middle English alliterative verses as *rising, falling, rising-falling,* and *falling-rising* to refer respectively to verses beginning with a dip and concluding on a lift, beginning with a lift and ending on a dip, beginning and ending with a dip, and beginning and ending with a lift. These categories, however, carry no real information for metrical interpretation or prediction (Kane 1981; Lawton 1988, 224). The same may be said of the category 'heteromorphic feet' (McIntosh 1982, 21–2),

---

[4] In rhythmic notation, a solidus indicates a lift, an 'x' each syllable in the dip, and the position of the caesura is marked by a double space. Thus, *For þe hede in his honde he haldez vp euen* would be represented by *xx/xx/ x/xx/x*. In descriptions of the alliterative patterning *a* stands for a full stave, *x* a blank stave and a solidus the caesura. Thus *His longe louelych lokkez he layd ouer his croun* would be *aaa/ax* and *Þat þe bit of þe broun stel bot on þe grounde* would appear as *aax/ax*. Mute staves are placed in parentheses, and when a second sound appears to alliterate within the line, the second pair is designated with *b*. Thus, the defective line *And wyth a countenaunce dryȝe he droȝ doun his cote* is represented as *ab/ba*.

for in the absence of any rules to predict when one or another form of the 'heteromorphic foot' is to appear or (more importantly) when it cannot appear, the term is trivially descriptive.

The Meter of Patience, Cleanness, and Gawain

The first three rules below govern the distribution of alliterating syllables in the long line, the fourth the caesura, and the last three describe the rhythmic structure of a-and b-verses:

Metrical Rule 1:

The poets wrote exclusively in the following combinations of alliterative patterns:

$$\left.\begin{array}{l} aa \\ aax \\ axa \\ xaa \\ aaa \end{array}\right\} : \left\{\begin{array}{l} ax \\ aa \end{array}\right\}$$

The minimum requirement of metricality is that two full staves must appear in the a-verse and the first stave in the b-verse must be full (Duggan 1986a).

Over 90 percent of lines in the three poems correspond to one of the following patterns of alliteration:

Þe tulk þat þe trammes of tresoun þer wroȝt	G 3	aa/ax
Þe coge of þe colde water, and þenne þe cry ryses	P 152	aax/ax
And steken þe ȝates ston-harde wyth stalworth barrez	C 884	axa/ax
THE grete soun of Sodamas synkkez in myn erez	C 689	xaa/ax
Fro riche Romulus to Rome ricchis hym swyþe	G 8	aaa/ax
He glydes in by þe giles þurȝ glaymande glette	P 269	aa/ax
Þroly þrublande in þronge þrowen ful þykke	C 504	aaa/aa[5]

Some exceptions to these rules governing alliteration cited in early studies of the meter are only apparent because the poet's fondness for elision alliteration obscures the pattern:

---

[5] This one instance is offered for the variant forms with aax/aa, axa/aa, xaa/aa. Though significant numbers of a-verses with three metrically stressed positions appear in the corpus, the minimal metrical requirement is that two stressed syllables in the a-verse should bear alliteration, and thus aax, axa, xaa, and aaa are all metrically much the same thing, though stylistically perhaps different in their effect.

/   x   /   x   / x x   x   x   x / x   / x
Nym þe way to Nynyue   wyth-outen oþer speche   P 66   axa/ax

This verse, identified by Oakden as alliterating aba/bx and by Sapora as
ax/ax, is in fact quite unremarkable, alliterating on /n/ at the juncture of '-en'
and 'oþer.'[6] The same is true of C 1779:

x   x   x   / x x   /   x / x x   / x
Withinne an oure of þe niy3t an entre þay hade.   aa/ax

This line alliterates regularly aa/ax on /n/ rather than on the vowels (*pace*
Sapora 1977, 110). Elision alliteration is common and does not distinguish the
Gawain-poet from any other poet in the tradition.[7] Rather more distinctive is
his tendency to write verses in which so-called 'little' words, normally
unstressed words from closed classes, are given metrical stress by dint of
being the sole word carrying alliteration in their quadrant of the line. This
feature occurs some three dozen times in the three poems:

x   / x x /x /   /   x x   / x
3et hym is þe hy3e kyng harder in heuen   C 50   aax/aa

x /   x x x   x / x / x   / x x x   / x
Hit weren not alle on wyuez sunez wonen with on fader C 112   aax/ax[8]

/ x   x   x x / x x   / x x x / x
Hit watz not for a halyday honestly arayed   C 134   aa/ax[9]

x   x   x / x   x   / /   x x   /   / (x)
And ay hatz ben and wyl be 3et   fro her barnage   C 517   aa/ax

x /   x x x   /   x x / / x
Þa3 I be not now he   þat 3e of speken   G 1242 aa/ax

[6] Oakden 1930, I. 191; Sapora 1977, 96. The latter's SWSW is more or less the equivalent of
ax/ax in other notational systems, though Sapora does not recognize the caesura as a
metrical feature.
[7] Elision is a stylistic option and does not always occur. For instance, alliteration on vowels
in *ende, any*, and *I* is more likely in G 660 than elision alliteration on the juncture of *withouten*
and *ende* and *noke*, though the text is insecure at this point:
x   x x   /   x / x /   / x x   / x
Withouten ende at any noke I oquere fynde
See Davis's textual note. In the case of G 1615, one would perhaps prefer to account for the
a-verse as scribal error than as an inept instance of elision alliteration:
x   x x / /   x   /   x x / x
Now with þis ilk swyn þay swengen to home.
[8] Though it would be conceivable to scan this verse with alliteration on *alle, on*, and *on*, the
last two being the numeral 'one' and thus capable of stress promotion, the head stave is
clearly *won-*, and the vocalic alliteration is incidental.
[9] Only the existence of this pattern in other of the poet's lines would suggest that 'Hit'
occupies a metrically stressed position.

```
   x   /   /                    x  x  /   x  x   /x  /(x)
And now nar (= 'ne are') ȝe not fer   fro þat note place        G 2092aax/ax
```

Some of these verses – most of them in *Gawain* – are probably not authentic, for we must remind ourselves that we have only the single witness to the texts, not the texts themselves. At the same time, some of these verses will be authorial, for the phenomenon, accounted for in metrical rule III, of stress elevation of function words in the absence of a competing word from a higher class is common in other poems where multiple attestation supports their authenticity.

Metrical Rule 2:
   Alliteration always falls on a stressed syllable. An ictus (a metrically stressed syllable) coincides with normal prose phrasal stress.[10]

Metrical Rule 3:
   A hierarchy of word classes determines which words may appear in ictus. Words from open classes (nouns, adjectives, most verb forms, adverbs with two or more syllables, pronouns ending in *-self*) take precedence over words from closed classes (prepositions, conjunctions, some verbs, auxiliaries, pronouns, monosyllabic adverbs). Alliteration falls on the latter only with syntactic inversion or in the absence of a word from the open class. (Duggan 1990a.)

Though in most metrical contexts any word from an open class may occupy a stave, the poet, like other alliterative poets, had at his disposal a large corpus of distinctively poetic words associated with alliterative verse. We may see something of the poet's range in a single eight-line sentence. Ictus positions in the first four lines are filled with common, colloquial words:

> Now neȝez þe Nw ȝere   and þe nyȝt passez
> þe day dryuez to þe derk,   as Dryȝtyn biddez;
> Bot wylde wederez of þe worlde   wakned þeroute,
> Clowdes kesten kenly   þe colde to þe erþe[11] . . .   (G 1998–2002)

Only 'Dryȝtyn' here might send a novice to the glossary, but the alliterating words in the remainder of the sentence are rather more typical of the poet's diction. The last clauses begin with relatively plain diction (though one

---

[10] Duggan 1990a. A variant of this rule applies only to *Piers Plowman*. When the alliterative staves are established clearly in the first half-line, a mute stave may appear in the initial or medial dip of a b-verse (Duggan 1987b).

[11] Line-terminal *erþe* here represents the poet's usual distinction between it as the common term and the more highly ranked synonyms *erde, folde, molde,* and *world* that appear in ictus positions. All thirteen occurrences in *Gawain* appear at the end of the line, and eight of 25 in *Cleanness* (Borroff 1962, 70–74).

should note the poet's characteristic use of the absolute adjectives *naked* and *wylde*) and swiftly moves to a more customarily ornate diction:

> Wyth ny3e innoghe of þe norþe, þe naked to tene;
> Þe snawe snitered ful snart, þat snayped þe wylde;
> Þe werbelande wynde wapped fro þe hy3e,
> And drof vche dale ful of dryftes ful grete. (G 2003–05)

Snart as adverb appears only here and (with *-ly*) in *The Awntyrs off Arthure at the Terne Wathelyne* 82: *þe sneterand snawe snartly hem snelles*, while the adjectival form appears only in *The Wars of Alexander* (Duggan and Turville-Petre 1989) 3761 and a few northern surnames. *Snitered* appears only in the same line from *The Awntyrs off Arthure*, while the verb *snaypen* appears both there and in *The Wars of Alexander* 3761, 4123, also in an ictus position, as well as in *Cursor Mundi* in a different sense. The final verb phrase returns the sentence to the plain, workaday diction of its opening. The fullest, most useful treatments of this aspect of alliterative verse are those of Borroff 1962; Benson 1965b, 110–43; and Turville-Petre 1977, 69–83.

Few lines in *Patience* and *Cleanness* fail to meet Metrical Rules I–III. J.P. Oakden (1930, I) found that 97.9% of the lines in *Patience* (520/531 lines) and 97.95% in *Cleanness* (1775/1812 lines) were metrically regular, and Robert Sapora (1977) found similar regularity in alliteration. The text of *Gawain*, on the other hand, manifests a greater diversity of alliterative patterns. Oakden found that 91.9% (1861/2025 lines) of the long lines in *Gawain* are metrically regular, Sapora some 89%. Such counts are difficult to make accurately, but the difference between 98% compliance with the alliterative rules and 89–92% is sufficient to suggest either that the poet's metrical practice changed or that the quality of the text of *Gawain* is relatively more corrupt. No convincing evidence establishes the relative dates of composition, and all attempts to establish the order of composition have rested upon impressionistic criteria. We can at best speculate as to whether differences in alliterative practice, if they were attributable to the poet, might reflect a movement toward greater regularity or the reverse. Attribution to the poet is unlikely. Though conceivably the greater concord between the metrical rules and the practice in *Patience* and *Cleanness* could reflect scribal hyper-correction, a spurious regularization of lines composed more roughly, the evidence derived from analysis of *Piers Plowman*, *The Siege of Jerusalem*, *The Parlement of the Thre Ages*, and *The Wars of Alexander* suggests that it is far more likely that the text of *Gawain* is corrupt. That is, in those other alliterative poems where the evidence exists to distinguish scribal *usus scribendi* in metrical matters from authorial, it invariably shows that the lections inconsistent with the alliterative rule are scribal.

David Lawton (1993) has recently argued against the homogeneity of alliterative patterning in unrhymed Middle English alliterative verse. Though readily granting that the evidence derived from the multiple witnesses to *The Siege of Jerusalem*, *Parlement of the Thre Ages*, and *The Wars of Alexander* shows those poets very close to absolute regularity in both alliteration and adherence to the b-verse rules, he nevertheless wants to defend the over two dozen lines in *Gawain* of the pattern aa/xa. As he notes, 'all these lines make reasonable sense' (152). Moreover, the pattern 'is just the pattern to show some influence from poetry with end-rhyme' (163). Lawton's point is sensible, and probability cannot, without additional manuscript evidence, be established one way or another. However, it is worth noting that this pattern does not appear at all in either *Patience* or *Cleanness*. In this instance, a cursory inspection of the variant readings of four manuscripts of *The Siege of Jerusalem* offers some insight into the issue of authorial versus scribal alliterative patterning. The pattern aa/xa appears ten times in manuscript A, only once in V, thirteen times in C, and seventeen times in U. Every one of those scribal lines 'makes reasonable sense' and we could, with Lawton, consider that in each it is still 'just the pattern to show some influence from poetry with end-rhyme' (1993, 163). Nevertheless, in the critical text of *The Siege of Jerusalem* prepared by Ralph Hanna and David Lawton (forthcoming), the editors do not treat a single one of those verses as authorial! In the case of *Gawain*, we lack the comparative evidence that permitted Hanna and Lawton to reject such verses as scribal. It is a question of probability, and diverse folk are likely to say diversely on this issue.

The remaining 140 or so lines in which alliteration in *Gawain* fails may well repay editorial attention if they are treated as erroneous. Though like the pattern aa/xa, the non-canonic patterns in the irregular lines conceivably represent a change in the author's concept of his form, they more probably reflect a defective text.

Metrical Rule 4:
The alliterative line is made up of two distinct half-lines (verses) divided by a caesura which usually corresponds to a phrasal boundary.

Though some recent metrists and editors have expressed doubt about the existence of the caesura and thus of the half-line, manuscript evidence strongly supports the notion that the long line is composed of two cola separated by a metrical caesura.[12] The a-verse is both syllabically and semantically heavier than the b-verse which tends to carry less of the meaning, to serve essentially reiterative, transitional, elaborative, or space-holding roles. With a handful of exceptions, one may cover up the b-verses, read only the

---

[12] Generative metrists have tended to deny the existence of metrically significant half-lines, following Keyser (1969; 1969–70, 77 n. 2). That view is supported by Schiller (1968, 276) and Sapora (1977, 24–25). They have been followed by traditional metrists such as Fussell (1979) either in rejecting the idea of the caesura entirely (45) or by dismissing it as 'by no means a constant feature,' as Hieatt does (1974, 128), a view shared by Peterson (1977, 30).

a-verses, and usually make very decent narrative sense. We may see this in Gawain's temptation by the servant guide who attempts to dissuade him from meeting the Green Knight:

> Forþy, goude Sir Gawayn, *let þe gome one*
> And gotz away sum oþer gate . . .
> Cayrez bi sum oþer kyth . . .
> And I schal hyȝ me hom aȝayn . . .
> þat I schal swere bi God . . .
> As help me God and þe halydam . . .
> þat I schall lelly yow layne *and lance neuer tale*
> Þat euer ȝe fondet to fle . . .
> 'Grant merci,' quoþ Gawain . . .
> 'Wel worth þe, wyȝe . . .
> And þat lelly me layne *I leue wel þou woldez*
> Bot helde þou hit neuer so holde . . .
> Founded for ferde for to fle . . .
> I were a knyȝt kowarde . . .
> Bot I wyl [cheue] to þe chapel . . . (For the emendation, compare G 1674.)
> And talk wyth þat ilk tulk . . .
> Worþe hit wele oþer wo . . .   G 2118–34)

The three b-verses needed to make sense of this passage of seventeen lines are supplied in italics. We should not dismiss the other b-verses as otiose or think the poetry would be more powerful without them, but their effects are different from those in modern foot-counted metrical forms.

Many scholars have noted this tendency toward phrasal aggregation as the principle of syntactic development in alliterative poetry. Mary Hamel (1984) has argued cogently that the line end and caesura constitute the alliterative poet's principal markers for syntax and meter. She points to the curious fact that modern editors, who generally supply full grammatical pointing, tend not to represent the only punctuation marks characteristically inserted by scribes – the solidus, punctus, or punctus elevatus to mark the caesura.[13] Middle English alliterative poets made their 'syntactical and metrical structures clear by the management of half-lines . . . Caesural and line end pauses, then, take the place of commas and periods, but offer more flexibility of interpretation than commas and periods would – and offer more flexibility of structure to the poet himself' (Hamel 1984, 23).

Though all extant alliterative poems are clearly the product of literate, even learned poets, their style reflects the probable origin of the poetic form in a tradition of oral composition. The excessive claims of the Harvard oral-

---

[13] The scribe of Cotton Nero A.x did not mark the caesura, but many others did. See Lawton 1982a. The most sophisticated work thus far on the relationships of syntax and metrical structure is the seminal essay of Joan Turville-Petre (1976).

formulaicists in the late fifties and sixties helped to discredit the notion that the formative stages of Old and Middle English alliterative verse lay in traditions of oral composition. The sound and scholarly work on grammatical/semantic formulaic patterns in Middle English alliterative poetry, what R.F. Lawrence usefully called 'grammetrical patterns', was frequently ignored or dismissed,[14] though Turville-Petre and I found it extremely useful for editing *The Wars of Alexander* (Turville-Petre 1987; Duggan 1976, 1996, 88–91; Duggan and Turville-Petre 1989, xliii–li). Alliterative poets shared a common grammar of composition, a set of grammetrical moulds, often accompanied by semantic collocations in more or less fixed formulae, from which metrical half-lines were generated. The poets' choice of words as well as of their order and placement was determined partly by what they wished to say, partly by considerations of alliterative collocations, and partly by rhythmic concerns. Such choices, of course, may well have been sub-conscious ones.

The strong tendency for the half line to coincide with a phrasal unit means that alliterative poets make infrequent use of strong enjambment. Only rarely does the central caesura or line end occur other than at the major syntactic juncture in the line, and much more rarely does it appear between an attributive adjective and its noun head. A small handful appear in *Patience*, *Cleanness*, and *Gawain*.

A. The caesura appears at a minor syntactic juncture:

Care-ful am I, kest out fro þy cler yȝen	P 314
So hatȝ anger onhit his hert, he calleȝ	P 411
When ho watz gon, Sir Gawayn gerez hym sone	G 1872

B. The caesura almost never separates a preposition from its head noun(s):

Þenne watȝ no tom þer bytwene his tale and her dede	P 135

C. The caesura separates an uncharacteristically stressed and alliterated auxiliary verb from an infinitive or past participle:

Þat so worþy as ȝe wolde wynne hidere	G 1537
As domezday schulde haf ben diȝt on þe morn	G 1884
Thenne þe knyȝt con calle ful hyȝe	G 2212

---

[14] For some of the sound scholarship based upon the Parry-Lord hypothesis, see Waldron 1957; Benson 1965b, 110–66; Lawrence 1966, 1970; Duggan 1976; Krishna 1982. Excessive claims for orality in Old English verse led to a sometimes not deeply rational backlash against the notion of residual orality, reflected variously by Turville-Petre 1977, 83–92; Pearsall 1981, 4; Lawton 1982b, 5–7. For a survey of the mid-century debate, see Parks 1986. For some evidence of renewed interest in the debate, see Lawton's recent 'The Idea of Alliterative Poetry' (1993).

Deficiency in alliteration in 1884a and syllabic structure in 1537b suggests that neither line is original, and 2212 is probably also inauthentic.

D. The caesura separates an attributive adjective from its noun head:

Þe gome glyȝt on þe grene graciouse leues	P 453
Syþen he is chosen to be chef chyldryn fader	C 684
And Mary, þat is myldest moder so dere	G 754
Syn we haf fonged þat fyne fader of nurture	G 919
And sayde he watz þe welcomest wyȝe of þe worlde	G 938
As hit is breued in þe best boke of romaunce	G 2521

Perhaps the oddest violation of our expectation for placement of the caesura occurs in *Cleanness* 1312 where the poet must have taken the name *Nabugode-nozar* to be 'Nabugo of Nozar,' an idea credited by the scribe who steadily wrote the name as *Nabugo de Nozar*: Neuer ȝet nas Nabugo de Nozar er þenne (see 192 above).[15]

The rules governing a-verse rhythms and the caesura are normative rather than categorical, though both are formidably regular in their application. The rules governing alliteration and the distribution of stressed and unstressed syllables, on the other hand, are categorical. That is, the evidence shows that apparent violations of rules 1–3 and 5 invariably represent scribal error. Not every metrically regular b-verse is authorial, but every unmetrical b-verse is scribal.[16]

Metrical Rule 5:

The b-verse consists of two lifts and one, two, or three dips. The verse requires a minimum of four syllables and permits a maximum of eight. One of the dips preceding either lift must be strong. Both initial and medial dips may not be strong. The line terminal dip is optional and is always weak. (Duggan 1986b and Cable 1991, 85–113.)

Metrical Rule 5a:

The requirement that either the initial or medial dip must be strong is waived in b-verses in which a dissyllabic adjective stressed on the first syllable immediately precedes a noun stressed on its first syllable. (Duggan 1988)

---

[15] Many of these verses are cited by Thomas (1908, 9). The most complete study of enjambment in the works of the *Gawain*-poet is Mills 1964.

[16] The issue is disputed. Evidence for the claim is laid out in Duggan 1986ab, 1988, 1990a. Cable offers a different theory of the meter in which alliterative patterning is largely ignored (1991, 66–113). I have offered evidence to contradict his eccentric view of the retention of final -e in late Middle English (Duggan 1994). See also Lawton 1993.

Metrical Rule 6:

> The a-verse consists of two or three lifts and from one to four dips. There are rarely more than six or seven syllables in an a-verse dip, and the most common rhythmical patterns involve three or fewer syllables in each dip. None to five unstressed syllables may occur before the first lift and from none to seven immediately follow it. None to three syllables may fall after the final stressed syllable. Though any two dips may have three syllables, the third dip in such lines tends to be light, and when any one dip contains four or more syllables, the other two dips tend to have two, one, or no syllables. (Duggan and Turville-Petre 1989, xx)

A-verse rhythms are far more flexible than those of the b-verses, and the rule is normative rather than categorical. Thomas Cable has argued that the a-verse must either contain two strong dips or three ictus positions (1989ab; 1991), but the evidence is plentiful that the *Gawain*-poet felt no such constraint.[17]

The Meter of Pearl

Pearl is frequently said to be an alliterative poem. Two of the poem's most recent editors have labored under the illusion that it is in the same meter as the other three poems in the manuscript (Moorman 1977, 197; Vantuono 1984, I. 368). The reasons for this confusion are not far to seek. Scribal spellings frequently disguise the metrical structure of the line, occasionally supplying unwanted syllables, sometimes omitting grammatically and metrically appropriate ones. So long as it was thought that virtually no rules governed the composition of alliterative verse, any poem with a high density of alliterating syllables and an average of four stressed syllables per line with a caesura was likely to be called 'alliterative verse.' If that term is reserved for poems written in accord with the metrical rules enunciated above, *Pearl* is not in the same metrical form as the three other poems but is written in a traditional form of late Middle English iambic tetrameter.[18] The metrical form was identified many decades ago by Clark Northup and remained largely uncontroversial until the middle years of this century.[19] Since then, scholars have perceived in *Pearl* a poem composed in half-lines of no predictably discernible rhythmic shape, with the full line varying between seven and fourteen syllables, with unpredictable alternations of iambic, trochaic, anapestic, pyrrhic, and spondaic feet.

---

[17] I have criticized Cable's claims in Duggan 1990b, 1994.

[18] For a perceptive statement of the differences in style and syntax between the *Pearl*-poet's tetrameter line and that of Chaucer's *Parlement of Foules*, see Stephens 1988.

[19] For a survey of the scholarship, see Duggan forthcoming.

The rhythmic patterns of *Pearl* are unlike those of the alliterative long line. Alliterative poets rigorously avoided alternating rhythms, both iambic and anapestic, in their b-verses. In *Pearl*, on the contrary, over 90% of the last two feet in any line are regular iambs. Moreover, though alliteration and metrical stress coincide in the alliterative long line, they clearly do not in *Pearl*, as its first line shows:

> /   x   / x   / x /
> Perle, plesaunt to princes pay.

Only those who take the distribution of syllables in the alliterative line to be without rule can think the *Pearl* line originated in alliterative verse.

The fundamentally iambic form of most verses can readily be seen in the many verses where syllable count or stress assignment is not ambiguous:

	/ x / x / x /
27	Blomez blayke and blwe and rede
	/ x / x / x /
29	Flor and fryte may not be fede
	x / x / x / x /
30	þer hit doun drof in moldez dunne
	x / x / x / x /
33	Of goud vche goude is ay bygonne

In the text as presently edited, however, many lines remain where too few or too many syllables appear. Recent editors have thought that the poet, though content to write regular iambic tetrameter verse most of the time, did not intend to restrict himself to the form. That, however, is to confuse the poet with the scribe and to attach unwarranted authority to scribal spellings and scribal choices from among synonyms or doublet forms. Evidence both from *Pearl* and from the other poems in the manuscript shows that this scribe's spellings and forms are not those of the poet. Essentially, the scribe tended to write dissyllabic *oþer, syþen, wheþer, neuer, euer*, and *ouer*, where the meter shows that the poet wrote monosyllabic *or, syn, where, n'er, ere*, and *o're*. That is as true of the three alliterative poems as it is of *Pearl*.

Furthermore, the rules governing the scribe's use of written final -*e* differed from the those governing the poet. The scribe clearly took final -*e* not to be sounded. His practice in this respect is not chaotic but subject to rule. Scribal <-*e*> tends to appear under the following conditions in this manuscript:

(1) after monosyllabic stems ending in a consonant cluster (e. g. *golde* < OE. *gold; grounde* < OE *grund; breste* < OE *bréost; corne* < OE *corn, honde* < OE *hond; towarde* < OE *tóweard; ofte* < OE *oft; foreste* < OF *forest*.) The spelling *fonte* at l. 327 for the past participle of *findan* shows that the *e* is motivated by the combination of vowel plus consonant cluster rather than a survival of inflectional -*en* since the *e* would have had to be reduced to zero for final -*d* to have

become -t (Gordon 1953, xlvi, 93, 95). This is only a strong tendency and not universal in the manuscript. Counter instances are *rert* 591, *bycalt* 1163, *flonc* 1165. For others, see Gordon 1953, xlvi.

(2) following a single consonant to indicate the length of the tonic vowel (e. g. *oute* < OE *út*; *sede* < OE *séd*, etc.).

This scribe steadily wrote final -e to convey phonetic features of the preceding syllable rather than to express grammatical function or to designate syllabic schwa. Though the poet himself did not habitually sound such -e's either within the verse or at verse end, he occasionally used historically motivated syllabic -e when the meter required it (Borroff 1962, 140–60, 182–89; Duggan 1988). Borroff (1977) has demonstrated that the poet did not routinely sound final -e in his rhymes in *Pearl* (33–35). Within the line, corroborative evidence for the loss of e appears in monosyllabic weak or plural adjectives when the meter suggests the silencing of an historical -e:

	x / x / x / x /	
15	Þat wont watz whyle *deuoyde* my wrange	inf.
	x / x / x / x /	
50	For *care* ful colde þat to me caȝt	etym. < OE *cearu*
	x /(x) x / x / x /(x)	
284	And wony wyth hyt in *schyr* wod-schawez	pl. adj.
	x / x / x / x / x	
597	Now he þat stod þe *long* day stable	wk. adj.

In each case, the metrical evidence suggests that neither the poet nor the scribe consistently sounded weak and plural adjective inflections.

On the other hand, we find a number of lines metrically regular only because an etymological -e is inscribed [e.g., *stylle* < OE *stille*, 20; *faste* < OE *fæste* 54 (stressed here, unstressed *faste* is monosyllabic in 150); *tonge* < OE *tunge* 100; *gemme* < OF 118, 289; *herte* < OE *heorte* 128, 176; *tenþe* < OE *ten* + ordinal -þa 136; *Bytwene* < OE *betwéonan* 140; *mote* < OF 142; *nwe* < OE *néowe* 155; *fayre* < OE *faeger* 169, 177; *sute* < OF *su(i)te* 203; *kynde* < OE *gecynde* 276]. Another set of lines, somewhat smaller, is metrically regular because a historically motivated inflectional -e is present [e.g. *fyrce* (pl. adj.) 54; *fyrre* (wk. adj.) 148; *wynne* (pl. adj.) 154; *aske* (inf.) 316; *oȝte* (pret. impersonal) 341; *for soþe* (petrified dative) 292].

Though iambic tetrameter verse tends toward greater rhythmic sameness than pentameter, it does not demand the monotonous alternation of iambic feet. Headless lines lacking the unstressed initial syllable are common in *Pearl* and in other poems written in iambic tetrameter: about 7 to 15 percent in *Pearl*, Chaucer's *The Book of the Duchess*, and other poems like *Octavian* or *Kyng Alisaunder*. Epic caesura occurs with greater frequency in *Pearl* than in *The Book of the Duchess* or *Cursor Mundi*, but no more than in other popular poems composed in the four-stress line. Predictably, dissyllabic occupancy occurs more often in the first foot than in the second, though many of these reflect scribal spellings.

The pervasiveness of the epic caesura in *Pearl* contributes to the illusion that its meter is based on that of the alliterative line and that it is composed in half-lines (Osberg forthcoming). Indeed, it is easy to cite many lines in *Pearl* in which a syntactic juncture occurs after the second stress and appears to coincide with metrical caesura, e.g.:

```
       x    /   x / x  x  /   x /
5      So rounde, so reken  in vche araye

       x   /   x  / x   x  /   x /
22     To þenke hir color  so clad in clot

       x   /  x   /  x  x   /  x   /
25     Þat spot of spysez  mot nedez sprede
```

Epic caesura appears in five to ten percent of *Pearl*'s lines.

As we have noted, epic caesura, though it appears less frequently in Chaucer's *Book of the Duchess* than in *Pearl*, is well attested in Chaucer's tetrameter verse and in other four-stress poems:

BD 113	Or how he fareth,	or in what wise
BD 134	To do hir erande	and he come nere
BD 136	Go bet quod Juno	to Morpheus
BD 147	And shewe hire shortly	hit ys no nay.

Though such lines superficially resemble the half-lines of alliterative verse – the metrical caesura corresponds with syntactic juncture, and each half-line is a metrical phrase – the resemblance is accidental. Other verses show clearly that the full line – and not the half-line – is the fundamental metrical unit. That is, the syntactic integrity of the colon in Middle English alliterative verse (and in the verses cited above) is frequently violated in *Pearl*. Lyric caesura appears in many lines where metrical and syntactic units are not coterminous:

```
       x    /   x / x    /   x  /
7      Queres['Je['Jer I jugged  gemmez gaye

       x /  x   /  x   / x   /
8      I sette hyr sengeley  in synglere

       x  /   x  /  x   /   x  / (x)
98     þat fryth þer fortwne  forth me ferez
```

Yet other lines show what would be the caesura occurring after the syntactic juncture:

```
         x   /  x       / x /  x  /
85    Th['̛]adubbement    of þo downez dere
```

```
       x   /  x      /  x /   x  /
411    þow wost wel    when þy perle con schede
```

```
       x   / x   / x / x  /
418    Hys lef is.   I am holy hysse
```

```
       x   /  x    / x / x  /
516    Ne knawe ȝe    of þis day no date?
```

```
       x    /       x  /  x  /  x  / x
544    And fyrre,    þat non me may reprené
```

```
       x   / x / x       /   x   /
737    For hit is wemlez,    clene, and clere.
```

A few verses sport two syntactic junctures, and the meter moves regularly without reference to either juncture:

```
       x     /    x /  x /    x    /
525    þay wente    into þe vyne   and wroȝte
```

```
       x  /     x / x  /     x   /
530    On our    byfore þe sonne   go doun
```

```
       /  x  /    x    /     x  /
569    þus schal I    quod Kryste   hit skyfte.
```

Because the poet used final -e's which were not part of the scribe's dialect, apparent clashing stress occurs in several lines because a historically justified final -e is omitted in the manuscript. In square brackets I have supplied the historically justified inflectional or etymological es that make each verse metrical:

17   Þat dotȝ bot þrych my hert[e] þrange
68   Where rych[e] rokkez wer to dyscreuen
122   Of wod and water and wlonk[e] playnez
225   I hope no tong[e] moȝt endure
286   Þat hatȝ me broȝt þys blys[se] ner[20]

The fit between the independent systems of grammar and meter lends credence to the theory that the poet used doublet forms. The case would be

---

[20] Other instances appear in 381 carp[e]; 486 fyrst[e]; 564 ask[e]; 586 long[e]; 678 hyȝ[e]; 683 step[e]; 825 wroȝt[e]; 999 fyrst[e]; 1036 rych[e]; 1046 self[e].

weakened if it were possible to find significant numbers of lines with clashing stress for which no historically motivated -*e* is available, but there are none.

Stanzaic and Strophic Structures

Though much Middle English unrhymed alliterative verse is stichic, that is, not arranged in stanzas, both *Patience* and *Cleanness* are composed in stanzaic/syntactic units of four lines. It is misleading to call these groups quatrains and perhaps misleading to think of them as metrical features. They are certainly structural units, and were recognized as such by the scribe who with remarkable consistency marked their first lines with small double virgules, the same signs appearing at the beginning of each stanza in *Pearl* and strophe in *Gawain*. The scribe's loss of a single line in *Patience* between lines 512–15 (or mistaken copying of cancelled lines in 513–15) and subsequent mis-marking shows that the structural pattern is the poet's and not scribal *ordinatio* (Anderson 1969, note 509–15). *Gawain* is composed in strophes of disparate length (as few as 12 long lines, as many as 37), though as Metcalf (1980) has pointed out, the average number of long lines per strophe (2530 ÷ 101) is 25 with a remainder of five lines. Each strophe is brought to a close with a five line bob-and-wheel rhyming *ababa*. The bob consists of a single iambic foot – the three bobs with two initial unstressed syllables (806, 1145, 2042) reflect scribal error[21] – and the wheel is made up of four irregularly iambic trimeter lines (Borroff 1962, 155–63). The stanza of *Pearl* is twelve lines of iambic tetrameter in the rhyme scheme *ababababbcbc*. The poet concatenates most stanzas by repeating the concluding words of a stanza as the first words of the stanza following.

Larger textual divisions in both *Patience* and *Cleanness* are further marked in the manuscript with three- and four-line colored ornamental capitals at what at first sight appear to be irregular intervals. Five such divisions appear in *Patience* with groupings of 15, 46, 15, 26, and 30 (or 31) stanzas. *Cleanness* has three major divisions marked at the beginning with an eight-line ornamental capital and two four-line capitals at 557 and 1157. Those large sections are further sub-divided with ten additional three-line capitals at 125, 193, 249, 345, 485, 601, 689, 781, 893, and 1357 (Spendal 1976; Crawford 1993). *Gawain* is also divided into four major fitts, marked in the manuscript with five- and six-line ornamental capitals, as well as by two- and three-line minor capitals at 619, 763, 1421, 1893, and 2259 (Hill 1946; Tuttleton 1966; Robertson 1982). Until recently, scholars have tended to agree with Norman Davis that the

---

[21] In two lines, the scribe has written a trisyllabic form for which a dissyllabic doublet is available in Middle English, *auinant* for *auaunt* (806) and *oþer* for *or* (2042). The definite article is perhaps scribal in 1145 *of þe best*.

minor capitals are part of a scribal *ordinatio* and that they are not 'systemati-
cally planned' (1967, xii).

However, intrigued by *Pearl*'s 1212 lines, its description of the 144,000
virgins of the heavenly Jerusalem, the repetition of the first line of *Gawain* at
line 2525 just five lines before the conclusion of the poem, the 101 stanzas of
both *Pearl* and *Gawain*, and the elaborate symbolism of the pentangle, scholars have attempted to determine whether the *Gawain*-poet shared Dante's
(indeed, the common medieval) interest in number symbolism and whether
the obvious structural symmetries of the plot of *Gawain* were reinforced by
subtle and complicated numerological schemata. The preponderance of evidence suggests that the poet carefully plotted his works so that part of their
meaning is carried by the order and position of elements within the larger
structures. The fullest discussion thus far has been of *Pearl* (Røstvig 1967;
Ovitt 1979; Fritz 1980; Hieatt 1976; Peck 1980, 44–51; Fleming 1981) and
Gawain (Hieatt 1968, 1976, 1980; Käsmann 1974; Metcalf 1980; Bachman 1980;
Robertson 1982), but perhaps the most convincing case for numerological
structures in the poems is Donna Crawford's demonstration that the manuscript divisions in *Cleanness*, itself usually taken to be something of a baggy
monster, are markers to a highly elaborated numerical structure based on,
among other things, the ratio of the golden section (Crawford 1993). *Cleanness*, a poem generations of readers had taken to be an architectonic failure,
is in fact as highly structured as the *Pearl*.

Vocabulary

Norman Hinton's recent interim reports on his ambitious research-in-
progress, a computer-based investigation of the poet's vocabulary, modify in
interesting ways the traditional accounts (1987; 1989). Such vocabulary studies are notoriously difficult – what constitutes a word? How accurately can
an etymology be determined? Is that etymology proximate or more distant?
– so it should not surprise us when different counters get different results.[22]
Oakden (1930, I. 85–86), Gordon (1953, 97–106), Anderson (1969, 73; 1977,
108), Davis (1967, 138–43), and Vantuono (1984, I. 373–74) all provide estimates of the constituents of the poet's vocabulary. Those estimates vary, but
only within a few percentage points, with the greatest number of words being
derived from Old English (60–70%), the next largest group from Old French
(22–30%), Old Norse (8–10%) and under one percent from other sources.

Hinton's preliminary findings are at odds with those studies, and we must
await completion of the project to evaluate his results. Hinton first established

---

[22] Rolf Kaiser's attempt to find lexical bases for dialect study differs from the editorial counts
of vocabulary items. Kaiser lists some 130 distinctively northern words appearing in the
four poems (1937).

a computerized database, initially consisting of a large sampling from *MED* from the letters A–M and eventually from A–SIM for the 1989 paper. Over 5,400 randomly selected words were entered with searchable fields for etymology, parts of speech, and the dates at which they are first attested in Middle English. Initially, two other databases were assembled, one from the Kottler-Markman *Concordance* (1966) and another from the Tatlock-Kennedy concordance to Chaucer's works (1927). For the second paper, the database was supplemented with glossaries to the *Alliterative Morte Arthure*, the Vernon manuscript of *Piers Plowman A*, and *William of Palerne*. Hinton found that the overall etymological makeup of Middle English as represented in his second and larger sample from the *MED* was as follows:

Germanic: 35.06%   Romance: 64.54%   Other: 0.35%

Chaucer's vocabulary sources were in the following distribution:

Germanic: 38.5%   Romance: 61.2%   Other: 0.09%

The poems in Cotton Nero A.x showed a much higher proportion of native terms:

Germanic: 58.7%   Romance: 41%   Other: 0.15%

As Hinton notes, this 'is hardly the 70–30% dispersal suggested by Gordon, and the percentage of items from Old Norse is far lower than is generally thought: 5.76% (as opposed to the 2.13% in Chaucer and 3.74% in ME)' (1989). Further analysis shows, somewhat surprisingly, that though the number of Scandinavian words in the *Gawain*-poet's works is higher than in the *Morte Arthure, William of Palerne,* or *Piers Plowman A,* the difference is not statistically significant.

Hinton's database permits him to compare the constituents of a poet's vocabulary with that of the language as a whole at various times. The distribution in Chaucer's works of Germanic and Romance words, for instance, more closely approximates the etymological mix obtaining in Middle English in 1460 than when he actually wrote, while the *Gawain*-poet's vocabulary reflects the etymological mix of Middle English as of 1390. Perhaps more interesting, determining the average and mean dates of Chaucer's and the *Gawain*-poet's lexicons suggests that the latter's poetic diction is seventy years older than the diction of Chaucer (Hinton 1987, 85). Hinton argues that this 'suggests a conscious effort on the part of the *Gawain*-poet to use an older stage of the language' (1987, 85). It is more likely that the alliterative poet's older lexicon reflects both the numerical preponderance of Germanic elements and the shaping of the tradition of grammetrical frames and semantic formulae in the century before the earliest extant Middle English long line poetry.[23]

---

[23] Blake 1979; Salter 1966–7; D.A. Lawton 1979, 1983 and Turville-Petre 1977, 15–17, 22–25

Dialect

The salient features of the phonology and morphology of the scribe who wrote Cotton Nero A.x are well catalogued and need not be repeated here. We shall, instead, concentrate upon differences between the scribe's dialect and the poet's. Though *LALME* has proved to be of great value in localizing manuscripts, it has, at least in the case of the *Gawain*-poet, proved less useful for locating the poet's dialect with any precision. McIntosh's early placement of the manuscript in 'a very small area either in SE Cheshire or just over the border in NE Staffordshire' (1963, 5), is maintained in the completed work (*LALME* 3.37–38, LP 26). That placement of the manuscript may well be accurate.[24] A few years after McIntosh's 1963 article, Charles Jones (1972), using *LALME* methods and materials, argued that the manuscript 'is likely to have been composed in the very small area in north Staffordshire shown on [his] Map II' (216, Map II is on 213). There is here more than a faint hint of confusion of poet and scribe in the verb 'composed.'

Indeed, from the beginnings of modern scholarship on these poems, editors have tended to assume essential identity between the scribal dialect and that of the poet. Richard Morris begins the tradition with the confident claim that 'there is no internal evidence of subsequent transcription into any other dialect than that in which they were originally written' (1869, viii), a view repeated by the most recent editor (Vantuono 1984, 235–36).[25] The claim is broadly true, in the sense that both the scribe's and poet's dialects were north-west Midlands.

The matter is complicated by the fact that the scribal dialect is more homogenous than that of the poet, since the *Gawain*-poet, like other poets who composed alliterative verse, made use of a variety of phonological, morphological, and stress doublets from other dialects to meet the demands of alliteration and verse rhythms. The poet, for instance, used both /g/ and /j/ forms of *give*, though the latter only once in 22 occurrences, while a more southerly poet, such as Langland, used the /j/ form more often than the /g/

---

have argued that the tradition of composition in this metrical form is historically shallow, an early mid-fourteenth-century creation, more or less contemporary with the extant poems. I have adduced syntactic, morphological, and metrical evidence that the tradition of composition in this form must have begun at least as early as the thirteenth century (Duggan 1988). However, differences in form and style make it improbable that the Middle English unrhymed alliterative long line descends in any direct line from the classical Old English line.

24 T.L. Burton's criticism of *LALME* (1992; responded to by Michael Benskin 1992) as severely flawed in both conception and execution is directed mainly to the southern dialect regions.

25 The tradition of linguistic scholarship continued in a series of (mostly German) dissertations in the late nineteenth century. For summary discussion of the most important of these, see Borroff 1962. In addition to the editions cited above, see Menner 1920, lviii–lxii; Oakden 1930, I. 72–78; Serjeantson 1940; McLaughlin 1963; Kottler and Markman 1966; Jones 1972, 213–16; Andrew and Waldron 1987, 45–50; and Vantuono 1984, I. 372–78.

(Duggan and Turville-Petre 1989, xxxvi–xliii). The scribe in this case was aware of the doublet form, spelling the /g/ forms with <g> and the /j/ with <ʒ>. A number of other rare forms are likely to reflect the poet's awareness of linguistic possibilities in adjacent dialects. For instance, he adopts the generally Northern *-ez* inflection for the first person singular indicative verb *byswykez* to achieve a perfect feminine rhyme (*Pe* 568) and first person plural *renowlez* (*Pe* 1080). Davis, noting northern *-es* ~ *-ez* plural forms in *Gawain*, points out that *hyʒes* (*G* 1351), though confirmed by rhyme is not, as it would have been in a northern poet's dialect, disjunctive with its pronoun subject (1967, 146). The prefix *i-* as a marker of the past participle appears but once in the poet's work. When he needed an unstressed syllable in *Pe* 904 to make the final iambic foot in the line, he wrote *ichose*. Similarly, though his ordinary form is *strete(z)* for 'street(s),' he used the rare form *stratez* in *Pe* 1043 to rhyme with *fatez*, *datez*, and *-whatez*. Rhyme evidence shows that the poet's usual form for words with OE, ON /a:/ was the rounded /ɔ:/, but he occasionally rhymed them with /a:/ (Davis 1967, 135; Gordon 1953, 96). Clearly, though the poet's language was 'founded in a North-West Midland dialect, . . . it is a literary language, with features which are unlikely to have been part of any local speech' (Anderson 1977, 73; Osgood 1906, xii; Davis 1967, xxvii; *et al.*).

As we have seen (233), the scribe was sometimes oblivious to the poet's forms, now substituting his own forms, now maintaining the poet's forms. These divergences are useful for distinguishing the poet's dialect from the scribe's. The most important of these appear in their different uses of final *-e*, their different forms of tonic vowels derived from of OE /y/ and /y:/, and their different realizations of OE /hw/ and /kw/. We have discussed the differences in their uses of final *-e* above (233–34). All suggest that the scribal dialect was one in which final inflectional and etymological *-e* was no longer an option, while the poet used historical *-e* when the context demanded an unstressed syllable. With the reflexes of /y/ and /y:/, the scribe's spellings indicate retention of rounding in many contexts in his dialect, while the rhyme evidence shows both had become unrounded to /i/ or /i:/ in the poet's speech. The scribe often spells the reflexes of OE /hw/ and /kw/ with <wh> and <qu>, and less frequently with <w> alone. As the alliteration shows, the poet used only the /w/ form (*C* 422, *P* 247, 421, *G* 1186, 1227, 1235, etc.), placing him well south of the *Wars of Alexander*-poet and the Cotton Nero A.x scribe. Moreover, though reflexes of OE, ON, and OFr /kw/ had in some northerly dialects developed to /xw/ and eventually to /hw/ and /w/, that had not occurred in the poet's dialect (Orton 1962, 130–34, 155–61; Whitehall 1930; Jordan 1974, §195; Kristensson 1967, 214; Davis 1967, 136–37; McLaughlin 1963, 124–26; Matsumoto 1993). Spellings such as *whene* (*G* 74, 2492), *whyssynes* 'cushions' (*G* 877), on the other hand, suggest that the scribe's usage was shaped in an area where that change had occurred. Though Davis is correct to say that the spellings <qu-> ~ <qw-> came to represent /w/ in a variety of Middle English dialects and that such spellings do not prove conclusively that the scribe was more northerly than the poet (1967, 132), that evidence added to the other indications of a discrepancy between scribal and authorial forms, especially final -*e*, suggests a provenance more southerly than that of the manuscript. Unhappily, it does not permit precise localization of the poet's dialect.

A few other minor differences between scribal and authorial forms are unhelpful for localizing the poems, but serve to distinguish the scribal dialect. For instance, parasitic glide vowels show up occasionally in all four poems in words like *bereste* 'breast' (*Pe* 854), *dowelle(z)* 'dwells' (*C* 1674, *G* 566, 1075, *P* 69) *boroʒt* 'brought' (*Pe* 628), *dewyne ~ dowyne* (< OE *dwϊnan*) (*Pe* 11, 326), -*selepe* 'sleep' (*P* 186). In most instances in all four poems the metrical evidence reveals the glide vowel to be the scribe's form and not the poet's.

Two anomalous instances in *Cleanness* of possible *he* forms of the third person nominative plural pronoun are probably better accounted for as scribal error or grammatical confusion than as evidence of relict forms. Anderson argues of *C* 62 *Alle excused hem by þe skyly he scape by moʒt* that '**Alle** is evidently thought of first as plural (*hem*), then as singular (*he*)' (Anderson 1977, 63). Similarly, at *C* 657, he emends manuscript *he* to *hit*, noting that 'MS *he* would be quite exceptional as a plural form in this MS' (79):

> For soþely, as says þe wryt, he wern of sadde elde.

The cumulative evidence of disjunction between the poet's dialect and the scribe's suggests that if the *LALME* localization of the manuscript is correct and if the poems are not substantially earlier than the manuscript (there is little reason to think so), then the poet's natal dialect is less likely to have been formed in Cheshire, Lancashire, or Derbyshire than further south in Staffordshire.[26]

---

[26] Though we may note that Derbyshire extends on the east almost as far south as Staffordshire, while Derby and Stafford are on virtually the same latitude.

9

Sources I:
The Sources of Sir Gawain and the Green Knight

ELISABETH BREWER

There is no single source for *Sir Gawain and the Green Knight*. Critics were at one time reluctant to attribute the complex unified structure of the poem to an English author, and so suggested that there must have been a lost original from which it derived. The ultimate origins of the story may well be Celtic, but the *Gawain*-poet seems to have been familiar with and may well have been influenced by a wide range of both English and French romances, in particular those of Chrétien de Troyes. The remarkable interplay between convention and invention is one of the most intriguing features of the poem, but the author's genius is nowhere more apparent than in the way in which he has brought together and synthesised into one story its three key elements, the Beheading-game, the Temptation theme, and the Exchange of Winnings. Ad Putter in a recent study (1995) shows that while the search for the origins of the poem has in the past centred mainly on earlier stories of beheading and temptation, the pervasive influence of French Arthurian romance has been largely ignored.

As in much traditional narrative the basic structure of the poem bears some resemblance to that of folktale. Claude Luttrell (1979) sees some similarities between *Sir Gawain and the Green Knight* and the narrative structure identified as Type 313 in Aarne and Thompson 1961. Tales conforming to this pattern, very popular in Ireland and known in Scotland, involve a challenger who in some versions is green, a feature probably deriving from the tradition in which the devil appeared in that colour. This type of tale begins with a youth playing a game with a stranger, losing, and promising to come to his castle in a year and a day. The narrative structure of *Sir Gawain and the Green Knight* involves the combination of some features of this tale, with the motif of beheading and of a beautiful girl coming to the hero's bed, both common in Arthurian romance. Luttrell suggests that the medieval popular tale included elements that had been particularly effective with 'a very wide range of audience over large tracts of time and space', so that, 'by a process akin to Darwin's "natural selection" ', it survived and could be refashioned by successive storytellers. He concludes that the author of *Sir Gawain and the*

Green Knight did not simply retell an old story, but exploited it by selection and adaptation, for his own sophisticated ends.

The poet's subtlety and ingenuity are clearly apparent in his handling of his hero, for the figure of Gawain controls the form that the story takes. The tradition in which he was writing begins with Geoffrey of Monmouth's *Historia Regum Britanniae* (c.1135) in which Gawain appears as Arthur's sister's son, a heroic and blameless warrior. His character is somewhat broadened in Wace's translation of Geoffrey, *Le Roman de Brut* (also of the twelfth century) in which he acquires a courtly aspect and a leaning towards love and chivalry rather than war. In the English tradition, culminating in such poems as the alliterative *Morte Arthure*, he is often referred to as Gawain the good, and is seen as a fearless warrior. English authors regarded him as a British hero.

With the earlier romances of Chrétien de Troyes, Gawain is assigned an important role as a friend of the hero and as an example for young knights to emulate. He is chaste, he is brave, he is honourable, he is renowned for his courtesy, modesty and wisdom; and in Chrétien's later romances he is often represented as the moral victor in the combats in which he engages. In the *First Continuation* of Chrétien's *Perceval* his virtue is such that, after an arduous search for the Grail castle, he is actually afforded a vision of the Grail and its mysteries.

However, in other narratives he begins to have a reputation as a lover, which frequently causes excitement when he approaches a castle, and an element of burlesque even enters into the stories. In such post-Chrétien verse-romances as *Le Chevalier à l'Epée*, *La Vengeance Raguidel* and *La Mule sans Frein* (*La Damoiselle à la Mule*) he is often depicted as amorous; indeed, *La Mule* may be seen as an anti-Gawain parody. Ladies gladly offer themselves to him and, as Whiting points out (1947), although he is not an adulterer, he is not celebrated for chastity in these tales.

In the post-Chrétien prose romances, such as the Vulgate *Queste*, in which the tone becomes more serious and more religious, Gawain is denigrated. He loses his position as Arthur's chief knight, and also his good faith. In the *Suite du Merlin* and the Prose *Tristan*, his character further deteriorates.

Since the French Arthurian romances were well-known outside France in the fourteenth century, we can be sure that the English poet would have known some of the texts in which Gawain appears, and that he might even have been able to assume that members of his audience would have heard other stories about his hero. In writing *Sir Gawain and the Green Knight*, he might thus have been able to choose whether to make Gawain heroic, as in Geoffrey, an exemplar of courtesy (Chaucer's 'Gawayne with his olde curteisye' (*Squire's Tale* line 95; Benson 1987)), or a Grail knight, or even a – possibly comic – figure with a taste for amorous adventure. The poet might, furthermore, have been able to exploit the uncertainty of his audience as to which Gawain they were about to encounter, just as he makes both the lord of the castle and the lady question Gawain's identity during his stay at Hautdesert.

To go back to the origins of the story itself, the earliest surviving example of the Beheading-game seems to be in the Middle Irish *Fled Bricrend* (*Bricriu's Feast*), of which there are two separate versions. At a great feast in hall Cuchulainn, the hero, accepts the challenge of the huge, shape-shifting Terror who descends on the company and beheads him, whereupon Terror departs, carrying his head. Next day Cuchulainn keeps his promise to submit to a return blow, but Terror spares him, after giving him three strokes of the axe with the blade reversed. He then praises Cuchulainn as the best of warriors.

In the second version, the shape-shifting Curoi in the form of a churl challenges the warriors at the court to behead him with a huge axe. As in the other version he then departs carrying his head. Though they succeed in beheading him, they do not present themselves the next night when he comes back, but Cuchulainn subsequently beheads him again, smashing his head with a second blow. When he returns the next night, Cuchulainn prepares to keep the covenant, but the churl then spares him and declares him the champion.

The motif of the Beheading-game is thereafter found in French romance where the *Gawain*-poet almost certainly encountered it. It seems virtually certain that he knew the episode in the *Livre de Caradoc*, part of the *First Continuation* of Chrétien's *Perceval*, of which there were three thirteenth-century metrical redactions (known as the 'Short', the 'Mixed' and the 'Long') all prior to *Sir Gawain and the Green Knight*, as well as the Prose Redaction of 1530, which may have been known earlier. In the *Livre de Caradoc*, a very big knight rides into Arthur's court at the feast of Pentecost. After taunting Arthur's knights with cowardice, he demands that one of them shall behead him with the sword that he carries. When no-one volunteers, Caradoc accepts the challenge and strikes off his head, whereupon the knight replaces his head and departs. A year later he reappears to claim his right to strike a return blow, to the consternation and distress of the whole court. He twice threatens Caradoc with the sword, provoking an angry outcry from him at the torment-ing delay so that, like Gawain in similar circumstances, Caradoc accuses the knight of cowardice. This knight then merely strikes him with the flat of his sword, after which he reveals that he is actually the young man's father.

Another example of the Beheading-game appears in the prose romance of *Perlesvaus: Le haut livre du Graal* (known in England from the early fourteenth century onwards), but with Lancelot as the protagonist in the 'game'. Here, Lancelot in the Waste Land encounters a very handsome young knight who insists that he shall behead him with his axe, and return in a year's time to put his head in the same jeopardy. Lancelot complies, keeps his covenant and returns on the appointed day; as a result the Waste City is restored. Elsewhere in *Perlesvaus*, Gawain is threatened with decapitation, but this time by a beautiful lady who welcomes him to her castle in which she has set up three tombs. She informs him that they are intended for Lancelot, for Perceval and for Gawain himself, all of whom she intends to kill and then to inter, richly shrouded, in her chapel. Fortunately no-one asks Gawain his name – it is not the custom of this particular castle – so after staying the night and attending mass in the morning, he gallops away, with no desire to return (cited from Bryant 1978, 54ff.).

Beheading is again associated with the keeping of a promise in *La Mule sans Frein*, where Gawain is invited to decapitate a churl, who intends to do the same for him next day. The morning after, the churl returns complete with head, but he spares Gawain, who has knelt down and uncovered his neck for the blow, because he is so loyal and has so well kept his word.

In *Hunbaut* (early thirteenth century) Gawain is involved in both a Temptation episode and a Beheading-game, but there is no connection between the two episodes and there are many differences between them and the corresponding ones in *Sir Gawain and the Green Knight*. For example, when Gawain has beheaded the hideous churl who bars his way and offers his neck, on the understanding that his antagonist is to deliver a return blow immediately after decapitation, he swiftly seizes him by his clothes so that he cannot reclaim his head, which has rolled more than ten paces away. The magic fails, and the double game is brought to an end, leaving Gawain free to go on his way.

Another analogue of the Beheading-game in the *Diu Crône* of Heinrich von dem Türlin probably owes its existence to the fact that Gawain as hero has drawn into the romance a number of features from other sources. Elizabeth Andersen (1987) comments that this work is essentially a biographical romance about Gawain.

In none of these beheading episodes is Gawain also subjected to sexual temptation. The folktale of Type 313, however, as Luttrell (1979) has pointed out, links the impossible task imposed upon the hero with a woman: he is helped by the daughter of his antagonist who with her magical powers enables him to perform his task, before eloping with her. *Sir Gawain and the Green Knight* conforms to some extent with this pattern in closely linking the beheading with the temptation theme. It reverses the latter in so far as the Lady is in league with her husband and apparently against Gawain, whose survival is dependent on his own merit, and in particular on his chastity, aided by the Virgin Mary. The motif of sexual temptation appears in Chrétien's *Perceval* and its *Continuations* and in *Perlesvaus*, and Gawain is several times represented in situations in which he does not succumb. In *Perceval*, for example, a girl is entreated by her brother to be generous, liberal and kind-hearted to Gawain when he arrives at their castle, and they immediately settle down to talk of love: 'if they had talked of anything else, what a waste of breath it would have been!' (Bryant 1982, 63). Love-talk is soon followed by kissing, but the scene is then interrupted by a vassal who denounces Gawain as the killer of the girl's father, before rushing out to organise an attack by the townspeople. The episode ends with Gawain embarking upon a search for the bleeding lance associated with the Grail. Somewhat similarly, in the course of his many adventures in *Perlesvaus*, while riding through a forest he comes across a magnificent tent to which he is welcomed by a dwarf who unarms him. Two beautiful maidens, arriving later, assert that there is an evil custom associated with this tent. They claim that Gawain will be able to remove it, if he chooses one of them to sleep with him. He absolutely refuses, later overhearing the indignant remarks of the maidens who consider themselves insulted. Next day, after he has destroyed the evil custom, they repeat their offers which are again rejected, and Gawain goes on his way despite their renewed disdain (Bryant 1978, 63–6).

In the *First Continuation* of Chrétien's *Perceval*, however, Gawain is once more associated with the theme of temptation but here he does not resist. After the seige of Brun de Branlant's castle, Gawain, who is recovering from his wounds, rides on and on until he comes upon a beautiful girl in a pavilion. When she hears who he is, she offers herself to him entirely and 'loses the name of maiden' (Bryant 1982, 119). He leaves her, promising to return, but is attacked first by her father and then by her brother, both of whom he kills, after being seriously wounded himself. While he is recovering the story moves on.

In Gerbert de Montreuil's *Continuation* of *Perceval*, as Ad Putter has shown (Putter 1995, 112 ff., quoting from Williams and Oswald 1922–75, II. 12418–639), there are a number of close correspondences with *Sir Gawain and the Green Knight*, when Gawain encounters a lady in a pavilion by a ford, but the outcome of the story is different in that he eventually makes love to her against her will. By making the sign of the cross at a crucial moment, he is enabled to detect and conceal the knife with which she had intended to kill him.

Sexual temptation in association with Gawain also appears in such burlesque romances as *Le Chevalier à l'Epée*, in which he is presented as a knight with a reputation as a womaniser. In this story, his host allows Gawain to go to bed with his daughter but twice, as he tries to make love to her, a sword descends, slightly wounding him, after which he abandons his attempts. Next day Gawain and the girl are married by her father, but the story ends with a misogynistic outburst when the girl abandons Gawain for another knight as they are leaving the castle some time later. Another, earlier feature of this tale may further remind the reader of *Sir Gawain and the Green Knight*, in that the host goes off to see his woods soon after Gawain's arrival, thus leaving him alone with the beautiful girl.

The motif of the lady visiting the knight's bed in these romances is found not only in association with Gawain and Lancelot, but also with Perceval, whose hostess goes to him in deep distress. He wakes to find his face wet with her tears and her arms tightly clasped round his neck, as she begs his help because her castle is under attack from Engygeron, the seneschal of

Clamadeu of the Isles. Perceval affords her comfort by drawing her into bed with him and they spend the rest of the night in each others arms, 'lip to lip', to their mutual satisfaction (Bryant 1982, 22–3). On this occasion he is more fortunate than when he finds himself in bed with a beautiful fiend 'in the semblance of his sweetheart', who vanishes taking both bed and pavilion with her when he makes the sign of the cross (in the *Third Continuation*, by Manessier; see Bryant 1982, 288).

The lovely temptress again features in *Yder*, the Vulgate *Lancelot del Lac*, and the twelfth-century Anglo-Norman *Lanzelet*, as well as in many medieval English texts such as *King Horn* and *Generydes*. J.A.W. Bennett (1972–6) points out that it also occurs in Book I of the *Roman de Troie*, in *Jason and Medea*, *Amis and Amiloun*, *Sir Launfal*, *Graelent*, *Lanval*, and *Ywain and Gawain*.

Although temptresses abound, it is not easy to find in romance earlier examples of the Exchange of Winnings, though the topos is familiar in folktale. It appears in the Latin *Miles Gloriosus* (see Vantuono 1984, I. 381) and is paralleled in some respects in *Yvain*. In Chrétien and the *Continuations* it can perhaps be said to take the form of making a promise, as Gawain does on several occasions. The exchange of winnings to which he agrees in *Sir Gawain and the Green Knight* enhances the effect of the motif, since the agreement, easy to fulfill on the first two occasions, makes so intolerable a demand of him on the third.

In addition to the major features or topoi of the narrative, there are a large number of others which may have sources and certainly have analogues in earlier or contemporary texts. *Sir Gawain and the Green Knight* begins with allusions to the tradition of Britain's Trojan origins, which, though a medieval commonplace, seems to have been of importance to the poet, who returns to it in the final stanza (thus making the total number of stanzas 101, as in *Pearl*). The belief in Britain's ancient Trojan ancestry goes back to Nennius, writing in the eighth century, and is taken up by Geoffrey in his *Historia*, in which he connected mythical history with authentic history as set down by Caesar. Geoffrey tells the story of the founding of Britain by Brutus, great-grandson of Aeneas, and of how he called his first city Troya Nova. In consequence of the general acceptance of this tradition in the fourteenth century, London was regarded as a happier Troy. An opening passage somewhat similar to that of *Sir Gawain and the Green Knight* occurs in *Wynnere and Wastour* (Trigg 1990):

> Sythen that Bretayne was biggede, and Bruyttus it aughte,
> Thurgh the takynge of Troye with tresone with-inn,
> There hathe selcouthes bene sene in seere kynges tymes.   (1–3)

The alliterative *Morte Arthure* (Hamel 1984) ends with a description of Arthur as being of 'Ectores blude, the kynge sone of Troye/ And of sir Pryamous, the prynce, praysede in erthe' who 'broghte the Bretons . . . Into Bretayne the brode, as the Bruytte tellys.' (4342–6).

Arthur's custom of awaiting a marvel at great feasts has its analogues in other texts, of which the Caradoc story in the *First Continuation* of Chrétien's *Perceval* is a good example. The marvel itself, in the person of the Green Knight, has no obvious precedents. He has some similarities with the hostile challenger in the *Livre de Caradoc*, where the knight, who is a very big knight in the *Mixed Redaction*, rides into Arthur's court, splendidly dressed, bringing the challenge. He also resembles the young man in *The Parlement of the Thre Ages* (Offord 1959, 112–23) who is equally shapely in form and similarly dressed in green adorned with gold. Benson (1965b, 56–95) sees the Green Knight as a combination of the Green Man of folklore and the 'wodwose' or wild man. But although according to medieval tradition green is the colour of fairies, of the dead and of the devil, as Burrow has suggested (1965, 14; though cf. Brewer above), since he commends Gawain to God at the end of the story, the Green Knight cannot here be seen as the devil. Bennett (1972–6, I. 20) suggests that his greenness may be simply the product of a tregetour's trick.

The description of the passing of the year after the Green Knight's visit to Arthur's court (Andrew and Waldron 1978, lines 495–535), though it has no single source, may owe its origins to some extent to earlier writers. Derek Pearsall has drawn attention to the influence of the 'artes poetriae' of the rhetoricians, Matthew of Vendôme and Geoffrey of Vinsauf, on medieval writers; their precepts may have been known to the *Gawain*-poet through the teaching of the schools or deduced from French literature (Pearsall 1955). Just as the Green Knight and his horse are described in conformity with medieval rhetorical practice, as are the ladies in Bertilak's castle, so the survey of the seasons belongs within a long and well-established tradition found in both narrative and lyric poetry. Though such description is often confined to spring, in such poems as *Kyng Alisaundre* the passing of time is marked by mention of the seasons, often accompanied by allusion to their characteristic practical activities, while such formulaic phrases as 'wylde wederez of the worlde' are found elsewhere in alliterative poetry. Silverstein points out that the 'cursus annorum', the endless cycle of the seasons, and by analogy the journey from youth to age, and from life to death, is in the tradition of Seneca and the Christian homilists. He attributes the 'monitory aphorisms on the shifting fortunes of the year' with which the second part of the poem begins to the poet's knowledge of the *Book of Proverbs* and to Cato's *Distichs*, a familiar medieval schoolbook (Silverstein 1984, 7).

Many other elements may have contributed to this particular passage. The 'conflictus' literature, in which summer and winter hold a debate, as well as medieval cosmologies also lie behind these verses which have their counterpart in the *Secretum Secretorum*. In this didactic work, supposedly composed by Aristotle for Alexander, and well known in the Middle Ages, the seasons are linked to the Four Ages of Man. The traditional association of the seasons with mutability and death inherent in this topos is given hauntingly powerful effect in *Sir Gawain and the Green Knight* 530–5, as the Michaelmas moon with its threat of oncoming winter causes Gawain to think of his 'anious vyage'.

Gawain's lamented departure after his carefully described arming (itself an ancient and familiar topos; see Brewer 1979a and above), his difficult and unpleasant journey, his arrival at Bertilak's castle and his welcome there, all have ample precedent in French romance and also to some extent analogues in English romance. In *Perceval*, Gawain's departure from the court is marked by demonstrations of grief far more violent than in *Sir Gawain and the Green Knight*:

> Before he had even left the court there was bitter grieving for him, as many beat their breasts and tore their hair and scratched their faces in despair; there was no lady, however cool-headed, who did not grieve for him desperately. Many men and women lamented bitterly as Sir Gawain departed. (Bryant 1982, 52)

The formal arming of the hero occurs many times in Chrétien and in the *Continuations* of his *Perceval*, traditionally preceding the hero's first significant enterprise. Erec, eager for the coming battle, is armed by Enide, and on a subsequent occasion by a squire. In the *First Continuation*, Gawain (after going to confession) is clad in his armour most splendidly, with a smooth padded doublet underneath:

> they equipped him at his leisure with all the arms he would need both for attack and for defence: everything was perfect . . . Gifflet and Yvain, who dearly loved him, armed him with their own hands, and with great skill. (Bryant 1982, 103–4)

Later, Gawain puts the finishing touch to his arming by fixing to his lance a pennon, richly worked especially for him by the lovely lady Guilorete, as a love-token which, says the author, 'would boost his courage when the time came' (106). Often, however, the arming is hasty and perfunctory rather than ceremonious, as the knight snatches up his accoutrements and dashes off to the fray.

The arming of Gawain in *Sir Gawain and the Green Knight* is the most elaborate and the most important of all the many occurrences of the topos in classical and medieval literature. Although, as Ad Putter has pointed out (1995, 178 n. 47), his armour could not preserve Gawain at the Green Chapel, in his encounters with the 'wormez', the wolves, the 'wodwos', the 'bullez and berez, and borez', not to mention the 'etaynez', he must have been thankful for it. The Pauline resonance of the arming-passage deepens its significance.

The poet's description of the Pentangle is of special interest, for not only is it a new device for Gawain (as line 636 suggests), but so elaborate a description of a shield is without precedent in the romances that the poet is likely to have known. The Pentangle is Gawain's device here only; and the word 'pentangel' appears for the first time in English here. Nevertheless the figure had long been associated with Solomon, and was believed to be effectual against evil spirits. Bennett suggests that it may have reached England via the Templars (1972–6, II. 7–8). To the Pythagoreans it was a symbol of health, to the neo-Platonists and Gnostics a symbol of perfection. Silverstein suggests that the poet may have come across the word in the dictionaries of Hugutio of Pisa and of Giovanni Balbi, both known in England in the fourteenth century, or even in Dante's *Convivio*, where it appears as 'pentangulo' (Silverstein 1984, 131). The number five according to orthodox Christian numerology is the number of Man, who sins by the five senses and is redeemed by the five wounds (De Bruyne 1946, II. 349; cited by Bennett 1972–6, II. 7). So the poet enhances the representation of Gawain as he appears in Chrétien and the earlier romances by associating him with the Christian virtues represented by his device, with their wide range of meanings. And perhaps Cicero's *De Officiis* may have suggested Gawain's 'fifth five', the secular virtues based on justice, 'Fraunchyse and Fela3schyp . . . Clannes and Cortaysye . . . And Pite' (Goold 1968, 652–3).

The image of the Virgin Mary on the inside of Gawain's shield reflects a traditional association of her figure with King Arthur, also to be found in Nennius and Geoffrey of Monmouth, where he carries her image on the inside of his shield.

After arming, the knight's departure may be ceremonious, if he addresses himself to some special task, as we see in the *First Continuation* of *Perceval* as well as in *Sir Gawain and the Green Knight*, or it may be somewhat perfunctory if his sojourn has been brief. The poets also have a formula for the departure of large parties, as when Bertilak's Christmas guests 'Tyffen her takles, trussen her males' (1129). In *Perceval* Chrétien tells us that:

> Then you might have seen sheets and blankets and pillows packed, coffers filled, packhorses loaded and carts and wagons piled high, for they were not sparing with the number of tents and pavilions they took. (Bryant 1982, 45)

A somewhat similar scene is described in the *First Continuation*: 'so many splendid chests and coffers loaded that day', 'many splendid wagons to carry the king's equipment, his provisions and his pavilions: his baggage train was of an astounding length' (Roach 1949, 100). The author of *Sir Gawain and the Green Knight* again demonstrates his genius in the economy with which he indicates the lively scene instead of counting the coffers.

Although there are many accounts of journeys in the romances with which the *Gawain*-poet must have been familiar and with which to some extent he conforms, he gives to Gawain's journey to Hautdesert and to the Green Chapel a degree of vivid and significant detail seldom found elsewhere. Very frequently in Chrétien Gawain is seen riding on and on through mountainous country, forests and meadows, usually of a rather featureless nature. In the

First Continuation, he rides all night without stopping, in dismay and fear, swept by gales and wind, with nothing to eat or drink (Roach 1949, 128). In *La Mule sans frein*, the terrain is more challenging: he has to pass through a forest full of wild beasts, before coming to a black and turbulent river – 'never was anything so ugly seen, nor so horrible, nor so cruel . . . the river of the devil in both appearance and actuality' (Brewer 1992, 47). Commending himself to God, he makes a perilous crossing by means of an extremely narrow plank. It is very seldom that any indication of weather conditions amplifies the descriptions of these travels in French romance: the snow on which Chrétien's Perceval sees three drops of blood, reminding him of his beloved's beautiful complexion, serves another purpose than to suggest the harshness and discomfort of his journey (Bryant 1982, 45–6).

Gawain's first glimpse of the castle on his way to keep his assignation with the Green Knight has many precedents in French romance. In the *First Continuation*, he joyfully catches sight of a tower at the edge of a forest after his anxious journey (110), while Perceval somewhat later sees one of which all the battlements were whiter than new-fallen snow (142), and later still, a castle 'strong and impressive indeed, built of limestone and white marble' (164). The *Gawain*-poet is to some extent using a conventional motif in describing Hautdesert as it appeared through the trees on Christmas Eve, but his description is unusually realistic and excels many earlier examples in richness of detail.

Gawain's arrival at Bertilak's castle and his reception there also has its counterpart in very many episodes in French romance, in which a set pattern of welcome is usually followed. Chrétien's Perceval on reaching the castle besieged by Engygeron is led to the great hall, helped to dismount and to unarm and given a grey cloak to wear, while his horse is carefully stabled (Bryant 1982, 20); later, and elsewhere, he is similarly welcomed and wrapped in a brand-new mantle of fine woollen cloth, his horse again receiving appropriate treatment (33). Gawain, too, in the same romance, arriving at a castle where there is not only a Wondrous Bed, but two elderly ladies who turn out, rather surprisingly, to be the mother of King Arthur and his own mother, encounters the same customs which include the provision of an extremely costly ermine robe (82–3). The ritual of welcome, including good stabling for the horse and a fine robe for the knight, is perhaps the most common topos in such romances.

The feast naturally follows the knight's arrival and accommodation as an honoured guest, and again it is clear that the customs of Hautdesert are in no way inferior to those familiar to Chrétien's characters. The topos of the feast is common in English romance, and there is an analogue of especial interest in *Cleanness* (1997–1424; see Brewer 1991 and above). Chrétien pays particular attention to detail in his description of the Grail feast in *Perceval*: warm water is brought for washing, the beautiful table is of ivory, the cloth whiter than white. A haunch of venison is served in hot pepper sauce, skilfully carved by a squire, with excellent wine from golden cups. Later, a wonderful array of fruits with spiced wine, old mulberry wine and clear syrup is brought in. Such detail indicates the special, indeed the superlative quality of the Grail feast, so plenteous that it causes Gawain to fall asleep when he should be awake (Bryant 1982, 35–6). A similar magnificence is displayed at the banquet offered to the Roman senators at the beginning of the alliterative *Morte Arthure*, where very many items of food and drink are enumerated (Hamel 1984, lines 176–205). But in *Sir Gawain and the Green Knight*, at Camelot and again at Bertilak's castle, the poet makes use of the 'inexpressibility' topos rather than detailing the dishes and drinks. The feast nevertheless conforms to convention in terms of the preliminary washing, the seating in pairs, and the serving of dishes in the same way, as well as in Arthur's desire for some marvel to occur or be reported before he addresses himself to his food. This custom of Arthur's is mentioned in many French romances such as *Perceval* and the *First Continuation*, as also in *Perlesvaus*, where again it is between the first and second courses that the important event takes place (Bryant 1978, 33).

Although hunting-scenes are often included in medieval romance, it would not seem that their presence in *Sir Gawain and the Green Knight* is due to the influence either of Chrétien or of the other earlier Arthurian authors to whose work so many features of the poem bear some resemblance. Geoffrey Shepherd (1970) draws attention to the didactic nature of these passages:

> In a society instructed by word of mouth, and by ear, any information or moralization is taken directly as it comes, in memorable and discrete parcels: the attention is directed simply to a succession of points; and if the points are sharp enough they will stick in the mind. Information is accepted within the frame of a story and extracted from it without discomfiture.

This suggests that – as many modern readers have felt – the hunting-scenes are more extended and more detailed than is strictly required by the narrative; and that the satisfaction derived from them by the medieval audience must have resulted, at least in part, from their recognition of their technical interest. (For a fuller discussion of the function of the hunting scenes, see Rooney above.) Shepherd suggests that though we can assume a general interest in hunting on the part of the audience, we cannot assume that more than a few members of the audience would have had a comprehensive and expert knowledge of the finer points and their terminology.

Although they are usually less technical and detailed than the passages in *Sir Gawain and the Green Knight*, there are nevertheless plenty of hunting scenes in other English romances (see Rooney 1993). In *Sir Tristrem* there is a very full account of how the hero, particularly renowned for his skill as a huntsman, demonstrates his expertise when breaking the deer (McNeill 1886, lines 441–510). Other English romances in which hunting episodes occur are the *Parlement of the Three Ages* which like *Sir Gawain and the Green Knight* has a detailed account of the breaking of the deer (Offord 1959, lines 60–100) and *The Awntyrs off Arthure at the Terne Wathelyn* which gives a succinct and spirited account of the deer-hunt itself (Gates 1969, lines 33–65). In the *Avowynge of King Arther* the king successfully engages in a ferocious battle with a tremendously strong, fierce boar (Dahood 1984, lines 69–272). Understanding the huntsman's art as he does, Arthur is able to undo the boar in the space of a few short lines. Guy of Warwick is another knight who is able to dispose of a boar with remarkable despatch. We are left with the question of where the *Gawain*-poet gained his extensive knowledge of hunting practices. He could have consulted William Twiti's *Art of Venery*, or the *Livre de Chasse* of Gaston Phoebus which discusses both the boarhunt and the undoing of the boar, though the *Gawain*-poet's treatment of this topic differs in some respects from that of Phoebus. No English manuals, it appears, treat of the boarhunt; and Bertilak's battle with the boar is described in terms of the romance tradition, since the use of a sword rather than a spear against so formidable an animal would have been impractical.

Again, even though the *Livre de Chasse* does mention the fox, since there are no analogues for the foxhunt in English romance, it seems probable that the poet relied upon personal experience coupled with invention.

The temptation to which Gawain's guide tries to subject him, to avoid the confrontation at the Green Chapel by taking another route, has its counterpart in the Vulgate *Lancelot*.

It can scarcely be wondered at that the outburst against women in which Gawain indulges after Bertilak's revelations at the Green Chapel is a familiar topos in medieval literature, often taking the form of a reflection on the power of love over the wisest and greatest of men. Such lists, occurring in for example, *Cursor Mundi*, *Confessio Amantis*, *Kyng Alysaunder* and a number of other contemporary texts, including *Le Roman de la Rose*, usually consist of names of men who have been brought low by love, whereas this list consists of those who have been deceived by women. Similarly in the Vulgate *Lancelot*, Gawain says 'que homme soy honnist qui croyt femme ne bonne ne malle' (cited by Silverstein 1984, 165 n.2414 ff.).

In so far as the material of the poem is concerned, the French sources and analogues predominate even though we have an English Gawain. The Englishness of the poem is reinforced by the fact that the poet writes here as in his other poems in forms of the alliterative verse which represent a peculiarly English tradition. There is no model among the possible French sources for the elaborate stanza-form which he used: most of them were written in octosyllabic couplets, which though a convenient free-flowing form for an extended narrative make subtle effects very difficult. The metre of the poem is discussed more fully elsewhere in this book, but here we may simply note that the poem is both much more elaborate in metre and more courtly in style than any other alliterative poem of the Middle English period, except the other poems *Cleanness*, *Patience* and *Pearl*.

The author of the *Second Continuation* of Chrétien's *Perceval*, telling what he claims is the true story of Perceval, complains of the 'many worthy fellows going round these courts as storytellers, who are twisting the good stories, distancing them from their sources and adding so many lies that the stories are killed and the good books dishonoured', making their hearers believe a pack of lies, and padding and stringing out the stories (Roach 1971, 162–3). But the *Gawain*-poet uses his material in such a way that we are left marvelling at the skill with which he has ordered it, enhanced its symbolic power and endowed it with profundity of meaning.

10

Sources II: Scriptural and Devotional Sources

RICHARD NEWHAUSER

It is altogether natural that the *Gawain*-poet would have drawn on Scriptural and other devotional materials when composing his works, given his interest in the relationship between God's plan for salvation and the human will which is so evident in *Cleanness*, *Patience*, and *Pearl*. Even the poet's adaptation of the primarily secular genre of the romance to write *Sir Gawain and the Green Knight* was guided in essential ways by similar questions of Christian ethics, integrated though they may be here, of course, within an Arthurian narrative with its affinities to folklore and myth. But the *Gawain*-poet's debt to the Bible and later devotional texts reaches beyond the vision of such materials as a storehouse of imagery and thematic suggestions, for they also provided him with guidance and models for the very structure of his poetry. The scholarship of the last few decades in particular has brought to light many sources which may have influenced the *Gawain*-poet in the conception and execution of his poetry. It must be emphasized, however, that a number of these homilies, treatises, and the like, represent indirect or 'ultimate' sources which can be taken as establishing a general framework for the poet's indebtedness, while many of the more direct influences on his works have yet to be identified, and some of the implications of his borrowings from already known sources have not yet been fully explored. The variety of material which affected the *Gawain*-poet's creative activity demonstrates the wide range of his reading in many of the genres of both English and Latin devotional texts. This diversity in the poet's sources has not always been as widely appreciated as it deserves to be.

The *Gawain*-poet's clearest and most enduring direct debt is to the text of Scriptures found in the Latin Vulgate (Weber 1975). Although some details have been identified in *Patience* which are derived from the Septuagint's treatment of Jonah – such as the prophet's noisy snoring in the hold of the ship during the storm which God sends to bring him back to his mission (cited from Anderson 1969, l. 186) –, there is no doubt that the poet had access to these details through intermediaries. Among the works which have been suggested for such a role are the commentary on this book of the Bible by Jerome, with its Latin version of the Septuagint text of Jonah (Nicholson 1988,

104–08; Vantuono 1972, 416–17), works in the tradition of Jerome's commentary (Szarmach 1971, 125–26), and, though this is much less likely, the poem *De Jona et Ninive* formerly attributed to Tertullian (Hill 1967; Emerson 1895, 244; cf. Anderson 1969, 6). However much Scriptural passages adapted from the Latin Vulgate suffuse *Pearl* and supply the essence of the narration in *Patience* and *Cleanness*, what is true for most other works in the tradition of Biblical paraphrases is valid for the *Gawain*-poet as well: the techniques he makes use of to render his Biblical sources in English are clearly not exhausted by a literal translation of these passages. Nevertheless, he frequently stays close to Scripture in his three explicitly religious poems, especially within the framework of direct speech, as when the pearl-maiden cites Biblical authorities in section 12 of the poem to support the doctrinal position that the innocent who die too young to have sinned will always be saved by right. The following use of the Psalms is indicative of the poet's more direct translation (Fowler 1984, 216):

> Þe Sauter hyt satȝ þus in a pace:
> 'Lorde, quo schal klymbe þy hyȝ hylle,
> Oþer rest wythinne þy holy place?'
> Hymself to onsware he is not dylle:
> 'Hondelyngeȝ harme þat dyt not ille,
> Þat is of hert boþe clene and lyȝt,
> Þer schal hys step stable stylle. . . .'   (*Pearl* (Gordon 1953), 677–83)

Ps 23:3–4: Quis ascendit in montem Domini, aut quis stabit in loco sancto eius? Innocens manibus et mundo corde, qui non accepit in vano animam suam, nec iuravit in dolo proximo suo. (Weber 1975, I. 794 [punctuation mine])

Three-fifths of *Cleanness* represent a more or less direct rendering of various passages from the Vulgate (Menner 1920, xxxix), while nine-tenths of *Patience* are adapted from the same source. As one might expect from any translation/adaptation of narrative material, in both works the poet's technique of close translation is used with greatest frequency not only within the framework of direct speech, but also in purely narrative passages, which depend for their effect on speed and logical development; in descriptive sections, the poet had greater leisure to elaborate on his subject by expanding his Latin source (O'Bryan 1985, 15). Thus, for example, in *Cleanness* the passages narrating Lot's offer of his daughters during the Sodomites' attempt to attack the angels in his house, and those relating the subsequent destruction of the cities (861ff.), follow the Vulgate account in Genesis 19 very closely. There are, to be sure, enough differences in the handling of some specific details to indicate that the *Gawain*-poet may also have had in mind some Latin literature of Biblical interpretation and paraphrase when composing this section of his poem, such as what one finds represented in the tradition of the anonymous *De Sodoma* (cf. Vantuono 1984, I. 383–84), but the vast majority of the poet's work on this section of *Cleanness*, as on other parts of his oeuvre which depend on Biblical sources, required no further intermediary between himself and the Vulgate than his own poetic abilities. The expansiveness which the poet allowed himself in descriptive passages may be illustrated from this same section of *Cleanness*. The Vulgate (Gen 19:1) mentions merely that 'duo angeli' entered the town, but on the basis of this simple phrase, the poet has included a detailed depiction of the two angels which emphasizes the purity and beauty of their appearance (Bennett 1986, 232):

> Bolde burneȝ wer þay boþe, with berdles chynneȝ,
> Royl rollande fax to raw sylk lyke,
> Of ble as þe brere-flour, where-so þe bare scheweed.
> Ful clene watȝ þe countenaunce of her cler yȝen;
> Wlonk whit watȝ her wede, and wel hit hem semed;
> Of alle fetureȝ ful fyn, and fautleȝ boþe;
> Watȝ non aucly in ouþer, for aungels hit wern.... (789–95)

This expansion is part of the poet's technique of rationalizing, or realizing (Spearing 1970, 55–65), the Biblical narrative by supplying psychological motivation for the action: the description of the angels' beauty provides an explanation for the Sodomites' response to the youths in *Cleanness* where one was lacking in the Vulgate (O'Bryan 1985, 17). But beyond this, the expansion is also thematically integrated into the rest of the poem, for the angels' pure exterior is an indication of their sanctified status as vessels of God's will (Morse 1978, 1971). In either case it is further important to note that here, and in *Patience* as well, the poet adapts Biblical narratives in a way which frequently does not deny their allegorical or typological potential, but which also demonstrates his great interest in their literal level, as stories of understandable human psychology (cf. Spearing 1970, 15).

The importance for the *Gawain*-poet of rationalizing Biblical narratives also accounts for many of his other techniques in adapting the Vulgate text. Expansions in his paraphrase of the Latin source by the addition of new passages or the specification of the characters' motives make up the majority of his changes to the Scriptural story line and amount to his particular 'signature' in translating from the Vulgate (Andrew and Waldron 1978, 19; Diekstra 1974). However, he also compressed the Biblical text where necessary, or rearranged passages from the Bible, in order to achieve a more logical development of his themes, more narrative economy in the progression of the stories he was using, or a greater amount of dramatic tension, even when this meant omitting indications of motivation. A few examples will make this process clear. In *Cleanness* 667–68, the poet drops the Vulgate's mention of Sarah's motive for denying she laughed at the thought of giving birth at such an old age, namely her petrified fear of the Lord (Gen 18:15), for in this section of the narrative the poet means to contrast the relatively venial nature of her fault, and its lack of punishment, with the uncleanness of the Sodomites and the dreadful end God has foreseen for them (cf. Anderson 1977, 4). In *Pearl* 989–1032, the poet inverts a sequence of five verses from the Vulgate which describe 1) the measurements and 2) the material used to build the heavenly Jerusalem (Rev 21:15–20), for he wishes to emphasize in his poem the striking effect the vision of Jerusalem's gold and precious jewels has on the dreamer, their permanent splendor in opposition to a world marred by transience (Stanbury 1991b, 22; Field 1986), before including the dimensions of the city in his description. The poet also alters the sequence of events from the Vulgate text during the storm in *Patience* in order to dramatize the desperation of the sailors', and Jonah's, situation. In the Latin text, the storm first brings the sailors to call out to their gods and then to throw all of their implements overboard (Jonah 1:5), whereas in Middle English the poet details a long list of the belongings which the sailors throw out, noting that their actions are to no avail, before he has them invoke their gods as a last resort:

> Þen þo wery for-wroȝt wyst no bote,
> Bot vchon glewed on his god þat gayned hym beste. (163–64)

In the Vulgate, the motive for the narrative sequence is unclear; the *Gawain*-poet has supplied this causality by inverting the chain of events so that the sailors' invocation of the gods follows from the futility of making the boat lighter in the water (Vantuono 1972, 408).

Patience is the closest the *Gawain*-poet comes to pure Biblical paraphrase, since most of the text is an adaptation of one book of the Bible. Source studies have long been used in approaches to some of the most important critical cruxes in this work: the form of the poem as a whole; the combination in the prologue (1–60) of a first-person account of the need for patient suffering in poverty with a paraphrase of the beatitudes as they are found in Matthew (Matt 5:3–10); and the connection between the virtue of patience, which is praised throughout the work, and the character of the prophet Jonah as it is developed in the body of the poem (61–523). A number of Latin works in the tradition of Biblical paraphrases and other forms of devotional and homiletic literature have been proposed as direct influences on the poet's composition of this work, although many of them represent at best only analogues to *Patience* or must be counted among its ultimate sources.

In formal terms, the poem is modeled on the simplest kind of structure used in preaching, the homily (Vantuono 1972, 402). This type of pulpit discourse developed in the early Middle Ages and remained in use even after the form of the modern, or university (or scholastic), sermon had become popular. The homily demanded of the preacher merely a retelling of the gospel pericope of the day and the addition of any exegetical or moral lessons he cared to draw from it. Homilies were not highly structured forms and at times contained only the gospel narrative followed by its exegesis (Wenzel 1986, 62). This simple form of the homily served as the foundation for the

Middle English work, for the poem's introduction contains praise for the virtue of patience within a paraphrase of Matt 5:1–12, the gospel for the feast of All Saints (1 November), and the body of the poem supplies largely a 'negative *exemplum*' (Moorman 1963, 90) of that virtue in the story of Jonah. There are, furthermore, striking parallels between the use of the beatitudes as a setting for this virtue in the introduction to *Patience* and the primacy of the beatitudes in the recommendations for a sermon on the same virtue found in Alan of Lille's *Ars praedicandi* (Scattergood 1992; Cairns 1987, 10–15; Fáj 1975–76, 21), a popular handbook on the composition of sermons dating from the late twelfth century (D'Alverny 1965, 109–19). These close parallels show that the suggestions for a sermon on patience in Alan's treatise, or perhaps even a preaching text which it had inspired, can be reckoned among the poem's sources, and thus the influence of homiletic literature can be adduced both to help demonstrate why the beatitudes are used as the framework for a presentation of patience in the Middle English poem and to more closely define the structural foundations of the poem itself.

The *Gawain*-poet clearly indicates in the prologue that the inspiration for this work came in church, probably on the feast of All Saints (Hill 1968, 103–04):

> I herde on a halyday, at a hy3e masse,
> How Mathew melede þat his mayster his meyny con teche.
>
> (9–10)

Yet this reference may only indicate that the poet heard the chanting of the gospel for the feast, although it is not improbable that the preaching on the gospel for this day may be meant here, as well. Nevertheless, however much homiletic literature such as Alan's treatise or preaching composed on the basis of it may have influenced the poet, this is not to say that he intended *Patience* as a homily itself, though this argument, or even a further one which finds the more elaborate features of the university (or scholastic) sermon represented in the poem, has been advanced on numerous occasions (e.g., Friedman 1981, 100; Vantuono 1972, 401–07; Anderson 1969, 16; Moorman 1963) and discounted almost as many times (e.g., Cairns 1987, 7–8; E. Wilson 1976, 49; Williams 1970a). Though the poem is modeled on the structure of the simple homily, the *Gawain*-poet still takes care to motivate the movement into the paraphrase of the book of Jonah on personal and narrative, not doctrinal, grounds, by wondering how he himself would react if his lord were to send him to Rome – as the prophet was sent to Ninive (51–60). The poem enforces the impression that the poet himself was hard at work learning the lesson of patience he projects onto his protagonist (Bowers 1986, 15). Such a motivation demonstrates the poet's participation in one of the most frequently used processes of medieval self-fashioning, for he, as many other writers, identifies his existence as significant to the extent that his life is guided by the design contained in a Biblical paradigm (Alford 1992, 16; see also Robinson 1986). The lessons of Jonah's life are those of his own.

The narrative of the prophet is developed in *Patience* in the tradition of other Biblical paraphrases such as the poems *De Jona et Ninive* formerly attributed to Tertullian, Prudentius' *Hymnus Ieiunantium* (Kelly 1967), and Marbod of Rennes' *Naufragium Ionae Prophetae*, though these works are merely analogues of the Middle English poem (Cairns 1987, 7; cf. Vantuono 1972, 411–16). The *Gawain*-poet was also clearly aware of the exegetical tradition surrounding this book of the Bible and may have been indirectly influenced by Jerome's *In Ionam Prophetam* and other commentaries in the tradition of Jerome's work (Cairns 1987, 7; Szarmach 1971, 125–26; cf. Nicholson 1988; Vantuono 1972, 416–18). Nevertheless, the exegetical tradition regularly emphasized Jonah's figural role as a type for Jesus, while the often fallible – angry, slothful, even foolish – prophet we meet in *Patience* does not conform well to this typological view (Prior 1994, 73; Schleusner 1971; Moorman 1968, 68–69; cf. Andrew 1973), for Jonah's opinion of God's purpose is an overly apocalyptic one (Prior 1986). Nor will exegetical literature on the whole help illuminate the poet's connection between patience and the story of Jonah, instead of the common exemplar of this virtue, Job. For such a connection, one must turn to the literature of the moral tradition, as scholars have frequently done who have analyzed Jonah's failings as due to anger (Andrew and Waldron 1978, 20; cf. Pohli 1991) or sloth (Stock 1991). While both of these sins are manifested in the prophet's behavior, the organizing principle in Jonah's fallibility as the poet sees it remains his lack of patience, and an invariable connection between patience and one, single vice is not at all what we find in the history of treatises on the sins in the later fourteenth century. On the other hand, treatises devoted primarily to the examination of the virtues have a prominent place among the burgeoning literature of moral analysis in England in the later Middle Ages, where one can detect, in fact, a growing number of works which concentrate precisely on the virtue of patience (Newhauser 1993, 149; Hanna 1978). Patience, indeed, held a place of honor in medieval ethics (Bennett 1986, 218). Many of these treatises on virtue depend on the analysis of William Peraldus, whose *Summa de vitiis et virtutibus* was in circulation by 1250 (Dondaine 1948). Peraldus, and the enormous number of works which ultimately depend on his, make the connection between (im)patience and Jonah quite clear, though Peraldus was surely not the first one to do so (Walls 1992). But his mention of Jonah in connection with patience is illuminating because it also contains a reference to the endurance of poverty, which the *Gawain*-poet emphasizes in the prologue and epilogue of *Patience*. As Peraldus says in the fifth chapter of his treatment of patience (contained in the sixth part of the treatise on fortitude in his *Summa* on the virtues):

Diabolus eos, qui sunt in deserto paupertatis, incitat ad iram vel impatientiam. Unde tentatio eius talibus est ventus urens. . . . Ione iiii: 'Precepit Dominus vento calido et urenti; et percussit sol super caput Ione, et estuabat.' . . . Quandoque vero diabolus Deo permittente hoc ad probationem et profectum amicorum suorum suscitat quasi ventum vehementem, ut videatur omnia concutere, Iob i . . . et Ione i: 'Misit Dominus ventum magnum in mare, et facta est tempestas magna'

(Summa, 3.4.6.5 (Peraldus 1512), 158vb).

(The devil incites to wrath or impatience those who live in the desert of poverty. Whence, his temptation is a parching wind to them. . . . Jonah 4: 'The Lord admonished him with a hot, parching wind, and the sun beat upon the head of Jonah, and he was faint' [Jonah 4:8]. . . . But sometimes, if God permits this as a trial and means of improvement for those who are His friends, the devil stirs up, as it were, a violent wind so that it might appear to shake all things to their very foundation, Job 1 . . . and Jonah 1: 'The Lord sent a great wind upon the sea, and there was a great tempest' [Jonah 1:4].) (My translation.)

One is far from asserting that Peraldus was a direct influence on the *Gawain*-poet, but the moral tradition on which Peraldus put his stamp surely formed part of the essential framework for the poet's conception of Jonah as an exemplar of patience.

Homiletic literature also plays an important role in the structural foundation of *Cleanness*, for if *Patience* is modeled on the relatively simple form of the homily, in *Cleanness* one finds the poet's reflection of the much more complex structure seen in the university (or scholastic) sermon (Brzezinski 1990; Kittendorf 1979; Means 1975; cf. also Schreiber 1981). Briefly described, the formal characteristics of this type of pulpit address included the statement of a theme (generally a Scriptural passage containing the message of the sermon) and the progressive development of the theme by various divisions and subdivisions. These elements could also be augmented at the beginning of the sermon by the addition of a protheme (often a further Scriptural authority expanding on the theme) (Wenzel 1986, 66–69; Owst 1926, 316ff.). As in *Patience*, the essential message of *Cleanness* is provided by the beatitudes – in this case only the sixth one – using the text in Matthew. As the poet notes, it is not a difficult task to praise cleanness, but the Lord abhors impurity:

> Kryst kydde hit hymself in a carp oneȝ,
> Þer as he heuened aȝt happeȝ and hyȝt hem her medeȝ.
>
> Me myneȝ on one amonge oþer, as Maþew recordeȝ,
> Þat þus of clannesse vncloseȝ a ful cler speche:
> 'Þe haþel clene of his hert hapeneȝ ful fayre,
> For he schal loke on oure lorde with a loue chere.' (23–28)

The structural counterpart to the sermon's protheme is found in *Cleanness* in the parable of the wedding feast and its implications (49–192; from both Luke and Matthew), which augment this message by demonstrating the rewards for purity or, more important to the narrative conception here, the punishment for impurity. The *Gawain*-poet's reflection of the sermon's division continues this same hortatory dichotomy, presenting three main *exempla* in support of the beatitude which emphasize the punishment for uncleanness: the story of the flood (249–544; Gen 6:1ff.), the destruction of Sodom and Gomorrah (890–972; Gen 19:12ff.), and Belshazzar's feast and demise (1357–1650, 1709–1804; Dan 5:1ff.). Summarizing this structure at the end of the narrative, the poet notes:

> Þus vpon þrynne wyses I haf yow þro schewed
> Þat vnclannes tocleues in corage dere
> Of þat wynnelych lorde þat wonyes in heuen. . . .
> *(Cleanness* 1805–07)

Cleanness is, thus, as thoroughly indebted to Scriptural sources as is *Patience*, though it does not concentrate on a single narrative, but rather on an assembly of Biblical stories which are all figurally related as types of the last judgement (Morse 1971, 202). Beyond this, the rationale for the poet's choice of narratives is essentially Scriptural, as well, for it is based on the mention of Noah, Lot, Lot's wife, and Sodom in the context of the coming apocalypse found in Luke 17:21–37 (see also 2 Peter 2:4–13 and Wisdom 10:1–7) (Brzezinski 1990, 172–74; Johnson 1984, 106–08). This combination and juxtaposition of Scriptural narratives in support of one theme is characteristic of the poet's treatment of the Vulgate in *Cleanness* (Gradon 1971, 122). Although he attributes the parable of the wedding feast to Matthew alone (51), for example, his paraphrase is in fact adapted from both Matt 22:2–14 and Luke 14:16–24 in a way which unifies their typological implications and emphasizes the punishment of the wedding guest in unsuitable clothing for his uncleanness (Johnson 1984, 99–105; Davenport 1978, 79–83). The *Gawain*-poet's treatment of his Biblical sources further illustrates his interest in the Christian understanding of the progress of spiritual history in *Cleanness*, from natural law, to revealed law, to the grace leading to the vision of God promised in the sixth beatitude (Stanbury 1991ab). Since Noah is used as an illustration of what was positive in natural law, for example, the poet interrupts his paraphrase of the Biblical narrative of the flood at 540 by omitting Gen 9:1–7, God's promulgation of the Noachic laws, substituting instead a series of admonitions about God's wrath for uncleanness (see the appendix). Only with the next stage of the narrative, that dealing with Abraham, does the poet present God's revelation of the law as the next step in spiritual history.

If the poet's essential inspiration for the narratives in *Cleanness* was drawn directly from Scripture, a number of the details of his composition show that he was also influenced by the literature of the moral tradition and treatises of Biblical interpretation and paraphrase, though one does not have evidence

for the poet's direct borrowing from such sources as can be adduced for two
secular works: the *Romance of the Rose* and Mandeville's *Travels*. The anonymous *De Sodoma* has been mentioned as a possible source for *Cleanness* from
Latin devotional literature, as well as Jerome's commentary on the Book of
Daniel, but they should more likely be considered analogues to the Middle
English poem (Vantuono 1984, I. 383–84). Although the lesson of Lot's wife
is mentioned explicitly in Luke 17:32, in medieval commentaries she also
came to exemplify the inability of some who had taken religious vows to
leave the world completely. Her punishment in *Cleanness* is an extension of
the opening image in the poem of pure or faithless priests, whose virtue, or
lack of it, will decide whether they are rewarded or chastised by the Lord
(7–16) (Twomey 1991, 126). The moral tradition provided a further reason for
the religious to avoid behaving as Lot's wife had by noting that the reward
for pure faith was contained in the sixth beatitude. The discussion in the *Book
of Vices and Virtues*, for instance, draws together Lot's wife, the beatitude, and
the virtue of cleanness, recommending the example of Paul's faithfulness for
those who want to attain endless joy:

> þis is þe blessyng whider þat þe ჳifte of cunnyng ledeþ hem þat kepeþ
> clennesse of herte and of body, as we haue schewed here-tofore; & þerfore
> seiþ oure lord þat blessed be þe clene of herte, for þei schulle see God.
> (Book of Vices (Francis 1942), 270)

> (This is the blessing to which the gift of knowledge leads those who
> maintain cleanness of heart and body, as we have demonstrated earlier,
> and therefore our Lord says, 'Blessed are the pure in heart, for they shall
> see God.')

Here again, as in *Patience*, it is the moral tradition which provides insight into
the framework of the poet's conception of an important homiletic detail in
his work, in this case Lot's wife as a negative *exemplum* of the cleanness
mentioned in the sixth beatitude. Other details show the poet's familiarity
with apocryphal material that had grown up around the Biblical text in the
course of the Middle Ages. In his treatment of humanity before the flood, for
example, the *Gawain*-poet draws on an apocryphal tradition which identified
fallen angels as the ones who had sired giants on the daughters of men (cf.
Gen 6:1–4). This tradition is represented in John Trevisa's translation of
Ranulf Higden's *Polychronicon*, completed in 1387 (Kennedy 1989, 2656), and
in other English works with legendary material (E. Wilson 1976, 90–92),
though the poet may more likely have found a source for his view of
ante-diluvian times in Peter Comestor's twelfth-century *Historia scholastica*
and that author's source for a number of details, the anonymous *Revelationes
sancti Methodii* (Twomey 1989), which was also available in English (Kennedy
1989, 2664–65). The monumental, fourteenth-century history of humanity in
English verse, *Cursor mundi* (Raymo 1986, 2276–78), also contains much
legendary material which parallels details in *Cleanness*: the behavior of the

animals which look to heaven for mercy at the time of the flood (387–96), the description of the properties of the Dead Sea (1013–51), and other passages, recall similar treatments of the same matter in the earlier poem (Vantuono 1984, I. 302, 307; Anderson 1977, 71, 88; Day 1940, xxxi; Menner 1920, 85), though it is not at all clear that the *Gawain*-poet is indebted directly to *Cursor mundi* in these verses (cf. Horrall 1985). Again, it appears likely that the *Gawain*-poet was familiar with the same legendary tradition used by the poet of *Cursor mundi*.

The confluence of a number of theological traditions in the conceptual framework of *Pearl* characterizes the *Gawain*-poet's treatment of his sources in this work, as well. These influences include devotional and moral works, but also lapidaries (Stern 1955), descriptions of the otherworld (Kean 1967, 89ff.), the liturgy, especially for Holy Innocents' Day (Bishop 1968), and works in the mystical tradition (Vantuono 1984, I. 379; Wilson 1968). Many of the doctrinal matters in which the pearl-maiden instructs the dreamer were commonplace and widely diffused in medieval Christian thought, such as the inappropriateness of grief for the dead, or the necessity of faith in God's grace. Other issues were current in fourteenth-century England and show that the *Gawain*-poet was in touch with the theological trends of his day as these have been identified in the works of Thomas Bradwardine (d.1349), the productions of Richard Rolle (d.1349) and related writers, the *Testament of Love* by Thomas Usk (d.1387), and other theological material. These issues include the special emphasis on grace in achieving salvation, or the efficacy of the baptism of innocents for gaining heaven (Spearing 1976, 112–13; Gordon 1953, xxxv). Though *Pearl*, too, is thus openly concerned with religious instruction, it is much more allusive than the direct didacticism of *Patience* or *Cleanness*, and its symbolic and dramatic procedures involve a more complete poetic transformation of its sources than the essentially homiletic structures of the other two works. The complexity of such a transformation can be seen in the formal and generic influence on *Pearl* of various types of theological literature, demonstrating the poet's reading of English and foreign material (cf. Gordon 1953, xxxv), as well as in the treatment of Biblical sources in the poem.

Formally, *Pearl* is a dream vision, as the dreamer notes after he awakens at the end of the poem and reflects on what he has seen:

> 'O perle', quod I, 'of rych renoun,
> So watȝ hit me dere þat þou con deme
> In þys veray avysyoun!'   (1182–84)

But as has often been pointed out, the dream vision is a large generic category which includes the *consolatio* tradition of philosophical/theological dialogue inspired by Boethius' *Consolation of Philosophy*; the vision of religious revelation, the most important example of which in Christian literature is *The*

Revelation to John; and the secular love vision, as well, established by the *Romance of the Rose,* which the *Gawain*-poet mentions explicitly in *Cleanness* (Prior 1994, 21–25; Andrew and Waldron 1978, 29; Spearing 1976). What is important to note for *Pearl* is that in fact all of these types of dream vision influenced the poet in the composition of this work. The beginning of the poem, in which the dreamer finds himself in a garden reminiscent of the *locus amoenus* and uses the language of courtly love, is indebted to the tradition of the love vision, and *Pearl* owes a number of central motifs and symbols to the *Romance of the Rose* (Pilch 1964). Yet the dreamer is also in a state of mourning, and though he is ravished with love for the pearl-maiden, he is in need of consolation for the loss of her.

Whether this loss must be understood as the death of the dreamer's young daughter is a topic which engaged critics a number of years ago. The evidence of source studies makes it moot. First of all, the poet's adaptation of an epistolary formula at the end of the work, when he takes his now resigned leave of the pearl-maiden at her grave and commends her to God 'In Kryste3 dere blessyng and myn' (In Christ's precious blessing and mine – 1208), is an almost invariable indicator of speech from a parent to a child (Davis 1970). It has also been shown that the *Gawain*-poet, as Dante, endows his central female protagonist with the characteristics of a resurrected body, as medieval theologians expected such a body to appear (Marti 1993). But even at the beginning of the poem, when the symbol of the pearl has not yet been identified with the pearl-maiden, there is evidence, in the poet's adaptation of the language of Middle English death poetry, that the dreamer must be consoled for the death of someone dear to him. Complaining of his loss of the pearl, the dreamer says:

> Allas! I leste hyr in on erbere;
> Þur3 gresse to grounde hit fro me yot. (9–10)

These lines recall a widespread tradition of lyrics on death which reflected the custom of moving the corpse from the bed to the floor immediately after death, a journey of descent which continued when the corpse was placed in the grave (Newhauser 1995). A thirteenth-century example, which inspired many variations to the end of the Middle Ages, begins in this way:

> If man him biðocte
> inderlike and ofte
> þu arde is te fore
> fro bedde to flore. . . . (Woolf 1968, 78)

(If humanity considered / inwardly and often / how hard it is to go / from the bed to the floor. . . .)

The point of the poet's adaptation of the *consolatio* tradition is that the dreamer must be provided with a Christian context for the suspension of his grief occasioned by this death (Means 1972, 49–59; Bishop 1968, 13–26; Conley 1955; cf. also Cherniss 1987, 151–68). As in Boethius' *Consolation of Philosophy*, the dreamer is first instructed by his mentor to abandon the very forms of secular literature with which he began the work. The pearl-maiden brings this about by redirecting the dreamer's language from the secular to the sacred realm (Prior 1994, 34–40; Clopper 1992, 235; E. Wilson 1976). This is to say that the influence on *Pearl* by the secular love-vision is a necessary first step in the dramatic and symbolic transformation of the dreamer himself and his understanding of the pearl-maiden. In the dialogues with his daughter, the dreamer is taught to give up his possessive, earth-bound love for her and to find sufficiency in God. The influence of the moral tradition can be observed here, for what the dreamer eventually learns is not to desire a materially valuated 'more and more,' to use the linking phrase in section 3 of the poem, a desire which moral theologians following Augustine identified as the sin of avarice understood in its broadest terms as the love for anything in this world, whether tangible or intangible, which detracts from the love of God (Prior 1994, 37–40; Newhauser 1989; for further influence from the moral tradition on the eucharistic imagery of the poem, see Ackerman 1964, 156–62). This same analysis of greed forms part of the protagonist's self-accusation in *Sir Gawain and the Green Knight*.

But the *consolatio* is not the framework for the last stage of the dreamer's knowledge. Ultimately, this tradition is superseded by the vision of revelation in which the dreamer completes his transformation from a merely material to a fully spiritual orientation and finds his final consolation in the vision of the new Jerusalem and its implications (Wimsatt 1970). Such a reorientation of the Christian in the ascent to God is what was envisioned by devotional writers concerned with the theory of the spiritual life from Bernard of Clairvaux and Hugh of St Victor (both twelfth-century) to Bonaventure (thirteenth-century) and the *Gawain*-poet's English contemporary, Walter Hilton (E. Wilson 1976; Blenkner 1968). It is, furthermore, what these contemplative thinkers, and a number of preachers as well, had in mind when they described a refinement of vision from merely literal seeing to anagogical sight (Clopper 1992; Chance 1991). It is, finally, also part of the narrative pattern of Dante's *Commedia*, the influence of which on the *Gawain*-poet has been detected in his conception of the pearl-maiden, in her pedagogic relationship with the dreamer separated from him by a stream (as Dante is separated from Beatrice by the Lethe), in the similarities between the dreamer's vision and the last cantos of *Purgatorio* and the *Paradiso*, and in a number of his other literary procedures as well (Shoaf 1990; Despres 1989, 107; Ginsberg 1988; Spearing 1970, 17–18; Wimsatt 1970, 122ff.; Kean 1967, 120–33). There are also, one can note, similarities between *Pearl* and Boccaccio's Latin eclogue 'Olympia,' but it remains unclear whether this work could have influenced the *Gawain*-poet (Carlson 1987; cf. Schofield 1904, 203–15).

In 983–84, the poet names Revelations as his direct source for the dreamer's vision of new Jerusalem near the end of *Pearl* (from Rev 21–22). He may also have been inspired by illuminated manuscripts of this book of Scripture available in England (Stanbury 1991b, 24–31; Stanbury 1988b; Field 1986; Whitaker 1981; Nolan 1977; see also Stanbury 1988a). Tapestries on the Apocalypse provide a further analogue to the poet's pictorial imagination (Bennett 1986, 238). This passage from Revelation and two others, the parable of the vineyard (Matt 20:1–16) and the procession of the 144,000 (from Rev 14), account for the poet's most extensive borrowing from Biblical sources in *Pearl* (see the appendix). The poetic transformation of these passages is more varied than the sole use of Biblical paraphrase as authoritative proof texts in the homiletic poems already examined. There are of course small changes to Scripture which the *Gawain*-poet has undertaken to make the quoted material a seamless part of his narrative: the 144,000 chaste men of Revelation, for example, have become maidens in the poem, among whom the dreamer discovers his pearl-maiden. The poet has also, as in his other works, rearranged and selected details from Biblical passages to suit his purpose. But even beyond this, he has allowed the dreamer to misinterpret texts from Scripture, because part of the plan of this poem is the instruction of the narratorial voice in the correct understanding of Scripture (Moorman 1955). Thus at the end of section 10, the dreamer objects to the pearl-maiden's contention that though she has only lately come to heaven, she has more bliss than many others. He quotes Ps 61:12 ('For you requite each person according to his deeds') as contradicting her, but she then points out that the Psalm verse accords with what she has said, for though each one is paid according to his merit in heaven, eventually all are paid equally (601–04) (Horgan 1981). This lesson on the difference between grace and deeds is a necessary part of the dreamer's education, and in her pedagogy the pearl-maiden has followed authoritative doctrine to instruct him in the correct interpretation of the passage, for in the Epistle to the Romans Paul had used the same verse from the Psalms in his teaching on the relationship between mercy and justice (Rom 2:6ff.).

Unlike the works examined so far, *Sir Gawain and the Green Knight* owes very little to the Bible by way of direct paraphrase. Only a few verses can be seen as dependent on the wording of Scripture (for examples, see Burrow 1965, 155, 40), and direct allusions to the Bible are not much more extensive. Gawain's misogynous outburst after Bertilak has forgiven him for retaining the green belt (2414–28) uses Adam, Solomon, Samson, and David as examples of great men who fell through the wiles of women, a traditional list in Latin and homiletic literature (Woolf 1972, 373n48; cf. also Owst 1961, 385–404). The list is also pointedly ironic in this passage of *Sir Gawain and the Green Knight*, where it does not seem strictly applicable to Gawain's situation, since he concealed the green belt on his own initiative. On the other hand, the allusion to Solomon does in fact make the idea of the contingency of human goodness, to which Gawain is referring here, all the more obviously fitting for his situation, because the poet had earlier mentioned Solomon as the patron of the pentangle, the symbol of Gawain's crowning virtue (Burrow 1965, 146–48; Green 1962; cf. Spearing 1970, 228–29):

> Hit is a syngne þat Salamon set sumquyle
> In bytoknyng of trawþe, bi tytle þat hit habbez. . . .   (625–26)

Gawain, too, as the narrator himself in *Patience*, is guided here by the design contained in a Biblical paradigm, and the *Gawain*-poet is equally aware of the possibilities for perfection and for failure which the model of King Solomon contains.

If these limited uses of the Bible in *Sir Gawain and the Green Knight* are quite distant from the extensive involvement with Scriptural narrative seen in *Patience*, *Cleanness*, and *Pearl*, one is nevertheless justified in maintaining that theological texts are as important as sources for the poet's conception of his material here as they are in the other three poems (Anderson 1990b; Besserman 1986, 229; Champion 1967), though, of course, they ultimately serve neither a doctrinal nor a homiletic function in the romance. This importance can be seen in a number of ways. Liturgical elements frame the events of the romance and add their own implications to these actions: the wounding of the Green Knight at Arthur's court and that of Gawain at the Green Chapel occur on New Year's Day, when the Feast of the Circumcision was celebrated, and these wounds suggest the action of circumcision itself (Shoaf 1984, 15–30). Furthermore, when Gawain sets out to find the Green Knight, it is on All Souls' Day after having attended with ominous suitability a requiem mass, all of which contributes an especially solemn note to the reminders of death which begin to accumulate at this point in the narrative (Barron 1980, 113–14). Gawain in particular is also shown frequently engaging in religious observances: when he crosses himself and says the Paternoster, Ave, and Creed just before Bertilak's castle appears (757–62), he is repeating material typically found at the beginning of primers or catechetical manuals for elementary instruction in the faith which circulated widely in England in the late Middle Ages (Anderson 1990a). This connection underscores the description of Arthur's court in the romance as being especially youthful. There are also hagiographic precedents for the three strokes from the Green Knight's axe to which Gawain must submit (Tkacz 1992). The Green Knight, too, is defined partially by the tension of the human and the superhuman (among other seemingly contradictory pairs of elements) in the Christian doctrine of the hypostatic union (Besserman 1986), though it seems unlikely that treatises such as Christine de Pisan's *Livre de la Mutacion de Fortune* (Eadie 1986) or Robert Holcot's *Moralitates* (O'Mara 1992ab) can account for the essential elements of this enigmatic character.

However, the most important sources for the Christian elements in the romance come from penitential and moral literature. The qualities summed up in the pentangle device on Gawain's shield invoke Christian ethics, not simply courtliness, to define his virtue (Arthur 1987; Benson 1965b, 104). The inclusion of purity in the five bodily senses among the pentangle's interlocking virtues may reflect the ubiquitous presence of treatises on the senses in penitential and catechetical manuals in late medieval pastoral theology (Ackerman 1958; cf. Bloomfield 1961, 45 n. 36), but in any case, in spite of his confession to and absolution by a priest before leaving Hautdesert for the Green Chapel, Gawain explicitly identifies his fault as a moral failure when confronted with his behavior by Bertilak at the end of the poem. In three different verses (2374, 2380, 2508) Gawain accuses himself of 'covetyse,' the common Middle English designation for the vice of avarice. Though some have doubted the appropriateness of the term Gawain uses here (Kaske 1984, 27; Silverstein 1977–8, 11; Waldron 1970, 19; Spearing 1970, 227; Tolkien and Gordon 1967, 128), the moral tradition illuminates its accuracy, for it denotes a specific type of the broadly understood greed for more examined already in *Pearl*, namely the greed for life (Johnson 1984, 86), rather than either a sin related to theft, identifiable in Gawain's retention of the green belt (Burrow 1965, 135–36; cf. Allen 1992), or a more general sense of cupidity which underlies all sin (Shoaf 1984, 66ff.; Reichardt 1984, 157; Hills 1963). Avarice is never represented in the poem by Gawain as the root of all evils in some speculative sense, nor as the greed for an object (the green belt) which is continually described as worthless in material terms (see Mann 1986), but as the effect of his fear of death, and it is intimately associated with deceitful lying. Precisely these qualities – untruthfulness, fear of death, and the greed to live longer than the amount of time which has been ordained – are the key elements in Augustine's analysis of *avaritia vitae* in his *Sermon 107*. This sermon, then, is the ultimate source for the poet's conception of Gawain's greed (Newhauser 1990), though the poet has not, of course, built this into a sermon, but made it part of Gawain's somewhat overwrought reaction to his lack of perfection.

What emerges from this analysis of the *Gawain*-poet's sources in all four of his works will confirm in general Gordon's observation that the poet had read theological treatises without himself being a systematic theologian (Gordon 1953, xxx). But those sources can also be seen to have been more varied than Gordon conceived, for they included English and Italian texts, as well as material in Latin and French. The *Gawain*-poet was at home in the homiletic and moral literature of the church, from which he drew much of the inspiration for the content and form of his poems; he was conversant with theological currents of the late fourteenth century in England, including doctrines on grace and mystical theology; and he was able to use his knowledge of Biblical commentaries and the legendary material which had developed around the text of Scripture in his poetic interpretations. Above all, he was thoroughly

versed in the Vulgate Bible (Spearing 1970, 13) and read its narratives with
an avid appreciation for the psychological subtleties of the text that remains
fascinating, and one of the chief sources of his poetic power, still today.[1]

APPENDIX

Major Biblical Sources Paraphrased or Translated
in *Cleanness, Patience,* and *Pearl*

C = *Cleanness,* J = *Patience,* P = *Pearl*

Gen	3.1–24	C235–48
	6.1–22	C249–342
	7.1–24	C343–434
	8.1–22	C435–540
	9.8–17	C564–70
	18.1–33	C601–780
	19.1–28	C781–1014
Exod	15.1–18	J237–38
	28.9–11	P1039–42
Deut	29.23	C956–58; C1028
2Chr	36.12–14	C1157–74
	36.17–20	C1245–92
Job	6.26	P313
Ps(LXX)	6.2–5	J282–88
	7.10	C592
	14.1–2	P678–83
	14.3	P687–88
	14.5	P678–83
	23.3–4	P678–83
	23.4	P687–88
	23.5–6	P675
	61.12–13	P595–96
	68.1–37	J305–36
	93.8–9	C581–86; J121–24
	97.1	P882
	142.2	P699–700
	145.8–9	J417–20

[1] For reading and commenting on an earlier draft of this essay, the author would like to
thank Larry Besserman (Hebrew University, Jerusalem, Israel).

Cant	4.7–8	P763–64
Wis	1.6	C592
	10.10	P690–92
	12.18	C748
Isa	1.3	C1086
	14.12–14	C205–34
	40.3	P819
	53.4–7	P826
	53.4–10	P805–16; P822–24
	53.7	P801–3
	53.8	P827–28
	53.9	P825
	53.10–12	P826
Jer	17.10	C592
	52.4–11	C1175–1224
	52.12–14	C1233–44
Dan	2.22	C1600
	3.28–33	C1157–74
	4.1–34	C1325–28
	4.27–33	C1651–1708
	5.1–31	C1357–1796
	9.5–14	C1157–74
Jonah	1.1–17	J61–304
	2.1–11	J305–44
	3.1–10	J345–408
	4.1–11	J409–516
Matt	3.3	P819
	3.13	P817–18
	5.1–12	J10–28
	5.8	C27–28
	13.30	P32
	13.45–46	P192; P730–35; P745
	15.19	C177–92
	18.1–3	P711–24
	19.13–15	P711–24
	20.1–16	P501–72
	22.2–4	C51–60
	22.8–14	C73–164
	26.53	P1121
	26.63	P803
	26.67	P805–16
	27.12	P803
Mark	1.4–5	P817–18
	1.9	P817–18

	10.13–16	P711–24
	14.61	P803
	14.65	P805–16
	15.5	P803
Luke	3.3–4	P817–19
	11.9–10	P727–28
	14.16–24	C51–108
	18.15–17	P711–24
	22.63–64	P805–16
John	1.23	P819
	1.28	P817–18
	1.29	P820–24
	12.24–25	P31–32
	19.34	P650, P654
Rom	1.27	C695–96
1Cor	6.9–10	C177–92
	12.12–27	P457–66
	15.36–37	P31–32
Gal	5.19–21	C177–92
Rev	2.23	C592
	4.2–10	P1051–54
	5.1	P835–40
	5.6	P1064; P1111; P1135–37
	5.6–8	P835–40
	5.8	P1119–20
	5.9	P1122
	5.11	P1121
	5.11–13	P1123–27
	5.14	P1119–20
	7.9–11	P1051–54
	7.14	P766
	8.3–4	P1122
	14.1	P786–89; P867–72
	14.2–5	P873–900
	19.7	P785; P791–92
	19.8	P163; P197
	19.9	C52
	21.2	P943; P985–88
	21.10	P976; P979–81
	21.11	P982
	21.12–13	P1034–42
	21.14	P989–94
	21.15–16	P1029–32
	21.16	P1023–24

21.18	P1017–18; P1026
21.18–20	P989–1016
21.21	P1036–38; P1106
21.22	P1061–64
21.23	P982; P1043–48; P1069; P1072–76
21.25	P1065–66
21.27	P966; P970; P972; P1067–68
22.1	P107; P1055–60
22.2	P1077–80
22.5	P1043–48; P1071–76
22.6	P1183–85
22.14	P766

More complete lists of the Biblical sources of these poems may be found in the following: C – Vantuono 1984 I. 385–86; J – Cairns 1987, 8–9; Vantuono 1984 II. 375–76; Vantuono 1972, 406; P – Vantuono 1984, I. 380–82; Gordon 1953, 165–67; Osgood 1906, 98–100.

11

The Supernatural

HELEN COOPER

The supernatural, a crucial element in all the works of the *Gawain*-poet, takes the form of the divine order beyond nature in the three religious poems, and of secular magic and marvel in *Sir Gawain and the Green Knight* (henceforward *Sir Gawain*). Both forms are marked by their otherness, their resistance to any kind of rational analysis: the green man who can pick up his head after it has been cut off, the talismanic girdle, the bejewelled land of the dead, the helpful whale, the bodiless hand that appears in the middle of a feast to inscribe on the wall words all the more threatening for being incomprehensible. Yet the poet insists that the supernatural is not finally 'other', alien or exotic, but rather stands for something within the protagonist of each poem, and therefore, given the poet's insistent moral concern, within the reader too.

It might sound as if reading the poems in this way would take all the fun out of them. The Green Knight is, after all, gripping in a way that no amount of psychological analysis, let alone moral homily, could ever be. In fact, the doubling of effect – narrative excitement, inward thoughtfulness – enables the poet to get the best of both worlds. It is a frequent complaint about the supernatural in medieval romances that it is boring. Chaucer introduces a giant into his own parody of such works, *Sir Thopas*, and has to give him three heads a couple of stanzas later in an attempt to stop the level of excitement from collapsing. A ring or a sword that confers invincibility on a hero has the effect of making him unheroic: *anybody* could win a battle if they had such a weapon. So in the Arthurian stories, the young King Arthur himself has to fight an opponent who is armed with the stolen Excalibur, which draws blood at every stroke, and its scabbard, which prevents its wearer from losing blood – and yet Arthur still wins.[1] The supernatural powers of the sword and scabbard become most telling when the hero is pitted against them: Arthur's achievement here is all the more significant, and exciting, because it is not supernatural, and the magic serves to highlight his courage and prowess. *Sir*

---

[1] The episode occurs in the French prose *Suite du Merlin*, and appears in Malory's translation of the *Morte Darthur* as Book IV chapters 8–11 (in Caxton's numbering, Vinaver 1971, 84–8).

Gawain would be much less exciting if the girdle were indeed what the lady says it is, a talisman of invulnerability. It is true that Gawain is not killed while he is wearing it; but if he, and we, really believed in its magical powers, his bravery in finally facing the Green Knight would dissolve, and the episode would lose both its suspense and its significance.

This kind of argument, that the most heroic hero is the one who pits his own human resources against supernatural odds, might seem much harder to make for the three religious poems. It is foolish, not heroic, to challenge God, and Jonah and the dreamer of *Pearl* emerge from their confrontation with the divine appearing belittled, fallible – human with all its connotations of weakness rather than potential. God, moreover, is always beyond human apprehension. Not only is He not bound by the natural world; He is also ineffable, beyond language, for language, as medieval religious writers well knew, is a bodily activity, spoken with the tongue, and designed to describe the physical world. Writers about God therefore face a particular problem. The poet has nothing but the earthly tools of language with which to speak about an order beyond nature, just as his protagonists encounter the divine equipped with nothing but their imperfect mortal understanding. It is none the less possible to speak about God through metaphor and symbol. The world of nature itself is God's creation and can be read as a book to reveal something of God's own supra-nature. The word *lamb* is a phonetic signifier for a young sheep; the animal *lamb* can in turn be read as signifying the meekness of Christ in the Passion, His sacrifice for mankind. How far one has travelled from the original concept in such a symbolic reading is shown up by the use in both Revelation and *Pearl* of the term *lamb* to describe the weird creature with seven horns of red gold sitting upon a throne in the midst of the New Jerusalem. By this stage, the natural world has given way to something very un-natural indeed.

It is thus possible to work outwards from something within the natural order towards an understanding of the supernatural, whether of secular marvel or of the divine. The trouble comes in that symbolic significance is not inherent in the physical object. Pearls or girdles may be just that (even Freud was prepared to admit that a cigar need not always be a phallic symbol); or even if one is prepared to 'read' them, to interpret them as signs of something beyond themselves, there are generous possibilities for misinterpretation. The men of Sodom take the beautiful figures who appear in their streets as belonging to the natural order – to be men, not angels. The revellers in the hall at Camelot have no way of knowing whether the Green Knight is man, giant, fairy, phantasm or devil. Gawain is persuaded that the girdle is not as simple as it looks (*Sir Gawain* 1846–50), and, as the criticism on the poem shows (Hanna 1983), it is not as simple as it looks, but probably not for the reasons the lady claims. The *Gawain*-poet repeatedly shows the protagonists of his poems getting things wrong, having to be trained to read the world they inhabit; and in that process, the central character also serves as a surrogate for the reader of the poem. Gawain's or Jonah's or the *Pearl*-dreamer's making sense of his world charts a parallel process in which the reader learns to 'read' the text properly.

In this process, however, the supernatural of the divine and the supernatural of magic work in somewhat different ways. In the religious poems, the reader may well have a head start over the characters in interpretation (we know what is happening to Jonah or Belshazzar long before they themselves do); but self-discovery for both readers and characters comes as a consequence of symbolic understanding, of apprehending more about the nature of God. The difference between God and humanity, the supra-natural of the divine order and the natural order of the created world, defines what it means to be human. With the secular magic and marvellous in *Sir Gawain*, the reader is likely to share Gawain's bewilderment, but for both a precise understanding of the supernatural nature of the sign matters much less than its human import. It is crucially important that the figures in Sodom are angels; it is hard to be entirely sure what the Green Knight is, and there is a sense in which it ultimately does not matter. That the Trinity appears to Abraham in the form of three persons is significant in itself as the three heads of the giant in *Sir Thopas* signally fail to be; and the Green Knight's ability to pick up his decapitated head would be as little gripping as Sir Olifaunt's multiple heads if his action did not threaten such nasty consequences for Gawain. The pentangle is not an apotropaic symbol to ward off evil:[2] it does nothing within the poem that Gawain himself does not do in his own person.

Part of the *Gawain*-poet's skill lies in the psychological accuracy with which he charts his protagonists' journey towards understanding: the dreamer's reorientation towards his place in God's order in *Pearl*, Jonah's acceptance of his dependence on God, Gawain's discovery that what he is up against is in the final analysis himself, the reader's own training in moral apprehension in *Cleanness*. In this process, the supernatural can appear at first as a distraction from psychological depth, which substitutes narrative excitement for moral alertness and invites the protagonist to focus on something exotic and alien to himself. Brought into closer focus, however, it changes what one thought one knew about one's own nature. The natural, the known, is itself defamiliarised and made strange, so that it can be seen as if for the first time.

Patience

Of the four poems in the manuscript, *Patience* has the least supernatural material in it. This might seem surprising, when the story tells of a man pursued by a vengeful God and swallowed and regurgitated by a whale; but

---

2 The primary medieval associations of the number five, and with that the pentangle, are overwhelmingly rational and mathematical rather than magical: see Davis 1993.

here the stress is very much on God's control over the natural world through natural processes, not on His intervention to overturn them. Jonah's first error is simply to underestimate God as a force within this world; given his unpalatable errand, to warn the Ninevites of impending doom, he believes he can escape God's notice just by moving away –

> I wyl me sum oþer waye þat He ne wayte after. (86)[3]

In fact, of course, God is omnipresent in His created world, and Jonah's belief is naive in the extreme:

> He wende wel þat þat Wyʒ þat al þe world planted
> Hade no maʒt in þat mere no man for to greue. (111–12)

The resulting storm is not the sort found in *Cleanness*, that floods the world or accompanies the destruction of sinful cities: it is a storm such as regularly overwhelmed the tiny wooden ships that sailed Jonah's Eastern seas or the English Channel. The sailors' initial response is strictly practical, to throw out everything they can spare to lighten the ship. Only when that fails to offer any hope of preservation do they cast lots and throw out their passenger as well.

That the whale is swimming past at the crucial moment is an act of Providence, 'as Wyrde þen schaped' (247), but a Providence that uses natural means: the creature has been disturbed from its normal habitat in the depths, 'þe abyme', by the storm. It is, all the same, a 'wonder' that Jonah is saved, and still more so that he does not die in the whale's stomach:

> What lede moʒt leue bi lawe of any kynde
> Þat any lyf myʒt be lent so longe hym withinne? (259–60)

This, the whale's failure to digest Jonah, is the one thing in the poem that is signalled as being against the 'law of kind', the laws of nature, but it is a suspension of a natural process rather than a shift to a different order of experience. If the whale's belly signifies 'hellen wombe' (306), the poet does not elaborate on the idea (in contrast to Biblical exegesis, which gave a standard interpretation of the episode as a type of Christ's descent into Hell); and the depths from which Jonah cries (308) are literal and psychological (the sea, his near-despair) rather than eschatological, a figure of the next world. Nineveh is not destroyed by the supernatural intervention of an avenging God. The woodbine that grows up to provide Jonah with shade both grows and dies by natural processes.

The setting of *Patience* is the ordinary world, which is itself the scene of God's actions within the normal bounds of nature. It is, perhaps, easy to be

---

3   All quotations from Andrew and Waldron 1987.

patient when one is faced with something that transgresses the limits of earthly experience; Jonah has to learn patience under rather extraordinary circumstances, but not ones that take him beyond this world.

Cleanness

Cleanness shows with particular clarity the principle of moral enlightenment through encounters with an order beyond the natural. The poem demonstrates repeatedly that outward appearance alone is inadequate as a means to understanding: correct interpretation has to look beyond the physical to find a trans-natural meaning, in a process analogous to the exegetical insistence that the literal level of the Biblical text was not enough. The idea is established in the opening lines, with their reminder that priests can be spiritually filthy beneath their fine vestments. Such a moral and theological commonplace hardly counts as a supernatural element in the poem; but the kind of gap that is opened here between outward form and inward significance repeatedly, as the poem progresses, allows space for the divine to enter. *Things*, in this poem as in *Sir Gawain*, are very often not what they seem.

The lack of necessary connection between outward physical appearance and inner meaning requires constant attentiveness from the audience. The ark is constructed without sails, rudder or oars (417–20), for God alone is its guide and pilot: its outward form appears to invite disaster, its divine control ensures salvation. Such connections between outer and inner can result in something akin to shape-shifting, where physical form is itself transmuted by a process that has its origins beyond the natural world. Nebuchadnezzar undergoes a transformation from man to the form of a beast, so that his outward shape becomes a true signifier of his inward state; not until he understands God's grace is he metamorphosed back from beastlikeness to humanity. Lot's wife, transformed into a pillar of salt, is the victim of metamorphosis as punishment, the fixedness of the pillar signifying her looking back, the salt as a terrible revenge for her salting the angels' food (999). The point of these episodes is a moral one, but the poet is fully alert to the narrative attractiveness of making theologically correct miracle look like seductive marvel: the outward form of the punishments is much more what one expects to find in Ovid's tales of the interventions in the natural world by the pagan gods, or in stories of enchantresses or fairies, than in Biblical homily. In this poem, the boundary between the human and divine worlds is very permeable indeed. God Himself comes walking down the road to Abraham's dwelling as he lies in the shade under a tree; the fallen angels engender giants on the daughters of men; a disembodied hand appears in the course of Belshazzar's feast to write inscrutable words on the wall. The natural and supra-natural interpenetrate as freely, and with much the same sense of wonder, as happens with the passage between this world and the

Otherworld of fairy in near-contemporary romances such as *Sir Orfeo, Sir Launfal* or *Thomas of Erceldoune*.

This drawing of analogies between God's world and the Otherworld, between miracle and magic, serves as a good rhetorical and narrative strategy – the poet can draw on his listeners' predisposition to find magic more attractive and exciting than theology; but it can also serve to define a misreading, to show a sign being taken in the wrong way. The process is most explicit in the episode of the writing on the wall, which is described both within the narrative and by Baltazar himself as a 'ferly', a marvel with strong connotations of other-worldliness about it (1529, 1629).

> In þe palays principale, vpon þe playn wowe,
> In contrary of þe candlestik, þer clerest hit schyned,
> Þer apered a paume, with poyntel in fyngres,
> Þat watʒ grysly and gret, and grymly he wrytes;
> Non oþer forme bot a fust faylande þe wryste
> Pared on the parget, purtrayed lettres. (1531–6)

The poem's readers know the origin of the terrifying hand and its enigmatic writing to be divine; the pagan Baltazar takes them as supernatural in a more black magic sense, calling on sorcerers, raisers of spirits, and 'wychez and walkyries' to come to read them (1576–9). No such 'clerkes' can understand them, however, for they have no true spiritual insight. It needs Daniel, prophet of the true God, to interpret the signs correctly.

As this episode demonstrates, the poet is thoroughly alert to the possibilities of borrowing elements from the secular supernatural to make a spiritual point, and there are a number of other passages where he exploits marvels or magic in a similar fashion. The fearful storms in his accounts of Noah and the destruction of Sodom and Gomorrah overgo those raised by enchanters as widely separated in time as Medea and Prospero, or, to take examples closer to the poet, by the fairy king Oberon in the French romance *Huon of Bordeaux*, and by the action of pouring water onto a stone in the *Yvain* of Chrétien de Troyes and its Middle English translation.[4] These enchantments, however, show only a partial and temporary control of the natural order; God's control is absolute, and He can intervene in it whenever and however He wishes. The natural world is His creation; He establishes its order in the Garden of Eden, and confirms it in His promise to Noah that seed-time and harvest shall not fail (523–39). It is a world of generation and regeneration; the animals are sent out from the ark to multiply, each to its own particular habitat, and God's great speech to Abraham on the joys of 'þe play of paramorez' (700) confirms its place in the human as well as the animal order. This is why the sin of Sodom and Gomorrah is so intolerable, because it breaks

---

4   See the Tudor translation by Lord Berners (Lee 1882), chs. xxi, xxiii, xliv (pp. 64, 67, 156); *Ywain and Gawain* (Friedman and Harrington 1964), 319–84, 621–4.

God's order for His own creation. The site of the destroyed cities, around the Dead Sea, is accordingly represented as a rupture in the fabric of nature. The poet's account is largely borrowed from Sir John Mandeville's highly-coloured description of the marvels of the East, but he stresses further how contrary to the natural order the place is, sometimes by contrasting it with the ordinary world familiar to the reader, sometimes by frightening details of further unnaturalness. The pillar formed by Lot's petrified wife was, supposedly, such a marked topographical feature that it appears on the Mappa Mundi, the great thirteenth-century map of the world preserved at Hereford Cathedral; the poet calls attention to its strangeness by noting the paradoxically mundane detail that cattle use it as a salt-lick. Mandeville reports that the waters of the Dead Sea cause barrenness rather than fertility; iron floats in it, while a feather will sink; and it will not swallow any living thing. The poet startlingly enhances this last property by claiming that any creature thrown into it will survive until the Last Judgement (1029–32). The point of all this is precisely that it is counter-natural, *contra naturam* as the Latin text of Sir John Mandeville's *Travels* puts it; 'alle þe costes of kynde it combrez vchone' (1024), for it figures the unnaturalness of the sin that called down God's anger.[5] The fruit that grows beside the Dead Sea similarly breaks right order by being beautiful in appearance but containing foul-tasting ashes within the rind, so recalling the inwardly defiled priests of the opening lines. Once again, the outward appearance is inadequate as a sign of what lies within; physical form belies the symbolic order of divine meaning.

Pearl

The sign system that represents the supra-natural in *Pearl* is not misleading in the way it can be in *Cleanness*; it is rather that the dreamer cannot understand it, that he takes it literally, reads the thing for the symbol, and has to be educated by the maiden to interpret in a supra-natural sense what appears to him to be physical. Much of this happens within their debate, at a conceptual level; he has to learn new and transcendent meanings for ideas and images such as pearls, courtesy, Jerusalem – even for words such as 'more', which in this disorienting world of God's infinite abundance stands for an absolute that allows of no comparison; there can be no corresponding 'less'. The intellectual qualities of the debate distance such transcendent meanings from most narrative supernatural: instead of participating in exciting events,

---

5 Seymour 1963, 60, 61. The surviving Middle English translations postdate the *Gawain*-poet, and he is likely to have been working from the French; some of the details of his account, however (survival until the Last Judgement, the pillar of salt that was Lot's wife being licked by cows), do not seem to be from any known version of Mandeville, though the salt-lick does figure in the *Cursor Mundi* (Morris 1874–93, 2855–6).

the dreamer has to learn to translate one sign system (words describing the physical world) into another (this-worldly concepts standing for spiritual or divine ones) in a strenuous mental process. Even here, however, the otherness of the supra-natural order is stressed by the distance, even the contradictions, between the physical sign system and its heavenly signified. The objections of the workers in the vineyard to the unfair system of payment are, in earthly terms, unanswerable, but earthly unfairness can point beyond itself to divine justice. Blood in this world stains indelibly; in heaven, it washes into spotless whiteness (766; Revelation 7.14).

The supernatural in the narrative outside the debate takes a more physical outward form than this intellectual variety, being based on things rather than concepts. The opening section portrays this world only, with its processes of seedtime and harvest such as define the natural order in *Cleanness*; the pearl at this point remains a physical object, and the narrator is completely bound up in earthly grief. It is not until the second section, when the dreamer-narrator announces a shift to a world that resembles one of romance adventure and marvel, that the supra-natural order of the divine takes over, and even then he does not recognise it for what it is. In contrast to the landscapes of most dream visions, which portray the natural world raised to an ideal level, this landscape is anti-natural, inorganic; its blue-trunked trees bear silver leaves that one cannot imagine withering or fading, the intensity of light is beyond the power of any sun. His suggestion that it is a world of 'mervaylez' (64) is inadequate, but he also has to learn that it is not exactly a world of anything else either. The maiden indicates to him that the landscape does not have any real existence at all (295–6), that his encounter with her is not happening in the spatial and visual form that is all his understanding can comprehend. The full supra-natural quality of his experience has to be translated back into terms that carry some physical properties with them if he is to apprehend anything whatsoever.

If the dreamer's understanding is relentlessly this-worldly, the content of his vision is as relentlessly 'other'. The sources for the poet's description of the New Jerusalem lie in the Book of Revelation, but the inspiration for the dream landscapes seems to have as much to do with fairy worlds as with the Bible. The jewelled land in which those who have been lost from the mortal world are preserved brings reminiscences of romances such as *Sir Orfeo*, with its crystal-walled castle and dwellings of precious stones; that such kingdoms are often entered through a hill or a rock means that they too get their light from some source other than the sun or moon.[6] The maiden herself, of beauty beyond the natural (as the dreamer himself notes, 749), recalls fairy mistresses such as that in *Sir Launfal*, though her role in the poem – as an instructress

---

6 *Sir Orfeo* (Bliss 1966), 347–72, 387–401 (Auchinleck version); see also Patch 1950, 232. The comparison works in both directions: the *Orfeo* poet compares his fairy world to Paradise (376).

who will turn the dreamer's love away from her and towards Christ – is the opposite of theirs. The city that can only be entered by those of complete purity (971–2) is also reminiscent of supernatural tests in the Arthurian legends, such as the drinking-horn devised by Morgan le Fay that spills wine on a woman of less than perfect chastity, or the ship that can only be entered by those of perfect faith.[7] Such associations are not developed by the poet, however; they remain almost at the subliminal level, to give the reader something of the same sense of disorientation and suspense that the dreamer experiences.

The supra-natural in *Pearl* requires not a mere adjustment to the rules of a fairy culture, but an entire reorientation of the mind, a rethinking of what constitutes the rational. This is a world in which everyone is queen or king, where the highest form of deserving is to have done nothing, and where a Lamb with seven horns of red gold practises polygamy on a telephone-number scale. It is no wonder that the dreamer has trouble adjusting. Yet the culmination of the vision is not any of these: it is the moment when the dreamer sees the Lamb's wound, and feels the quintessentially human emotion of pity, compassion. The order of God may be alien to the mortal order, the 'worlde wete' of nature (761), but in the Incarnation and the Passion He stepped across the divide between the two to identify with suffering humanity. What the dreamer finally has to learn is that Christ suffered as man; the marvellous vision gives way in the final stanza to the everyday miracle of transubstantiation, the Real Presence of Christ in the Eucharist,

> Þat in þe forme of bred and wyn
> Þe preste vus schewez vch a daye. (1209–10)

It is immensely important that the poem should not leave the dreamer in his otherworld country, or end at the moment of his waking. It takes him back from the 'so strange a place' of his dream (175) to the vale of tears, the 'doel-dongeon', of the mortal world, but with a new understanding of the order of nature in which he lives. The poem is about what it means to be mortal; ultimately that meaning will embrace the New Jerusalem, but for the narrator, and for all readers of the poem, the lessons of the work have to be put into practice in this world.

Sir Gawain

Sir Gawain is a Christian poem, but it is not a religious one. Its affiliations lie with romances rather than with theological or homiletic literature. Its hero has to confront, not the disorienting and absolute Other of God, but a series

---

[7] These occur in the French prose *Tristan* and the *Grail*; for Malory's versions, see VIII.34, XVII.2 (Vinaver 1971, 270–1, 579–80).

of adventures that are never quite what they seem, and in which neither he nor the reader is quite sure what elements belong to the natural world and what to the worlds of magic and the supernatural. As in *Cleanness*, there are plenty of signs, and very little certainty as to how they might mean; but at least in *Cleanness* there is finally an unequivocal moral import behind them all. It is far from clear in *Sir Gawain* when something stands merely for itself and when it might be a sign for something else, nor whether that something else might be good or bad.[8]

A good deal of earlier criticism on the poem was devoted to uncovering the distant pagan origins and antecedents of those elements in it that do appear to be supernatural – green men who renew their lives at the New Year, Morgan le Fay's reputed origins in the Irish pantheon,[9] Gawain's own possible origins in a Celtic sun-god. Such sources can never be more than hypothetical, not only because it is highly unlikely that the *Gawain*-poet could have known them, but because they were almost entirely reconstructed, or invented, on the basis of scraps of evidence that are mostly widely separated from the poem temporally and geographically. They have none the less been taken as providing the meaning of the poem: what other medieval green men might be hypothesised to have been, the Green Knight must also be. The results, unsurprisingly, fail to illuminate the poem much, and recent scholarship has tended to move away from seeking out pagan parallels to reading the poem rather as if it were another moral homily like *Patience*, a cautionary tale about a man who failed to trust the Virgin and instead placed his faith in a supposedly magic girdle that had no power to protect him. This is, however, still not how the poem is written, and it leaves large areas of it unexplained. The Virgin specialises more in the salvation of souls than in the life-saving that Gawain so desperately wants. She is particularly powerful in protecting humankind from the assaults of the devil; but although Gawain does begin to wonder at one stage whether the Green Knight might be the devil, he is wrong. The poem is not pagan, whatever elements of fertility figures the Green Knight may retain; but its Christianity does not bring with it a defined theological meaning. As a romance, its connotations and range of reference belong with other romances, Arthurian in particular, where challengers arrive at the great feasts of the annual cycle, where Morgan le Fay is the implacable enemy of the renown of Arthur's court, and where magic objects may not be commonplace but are not impossible either.

The work portrays a clash between the ordinary human and knightly world of Arthur's court, and something that presents itself as profoundly other. The Christmas festivities at the start show the court enjoying a very good party, but not an implausibly exotic one; similar events would take place

---

8   Arthur 1987, 3 discusses how the poem both invites and resists decoding.
9   Attempts to link Morgan with the Irish Morrìgan, goddesses of war, are misguided, as the words are not cognate: see *Contributions* 1973–6, s.v. Morrìgan.

at Christmas in the contemporary royal court. The appearance of the Green Knight is all the more shocking by the contrast; this has not seemed to be a world where such things could happen. Even the adventures that Arthur is waiting for before he starts to eat, a traditional motif in Arthurian romances, are of the commonplace and possible variety: stories of combats, requests for jousts and so on. Coloured knights in other romances take their names from the colours of their armour and trappings alone: the Red Knight who is the novice Perceval's first opponent, for instance, or the various knights, including a Green Knight named Sir Pertholepe, whose defeat establishes the chivalric reputation of Gawain's young brother Gareth.[10] No one in *Sir Gawain* is prepared for a man and horse whose greenness extends to flesh and hair. Still more disturbing are the contradictory signs as to what he might be, and his refusal to fit into any possible categories (Spearing 1970, 179–80, 223; Arthur 1987, 3–4). The poet indicates that he is not a giant, but a man (141); but men do not have green skin and beards. He is not a wild man, a *wodwos*; those are savage creatures, unclothed and covered with hair, who live in the deep woods (Bernheimer 1952), where Gawain will encounter them later. Nor, despite his beard as big as a bush (182), is he a 'green man' of the kind it was currently fashionable to portray in church carvings, their heads emerging from and merging into foliage or with tendrils twisting out of their mouths (Basford 1978, esp. plates 48–80). Devils sometimes wear green, as the devil does in Chaucer's *Friar's Tale* (*Canterbury Tales*, Benson 1987, III. 1382; Robertson 1954; and see Brewer in this volume); but such an idea does not seem to occur at this point to the onlookers, though they do wonder whether he might be 'fantoume and fayryȝe' (240). One of the most disturbing things about the Green Knight, however, is the fact that he cannot easily be classed even as 'other'. His clothes are fine and of rich materials, such as any knight might value. He carries an axe, an obvious metonymy for destruction, in one hand, and in the other a holly bob, 'þat is grattest in grene when greuez ar bare' (207). As it stands, that line is a mere statement of fact; it may invite interpretation of the holly as a token of continuing life or a fertility symbol, but it falls well short of committing the poet to authorising such a meaning, and announces nothing about the Green Knight's nature or intentions. It does not suggest hostility, especially as messengers often carried branches to indicate their good intentions; but neither does the axe suggest peace. He asks for a Christmas game, which is to consist of having himself beheaded in exchange for a return blow – if it could ever happen – in a year's time. Malory's Gareth too has to face what seems to be a knight armed with an axe, who can also be dismembered and reconstituted; but he is a creation of 'subtyle craufftes' (Vinaver 1971, 205), and we are given a privileged view

---

[10] Chrétien de Troyes, *Le conte du Graal* (Lecoy 1975), 869–70, 948 etc. (Kibler 1991, 392–3), and its free Middle English adaptation, *Sir Percevall of Galles* (French and Hale 1964, 531–603), 603, 665 etc.; Vinaver 1971, 184–207, esp. 192 (VII.7–23, esp. 12).

of both his creation and his resuscitation. That the Green Knight's decapitation makes no difference to his behaviour, speech or control of his own actions makes him much more terrifying.

That irreconcilable variety of the signs concerning the Green Knight, and their contradictory meanings, continues throughout the work. His assurance to Gawain that he cannot help but find him sounds very like a periphrasis for death; the Old Man in Chaucer's *Pardoner's Tale* gives a similar assurance to the rioters who are seeking Death to kill him – 'Noght for youre boost he wole him no thyng hyde' (*Canterbury Tales*, Benson 1987, VI. 764). The guide's words to Gawain about the denizen of the Green Chapel, that he kills everyone who comes by, whether knight, priest or churl (the three estates that composed medieval society), similarly suggest that Gawain is on his way to meet a personified Death, with whom no one can survive an encounter. The Green Chapel itself, which sounds godly though odd (chapels are not normally green), turns out to be a barrow, a mound of no great distinctiveness; but the threat it contains enlarges any superstitious associations it might carry to make it diabolical in Gawain's eyes, to the point where he wonders if he might be about to encounter the devil. That cannot be right, given that the figure he is about to meet is his host in a different shape, and he has celebrated Mass in his household every morning (one of the standard tests for devils being whether they can endure the presence of the Eucharist);[11] but neither Gawain nor the reader as yet knows that the two are identical. Other suggestions as to interpretation, less explicit in the poem and therefore less likely though not necessarily impossible, have also been made: that the Green Knight is associated with Christ, for instance, through his appearances at Advent and the Judgement of his second coming; or that he represents the Old Law, an argument related to the fact that New Year's Day, the cusp of the year when Gawain has to go to meet what he expects to be certain death, is also the Feast of the Circumcision (Shoaf 1984, 49–54).

The possibilities are too many, and too contradictory: death and life, God and the devil. What they all have in common – and what Gawain himself never seems to doubt – is that the Green Knight must mean something beyond himself: he cannot simply be a knight who is green. Yet when he gives his own summary explanation of who he is – that he is called Bertilak de Hautdesert, and that he had been sent in such fashion to Arthur's court by Morgan le Fay in order to scare Guinevere to death – that is just what he asks Gawain to believe. The poet does not necessarily endorse Bertilak's statement: the last view he allows us of him is in his shape as Green Knight, not as Bertilak, riding off to an unknown destination, 'whither-so-euer he wolde' (2478). The poet never commits himself in his own voice as to whether the

---

11   There is an example of such a test for theological acceptability in one of the lais of Marie de France, *Yonec*, in which a lady has the Eucharist administered to a suitor who shape-shifts between man and bird.

Green Knight 'really' is Sir Bertilak under enchantment, or whether he really is primarily the Green Knight (as the guide suggests, with his account of the grisly inhabitant of the Green Chapel) who is merely playing the host as a means of waylaying Gawain. Since the poet is creating a fiction, he has no need to explain or define. He need not worry about the 'reality' behind the story, because it is story, not fact. The very lack of explanation, much of the time, is what makes for most of the suspense, and for the final moral force of the poem.

The role that the Green Knight assigns to Morgan le Fay would on first reading seem to militate against such mysteriousness. Her habits, familiar from other romances, define her as a specialist in magic and the supernatural, so she should be ideally cast to be the motive force of the action; but neither in narrative detail nor in import does his explanation fit with the rest of the poem. She may have intended to test the reputation of Arthur's court, but Bertilak is very clear that it was he himself who put his wife up to wooing Gawain, and there is no suggestion that Morgan even knows about his testing. It can hardly be her skills in necromancy that have created the girdle, since its magic properties turn out to be non-existent. The most shocking of all the Green Knight's revelations to Gawain, however, has nothing to do with Morgan's supernatural powers, but everything to do with Gawain's own nature: that she is his aunt. His prime antagonist has been, not a strange green challenger who has seemed to represent everything that Arthur's court is not, but one of his own kin.[12] In the meticulous mirror-symmetry of the poem's structure – the Troy references at the beginning and end framing the scenes at Camelot, the arming and the blows inside those, the three hunts and bedroom scenes at the centre – this revelation is reflected exactly by Gawain's claim at the start that the only good thing about him is Arthur's, his uncle's, blood in his body (357). It may indeed have been Gawain's position between the two, equal kin both to his mother's chivalric brother and to her necromantic sister, that suggested to the poet Gawain's peculiar potential as the central character. The Gawain of the Arthurian romances is always associated with Arthurian knightliness; but this Gawain also has, quite literally in his blood, the strains of his subversive and imperfect kinswoman. Here, it is not her supernatural powers that matter so much as their kinship, their shared nature.

None of this amounts to a denial that there is a supernatural element in the poem: it is undeniably there in the Green Knight, whether he is Bertilak turned green or the Green Knight turned human. Such shape-shifting, and his survival of decapitation, lie decisively outside the normal limits of the physical world. There are plenty of other places in the romance, however,

[12] For an interpretation of Morgan as a character in the hero's family romance in a more psychoanalytical sense, see Brewer 1988c.

where one cannot tell whether something is supernatural. Gawain comes upon the castle, for instance, when he has been praying for somewhere to take shelter and hear Mass (736–9, 754–6). The rhetorical construction of the scene allows for three explanations of its sudden appearance: the natural one, that when riding through a forest it is impossible to see more than a few yards ahead; the miraculous one, that the castle appears as an answer to Gawain's prayer; or the supernatural one, that it is in some sense an other-worldly castle that can materialise when required. The first of these does not necessarily exclude either of the other two, and so leaves the question of what the castle is, how Gawain or the reader should interpret it, or indeed whether it requires any interpretation at all, completely unresolved. That it turns out to be the site of Gawain's temptation suggests retrospectively that the second explanation must be wrong, unless the Virgin is given to answering prayers in very backhanded ways; Gawain would have been better off without any answer at all. The third possibility, that it is in some sense a supernatural manifestation, does not occur to Gawain, but it is a meaning made available to the reader by other romances. The Grail castle appears to Perceval in Chrétien de Troyes' *Conte del Graal* when there similarly seems to be no shelter to be seen, and he is told later that there is none for miles around (Lecoy 1975, 3029–45, 3452–9; Kibler 1991, 418, 423); and in *Huon of Bordeaux*, Oberon creates a fairy castle with an abundance of towers, and later a palace too, for the sake of the hero (Lee 1882, chs. xxii, xxv (pp. 64, 67)).

The same question as to whether or not something is supernatural arises, much more crucially for the meaning of the poem, in relation to the girdle. The lady assures Gawain that he will not be killed while he is wearing it, and he does indeed survive; and again romance expectations are on the lady's side, since it is common for heroes to have some kind of magic assistance, and not infrequent for them to complete apparently impossible tasks through the help of women (Jason's achievement of the Golden Fleece with the aid of Medea was one example widely known in the Middle Ages; and in one of the Charlemagne romances, the *Sowdone of Babylone* (Hausknecht 1881), the heroine's magic girdle keeps the Peers from starvation (2299–318). Finally, however, the girdle too works in a way that says more about the human than the supernatural. It raises the problems associated with any talisman of invulnerability: there is nothing heroic about being incapable of injury, no courage where there is no reason for fear. Gawain, indeed, never quite seems to trust the girdle despite the lady's assurances as to its magical powers: he spends a grim night after he has taken it, thinking on what is going to happen to him the next day, rather than sleeping the sleep of security. The poet's solution to the problem of reconciling magic with heroism is peculiarly radical. For long, in the more thoughtful romances, writers had used magic in surprising ways – used it, in particular, non-magically, or against the hero, or as a way of bringing out something in himself. So Arthur fights against Excalibur; Horn, hero of one of the earliest English romances, can only activate the 'magic' in his ring that will enable him to win battles against fearsome odds if he also thinks of his beloved who gave it to him; the lovers Floris and Blauncheflour, condemned to be burned after being found in bed together, each refuse to take the ring that will give its bearer magic protection, and are saved instead by the pity engendered in their judge by such strength of love (Cooper 1976). In none of these cases is the magic seen to work magically, yet the audience is never invited to be sceptical, to doubt its capacity. In one instance, when it does visibly work, it is immediately put out of action as unwanted: the Isolde of Gottfried von Strassburg's version of the Tristan story is sent by her lover a magic dog with a bell round its neck, the sound of which makes it impossible to feel unhappy. Isolde's reaction is to keep the dog for the sake of the giver, but she removes the bell so that she will not be happy while Tristan grieves over their separation.

The green girdle is the precise opposite of those. Horn's and Floris's rings, Isolde's bell, Arthur's sword, all show up something beyond the common-place in their owners: supra-human love in Isolde and Floris and Blauncheflour, extraordinary courage in Arthur, something of both in Horn. The poet never excludes the possibility that the girdle should be taken as magic, though there must be few readers who would finally accept the lady's statement, that the girdle will protect Gawain from death, rather than Berti-lak's, that it alone is the reason for his injury. The girdle's lack of supernatural qualities finally serves to measure, not how far Gawain has progressed beyond what any mortal could manage, but his failure to advance, to become supra-human. The pentangle in its entirety was a 'bitoknyng of trawþe' (626), *trouthe* being a quality that, as both Chaucer and Langland note, humankind can share with God, and that Langland further insists belongs particularly to knights.[13] The girdle, by contrast is a 'token of vntrawþe' (2509), of a failure on Gawain's part to live up to the highest chivalric standard that also has the potential to reflect God's image in man. Gawain may, as the Green Knight tells him, be like a pearl among white peas, but in his own eyes and so far as his own standards proclaimed in the pentangle are concerned, he is a failure. What catches him out is not even the striking sins he accuses himself of and from which the poet is so careful to exonerate him – covetousness, cowardice – but sheer love of life, instinct for survival: an instinct he shares with the animals on the hunt, and which is the lowest common denominator of being alive, of belonging to the order of *kynde*. Even in *Sir Gawain*, it is in the natural order, not the supernatural, that the most important things happen.

---

[13] See e.g. Chaucer's *Balade de Bon Conseyl* ('Trouthe'), and Schmidt 1978, I. 85–104.

12

The Gawain-Poet as a Vernacular Theologian

NICHOLAS WATSON

Introduction

When Gawain returns to Camelot wearing his 'token of vntrawþe' (G 2509), the green belt that has saved his life at the cost of a nick in the neck, he finds the symbol of his humiliation turned into a badge of honour by a brotherhood of knights pleased by his survival and less scrupulous than he now wishes he had been about how he managed it. Forgiven by everyone, even Bertilak, who pardons him without imposing any further penance (G 2390–94), Gawain's continuing remorse so closely resembles injured self-esteem as to be hard for most readers to take seriously. After all, while it may be that he has not entirely lived up to the ideals figuratively inscribed on his shield, he has only 'lakked a lyttel' (G 2366); if he has lied by omission, he has also heroically resisted sex with Bertilak's wife. The green belt which Arthur's company will now wear offers an ironic comment, certainly, on the extent to which the pentangle's 'endeles knot' (G 630) is translatable into reality. But the reconciliation of Christian and chivalric ideals the pentangle represents remains basically unthreatened.[1]

From the viewpoint of medieval Christian theology, there is little wrong with the court's reaction to Gawain's sin. As 'active' rather than 'contemplative' Christians – lay people who live 'in the world,' rather than being separated from it like monks or hermits – Gawain and his colleagues can never in practice achieve the perfection to which they must aspire, but must expect to live their lives in a cycle of venial sin, repentance and penance, and perhaps spend time in purgatory before finally attaining heaven. Despite his high ideals, Gawain, by the nature of his profession, belongs to a group theologians termed the *mediocriter boni*, rather than the spiritual elite known as the *perfecti*.[2] Indeed, his real error (like that of his more judgmental critics) may be his failure to recognize this fact: to realize that, having confessed his

---

[1] All citations from the poems are to the edition of Andrew and Waldron (1978).
[2] For this terminology, which was widespread in Latin discussions of the relative levels of spiritual perfection which were thought to pertain to different states of life, see Watson 1991, 9–15.

sin to Bertilak and been forgiven (in a scene which makes heavy use of the language of sacramental confession), he cannot continue to treat his sin as unforgivable. Yet from the viewpoint of the rest of the *Pearl* manuscript, the ending of *Sir Gawain and the Green Knight* (*Gawain*) can seem peculiar in its relative indulgence towards imperfection: an indulgence which seems at odds with the fierce insistence on purity found in *Cleanness* and *Pearl* itself. If the pearl of salvation is so 'wemlez, clene and clere' that only those who 'forsake þe worlde wode' can hope to 'porchace' it (*Pe* 737, 744–5), or if 'On spec of a spote may spede to mysse/ Of þe syȝte of þe Souerayn þat syttez so hyȝe' (*Cl* 551–2), then it seems odd that the court of an earthly sovereign, Arthur, can be represented as making Gawain's sin, however slight, into 'þe renoun of þe Rounde Table' (*G* 2519), without attracting criticism from a poet who is elsewhere so stern. It is not surprising that *Gawain* has sometimes been thought of as so different from the more didactic poems that accompany it as to contradict many of their arguments.

This chapter takes another look at the theology of the *Gawain*-poet, using the topic of purity as the focal point of a broader enquiry into the poet's role as a communicator of religious teaching in the vernacular to an audience of lay (and perhaps primarily male) aristocrats: an audience which saw itself flatteringly embodied, I suggest, in the figure of Gawain himself. By thinking of *Pearl*, *Cleanness* and *Patience* as written for readers whose ideals were more or less Gawain's, I hope to bring out something both of the theological strangeness of these poems (not only from the viewpoint of most kinds of theological writing in Latin but from that of the most nearly comparable vernacular materials as well) and of the logic underlying that strangeness. The poems do, so I believe, advance a common set of theological positions, which are better adapted for a lay readership than appears if we take their emphasis on radical purity at face value. Indeed, they represent one of the most interesting of all the fourteenth-century attempts to direct religious instruction at the laity in general and the aristocracy in particular. Yet we shall see that both the form and content of this instruction often represent choices on the part of the poet which cannot readily be paralleled elsewhere. An important part of my task here is to describe and, if possible, attempt to account for these choices.

To think of *Pearl*, *Cleanness* and *Patience* in relation to their theological views is to see them within the larger context of late-medieval English religiosity, and particularly of the rapid development, from 1350 on, of a body of vernacular writing which was more and more aware of, anxious to shape, and in turn shaped by the needs of lay readers: a body of writing which includes pastoral or devotional works (*Pore Caitif*, *Dives and Pauper*, Hilton's *Scale of Perfection*), a large and varied body of writings associated with the Lollards, and much else, from Passion meditations, to Lives of Christ, to religious polemic. To the extent that all the poems incorporate biblical para-phrase, they can be situated within a tradition which looks back to narrative poems like *Cursor Mundi* and the *Northern Homily Cycle* (both written c.1300), and alongside a number of little studied late fourteenth-century expositions of 'God's law': *The Book to A Mother*, *The Lyfe of Soule*, a work edited as *Fourteenth-Century Biblical Versions* and, longest of all, the enormous paraphrase that forms the prologue to the Wycliffite Bible itself.[3] All this religious writing is remarkably diverse and shows the extent to which the simple model of pastoral instruction first derived from the Fourth Lateran Council of 1215 – which assumed that the clergy's job was largely to *catechise* the laity – was giving way to more conflicted ideas of what it was appropriate for lay readers to know, and how the relations between such readers and the clerics who wrote for them should be articulated. For reasons I explore in detail elsewhere (Watson 1995), much of the religious writing of the time displays a new respect for the laity (particularly the aristocratic laity), and uses the vernacular not only in the way we would anticipate, as an instrument for conveying already formulated teachings, but also as a tool for exploring Christian truths from the often distinct perspective of the 'mother tongue': increasingly (as the use of French declined) a language of universal access, which also came to *symbolise* such access. From Chaucer's *Parliament of Fowles* and *Canterbury Tales*, to Langland's depictions of the 'field full of folk,' Piers's half-acre, and Truth's pardon, the poetry of the period is full of images of communality which can be seen as symbols for fourteenth-century English society, bound together not only by a common (if bitterly contested) faith and social structure but now also (despite dialect differences) a common language. Similar images, implicit or explicit, lie behind much of the religious prose of the period, whatever its theological emphases, and express a major preoccupation of the time. The parable of the vineyard in *Pearl*, the doomed cities of Sodom and Babylon in *Cleanness*, and the pardoned Nineveh in *Patience* are part of a much more extensive body of thinking about communal faith and morality.[4]

Pearl, *Cleanness* and *Patience* are thus part of a broad contemporary movement in which religious ideas of all kinds were quickly becoming accessible to vernacular readers; and we shall see that all three poems also have a number of more specific points of contact with different parts of that movement. But for every similarity we note between the poems and the larger world of late medieval English religious writing, it is possible to point to an equally suggestive difference – and here I will outline two which are to be of special importance in what follows. First, if the direction of much of the

---

3   For these and other vernacular theologies mentioned in this chapter, see the relevant chapters of the *Manual of Writings in Middle English*, especially Talbert and Thomson 1970 ('Wyklif and His Followers'), Raymo 1986 ('Works of Philosophical and Religious Instruction') and Lagorio and Sargent 1993 ('English Mystical Writings'). A list of religious writings in English written between c.1300 and c.1500 is given as the Appendix to Watson 1995.

4   For a study of notions of community in fourteenth-century England, see Aers 1988.

period's vernacular theology is set towards opening religious thinking up to a wider audience, this is true of these poems (despite their composition in the English vernacular, rather than in French) only in a special sense. When the Wycliffite Bible and its orthodox 'reply,' Nicholas Love's *Mirror of the Blessed Life of Jesus Christ*, were copied in the early fifteenth century, the dialect in which copies were made (that of the Central Midlands) was selected to be as widely comprehensible as possible (Sargent 1992, lxiv); when Hilton wrote book II of *The Scale*, Julian of Norwich the long text of her *Revelation of Love*, and Langland the B-text of *Piers Plowman*, each writer showed a similar concern to speak, if they could, to what Julian calls 'al myn even cristen' (Glasscoe 1978, 10.7–8). The *Gawain*-poet's dialectal and stylistic choices point in the opposite direction, towards establishing close contact with a lay audience able to understand (perhaps even in part *constituted* around their ability to understand) an ornate, and regionally specific, vocabulary. For all his interest in communality, he writes for a provincial aristocracy: not for the notionally universal audience of 'simple men and wymmen of gode wille' (as the prologue to *Pore Caitif* has it) addressed by other religious writers of his time but for a small, socially particularised part of that audience. As we shall see, this orientation has clear implications for his theology.

Second, a dominant element in the more sophisticated forms of late medieval English religiosity is the importance given to affective religious experience, the emphasis on the inner life of intentions, feelings and thoughts. English affectivity comes in many guises, from Rolle's famously fervid optimism, to the devout intensity of meditative writings like *A Talking of the Love of God* or *The Prickynge of Love*, to the abjection of Henry of Lancaster's *Livre de Seyntz Medicines*, or the *Instructions to A Devout Layman*. But even works whose major emphasis is on public practice, not private devotion – as seems the case, for example, with *Piers Plowman*, *Dives and Pauper*, and Lollard treatises like *The Lantern of Light* – tend to acknowledge at some level the primacy of the interior life over the exterior; if the Lollards generated little by way of devotional literature, they had as firm a sense as anyone of the importance of a proper interior disposition. The *Gawain*-poet, I shall argue, is deeply unusual among the more sophisticated religious writers of the time in his indifference to interiority and his insistence (despite his writing a whole poem on the virtue of patience) on the primacy of word and deed over thought and feeling – of what Gawain says and does with Bertilak's wife as she tries to seduce him over the (wholly undescribed) inner struggles her desirability might be assumed to generate. In this respect, the poet's closest points of contact are less with either the Lollards or with the spiritual traditions represented by the English 'mystics' (with whom he has often been compared in discussions of *Pearl*) than with the more matter-of-fact religiosity embodied in pastoral works such as those being produced in almost the same part of England, no more than two decades after his time, by John Mirk (the influential *Festial* and *Instructions for Parish Priests*). Such a view needs, of course, to be coordinated with an assessment of the poet's awareness of many different traditions (the theology of virginity and of visions, medieval sign theory, exegetical writings, and so on), and especially, I think, of his striking articulation of the nature of divine power and covenant, whose roots seem to lie as much in fourteenth-century academic theology as in the world of pastoralia. But for all the complexity of his artistry and the sophistication of his personal educational background, the view of the Christian life to which he gives expression is for the most part conscientiously simple.

All this talk of the *Gawain*-poet as a theologian may seem to be ignoring what most readers find the central fact about his works: their deep self-consciousness as highly wrought aesthetic entities, whose theological and didactic arguments are subordinated (especially in *Pearl* and *Gawain*, the poems most modern readers prefer) to a positively obtrusive sense of craft, of verbal 'coyntyse.' But in fact it is this aspect of the poems around which their specifically aristocratic articulation of the Christian life is formed and which must be a major concern of this analysis. *Pearl*, *Cleanness* and *Patience* represent a sustained attempt to translate an ancient tradition of thought concerning the centrality of purity in the Christian life – a tradition going back at least to the virginity literature of the fourth and early fifth centuries – from its old context in monastic and anchoritic writing to address the needs and aspirations of a lay elite. This act of cultural translation has both ethical and metaphysical dimensions. In ethical terms, we shall see that the idea of purity itself is redefined, so that a concept which had long been associated (on the level of the body) with virginity and (on that of the soul) with an attitude of abject humility comes to signify, at least in part, a set of rules for decorous conduct, which fuse Christian and courtly into a self-consistent code whose manifestations are public, not private, and which is designed for socially and sexually active laypeople. In metaphysical terms, we shall see that this redefinition depends on the creation of a structure of associations between the aristocratic society for which the poetry was devised, the complex aesthetic mode in which it was written, and the harmony of the cosmos – crafted, as it is thought to be, by a supremely complex and thus perfect divine creator, a creator who is at once ultimate poet and ultimate ruler. Rather as Hildegard of Bingen viewed both the convent she governed and the synaesthetic visionary works she wrote there as microcosms of heaven, paradises brought down to earth (Newman 1987), so the *Gawain*-poet seems to have perceived both his own intricate verbal creations and the self-consciously rarefied court culture within which they position themselves as earthly images of heavenly reality. This perception is not without an ironic sense (one absent in Hildegard) that earthly images are radically imperfect: a sense that often surfaces in these poems, from the jeweller's expulsion from Paradise at the end of *Pearl*, to the accounts of the pervasiveness of human sin in *Cleanness*, to the chapter of accidents which besets Jonah in *Patience* and the final scene of *Gawain* with which I began. Indeed, we will be seeing in this irony a quite different view of the relation between a sin-stained earth and heaven, in which the emphasis is on the virtual incommensurability of the two orders of being, which can be brought together only by divine grace or, fictionally, poetic craft. But by focusing as far as possible on the surfaces of things – on the public life of religious and secular observance, rather than the inner world of shifting thoughts and feelings – it does seem that the poet unites earthly and heavenly forms of courtliness in more than an *ad hoc* way: making the ideals represented by Gawain into a ladder by which readers (in the words of *An Ureisun of God Almihti*) can 'stihen [. . .] to þe steorren' (Thomson 1968, 76–7). In the following sections, which offer readings of *Pearl*, *Cleanness* and *Patience* in turn, I shall attempt to show how each of these poems offers a distinct, but closely related contribution to this over-arching didactic project.

Pearl

> To pay þe Prince oþer sete saȝte
> Hit is ful eþe to þe god Krystyin;
> For I haf founden Hym, boþe day and naȝte,
> A God, a Lorde, a frende ful fyin.
> Ouer þis hyul þis lote I laȝte,
> For pyty of my perle enclyin,
> And syþen to God I hit bytaȝte,
> In Krystez dere blessyng and myn,
> Þat in þe forme of bred and wyn
> Þe preste vus schewez vch a daye.
> He gef vus to be His homely hyne
> Ande precious perlez vnto His pay.
>   Amen. Amen. (*Pe* 1201–12)

There is initially something unexpected about the way that *Pearl*, the most intricate poem in Middle English, completes its highly symmetrical, indeed notionally spherical, design with a stanza asserting that pleasing God is 'ful eþe to þe god Krystyn': leaving us with a one-line commendation of the pearl to Christ and an equally perfunctory, but apparently confident, gathering in of all the poem's Christian readers to the household of God.[5] It is not plausible

---

[5] This discussion of *Pearl* has in part grown out of an attempt to respond to issues raised in David Aers's fine essay, 'The Self Mourning: Reflections on *The Pearl*' (1993), whose emphasis on the consolatory aspects of the poem provides a counterbalance to the didactic reading offered here. Readers should be aware that my argument differs sharply from most attempts to read the poem theologically, which in general terms assume that it has been heavily influenced by the literature of mysticism, and often take the poem (in my view wrongly, see further note 13) as a fictional account of an *itinerarium mentis in deum* (a journey of the soul to God). For this scholarly tradition, see, e.g., Blenkner 1968; Bogdanos 1983; Astell 1990 (chapter 5).

to assume that we are meant to view the stanza with irony, as giving yet more evidence of the jeweller's inability to learn. After all, he does here relinquish the pearl at last, transferring his layman's gaze from the 'hyul' which hides his daughter's rotting body to the hands of a priest as they mysteriously reveal, 'in þe forme of bred and wyn,' the resurrected body of her spouse (who now appears as the jeweller's own 'frende ful fyin,' no longer, as before, a pitiless and impersonal 'Wyrde' (*Pe* 249)); and the structural parallel between his submission to God and the poem's to its own finitude makes it impossible for us not to take his closing words as constituting, in some sense, its moral. Yet it is not immediately obvious how the jeweller can derive so comforting a lesson from his bruising encounter with eternity, nor how the poet can reconcile this picture of the 'eþe' of Christian living with his analysis of the profound gap between earth and heaven, which at some points appear as directly opposed orders of reality (see, e.g., the threefold use of 'kynde' in *Pe* 265–76). As a result, there is a temptation to ignore or resist this conclusion: a temptation felt especially strongly by a critical tradition which tends to extremes of interpretative complexity unparalleled in non-Chaucerian Middle English studies. It is admittedly true that an account of the poem that takes its ending seriously fails to support readings of the poem as a mystical journey, a meditation on Christian sign theory, or a study of the process of grieving (see Blenkner 1968; Baldwin 1984; Vance 1991; Aers 1993); and the reading offered here is doubtless in some ways reductive. As we shall see, however, such a reading does have the advantage of making sense both of what we can guess of the poem's aristocratic context and of the particularity of its theology.

Like most of the poem's readers, I take it that *Pearl* was probably occasioned by the death of a young girl, perhaps named Margaret, for whose father the poem was written (see, e.g., E. Wilson 1976, 1). Because I believe that the author of *Pearl* also wrote *Cleanness* and *Patience*, both of which (in view of their status as versified homilies) must surely be the work of a celibate cleric, I doubt the more romantic possibility that the dead girl was the poet's own daughter. Like those works, we shall see that *Pearl* makes sense as the product of a relationship between the poet and his first reader in which the latter is both the poet's patron and his spiritual charge – a relationship consistent with a situation in which the poet was a secular priest or friar working in an aristocratic household, now as secretary, now as confessor. Such a situation is much more complex than Chaucer found himself in when penning *Pearl*'s closest English analogue, *The Book of the Duchess*. Involving the poet as it does in a relationship with his audience which is both deferential and authoritative, some such situation may explain the unusual interplay in the poem between its consolatory and instructive functions: an interplay which, whatever its cause, is responsible for some of the most doctrinally idiosyncratic verse in Middle English.

As consolation, the poem (fictionally) works, first, by reassuring the jeweller that his pearl is not dead but glorified in heaven; second, by forcing him to confront the selfishness of his grief, concerned as it is with his loss, not with his daughter's gains. The reader is expected to have various attitudes to this process, sometimes identifying with the jeweller, sometimes feeling that sense of superiority to his failings which the *Gawain*-poet always offers us in our attitudes towards all his main characters (including, in *Cleanness*, even God; *Cl* 561–2). Like the narrator in *The Book of the Duchess*, who fails to understand the man in black's densely metaphorical courtly language and so is puzzled as to the cause of his grief, the jeweller at first cannot grasp how the language of heavenly *courtesie* is meant, making a series of crude assumptions about his daughter's situation and what he himself can now expect from her. It was often asserted by the more elitist clerical theorists of the religious life that uneducated lay people were incapable of thinking except in this naively 'carnal' fashion (Watson 1995, 840–6); and we could see *Pearl's* portrayal of the jeweller as invoking such a view only to work against it by holding it up to his lay audience's scrutiny. If so, however, we must also see the poem as making significant theological concessions to readers whose apprehension of heavenly reality remains dominated by images of social status, and who (despite their social superiority to him) have by no means left all aspects of the jeweller's point of view behind. For it is just those images, wrapping the pearl maiden as they do in the vague splendour of her role as a debutante heavenly queen, around which both the poem's consolatory and its instructive functions revolve.

One of the less often noted sources of the poem's depiction of the pearl maiden is the specialised kind of writing aimed at career virgins (e.g., anchoresses and nuns) known as the virginity treatise, of which the most notable English example is the thirteenth-century West Midlands work *Hali Meiðhad*.[6] At least in general terms, it is from the virginity tradition that *Pearl* derives its emphases on the relationships between heavenly purity, sexual 'intactness' and mystical marriage and to which, I suggest, it owes its deep sense of the beauty of the unsullied and pure. If it is because of her innocence that the pearl maiden is so early crowned a queen in heaven (*Pe* 613–36), it is because she is 'coronde clene in *vergynté*' (*Pe* 767, my emphasis) that she becomes not only a queen but a spouse of Christ, one of those select souls 'to Krystez chambere þat art ichose' (*Pe* 904), to whom he says ' "Cum hyder to Me, My lemman swete,/ For mote ne spot is non in þe" ' (*Pe* 763–4; see Canticles 4:7–8). As a good deal of the first part of the jeweller's dialogue with his daughter is designed to establish (VIII–XI), all the saved are crowned kings and queens 'of alle þe reme' of heaven (*Pe* 446–8), and in that sense are given the equal reward (the 'peny') the lord of the vineyard offers his labourers (the 'homly hyne' of the poem's final stanza, *Pe* 1211). But, as the

---

6   The best succinct study of the genre is in Millett 1982; for an edition and translation of *Hali Meiðhad* and further bibliography see also Millett and Wogan-Browne 1990.

later phases of that dialogue (XIII–XV) make equally clear, only a perfect soul – one 'þat hade *neuer* teche' – can be not simply a queen but 'a worthyly wyf' to the Lamb of God (*Pe* 845–6, my emphasis): a member of the 144,000 'maydennez,' or God's 'newe fryt,' who alone can sing his 'nwe songe' (*Pe* 869, 894, 882; Rev. 4, 14) because they alone are truly 'lyk to Hymself of lote and hwe' (*Pe* 896).[7] In referring to the martyrs of Revelation as 'maydennez' (a word which in Middle English predominantly refers to women), *Pearl* is clearly (*pace* Robertson 1950a, b) drawing on the virginity tradition's interpretation of Revelation 14 as referring to female virgins in particular, since it is this group of whom the language of marriage to Christ can be used with special appropriateness. 'ȝef [meiðhad] is Godd leof þet is himself swa ilich, hit nis na wunder, for he is leoflukest þing, ant buten eauereuch bruche, ant wes eauer ant is cleane ouer alle þing, and ouer alle þinge luueð cleannesse' (*Hali Meiðhad* 10.10–12).[8] In *Pearl*, as in *Hali Meiðhad*, virginity and the absolute purity it symbolizes is more precious to Christ than anything.

Part of *Pearl*'s function as a consolatory poem is thus fulfilled by informing its reader not only that the pearl maiden is in heaven but that the very fact of her early death has caused her to become someone special there, a figure of surpassing power in the eternal courts; and it does this by invoking a tradition of thinking about female virginity in which sexual 'intactness' in this life is given a highly elevated spiritual interpretation in regard to the next. Yet for all the importance this tradition assumes in thus elevating the pearl maiden, the poem's line of argument about her status also constitutes a major disruption of a millennium of thought about virginity and its rewards. Treatises like *Hali Meiðhad* were written to assure career virgins that their heroic, lifelong abstinence is worthwhile, since it earns them a special place at the side of Christ as his spotless spouse. Despite the great importance they attribute to physical virginity in and of itself, such treatises are clear that virgins deserve their reward because they *endure*, living their lives in a state of suffering somewhat akin to martyrdom (Millett and Wogan-Browne 1990, xv–xx). In *Pearl*, however, the whole notion of heroic suffering which is basic to the medieval ideal of virginity has gone, to be replaced by an ideal of innocence which is no more than an extension of the concept of physical 'intactness' to the rest of life. Here, the brides of the lamb are no longer career virgins but children, who are claimed to be superior to everyone precisely because they

---

7 I take it that the first stanza of section VIII, in which the jeweller questions the pearl maiden's claim to be a queen ('Art þou þe quene of heuenes blwe?' 423), is intended to initiate one phase of the discussion, to do with equality of reward, while the similar (and apparently repetitive) question at the end of section XIII ('What kyn þyng may be þat Lambe/ Pat þee wolde wedde unto Hys wyf?' 771–2) initiates a separate phase, this one to do with mystical marriage.
8 'If what is so like God is dear to him, it is no wonder, for he is more beautiful than anything, and without any sin, and always was and is pure above all things, and above all things loves purity' (translation in Millett and Wogan-Browne 1990, 11).

have *done nothing,* and have therefore retained all the pristine integrity with which they came forth from the baptismal font (*Pe* 657–60): an integrity which everyone else, without exception, is deemed to have lost. This is why the 'pakke of joly juele,' Christ's spouses, among whom the jeweller at last sees his 'lyttel quene'(*Pe* 929, 1147), do not apparently even include career virgins, consisting not partly but *solely* of baptized infants (*Pe* 841–52): a group who do not figure in most discussions of virginity. In view of the way these infants replace the career virgins the virginity treatises describe as Christ's brides, the jeweller's claim that the pearl maiden has supplanted 'so mony a comly onvunder cambe,' religious women who 'for Kryst han lyued in much stryf' (*Pe* 775–6), is less naive than is usually assumed.[9]

The poet's version of the mystical marriage of virgins to Christ can be defended in various ways, most convincingly as a consequence of his reading of Revelation 14 in its liturgical context as the epistle for the feast of the Innocents (Hart 1927; Bishop 1968; 104–12). Yet the poem's deliberate distortion of an ancient and, in the fourteenth century, still established body of thinking about virginity remains extremely unusual. While we, of course, must not assume that something has to be drastically amiss when a literary fiction like *Pearl* fails to operate according to the logic of a religious treatise, it is proper that we ask what the significance of its treatment of the theological issue of divine reward may be, and particularly what effect it has on the poem's role not simply as consolation but as a work of religious instruction for secular aristocrats. After all, the specific question over which the poem commits its conscious theological solecism – the question of just which virgins can properly be described as brides of Christ, and why – is a relatively abstruse one to occur in a vernacular work written for laypeople, and might indeed be thought irrelevant to them. That the poem is prepared to 'speke errour' (*Pe* 421) over such a matter at least suggests that something of real importance is at stake.

What I believe the redefinition of mystical marriage in the second half of *Pearl* does, for reasons I explore below, is to complete the divorce between heavenly reward and human desert which has been a major concern of much of its first half, by redefining not only purity but every aspect of human salvation in essentially formalistic, even ritualistic terms: terms, that is, which have more to do with a person's external and 'objective' state than with her or his internal or moral one. Virginity treatises sometimes put forth a formalistic view of heavenly reward where the states of virginity, widowhood and marriage are seen as by definition meriting variable rewards, which are

---

9 The jeweller, that is, has a standard late medieval understanding that nuns and anchoresses, like monks and hermits, can expect a special reward in heaven. The importance of the poem's clear reference here to 'spiritual athletes' such as anchoresses (paralleled by a reference to their male equivalents in 477–8, see below) has not, to my knowledge, been previously noted.

equated with the hundredfold, sixtyfold and thirtyfold fruit brought forth by the 'good seed' in the parable of the sower (e.g., *Hali Meiðhad* (Millett 1982) 20.17–21, Matt. 13:23). But by the late middle ages, the dispute which was always latent in the treatises between this view of reward and a growing emphasis on the inner disposition of individuals was well on the way to resolution. Reflecting the increased importance of affective spirituality, which conceptualises reward very differently, Rolle's *Ego Dormio*, for example, takes its reader's virginity as having little inherent significance, and assumes that her state in this life and the next depends entirely on how far she is able to transform her interior self so that she can become Christ's bride not in a formal but a mystical sense. From here it is but a step to Margery Kempe's rejection of the very idea that only virgins are eligible to be brides of Christ (*Book of Margery Kempe*, ch. 21): a development in the theology of spiritual marriage which completes its transformation from an exterior to an interior state.

Pearl, with its insistence that the pearl maiden is Christ's spouse as an automatic concomitant of her unsullied innocence, represents a reaction against this process of transformation: a reaction which has much to do with the poet's desire to formulate a version of Christian belief which is applicable not to contemplatives (like Rolle), whose energies are given over to the processes of inner reformation, but to laypeople who continue to be preoccupied with life in the world. In place of the hierarchies of reward which most medieval accounts of heaven assume, and in which different levels of commitment to God receive different rewards, *Pearl* substitutes a system in which all the saved are divided into two groups:

'Ryȝt þus I knaw wel in þis cas
Two men to saue is God – by skylle:
þe ryȝtwys man schal se Hys face,
þe harmlez haþel schal com Hym tylle.' (*Pe* 673–6)

This system preserves at least the principle of hierarchy, by distinguishing between those who 'se Hys face' (i.e., from afar?) and special souls, the 'harmlez,' who 'com Hym tylle' as his spouses; as I have implied, the longstanding idea that *Pearl* presents an egalitarian picture of heaven is wrong.[10] But by defining the latter, superior group not as those who have worked hardest to attain salvation but precisely as those who have almost 'com to late' to work at all (*Pe* 615), the poem can do away with the whole concept of Christian living as a spiritual struggle in which people attain

---

[10] For this view, see Robertson 1950a, b; Bogdanos 1983, 91–6. It should be added that the controversy over the *orthodoxy* of the pearl maiden's exposition here has tended to cloud what is the most important fact about that exposition: that it is unique in Middle English and runs directly contrary to the particular theological traditions the pearl maiden herself embodies.

different states of blessedness in the next life according to how they live in this: a concept basic to so much fourteenth-century vernacular theology, including theology written for the laity. Here, the heroic Christian (whether monk or hermit) who 'lyued in penaunce hys lyuez longe/ With bodyly bale hym blysse to byye' (*Pe* 477–8) appears to be in just the same situation as the most ordinary laypeople who barely fulfil the minimum requirement for salvation, 'þat takez not her lyf in vayne/ Ne glauerez her neiȝbor wyth no gyle' (*Pe* 687–8). Both groups must wash themselves with repentance for the sins they inevitably commit, and can attain salvation only through the surrogate 'innocens' provided by Christ's blood (*Pe* 697–708). But having performed this sacramental ritual, both can equally enter God's kingdom in a spiritual state which is a version of their original innocence. Like children, both are ritually pure, 'harmlez, trwe, and vndefylde,/ Withouten mote oþer mascle of sulpande synne' (*Pe* 725–6), and are presumably deemed to have forsaken 'þe worlde wode' to purchase the pearl of salvation (*Pe* 743–4).[11] Thus both, so the poem implies (and despite their functions as different limbs of Christ's body, *Pe* 457–68), receive a single reward. (If there is a difference between them, it is that heroic Christians are in more danger of protesting at the arrangement, and thus falling out with Christ at the last; see *Pe* 553–67).

In the economy of salvation which results from *Pearl's* remarkable transformation of the theology of virginity, then, the lifelong commitment to spiritual labour undertaken by hermits, anchoresses, monks and others achieves no more than does the rectitude of the righteous layperson. Indeed, the idea that God's favour can be earned – an idea at first endorsed by the mercantile jeweller, and which parallels the notion of reward found in the virginity tradition – is revealed as deeply vulgar, lacking in both courtesy and due subservience to a lord of whose power over his servants it can be said:

'For þouȝ þou daunce as any do,
Braundysch and bray þy braþez breme,
When þou no fyrre may, to ne fro,
Þou moste abyde þat He schal deme.'   (*Pe* 345–8)

The God revealed in *Pearl* takes no notice of how hard individuals have laboured, only of the 'couenaunt' (*Pe* 562) he established with them through the sacerdotal machinery of baptism, confession, penance and mass: a covenant by means of which those who live below the sphere of the 'spotty' moon, 'mokke and mul' though they are (*Pe* 1070, 905), can attain miraculously to the 'wemlez, clene and clere' pearl of salvation, so pure and precious that it

---

[11] Compare the account of how virginity preserves the flesh's purity given in *Hali Meiðhad*: 'Þis is ȝet þe uertu þe halt ure bruchele ueat, þet is, ure feble flesch, as Seinte Pawel leareð [I Thess. 4:3–5], in hal halinesse: ant as þet swote smirles and deorest of oþre þet is icleopet basme wit þet deade licome þet is þerwið ismiret from rotunge, alswa deð meidenhad meidenes cwike flesch wiþute wemmunge' (Millett 1982, 10.31–5).

resembles 'þe reme of heuenesse clere' (*Pe* 737, 735).[12] This God does not acknowledge the distinction I described at the outset between contemplative and active Christians, *perfecti* and *mediocriter boni*, and takes no more interest in most aspects of the inner lives of his servants than a hunter takes in the death-agony of the deer. When the pearl maiden compliments her father on how well he has rephrased his first outraged questions to her, she does not do so because he shows any signs of profound inner change but because his *speech* is different, no longer full of 'maysterful mod and hyȝe pryde' but now properly imbued with the meekness that God demands appear in the attitude of all his servants: 'My Lorde þe Lambe louez ay such chere' (*Pe* 401, 407). This God is not primarily concerned with inner transformation, but with outer submission. Even at the end of the poem, the jeweller feels none of the joy which might be associated with the achievement of a state of mystical transport, only the resignation which comes from surrendering his daughter to her divine husband. This is, indeed, why he can assert – only a few lines after he has plunged headlong after her, all he had ostensibly learned clean forgotten (*Pe* 1153–60) – that pleasing God is 'full eþe to þe god Krystyin' (*Pe* 1202). Submission to the demands God makes of his 'homely hyne' *is* simple when compared to the arduous journeys to God described by some of the *Gawain*-poet's contemporaries. The jeweller does not have to sacrifice his desire for his daughter, or his sorrow at her death. As he has now learned – in a vision which is closer to otherworld visions such as those associated with St Patrick's Purgatory than it is to the experiences of visionaries of the more mystical sort[13] – he has only to submit to what his lord has decreed and follow God's commands to take his place among the 'precious perlez vnto His pay' (*Pe* 1212).

---

[12] It is here that my reading parts company with that of Aers (1993, 72–3), who argues that the poem is individualistic and indifferent to the community of the Church. While it is true that the jeweller remains an isolated figure at the end of the poem (by contrast, for example, with Will at the end of *Piers Plowman* B XVIII (Schmidt 1987b), who summons his wife and children to pray after his vision of the Harrowing of Hell), on the level of theological argument the poem is deeply and conservatively sacerdotal.

[13] Otherworld visions were especially beloved of the medieval English, who made important contributions to the genre; Easting 1991 edits several of these associated with St Patrick's Purgatory (with an outstandingly useful introduction and apparatus), the latest of which records the experiences of a Durham man (William Stanton) as late as 1406. The vision in *Pearl* resembles these otherworld journeys inasmuch as the jeweller not only travels to the other world (or at least, to a place from which he can glimpse it) but also learns new information there about the nature of salvation and the eternal state of a particular soul. I suggest, then, that there may be a connection between the singularity of the poem's theology of salvation and its use of the vision genre. As Aers suggests (1993, 67, n. 50), the fact that in the poem's visionary climax the jeweller only looks briefly at the Lamb before returning his gaze to his daughter, at whom his plunge into the water is aimed, surely makes nonsense of attempts to read section XIX as an account of mystical union. Otherworld visions, however, do sometimes focus on particular individuals; see, e.g., the vision of a Winchester nun edited by Harley (1985).

Cleanness and Patience

In its extraordinary evocation of the perfect purity of heaven and its embodiment of that purity not in the traditional figure of the adult virgin but in the transfigured innocence of a resurrected child, *Pearl* is, among other things, a meditation on (as well as, paradoxically, a mediation of) the otherness of God. In *Pearl*, heavenly reality can to a considerable extent be described in human language; the poem is no fictionalized version of *The Cloud of Unknowing*. But to describe heaven, human language cannot continue to signify in human terms; confronted with the transcendent versions of earthly phenomena, it has to work in contradictory ways, sometimes affirming, sometimes denying continuity between earth and heaven in its attempt to convey the singular strangeness of the divine nature. (This is why the poem must work so hard, in its highly-wrought formal complexity, to show us fallen language, sullied with earthliness, being made into a fit instrument for the divine by a process of shaping which is an aesthetic equivalent of the sacraments.) Like any powerful lord, God has his idiosyncrasies, which must be carefully kept in mind by those who serve him, since he insists on obedience, tolerates no criticism (e.g., *Pe* 565–8), and 'lauez Hys gyftez as water of dyche,' whether they be 'nesch oþer harde' (*Pe* 607, 606); to that extent, the gap between humans and God is similar to that between earthly rulers and their subjects. Yet God's otherness is also more alarming, for it consists in part of an absolute sinlessness which humans who are not baptized infants cannot hope to emulate, but which they must overcome if they are to avoid eternal damnation. It is indeed fortunate that, despite the chilling perfection of his nature, God has entered into a covenant with humans which enables them to do by grace (through participation in the sacraments) what they cannot by effort.

The nature of this covenant and of the God who made it forms, in general terms, the subject of the two poems which follow *Pearl* in Cotton Nero A.x, *Cleanness* and *Patience*, which my brief discussion here treats as a lopsided diptych. *Cleanness* is surely the most frightening poem in Middle English in its evocation of God's anger and of the violent alternation between anger and love in his dealings with humanity. David Wallace (in his fine article, '*Cleanness* and the Terms of Terror,' 1991) is correct to see in it a reflection of late medieval scholastic discussion of divine omnipotence (*potentia absoluta*): the unconstrained power of God to create, destroy, change his mind, and enter into a series of agreements with humanity, is a theme running through all the poem's *exempla*. But where Wallace treats the poem as an expression of the final unpredictability of God – so that, for all the efforts people make to gain salvation, 'those are righteous whom God deems to be righteous' (100) – I suggest that, on the contrary, *Cleanness* exists to give its readers the information they need to avail themselves confidently of his mercy. God is presented as unpredictable in the poem only when not operating within a covenant which constrains him to pity for his creation, at which times he is liable to exhibit a terrifyingly destructive purity. *Cleanness* describes parts of the historical process by which God sets such a covenant in place. More important, the poem describes both what it is and why it takes the form it takes, that is, what aspects of the divine 'personality' (to use a term which is readily applicable to God in this poem) the covenant expresses. It is to engage the reader more effectively and further his or her salvation that the poem does all this in a narrative context that makes so vividly clear the dire consequences of confronting that personality outside the limits it has set on the expression of its own disapproval.[14]

The argument of *Cleanness* is both simple and coherent if one takes it at face value, and I do not share in the commonly expressed view that there is a disparity between the expository sections of the poem and its *exempla*, or any other particular structural problem (see, e.g., Davenport 1978). God is 'scoymus and skyg,' and requires purity in his servants, being unable to tolerate 'fylþe' in his vicinity, either in the next life or in this (*Cl* 21, 31). Despite his willingness to welcome all who will come to the eternal banquet, there can be no relaxing of standards for anyone (*Cl* 165–8). Anyone forfeits heaven who commits one of a number of sins: pride, covetousness, lying, treason and so forth (a list is provided, *Cl* 179–88). God dislikes all impurity; but he reserves his anger for one particular sin, 'fylþe of þe flesch' (*Cl* 202), which almost alone of all sins can cause him to destroy what he has created. While Lucifer was only cast down for his pride, life on earth was all but wiped out by the Flood when people 'controeued agayn kynde contraré werkez' (*Cl* 266). Although God promised not to repeat this punishment, foregoing for all time his right to punish fleshly sin by destroying 'al þat flesch werez' (*Cl* 287), readers should still take note. God searches out the 'reynyez and hert' (*Cl* 592), and his promise does not preclude him from destroying those with whom he is angry (*Cl* 570–2), as he did the Sodomites. God's cleanness was demonstrated at the incarnation and during Christ's life, where all he touched became clean (*Cl* 1088–109). How, then, can readers approach him, once baptismal purity is lost? By washing themselves with penance, as a pearl is washed with wine:

> So if folk be defowled by vnfre chaunce,
> Þat he be sulped in sawle, seche to schryfte,
> And he may polyce hym at the prest, by penaunce taken,
> Wel bry3ter þen þe beryl oþer browden perles. (*Cl* 1129–32)

---

[14] Wallace's reading of *Cleanness* is based largely on the exempla, and draws on the accounts of the late medieval scholastic division between the *potentia absoluta* and the *potentia ordinata* developed by Janet Coleman (1981a, 1981b). His analysis may, however, take too radical a view of the theology of divine omnipotence which the *potentiae* were used to develop. For a more conservative understanding of the *potentiae* than Coleman's, see Courtenay 1984, and for references to studies dealing with their dissemination in late medieval vernacular texts, Courtenay 1987, 377, n. 50.

Having done this, though, there must be no repetition of the sin. Backsliding is the other sin that makes God angry, 'entyses Hym to tene more trayþly þen euer' (*Cl* 1137). When what has been purified is soiled again – 'þaʒ hit be bot a bassyn, a bolle oþer a scole,/ A dysche oþer a dobler, þat Dryʒtyn onez serued' (*Cl* 1145–6) – God considers a covenant broken and punishes as he did Belshazzar for abusing the sacred vessels. People should therefore take care to keep their spiritual clothes clean (*Cl* 1811).

Cleanness thus operates at once as a sermon and as a history lesson about how God has evolved a covenant with humankind through a process, remarkably, of trial and error, gradually imposing restraints upon himself while at the same time making ever more specific demands upon his people. The first humans live without either social hierarchy or marriage, constrained only by the law of 'kynde' (*Cl* 252, 263), and this lack of controls gives God an equivalent freedom when punishing them: a freedom he still enjoys more locally when destroying the Sodomites (who disobey the more specific rules God expounds to Abraham, *Cl* 697–712) and overthrowing Belshazzar (who defiles him by defiling his vessels). Since the time of Christ, the covenant has changed again, functioning on an individual basis according to yet more specific rules. But God himself is the same as he always was, and readers must therefore also understand the lessons of the past tropologically and anagogically, referring them to their own moral condition and the threat that hangs over them if they fail to follow his commands.

The poem's emphasis upon purity, as pronounced as in *Pearl*, no doubt has a number of reference points, among them the pastoral writings and legislation concerned with the proper performance and meaning of the Eucharist (see Rubin 1991, 83–107). It is surely to such writings that the poem owes its emphasis on specifically *ritual* purity, as expressed through the imagery of clean and dirty vessels and the hands that touch them (*Cl* 1–16, 1089–108, 1143–6ff., see Morse 1971), as well as through the incident in which Lot's wife is punished for her ritual *faux pas* in serving salt to angels (*Cl* 817–28, 996–1000). As has often been remarked, there is influence from the literature of penance too, which supplies, for example, one basis for the interpretation of the parable of the wedding feast, as well as the metaphor of clothing used at beginning and end.[15] But much of the poem's emphasis on purity is again traceable to virginity literature, whose presence is discernible, for example, in the idea that fleshly sin is especially hateful to God – rather than being treated as less serious than sins like pride, as in the scholastic schema familiar to modern readers from the *Inferno*. Again, the process of daring adaptation of this tradition, which we saw in *Pearl*, is in evidence here. Virginity treatises prohibit all physical sexual expression, treating sexual sin as a symbol for everything that offends God, and seeing God's hatred of such sin as

---

[15] *Cl*, 133–70, 1811; compare, e.g., *Piers Plowman* B XIII.271–XIV.332 and see Alford 1974.

motivated in part by a lover's jealousy; the bride of Christ must, above all, avoid making him (to put it bluntly) a cuckold. Despite its moving evocation of the virgin birth of Christ (*Cl* 1069–77), *Cleanness* has a very different view of some forms of sexual activity, and recasts the notion of sexual purity for its lay audience to include the 'kynde crafte' of heterosexual intercourse (*Cl* 697), here presented not as a grudging second best to virginity but as fully its equivalent, 'welny3e pure paradys' (*Cl* 704). God's anger against sexual sin is reserved for sex 'agayn kynde,' invented ('controeued') by the antediluvians and notoriously practiced by the Sodomites (*Cl* 266, 694–6; Frantzen 1996). And this anger is not that of a lover but of an artist-father, outraged engenderer of a creation which has perverted itself and so, implicitly, defiled (even unmanned) him (*Cl* 540–2), destroying the aesthetic unity of the natural order so that the one satisfaction left him is to complete this work of undoing with a finality that has its own terrible beauty: a beauty the poem invites the reader to appreciate. In a move which suggests that Chaucer's *The Parliament of Fowles* is not the only Middle English poem to be influenced by Alain of Lisle's *De Planctu Naturae*, purity is here made coterminous with the natural order, redeemed as it is by a covenant which, through participation in the sacraments, allows Christians to remain in the world and still remain acceptable to God. For all the language of absolute purity, and the emphasis on how the 'gropande God' searches out all humanity's hidden secrets (*Cl* 591), this is not a covenant which should be hard for the poem's readers to keep. Exactly as we found in *Pearl*, basic moral rules (adapted here for an aristocratic readership; see, e.g., *Cl* 185–6), an attitude of submission, and the willingness to repent of any sins one may commit, are adequate to render the sacraments efficacious and leave the soul jewel-bright before God.

One of the ways in which both *Pearl* and *Cleanness* are able to bring about their striking union of frankly rudimentary spiritual standards with a rhetoric of perfection is by rigorously excluding mention of the saints and martyrs whose heroism is regularly invoked by other religious texts. Apart from Christ, the Virgin Mary and the pearl maiden, the nearest thing to saints in the poems are the figures of Noah and Abraham, both of them comfortably married property-owners, who are not seen as people of exceptional virtue but as dutiful servants of God. Nor does the narrator of *Cleanness* present himself as speaking from a viewpoint in any sense (either morally or in terms of his formal spiritual authority) above his audience. On the contrary, he is deferential, 'counselling' his readers rather than overtly commanding them, and at one point even referring obsequiously to any sin his readers might commit as an 'vnfre chaunce' (*Cl* 1056, 1129), a churlish accident, easily remedied by a prompt application of priestcraft (the penitent can 'polyce hym at the prest,' *Cl* 1130). The same deference, combined with the same note of anti-heroism, is evident in *Patience*: a poem whose position in the manuscript seems to be intended to demonstrate that God does, despite *Cleanness*, display mercy as well as anger, but which might also have been designed to reassure aristocratic readers that the didactic poetry they are reading has not been written from any position of implied moral superiority. Sent to preach wrath to the secular community of Ninevah, Jonah – a figure who is directly paralleled with the preacher-narrator (*Pat* 49–56) – fails ludicrously and at every stage to do or think what he should, measuring up as badly as can be against everyone else in the poem, from the sailors who do all they can to avoid throwing him overboard (*Pat* 215–30), to the king and people of Nineveh who know better than Jonah when God means business (*Pat* 371–406). Jonah does worse than the jeweller in *Pearl* and much worse than Gawain. As a figure of the preacher he is wholly unthreatening except in his message; and even this is overtaken by events, since his commission to preach damnation – as the poet has done in much of *Cleanness* – proves, to his great annoyance, to have been intended by God as a means, rather, of saving the Ninevites. Like its predecessors in the manuscript, *Patience* shows how easily God forgives those who do penance, how he must be obeyed, and how his ways (like his sense of humour, *Pat* 443–78) are strange. What it adds to its poetic partners is this implicitly self-deprecating picture of a prophet of wrath, who himself makes as great a demand on the divine patience as anyone because he has failed to learn the simple moral lesson he must preach. Given the parallel the beginning of the poem sets up not only between Jonah and the narrator but also between the narrator's 'lege lord' and God, it is hard not to see *Patience* as a kind of apology for the position of authority in which the poet, despite his status as a secular lord's employee, is situated. As David Benson has pointed out (1991), the poem places readers exactly in the position of judge over Jonah, obliging us to exercise the godlike quality of patience towards a figure whose role in the poem is nonetheless that of the mouthpiece of the divine will. From the viewpoint of aristocratic lay readers, who learn here that the spiritual authority of the preacher entails neither special status before God nor any claim to earthly power – Jonah's direct influence over the lives of the people of Nineveh is shortlived – nothing could be more reassuring.

Conclusion

If space permitted, it would be interesting to conclude this discussion of the theology of Cotton Nero A.x with a detailed account of *Gawain* along the lines I have traced for the other three poems. I would try to show what I can here only state, that *Gawain* reintroduces on a secular level the sense of both hierarchy and heroic effort which have been kept out of its predecessors, and thus valorizes the difficulty of its hero's high ideals in a way we do not find elsewhere in the manuscript. On a religious level, there is no sign that Gawain aspires to any spiritual state more elevated than those depicted in *Cleanness* or *Patience*. But as an aristocrat, the standards of sheer *manners* (especially in speech, 'þe teccheles termes of talkyng noble,' G 917) of this 'fyne fader of nurture' (G 919) are elevated indeed, bound up as they are in intricate pattern with a moral system whose absolutism they must seek at all costs to veil. However one treats Gawain's flawed demonstration of the marriage of manners and morality, this pattern does help make a larger pattern in the *Gawain*-poet's thought and aesthetics as a whole, by completing the triangular link I mentioned at the outset between poetic craft, the intricate harmony of heaven and the self-conscious complexities of courtliness. From a religious point of view, Gawain's sheer well-bred gloss could be seen as a worshipping attempt to imitate the harmony of heaven. (The fact that this act of imitation, unlike the efforts of virgins and saints, carries with it, according to *Pearl*, no final reward renders it the more praiseworthy in its disinterestedness.) Thus in *Gawain*, the graciousness of the life of courtesy is finally allowed to suggest (in the context of the other poems) the special ties which link the secular aristocracy with heaven, and to complete what I see as this poet's project: the displacement of the traditional categories of Christian heroism (embodied in virgins, martyrs and preachers) to make way for a new set, embodied in a figure closer to the aspirations and capacities of the poet's audience, Gawain himself.

Such a reading of *Gawain* needs, of course, much fuller attention than I can give it here. Enough has been said, though, to convey a sense of the place the *Gawain*-poet holds among vernacular theologians of his era and to suggest something of what makes him so unusual. Sharing with a number of writers (the author of *Dives and Pauper* and the Hilton of the *Epistle on Mixed Life* among them) the aim of adapting aspects of Christian belief for an audience of aristocrats, the *Gawain*-poet seems partly to have followed (at least, in *Pearl*) a traditional route of working outwards from an existing body of vernacular religious material, including especially the virginity treatise. Rather as *Ancrene Wisse* was at about the same time finding its way into the Vernon manuscript and being adapted for new readerships (Allen 1923, 1929; Gillespie 1984), or as the two books of *The Scale of Perfection* move from addressing a single, anchoritic reader to a broad lay audience, so *Pearl* can be seen as an adaptation of the theology of virginity. But where Hilton, the compilers of Vernon and many others saw what they were doing as seeking to make available to the laity some of the practices, principles and benefits of the contemplative life, educating them both intellectually and spiritually to the point where they could attain at least to its lower rungs, the *Gawain*-poet attempted something (from an ecclesiastical viewpoint, if not a theological one) more radical. Focusing not on his sources' emphasis on the inner life nor on their devotionalism but on their use of the *rhetoric* of purity, their spiritualised aestheticism, this writer sought to undo the theological system which consigned his lay readers to the status of *mediocriter boni*, and make them equal to contemplatives in the acceptability of their lives to God. Most striking, he did this less by trying to change the lives of his readers than by rethinking the way in which theology perceived them, portraying the experience of the aristocratic laity as normative for all Christians.

In the process of constructing his aristocratised theology (not only from virginity treatises but from many other materials whose importance I am compelled to gloss over here), the *Gawain*-poet thus showed himself unusually willing to ignore or challenge what most of his contemporaries would have regarded as givens: to the point, indeed, where his work would surely have encountered fierce disapproval if it had been written in a more accessible style. While the formal orthodoxy of the poetry can no doubt be defended – if on no other grounds then, at least, by arguing that it is, after all, only poetry – its view of heavenly reward, its depiction of God (especially in *Cleanness*) and perhaps (again in *Cleanness*) its vivid descriptions of various sexual acts are all questionable, even from the relatively tolerant viewpoint of pre-Lollard English religiosity. Equally startling to some of the poet's contemporaries would have been the poetry's deference to its readers on a tonal as well as theological level. Offering their instruction in the form of coterie entertainment, and pressing their claim to homiletic authority only in the most painfully oblique manner, the poems present a view of the sacramental system they expound as existing purely for the convenience of aristocrats who employ priests to see to their salvation in much the way they employ stewards to see to their households. Where religious writings by fourteenth-century aristocrats and gentry themselves (from Henry of Lancaster's *Livre de Seyntz Medicines* to Sir John Clanvowe's *The Two Ways*) are full of expressions of unworthiness and pleas for divine mercy, the poems of Cotton Nero A.x remake the faith in a shape which seems to demand – except in a purely ritual context, such as when using a priest to polish their souls in confession – as few as possible of these indignities from its readers.

In his popular theological compendium, the *Elucidarium*, Honorius of Autun (a pupil of Anselm of Canterbury, writing in the first half of the twelfth century) at one point asks whether knights (*milites*) are virtuous enough to expect salvation, and answers the question with all the contempt of a professional contemplative for powerful worldlings: 'Pauci boni [. . .] de his dicitur, *Defecerunt in vanitate dies eorum* [. . .]; *ideo ira dei ascendit super eos* (Ps 77:33, 30)' (II.18: 'Few of them are any good; of such people it is said "they consume their days in vanity – and so the anger of God will overwhelm them" '). While so severe a view would never have been universal, the works of the *Gawain*-poet are among those vernacular theologies which show how much had changed, two and a half centuries later, in the relationship between the Church and the aristocratic laity. In their concern for lay readers and their deference towards aristocratic power and priorities, these poems are part of a larger movement of laicization, whose effects can be felt in a multitude of other works written in the seventy years or so after 1350, and which was eventually (*mutatis mutandis*) to lead to the still more thoroughly gentrified

Church of England of the post-Reformation era (Duffy 1992). We could compare the poems not only to the literature of interiority (as has been my practice here) but to different kinds of text in which this development is also felt: the works John Trevisa translated for Thomas of Berkeley (especially the *Dialogus inter Militem et Clericum*; see Edwards 1984), or the moral poetry composed by the Kentishman John Gower, as well as the more explicitly anticlerical polemics produced by the Lollards. Nowhere in medieval English writing, though, do we to my knowledge find a body of work (whether composed by a cleric or a layperson) in which the life of the aristocracy is so thoroughly idealised in quite this way, so carefully presented as coterminous with Christian life in general. Nowhere does a clerical author refashion his role as homilist to the point where his writing is so fully taken over – on a moral, social and aesthetic level – by the mores of his audience.

13

Allegory and Symbolism

PRISCILLA MARTIN

The author (or authors)[1] of the poems in the *Gawain*-manuscript inhabited a Christian culture which interpreted human life sacramentally, viewed Nature as a book by God to be 'read' by his creatures, and inherited allegorical methods of understanding Scripture. Theologians and poets repeatedly caution – in such images as nut and shell or fruit and chaff – against concentrating merely on the letter and neglecting the spirit. Allegorical interpretation could be multilevelled: as well as the literal sense, a passage of the Bible might yield 'spiritual' senses, the moral or tropological, allegorical and anagogical. These applied the text to, respectively, the soul, Christ and the Church Militant, heaven and the Church Triumphant. Typology juxtaposed characters and episodes from the Old Testament with the New, 'proving' that the Christian revelation was inherent in the Hebrew Scriptures. Much religious literature – sermons, poems, morality plays – presented life allegorically: for example, as a pilgrimage towards the true Jerusalem, as a psychomachia between warring vices and virtues, as an arena for debate between personified abstractions or for processions of the Seven Deadly Sins. Secular literature, especially love poetry, also employed allegory and shared many motifs with religious art. The *Roman de la Rose* was particularly influential with its Garden of Love, the *locus amoenus* which, in Christian tradition, draws upon the Garden of Eden and an allegorical reading of the *Song of Songs*, and its cast which includes the personified feelings of its heroine, the Rose.

The *Gawain*-poet had read allegories and allegorical interpretations. As well as the Bible, he knew Biblical exegesis and the *artes predicandi*. The narrator of *Cleanness* says: 'I have herkned and herde of mony hyghe clerkes, / And als in resouns of ryght red hit myselven . . .' (193–94)[2] and the poem shows considerable learning in Scriptural commentary. The poet was acquainted with other European literature. He knew the *Roman de la Rose* and refers to it in *Cleanness*. *Pearl* may also be influenced by Dante and Boccaccio.

---

[1] Single authorship and male authorship of the poems seem probable to me. Cf. Andrew above.

[2] Quotations from *Pearl*, *Cleanness* and *Patience* are from Cawley and Anderson 1976.

The lexical range and allusive subtlety of the poems point to sophisticated and self-conscious authorship.

All four poems insist on allegorical, symbolic or analogical understanding. They encourage their readers and their characters thus to interpret the inner meaning of their experience. The jeweller can reconcile himself to the loss of the pearl only by a painful education in its symbolism. Jonah has to make the analogy between his feeling for the woodbine and God's for Nineveh, to see himself in God's likeness and imagine what the world would be like if God were in his. *Cleanness* founds its argument on parables which depend on the analogies between inner and outer purity and between the duties owed to an earthly lord and to the King of Heaven. Gawain has to revise his understanding of Green Knight, Green Chapel and green girdle.

Yet they are not consistently allegorical narratives. Their characters are exemplary, representative, rather than personifications. The poet draws on the resources of more extended allegories to analyse or clarify their stories but does not write extended allegories himself. A sketchy psychomachia appears in the spiritual conflict at the opening of *Pearl* – 'Thagh kynde of Kryst me comfort kenned,/ My wreched wylle in wo ay wraghte' (55–56) – and its secular versions, such as the *Roman de la Rose*, in the complex emotions roused by the sight of the transformed Pearl-maiden: 'To calle hyr lyste con me enchace,/ Bot baysement gef myn hert a brunt' (173–74). The ladies who greet Gawain at Hautdesert freeze briefly into a tableau of Youth and Elde, a *memento senescere* or disincentive to concupiscence. The virtues of the Beatitudes are tersely personified in *Patience* as 'thise ladyes . . . / Dame Povert, dame Pitee, dame Penaunce the thrydde,/ Dame Mekenesse, dame Mercy and miry Clannesse,/ And thenne dame Pes and Pacyence . . .' (30–33) and typology illuminates the relationship between Jonah and Christ. Traditional exegesis supplies the Trinitarian reading of the episode in *Cleanness* when three men visit Abraham and he goes to them 'as to God' (611), setting them in a context of providential history. But most critics have emphasized the author's interest in the literal texture of Scripture: e.g. 'what most interested him was the literal sense of his Biblical sources rather than their typological or allegorical significance' (Spearing 1970, on *Cleanness* 13); 'rejection of the traditional exemplar of patience, Job, in favour of this equivocal tale suggests that the literal interest of the story itself was more important than its exemplary force' (Davenport 1978, on *Patience* 105).

A striking feature of all four poems is their vivid concreteness and their intensity of abstraction. Their titles, though editorial, are appropriate. *Pearl* could be called nothing else: the poem opens with the word and develops through the narrator's and reader's growing understanding of its meanings. The titles *Cleanness* (sometimes called *Purity*) and *Patience* are also the opening words, announcing the author's interest in general moral questions. The individual and the symbolic meet in *Sir Gawain and the Green Knight* (*Sir Gawain*). 'If the poem were to be called any such [abstract] thing, it should be called *Truth.*' (Burrow 1971, 86). Yet although the poems overtly discuss abstractions – divine justice, purity, patience, the theological implications of the geometric symbol of the pentangle, the tensions between courtesy and chastity – they instantly impress all readers with their sensuousness: the warm fragrance of the graveyard in August, the radiance of the other world, the smoky destruction of Sodom and the sulphurous Dead Sea, floods and storms, the slime of the whale's belly, the feasts with their elaborate food and architectural tableware, the cold and damp of the winter journey, the sound of an axe being sharpened. The vivid perceptions are not merely sensory: as in the title virtue of *Cleanness*, physical and spiritual are interconnected. All creation is God's material and the vehicle of his purpose, as he points out to Jonah: 'I made hem myself of materes myn one' (503). The 'gostly drem' of *Pearl* is not abstract in being disembodied but more intense than waking physical experience. The opening stanza emphasizes the smooth touch of the pearl as much as its appearance and value: the perfection of its shape and surface can be felt as well as seen and analysed. The first of Gawain's virtues symbolised in the pentangle is that 'he watz funden fautlez in his fyve wyttez' (640): sensitivity contributes to sinlessness. God himself is seen as supremely sentient and this should be an inspiration to moral awareness:

> Hope ye that he heres not that eres alle made?
> Hit may not be that he is blynde that bigged uche yye.
>
> (*Patience* 123–24)

There is powerful use of natural symbolism in the poems. The 'erber' of *Pearl* manifests the life, death and rebirth of nature, suggesting two opposed interpretations: that we die more decisively than the fruits and flowers or that their renewal suggests ours. The barrenness of the Dead Sea mirrors the spiritual sterility that it punishes. The storm at sea in *Patience* is one of the most terrifying images of human helplessness. Jonah's prayer from 'the dymme hert' of 'the depe se' (307) (the most powerful passage in the Hebrew original and the Vulgate translation) rises from an archetypal abyss. The natural is also contrasted and counterpointed with the city and the civilised, raw and cooked, isolation and community. In *Pearl* the natural world of the 'erber' (38) modulates into the brilliant 'artifice of eternity' of the Earthly Paradise and the Celestial City. The Green Knight's body, clothes, trappings and demeanour seem both elegant and elemental, suggesting culture and nature, the sophisticated and the barbaric, the golden age and the green world. Gawain's journey takes him from the consciously superlatively civilised court of Camelot into the savage and monstrous world of the journey north and back to Christian civilisation at `Hautdesert. There the hunting scenes blazon the claim to order the savage, elaborating the rules, decorum, hierarchy and property rights imposed on the blood-lust which predates civilisation, and they pointedly enclose the seduction scenes in the castle with their own complexities of lust and etiquette. The poems are full of images of community: the blessed souls in the procession of the Lamb, the wedding feast of the parables and the doomed, ironic banquet of Belshazzar, the Christmas celebrations at Camelot and the Christmas 'fast' at Hautdesert, the earnest collective penitential fast which the king of Nineveh imposes even on children at the breast and animals in the fields. Outside the city walls Jonah makes his own poignant attempt at domestic architecture, 'he busked hym a bour, the best that he myght', (437) and settles down gratefully under the woodbine, 'a hous as hit were' (450).

As well as their natural associations, time and place are symbolically structured for the poet by literary and theological tradition. The late summer opening immediately sets *Pearl* slightly at odds with the love-visions, despite its garden setting and romantic vocabulary. It is not spring, the mating time, the season of romance. It is 'Auguste in a hygh seysoun/ Quen corne is corven wyth crokes kene' (39–40), the time of harvest, suggesting both the fruits of labour and the work of Death the reaper. The natural rhythm of the seasons is endowed with Christian significance by the 'hygh seysoun', most probably the Feast of Lammas, 1st August, which is associated with harvest time, though the Transfiguration of Christ, 6th August, and the Assumption of the Virgin, 15th August, have also been suggested and would underline the transformation of the Pearl-maiden in Heaven. The sequence of biblical *exempla* in *Cleanness* parallels the pericopes (i.e. the Biblical readings) for the divisions of the liturgical year (Lecklider 1994). *Patience* also opens with a reference to the liturgical year: 'I herde on a halyday, at a hyghe masse,/ How Mathew melede that his mayster his meyny con teche . . .' (9–10). The teaching is the Beatitudes, the Gospel for the Feast of St Boniface and for the Feast of All Saints. The former association would link and contrast Jonah, terrified of torture and death if he carries God's word to the Ninevites, with St Boniface, whose missionary work in Saxony culminated in his martyrdom. The latter would, as in *Sir Gawain*, allude not only to All Saints but to All Souls, an ominous time to set out on a dangerous journey. The time scheme of *Sir Gawain* is structured by the natural and the liturgical year. The action of the poem begins on New Year's Day, a symbolic new beginning, with the Green Knight's visit to Camelot and ends exactly a year later with Gawain's promised visit to the Green Chapel. One of the most striking passages of the poem tells the passage of the seasons during this year, which seems to accelerate as Gawain draws nearer to that grim journey. It takes him into the coldest and darkest time of year but also the time which heralds the Nativity. Conversely, the interlude of warmth, leisure and comfort in the castle is the time of real danger. The spiritual meaning of events may be hidden from the senses. And their obscurity and the ambiguity of the Green Knight are aptly symbolised at the year's beginning by the double-faced god Janus. (A similar configuration of season and paradox occurs in Chaucer's *Franklin's Tale*.) New Year's Day is the Feast of the Circumcision: it has been argued that the Green Knight 'circumcizes' Gawain with the nick on the neck, that he symbolizes both the Old Covenant with his rules, threats and bargains and the New Covenant with his power to hear confession, impose penance and absolve (Shoaf 1984).

The poet draws on other symbolic schemes to structure and convey meaning. One is numerology, a scheme which feels 'natural', God-given, because it is ancient, arithmetical, classical and Scriptural. Some numbers are sacred: three suggests the Trinity (*Cleanness*) or the three days from Crucifixion to Resurrection (*Patience*). Five suggests perfection and occurs in natural and spiritual taxonomies, such as the five fingers, the five senses, the five wounds of Christ, the five joys of Mary (*Sir Gawain*). Five is a 'circular' number. The *Gawain*-poet is fascinated by beginnings and endings, sequences, circles and symmetry. Peace and Patience are said to be first and last, enclosing the other virtues. The pearl, a circle or sphere, symbolizes perfection. The elaborate patterning of *Pearl* is, among other things, numerical, based on the number 12. Its stanzas are 12 lines in length; the poem is 1212 lines long; 12 multiplied by 12 comes to 144 and the number of the elect in the Apocalypse and in *Pearl* is 144,000; in the heavenly Jerusalem there are 12 foundations of stones, 12 gates of pearl and the sides of the squares are 12 furlongs long. *Pearl* and *Sir Gawain* have the same number of stanzas, 101, perhaps a deliberate asymmetry (like the year-and-a-day time scheme of *Sir Gawain*) to suggest that perfection has not been achieved.

The *Gawain*-poet is not particularly interested in argument from etymology, and probably believed that the meanings of words are assigned by convention but words, like numbers, can suggest numinous significance to him. He exploits formal resources, such as alliteration, rhyme, homophony (same sound) and paronomasia (repeated similar sound, serious pun), to emphasize or even symbolize his argument. The 'poyntes' of Gawain's pentangle are both 'points' and 'virtues'. The sections of *Pearl* are bound together and to each other by *concatenatio*, a system of key words which occur in the first and last lines of the stanzas, until the 'perles' of the last line recapitulate and multiply the 'perle' which is the first word of the first line. The stanzas, linked by concatenation, are like a string of pearls or a rosary, to be read and revolved, meditating on different senses as they change and grow in meaning. Human limitations are set against divine infinity in the sections which develop through the words 'more', 'date' and 'ynogh'. In the New Jerusalem the Lamb is the lamp, the 'lombe-lyght' (1046). Alliteration encourages us to suspect that 'blysse' and 'bale' may not be the absolute contraries the narrator assumes. It underlines the explication of the parable of the wedding garment: 'wedes' are 'werkes' in *Cleanness* (169–71). In *Patience* it suggests the one-damn-thing-after-another-ness of life, to which resignation is the only prudent response: 'Yif me be dyght a destine due to have,/ What dowes me the dedayn other dispit make?' (49–50). Poetic forms and figures seem to embody virtues in themselves: the intricate virtuosity of the *Pearl* stanzas is the author's earthly compliment to the dazzling symmetry of the New Jerusalem, the fitting 'wedes' for his 'werkes'; the 'lel letres loken' (35) of the literary tradition behind *Sir Gawain* describe alliteration as the loyalty of one letter to another, an apt vehicle for an exploration of truth and fidelity.

Cleanness and *Patience* employ a narrative method familiar from medieval sermons, the exemplum, which teaches moral lessons or Christian doctrine through instances of human behaviour. The examples may be fictional, as in the parables of Christ, or they may be (or be thought to be) historical. They may be positive or negative. *Patience* and *Cleanness* both use negative examples to define Christian virtues. The poet actually presents *Patience* as being inspired by the reading or the sermon 'on a halyday, at a hyghe masse' about the Beatitudes. He applies the lesson to his own life before turning to the story of Jonah. Since he is poor, he had better be patient: his poverty will be even harder without it. Jonah, after all, made everything worse for himself by his impatience. We cannot get away from God's meanings any more than he could. His attempt to escape his mission to Nineveh lands him in the whale's belly; his escape from that lands him in 'the regiounes ryght that he renayed hade' (344). He is perversely indignant at the success of his preaching when the Ninevites repent; God instructs him by withering the woodbine that the Ninevites are dear to their maker. The representative character is not exactly allegorical but the exemplum does have something in common with allegory. It deals in the ruling passion, the exactly characteristic vignette, like the 'humours' in Renaissance drama. Jonah resents the Ninevites for being more flexible than he is himself, for stepping out of the roles he assigned them, the personifications he imposed on them. Auden noted: 'We enjoy caricatures of our enemies because we do not want to consider the possibility of their having a change of heart, so that we would have to forgive them' (1948, 383). Jonah, who likes to enclose himself in spaces – the hold of the ship, the 'bour' of the woodbine – as well as attitudes, is symbolically punished in two complementary ways, by imprisonment in the whale and exposure to the elements. He has no right to enclose God's teaching: 'Lo, my lore is in the loke, lauce hit therinne!' (350). The poet knows traditional allegorical readings of the story. Jonah's improbable sleep during the storm at sea could be interpreted as the spiritual torpor of the sinner who ignores the judgment to come. Typological reading originates in the New Testament, when Matthew compares Jonah's three days in the whale's belly with Christ's three days in the heart of the earth (Matthew 12:40. See also Luke 9:30). In *Patience* Jonah's fear of being crucified in Nineveh clearly alludes to the Passion: 'Our Syre . . . gloumbes ful lyttel/ Thagh I be nummen in Nunniue and naked dispoyled,/ On rode rwly torent with rybaudes mony' (93–96). A.C. Spearing mentions both interpretations but emphasizes the realism with which Jonah's sleep is described and finds the allusion to Christ 'almost shocking . . . [it] serves to belittle him still further. In the Bible he is a type of Christ; in the poem, an antitype.' (1970, 82–83, 87). Jonah is an 'antitype' in the sense of being an anti-hero but the poet is not reversing standard allegorical method. The relationship between Old Testament type and New Testament antitype may in part be contrast, as in the fundamental Adam/Christ relationship. The line 'On rode rwly torent with rybaudes mony' recalls the Passion plays in the mystery cycles, which dramatize the pattern seen in Old and New Testament and draw into it the members of the contemporary community. Three times are simultaneously present: the time of Jonah's story, the time of the Incarnation and the time of the fourteenth-century author and audience, on whom patience is again impressed in the closing lines of the poem.

Cleanness also presents a virtue through exempla placed in the context of providential history. It is no trouble, assert the opening lines, to think of positive examples of purity: 'Clannesse whoso kyndly cowthe comende,/ And rekken vp alle the resouns that ho by right askes,/ Fayre formes myght he fynde in forthering his speche . . .' (1–3). However, the poem mainly engages with the 'kark and combraunce huge' of the 'contrare' (4). It presents three dramatic examples of God's vengeance on uncleanness: the Flood, the destruction of Sodom and Gomorrah and Belshazzar's Feast. In the first two cases God's wrath was especially provoked by sexual impurity, in the third by the defilement of the sacred vessels of the Temple. Each story is a type of the Apocalypse. They are prefaced by the parable of the wedding feast, or rather a conflation of the parables in Matthew 22:2–14 and Luke 14:7–24. Matthew's story is more punitive than Luke's and this composite version more punitive than either, culminating in the savage incarceration of one of the down-and-outs for being shabbily dressed. 'The suggestion that peasants and tramps in "gorstes and grevez" should have a clean garment handy in case somebody forced them to go to a wedding is an idea that one can only accept if one abandons the literal fable and translates the garment into its allegorical equivalent, but the poet, by being realistic and dramatic, does not encourage one to make this desperate breach of decorum.' (Davenport 1978, 82–83). On this view the poet is more indecorous than the wedding guest but medieval texts do often breach later ideas of decorum. The allegorical test case, shocking at the literal level, occurs elsewhere, for example in the *Clerk's Tale*. To see beyond this level to the *sentence* might prove the reader one of the few chosen to come to the Lord's banquet. However, the emphasis on destruction in the parable and the examples is a disturbing contrast to the forgiveness shown in *Patience* and *Sir Gawain*. Still, the narrative order may suggest the progress of the liturgical year towards Advent and redemption (Lecklider 1994), God is generous to Abraham and Noah and clement to Nebuchadnezzar, he is angry at sexual perversion because he created love between the sexes to be the greatest pleasure ('a maner myriest of other . . . Bytwene a man and his make such merthe schulde come,/ Welnyghe pure Paradys moght preve no better', 701–704) and the climactic destruction of Babylon is preceded by the supreme example of purity, the Nativity and ministry of Christ. The opening parable and the three apocalyptic exempla show God's vengeance but much in *Cleanness* demonstrates or symbolizes his mercy: Sarah's miraculous pregnancy prefigures Mary's, Noah's ark is a type of the Church and, like the kingdom of heaven, has many mansions, the lord longs to be hospitable. Belshazzar's feast is like a malign parody of God's wedding banquet, as if sin is perverted symbolism. The earthly should symbolize the heavenly and the poet even produces the advice given to wooers in the *Romance of the Rose* as a fit analogy of the courtesy Christians should show to God (1056–68).

Pearl is evidently an allegorical poem, though there has been disagreement about how allegorical it is. In the simplest terms, it is not about a literal jeweller who has lost a literal pearl. The lost pearl has usually been understood to signify a child who died in infancy, the narrator's daughter, perhaps the poet's daughter, perhaps called Margaret. There has been critical disagreement about whether to identify narrator with poet and whether the pearl carries other or additional allegorical senses: spiritual consolation, innocence, immortality, the kingdom of heaven. D.W. Robertson applied the fourfold method of interpretation to it: 'The symbol of the pearl may be thought of on four levels. Literally, the pearl is a gem. Allegorically, as the maiden of the poem, it represents those members of the Church who will be among the "hundred" in the celestial procession, the perfectly innocent. Tropologically, the pearl is a symbol of the soul that attains innocence through true penance and all that such penance implies. Anagogically, it is the life of innocence in the Celestial City. The allegorical value presents a clear picture of the type of innocence; the tropological value shows how such innocence may be obtained, and the anagogical value explains the reward for innocence. To these meanings the literal value serves as a unifying focal point in which the other values are implied to one who reads the book of God's work on the level of the *sentence*.' (Robertson 1950b). Jane Chance develops a linear reading of the fourfold interpretation: in the first section of the poem (stanzas 6–33) the narrator is morally educated out of his selfish and literal understanding of his loss; in the second (34–64) his problems about the salvation of the pearl are addressed by allegory; in the last anagogical section he is granted a vision of the celestial kingdom. (Chance 1991)

Some of these interpretations do not now look like such stark alternatives as they once did. Narrative voices sound less unitary: the narrator of *Pearl* inhabits several time-frames. The author seems less unified, especially such an anonymous one (or four). He (or she) works with the codes, conventions and traditions of late medieval poetry. Poet and audience bring to the poem many associations with the image of the pearl and standard interpretations of it. They are familiar with it as a beautiful and expensive stone for ornamental use. The ornamental uses may create their own symbolic contexts. Its whiteness easily suggests purity, innocence or virginity. Medicinal powers are ascribed to it in the lapidaries popular at the time. Jesus used the image in a prohibition and a parable, which apply very aptly to the method and the meaning of *Pearl*. 'Give not that which is holy unto the dogs, neither cast ye your pearls before swine' (Matthew 7:6) can be used as a defence of allegory itself, which puts a figurative barrier between the pearls of sacred import and any swinishly unappreciative reader. Nonetheless, the parable spells out its interpretation immediately: 'the kingdom of heaven is like unto a merchant man, seeking goodly pearls; Who, when he had found one pearl of great price, went and sold all that he had, and bought it.' (Matthew 13:45–46). Despite its clarity, the parable is not an absolutely schematic allegory: the kingdom of heaven is presumably like the pearl of great price rather than like the merchant. Perhaps one should not demand a rigid scheme or neat equations between tenor and vehicle in the polysemous depth and complexity of *Pearl* either. The meanings of the pearl are meditated and revealed throughout the poem, not as one-for-one correspondence but in a developing apprehension of significance. Perhaps the purpose is to expand the meanings rather than define them with allegorical precision. The Pearl-maiden does not have to represent either the soul of a dead child or innocence or immortality or the kingdom of heaven. All these meanings are simultaneously present in the figure of the immortal soul of an innocent child in heaven.

There is a profusion of symbolism in the opening section, both of suggestions to be developed and associations to be questioned. The poem opens with an apparently literal and worldly celebration of the 'perle, plesaunte to prynces paye' (1): the pearl valued in earthly terms and in the social hierarchy, ready to be set in gold. It will close with a spiritual understanding of the same words: we are to be 'precious perles' to the 'pay' (1212) of the heavenly Prince. In the first stanza the jeweller regards himself as the judge: he has never 'proved' any other pearl her equal and has 'sette hyr sengeley in synglere'. By the end of the poem he has learned to place himself in the judgement of God and in the community of Christians, rather than emphasize the singularity of his own possessive affections: in this first section the pearl is twice his 'privy perle'; in section VI the concatenation word is 'deme', the subject varying between the jeweller, the daughter, man's 'one skyl', men and God until the final affirmation: 'Al lys in hym to dyght and deme' (360). The pearl has been lost in an 'erber' (38), slipping through the grass to the ground. The pearl is 'hyr', is smooth and rounded both like the jewel and the beloved ladies of courtly poetry. We begin to see the pearl as a person rather than a jewel, perhaps the mistress in a love poem, an impression strengthened by the narrator's description of his grief as 'luf-daunger'. Her identification as his child will be made gradually during the poem, through such details as 'Thou lyfed not two yer in oure thede;/ Thou cowthes never God nauther plese ne pray,/ Ne never nawther Pater ne Crede' (483–85) and the use in the last stanza of a conventional blessing by parent to child. The 'erber', literally the graveyard, is a scene of bitter grief and yet overpowering beauty for the narrator. It has natural, romantic and spiritual connotations: gardens, Gardens of Love, the Garden of Eden. Death was the punishment for the original sin; the narrator has been perceived as repeating that disobedience in trying to reach his pearl in heaven and bypass death at the end of the dream. Yet the buried pearl is in a setting of flowers and fruits, colours and spices and through the overwhelming synaesthesia of sights and scents we hear images used in the Gospels to promise resurrection: grain, wheat, seed. The Pearl-maiden will use this symbolism herself: he has lost only a rose, which flowered and failed, as was natural; now she is a pearl, unchanging, immortal. Yet the rose, symbol of earthly beauty, love and mutability, is also a symbol of Christ, his Passion and divine love, and the dreamer is later to describe the pearl as a 'reken rose' (906) in contrast to his own doomed earthiness. The central images – pearl, rose, coffin, garden, garland, prince – are transformed during the course of the poem.

The dreamer's meeting with his transformed pearl is as vexing as rapturous. He brings to it all his human feelings of bereavement, relief, possessiveness and desire. He sometimes sounds, like Jonah, disappointed that things have turned out so perfectly for her. We understand his reactions completely. By definition, we cannot understand the pearl, though she spells her meaning out in pedagogic tones. She can seem distant, didactic and cold. Precisely in the middle of the poem she addresses herself to one of his problems in the terms of a traditional allegory, expanding allegory by allegory. She retells the parable of the labourers in the vineyard to convince her father that she merits reward in heaven as much as (or even more than) those who lived longer and worked and suffered and sinned more. The parable was more often applied to those who die after an 'eleventh-hour' conversion but it was also used of children who died in infancy. It has dominical authority and the pearl narrates it vividly. Its imagery of harvest echoes the opening 'erber' and clarifies its symbolic suggestiveness. One of the terms – 'hyne' (505, 632) labourers – will finally express the narrator's acceptance of God's will in the penultimate line of the poem: 'He gef vus to be his homly hyne' (1211). For the earthbound reader the parable gains much of its power from the aggrieved tones of the workers and from a tinge of melancholy in the passing of time and the approach of night. Time does not pass in Heaven and there are no shadows in the New Jerusalem. The pearl sets out its munificence with a kind of hard clarity which is to dominate the rest of the vision.

Earlier critics of the poem tended to be rather deferential to the pearl and her teachings, to accept her 'rightness' and to dismiss its harsh impact as proof of our 'wrongness'. More recent accounts have focused on the problematics of discourse as well as the problems of theology in the poem. Several have found the central passage of the dialogue with the pearl less rich and suggestive than the beginning and the end: 'the work has modulated from a symbolic to a discursive mode of presenting divine truth' (Bogdanos 1983, 82); 'for more than four hundred lines the pearl symbol undergoes no further development, and simpler, more explicit forms of exposition take its place' (Spearing 1970, 152); 'between the two peaks lies a tract of stony ground, the enclosed, "intellectual" portion of the poem, which is, in parts, prosaically presented and rigid in effect' (Davenport 1978, 50). Davenport concedes that 'from this combination come the poem's different levels of meaning, and the sense that *Pearl* includes contradictory or antithetical qualities' (53). One critic sees the poem as attempting the inexpressible and exposing its inexpressibility: 'the obvious involvement of similitudes and their failure, despite their familiarity and logical coherence, are part of the pattern of symbolic failure that builds up through the poem to its dramatic climax – the hero's encounter with the New Jerusalem.' (Bogdanos 1983, 94).

The vision of the New Jerusalem has to be seen in terms of another discursive mode, the apocalypse, as the narrator's frequent allusions to St John underline. Allegory was often linked to *aenigma*, the term used by St Paul to describe the condition of our imperfect knowledge in this life: 'For now we see through a glass darkly . . .' (I Corinthians 13:12) This was contrasted with the direct knowledge which the pearl now claims: 'We thurghoutly haven cnawyng' (859). It can be reported by the narrator to the reader only indirectly by recourse to the authority of the *Apocalypse*. And the clarity and radiance of this vision can daze or even repel: 'The kingdom of heaven withdraws into an icon, a frozen image of ideal ritualistic stasis.' (Bogdanos 1983, 142). The sun and moon (the concatenation word of section XVIII) are not needed in that perfect light but the sublunary reader may be more moved by the simile of the 'maynful mone' (1093) which opens section XIX than by the description of the procession in which the narrator suddenly sees his 'lyttel quene' (1147). His attempt to cross the river to her wakes him, back in the graveyard, knowing his violent desire prevented him from seeing more, commending his pearl to God and accepting that he is shown Christ in the sacrament of the Eucharist. The poem ends where it began, with more understanding of its nature, describing its own circle. The jeweller has to acknowledge that it is only God who creates 'oght of noght' (274) and owns his pearl but he creates his own pearl, the poem.

Sir Gawain is structured by repetitions, parallels and contrasts. The opening stanza seems to place the story within a purposeful and linear view of European history since the Trojan War but its first line will virtually be repeated at the end of the poem and its wheel presents a cyclical picture of 'werre and wrake and wonder . . . blysse and blunder' alternating 'bi syþez' (16–18). In this story we have two Christmases and New Years at the two courts of Camelot and Hautdesert, two great lords in King Arthur and Bertilak, two beautiful hostesses who are specifically compared ('Ho watz . . . wener þen Wenore, as þe wiȝe þoȝt', 943–45), two brave champions in Gawain and the Green Knight, three journeys from Camelot to Hautdesert, from Hautdesert to the Green Chapel, from the Green Chapel to Camelot. There are 'games' at both courts, the blow and the return blow, the three hunting scenes and the three seduction scenes, three exchanges of the winnings in each. The commercial vocabulary in which the agreements are made, the parties appraised and their achievements assessed encourages us to evaluate and to question them. For example, is Gawain's confession to the priest at Hautdesert 'worth' as much as his confession to the Green Knight at the Green Chapel? Gawain represents, so in a sense symbolizes, Camelot. But what does the Green Knight symbolize? Does Gawain still symbolize Camelot on his return as on his departure?

The symbolic contrast between the pentangle and the green girdle is obvious, though what the girdle symbolizes is less obvious. We are told at length what the pentangle symbolizes: 'And qhy þe pentangel apendez to þat prynce noble/ I am in tent yow to telle, þof tary me hyt me schulde' (623–24). The scene of the arming of the knight is already highly symbolic. The knight sets forth representing more than himself: his king, his court, his country, his family, their values, faith and reputation. Some of this signifi-cance is outwardly identified by heraldry. Spiritually, the symbolism of the arming applies to all Christians: the Christian 'soldier' is to 'put on the whole armour of God' (Ephesians 6:11–17). The five-pointed star on Gawain's shield

> is a syngne þat Salamon set sumquyle
> In bytoknyng of trawþe, bi tytle þat hit habbez,
> For hit is a figure þat haldez fyue poyntez,
> And vche lyne vmbelappez and loukez in oþer,
> And ayquere hit is endelez; and Englych hit callen
> Oueral, as I here, þe endeles knot. (624–30)

The sign betokens truth, the central virtue in the poem, because it has five points, it is composed of interlacing and interlocking lines, and the total figure can be drawn in one continuous line. Five is a sacred number. Mathematically, it produces a number ending in itself whenever it is squared. It suits Gawain because he was known to be ' For ay faythful in fyue and sere fyue syþez' (632): he was faultless in his five senses, he never failed in his five fingers, all his trust was in the five wounds of Christ, all his prowess came from the five joys of Mary and the 'fyft fyue' were his 'fraunchyse . . . fela3schyp . . . clannes . . . cortaysye . . . and pite' (652–54). The interconnected and continuous nature of these qualities are symbolized by this figure. (We may be reminded of the Beatitudes at the opening of *Patience*, envisaged perhaps as a circle of ladies, with Poverty and Patience first and last and so next to each other.) The view that all virtues are interconnected and involve each other had been put forward by various philosophers, including Aquinas. Ideally, this should be so, yet there is tension at Hautdesert between the claims of 'clannes' and 'cortaysye' and at the exchange of winnings between 'trawth' to the lady and to her husband.

Gawain leaves Camelot armed with the golden pentangle. He leaves Hautdesert armed with the green girdle. It is harder to say what the girdle symbolizes. It proves definitely only not to be what Gawain was told. It does not protect him but causes the slight injury dealt him in the return blow. It is not a 'sygne . . . of trawþe': the lady lied about it and it leads Gawain into telling a lie to her husband (and perhaps 'acting a lie' to the priest). The Green Knight offers it to Gawain, after he has 'confessed so clene' (2391) and 'hatz þe penaunce' (2392), as a 'pure token/ Of þe chaunce of þe grene chapel' (2398–99); Gawain accepts it as a 'syngne of my surfet' (2433); on his return to Camelot the whole court adopts it as a badge of honour. It can mean different things to different people. Different people can impose different meanings upon it.

Both pentangle and girdle are described as 'syngne', foregrounding the problem of signification. Initially it looks as if the pentangle is 'good', the sign of Gawain's virtue, and the girdle is 'bad', the sign of his compromise. The pentangle, logically and geometrically, has a claim to be eternally true; the girdle, sartorially, morally and epistemologically, can be arranged in various ways. There was contemporary interest in the theory of signification. A standard distinction was between natural and imposed signs. At first the pentangle seems to be a natural sign 'bi tytle' (626) because of its mathematical basis. The girdle, in contrast, is arbitrary: it bears the various meanings imposed on it by the Green Knight, Gawain and Camelot. However, we are also told that Solomon imposed the meaning on the pentangle ('Hit is a syngne þat Salamon set sumquyle/ In bytoknyng of trawþe', 624–25); most of the symbolism here ascribed to the figure seems to be the poet's own, and both Solomon and pentangle can have adverse as well as favourable associations. Furthermore, if human signification is largely arbitrary, the pliable girdle might be a 'truer' sign than the rigid pentangle in admitting the arbitrary nature of its significance. Some of the more recent readings of the poem raise doubts about the ideal pentangle and its application to Gawain. 'Piece by piece he is himself built up as a chivalric emblem . . . active expression of its meaning can hardly avoid reliance on false pride in a false projection of himself arrived at by false logic' (Watson 1987). Its replacement by the girdle is seen as realistic, a salutary education in humility. 'The poem's view of Gawain follows the same pattern as his signs. From the idealized Christian knight . . . [to] a fallible human being, whose goodness is a matter of dispute' (Prior 1994, 123). Or the girdle can be seen as open to false projection of the opposite kind: 'Gawain would like to use the green girdle as a sign for his own personal and permanent *untrawth*. He is unsuccessful . . . since he cannot establish it as a stable sign even for its first intended audience, the people of Arthur's court. This failure arises from the fact that the intended meaning is not something that is possible in the world of living humans: no man is in a state of permanent *untrawth*.' (Arthur 1987, 126). The poem, 'composed in a world where the armour of Platonic idealism had begun to show chinks', 'moves from a theory of inherent value, evinced chiefly in the pentangle, to a theory of ascribed value, evinced chiefly in the green girdle', from youthful idealism to a mature recognition that 'all signs of human institution are arbitrary, relative, comparative, ascriptive' (Shoaf

1984, 29–30). With this revaluation of the girdle goes a revaluation of Gawain and the Green Knight, Camelot, Hautdesert and the Green Chapel.

The girdle, in Shoaf's perception, becomes an image for the poem itself. One of its most haunting assertions, 'Þe forme to þe fynisment foldez ful selden' (499), suggests that experience rarely corresponds exactly to an 'endeles knot' such as the pentangle. Time and change are at work to qualify the symmetry of the New Year opening and close. Yet, as in *Pearl*, the poem partly satisfies the human desire for perfect form. It *almost* ends with its first line.

The circularity of these two poems alludes to the perfect forms of the pentangle and the pearl, images of eternity. Their linearity insists that they develop within time and return, changed, to their beginnings. Art is our best – or only – image of eternity and art is created and received within time. J.A. Burrow connects the structural circularity of much Ricardian poetry with an unheroic vision of humanity: 'Where epic moves forward to a triumphant or tragic close in which the achievements of the hero are celebrated, these poems turn back towards their starting place and reach there a muted and often doubtful conclusion.' (Burrow 1971, 100–101). A recurring theme in all four poems is that of home and exile, in Christian tradition central images of heaven and this life. At the beginning of *Pearl* the narrator accepts that the grain must die or 'No whete were elles to wones wonne' (32) but fails to see the spiritual application to his own loss: he believes that his pearl's home is the graveyard ('Ther wonys that worthyly', 47). By the end of the poem he knows that their true home is heaven, grieves to be exiled ('outfleme', 1177) from it but perceives himself as one of Christ's 'homly hyne' (1211) in this life. *Cleanness* culminates in the period of the Babylonian exile in which the exiled Daniel is the only person who can decode the writing on the wall. In *Patience* the whale's belly is Jonah's ironic home 'his bour' (276) and he tries to turn the woodbine into his ideal home ('Iwysse, a worthloker won to welde I never keped', 464). *Sir Gawain* opens and closes with the great story of exile at the beginning of European literature. Within this frame Gawain makes his circular and linear journey, returning to a Camelot which is home and yet not home in its different interpretation of his symbol.

14

Narrative Form and Insight

NICK DAVIS

The *Gawain*-poet[1] writes as one who wishes to convey the force of certain ethical teachings: 'Be patient', 'Fear and trust God', 'Practise courtesy', to single out but a few. One might have thought that precepts of the kind were best handled in an expository, teacherly form of instruction: 'This is what the virtue of Patience is and here are the reasons why one should be patient . . .'. Our author has, however, chosen to address the reader or hearer in a considerably more subtle way. Although the orderly exposition of moral precepts has a certain place in these poems – one thinks for example of the commendation of penitence in *Cleanness* – they consist mainly of densely-wrought accounts of particular actions and events, whose significance will emerge only on reflection. And in encountering the individual poems, *Patience* for example, we quickly discover why this should be the case. A moment's reasoning, this poem tells us, can inform anyone that Patience is a quality of which human beings stand in need: in a hypothetical instance, 'If my master sends me on an errand to Rome, I'd do better to go without complaining than complain, giving him offence, and have to go anyway' (compare 49–56).[2] This can be taken as self-evident. But – so the thought of the poem runs – there is a great difference between knowing *that* Patience is a necessary quality or virtue, and coming to know Patience *as* the noble (531) virtue that it is. Most of the time being patient doesn't look or feel at all noble. In order to come to know Dame Patience (see 29–45) in the more worthwhile sense it is necessary to reflect hard on processes of lived experience in which both the difficulty of being patient and the need to be patient become apparent; only then might one claim to have gained some genuine acquaintance with Patience, as distinct from possessing a more or less abstract and theoretical concept of its/her value. *Cleanness* is, as I shall argue, much preoccupied by this sort of

---

[1] I assume throughout that *Sir Gawain and the Green Knight* and its companion pieces in the Cotton Nero manuscript come from the hand of a single writer, or possibly of writers who worked in close association.

[2] For *Cleanness*, *Patience* and *Pearl* all references are to Andrew and Waldron 1978; for *Sir Gawain and the Green Knight*, to Tolkien and Gordon 1967.

distinction between the abstract and the concrete or intuitive understanding of a moral condition, in this case the condition of being 'clean'. The distinction, inconclusively explored in *Cleanness*, is still more integral to the structure and meaning of the other poems of the group, which address the dividedness of human experience between these contrary forms of understanding.

Telling stories is our usual means of presenting to thought and attempting to make sense of the processes of lived experience, actual or imaginable. A story offers to explain why event Y followed event X, and so implies something about the nature of a world in which event Y can follow event X. The framing of stories seems to be fundamental to human self-understanding; without it we would probably have little sense of identity, individual or collective ('We are the ones who did this and to whom this happened'). As well as being, largely, works of narrative, the poems of our group also show a considerable critical interest in this very human activity. Acceptable story-making is never pure observation or entirely random fantasy: we expect stories to string events together in more or less coherent sequences, possessed of a beginning, a development out of this beginning, and an end, so presenting the image of a world that makes cumulative sense. We tell stories about our lives in order to find meaning in what we have done and undergone, and one could hardly wish it otherwise (in a characteristic instance, our administration of justice usually and necessarily involves the piecing of scattered data together as coherent narrative material). Nevertheless, the ordinary human reliance on story-making incurs certain risks. Perhaps most characteristically it over-interprets the world, producing coherence and intelligibility where there may be none, or at least none of the kind envisaged (a convincing story can convict an entirely innocent person). Story-making can represent failure to adapt to reality as well as a form of responsiveness to reality's exacting demands. To piece together experienced and anticipated events in coherent, self-explanatory narrative sequences is to assume that one can interpret the world adequately from the position in which one happens to be standing, which is to assume that the world more directly corresponds to the material of one's own imagination, and so is more directly fashioned out of one's own wishes and anxieties, than is likely to be the case. *Patience*, *Pearl* and *Sir Gawain and the Green Knight* have centrally-placed narrative agents who attempt to make their experiences understandable to themselves by piecing them together in ways which they find convincing but which also prove to be wholly or partially inadequate (the most flagrant case is that of Jonah, who at a climactic moment attempts to regain his interpretative grip on the present by falsifying his image of the past). These central figures ultimately fail to remain at the centre of their own narratives, in the sense of holding on to a position from which they can see their component events whole and interpret them adequately. Critical discussion of *Pearl* has striven to define the role and function of the Dreamer-narrator in a story that mainly defines, against the grain of its narrator's understanding, the relationship between the Pearl and God; and recent criticism of *Sir Gawain and the Green Knight*, not dissimilarly, to give a stable account of Gawain's role as foregrounded narrative agent in a story that emanates, though invisibly, out of the designs of Morgan le Fay. The poems' approach to narrative composition has been influenced, I shall suggest, by the critique of what one might call human narrative egocentricity found in the scriptural books of Job and Ecclesiastes: the general burden of this critique is that the sense which we most spontaneously give to our life, under the pressure of experience, is probably not the sense that it has. *Pearl* and *Sir Gawain and the Green Knight* also associate inflexibility of narrative mind-set with the distinctively masculine consciousness of their central figures, foregrounded in encounters with bearers of a considerably more elusive female consciousness. The association is, however, made sympathetically and with an entirely uncondescending sense of what offers resistance to understanding in the reality which these male figures confront.

As thought-provoking narrative compositions, all of the poems of the group have been affected by the assertion, characteristic of later medieval philosophy, of 'God's infinite and absolute creative and causative power against those who thought to circumscribe it by the principles of natural philosophy' (Grant 1982, 537–38). Broadly, where earlier scholasticism in the manner of Aquinas and others had constructed a self-consistent and knowable divine order by analogy with and in relation to a (more or less Aristotelian) order of Nature and morality, later medieval thinkers tended to stress God's absolute transcendence of human, naturally-derived structures of inference; while not entirely rejecting the earlier scholastic synthesis, they viewed its account of the relationship between man and God as being in certain respects inadequate. As *Cleanness*, like *Patience*, forcefully reminds us, God's creative or destructive power is not limited by the requirements of human comprehension, and Nature is merely a local, conditional order which can be radically altered in pursuit of God's purposes: Jonah's retention of life when the whale swallows him in *Patience* (see esp. 258–59) and God's first two acts of vengeance in *Cleanness* (see esp. 363–72, 947–1052) are presented as clear affronts to that sense of the stability of things which human beings might derive from their ordinary experience. In its own way each of the poems is much concerned with a speculative issue which could be stated as follows: how is it possible for finite beings to live in given relation to an infinite one? This suggests another way of looking at the inadequacy of human story-making in the poems' conception of it. Perhaps the only sense genuinely possessed by events is the sense that God produces and perceives. This is not, however, a sense that human beings are well-equipped to grasp; their approach to participation in a history that God ordains is thus more properly one of faith and trust than one that assumes sustained capacity for insight and understanding. *Cleanness* also seems to be exploring the idea that

God, for his part, finds certain aspects of human behaviour unintelligible, and by the same token intolerable: signal acts of divine vengeance have occurred where divine and human understandings of the real have moved in entirely contrary directions. *Cleanness* is in most modern judgements a less aesthetically-honed piece than the other poems of the group. I suggest that it be viewed as a somewhat experimental broaching of issues which the other poems handle with greater assurance.

Cleanness as narrative and argument pivots around three memorable acts (presumably the 'þrynne wyses' of 1805) of divine vengeance on erring human beings – the extermination of virtually all living creatures in the Flood, the obliteration of Sodom and Gomorrah (which turns a once beautiful landscape into an imaginatively haunting anti-Nature; see 1013–48), and the destruction of Belshazzar and his regime at the hand of foreign invaders. These acts, we are informed at the start, represent departures from God's customary courtesy. Ordinarily, God practises 'mesure' (215) or moderation in dealings with his creatures, accepting their creaturely limitations; that is, he shows mercy to wrongdoers, and even in punishing them acts within the compass of their understanding (even Satan, in an example given, could in principle have recognized the justice of the punishment that his rebellion incurred). But the poem's acts of vengeance – seen as being elicited by a particular kind of wrongdoing, namely 'filth' – display on the other hand God's 'malys mercyles' (250); a rough modern equivalent would be phobic hatred and the, to an observer, irrational or excessive behaviour that goes with it. In these cases, I am trying to suggest, even the possibility of human and divine mutual comprehension has broken down. The drama of the poem unfolds at two levels. Its narratives vividly present the sets of mind which either bring human beings into the scope of God's malice (the determination of the Sodomites to get their hands on Lot's young male guests, the folly which Belshazzar and his concubines show in drinking from the Temple vessels) or result from their experience of it (the anguish, sympathetically conveyed, of Noah's contemporaries as they realize that the waters are about to engulf them). The sets of mind admit of no alteration or, in the case of the Flood's victims, are allowed none: more or less unwittingly, human beings have entered into terminal confrontation with God. At the same time the argument of the poem, which has these and a number of historically contiguous narratives at its service, attempts to explain how human beings can be 'clean' (this is conflated with the purity of heart commended in the Beatitudes), and so avoid incurring God's utter hatred.

Charlotte Morse has offered a map of the poem's design which shows clearly enough why the brief inset narrative of Christ's Incarnation, Nativity and Ministry should achronologically precede the third large-scale narrative of divine vengeance. This final narrative, though still dealing with Old Testament subject-matter, is implicitly concerned with the condition of modern followers of Christ who can make themselves 'clean' by having recourse to the sacrament of confession (Morse 1978, 129–99); that is, the emphasis has shifted from the need to know what 'cleanness' is to a practical means of achieving 'cleanness' in the sight of God, regardless of the limitations of human understanding. This shift of emphasis must, however, come as a surprise to the reader or auditor, since the poem has developed in such a way as to suggest the capacity of human beings to recognize and participate spontaneously in the condition of 'cleanness'. Like the other poems of the group, but at some cost of inconsistency (as in the case of the near-contemporary poem *Piers Plowman* we may be dealing with a controlled breakdown of orderly structures of exposition), *Cleanness* squarely addresses the difficulty of achieving positive knowledge of those aspects of the human that most directly concern God. As we follow the poem's progress, the idea of Nature is the first raft of security that it offers to the inhabitants of a dangerous world: to live by Nature is to be clean (the only 'law' imposed on Adam and Eve's immediate descendants, similarly, was 'loke to kynde'; 263). But this advice is not as easy to follow as one might have thought. It is not enough to know that Nature is good ('exposition'); one must know Nature as good ('intuition'), or in other words be able to implement this good in suitable actions and recognitions as a condition of being natural (cf. the more or less unwitting character of the offences that provoke God's ruthless vengeance) – the general aim of the poem as argument directed to an auditor or reader is to close, or at least narrow, the yawning gap between 'knowledge that' and 'knowledge as'. Assistance is at hand, however, in properties of the poetic medium itself: we are informed that praise of 'cleanness' is natural to it, and that 'fair forms' offer themselves spontaneously for the purpose; if on the other hand one tried to praise uncleanness the very medium would offer strong resistance (see 1–4). The idea seems to be that in dealing with poetry (writing or reading it) one is, as it were, making direct acquaintance with the good and the natural, and not just being told about it.

A major problem bound up with this idealization of the medium,[3] however, and one that fully emerges in the poem, is that art best provides acquaintance with the artful, while its commendations of the simple and intuitive remain a form of 'knowledge that'. Nature in its posited simplicity can be celebrated best by elaborate rehearsals of departures from it which most fully tax and display the writer's skill: the poem's ingenuity thus uncomfortably resembles that of its malefactors, who are convicted of a failure to rest content with the simple and obvious. In the narrated action of the poem God's first two acts

---

3 The poem seems to be aligning itself with the literary tradition of Alain de Lille's *Complaint of Nature*, which associates over-ingenious use of language with deviation from Nature's requirements, and specifically with sodomy (i.e. male homosexuality). The *Romance of the Rose*, commended as 'clean' at 1057, recapitulates many of Alain's arguments. For overviews of the tradition, see Curtius 1953, 106–27, and Wetherbee 1972, 128–266.

of vengeance deal with human 'filth', or straying from Nature's law, by disarranging natural order on a much larger scale; we are not speaking merely of the destruction of things, but of making the world operate by entirely anomalous physical principles (Spearing 1980). We also find that key passages pay homage to the idea of 'cleanness' by describing Nature wrought – through the 'craft' of Solomon as applied to the making of the Temple vessels (see 1451–88), and in the miracle of the Incarnation (see 1069–88) – to barely imaginable forms of aesthetic perfection. Moreover, the 'clean' style of art at which Soloman arrived in his wisdom seems hard to distinguish, except in elaboration of detail, from the, in context, over-fanciful and excessive style of art (musical, culinary) which is in vogue at Belshazzar's court (see 1401–16). Consciousness continues to encroach on the assumed spontaneity of intuition, as in the life-history of Belshazzar's father Nebuchadnezzar. A leader of ruthless capability, he has the good sense to honour God's Temple vessels and to listen to Daniel; his power becomes such that he is known as a god on earth ('þe god of þe grounde'; 1324). When on the other hand he *calls* himself 'god of þe grounde' (1663) God reduces him to madness: 'Þus he countes hym a kow þat watz a kyng ryche' (1685). The raft of Nature appears not to be as secure as one might have hoped. But, as has been said, the poem does push out another raft: an explicit sense of obligation to God would have prevented the destruction of Jerusalem and the Babylonian captivity (see 1161–68); the same sense of obligation instructs us in the present to keep ourselves metaphorically and spiritually 'clean' by going to confession, an institution adapted to man's lack of natural 'cleanness' (see 1110–48); at 1114, evocatively enough, human beings are 'fenny' – our ordinary disposition is towards mud and mire.

The gap between 'knowledge that' and 'knowledge as' is not to be closed by these means, or perhaps at all; Lot's bizarre attempted persuasion of the Sodomites to try his daughters in place of his guests (see 861–72) might be seen as acknowledging the theoretical impasse. I have spent a little time on the argument of *Cleanness* in order to show that it conducts a kind of logical harassment of its reader or hearer: we are drawn into a drama of (in)comprehension, where the very attempt to arrive at fullness and clarity of understanding is apt to function as a barrier to it. The remaining poems of the group bring this readerly predicament to a more satisfactory crystallization for thought as the predicament of the central figure *in* a narrative. Consideration of certain key terms from *Patience*, *Pearl* and *Sir Gawain and the Green Knight* will help to explain how the predicament takes form specifically as a narrative predicament – that is, as one of which only story-making can render adequate account. The poems might be compared with the thought-world of Kierkegaard and Kafka, shapers of an admittedly different modern sensibility, where reflective narrative nevertheless addresses somewhat comparable problems.

In lines 413–28 of *Patience* (a considerable amplification of Jonah 4.2–3)

Jonah attempts to become the masterly interpreter of his story to date. Jonah has been infuriated by God's failure to destroy Nineveh as threatened, which makes him (Jonah) a liar. I excerpt:

> Wel knew I þy cortaysye, þy quoynt soffrance,
> Þy bounté of debonerté and þy bene grace,
> Þy longe abydyng wyth lur, þy late vengaunce;
> And ay þy mercy is mete, þe mysse neuer so huge. (417–20)

– 'Didn't I say this would happen?' (To which the simple answer would be 'No', since the Jonah of the poem has not thought in these terms before.)[4] Interestingly, Jonah does not accuse God of inconsistency, but of having had the consistent purpose of making a fool of him. In his recent adventures Jonah has at different times acted in the explicit knowledge of dealing with a God who inexorably enforces his justice (see his words at 209–12) and who responds to sincere pleas for mercy (he accepts at 305–7 that his prayer from the whale's belly at 282–88 has been answered). Justice and mercy are both, so far as Jonah is concerned, available modalities of divine behaviour. But what he cannot bear is the service of a God who shifts beyond anticipation from one modality to another: Jonah thought that he was implementing God's justice but has been, as it turns out, implementing his mercy; he therefore claims that he knew all the time that he was dealing with a merciful God, as an alternative to confronting the more disturbing idea that his dealings are with a God who can elude his understanding altogether. The accusation of 'courtesy' appears to encode a fear of God's large-spirited unpredictability or spontaneity, cultivated as an ideal of aristocratic behaviour in the later medieval period (cf. the Theseus of the *Knight's Tale*). Jonah for his part lays no claim to courtesy or to an insider's understanding of its ways, and opts spontaneously for the image of a God who, however 'courteous', has played a petty-minded trick on him.

Jonah knows that God can be just, and that God can be merciful, but what he cannot make recognizable to himself – understandably enough in view of the given scope of his vision – is a consciousness in and for which justice and mercy coexist (at 93–96 he has ironically anticipated the Crucifixion, for God a point of coincidence between justice and mercy, imaged as the end of a course of action which no sensible person would take). In the following episode of the woodbine God therefore rather contemptuously offers him a valid anthropomorphism that he can intuit, and in that sense has to accept: 'If you feel so upset about the destruction of the woodbine, how do you suppose that I would have felt about the destruction of Nineveh?' With

---

4 As Spearing notes (1970), the poem has given Jonah an entirely different motive for attempting to flee the role of prophet, whereas the scriptural text does not make his motivation explicit; the poem, in other words, has closed off the possibility that Jonah here is speaking the truth.

regard to the virtue of patience the poem makes, as has been said, a similar distinction: although we can intellectually infer the human need for patience, and esteem the virtue on that somewhat abstract basis, our plight resembles Jonah's in that life does not usually allow us to know patience *as* the excellent virtue that it is. The poem's suggestive framing of the idea occurs in the statement with which it begins and ends: 'Patience is a poynt [concluding line: nobel poynt], þaȝ hit displese ofte.' 'Poynt' here is usually, and rightly, understood as 'virtue', though this meaning was not very common (information about Middle English usage is drawn from *MED*). 'Point' in Middle English carried a wider range of potential meanings than it does for us, all derived through obvious kinds of semantic extension from the basic meaning, 'dot marked on a surface' (cf. Latin *punctus*). In its exposition of Gawain's Pentangle emblem *Sir Gawain and the Green Knight* makes the meaning 'virtue' overlap significantly with another available meaning, 'point defined by a convergence of lines (as in an angular figure)': through tracking the form of the Pentangle as five-pointed linear construction we come to understand an exemplary practice of virtue (see 619–65; more on this later). As Laurence Eldredge has suggested (1979), the poems' handling of the idea of a point seems to have as its context the period's intense speculative interest in the nature of a geometrical point;[5] for enquiring laypeople as well as the academically learned concern with this apparently arcane matter brought a wide range of philosophical and theological issues to a suggestive focus (see also Molland 1983). A dot marked on a surface is, plainly, something that we can see in the ordinary sense, knowing that it is there as a fact of apprehension. The geometricians' point, conversely, is not something that we can see, since strictly speaking it has no parts or dimensionality; our intellect, however, reliably locates it for thought at a determined angle of convergence between lines – in the period's language it exists for the 'mathematical imagination', as distinct from ordinary or imaginable seeing.[6] The mystic Julian of Norwich is thus being entirely precise when she explains that 'I saw God in a poynte, that is to sey, in myn vnderstondyng' (Glasscoe 1978, 13). The statement refers to an exclusively intellectual act of 'seeing' – the intellect formed a genuine idea of God which otherwise had no intuitive basis. Julian distinguishes clearly between such 'seeing' and those visions of the Passion, perceived as if spread out in space and time, which were given to what she terms her bodily sight. In this same way one might distinguish between what can take form in the intellect alone, and what can be grasped by intuition, in the sense

---

5 My understanding of this context's relevance differs, however, from Eldredge's.
6 The fourteenth century saw recurrently fierce academic dispute on the issue of whether the geometrical *punctus* existed *in re* or purely as a creature of the 'mathematical imagination'; the real measure of line, albeit measurable by God alone, might for example be the number of points of which it consists. Our poems appear to take the view that the *punctus* has a real existence.

of thoroughly organized as or in relation to a familiar structure of experience. One of the leading ideas framed by *Patience*, as thought-provoking narrative, seems to be that the coincidence of justice and mercy in God can be given to human intellection, but not satisfactorily to human intuition.

We can infer more about this rift in experience from *Pearl*'s handling of the term 'spot', which receives considerable emphasis as the refrain-word of the first five stanzas and recurs in what develops out of them. It can carry both the meanings of 'bounded location in space and/or (an important difference from modern usage) in time', and of 'mark or stain'; but the poem is organized in such a way as to produce a significant and provocative overlapping of the two. Reflection on the lost pearl produces the necessary conceptual mobility: it is remembered as spotless or immaculate, the place and time in which the Dreamer mourns it define a cosmically locatable spot (see 61; the temporal and physical co-ordinates of the scene have been carefully established), it or its place of interment is a spot of physical matter (see 25); but its lack of a spot, as in the refrain, also latently implies the impossibility of making any physical discovery of it – the instability of the term 'spot' becomes a way of capturing important aspects of the human for thought. At one level, a spot is a dot that does not exist for the intellect as a point: we might say that it is too spread out, though at the same time that it is the intuition's only means of approach to apprehension of a point. But 'spot' understood as temporal and/or physical location also indicates a condition of confinement and suffering (cf. the 'doel-doungoun' of 1187). Human beings inhabit a spot on the earth, and indeed the earth itself as spot set on its course between Creation and Dooms-day, where spottedness (unclarity, stainedness, disposedness to sin) is an intransigent material condition of life. This spot is the place in which we aspire to the 'cleanness' (with connotations of sharpness; cf. *Cleanness* 1099–108) of the point; the given human condition is spotted – which we need to hear partly as 'located' – but at the same time the point is the intellect's object of affinity. After his death Chaucer's Troilus, or rather his spirit, looks down on 'This litel spot of erthe' (Benson 1987, 584; V, 1815) with the new-found clarity of vision which ascent through the spheres affords him, and laughs at his mourners' unhappiness; this insight, we are to understand, would not have been available to him before. In the poems of our group, however, the effect is different: their narrative construction emphasises the close, continuing intertwinedness of genuine perception and misperception in mortal human experience.

Patience, Pearl, and *Sir Gawain and the Green Knight* deal with individual projects of identity where one obvious purpose is to preserve a sense of what one is, before oneself and before others, unimpaired across time; the result of such aspiration can be seen at its simplest in Jonah's ill-founded attempt to convince himself and/or God that he knew what was happening all along. These three poems are shaped towards concluding statements which closely echo those with which they began. The two last-mentioned poems have 101 stanzas, a numerical quantity unlikely to have been arrived at by chance; viewed in relation to the poems' large-scale recapitulative structure, this feature suggests that the ending of one cycle ('100', with its connotations of completeness) which the narrative has tracked is to be understood as precipitating the beginning of another that will have many of the same properties. The apprehension of cyclical patterns of recurrence in the human experience of time is an ancient one, no doubt derived by inference from such obvious periodic phenomena as seasonal progression and the sequence of the lunar phases (Eliade 1955; Morris 1984). This apprehension is, however, profoundly ambivalent in what it might imply for the sustaining of a project of identity. It is convenient to consider the negative implication first, explored in an individual manner in *Sir Gawain and the Green Knight*'s well-known account of the seasons' annual progression, since to do so is also to bring out certain features of the positive one.

The passage (500–35), which in its narrative positioning follows Gawain's mid-winter acceptance of the Green Knight's challenge, presents a procession ('vche sesoun serlepes [in turn] sued after oþer'; 501) of somewhat anthropomorphized figures, including 'crabbed Lent', spring weather that 'contends' (*þrepez*; 504) with Winter, a West Wind (Zephyrus) whose whistling on plants marks the summer, a Harvest who hurries on to the scene as if to interrupt this idyll, and an angry late-autumnal wind who wrestles with the Sun, thereby causing or hastening the Sun's decline. It also describes the humanly evocative behaviour of birds and plants, among them the crop-plants which are Harvest's concern, to the changing weather conditions which these figures represent: the birds, for example, make noble music on summer's full arrival, the crop-plant listens to Harvest's advice and hardens himself against the winter (and/or this is Harvest's self-hardening, since the 'hym' of 521 is ambiguous). The whole passage ends with an explicit act of human consciousness, the worried turning of Gawain's mind to his impending, probably fatal journey. But such acts of consciousness have been implied throughout in the omnipresence of man-like thoughts and feelings. In the passage we encounter a mentality caught up in the seasonal progression, which substantially shapes what it is at any given phase or moment. The impulse of this mentality is to consolidate itself and flourish in given circumstances, but these movements of self-assertiveness are oddly counter-productive. Harvest, for example, forward-looking as well as pugnacious like most of the other agents of change, suggests the making of a stand against winter's coming. As a consequence the duly hardened plant will fall under the reaper's sickle; this is Harvest's deceit, or perhaps a deceitfulness built into the conditions of life.

The passage is indebted to the Old Testament books of Wisdom, and particularly to the internal critique of Wisdom provided by the books of Job and Ecclesiastes. Wisdom according to the scriptures derives, or ought to derive, from reflective attention to the course of things; it suggests a mode of human self-adaptation to the world as we have it. As a matter of common opinion there is, for example, a proper time for everything, and the wise individual will know how to recognize and make use of it (cf. for example Psalms 1.3, 31.15, 104.27). The famous list of 'times' provided by Ecclesiastes – 'a time for being born, a time for dying, a time for planting, a time for uprooting what has been planted',[7] and so on (see 3.1–8) – points to the availability of such wisdom. The list issues, however, into the following series of puzzled statements:

> What profit does a man gain from his labour? I have seen the affliction that God sends to the sons of men, with the result that they are divided [more literally, 'stretched apart'] between its requirements (*ut distendantur in ea*). He has made everything good in its own time, and he has handed the world over to their disputation, with the result that man does not keep track of (*non inveniat*) the work of God from its beginning to its end. (3.9–11)

The speaker gains no satisfaction from his masterly survey of 'times'. It merely shows the diversity of the tasks to which human beings necessarily give themselves, to the detriment of lasting self-possession or encompassing awareness. What is voiced in Ecclesiastes is not a confidence in shared tradition and accumulated knowledge, but rather the commitment of an individual to an uncomfortable insight which the optimistic, collective vision fails to accommodate; this individual has discovered – ironically, by having recourse to such shared 'wisdom' – that he, like other men or indeed like the animals (see 3.19–20), possesses no adequate control over his own destiny (Williams 1987). The last sentence of the just-quoted passage, with its suggestion of a resistance to continuous (self-)understanding which forms part of the very structure of things, offers a context for one of the dark statements with which the poem introduces its account of the seasons: 'Þe forme to þe fynisment foldez ful selden' (499). The seasons passage as a whole echoes the reflective, sceptical poem about cosmic process with which Ecclesiastes begins (see 1.1–11). From one point of view, of course, a cyclical progression like that of the seasons does precisely produce a recurrence of the same; but this detached, spectatorial vantage-point on the cycle is not that of the individual caught up in it, experiencing the onward movement as disorientation and loss of envisaged purpose: 'A ȝere ȝernes ful ȝerne, and ȝeldez neuer lyke' (498). 'And þus ȝirnez þe ȝere in ȝisterdayez mony' (529) most directly evokes Job's 'We are surely of yesterday, and do not know how long the shadow of our days will be upon the earth' (8.9), but (like Macbeth's famous soliloquy) has been affected by Ecclesiastes' proof that in attempting

---

7 All scriptural passages are translated from the Vulgate (Weber 1975).

to grasp and make use of the present we encounter what has existed before, and therefore a reminder that nothing lasting was achieved (see 1.9–11).

The seasons passage also brings out assumed features of common human experience which are not strongly emphasized in these scriptural texts, but which help to confirm their drift of argument. Like the rest of the poem and the other poems of its group, it is written in a style which suggests the power of given, transient sensory phenomena to shape awareness from moment to moment. There is typically an excess of 'phenomenon' over 'interpretation', making for a dramatic sense of immersedness in ongoing events. The human predicament as represented is that of Marvell's body-tormented soul, 'blinded with an eye; and (. . .) Deaf with the drumming of an ear' ('A Dialogue between the Soul and Body'). We find that the poems adopt metres and a narrative-descriptive method which emphasize the sheer impact of phenomena on the consciousness to which they are exposed. In *Sir Gawain and the Green Knight* the long alliterative line might be heard or felt as a series of such 'impacts', whereas the rhymed and less insistently alliterative lines suggest a certain standing back from the phenomenal rush. In all the poems descriptive detail is not merely accumulated, but selected and arranged in such a way as to create a strong sense of participation and local vantage point. Human beings are, no doubt, often in a position to select or modify their perceptual environment. What the poems of the group primarily stress, however, is sheer human responsiveness to a given environment and its pressures – vivid experiences, in particular, take over much of what we are. Gawain is a refined individual (we are told that he 'watz funden fautlez in his fyue wyttez', 640, which seems to mean that he had his responses to sensations under exemplary control) who makes intelligent use of this human proclivity: wrung by suffering on his first winter journey, he embraces the suffering as a form of penitential self-denial and self-emptying (see 750–62); later, on the Lady of the Castle's third approach, he accepts her attentions partly as a welcome distraction from anguished thoughts about imminent death (see 1750–65; as the narrator points out, this is in fact a moment of great danger). The prophet Jonah, conversely, a less civilized type, seems all too readily deflected from wider concerns by the comforts of his lately-sprouted woodbine (see *Patience*, 457–64). But the same aspect of humanness is being put in evidence; this is what it is to inhabit a spot. Susceptibility to the disorientating but also addictive effects of strong sensations is perhaps most clearly displayed and described by the narrating figure of *Pearl* (see esp. 129–32). In the poems' representation of it human awareness is anchored with unusual firmness to the perceptual field in which it happens to take shape (Stanbury 1993 concentrates helpfully on the importance and problematics of seeing), another aspect of our common subjectedness to the processes of time.

Anti-Wisdom of the kind or kinds that I have been describing might be strikingly inimical to the cultivation of narrative. It tends to erode the difference, or settings apart of persons, things, events, which narratives of their nature produce, and are valued for producing. One of the seasons passage's proposed linkings of itself, for example, with the episode of Challenge and Beheading at Arthur's court which precedes it is the rueful observation that men who have had a lot to drink behave much alike (see 497). Moreover, as an aspect of this erosion it disrupts the sequentiality of expectation and consequence on which narrative's understood coherence depends. Here is anti-Wisdom in one of its characteristic scriptural formulations:

> A good name is better than precious ointment; and the day of death better than the day of birth. (Ecclesiastes 7.2)

It is difficult to hear this through without bewilderment. The first part of the verse speaks of purpose and tangible achievement; the second part, of their vanity or lack of enduring substance ('vanity', from the Vulgate Bible's *vanitas*, familiarly translates Hebrew *hevel* = 'breath', 'vapour'). The *Gawain*-poet's 'Þe forme to þe fynisment foldez ful selden' taxes thought in a similar way: if nothing that human beings value survives the test of time, all stories will collapse into a single story of defeat.

I stress the point, however, in order to take due measure of the conceptual distance that separates *Sir Gawain and the Green Knight*'s account of the seasonal progression from the much more optimistic account of a human relation to time which is given near the poem's start:

> Bot of alle þat here bult, of Bretaygne kynges,
> Ay watz Arthur þe hendest, as I haf herde telle.
> Forþi an aunter in erde I attle to schawe,
> Þat a selly in si3t summe men hit holden,
> And an outtrage awenture of Arthurez wonderez.
> If 3e wyl lysten þis laye bot on lyttel quile,
> I schal telle hit as-tit, as I in toun herde, with tonge,
> > As hit is stad and stoken
> > In stori stif and stronge
> > With lel letteres loken,
> > In londe so hatz ben longe. (25–36)

This declaration of purpose points to, and tends to superimpose as a single object of reflection, several different forms of linkage across time making for the endurance of stable form. At the level of the smallest temporal unit we have the internal connectedness of the alliterating line, locked together by means of 'loyal' letters – I assume that each acts loyally to its predecessor by maintaining this predecessor's form. Over a somewhat wider span of time we have the similar internal connectedness of a 'stiff and strong' narrative, commending itself to attention and memory as a firm, self-consistent pattern. The narrator presents himself as repeating something already set down and made firm ('stad and stoken'); an aspect of the firmness is that well-wrought

story-making in this style, or perhaps this particular story, and/or alliterative
line-construction has/have long existed in the land. Historical events set
down in such solid material are likely to go on being recalled, and recalled
correctly. But then Arthur is already, for us, singled out from a sequence of
British kings who can go unnamed by the currency of his reputation for noble
accomplishment: 'Ay watz Arthur þe hendest, as I haf herde telle' (26). In the
long view of British history taken at the beginning of the poem, this history
is a rapid, confusing alternation of 'blysse and blunder' (17), the turmoil
produced over time by bold men who loved fighting (see 21). Arthur's
reputation as we now receive it points, however, to a solidity of achievement
which, at least as remembered, stands out against the monotony of repeated
flourishing and collapse. The structure of the whole passage tends to conflate
the attributed project of Arthurian civilization with the empirical projects of
the poem as integrated composition, and of the regional or national artistic
traditions with which it aligns itself – all are the attempted making of a form
and identity self-preserved across time and therefore, figuratively, the completion of the cyclical as unbroken circle. The Pentangle in its character of
'endless knot' (see 628–30) is thus an appropriate heraldic device to be borne
by the member of Arthur's court which the action of the poem singles out as
the court's representative. On the other hand, the Green Knight's performance at Arthur's court counts as a spoof, if a terrifying one, on the theme of
endurance at the cost of radical self-discontinuity – going on speaking
through one's own severed head makes the shape of the idea disturbingly
clear. The Pearl, rather similarly, can go on being recognized as the Pearl by
dint of appreciation that she exists in radical discontinuity with her earthly
self; the Dreamer is able to work this out by inference and under her
instruction, but goes on finding it deeply counter-intuitive. In both poems
intellective apprehension of an order that transcends time co-exists discon-
certingly with intuitive recognition of mortal human subjectedness to time.

 Pearl and *Sir Gawain and the Green Knight* may be compared as poems in
which male narrative agents' projects of identity that have both an intellective
and an intuitive dimension are defined and put to the test of events. In their
intuitive dimension the projects are kept in place for the poems' central
figures by well-defined acts of projection: the Dreamer in *Pearl* and Gawain
attempt, very understandably in context, to fashion out of the reality that
confronts them a world corresponding to their own most immediately felt, if
not necessarily acknowledged, psychological needs. At the beginning of *Pearl*
the narrator recalls a situation in which the Pearl existed for him as an entity
objectively known. In his character of jeweller he was able to assess the Pearl's
worth by reference to shared, public standards of evaluation (see Davis 1995);
knowing, by these (ostensibly) unimpeachable standards, the Pearl's pre-
eminent worth, he attached much of his sense of his own worth to it.
Relationship to the Pearl has been, and therefore continues to be, a vital means
of understanding what he is; he experiences her loss as a loss of much of the

selfhood that he thought he possessed. The poem, accordingly, takes shape as a series of attempts to reach an apprehension of what the Pearl now is to him, in or despite her loss, and so reclaim a degree of self-possession; in the poem's plausible account of processes of mourning affective denial of loss is closely bound up with the bid for clarity of thought concerning loss. The first attempt, which the narrator performs in waking life and which precipitates his dream, can be taken as characteristic. As we encounter him he is seeking to assign the loss to a typical sequence of loss and gain in which he, like other human beings, participates, and which he can therefore understand and accept. Collective wisdom offers him the successive activities of wheat-cultivation as a suitable object of thought, and he enters an actual scene of harvesting at line 37: kinds of loss (evidently mapping utterly serious human loss through death) – preparation of the ground with valued materials, burial of seeds, and burial of good seeds at that (see 25–36) – must be incurred before the wheat will grow. In New Testament contexts (see John 12.24–25 and 1 Corinthians 15.35–38 on the theme of resurrection) the scene has large and obvious figurative potential. We can infer that the aspiration to wisdom is valid, and will find that the seeds (a metaphor which the passage supports) of much of what will develop in the ensuing dream have already been present here in an artful disposition; for example, the narrator's sense that the Pearl lives on in an appropriately rich dwelling-place (see 41–48), a fantasy as applied to a burial-mound, will nevertheless bear fruit in his vision of the Pearl as an inhabitant of Heaven, numbered among the brides of Christ. What the passage stresses, however, is the narrator's inability to stand at the vantage point on loss and gain in their ordered relationship which wisdom rightly commends to him; the immediate pressures of grief, especially as intensified by the beauty and other sensuous properties of the scene, are simply too great. Or, figuratively, the setting of things in order which precedes harvesting has been well accomplished, the capacity to harvest is limited or lacking. He summarizes his predicament in these words:

> Þa3 kynde of Kryst me comfort kenned,
> My wreched wylle in wo ay wra3te. (55–56)

The first-quoted line is, perhaps purposively, ambiguous ('Although Nature instructed me in a comfort deriving from Christ', 'Although Christ's nature was present to my intellect as a bringer of comfort'), but asserts the basic correctness of the narrator's intellectual apprehensions of order; the second line, alarmingly, speaks of currents of mental life which these apprehensions have absolutely no power to direct – what the intellect (rightly) presents as being the case remains in important respects unthinkable or ungraspable.

Modern commentators have differed on the question of whether the narrator of *Pearl* moves towards enlightenment in the course of the dream, which is called a space of 'auenture' (64): the stages of his physical movement and of his dialogue with the Pearl define a spiritual progress (see e.g.

Finlayson 1974); he remains enmeshed throughout in entirely earthbound categories of understanding, and so no progress of the kind is made (see e.g. Kean 1967). But a good deal of the poem's intriguingness as narrative composition seems to have to do with the fact that both are the case. The narrator confronts intellections of increasing revelatory power: a particularly important transition comes at the point where the Pearl explains (by reference to Matthew's parable, 13.45–46) that the pearl of which he is properly in search is that of salvation (see 721–44); his final vision is of the Heavenly Jerusalem, and of the apocalyptic Lamb to which/whom he is inexorably drawn. The intuitions which support these intellections remain, however, inadequate and basically fixed, since their tissue is that of ordinary experience: 'the textual space we inhabit as we read the poem is principally constructed of the dreamer's visual universe'; one consequence is that his vision of the heavenly city affects us as 'a powerful dramatization of the experience of not knowing or of seeing that which cannot fully be grasped' (Stanbury 1993, 35). Crucially, the figure of the dreamer's longing remains the lost Pearl, imagined as that being in union with whom he would again find his wholeness (Spearing 1970, 110–17). Although the most solid natural identities offered for the narrator and the Pearl are, respectively, those of grieving father and of daughter lost through death, it is important that the Pearl should have been in her first evocation Woman as a projection of the masculine imagination, spanning a much wider range of cultural meanings (cf. the 'luf-daungere', or mistress's stand-offishness, of 11, and the erotically-inflected language of 6). We are aware simultaneously of a compelling, human directedness of desire towards an imaginable though ultimately elusive object, and of those remorseless acts of intellection which refer all desire finally to a God who cannot be imagined.

Pearl as narrative of 'adventure' develops through repeated breaching or disruption of those forms in which the narrator spontaneously organizes the experiences of his dream. The landscape in which he first finds himself, a version of the Earthly Paradise in which trees have indigo trunks and birds sing an improved human music, lies at the limits of the imaginable. On the other hand the content of the landscape that he sees on the far side of the river is not, strictly speaking, imaginable at all; or to put it another way, composable for thought in a 'landscape' as given to the objectivity of natural perception. Here, says the Pearl, 144,000 virgins including me are simultaneously wedded to a lamb. Here absolute equality and absolute hierarchy both prevail, as reflected in the fact that my companions and I all have the rank of Queen; but of course the Virgin is also our Queen. Objectively viewed, a queen might be said to be someone who ranks higher than, say, a countess (as the Dreamer observes at 489–92); a principle of comparison seems to be intrinsic to the idea of 'queen' in its ordinary currency (the jeweller-narrator's first estimation of the Pearl's high worth was obviously reached through comparison; see 7–8). To this going and convincing objectivity, however, the

Pearl responds with the unyielding statement that she as entity is quite different from anything that the narrator can possibly imagine – a principle that he formally embraces in declaring that Pygmalion could not have succeeded in portraying the Pearl, and that Aristotle could not have incorporated her properties into his philosophy of Nature (see 750–52). The dream-adventure of *Pearl* proceeds as a ratcheting up, finally to breaking-point (see 1153–64, where the dreamer's mind has passed beyond the limit of what it can even imagine containing for thought), of what can be inferred concerning the Pearl and salvation, and what can be given to natural perception. The conflict announced at the start, between 'kynde of Kryst' and the 'wrechyd wylle', has not been resolved in any sense: on the contrary, the authority of both has been very powerfully instated. It would be beside the point to convict the narrator of blindness under circumstances where seeing as such could not yield results different from the ones he obtains.

The narrative progression of *Sir Gawain and the Green Knight* might be said to be the opposite of *Pearl*'s, in so far as its stages are marked by Gawain's strengthening (though partly erroneous) conviction that he understands what is going on. The passage which describes Gawain's ceremonious arming in preparation for his quest (566–69) throws a good deal of light on the poem's larger narrative structure. Three components of the arming – all loops of various kinds, representing bonds of human connectedness and obligation – are singled out for our attention as the passage progresses (Watson 1987). They are in presented sequence the 'vrysoun' (608; cf. modern 'horizon'), a silk band which attaches the rear of Gawain's helmet to the backplate of his armour; embroidered by female hand with turtle doves, love-knots and the like, this is significant of courteous and erotically-inflected relations between the sexes. Next-mentioned is the 'cercle', a flat metal crown studded with brown (= 'male') diamonds, projecting the bonding of chivalric brotherhood and of a society of (male) equals (cf. the form of the Round Table, mentioned several times in the poem); we are told that this possessed more worth (615–16). Last comes Gawain's Pentangle emblem, which receives its own passage of complex exposition. It is generally agreed that this passage places courteous and chivalric commitment in a wider context of Christian commitment (see especially Burrow 1965, 37–51). I have argued that, as a geometrical figure with a very recognizable profile in the speculative mathematics of the period, the Pentangle as glossed here offers precise theoretical guidance in reconciling – in the terms of the figure's topology, joining in a continuous though intricate bond – kinds of ethical commitment that might well pull in different directions (Davis 1993); it signifies both inter-human bonds and the human bond with God, on the principle that these are indissolubly connected (cf. Luke 6.83). The reference in the passage as a whole is to moral choices which recurrently confront the member of a Christian and courtly culture (cf. the 'Maying' passage from Malory's *Morte D'Arthur* (Vinaver 1971, 648–49), which in context acknowledges the delicacy of the situation in which

Guinevere and Lancelot find themselves; our poem is more specifically concerned with male moral agency). The passage clearly arranges its physical loops – i.e. 'bonds' – in ascending order of importance. Viewed in its appropriate mathematical context, the Pentangle defines a proportion (the one known in our own times as the Golden Proportion, out of which the figure is built at every level) which brings unequal quantities into a harmonious and mutually-supportive relationship; that is, it characterizes an ideal pattern of good moral proportionality such that the perceived relation of commitment A to commitment B already yields that of commitment B to commitment C (the period's study of Aristotle forms the background to the poem's preoccupation with the achievement of good proportion in ethical dealing). As much of the action of the poem demonstrates, Gawain is amorously committed to Woman (an important obligation) as one already committed by loyalty to fellow males (treated as being of greater ethical significance), and committed to fulfilling obligations to males, where obligations to Woman are also at stake, as one already devoted to fulfilling his obligations to God, the most binding of all. Gawain's practice of virtue, the arming passage gives us to understand, conformed with unusual closeness to the ideal pattern (an intellection of 'Truth' in a Christian-philosophical understanding) set forth in the Pentangle, hence his right to bear this figure as his heraldic emblem; the passage makes high claims on Gawain's behalf, though not exactly a claim to perfection.

This theoretical structuring of the moral life lends support to and is supported by a narrative design of beautiful formal clarity. The design takes shape for us as an 'imagined sequence of events' or our sense of 'what is really happening' (in the Russian Formalists' language, *fabula*), prompted by 'features of selection, presentation and ordering which we do not take to be determined by *fabula*' (*szujhet*). At both levels we are made aware of Gawain's own attempted conceptual ordering of his experiences and of his various moral obligations; one aspect of the poem's artful presentation of its story-matter is, of course, that its implied vantage-point on much of what transpires is Gawain's own. Somewhere between our own perceptions and Gawain's there takes shape a story whose matrix is two successive years' celebration of Christ's Mass, an act of serious devotion to God which characteristically issues into acts of human conviviality (see 63 et seq., 748 et seq., 995 et seq.). As an upshot of Christmas merrymaking Gawain finds himself under a formal obligation to two men (as it transpires one man), which leads to the playing out of (what seems to be) the mortally serious Beheading Game with the Green Knight and of (what seems to be) the light-hearted Exchange of Winnings Game with the Lord of the Castle; the two rounds of the Beheading Game frame or bracket the three rounds of the Exchange of Winnings Game. This last defines an external purpose or upshot, in the forms of 'winnings' to be publicly exchanged with the Lord of the Castle, for Gawain's (apparently) secret amorous encounters ('love-talking'; see 927) with the Lady; as presented (the two actions are partly simultaneous) the Lord's acquisition of 'winnings' in three days of hunting frames Gawain's acquisition of 'winnings' – kisses and finally the green girdle – in three playfully-managed encounters. In other words, a Gawain-centred *fabula* and *szujhet* arrange the following forms of human bonding in a sequence embedded according to descending order of perceived importance: human to God, precipitating human to human in a setting of Christmas celebration, framing Man (male) to Man exclusively, framing Man to Man as mediated by dealings with Woman, framing Man to Woman as mediated (at Gawain's insistence) by dealings with Man. Gawain accepts that he has obligations to the Lady, roughly a matter of respecting her feelings and privacy. But at a crucial moment of ethical decision (see 1773–75) he declines her sexual advances in explicitly subordinating his obligations to her to his obligations to her husband, and to his even more serious obligations as a devout Christian. This hierarchical arrangement of moral bonds receives seeming confirmation when the Lady, as if motivated by love, unexpectedly produces the seemingly magical gift which may well enable Gawain to fulfil what he sees as his overriding obligation to a fellow man, and to the still more inclusive ideal of Truth projected in the Pentangle; specifically, what were at first the exclusively Man to Man dealings of the Beheading Game turn out, like the Exchange of Winnings, to have Woman as their concealed mediator.

The Pentangle undoubtedly 'works' as a template of choice and perception – at the most practical level it helps to save Gawain's life, as well as protect his soul from 'Gret perile' (1768; though a role may also be played, as it were out of sight, by the Virgin whose image is depicted on the inner side of Gawain's shield, and whose aid the narrator directly implores with a striking shift of tenses in this same line). Gawain's dealings with Man, in the second encounter of the Beheading Game, are indeed mediated by his dealings with Woman, if not at all in the way he had supposed. At the same time, however and needless to say, more or less everything that is gratifying to Gawain in the understanding of 'what is really happening' that he has constructed by implicit reference to the Pentangle collapses at the touch of Bertilak's final revelations, a very crushing experience. But we are not quite as surprised by this as Gawain, in view of the psychological projectivism that has gone to the shoring up of an intrinsically valid or wise practice of virtue. Bertilak's revelations give form to what we have already inferred as sub-text, namely that neither Man nor Woman has been in the place where Gawain has intuitively sought to locate them; we have been dealing with projections of masculine and feminine identity that correspond to Gawain's thoroughly-motivated anxieties concerning himself. Gawain seems to discover in the Lord of the Castle, and before learning of their common identity, a sort of benign counterpart to the Green Knight who seems set to cut his head off. Particularly as masked by the delayed arrival of explicit or conscious recognition, this tale of unresolved rivalry for possession of a desired woman

played out with an older man hugely admired and hugely feared stirs up rich
Oedipal material (Brewer 1980; E. Wilson 1976). Bertilak himself is, however,
an unusual, projectively-elusive being who seems to have little interest in
stories or sustained projects of identity: his performance at Arthur's court is
a self-contained and explosive dramatic interlude, albeit one that does not
confer the usual assurance that it was all pretence (Arthur's words at 470–77
are clearly meant to cheer people up); we see him hunting and otherwise
taking part in experiments on the world, accepting the largely contingent
results. Gawain's well-known anti-feminist outburst (2407–28) might be seen
as a wishful attempt to hive off his relations with Man – where, the idea seems
to be, he is at least dealing with what he can understand – from his relations
with Woman, now placed as radically other and unknowable. What Bertilak
goes on to say, however, denies him even this epistemological comfort: he
(Bertilak) has merely been what a woman – 'þyn aunt', in fact – has required
him to be, meanwhile pursuing some schemes of his own. Bertilak's account
of the real, underlying *fabula* (2456–62), stemming it would seem from Morgan's (unexplained) wish to kill Guinevere, is flippant in manner and under-
informative; but it reveals a Gawain, and a Bertilak, inextricably caught up
in dealings with and between women, so thoroughly disabling Gawain's
final attempt to take command of the interpretation of his own story (compare
Fisher 1989 and Heng 1991). This is our problem as well as Gawain's, since
the going sense of 'what is really happening' slips at the same time out of
final narratorial control.

The narrative of *Sir Gawain and the Green Knight* shares a distinctly uncanny
property with that of *Pearl*. 'Woman' seems to be the psychological figment
that the hero most strongly needs to give meaning and direction to his
adventure; the Lady of the Castle's presumably tongue-in-cheek rehearsal of
the theme comes at 1508–27. Modern commentators have no doubt been
right, for example, to see the green girdle as tending to displace the Pentangle
as the object of Gawain's implicit trust: a looser and more accommodating
circle or 'bond', one strongly suggestive of knowing intimacy with Woman
and even a certain self-feminization, 'þe ladies gifte' (2030) and supposed
magic talisman reassures Gawain as his tryst with the Green Knight approaches in a way that no moral theory could. When Gawain perceives in the
Lady of the Castle a woman fairer than Guinevere (see 945), we know that he
is feeling at home; conversely, Morgan as seen but not recognized at the
unfamiliar court becomes the embodiment of Gawain's anxieties about mortality and subjection to time's effects (see 947–69). Meanwhile, however, both
poems open up and maintain a considerable distance between Woman as
figment of thought, and the posited reality of the women who, invisibly even
to the poems, exist and act outside the scope of the masculine imagination;
as has been said, the Pearl's defining relationship is with God, not with the
Dreamer-narrator; in *Sir Gawain and the Green Knight* it would make a difference if we were told *why* Morgan wants to kill Guinevere (French romance

offers a skein of narrative material that would account for this), but we are not – Morgan has the unaccountability of a 'goddes' (2452), whatever the Virgin does lies outside the poem's purview. Both poems invite us to distinguish between their heroes' spontaneous projection of Woman, and another more disconcerting projection which arises in its place and with its obvious failure, such that Woman becomes the bearer of the poems' own will to probe inadequacies in human acts of consciousness. This is, by analogy with Gawain's shield, the inner side of narratives which more overtly deal with masculine struggles to preserve stability or rigidity of identity against the flow of time.

15

Courtesy and Chivalry
in Sir Gawain and the Green Knight:
the Order of Shame and the Invention
of Embarrassment

DEREK PEARSALL

When Gawain returns to Camelot after his unfortunate adventure at the Green Chapel, he is warmly greeted by the king and court, who are glad to see him 'al in sounde' (2489). The girdle of bright green that he bears diagonally over his right shoulder and under his left arm (2487) is for them a badge of honour which all will wear as a 'bauderyk' (2516) for the sake of Gawain and as a mark of the renown that he has brought to the Round Table. But for Gawain it is a mark of shame, the ribbon of an order of which he is the shameful founder; it is the outward token of an inward fault, the only visible sign of it now that the wound in his neck has healed (2484). Gawain, after rehearsing the story, describes the state of shame in which he must now, like Lord Jim in Conrad's novel, for ever live:

> 'Lo! lorde,' quoþ þe leude, and þe lace hondeled,
> 'Þis is þe bende of þis blame I bere in my nek,
> Þis is þe laþe and þe losse þat I laȝt haue,
> Of couardise and couetyse þat I haf caȝt þare;
> Þis is þe token of vntrawþe þat I am tan inne,
> And I mot nedez hit were wyle I may last;
> For mon may hyden his harme, bot vnhap ne may hit,
> For þer hit onez is tachched twynne wil hit neuer.' (2505–12)

This speech is an index to the problems of honour that the poem presents; it contains reminders of all the strands in the delicate fabric of chivalric idealism that the action of the poem has teased out. The contrivance of the story allows the contradictions within the system to emerge, reveals the fragility of the weave, the manner in which a multiplicity of different impulses and ideals, appetites and codes of restraint, are held in precarious orbit. It only needs one break in the circuit for the circuit to fail, for chivalry, like the pentangle, is an 'endeles knot' (630).

Gawain's speech of self-blame has often caused puzzlement because the language that he uses seems so redolent of the Christian formulae of confession and yet, it is argued (e.g. Burrow 1965, 155), he seems not to understand the Christian ritual of forgiveness. The puzzlement is natural enough, in a poem that seems so thoroughly imbued with Christian values and language, but it is the result of a mistake. If Gawain's 'harme' (2511) were a sin, he could of course be relieved of the burden of it by confession, but it is not a sin in the strict or indeed in any sense. The language that he uses bears a resemblance to the language of the confessional – any attempt to talk seriously about human behaviour in late fourteenth-century English poetry is bound to take on a Christian colouring, since Christianity dominated the vernacular language of ethics (compare the language Chaucer has to use when he wants to talk about 'tolerance' in the *Franklin's Tale*, V.761–90 (Benson 1987)) – but the resemblance is superficial. In fact, religion is not very important for Gawain, as Benson (1992) makes clear in a brisk essay. He is dutiful and pious, and has a care for his 'costes' (750), or observances, when he finds himself apparently far from human habitation and praying-places on Christmas Eve, but he has no inward sense of religion, of the reforming or re-forming power of faith. At its most spectacularly demonstrative, in his adoption of the device of the pentangle, Christian faith is little more for him than a sentimental or even superstitious attachment to *objets de foi*, hardly different from the attachment to the green girdle which so swiftly replaces his reliance on the pentangle and the Virgin Mary. Christian belief has not penetrated to that central identity that is constituted in honour and shame – the pride in honour and the fear of shame that spurs men to honourable action. (This identity, particularly in its social manifestations, is well-mapped by Burrow (1984), modifying his earlier reading (1965), and drawing on an important essay by Pitt-Rivers (1966) and previous discussion by Larry Benson (1965b) and D. Brewer (1968, 1973).)

In the place that he allocates to religion, Gawain is little different from the chivalric culture that is represented as shaping him. Christianity played its part in chivalric literature, probably not much different from that which it played in upper-class life: bishops are wheeled on to preside over certain rituals, and hermits are always on hand to dispense advice and provide medical treatment. Religion more generally has its role in reinforcing certain restraints, necessary to the chivalric code, and in endorsing certain forms of behaviour, and of course it is an important ally of knighthood in convincing the common people of the inevitability of their subservience and the need for patient resignation to their lot. But no self-respecting knight would be swayed by religious considerations from a course of action on which he had worshipfully determined, unless those considerations could be perceived to add some lustre or advantage to the action. Where considerations of a religious kind come to play any seriously important part in a narrative of

chivalric action, they change its nature, as with the story of the Grail in the
Vulgate Arthurian cycle or the many popular English romances that draw
towards the hagiographical (see Hopkins 1990).

Sir Gawain and the Green Knight is not a romance of this kind, which is why
the considerable discussion there has been of its significance as a Christian
poem (e.g. Engelhardt 1955; Morgan 1979; Barron 1980; Bennett 1986, 213–17;
Johnson 1984, 37–96) seems misplaced. Religion functions in the poem as it
functioned in chivalric life: it provides the rituals that structure the day and
year, a range of mantras and charms that give reassurance in times of danger,
and opportunities for a strictly codified version of the inner life to be hauled
to the surface for inspection and dismissal. Gawain's confession to the priest
has played a notable part in the discussion of the poem (e.g. Burrow 1965,
104–10; Morgan 1985), but it plays no large part in the poem. It is what he
expects and is expected to do before setting out on a dangerous mission, and
it all goes off perfectly satisfactorily: Gawain makes his confession, the priest
absolves him (1883), and that is that. We are not told what Gawain said,
because of course the confessional is private and in any case we *know* what
he said and that it had nothing to do with any of the things that were
happening to him that were to turn out to be of such serious importance. The
irony of the confession scene is in the deliberate juxtaposition of the priest's
confession with that offered by the Green Knight, the penance of his blade's
edge (2392). Of the priest it is said,

> And he asoyled hym surely, and sette hym so clene
> As domezday schulde haf ben di3t on þe morn.   (1883–4)

The Green Knight says,

> I halde þe polysed of þat ply3t, and pured as clene
> As þou hadez neuer forfeted syþen þou watz fyrst borne.
>
> (2393–4)

The echo is striking, and somewhat mischievous, since what is clear is that
neither the priest nor the Green Knight have any idea of the irrelevance of
the absolution they are offering to the condition Gawain is in. Gawain's
shameful deed cannot be confessed and absolved; there is no-one else who
can take the blame or bear the burden, neither Jesus Christ nor his own body:
'knyghtes ons shamed recoverys never', say Sir Clegis and Sir Bors, agreeing
with Sir Launcelot (*Morte Darthur* (Vinaver 1971), 130). Dead to honour,
Gawain chooses death by a thousand self-narrations.

Gawain's final speech of self-blame, in addition to indicating something
of the importance and unimportance of religion in his system of understanding, also exposes one of the 'points' (*points d'appui* but also points of
weakness) in the chivalric pentangle of forces. Gawain seems to want to find
some way of externalizing his shame: he uses the green girdle, 'þe bende of

þis blame I bere in my nek' (2506), but he also uses the wound inflicted by the Green Knight, seeming to accept the Green Knight's view that 'þe nirt in þe nek' (2498) he received from him is a form of bodily penance. Unfortunately the wound has already healed (the body has no shame, apart from the transitory moment of the blush, e.g. 2504), which empties Gawain's gesture of much of the significance he tries to attach to it.

The Green Knight clearly thinks the imperatives of the body are more powerful than any others. Whether he thought them up or not, the bedroom temptations were a routine and on the whole routinely repulsed attempt to arouse Gawain's body to disobey his purpose of honour; and when he rebukes Gawain for his lack of 'lewte' he does offer him the excuse that he was after all only thinking of his body and trying to save his life:

> 'Bot here yow lakked a lyttel, sir, and lewte yow wonted;
> Bot þat watz for no wylyde werke, ne wowyng nauþer,
> Bot for ȝe lufed your lyf; þe lasse I yow blame.'   (2366–8)

The Green Knight seems, wilfully or not, to miss the point. Losing one's life is not a fear to be entertained, but a risk or even a certainty to be embraced in the pursuit of honour, and the sentiment gains force from the echo of scripture – 'For whoever would save his life will lose it; and whoever loses his life for my sake, he will save it' (Luke 9:24). The manner in which the chivalric principle of conduct draws close to the Gospel exhortation (because of the permeability of the vocabulary of social conduct to the surrounding pervasively Christian language of moral and spiritual conduct) is illustrated in a familiar proverbial couplet (*IMEV* 3985) that appears thus in Huntington MS HM 744 (fol. 11v):

> Whan lyf is most loued and deeþ most hated
> þane deeþ drawiþ his drauȝt and makeþ man ful nakid.

But the Green Knight, though he misses the point, seems to understand Gawain, who has been shown throughout, in an unusual twist that the poet gives to the telling of the story, to be unchivalrically susceptible to bodily impression. It was winter that troubled him most his journey north, we are told, in a sympathetically reductive aside (726), not the routines of battle against giants and dragons and monsters, and there is a similar generosity to young blood in the picture of Gawain luxuriating in the new comfort of his unexpected Christmas quarters, or, flushed with wine after the privations of his journey, pursuing the young chatelaine a little too eagerly into the chapel (935–6). The temptations of the bedroom are real, and felt through the body ('Wiȝt wallande joye warmed his hert', 1762), though I take it that no-one, inside the poem or out, ever thought for more than a moment that Gawain would succumb. The imperatives of the body can be circumvented, in the code of honour, by various strategies; they do not have to have their way.

Thinking on higher or more urgent things is one strategy for withstanding the temptations of the body, and Gawain finds thoughts both of his coming journey (1284–7) and of his obligations to his host (1773–6) efficacious in this respect. As for bodily fear, the fear of death, it counts for nothing, when it comes in its own guise, beside the pride in being courageous in the face of death, which is no different from the fear of shame in being thought fearful in the face of death. Gawain flinches instinctively as the axe descends ('schunt', 2280, like the fox, 1902), but then, partly out of shame at being seen to flinch and partly out of anger at the Green Knight's theatricals, he stands firm:

> Gawayn grayþely hit bydez, and glent with no membre,
> Bot stode stylle as þe ston, oþer a stubbe auþer
> þat raþeled is in roche grounde with rotez a hundreth.   (2292–4)

This is Gawain's great moment in the poem, and his display of courage is not, I take it, meant to be understood to be due to the presence on his person of the green girdle. Our view of his behaviour is not, in this instance, made ambiguous by the question one has to ask throughout this last Fit: is Gawain's courage in finding and facing the Green Knight to be understood to be compromised by his belief in the life-saving properties of the green girdle? The poet never resolves this enigma, perhaps because the enigma is too deeply embedded in Gawain's own motives, but there is a difference between his behaviour here in the presence of the executioner (though cf. 2226) and the possible hypocrisy of his answer to the guide (see Delany 1965).

The body has its reasons, therefore, and there is comedy in the operation of their powers, but the body does not compel the will nor usurp it except in moments of relaxation or absent-mindedness or, as St Augustine would wish to remind us, sexual excitement (*The City of God*, xiv.24). Higher purposes can always be invoked. But again, to return to Gawain's speech of self-blame, our index to the order of shame, there seems to be no clear indication by Gawain of what those higher principles of conduct may be that he has violated. Gawain's response to the Green Knight's revelations was characterised from the start by the undiscriminating nature of his self-accusation, as if he had reached for a blunderbuss because he was unsure of his target – or in order to make sure that he missed it. 'Cowarddyse and couetyse' are the first names he gives to his offence (2374), or the 'cowardyse' that leads to 'couetyse' (2379–80), but also lack of 'larges and lewte' (2381), and 'trecherye and vntrawþe' (2383). Later, when he has gathered himself somewhat, and is prepared to bluster, he turns on women and blames them, and blames himself for 'þe faut and þe fayntyse of þe flesche' that made it susceptible to thoughts of (sexual) sin, 'teches of fylþe' (2435–6). Subsequently, the poet speaks of the 'vnleute' (2499) which earnt Gawain the nick in the neck. In Gawain's own final speech, 'couardise and couetyse' and 'vntrawþe' (2508–9) are all invoked again. Much of this seems not immediately to the point, and sexual sin is clearly irrelevant. 'Couetyse' is a general all-purpose sin, the root of all sins (*radix malorum est cupiditas*), which makes it useful for confessional purposes but not very helpful in understanding what precisely has been going on (and maybe all the more useful therefore for confessional purposes). Considerable attention has been devoted to 'couetyse' (e.g. Hills 1963; Burrow 1965, 135–6) but all it has done is to inflate the emptiness of the term in the present context. 'Couardyse' has apparently more relevance, but it is again vague and misleading. Fear of bodily hurt and fear of death are inseparable from being human, and knights are under no obligation to risk their lives wantonly. Life is not to be loved – the Green Knight was wrong there – but it is not to be wasted, and the green girdle offered an apparently honourable alternative to certain death. There was no cowardice at the Green Chapel.

The acceptance of the girdle, or at least the failure to render it to Bertilak as the day's winnings, seems to be the basis of the accusation of 'vntrawþe' or 'vnleute'. One meaning that has been ascribed to 'untruth', that is, the lack of Christian faith exhibited by Gawain in accepting a magic talisman, is surely to be rejected. Magic swords, shields, armour, clothing, rings, amulets, gloves, keepsakes, are the common currency of medieval romance (see Clein 1987, 119), and no-one ever accuses the bearers of a betrayal of faith, or of putting magic before Mary. Such things are accessories to the systems of protective agency offered by the Christian religion and not, or not necessarily, in conflict with them. Formal trial by combat forbade the use of magical talismans on the body as a means of helping to overcome an opponent, but the adoption of such magical safety precautions in the context of the present romance is hardly to be considered a form of underhand practice, as if Gawain had acted dishonourably in changing the rules of the beheading-game without telling the Green Knight; after all, the Green Knight had not told him all the rules in the first place, as Gawain quite pointedly remarks (2282–3).

Normally, however, Gawain's 'untruth' is taken to be his failure to keep to the exchange of winnings agreement by returning the green girdle to Bertilak. This argument has its value, though there is a precious legalism about it that is unsatisfactory. It has been argued (e.g. Fox 1968, 9; Morgan 1986, 293) that the keeping of vows and promises is to be regarded as a fundamental principle of obligation in medieval romance and that persons who fail to keep their promises, even to the letter, are to be condemned. Arveragus is often quoted on the subject ('Trouthe is the hyeste thyng that man may kepe', *Franklin's Tale*, V.1479 (Benson 1987)), though it is not clear that Arveragus's remark, in the context of Chaucer's very different conundrum of conduct, has an immediate relevance to *Gawain*. The relevance of searching through Aquinas and the Church Fathers for authoritative views on the keeping of promises, as Morgan (1986, 290–94) and Gaylord (1964, 321–7) do, is even less clear. The context of expectation must be the context of medieval chivalric romance, and in that context there is some variety of practice. Malory's King

Mark – not perhaps the most reliable of witnesses – insists that a promise, even if made in haste, must be kept (Vinaver 1971, p. 264). Elsewhere, the very respectable knight Alysaundir keeps his oath successfully on a technicality (Vinaver 1971, p. 396). Generally speaking, within reason (and sometimes without), promises are to be kept. The problem with Gawain's confession of 'vntrawþe' is that it seems to fit too easily with the determination of the poem to conceal its real subject and to schematize and clarify issues in a quasi-legal way. Human conduct is too muddily and complexly motivated: it can be represented but not explained, and so, when explanations are called for, as in the confessional or the law-courts, it is best to have some formula available – 'I have committed a sin of untruth', or 'Guilty as charged'. The transparency and consequent impenetrability of the language is what keeps the subject pinioned: Cresseid, in Henryson's poem, is not represented as really 'guilty' of blasphemy but that is the charge that the gods (the 'system') frame in order that she may be punished. In a way, it is like convicting Al Capone on an income-tax violation.

In *Gawain*, too, we read what the words say but also understand that what the poem means has to be read between the lines. To go back to Gawain's final speech, we find in it a strange wavering in the attribution of responsibility. He speaks of 'þe laþe and þe losse' that he has 'laȝt' (2507), which means 'obtained', but in the sense of 'received' rather than 'obtained as a result of seeking to obtain'. He speaks of the 'couardise and couetyse' that he has 'caȝt' there (2508), presumably at the castle of Hautdesert, as if these were vices that he unfortunately got infected with during his stay there. And he speaks of the green girdle as 'þe token of vntrawþe' that he has been 'tan inne' (2509). There is in the first two verbs a displacement of agency, so that whatever has gone wrong seems to be the responsibility of circumstances beyond Gawain's control, though he acknowledges that he has to bear the blame. The expression 'tan inne' gets us closer to Gawain's understanding of what has happened to him. He has been detected in an act that he presumed to be private but that has turned out to be very public. He has been, not 'taken in' (though it makes an interesting pun), but 'found out'. His shame is not in the act but in the making public of what he thought was private. This is what he can never live down, and the pain of it is greater than the suffering caused by any guilt.

The worlds of the private and the public are interestingly confused in *Gawain*, and there has been some excellent writing on the blurring of the one into the other and the discoveries that are made for the enlargement of the sphere of fiction in the process (see e.g. Mann 1986, 307–11; Aers 1988; Spearing 1994). Chivalric culture had always been in theory a world in which the public and the private were the same; there was no such thing as 'privacy'. This was true too of the world of political theory, where the 'mirror for Princes' saw the actions of the public man as those of the private man writ large, and of the kind of psychological theory that underwrote the institution of confession. The sinner, says the sermon-writer, 'may not hide himself wiþinne himselfe, for þere is þe worme of conscience remorsing' (Cigman 1989, 226). The private self is known to itself, through the implanting of the detection mechanisms of conscience, to be always on display on the vast monitors of God, every word, thought and action recorded ready for replay at the Last Judgment. Gawain, as we have seen, seems to be unaware of these worms of conscience, or that he is being watched and recorded, and when he goes to confession he does not seem to have been aware or to have been made aware that he was doing anything wrong, if indeed he had been. Gawain has a conscience, one presumes, but it is nothing beside his capacity for shame and for embarrassment.

So, in chivalric culture and literature, what exists only in private does not exist, and it only begins to exist, and to be a cause of shame, if it is made public (see Burrow 1984, 126). Arthur, Malory tells us (Vinaver 1971, p. 674), 'had a demyng' of the adulterous liaison of Lancelot and Guenevere, 'but he wold nat here thereoff' and therefore he did not have to act on it, since the relationship did not exist until it was made public by the malice of Agravaine and Mordred. Malory on the whole is very content with the occlusion of the private, and it is interesting to see the way his modern imitators, such as Tennyson, T.H. White and John Steinbeck, are constantly urged to occupy the spaces he leaves vacant, supplying conversations for every private occasion that make everything explicable (in a manner that Mann (1991) shows to be inappropriate for Malory) and change the whole nature of the story.

Gawain is an inhabitant of the world of Malory's Arthur. He understands the public forms of display in which a knight's identity is constituted, and the desire for renown and the fear of disworship that motivate the asserting and reinforcing of that identity. His first speech in the poem, when he emerges from the background of the court to address Arthur, is an example of his perfect command of these forms of display: it could have been written, as Stevens says (1973, 173), 'as a model in a handbook of "cortaysye" ' (and is expertly analysed in Spearing 1964, 38–43). The court is shamed by its failure to respond to the Green Knight's challenge, as the poet politely intimates (246–7, 301–2), and Arthur is shamed in having to take it upon himself, because it is an not an appropriate responsibility for a king to take on (Burrow 1984, 121). Gawain alone may be presumed to have refrained out of 'cortaysye' (246) from acting earlier. His speech is a masterpiece of courtly rhetoric, in which he releases Arthur and the court from shame, takes upon himself the foolish challenge ('þis note is so nys', 358), and reassuringly proposes himself uniquely qualified to take it up, since he will not be missed, and the only virtue in him is that Arthur is his uncle. One should not mistake this for humility: it is as proud as any boast, but it is phrased with beautiful and nonchalant courtesy. This is what Gawain is good at, and at first apparently the only thing he needs to be good at.

He is the perfect knight, for his inner is his outer, just as he proclaims himself united in himself in the pentangle and equally in the inside and outside of his shield. There is no suggestion that he has any fears or qualms or inner debate about the quest he has undertaken. The fears are explicitly displaced from his person by being made the subject of malicious and trivial insinuations by the narrator (487–90, 497), while the questioning of the wisdom of the undertaking is left to the inveterate court complainers, who of course want to blame the government (682). Gawain has his problems on the journey but they are not the product of any inner debate: we never imagine him, in the moments the narrator doesn't tell us about, saying to himself, What am I doing here? Why am I doing this? Who am I? If he wants to talk to anyone, he talks to God (696), which bespeaks a mind at ease with itself. His outer life is his inner life.

The embarrassment of the lady's bedroom visits is an acceptable embarrassment. Gawain could have talked about it to his friends. It is what knights of the Round Table are used to, as the parallels collected by Elisabeth Brewer (1973, 1992) show, though they do not always behave in the same way. 'Be ye a pusell or a wyff?' says Gareth when the daughter of Sir Persaunt turns up in his bed (as part of a test); on hearing that she is a maiden he tells her to leave, as he will not shame her father (Vinaver 1971, p. 192). One assumes that he would have behaved differently if the answer had been otherwise, which suggests an exceptional propriety and restraint in Gawain's behaviour. The only time he shows signs of discomposure is when the lady stands to leave after her first visit:

> And as ho stod, ho stonyed hym wyth ful stor wordez:
> 'Now he þat spedez vche spech þis disport ʒelde yow!
> Bot þat ʒe be Gawan, hit gotz in mynde.'
> 'Querfore?' quoþ þe freke, and freschly he askez,
> Ferde lest he hade fayled in fourme of his castes.   (1291–5)

Gawain is shocked to think that he may have failed in some courteous observance, because to fail in observance for a knight whose inner and outer are one is to cease to be (see Benson 1965b, 220–24). If he is not recognisable as Gawain, with all the appurtenances of that constructed self, he is nobody. Fortunately the lady's complaint is of an omission which can readily be rectified, for we have Lancelot's word for it that a kiss is no disworship (Vinaver 1971, p. 661). When she tries the trick a second time (1481), he is much better prepared.

The bedroom temptations are real enough, and rendered with warm physicality, but they are not seriously threatening. The embarrassments are all outward and manageable, have nothing to do with any hidden self that might be secretly and painfully embarrassed (in a modern novel, it might be fear of impotence or inadequate sexual performance or the exposure of some secret blemish). Gawain is on occasion angry with himself for being so pleased to be seduced (1660), but it does not seem like an ungovernable torment of conscience. Even the debate that he has with himself about his conduct is consciously staged as a little drama with a swift denouement:

> For þat prynces of pris depresed hym so þikke,
> Nurned hym so neȝe þe þred, þat nede hym bihoued
> Oþer lach þer hir luf, oþer lodly refuse.
> He cared for his cortaysye, lest craþayn he were,
> And more for his meschef ȝif he schulde make synne,
> And be traytor to þat tolke þat þat telde aȝt.
> 'God schylde,' quoþ þe schalk, 'þat schal not befalle!'   (1770–76)

This glimpse of Gawain's 'interior consciousness' is of a subjectivity almost public in its availability for inspection.

Gawain's truly private self is revealed for us when he accepts the girdle as a life-preserver. There is no self-consciously staged inner debate here, but a slithering of fear and desire into self-justification and willed but un-self-aware act:

> þen kest þe knyȝt, and hit come to his hert
> Hit were a juel for þe joparde þat hym iugged were:
> When he acheued to þe chapel his chek for to fech,
> Myȝt he haf slypped to be vnslayn, þe sleȝt were noble.   (1855–8)

The slipperiness of the planned escape from death is well conveyed in the consonants of 'slypped to be vnslayn', while the queasiness of the self-justification is present in the stubborn oxymoron of 'þe sleȝt were noble'. For the first time a fault-line opens or is revealed between Gawain's public self and his private self. He has done something which he would be very embarrassed to talk about to anyone, even to God. It was the apparent privacy and secretness of the occasion, Gawain's aloneness with his fear, and also, one must admit, the rather unusual circumstances of the test to which he was being subjected, that made him temporarily oblivious to shame. Like Conrad's Jim, he was a young man of perfect composition and steely resolve to be fearless who was 'taken unawares' (Conrad 1900, 9, 95).

It is finding out that what he has done was already being talked about, and indeed was planned to happen just as it did, that drops Gawain into the abyss. It is not what he did that so fills him with embarrassment, but that he was found out in the way that he was; as Burrow says, 'Only when he is actually dishonoured by the censure of a fellow knight does he feel its shame' (1984, 126). He was apparently quite happy with his chosen course of action until then, or rather he was content to act as if he did not realise what he was doing: 'as for many chivalric heroes', says Spearing (1970, 226), 'the criteria of conduct are not fully internalized'. Once he had accepted the girdle, he behaved with the noble courtesy and courage that was customary to his public self and that constructed also his private self. Now he is aware of the gap between the two that existed all the time, of the lies that he has told to himself, of the disunity of his personality; he is 'ashamed of himself'.

To show a fictional character capable of being embarrassed and humiliated (very different from being humble, which Gawain is good at) in the way that Gawain is embarrassed and humiliated is a new art of the interior self (though not, one presumes, a new experience for human beings) that is being disentangled from the fictions of chivalry that had prevailed. Yvain, faced with the shame and humiliation of having forgotten his promise to Laudine, in Chretien's *Yvain*, can only run mad in the woods. This is the customary response to extreme embarrassment in medieval romance: it constitutes a kind of mental suicide, a revulsion against the pain inflicted on the inner self so violent that mental life must be suspended, blocked off, until some form of redemption becomes available. Gawain goes through all the painful stages of self-recognition when he finds that he has been the unwitting subject of a kind of research experiment to determine whether the 'surquidre' of the Round Table (2457) is all that it is renowned to be. He feels anger, irritation, dismay, shame, self-loathing, and it is no comfort to him that the experiment is said to have been largely positive in its results, and that he is thought to have done fairly well (2364–8). But Gawain does not go mad, or run wild in the woods. He shows a capacity for bearing his shame and turning it into the story of his life that puts him with the Ancient Mariner rather than with Yvain or Lancelot or Tristram.

William Ian Miller, a scholar of Icelandic literature and law, argues in a recent book (1993) that humiliation, shame and embarrassment are 'the central emotions of everyday social existence', and quotes the view of the philosopher Richard Rorty that 'the *humiliatibility* of human kind' is a social-psychological universal that transcends differences between cultures. These are large claims, but in a discussion of *Gawain* Miller makes the interesting argument that 'shame' was once used to cover much of the ground now assigned to 'embarrassment' and 'humiliation'. The words did not exist, but the feelings did, and the poet of *Gawain* knew about them. This argument I take to be the basis of a possible distinction between the public nature of 'shame', as part of a system of values, able to be expiated, exploited or revenged, and the private nature of 'embarrassment', which is an inseparable part of one's private being, a permanent blush. This distinction between public 'shame' and private 'embarrassment', though customary usage of the two terms will not allow it to be strictly maintained, may help to provide some consolation for Gawain in his newly discovered solitariness. There is nothing to be done, no action which will cleanse and renew his humiliated self, no person, however well-disposed, who will properly understand what has happened to him, but the quality he has found in himself is the quality in individuals that we have become accustomed to believe constitutes them in their essential individual humanity as distinct from their animal or their social being. Ricks (1974, 2) quotes Erving Goffman: 'By showing embarrassment . . . the individual . . . demonstrates that, while he cannot present a sustainable and coherent self on this occasion, he is at least disturbed by the fact and may prove worthy at another time'.

16

Sir Gawain: *Some Later Versions*

The Grene Knight

GILLIAN ROGERS

The short 6-line tail-rhyme romance, *The Grene Knight* (*GrKn*), is one of a group of eleven Arthurian pieces in the Percy Folio Manuscript (BL Add. MS 27879), compiled in the 1640s by an unknown scribe of strongly antiquarian leanings, with an interest in the popular literature of the past. Ballads, historical, 'traditional', 'outlaw', and broadside, rub shoulders with medieval romances, contemporary Cavalier lyrics, popular songs, alliterative poems and political satires. The Arthurian pieces include lengthy romances such as *Libius Disconius*, clearly related to medieval ancestors, brief ballads such as the fragmentary *The Marriage of Sir Gawaine*, of which a romance version also exists, and interesting oddities such as the unique *The Turke & Gowin*, also fragmentary, occupying a midway position between ballad and romance.

This large and battered manuscript was discovered by Thomas Percy, editor of the *Reliques of Ancient English Poetry* (1765) in the late 1750s, lying beneath a bureau in his friend, Sir Humphrey Pitt's, parlour, where it was being used to light the fire. This household economy resulted in missing half-leaves in several of the texts at the beginning of the volume, including four of the Arthurian items. Percy himself annotated it copiously, but often very appositely (see St Clair-Kendall 1988, 1–32; Rogers 1991, 39–64; Donatelli 1993, 114–33, for fuller descriptions of the manuscript, its state, its contents, and Percy's treatment of it.)

Were it not for the fact that the first citations in the *Middle English Dictionary* of some dozen or so words in *GrKn* date from the first half of the fifteenth century, one might almost be tempted to place *GrKn* in the late fourteenth century, since, as Fowler (1968, 140) pointed out, it strikingly resembles Chaucer's *Sir Thopas* (*ST* in style), and might almost have been the romance he was parodying, so close are some of its effects to those of *ST* (compare *GrKn* 271–6, with *ST* 875–80, for instance). *GrKn* contains no words that do not appear until after 1500. A mid-to-late fifteenth-century date for it therefore seems reasonable.

As for where *GrKn* was written, opinions range from the south Midlands (Ackerman 1959, 497, and others) to north/north Midlands (Speed 1993, 237). Words such as 'kayred' (117) and 'gate' (290), are Northern in origin. The issue is clouded by the scribal habits of the seventeenth-century compiler, whose dialect, according to the *Linguistic Atlas* (McIntosh, Samuels and Benskin 1986), belongs to Cheshire.

For anyone interested in the way stories get transmitted and transmuted, *GrKn* makes instructive reading. From its earliest editors on (Madden 1839, 224–42; Child 1857, 35–57; Hales and Furnivall 1867–8, II. 56–77), it has been recognised as an adaptation of *Sir Gawain and the Green Knight* (*SGGK*). Kittredge (1916, 134, 126, 127), saw it as 'a condensed *rifacimento* . . .', 'much confused and somewhat defective', and the Percy text as a 'faulty transcript, perhaps written down from memory'; Ackerman (1959, 497) thought it a 'condensation . . . based on a very hazy memory'. Most other comments tend the same way. It has not had a good press. Its most recent editor, Speed (1993, 236–59), however, from whose edition the quotations in what follows are cited, is markedly more ready to see it on its own terms than were her predecessors.

Kittredge, in his still important study, did take *GrKn* seriously enough to list forty examples of close correspondence between the two versions (282–9), but he was not impressed by them. A close examination of the two, however, reveals that the *GrKn*-redactor must at one time, in whatever circumstances, have known *SGGK* very well indeed, however much he had forgotten in the meantime. Admittedly, the effect is rather like viewing a familiar landscape through drifting patches of fog, but it *is* a familiar landscape. The direct verbal parallels extend throughout the fabric of the poem, constant echoes, clusters of resemblances, all in approximately the same parts of the narrative, which follow the intention of the original, albeit often in a somewhat confused manner. On occasion, the redactor picks up on ideas spread over many lines in *SGGK* and condenses them into a few brief ones as, for example, in the Green Knight, Bredbeddle's, challenge to the court (133–50), which contains all the essential elements of the exchanges between Bertilak and Gawain in *SGGK* at the same point in the proceedings. And, habitually, this highly compressed, swiftly-moving poem makes one or two lines serve for many, sometimes with disastrously impoverished effect – as in Gawain's winter journey, where:

> Many furleys he there did see;
> Fowles by the water did flee,
>   By brimes and bankes soe broad.   (280–2)

has to make do as a substitute for the marvellously rich description of the winter landscape Gawain journeys through in *SGGK*; sometimes with a quite effective brevity – as in the description of Gawain's warm welcome at Bredbeddle's castle:

> Fier in chambers burning bright,
> Candles in chandlers burning light;   (310–11)

Nonetheless, the redactor has included features of the original descriptions into his own in both cases.

To give a clearer idea of the way in which this redaction is, and is not, like *SGGK*, I will briefly discuss two passages, both concerned with the Beheading Game, which in *GrKn* is the most prominent part of the plot rather than the framework for a more serious test, as it is in *SGGK*. The first, Bredbeddle's challenge, is a good example of the redactor's failure to exploit the inherent drama of the situation, while at the same time managing both to include most of the elements that appear in *SGGK* at the same points in the narrative, and to misunderstand the underlying significance of the action.

Where Bertilak arrives with demonic suddenness in the midst of the Christmas celebrations, Bredbeddle's demeanour, politely waiting for the Porter to announce him, rather suggests that he has dropped in for afternoon tea. The reaction to his announcement that he has come to test Arthur's knights is a sad travesty of the 'swoghe sylence' of the court in *SGGK*, conveying its stunned reaction to the intruder; Arthur simply sits 'full still' (121), waiting for Bredbeddle to finish speaking. His initial thought, that Bertilak wishes for a combat, is taken up by the *GrKn*-redactor, who then misinterprets Bertilak's reply, that if he had wanted a fight he would have come armed, and makes Arthur offer Bredbeddle some of his own armour, 'If and thine armor be not fine' (130). Bredbeddle's reply well demonstrates the bathetic effect the redactor can produce in a tail-line: ' "Godamercy, lord", can he say'. (132).

Bredbeddle then makes his challenge. And again, in place of the *Gawain*-poet's description of the stillness that falls upon the court at Bertilak's words, we are given the King sitting at ease 'full still' (151), and his lords saying 'but litle' (152), until Bredbeddle has finished (an example of the way in which, compressed though it is, *GrKn* nevertheless repeats an action, or reaction, where it occurs twice in *SGGK*).

Immediately following this, Kay boasts that he will strike off Bredbeddle's head. This traditional motif, of Kay's boorish intrusion into a scene, is normally rounded off by a rebuke from Gawain, but here, Kay is shouted down by the whole court, who *all* want to take on the challenge. This incident is of interest, however, since it replaces the scene in *SGGK* in which Arthur himself takes up the challenge, an instance of the redactor replacing a motif not perhaps familiar to him with one that is.

Gawain claims the challenge. Again, the redactor has picked up two clues from his original, but has misunderstood the purpose of both. In *SGGK* Gawain asks Arthur if he may 'wythoute vylanye' (345) leave the Queen's side to stand by him. Later when he asks to be allowed to accept the challenge, he refers to his blood-kinship with Arthur, his only claim to praise. In *GrKn* he says:

> ... That were great villanye
> Without you put this deede to me,   (166–7)

and claims the contest on the grounds that he is Arthur's 'sisters sonne'. The point about 'vylanye' in *SGGK* refers to the possible breach of etiquette that Gawain might commit were he to leave the Queen's side without permission; Gawain's abrupt plea of kinship transforms his self-deprecatory speech in *SGGK* into a belligerent demand to be given the contest simply *because* he is Arthur's nephew. In another fatal departure from his original, the *GrKn*-redactor has Arthur agree to this, but then immediately call for dinner, dismissing the coming beheading as if there were no more to it than a friendly joust after dinner.

The second incident concerns the return blow at the Green Chapel. Here, the *GrKn*-redactor reduces the three strokes that Bertilak offers Gawain to one (just as the three days of Gawain's Temptation by Bertilak's wife, are reduced to one, the last, with its three kisses, and the three hunts for deer, boar, and fox, become one, in which Bredbeddle hunts and kills all three kinds of beast – in this, at least, the redactor is consistent). Nonetheless, he has retained elements of all three strokes in his extremely compressed account.

The main feature of the third blow, of the stroke barely cutting the flesh, is well preserved in *GrKn*, and is immediately followed by the line: 'Then Sir Gawaine had noe doubt' (459), which looks like an attempt at line 2257 in *SGGK*: 'And lette as he noȝt dutte'. Then comes the element from the first feinted blow in *SGGK*, Bredbeddle's accusation: 'Thou shontest!' (460), clearly a memory of Gawain's admission 'I schunt onez' (2280). This is immediately followed by Gawain's anger, from the second feinted blow. The redactor then reverts to the aftermath of the third blow, with virtually the same reactions from Gawain, who leaps to his feet, draws his sword, and speaks fierce words. The lines:

> I had but one stroke att thee,
> And thou hast had another att mee;   (466–7)

seem to be an attempt to follow Gawain's argument in *SGGK*:

> I haf a stroke in þis sted withoute stryf hent ...
> Bot on stroke here me fallez   (2323, 2327)

and his exclamation, 'Noe falshood in me thou found' (468), appears to reflect his statement that he has kept the:

> ... couenaunt schop ryȝt so,
> Fermed in Arþurez hallez –   (2328–9)

One could demonstrate the same sort of pattern of close verbal resemblances and a firm grasp of the general sense of certain passages, together with curious misunderstandings and displacements, throughout the whole romance, and though some of the resemblances may, in themselves, be of small account, their cumulative effect adds weight to the idea that the GrKn-redactor must have been acquainted with SGGK, not merely at several removes, but very closely indeed.

But this intriguing redactor is nothing if not contradictory in his methods for, despite his adherence to the main Beheading-Temptation-Beheading outline, he introduces three major structural changes into his version which, in effect, reduce the carefully-wrought, finely-detailed architecture of the plot of SGGK to rubble.

The most serious change lies in the motives that drive the respective Green Knights to Arthur's court in the first place. In SGGK, after he has delivered the return blow, Bertilak tells Gawain that he was sent to court by Morgan le Fay with instructions to test the proud renown of the Round Table, to rob its members of their wits, and, if possible, to frighten Guenevere to death. He reveals that Morgan is the old beldame that Gawain had met in his castle, Arthur's half-sister, and Gawain's aunt. It is thus very much a family affair, and Gawain is very much the appropriate person to undertake the challenge on these grounds as well as for his personal qualities. The GrKn-redactor, not apparently liking this motive, substitutes for it a well-known Gawain-theme, that of the lady who loves Gawain, without ever having seen him. Bredbeddle therefore, is sent to court by his mother-in-law, the witch Agostes, to lure Gawain to his castle to satisfy his wife's love-longing, although he himself claims that he is going there to prove Gawain's 'points 3' (70). With this change, at a stroke, the redactor renders the whole test an impersonal one, devoid of the resonances which the family ties between tester and tested set up in SGGK.

The second major change that the GrKn-reactor makes is to turn the Exchange of Winnings Bargain into the Division of Winnings. Thus, Gawain, having won, within the course of a single day, three kisses from his host's wife and a talismanic white lace, renders up to his returning host only the three kisses, keeping the life-saving lace for himself.

The third change concerns the ending. Bredbeddle cuts short his somewhat confused explanation of the deceit that has been practised upon Gawain with an abrupt request, in mid-sentence, to be taken back to court with him. And off the pair of them go, 'with harts blyth and light' (498), pausing only to spend the night at Hutton Castle. Again, the motif of Gawain taking his erstwhile opponent back to court with him, to be integrated into the close-knit society of the Round Table, is a common one in English Arthurian romance, occurring also in The Turke & Gowin and Carle off Carlile, both in the Percy Folio, and in The Avowynge of King Arther and Golagros and Gawane.

It is easy to see what damage these changes do to the plot. Bredbeddle is reduced to the status of procurer for his own wife, apparently in full knowledge of what he is doing. His wife, who appeared to be dying for love of Gawain ('Without I have the love of thee, / My life standeth in dere' (380–1)), is in fact no more stricken than Bertilak's wife and, when Gawain rejects her on the grounds that her husband has been kind to him and that it would ill-become him to 'doe him any grame' (386), she merely offers him her assistance and the white lace, which she says will render him invulnerable – all this in a markedly cheerful manner. She does not bind him to secrecy about it. Because Bredbeddle's real intention is to lure Gawain to his wife on his mother-in-law's instructions, there seems little reason to go on with the other half of the Beheading Bargain once Gawain has rejected his wife's advances. His ostensible purpose, to test Gawain's 'points 3', would seem to have been more than adequately fulfilled, both by Gawain's rejection, and by the mere fact that he has turned up ready and willing to undergo the return blow. Bredbeddle's accusation of disloyalty after the return blow, appropriate enough in *SGGK*, here becomes doubly inappropriate. Gawain has amply proved his loyalty to his host by rejecting his wife and, because the Winnings Bargain was a division and not an exchange, he shows no disloyalty in keeping the lace either – indeed, it might be said that he adopted the most honourable course by rendering up the kisses, which surely touch his host more nearly, rather than the lace.

Because of Bredbeddle's abrupt change of subject in mid-explanation, Gawain does not react in any way to his host's revelations. This, one feels, is the greatest betrayal that the *GrKn*-redactor perpetrates upon his 'received' text, wreaking as much havoc on the moral level as it does on the structural level. Why this change, we may ask? Did the ending that the redactor found in his source simply baffle him, or did he feel that it was inappropriate that a tale about a knight who was, after all, the most popular of Arthur's knights in England, should end in that knight's discomfiture? Part of the oddity of the effect produced by this romance is that the redactor at no time seems to be aware of the damage his changes cause to either the structure of the plot or the motivations of his characters, and proceeds exactly as if he had not made them.

Perhaps surprisingly in the face of all this, the *GrKn*-redactor's technical abilities are somewhat greater than has usually been granted. The narrative, though sparse and bare, drives on from stanza to stanza with scarcely a pause; interestingly, some 75% of the tail-lines fulfil a functional role, rounding off the three-line unit and carrying the action forward, rather than being simply 'fillers', although 'fillers' there are in plenty, in couplets as well as in tail-lines.

The writer has a certain facility with alliterative and patterned lines, but habitually falls back on stereotyped phrases. A charitable interpretation may suggest that here we have the difference between something that is genuinely written for oral delivery, and conditioned by the needs of orality, *GrKn*, and something much more sophisticated and literary, *SGGK*. The comparison brings out again, in a rather unexpected way, what a subtle, complex poem *SGGK* is, even in the apparently simple matter of its story-line. And it also brings out, in their starkness, some aspects of *SGGK* that modern criticism sometimes overlooks. What other, for example, than a procurer for his own wife, *is* the Green Knight? What if Gawain had succumbed to temptation? And indeed in *SGGK* Bertilak's wife is, it turns out, no more in love with Gawain than is her *GrKn*-counterpart, but is apparently a willing pawn in her husband's attempt to kill Gawain, as would have happened, we must presume, had she succeeded in seducing Gawain. It is not, perhaps altogether surprising that the *GrKn* redactor changes the end of the story, and not necessarily a mistaken view that Gawain has after all succeeded. And the poet rightly takes the Beheading Game seriously, even if he simplifies the action. None of this makes *SGGK* a worse poem, or *GrKn* a better, but the conjunction of the two throws some new light on *SGGK*.

Bredbeddle on the whole emerges as the most positive, and indeed sympathetic, character, principally because the redactor backtracks from his description of Arthur's court to introduce him and his motives for making the challenge, and, throughout, keeps the focus upon him as well as upon Gawain. However, this backtracking removes all mystery from the figure.

The redactor evidently knew more about the English Arthurian tradition than he could have gleaned simply from *SGGK*. He knew, for instance, that Gawain and Kay usually exchanged sharp words; he knew of Arthur's wars with 'allyance', and of his bringing together the island of Britain under his rule; he knew of the tumultuous circumstances which led up to the making of the Round Table; and he set the tale in the interval of peace between the end of the wars of rebellion and the Roman War.

The reader is left with a somewhat baffling picture of a redactor who, at one and the same time, seems both to have known his original very well on one level and followed its main outlines with some fidelity, and to have understood it scarcely at all on the other, deeper, level of moral significance. There are some other incidental puzzles. Where does the name Bredbeddle come from? It is intrinsically absurd and comic enough in itself to destroy any serious effect. (It also occurs in the fragmentary sixteenth-century ballad *King Arthur and King Cornwall* (Child 1857, I. 274–88; Hales and Furnivall 1867–8, I. 59–73).)

The redactor's lack of comprehension of what was really going on beneath the surface enabled him cheerfully to alter and substitute where and as he pleased, to suit the taste of his prospective, possibly less sophisticated, audience, with absolutely no regard for the consequences. In the process, he reduced the immensely rich, intricately patterned and dense texture of *SGGK* to the bare bones of narrative, dispelling, by his predilection for revealing all prematurely, all sense of mystery, of impending fate, and falling back on the old formula of the happy ending, with Gawain's opponent reconciled with the court in an atmosphere of sweetness and light in place of the more sombre and uncertain ending of *SGGK*. It is storytelling reduced to the most basic level.

Thus we see how tradition may decay. To know great literature well is not at all to receive a guarantee of passing on great literature. In this case orality may have destroyed a great literate achievement. We also have a demonstration, nevertheless, that *SGGK* was known, perhaps widely, for long after it was composed. Inadvertently we also have a demonstration of how it came not to be understood – that it is a peculiar poem, arising out of an unusual poetic mind. Perhaps too we have evidence of the decay of a supportive cultural environment, out of the mainstream of courtly life and literature. It may even be out of that other mainstream; that of popular literature, which allowed, or supported, the production and reception of tail-rhyme romance far into the sixteenth century, up to Shakespeare's time.[1]

[1] A collection of eleven romances about Sir Gawain in English has been edited by Thomas Hahn, with valuable introductions, but was available too late to be considered here (Hahn 1995).

Sir Gawain *at the* fin de siècle: *Novel and Opera*

BARRY WINDEATT

> But was there not perhaps a deeper meaning, was there not some Middle
> English poem about a Green Knight? He now thought he recalled reading
> a translation of it when he was at Cambridge. What was the story? . . .
> Why does all this suddenly come upon me . . . why is it suddenly so
> significant? . . . Pieces of the story are there, but aren't they somehow
> jumbled up and all the wrong way round?   (Murdoch 1993, 431).

In Iris Murdoch's novel *The Green Knight*, and in the opera *Gawain* by Harrison
Birtwistle to a libretto by David Harsent (Harsent 1991; first performed at the
Royal Opera House, Covent Garden, in 1991; revived 1994), the 1990s have
already seen two significant contemporary works of art concerned – in their
differently original method and forms of allusion – to 'make new' something
of the medieval poem *Sir Gawain and the Green Knight*. The opera dramatizes
an interpretation of the medieval narrative of Gawain's temptation. The
novel's narrative does not retell the poem's but alludes selectively to the role
of the Green Knight within a narrative of events set in modern London (and
despite hints the potential connection with a reading of *Sir Gawain and the
Green Knight* is only made explicit just before the novel's close). Although
Harsent's libretto directly uses little of the original's text, the plot, structure
and setting of the opera correspond in outline with that of the medieval poem,
albeit with important shifts of emphasis, particularly in the intriguing development of the role of Morgan le Fay. In the novel, through transposition of
motifs from the poem, especially the beheading game ('somehow jumbled
up and all the wrong way round?'), Murdoch can recreate and reinterpret in
a latterday setting the mysteriousness of the Green Knight in a way that
challenges characters and readers.

Before Murdoch's *The Green Knight* begins, Professor Lucas Graffe, a historian, defending himself with his umbrella against a nocturnal assailant in
a park, has apparently killed him, endured an ensuing court case and
subsequently disappeared. The novel's main characters are an extended
network of longstanding friends, intelligent and civilized, and living in a
London where it seems most often to be rainy, dark and wintry. Apart from

the icily cerebral Lucas and his warmhearted brother Clement (who works in the theatre), the group includes the widowed Louise Anderson and her three teenage daughters – variously intellectual, idealistic and artistic – and another idealistic friend, Bellamy James, a former social worker, who has given away all his possessions and is intent on leaving the world and going into a monastery (but doesn't, and by the end of the novel 'comes out').

As the friends await Lucas's reappearance, the Andersons notice a tall, well-built man with a green umbrella taking an undue interest in their house. This proves to be the man Lucas Graffe was thought to have killed but who turns out to have survived. Events allow him to introduce himself as Peter Mir, of Russian Jewish ancestry (*mir* being the Russian for 'peace'), and by profession a psychoanalyst. Throughout the novel Mir is associated with the colour green by recurrent references to his green items of clothing or green accessories. In conversation at the Anderson house, Mir declares himself a vegetarian, interested in ecology and a member of the Green Party, at which Louise's daughter nicknamed 'Aleph' remarks: "That's why you dress in green . . . you've got a green tie and a green umbrella, and your suit is a sort of green too" (194). After Mir leaves, the Andersons play the game of what character in fiction he reminds them of: Mr Pickwick and Prospero are suggested, but then ' "I think he's the Green Knight," said Aleph' (195).

As Clement much later reflects: Mir 'had entered their lives as an accuser before whom they were to be judged guilty – and indeed did they not all of them feel guilty?' (270). When Lucas Graffe reappears, it is asserted by Mir that their previous, nearly fatal encounter was not how Lucas has subsequently represented it – namely as his self-defence with his umbrella against someone he took to be a mugger. Mir's version reveals – what had previously been concealed – that Clement had been with Lucas. Mir claims that he saw Lucas about to strike his brother on the head with their childhood baseball bat ('an accusing reminder . . . a magical object'; 293), and interposing took the force of the blow on his own head. (Lucas – an adopted child – coolly admits that he intended to kill his brother, because their mother always preferred her younger, natural son.) As a result of his head injury Mir can no longer pursue his work as a psychoanalyst and feels his life in that sense is over ('I saved you from the sin of Cain – and in return you have ruined my life'; 123). From Lucas Mir insistently demands justice and restitution. What he demands – since he neither wants nor needs money – is that Lucas should submit to receiving a return blow on the head delivered with equal force. Throughout there is a contrast between the reptilian coolness of Graffe ('I see him as something of an artist – and a gentleman. He doesn't want my money, he wants my head. . .' 199), and the passionate demand for justice from his inconveniently resurrected victim. Both Graffe and Mir mention the devil in connection with each other and with Mir's role, and the theme of the journey is evoked when Graffe claims of their negotiations 'I have come a long way to meet you' and Mir retorts 'I do not see that you have "come a long way", you have not moved from your first position, you have not *understood*' (126). Yet from Lucas's circle Mir – confessedly quite alone in the world, without family and friends – wants love, wants to be received by them and enjoy their friendship: to a masked party at the Andersons on a foggy night Mir turns up wearing a huge and startling bull's head mask ('Is he sane? I heard you saying just now that he was something out of *Beowulf'* . . . 'He has come out of the darkness. I think he is sane'; 215). No wonder Clement thinks of this 'Green Knight': 'What a nightmare it is, oh God if only he could *go away* and be just a dream' (125).

In his negotiations with Graffe, Mir wavers – not without allusion to Old and New Testaments – between desire for vengeance and punishment, and a willingness to be satisfied with reconciliation ('Perhaps it is more gratifying, as well as more blessed, to forgive rather than to punish'; 248). Eventually they agree on a kind of reenactment – at the same place one night – of the striking of the blow, albeit without intent to injure. The hope is that such a second playing out of the event will jolt the head-wounded psychoanalyst into regaining his memory of what he can only remember that he has forgotten (as Mir says to Graffe: 'You said earlier that you could not be my therapist. But you *can* be and you must be, you and you only, I require it of you'; 126). Attended by Clement and Bellamy, the second, mimed giving of blows has an eerie ceremoniousness ('He was holding up his green umbrella as if in a ritual'; 278) which means various things to different characters ('a duel – no – I would prefer something rather more – refined'; 124). Clement, the theatre director, remarks 'Peter thinks of it as a mystery play. I certainly think of it as theatre' (277), and for Bellamy it can be 'a sort of purification, like a sort of redemption', not unrelated to psychoanalytical method, 'miming it, to disperse, to melt away all your anger and your hate' (225). Although the botched re-enactment is partly seen through the confused panic of Bellamy, who thinks he has seen a religious vision, Mir does feel he has through the rehearsal remembered God, and found again both himself and his place in a spiritual journey (of which this 'Green Knight' speaks – for this is the 1990s – as a Buddhist). By this stage Graffe and Mir have greatly advanced in a rivalrous mutual respect: as Peter says to Lucas 'We have reached, may I say, a great high peak, or plateau, an open space, in our – contest – I mean our relationship' (316), and the watching Clement has a 'sense of them as two great rival magicians' engaged in some mysterious dance (317). The climax of their encounter is that Mir draws out a knife concealed in his green umbrella and with it nicks the flesh of the unruffled Graffe so as to draw blood – but because Clement, the other person present, faints with shock, this mysterious scene is only partly seen. And the departure of the Green Knight 'whiderwarde-so-euer he wolde'? During a party given by Mir for his new circle of friends, a psychiatrist arrives with his staff, to insist that Mir return to the hospital from which he has some while before escaped. Revealing that he was never a psychoanalyst, but actually a wealthy butcher ('Dr Fonsett kindly said I have had a fantasy. In fact I had simply told a lie'; 351), Mir agrees of his own free will to return to hospital with his psychiatrist for treatment. Not long afterwards his new friends hear that he has died there.

Not surprisingly, for the remainder of the novel some of its characters attempt to interpret the significance of this disconcerting visitant and the mysterious challenge that he posed to their sense of themselves (although Professor Graffe has again disappeared, this time 'eloping' to a new life on American campuses with Aleph, that daughter of Louise in whom Mir had apparently been most fondly interested). For Bellamy's spiritualizing cast of mind Mir must be 'an avatar, I mean an incarnation, a pure sinless creature, a very special visitor to this awful scene, like an angel – I can't express it' (450). Clement, brooding on the whole sequence of events, recalls how that evening:

> when Peter had gone they had all said who he reminded them of, and Aleph had said 'the Green Knight'. At the time Clement had vaguely assumed that she was referring to the green umbrella with which he had first appeared to them. But was there not perhaps a deeper meaning, was there not some Middle English poem about a Green Knight? He now thought he recalled reading a translation of it when he was at Cambridge. What was the story?

After recollecting to himself the narrative outline of *Sir Gawain and the Green Knight* Clement concludes:

> Pieces of the story are there, but aren't they somehow jumbled up and all the wrong way round? ... It isn't really like the poem, yet it is too, and it is something much more terrible ... Yes, it's all mixed up ... What had Aleph meant when she called him the Green Knight? She may have intuitively seen farther, seen him as a sort of instrument of justice, a kind of errant ambiguous moral force, like some unofficial wandering angel ... Only now, things are all confused, said Clement to himself inside his wild thoughts, and *I'm* getting confused ... *There* the first blow was struck as a provocation to a mysterious adventure, *here* the first blow was struck by an evil magician whose victim reappeared as another, ultimately good, magician ... And what about the temptress who in the story was the good magician's wife? ... Now the good magician has gone, receding into his mystery, and the beautiful maiden has been awarded to the evil one. Is this the end of the story? ... Only I am not a hero, not a chevalier, not a demon, not even a small demon, just a wretched sinner and a *failure*. A dispensable object. I have no courage. I have failed two women, no, three, and must wear the badge of failure for the rest of my life ... (431–2).

Somewhat later, after Clement's own sense of aimlessness and failure has been dispersed by the happiness of his marriage to Louise, his thoughts again return to the significance of the intervention in their lives of this latterday

Green Knight. In this, one of the last allusions to the 'Green Knight' in Murdoch's work, Clement's interpretation seems to equate the role of Mir in the novel with much modern evaluation of the Green Knight's role in the medieval poem: as something quintessentially from outside our mundane experience, strange and hence frightening – yet possessed of an intrinsic nobility, and functioning as an instrument of justice through which may be attained a self-knowledge more valuable than any glittering prize:

> And so, thought Clement, we betray him, we explain him away, we do not want to think about him or puzzle about him or try to make out what he was in himself . . . We may indeed diminish Peter and make him into a mere nightmare or a retired butcher – but really he is something alien and terrifying. After all, the Green Knight came out from some other form of being, weird and un-Christian, not like Arthur's knights. But he was noble and he knew what justice was – and perhaps justice is greater than the Grail . . . And he thought, I shall go on blindly and secretly jumbling all these things together and making no sense of them as long as I live. May be every human creature carries some such inescapable burden. That is being human. A very weird affair . . . (456).

For Birtwistle it was the wealth of formal patternings in *Sir Gawain and the Green Knight* – and its capacity for the inclusion of more – that drew the composer to the medieval poem for the subject of a contemporary opera (Samuel 1994, 24). One aspect of his librettist's task was to dispose the poem into 'parts' in the theatrical sense. In the poem the arrival and reception of the Green Knight in Fitt I, the exchanges between Gawain and the Lady in the bedroom in Fitt III or between Gawain and the Green Knight in Fitt IV, are already written in a highly dramatic form, involving much exchange of dialogue, and hence lend themselves to being staged. Other thematically very significant description of action, such as Gawain's lonely journeyings or the hunts, although cinematic in the way they communicate themselves to the mind's eye, will need to be represented on a stage in some stylized form. Then again, thematic aspects of the narration – such as the description of the seasons of the year passing from New Year to All Souls Day – will need, if retained, to be transposed into some kind of actable representation. In the event, Harsent seized the opportunities so offered for intrinsically operatic set-pieces in the arming of Sir Gawain, in the knight traversing the landscape, and in the seduction/hunt. Harsent's libretto effects 'an opening out of the poem: it follows the poem, but it turns description into action' (Harsent and Porter 1994, 31).

The action of the two-act opera's first act comprises in essence: an opening at Arthur's court and the entry of the Green Knight, the exchange of blows agreement with Gawain, and the Green Knight's decapitation and departure. (The staging of the Green Knight's entry on horseback, his beheading and his holding up of his still singing head were of course the *coups de théâtre* of the original Covent Garden production, although inevitably they may not have satisfied the imaginations of all readers of the poem). There follows a masque-like sequence (abbreviated for the 1994 revival), in which concurrently Gawain is ceremonially armed for his mission while the cyclical passage of the seasons is represented. This sequence – bringing the first act to a close – lies near the centre of the audience's experience of the opera. The second act, mirroring the first, begins with Gawain's entry into the home of Sir Bertilak, centres around the series of three attempted seductions and three parallel hunts (the latter represented through mime and dance), continues with Gawain's appointment with the Green Knight, and concludes with Gawain's wintry return into Arthur's court, his greatcoat and features thick with snow – an entry stipulated by stage directions to parallel the Green Knight's entrance in Act I ('Are you still king?' Gawain asks Arthur, shocking the court; 76). At first Arthur's courtiers simply do not recognize Gawain. Even when they do so, the change that has come over Gawain means that – neither for himself nor for them – is he the hero the courtiers want to 'recognize'.

Beyond such structural redisposition of the poem into opera libretto, there is the need to 'translate' the poem's way of accounting for character and motive into something that may be conveyed not simply through drama but through the distinctive medium of opera. There is a need for various 'devices' that may translate into stage action what – with its different resources – the poem could imply. One such device is the symbolic distinction of the indoors and outdoors worlds in the emblematic stage picture conveyed to the audience through the stage-set and the stylization of action within that set. The outdoors world is the outermost rim of the circular stage surface with its revolve (tilted so as to rise away from the audience up towards the back of the stage). The indoors world, within that outer rim, is hence always seen as completely surrounded, even besieged by the world without. The hunting sequence can be enacted on the outer rim of the circular stage area, apart and yet in conjunction with, and containing, the bedroom sequences. Hunt and seduction are related together through highly differentiated music, cutting 'back and forth, montage-like', while – reminiscent of Purcell's *Dido and Aeneas* – a hunt motif on off-stage horns accompanies the seduction scenes (Samuel 1994, 21). It is with the title *Gawain's Journey* that Birtwistle has drawn an orchestral synthesis from the larger opera score, pointing to the significance of the journey theme in the opera's reading of the poem. Within the indoors/outdoors conventions of the staging, journeys – fittingly circular – may be represented as taking place on the stage's outer rim, yet very close to their destination, and the upstage area of the revolve can be made to seem quite remote and mysterious. Associated with this 'outdoors' stage area is the 'figure' of the journeying, questing knight (referred to in Harsent's libretto as 'the "other" Gawain'), who can represent in mime, and silently comment upon, the journeys of Gawain: when Gawain moves to behead the Green

Knight there is the stage direction 'Gawain *begins to raise the axe. We see the figure of a knight travelling through the landscape of the "world outdoors"'* (31). This stylization of space and distance – opening doors and passing through, opening and not seeing who enters – only draws attention to the reality of inward, emotional movement and change, and to the way in which Gawain, for all his journeyings, finds sin and betrayal in himself quite close at hand. In Harsent's own synopsis of the action for the Covent Garden programme, Gawain hence with special force 'feels an outsider' after his return into a court with which, after his experience, he no longer feels at one.

That the opera's action occurs – or recurs – within circles is a significant aspect of Birtwistle and Harsent's reading of the poem, in which the rehearsal of time is an informing theme. The mirroring of events across the two acts builds this into the opera's action, as does the pivotal role of the 'seasons' sequence. Here the linear experience of an individual knight's preparatory rite is contained (even belittled) within an evocation of the essentially cyclical passage of five seasons, from winter to winter, and in each season a transition from night through day to night again. Here too arises a contrast between the cycle of nature and the knight's arming himself with material accoutrements and extensions of his bodily nature. After ritual cleansing comes the ceremonious donning of what are invoked by Arthur's knights as a 'second flesh' (the cuirass), a 'second skin' (the hawberk), a 'second skull' (the morion) and a 'second arm' (the sword), but there come too their unsettling rhetorical questions: 'Which is the false flesh, which the real?' . . . 'Which is the live skin, which the caul?' . . . 'Which is the strong arm, which the true?' (36–9). Overarching the circular stage during the masque of the passing seasons are some concentric arcs bearing stars, suggesting the zodiac, and further invoking the circles and cycles of time at the end of the first act. At the close of the second, final act, Morgan le Fay, seated within her huge bright hoop of blue neon light, ascends skywards singing 'Then / with a single step / your journey starts' (86), and so restating the opera's repeated thematic motif of endless journeys endlessly and everywhere beginning.

The role of Morgan le Fay – as dramatized through score and libretto – is one of the opera's most prominent 'devices'. In the opera Morgan is seen from the start as the controlling force whose magical conspiracy engenders and shapes the whole action, weaving a web of magic around the characters that holds Bertilak, his wife and Gawain in her thrall. As a stage presence, initiating, shaping and concluding the process, Morgan frames the opera's action: her voice is the first we hear, and also the last. The opera opens with Morgan and Lady de Hautdesert (the title given in the opera to Bertilak's wife), both invisible except to the audience, but present and watching at Arthur's court ('unseen, untouchable, my breath dousing their faces . . .' as Morgan sings; 14). The Green Knight's entry may thus be seen as the fulfilment of Morgan's designs against the Round Table: as the door opens to reveal the Green Knight Morgan sings 'Now I shall test his strength with mine, / his purpose with mine, his appetite with mine – ' (22). Morgan's sorcery is hence translated into action and presence as she plays the role of puppet master and director of the play. The music of the opening scene closely interrelates Morgan and her companion Lady de Hautdesert, while Morgan 'prompts' Bertilak and his wife in their speeches to their guest, so that they echo to Gawain phrases that Morgan has sung to them like cues just before (MORGAN: 'Tell your name . . .' BERTILAK: 'Will you tell your name?' . . . MORGAN: 'Help us to learn . . .' LADY: 'Help us to learn / the proper pace of passion . . .'; 49–50). Instead of the poem's notoriously belated few lines from the Green Knight to Gawain acknowledging Morgan's role, in the opera Morgan's motive is dramatized throughout as a hostile determination to test Camelot, and Harsent describes Morgan as the 'principal driving force of the piece' (Harsent 1994, 36). Yet that hostility, although rendered so much more overt ('My enemies under my hand, the old wounds opening' as Morgan sings; 48), is in itself no more expanded upon or explained in the opera than in the poem, which suggests that it cannot be. Morgan's hostile motive seems to be as much in the nature of things as everything else.

The other *dramatis personae* do however variously gain kinds of awareness and tokens of motivation that their counterparts in the poem do not have. Bertilak comments explicitly to Morgan on her motives before Gawain arrives at Hautdesert: 'Morgan . . . Your purpose chills me and excites me: the bonds of treachery and kinship' (48); his words echo his wife's first words in response to Morgan at the opera's opening. Bertilak's proposal of an exchange of winnings to Gawain becomes in the opera the ploy of a jealous husband to control his wife in his absence (a stage direction comments here: 'Lady de Hautdesert *is amused by her husband's jealousy and by the implications of the pact. Clearly it's a device to keep her faithful* . . .'; 53). Another stage direction stipulates that the hero should not be oblivious of the tensions between husband and wife or of Bertilak's difficulty in proposing that Gawain should keep his wife company. The stage direction carefully prescribes demeanour and gesture: Bertilak '*tries to say it lightly, but apprehensiveness betrays him.* Gawain *detects some of this. He looks first at* Bertilak, *then at* Lady de Hautdesert, *whose eyes are on her husband*' (52). In proposing such an exchange Bertilak seems for a moment to disconcert and irritate Morgan, who is prompting Bertilak and his wife through this scene; a stage direction says '[Morgan] *seems angry, as if she suspected he might be about to displease her*' (52). Bertilak's will is hence not altogether subservient to that of the sorceress. His wife is comparably represented as having feelings of her own, within her role of serving Morgan's ends through the attempted seduction of Gawain: stage directions (62) for the third seduction attempt include the informative parenthesis '(Lady de Hautdesert *is now in love with* Gawain)'. Needless to recall, in the poem the states of mind of Bertilak and his wife remain opaque.

As for Gawain, the unhidden source of the test in the opera alters perception of its hero from that of the poem. In the poem, where what lies behind the challenge is not disclosed until after the test, the experience of being 'in the dark' is one that the reader importantly shares with the hero. In the opera we watch with more knowledge of our own as a victim is 'set up', while the stripping, washing and arming of Gawain for his ordeal project a vivid tableau of the hero's vulnerability. Yet when the exchange of winnings is proposed, the operatic Gawain has the quickness to wonder immediately what he could gain at Hautdesert which would not already be Bertilak's? ('Gain? What could I gain? / . . . And how can I lose – / since whatever falls to me / must first be yours?'; 53). Medieval heroes are famously more backward in framing the obvious question. And if, in the libretto, Gawain's acceptance of the girdle is not especially highlighted, the terrors of the predicament that weighs on him are more palpable to us because of the three mimes on each night which manifest to the audience the nightmares that Gawain has about his impending death. The onset of Gawain's sleep is thrice accompanied (and implicitly controlled) by Morgan's singing of a lullaby, with the stage direction: 'During the lullaby we see an image from a nightmare as if Gawain were dreaming it. The image should be drawn from what has gone before: The Green Knight's head being severed, perhaps, or the axe being lifted' (54). In the opera, an astonished Gawain witnesses Morgan transform the Green Knight back into Bertilak after he has nicked Gawain's neck, which enables Morgan to explain: 'My power shape-shifted him / from man to hero – from hero back to man', and then to apply the point about change to Gawain as hero: 'I've done the same to you. / Become yourself; your purpose has just begun . . .' (72).

The 'reading' signalled through score and libretto largely conforms to the consensus of modern academic readings. Whatever may be the malign motive of Morgan le Fay, her role is seen as essentially virtuous in outcome, because of the morally improving effect the test has upon Gawain, who grows more vulnerable, more honest and substantial (GAWAIN: 'Now I'm home again, / sullen, empty-handed, feverish / with knowledge / . . . bringing news / no one hoped to hear. / I'm a spoiled reputation / . . . a symptom of sorrow'; 85). Through self-doubt is seen to come greater self-knowledge. What Gawain learns from his experience in the opera (according to Harsent) 'spoils him forever as far as the court conventions are concerned – and that was Morgan's intention all along' (Harsent and Porter 1994, 31). As Harsent admits: 'The poet doesn't say this, but he shows it. In my libretto I say it' (ibid.), and so the intriguingly equivocal balance that the poem could strike has to be tilted more heavily to draw out the modern reading. In Harsent's account of Morgan, the events of the poem are 'a woman's plot against Arthurian clubland', his King Arthur is 'weak and smug', and his Knights of the Round Table are 'full of childish emotions . . . beardless boys with nice suits of armour and a tiresome liking for male bonding' (Harsent and Porter 1994, 32). In the opera the knights of Camelot are listless and colourless, diverted by a riddling Fool, while Arthur is bored and petulantly impatient for distraction ('Who's brave? . . . Some traveller's tale / to make me mad, to bleed into my sleep'; 16–17). In the operatic version of Gawain's return, courtiers who helped arm the hero during the arming sequence now greet him again, each alluding to the piece of armour they once handed him and hoping to hear tales of knightly deeds in those arms – only to be rebuffed and irked by Gawain's irritable impatience with what to him now seem their irrelevant concerns (BALDWIN: 'Tell me of victories!' . . .; AGRAVAIN: 'Tell me of honour!' . . .; YWAIN: 'Tell me of courage!' . . .; GAWAIN: 'Why do you ask / for someone who isn't here? / Who do you want me to be? / I'm not that hero'; 81). This denial by Gawain of his role as hero only echoes his earlier denials to the Lady during her first attempted seduction ('Does the world adore me? / Is it true? / I'm not that hero. / No one has ever said so, except you'; 55), and at his return encounter with the Green Knight ('I'm not that hero. / No one ever said so'; 70). At his return to Camelot, only Queen Guinevere seems to discern Gawain's suffering and alienation sympathetically ('Now you are more yourself, / let's speak again'; 83). But then, it was Guinevere who kept up a sardonic commentary of deflating interjections during the knights' arming of Gawain for his knightly exploit ('Here is the court's darling, / dazzled by distances' . . . 'Here is the warrior, charmed / by his own recklessness' . . . Here is the only hero, / foxed by his own courage' . . . 'Here is the Golden Boy, / in love with his journey'; 38–41).

It is also in its allusions to dreaming – and to time as it might be understood by the subconscious – that the modern opera reinterprets the medieval poem's narrative. In part this encounter of Gawain and the Green Knight is suggested to occur within the dreams of the enchantress: Morgan sings in the first lines of the opera: 'Night after night the same dream . . . / Now at the year's dead end, / the dream quickens', while Morgan's companion, Lady de Hautdesert, sings of 'Day after day, the same promise – / a figure crossing a landscape, / travelling towards me . . . / A face I could almost see, / a meeting already rehearsed' (14–15). Casting about for a tale of bravery, the bored Arthur associates adventure with self-encounter through the dream world ('Who'll make the journey / over the badlands of sleep . . . / to meet himself there / waiting for the worst dream to begin?'; 18). Twice – when the Green Knight seems about to appear, and when Gawain raises the axe to behead him – Morgan and the Lady sing the same lines that associate dreams, journeys and an uncanny idea of the moment that attends us: 'This is the moment that waited for you / as you travelled towards it. / This is the moment you carried with you / from the worst dream'; 21, 31). Within this – for Gawain – worst dream his supremely threatening encounter with the Green Knight entails both knowledge and a resemblance that the hero might prefer not to discover: the Green Knight tells him as they make their agreement 'Now we shall come / to know each other. Now we shall grow / more like each other' (29). As the hero prepares to set out after his arming ('All Souls Day. The moment / waited for me'; 42), and as both Gawain and

Guinevere link his coming trial with dreams ('I dreamed my enemy kneeling before me'. . . 'He dreams himself / taking the last few steps'; 41), the Fool poses a series of four riddles ('Look . . . You might see . . . Who is it?') which baffle ordinary presumptions about perception and identity. Each riddle – a shadow moving (without anyone to cast it); opening a door in a hallway, only to see another just closing; a rider approaching over a moor who never gets any closer; seeing in a mirror 'the image of someone retreating before your face' – is accompanied by Morgan's four-times repeated half-line 'Now, with a single step – ', which she finally completes as 'Now, with a single step, your journey starts', the same line with which she opens the second act. It is this recurring idea of any single step as potentially the beginning of a journey that can enable the second act to complete the circle. Morgan sends Gawain back from the Green Chapel to Camelot with the words: 'Now you must go back, / taking with you everything you've gained: / greed, self-love and coward-ice. / Now you must go back; your journey starts . . .' (72). For Arthur the returned Gawain has escaped dream ('Now here you stand / delivered from the dream'), and the King complacently declaims 'All as it was, nothing changed', only for Morgan to turn his words back 'All as it was . . . except for dreams / of fear and fame, except for lies / . . . except for this man with dirty hands' (77). It is for the Fool to turn Arthur's words into a riddle that better fits Gawain now ('All as it was, all completely changed . . . / like a man returned from a journey / with nothing familiar about him / except his name'; 84). It is also the Fool's riddling idea of seeing 'in your mirror / . . . the image of someone retreating before your face' that Morgan le Fay echoes as she ascends in her bright hoop of light at the opera's close, before singing her departing injunctions 'Think only of dreams and promises' and 'Then / with a single step / your journey starts . . .' (86).

Sir Gawain in Films[1]

DAVID J. WILLIAMS

We are concerned here not only with the three films based on *Sir Gawain and the Green Knight* itself, but also with a number of others in which Gawain appears. A study of these adaptations must not be undertaken in a mood jealously protective of the text and character. An adaptation is in effect a critical reading, and can teach us, if only by contrast, about the nature of the original, but can tell us too about the fate of this long-lived figure in the wider world of popular culture, about the significance of such medieval fictions for the twentieth-century imagination.

Gawain is rarely a starring role. Thirty-odd films in the hundred-year history of the medium have an Arthurian theme, of which our hero appears in only a third. On the other hand, those few films are for our purposes usefully representative of the range of cinema itself, from lavishly spectacular productions to the intimacies of the television screen, from routine products of the industry to the work of individual *auteurs* at the boundaries of film art.

The specificity of the medium means that we must become accustomed to seeing a living Gawain, and the cinema offers us a sometimes baffling conglomerate image. Usually he is young (even when the actors are now perhaps better known to us in their middle years): humorous but genteel as Robert Urquhart (*Knights of the Round Table* 1954) or rash as George Baker (*Lancelot and Guinevere* 1963); Liam Neeson's Gawain is bearded, his hair in a trimly barbaric plait, and has an Irish accent (*Excalibur* 1981). Occasionally he is older, as a mustachioed Sterling Hayden, avuncular coach to the adolescent Prince Valiant (*Prince Valiant* 1954); or altogether the wrong generation in John Le Mesurier, a dim adviser to Kenneth More's Arthur in *The Spaceman and King Arthur* (1979), a Disney variation on Mark Twain's *A Connecticut Yankee at the Court of King Arthur*.

Unlike a medieval author, the filmmaker cannot expect in his audience, even if he would like to, a knowledge of traditional representations of Gawain, which can make the hero's role in modern versions of the legend seem arbitrary. But traditions do survive, even if transformed: Gawain the

---

[1] I am grateful to David Rudkin for his help when writing this essay.

accomplished foil for the wilful Perceval; the unhappy Gawain of the last days, friend and reluctant foe of Lancelot. Popular Arthurian films are concerned still with ancient themes: courage, love (especially in conflict with honour and knightly duty), chastity even, and truth itself. Particularly persistent is an interest in youth and its education through experience, or in contrast to age as an agent of renewal. On the other hand, film is itself a medium with deeply ingrained traditions, conventions, and genres, as inclined to the formulaic as any medieval text. One example of this is the very look of Arthurian films. Apart from rare attempts to approximate the period of a particular text, they inhabit their audience's expectations of a medieval fantasy world, familiar (castles, tournaments, horses, plate armour, trailing dresses) yet infinitely variable, and always with a strong contemporary colouring. Not unlike their medieval literary and pictorial forbears, films of Arthur's days are dateable by their allegiance to current fashion in dress and setting. The cinema's history is long enough to make some of its early Arthuriana seem as alien now as the medieval texts themselves.

Three films typify the spectacular approach to Arthurian legend taken by American productions in Europe during the fifties and sixties. Two of these, *Knights of the Round Table* (*Knights*) and *Sword of Lancelot* (*Sword*) remake recognizable stories from the tradition, while reducing the role of Gawain to near insignificance. The third, *Prince Valiant*, in cheerful disregard of all the medieval stories and most of the characters, nevertheless manages to be a more striking and self-assured continuator of tradition, and to give King Lot a vigorous new son. These are films of escape, made in a time of crisis for the American cinema, competing with the new rival of television. In 1954, *Knights* (MGM's first film in Cinemascope) and *Prince Valiant* in particular offered, to a world preoccupied with Korea, Senator McCarthy, and Dien Bien Phu, never-never lands of known, secure values, where an enemy, even when concealed, could be simply known and punished.

Knights and *Sword* may be taken together as examples of a process of extreme compression of the history of Arthur, discarding and conflating stories in the interests of concentrating on Lancelot and the love triangle. The richly ambivalent role of Gawain in the matter is the first to suffer. Even in *Sword*, where he eagerly pursues revenge against Lancelot for the death of his brother Gareth, the conflict is resolved simply as a mistake when he discovers that Modred was really responsible, all in time for Gawaine (sic) to support Lancelot in his final defeat of the villain. In *Knights*, Gawain is hardly more prominent than his harpist brother, as a loyal young lieutenant in Lancelot's entourage, comforting Elaine while her husband is away fighting Picts. The marriage of Lancelot matches the courtly restraint of his love for Guinevere: accusation there is, and emotional conflict, stuffily expressed by the three principals, Robert Taylor, Ava Gardner, and Mel Ferrer, but simply no adultery. As Taylor says in his defence, 'A man and a woman may love each other all their lives with no evil between them. And I dare as say such love is good, for by denial and suffering the heart is purified.' (The linguistic eccentricity is typical of an attempt here to devise a distinctive 'antique' tongue.) The tone, as well as language, of *Sword* almost a decade later is quite different: we see the lovers in bed together. And yet the underlying values are little changed. Lancelot at first resists Guinevere in the cause of 'honour', and when Arthur is dead and the field, so to speak, clear, finds no reward for adultery. To his dismay, the guilty Guin (as he calls her) has turned religious.

The most recent version of the love-triangle story, *First Knight* (1995), takes a stage further the process of compression, reducing familiar complexities, as Malory's Meleagant becomes the simplified villain Malagant. Sean Connery's Arthur is king merely of a country called Camelot (although, in blandly imperialist style, the 'freedom' it stands for he wants to give to the world); as Lancelot Richard Gere is an outsider, the kind of lone fighter familiar in Westerns. There is no time for adultery. Arthur's discovery of Lancelot and Guinevere embracing initiates the briefest of crises for the lovers, resolved by Arthur's convenient death, handing on country and wife to the younger man. As for Gawain, he scarcely registers, a mere spear-carrier, unidentified by name except in the cast list. For, despite the title, these are not knights at all but soldiers who wear blue uniforms and fight in 'brigades'.

In *Prince Valiant* the name of Gawain (pronounced 'G'wain') is restored to strange prominence. As mentor to the eponymous young hero, Gawain's bluff manliness is at the heart of the film's values. The source is not medieval but the comic strip stories of Hal Foster, begun in 1937 in the *New York Journal*. The context is a mythic adventure world of boy-scoutish morality, incorporating many loosely medieval times and places, and set, in the film, in a Britain of constant sunshine and evocative castle ruins. 'Val' is a Christian Viking who seeks to become a knight of the Round Table, which means, as Gawain tells him, being 'sworn to lay down his life for our king, and to defend truth, the weak, and the helpless'. Amusingly for readers of our poem, Gawain spends a large part of the film in bed recovering from injuries, where, for all his experience, he proves to be no ladies' man, embarrassed by their mere presence in his sick-room. He falls speechless at the sight of beauty (a radiant Janet Leigh). Through misunderstanding, he has fallen in love with his young squire's lady. But love here is nothing if not courtly; there is no sex, and marriage no more than a hint. The mistake is resolved and Gawain sums up: 'You were a young fool and I was an old one, which is worse. We both had things to learn. The truth hurts sometimes but it's the only thing to build happiness on.' One often hears such blurred echoes of medieval themes.

Three notable directors have given characteristic personal readings of the Arthurian material, and in the process arresting portrayals of our hero. In *Excalibur* John Boorman embraces the received imagery of Arthurian movies, but transmutes it with new expressiveness. In *Lancelot du Lac* Robert Bresson turns the genre's motifs against themselves in a bleak vision of the end of things. Eric Rohmer rejects the conventional realism of the genre in order to create for the text of Chrétien's *Perceval* a new cinematic voice (*Perceval le Gallois* (1978)).

Excalibur interprets the myth as a kind of world history, rearranging and conflating stories and characters in startling but often effective ways. Again for Gawain this has meant a role severely curtailed, yet of great importance, since in effect all the accusers of Guinevere have been compressed into this one knight. With no preparation, he explodes into the story when, feasting at the Round Table, seduced and goaded by Morgana, he questions the absence of Lancelot 'driven from us by a woman's desire!' A simple warrior, wild eyed, shaking with conflicting emotions, he overturns Guinevere's offered cup of reconciliation, and in consequence fights and loses to his beloved Lancelot in a noisy and damaging encounter. We last see him dead, tied half-naked to the back of his straying horse, defeated in his quest for the Grail. He had been present, we might note, a mere bystander at court, when the qualities of knighthood were being discussed. A cross is prominent in the background here between Arthur and Guinevere, as Merlin, after some hedging, decides for truth: 'When a man lies, he murders some part of the world.'

Bresson's *Lancelot* too addresses the present with ancient myth, using 'constant anachronisms' (Baby 1985, 4) as a deliberate signal. Its chief source is *La Mort le Roi Artu* (Frappier 1936, translated Cable 1971), but it also preys with ironic negation on our awareness of the standard trappings of medieval spectaculars. Most scenes are set at night, or in the dark forest, the camera keeping us at a constant distance from the actors, or confining us to fragments of a scene, typically details of armour or horses. That odd inclination among cinematic knights to wear armour at all times is here given meaning, when Arthur enjoins it as a mark of preparedness. The ruined habitations, bare-walled rooms, unadorned tents, are appropriate also to the monastic dedication of knighthood in an age of decline.

At the heart of this austere narrative, with its frequent ellipsis and stylization (repetitions of sound as well as image: clattering armour, neighing horses, croaking crows) emerges the most poignant portrayal of Gauvain. As 'modelled' (Bresson's term referring to his use of non-professional players) by Humbert Balsan, he is young, despite the late age of the world; restless, impatient, even optimistic, he is the only one who smiles, unless Guenièvre does, hesitantly, when in his company, the only place she seems at ease. Like our poet's hero, and as the queen suggests, he loves his life. In an extraordinary coup of narrative conflation, Lancelot kills him, not in a grand final combat, but unknowingly at the capture of Guenièvre. This short-circuiting of the source story is singularly successful as an expression of the tragedy, and of the film's sense of fated events coming to pass in darkness. Ever outspoken, the dying Gauvain tries to offer advice to his grieving uncle, but the noisy departure of an armoured knight drowns his words and ends the scene. Like Lancelot, we never see him again, but his absence haunts the film.

In *Perceval le Gallois* we find none of the customary paraphernalia of filmed Arthuriana: 'authentic' locations, ruined castles, real forests, spectacular action; but instead an ambiguous, perspectiveless space, where knights journey among gleaming miniature castles and symbolic trees. Although the aim is to make Chrétien's text accessible to a modern audience, that does not mean demystifying it and making it less medieval. It is precisely the alterity of the period as it idealized itself that interests Rohmer. He trims Chrétien's story but still mimics its fragmentary state, refusing the continuations, and giving us only the first of the Gauvain episodes (the tournament at Tintagel, then the amorous knight besieged by the townspeople of Escavalon), and breaks off even more suspensefully than the original. Justifying the inclusion of the episode at all, which some see as a mere accident of the text's transmission, Rohmer points naturally to the interesting contrast it suggests with Perceval himself, but admits that his real reason is 'la séduction de ces pages, les plus brillantes du livre' (Rohmer 1979, 7). Instead of the usual cinematic treatment of a literary text, where pictorial narrative replaces the original's words, we are given those pages through a combination of visual enactment and spoken narration, with the words (modern octosyllables) distributed between a chorus of speakers and singers, as well as the characters themselves.

When the wide-eyed, eager Perceval meets the famous Gauvain, we see at once the difference. Gauvain too is young enough, and blond, but with his shorter hair, drily intelligent face, and calm of manner, this is clearly the celebrated model of courtesy, who, as the chorus tells us, illuminated chivalry as the sun does the world. The actors (Rohmer too uses non-professionals, with André Dussolier as Gauvain) converse (and narrate) with a marked formality of gesture and tone, that conveys a convincing sense of the courtly social game, at once alien and appealing.

Of the three films based on our poem, neither of those by Stephen Weeks, *Gawain and the Green Knight* (1973) nor *Sword of the Valiant* (1983), shows much allegiance to the original. Rather the story has been ransacked for some features of medieval romance that have appeal in the late twentieth century, and where those have not been found, they are supplied from elsewhere. The script, of the earlier film at least, is animated by a certain enthusiasm for the world of medieval romance. We recognize motifs from the poem, despite the new guise, and accretions from other sources, including Chrétien's *Yvain* and Sleeping Beauty: the final encounter with the three blows survives, but turns into a conventional combat (of which both films are full); gone is Bertilak's lady, replaced by Linet, a sort of phantom lover who nevertheless has a green sash to offer; there is a black knight at a green stone, a Land of Lyonesse restored to life with a kiss, and even a unicorn. The dispiriting jumble of contents is much the same in each film, with the emphasis so much on individual motifs that all sense of narrative line is lost, whether the original's or any other; rather as if we had insisted on hearing in detail those adventures of Gawain the poet denies us. Despite the distance from the original, we can recognize the tracks of familiar critical responses to the poem itself. These Green Knights, whether Nigel Green or the more charismatic Sean Connery, are mystic wild men, representative of the 'nature gods' who, we are told, have an interest in Gawain's acquiring 'the courage and purity of heart that befits a man'. The desire to see Gawain as exceptional in Camelot reaches an extreme. The court is decrepit, the aged Arthur enraged at its decline. Only Gawain, who is not yet a knight, has the courage to answer the challenge. Thus the poet's subtle themes are simplified to the conventional story of a young man's trials in love and combat. The more expensive remake was an attempt by the new producers Golan-Globus to exploit a fashion then current for 'sword-and-sorcery', and hoped to appeal to a wider audience. The Gawain of 1973, played by singer Murray Head (Jesus in the original record- ing of *Jesus Christ, Superstar*), is a moody adolescent capable of tears. Ten years later the muscular and expressionless Miles O'Keeffe (a recent Tarzan tamed by a blond wig) is altogether more detached, a worldly-wise adventurer happy to go to bed with any lady, and always ready with a quip: 'This isn't such a bad place to be lost', he smirks appreciatively at the available Linet.

The one conscientious attempt so far to adapt *Sir Gawain and the Green Knight* for the medium of film is Thames Television's production, written by David Rudkin and directed by John Michael Phillips (transmitted 3 January 1991). The intelligence of its approach makes it instructive both about the nature of the poem itself and about what might in general be expected of film versions of a text whose visual qualities seem to invite filming. Readers have often found something cinematic in the poet's writing. Spearing, for example (1970, 37–38, referring to earlier examples), remarks on the mobile point-of- view that conveys a sense of spatial reality. The analogy is revealing about effects in the poem, but is dangerously misleading if it encourages the notion that a verbal text translates simply into a visual; as if to make a film all one has to do is photograph those social and topographical spaces, following the directions about close-ups on severed heads, and slow-motion shots of descending axes seen from below. What the poet's verbal close-up of 'lippez smal laȝande' (Tolkien and Gordon 1967, 1207) causes us to 'see' in our mind's eye is quite different from the relentlessly specific image of a particular actress, and the part that plays in the unavoidably visual sequence that is film narrative.

Still, much of the pleasure (as well as pain) to be gained from an adaptation comes precisely from observing the familiar, if not realized, then reinvented in the new medium, and the filmmakers have followed many of the writer's 'directions'. The film preserves the main lines of the story, following a reading of the Green Knight as a 'green man' with unkempt hair and a costume resembling huge veiny leaves. His identity with Bertilak is well concealed while allowing many dark hints, visual as well as verbal. At the Chapel, of course, the film faces a problem the poet could happily ignore, but the gradual transformation of Knight into host is amusing to observe. The temptation scenes work well, Valerie Gogan's performance as the lady conveying at times a delightfully dangerous feeling of commitment to her task. Gawain, contrary to some readings, appears happiest and most pleased with himself on the second day, although in general Jason Durr's blond hero is a glum and self-absorbed young man, too preoccupied by a sinister unease to display the easy grace of the 'fyne fader of nurture'.

The presence in the film of the real English landscape is affecting, even though the essential seasonal extremes are muffled by too much green leaf and an absence of snow. Perhaps our realization that the Green Chapel is in Goredale disturbs and flatters in a way analogous to the response of the original audience to recognizable topography. The courtly settings disappoint (although the fire- and torch-lit Hautdesert is a lively place), not because they follow the convention of using real medieval buildings in their modern condition, but because a much more generous budget would be required to represent such splendour. The production makes some attempt to match the stylization of the poem. Rudkin has devised a kind of clipped alliterative free verse that gives the dialogue a slightly ponderous but appropriately formal and coded feel, which is matched by the acting style, and editing which draws attention to the patterning in the story.

The filmmaker faces a serious problem when translating *Sir Gawain and the Green Knight* into the kind of visual narrative usual in film: how to deal with a gap of one year so early in the action. That essential hiatus, managed with such panache in two stanzas by our poet, is possible only for a speaking narrator, whereas in visual as in dramatic narrative, either some such figure as 'Time' must appear to explain, or a more 'realistic' way must be found. The difficulty is compounded by the further restriction imposed by the ninety-minute commercial television slot, divided into three by advertising breaks, which necessitates a modification of the poem's fourfold movement. (The breaks come during Gawain's arrival at Hautdesert and between the second and third day of his stay.) Rudkin's solution is to present the first episode as a series of recollections in Gawain's mind as he makes his way northward. It works well locally, with imaginative expansion of the journey stanzas into vignettes of the hero's hardships. But the device compels a changed point of view. Where the narration in the poem is designed, while showing much through Gawain's eyes, to lend distance and objectivity to the story, in the film, despite the medium's natural affinity with the literary third person, we are left with only the hero's perspective. It is a striking translation of the medieval narrative into something distinctively modern, where the story takes place, as it were, in Gawain's head. Gawain addresses us in voice-over, not only in the flashbacks, but at the end, where he interprets for us (rather than for his peers) his wearing of the girdle 'in honour of no exploit and no excellence, but in memoriam how one midwinter morning I met my master on a mountainside, and he invested me with emblem of the order of imperfect man'. This message lacks context because the absence of a genuinely exterior viewpoint has removed a whole dimension from the fiction. The pentangle comes to seem like the personal whim of a now faintly priggish hero, since we learn its meaning only because we hear Gawain himself meditating upon it. The reduction to the personal is compounded by a pre-title prologue which implies that Gawain is setting out for his own reasons, rejecting the entreaties not merely of some misguided 'segges' but of Arthur himself.

Is there another solution? For that particular context in commercial television probably not, but can we imagine an ideal film version of *Sir Gawain and the Green Knight* (other than a scholar's fantasy at limitless expense with Middle English dialogue and no audience)? By translating the poem into a psychological narrative, the film not only adopts the normal procedure for the medium, it also responds to something genuinely present in the poem. The realism of the writing has proved dangerously appealing, not only to filmmakers, but to readers, distracting them from the rhetorical and abstract structure of which it is part, emphasizing the familiarity and accessibility of the text at the expense of its medieval otherness. Perhaps that is what we want a film to do, and we have seen a number of Gawain films doing it, continuing a tradition by reinterpreting Arthurian stories and themes for new times and audiences. But the work of Rohmer and Bresson suggests more complex possibilities. If it is the very strangeness, the alterity of *Sir Gawain and the Green Knight* (or medieval romance in general), that appeals, then we might look for a version analogous to Rohmer's *Perceval* in which the verbal narration is foregrounded, which does not seek to conceal gaps, resolve contradictions, but allows what is awkward to stand. If we could imagine a Bresson version, we should expect so thorough a reworking that we might recognize no more than the bones of story and theme. In any case, what both these directors display, in different ways, is an approach to narrative that is not realistic, centred in a single consciousness, but is dispersed or impersonal, and formalized, however full of feeling. Paradoxically, as Jordan suggests in the case of Chaucer (1987), the post-modern and the medieval have much in common.

The small number of attempts at a filmed *Sir Gawain and the Green Knight* may be disappointing, although such films are but one manifestation in recent times of a continuing interest in the Arthurian romance tradition. On the other hand, the mere existence of the Thames Television version, despite its ephemerality, rather implies the canonical status of the poem. Commissioned in order to advertise the company's cultural ideals when TV franchises were due for renewal, transmitted on one night, after the ten-o'clock news, and now known only through unofficial copies, its origin and fate seem curiously similar to those of the original poem, whose existence it helps to perpetuate.

Bibliography

EDITIONS CITED

Anderson, J. J., ed. 1969. *Patience*. Manchester.

———, ed. 1977. *Cleanness*. Manchester.

Andrew, M. and Waldron, R., eds. 1978. *The Poems of the Pearl Manuscript*. London.

———, eds. 1987. *The Poems of the Pearl Manuscript*. 2nd rev. edn, 1996. Exeter.

Borroff, M., trans. 1977. *Pearl*. New York.

Cawley, A. C. and Anderson, J. J., eds. 1976. *Pearl, Cleanness, Patience* and *Sir Gawain and the Green Knight*. London.

Davis, N., revised. 1967, 1972. See Tolkien and Gordon below.

Gollancz, I., ed. 1891. *Pearl, An English Poem of the Fourteenth Century . . . with a Modern Rendering*. London.

———, ed. 1913. *Patience*. London. 2nd edn, 1924.

———, ed. 1921. *Cleanness*. London. Pt 2, 1933

———, introd. 1923. *Pearl, Cleanness, Patience and Sir Gawain*. Facs. edn. London. EETS os 162.

———, ed. 1940. *Sir Gawain and the Green Knight*. EETS os 210.

Gordon, E. V., ed. 1953. *Pearl*. Rev. I. Gordon. Oxford.

Greenwood, O., trans. 1956. *Sir Gawain and the Green Knight*. London.

Jones, R. T., ed. 1972. *Sir Gawain and the Grene Gome*. London. 2nd edn.

Madden, F., ed. 1839. *Syre Gawayne: A Collection of Ancient Romance-Poems*. London.

Menner, R. J., ed. 1920. *Purity* [*Cleanness*]. New Haven. Yale Studies in English 61.

Moorman, C., ed. 1977. *The Works of the* Gawain-*Poet*. Jackson, Miss.

Morris, R., ed. 1864. *Sir Gawain and the Green Knight*. London. EETS os 4.

———, ed. 1869. *Early English Alliterative Poems from MS Cotton Nero A.x*. London. EETS os 1.

Osgood, C. G., ed. 1906. *The Pearl: A Middle English Poem*. Boston.

Silverstein, T., ed. 1984. *Sir Gawain and the Green Knight*. Chicago.

Tolkien, J. R. R. and Gordon, E. V., eds. 1925. *Sir Gawain and the Green Knight*. Oxford.

———, eds. 1967. *Sir Gawain and the Green Knight*. Rev. N. Davis. Oxford. 2nd edn. [See Davis above]

Vantuono, W. 1984. *The Pearl Poems: An Omnibus Edition*. New York. The Renaissance Imagination 5–6. 2 vols.

Waldron, R. A., ed. 1970. *Sir Gawain and the Green Knight* London.

TRANSLATIONS WITH INTRODUCTIONS AND NOTES

FLEMISH
Heer Gawein en de Groene Ridder, vertaling Erik Hertog, Guido Latre, Ludo Timmerman. Utrecht/Antwerpen. 1979

FRENCH
Sire Gauvain et le chevalier Vert, trans. E. Pons. Paris. 1946
Sire Gauvain et le chevalier vert, trans. J. Dor. Paris. 1993

ITALIAN
Sir Gawain e il Cavaliere Verde, a cura di P. Boitani. Milano. 1986
Perla, a cura di E. Giaccherini. Parma. 1989

JAPANESE
Cleanness, with Japanese translation, edited by M. Taguchi and S. Yokoyama. Tokyo. 1993

TURKISH
Sir Gawain ve yesil sövalye. Tr. A. Cebesoy. Istanbul. 1947

OTHER WORKS CITED

Aarne, A. and Thompson, S. 1961. A. Aarne, *The Types of the Folktale: A Classification and Bibliography*. Trans. and enlarged by S. Thompson. Helsinki.
Ackerman, R. W. 1952. *An Index of the Arthurian Names in Middle English*. Stanford, NJ. Stanford University Publications University Series: Language and Literature 10.
———— 1958. 'Gawain's shield: penitential doctrine in *Sir Gawain and the Green Knight'*. *Anglia* 76. 254–65.
———— 1959. 'English rimed and prose romances'. In *Arthurian Literature in the Middle Ages: A Collaborative History*. Ed. R. S. Loomis. Oxford. 480–519.
———— 1964. 'The pearl-maiden and the penny'. *Romance Philology* 17. 615–23. Repr. in Conley 1970. 149–62.
Adam, K. L. 1976. *The Anomalous Stanza of* Pearl: *Does It Disclose a Six-Hundred-Year Old Secret?* Fayetteville, Ark. Medieval Series 1.
Adams, A., ed. and trans. 1983. *The Romance of Yder*. Cambridge.
Aers, D. 1980. *Piers Plowman and Christian Allegory*. London.
———— 1988. *Community, Gender and Individual Identity: English Writing 1360–1430*. London.
———— 1993. 'The self mourning: reflections on *Pearl'*. *Speculum* 68. 54–73.
———— 1994. 'Justice and wage-labour after the Black Death: some perplexities for William Langland'. In *The Work of Work: Servitude, Slavery and Labor in Medieval England*. Eds. A. J. Frantzen and D. Moffat. Glasgow. 169–90.

Alain de Lille. *Texts inedits*. See under D'Alverny, M. T.

Alexander, J. and Binski, P. 1987. *Age of Chivalry: Art in Plantagenet England, 1200–1400*. London.

Alford, J. A. 1974. 'Haukyn's coat: some observations on *Piers Plowman* B XIV 22–27'. *Medium Ævum* 43. 133–8.

—— ed. 1988. *A Companion to* Piers Plowman. Berkeley.

—— 1992. 'The scriptural self'. In *The Bible in the Middle Ages: Its Influence on Literature and Art*. Ed. B. S. Levy. Binghamton, NY. 1–21. Medieval and Renaissance Texts and Studies 89.

Allen, H. A. 1923. 'On some fourteenth century borrowings from *Ancrene Riwle*'. *Modern Language Review* 18. 1–8.

—— 1929. 'Further borrowings from *Ancrene Riwle*'. *Modern Language Review* 24. 1–15.

Allen, V. 1992. '*Sir Gawain*: "cowardyse" and the fourth pentad'. *Review of English Studies* ns 43. 181–93.

Allmand, C. T. 1988. *The Hundred Years War: England and France at War, c.1300–c.1450*. Cambridge.

Amis and Amiloun. See under Leach, M.

Amours, F. J., ed. 1906. *The Original Chronicle of Andrew of Wyntoun*. 4. Edinburgh. Scottish Text Society 54.

Andersen, E. 1987. 'Heinrich von dem Türlin's *Diu Crône* and the prose *Lancelot*: an intertextual study'. *Arthurian Literature* 8. 23–49.

Anderson, J. J. 1969. See list of editions.

—— 1977. See list of editions.

—— 1990a. 'Gawain and the hornbook'. *Notes and Queries* ns 37. 160–3.

—— 1990b. 'The three judgments and the ethos of chivalry in *Sir Gawain and the Green Knight*'. *Chaucer Review* 24. 337–55.

Anderson, W. 1990. *The Green Man: The Archetype of our Oneness with the Earth*. London.

Andrew, M. 1973. 'Jonah and Christ in *Patience*'. *Modern Philology* 70. 230–3.

—— 1979. *The* Gawain-*Poet: An Annotated Bibliography, 1839–1977*. New York. Garland Reference Library of the Humanities 129.

Andrew, M. and Waldron, R. 1978, 1987. See list of editions.

Antilla, R. 1969. 'Sound preferences in alliteration'. *Statistical Methods in Linguistics* 5. 44–8.

Aquinas, Thomas 1894. *Summa Theologica . . . editio altera romana ad emendatores editiones impressa et noviter accuratissime recognita*. Rome. 4 vols in 6.

Armitage-Smith, S. 1904. *John of Gaunt*. Westminster.

Arnold, I., ed. 1938–40. *Le Roman de Brut de Wace*. Paris. 2 vols.

Arnold, J. 1993. 'The jupon or coat-armour of the Black Prince in Canterbury Cathedral'. *Church Monuments* 8. 12–24.

Arthur, R. G. 1987. *Medieval Sign Theory and* Sir Gawain and the Green Knight. Toronto.

Assumption of Our Lady. See under McKnight, G. H.

Astell, A. W. 1990. *The Song of Songs in the Middle Ages*. Ithaca, N.Y.

Auchinleck Manuscript. See under Pearsall, D. and Cunningham, I. F.

Audelay, John. *Poems*. See under Whiting, E. K.

Auden, W. H. 1948. *The Dyer's Hand and Other Essays*. London.

Augustine 1945. See under Tasker, R. V. G.

—— 1950. *The City of God*. New York.

Avowing of King Arthur. See under Brookhouse, C.; Dahood, R.

Awntyrs off Arthure. See under Gates, R. J.; Hanna, R. 1974.

Baby, Y. 1985. 'Metal makes sounds: an interview with Robert Bresson'. Trans. N. Jacobson. *Field of Vision* 13. Spring. 4–5

Bachman, W. B. 1980. 'Lineation of the bobs in *Sir Gawain and the Green Knight'*. *English Language Notes* 18. 86–8.

Baillie-Grohman, W. A. and Baillie-Grohman, F., eds. 1904. Edward Plantagenet, *The Master of Game*. London.

Bakhtin, M. 1968. *Rabelais and his World*. Trans. H. Iswolsky. Cambridge, Mass. and London.

Bal, M. 1985. *Narratology: Introduction to the Theory of Narrative*. Trans. C. van Boheemen. 2nd edn. Toronto.

Baldwin, A. P. 1984. 'The tripartite reformation of the soul in *The Scale of Perfection, Pearl*, and *Piers Plowman'*. In *The Medieval Mystical Tradition in England: Papers Read at Dartington Hall, July 1984*. Ed. M. Glasscoe. Cambridge. 136–49.

Barber, C. L. 1957. *The Idea of Honour in the English Drama, 1591–1700*. Gothenburg. Gothenburg Studies in English 6.

Barber, R. and Barker, J. 1989. *Tournaments: Jousts, Chivalry and Pageants in the Middle Ages*. Woodbridge.

Barnes, G. 1993. *Counsel and Strategy in Middle English Romance*. Cambridge.

Barnie, J. 1974. *War in Medieval Society: Social Values and the Hundred Years War 1337–99*. London.

Barron, W. R. J. 1980. *Trawthe and Treason: The Sin of Gawain Reconsidered. A Thematic Study of* Sir Gawain and the Green Knight. Manchester. Publications of the Faculty of Arts of the University of Manchester 25.

Barthes, R. 1979. *A Lover's Discourse: Fragments*. Trans. R. Howard. London.

Bartholomaeus Anglicus. *On the Properties of Things*. See under Seymour, M. C. *et al.*

Basford, K. 1978. *The Green Man*. Ipswich.

Batman, S. 1582. *Batman vpon Bartholome his Booke De Proprietatibus Rerum*. London. Facs. repr. Hildesheim, New York. 1976. See also Seymour M. C. *et al.*

Beckwith, S. 1992. *Christ's Body: Identity, Culture and Society in Late Medieval Writing*. London.

Bedingfeld, H. and Gwynn-Jones, P. 1993. *Heraldry*. Leicester.

Bennett, J. A. W. 1972–6. 'Supplementary notes on *Sir Gawain and the Green Knight'*. Typescript. English Faculty Library, Cambridge.

—— 1986. *Middle English Literature, 1100–1400*. Ed. and completed D. Gray. Oxford. Oxford History of English Literature 1. Originally numbered 1.2.

Bennett, M. J. 1973. 'The Lancashire and Cheshire clergy, 1379'. *Transactions of the Historic Society of Lancashire and Cheshire* 124. 1–30.

—— 1979. '*Sir Gawain and the Green Knight* and the literary achievement of the north-west midlands'. *Journal of Medieval History* 5. 63–89.

—— 1982. 'John Audley: some new evidence on his life and work'. *Chaucer Review* 16. 344–55.

—— 1983. *Community, Class and Careerism: Cheshire and Lancashire Society in the Age of* Sir Gawain and the Green Knight. Cambridge.

—— 1992. 'The court of Richard II and the promotion of literature'. In Hanawalt. 3–20.

Benoit de Sainte Maure. *Le Roman de Troie*. See under Constans, L.

Benskin, M. 1991. 'The "fit"-technique explained'. In *Regionalism in Late Medieval Manuscripts and Texts: Essays Celebrating the Publication of* A Linguistic Atlas of Late Mediaeval English. Ed. F. Riddy. Cambridge. 9–26.

—— 1992. 'In reply to Dr. Burton'. *Leeds Studies in English* 23. 209–62.

Benskin, M. and Laing, Margaret 1981. 'Translations and "misprachen" in Middle English manuscripts'. In *'So Meny People Longages and Tonges': Philological essays in Scots and Medieval English Presented to Angus McIntosh*. Eds. M. Benskin and M. L. Samuels. Edinburgh. 55–106.

Benson, C. D. 1991. 'The impatient reader of *Patience*'. In Blanch, Miller and Wasserman. 147–62.

—— 1992. 'The lost honor of Sir Gawain'. In De Gustibus: *Essays for Alain Renoir*. Ed. J. M. Foley. New York. 30–9.

Benson, L. D. 1965a. 'The authorship of *St. Erkenwald*'. *Journal of English and Germanic Philology* 64. 393–405.

—— 1965b. *Art and Tradition in* Sir Gawain and the Green Knight. New Brunswick, NJ.

——, gen. ed. 1987. *The Riverside Chaucer*. Boston.

Bernheimer, R. M. 1952. *Wild Men in the Middle Ages: A Study in Art, Sentiment and Demonology*. Cambridge, Mass.

Besserman, L. 1986. 'The idea of the green knight'. *ELH* 53. 219–39.

Biblia sacra iuxta vulgatam versionem. See under Weber, R.

Bishop, I. 1968. Pearl *in its Setting: A Critical Study of the Structure and Meaning of the Middle English Poem*. Oxford.

—— 1984. ' "Solacia" in *Pearl* and in letters of Edward III concerning the death of his daughter, Joan'. *Notes and Queries* 229. 454–6.

Blair, C. 1958. *European Armour, circa 1066 to circa 1700*. London.

—— 1982. Notes on armour from Chalcis'. In *Arms and Armour in the Dorchester Arms Fair*. Dorchester.

Blair, J. and Ramsay, H. 1991. *English Medieval Industries: Craftsmen, Techniques, Products*. London and Rio Grande, Ohio.

Blake, N. F. 1979. 'Middle English alliterative revivals'. *Review* 1. 205–14.

Blanch, R. J., ed. 1966. Sir Gawain *and* Pearl: *Critical Essays*. Bloomington, Ind.

—— 1983. Sir Gawain and the Green Knight: *A Reference Guide*. Troy, NY.

Blanch, R. J., Miller, M. Y. and Wasserman, J. N., eds. 1991. *Text and Matter: New Critical Perspectives of the* Pearl-*Poet*. Troy, NY.

Blanch, R. J. and Wasserman, J. N. 1995. *From* Pearl *to* Gawain: *Forme to Fynisment*. Gainesville.

Blenkner, L. 1968. 'The theological structure of *Pearl*'. *Traditio* 24. 43–75. Repr. in Conley 1970. 220–71.

—— 1977. 'Sin, psychology, and the structure of *Sir Gawain and the Green Knight*'. *Studies in Philology* 74. 354–87.

Bliss, A. J., ed. 1960. T. Chestre, *Sir Launfal*. London.

————, ed. 1966. *Sir Orfeo*. Oxford. 2nd edn.

Bloomfield, M. W. 1961. '*Sir Gawain and the Green Knight*: an appraisal'. *PMLA* 76. 7–19. Repr. in Howard and Zacher 1968. 24–55.

Boccaccio. *Eclogues*. See under Massera, A. F.

Bogdanos, T. 1983. Pearl, *Image of the Ineffable: A Study in Medieval Poetic Symbolism*. University Park, Pa.

Boitani, P. 1982. *English Medieval Narrative in the Thirteenth and Fourteenth Centuries*. Trans. J. K. Hall. Cambridge.

Boitani, P. and Torti, A., eds. 1988. *Genres, Themes and Images in English Literature from the Fourteenth to the Fifteenth Centuries: The J. A. W. Bennett Memorial Lectures, Perugia, 1986*. Tübingen. Tübinger Beitrage zur Anglistik 11.

Boke of Huon of Burdeux. See under Lee, S. L.

Book of Vices and Virtues. See under Francis, W. N.

Borroff, M. 1962. Sir Gawain and the Green Knight: *A Stylistic and Metrical Study*. New Haven. Yale Studies in English 152.

———— 1977. See list of editions.

Bossy, J. 1985. *Christianity in the West, 1400–1700*. Oxford.

Boswell, J. 1980. *Christianity, Social Tolerance and Homosexuality: Gay People in Western Europe from the Beginning of the Christian Era to the Fourteenth Century*. Chicago.

Bowers, J. M. 1986. '*Patience* and the ideal of the mixed life'. *Texas Studies in Literature and Language* 28. 1–23.

———— 1995. '*Pearl* in its royal setting: Ricardian poetry revisited'. *Studies in the Age of Chaucer* 17. 111–55.

Brault, G. J. 1972. *Early Blazon: Heraldic Terminology in the Twelfth Century with Special Reference to Arthurian Literature*. Oxford.

Brennan, T., ed. 1989. *Between Feminism and Psychoanalysis*. London and New York.

Brewer, D. S. 1948. 'Gawayn and the green chapel'. *Notes and Queries* 193. 13.

———— 1966. 'Courtesy and the *Gawain*-poet'. In *Patterns of Love and Courtesy: Essays in Memory of C. S. Lewis*. Ed. J. Lawlor. Evanston. 54–85.

———— 1967. 'The *Gawain*-poet: a general appreciation of four poems'. *Essays in Criticism* 17. 130–42.

————, ed. 1968. Thomas Malory, *The Morte Darthur Pts. 7 and 8*. London. Introduction. 23–35.

———— 1973. 'Honour in Chaucer'. *Essays and Studies* 26. 1–19. Repr. in Brewer 1982. 89–109.

———— 1974. 'Some observations on the development of literalism and verbal criticism'. *Poetica* 2. 71–95.

———— 1976. 'The interpretation of dream, folktale and romance with special reference to *Sir Gawain and the Green Knight*'. *Neuphilologische Mitteilungen* 77. 569–81.

———— 1979a. 'The arming of the warrior in European literature in the fourteenth century'. In *Chaucerian Problems and Perspectives: Essays Presented to P. E. Beichner C.S.C*. Eds. E. Vasta and Z. P. Thundy. Notre Dame, Ind. 221–43. Repr. in Brewer 1982. 142–60.

———— 1979b. 'The gospels and the laws of folktale'. *Folk-lore* 90.1. 37–50.

————— 1980. *Symbolic Stories: Traditional Narratives of the Family Drama in English Literature*. Cambridge.

————— 1982. *Tradition and Innovation in Chaucer*. London.

————— 1983. *English Gothic Literature*. London.

————— 1984. *Chaucer: The Poet as Storyteller*. London.

—————, ed. 1988a. *Studies in Medieval English Romances: Some New Approaches*. Cambridge.

————— 1988b. 'Escape from the mimetic fallacy'. In Brewer 1988a. 1–10.

————— 1988c. *Symbolic Stories: Traditional Narratives of the Family Drama in English Literature*. Paperback edn. Harlow.

————— 1991. 'Feasts in England and English literature in the fourteenth century'. In *Feste und Feiern im Mittelalter: Paderborner Symposon des Mediavistenverbandes*. Eds. D. Altenburg, J. Jarnut and H.-H. Steinhoff. Sigmarigen. 13–26.

—————, ed. 1996. *Medieval Comic Tales*. Cambridge. New edn.

Brewer, L. E., ed. 1973. *From Cuchulainn to Gawain: Sources and Analogues of* Sir Gawain and the Green Knight. Cambridge.

—————, ed. 1992. Sir Gawain and the Green Knight: *Sources and Analogues*. Cambridge. 2nd edn. Arthurian Studies 27

Briggs, K. 1976. *A Dictionary of Fairies, Hobgoblins, Brownies, Bogies and other Supernatural Creatures*. London.

Brink, A. 1920. *Stab und Wort im* Gawain: *eine stilistiche Untersuchung*. Halle. Studien zur englischen Philologie 59.

Brookhouse, C., ed. 1968. *'Sir Amadace' and 'The Avowing of Arthur'*. Copenhagen. *Anglistica* 15.

Brown, D. C. 1987. *Pastor and Laity in the Theology of Jean Gerson*. Cambridge.

Brown, J. T. T. 1897. 'The poems of David Rate, confessor of King James the first of Scotland'. *The Scottish Antiquary* 12. 5–12.

Brownlee, K. 1984. *Poetic Identity in Guillaume de Machaut*. Madison.

Brundage, J. A. 1987. *Law, Sex and Christian Society in Medieval Europe*. Chicago.

Bryant, N., trans. 1978. *Perlesvaus: The High Book of the Grail*. Cambridge.

—————, trans. 1982. *Perceval: The Story of the Grail*. Cambridge.

Brzezinski, M. 1990. 'Conscience and covenant: the sermon structure of *Cleanness*'. *Journal of English and Germanic Philology* 89. 166–80.

Bullock-Davies, C. 1978. *Menestrellorum multitudo: Minstrels at a Royal Feast*. Cardiff.

Bumke, J. 1991. *Courtly Culture: Literature and Society in the High Middle Ages*. Trans. T. Dunlap. Berkeley.

Burrow, J. A. 1965. *A Reading of* Sir Gawain and the Green Knight. London.

————— 1971. *Ricardian Poetry: Chaucer, Gower, Langland and the* Gawain-*Poet*. London.

————— 1984. 'Honour and shame in *Sir Gawain and the Green Knight*'. In his *Essays on Medieval Literature*. Oxford. 117–31.

————— 1988a. 'The poet and the book'. In Boitano and Torti. 230–45.

————— 1988b. 'Problems in punctuation: *Sir Gawain and the Green Knight*, lines 1–7'. In *Sentences: Essays Presented to Alan Ward on the Occasion of his Retirement from Wadham College, Oxford*. Ed. D. M. Reeks. Southampton. 75–88.

Burton, T. L. 1992. 'On the current state of middle English dialectology'. *Leeds Studies in English* 23. 167–208.

Busby, K. 1980. *Gauvain in Old French Literature*. Amsterdam. Degré second 2.

Busnelli, G. and Vandelli, G., eds. 1934. Dante Alighieri, *Convivio*. Florence.

Butler, J. P. 1990. *Gender Trouble: Feminism and the Subversion of Identity*. New York.

Buttin, F. 1971. *Du costume militaire au moyen age et pendant la renaissance*. Barcelona.

Bynum, C. W. 1982. *Jesus as Mother: Studies in the Spirituality of the High Middle Ages*. Berkeley.

———— 1988. *Holy Feast and Holy Fast: The Religious Significance of Food to Medieval Women*. Berkeley. The New Historicism: Studies in Cultural Poetics 1.

———— 1991. *Fragmentation and Redemption: Essays on Gender and the Human Body in Medieval Religion*. New York.

Cable, J., trans. 1971. *The Death of King Arthur*. Harmondsworth.

Cable, T. 1989a. 'Old and middle English prosody: transformations of the model'. In *Hermeneutics and Medieval Culture*. Eds. P. J. Gallacher and H. Damico. Albany. 201–11.

———— 1989b. 'Standards from the past: the conservative syllable structure of the alliterative revival'. In *Standardizing English: Essays in the History of Language Change in Honor of John Hurt Fisher*. Ed. J. B. Trahern, jr. Knoxville. 43–56. Tennessee Studies in Literature 31.

———— 1991. *The English Alliterative Tradition*. Philadelphia.

Cairns, F. 1987. 'Latin sources and analogues of the M.E. Patience'. *Studia Neophilologica* 59. 7–18.

Calendar of Close Rolls 1896–1947. *Calendar of Close Rolls, Edward III to Henry VI*. London. 33 vols.

Calin, W. 1994. *The French Tradition and the Literature of Medieval England*. Toronto.

Cameron, E. 1984. *The Reformation of the Heretics: The Waldenses of the Alps, 1480–1580*. Oxford.

Cameron, K., ed. 1959. *Place-Names of Derbyshire*. Cambridge.

Campbell, M. 1991. 'Gold, silver and precious stones'. In Blair and Ramsay. 107–66.

Camporesi, P. 1989. *Bread of Dreams: Food and Fantasy in Early Modern Europe*. Trans. D. Gentilcore. Cambridge.

Cargill, O. and Schlauch, M. 1928. 'The Pearl and its jeweler'. *PMLA* 43. 105–23.

Carlson, D. 1987. 'The *Pearl*-poet's *Olympia*'. *Manuscripta* 31. 181–9.

Cato, *Distichs*. See under Chase, W. J.

Cawley, A. C. and Anderson, J. J. 1976. See list of editions.

Chadwick, N. 1946. 'Norse ghosts: a study in the *draugr* and the *langbir*'. *Folk-Lore* 57. 50–65; 106–27.

Chambers, R. 1866. *The Book of Days: A Miscellany of Popular Antiquities, in Connection with the Calendar*. London.

Champion, L. S. 1967. 'Grace versus merit in *Sir Gawain and the Green Knight*'. *Modern Language Quarterly* 28. 413–25.

Chance, J. 1991. 'Allegory and structure in *Pearl*: the four senses of the *ars praedicandi* and fourteenth-century homiletic poetry'. In Blanch, Miller and Wasserman. 31–59.

Chapman, C. O. 1932. 'The authorship of *The Pearl*'. *PMLA* 47. 346–53.

Chase, W. J., trans. 1922. Dionysius Cato, *The Distichs: A Famous Medieval Textbook*. Madison, Wisc. Wisconsin University Studies in the Social Sciences and History.

Chaucer, Geoffrey. See under Benson, L. D. 1987.

Cherniss, M. D. 1987. *Boethian Apocalypse: Studies in Middle English Vision Poetry*. Norman, Okla.

Cherry, J. 1969. 'The Dunstable Swan Jewel'. *Journal of the British Archaeological Association*. 3rd ser. 32. 38–53.

—————— 1992. *Medieval Craftsmen: Goldsmiths*. London.

Chestre, T. *Sir Launfal*. See under Bliss, A. J.

Child, F. J., ed. 1857–9. *English and Scottish Ballads*. Boston. 8 vols.

——————, ed. 1882–98. *The English and Scottish Popular Ballads*. Boston. 2nd edn. 5 vols in 10.

Chrétien de Troyes. *Arthurian Romances*. See under Kibler, W. W. 1991.

—————— *Cligés*. See under Gregory, S. and Luttrell, C.

—————— *Le Conte du Graal*. See under Lecoy, F.

Chronique de la Traison et Mort de Richart Deux Roy Dengleterre. See under Williams, B.

Cicero. *De officiis*. See under Goold, G. P.

Cigman, G., ed. 1989. 'Sermon of dead men'. In *Lollard Sermons*. Ed. G. Cigman. London. EETS os 294. 207–40.

Clanvowe, Sir John. *Works*. See under Scattergood, V. J., ed. 1975.

Clark, J. 1949. 'Observations on certain differences in vocabulary between *Cleanness* and *Sir Gawain and the Green Knight*'. *Philological Quarterly* 28. 261–73.

—————— 1950a. 'Paraphrases for "God" in the poems attributed to "the *Gawain*-poet" '. *Modern Language Notes* 65. 232–6.

—————— 1950b. ' "The *Gawain*-poet" and the substantival adjective'. *Journal of English and Germanic Philology* 49. 60–6.

—————— 1951. 'On certain "alliterative" and "poetic" words in the poems attributed to "the *Gawain*-poet" '. *Modern Language Quarterly* 12. 387–98.

Clarke, M. V. 1937. 'Forfeitures and treason in 1388'. In her *Fourteenth-Century Studies*. Eds. L. S. Sutherland and M. McKisack. Oxford. 115–45.

Clein, W. 1987. *Concepts of Chivalry in* Sir Gawain and the Green Knight. Norman, Okla.

Cloisters Apocalypse 1971. *The Cloisters Apocalypse: An Early Fourteenth-Century Manuscript in facsimile*. New York.

Clopper, L. M. 1992. '*Pearl* and the consolation of scripture'. *Viator* 23. 231–45.

Cocheris, H., ed. 1860. *Les couleurs en armes livrées et devises par Sicille, hérault d'Alphonse, V., roi d'Aragon*. Paris. Trésor des pièces rares ou inédites 18.

Cockcroft, R. 1978. 'Castle Hautdesert: portrait or patchwork'. *Neophilologus* 62. 459–77.

Colby, A. M. 1965. *The Portrait in Twelfth-Century French Literature: An Example of the Stylistic Originality of Chrétien de Troyes*. Geneva.

Coleman, J. 1981a. Piers Plowman *and the 'moderni'*. Rome. Letture di Pensiero e d'Arte 58.

———— 1981b. *English Literature in History, 1350–1450: Medieval Readers and Writers*. London.

Colley, C. B. and J. J. Anderson, eds. forthcoming. *English Historical Metrics*. Cambridge.

Colvin, H. M., gen. ed. 1963. *History of the King's Works* 1–2. London.

Conley, J. 1955. '*Pearl* and a lost tradition'. *Journal of English and Germanic Philology* 54. 332–47. Repr. in Conley 1970. 50–72.

————, ed. 1970. *The Middle English* Pearl: *Critical Essays*. Notre Dame, Ind.

Conrad, Joseph 1900. *Lord Jim*. London.

Constans, L., ed. 1904–12. Benoit de Sainte Maure, *Le Roman de Troie*. Paris.

Contamine, P. 1980. *Warfare in the Middle Ages*. Trans. M. Jones. London.

Continuations of Perceval. See under Roach, W.; Williams, M. and Oswald, M.

Contributions 1913–76. *Contributions to a Dictionary of the Irish Language*. Dublin.

Cooke, W. G. 1989. '*Sir Gawain and the Green Knight*: a restored dating'. *Medium Ævum* 58. 34–48.

Coomaraswamy, A. K. 1944. '*Sir Gawain and the Green Knight*: Indra and Narnucci'. *Speculum* 19. 104–25.

Cooper, H. 1976. 'Magic that does not work'. *Medievalia et Humanistica* ns 8. 131–46.

Cooper, R. A. and Pearsall, D. A. 1988. 'The *Gawain*-poems: a statistical approach to the question of common authorship'. *Review of English Studies* ns 39. 365–86.

Cosman, M. P. 1976. *Fabulous Feasts: Medieval Cookery and Ceremony*. New York.

Coss, P. R. 1993. *The Knight in Medieval England, 1000–1400*. Stroud.

Cosson, Baron de and Burges, W. 1881. *Ancient Helmets and Examples of Mail: A Catalogue of Objects Exhibited in the Rooms of the Royal Archaeological Institute of Great Britain and Ireland, June 3rd–16th, 1880*. London.

Courtauld Institute n.d. 'The Commentaries of Lorenzo Ghiberti'. Trans. members of the Courtauld Institute. Typescript.

Courtenay, W. J. 1984. *Covenant and Causality in Medieval Thought: Studies in Philosophy, Theology and Economic Practice*. London.

———— 1987. *Schools and Scholars in Fourteenth-Century England*. Princeton.

Crawford, D. 1993. 'The architectonics of *Cleanness*'. *Studies in Philology* 90. 29–45.

Creton, J. 1824. 'Histoire du roy d'Angleterre Richard'. Ed. J. Webb. *Archaelogia* 20. 1–423.

Cross, F. L., ed. 1958. *The Oxford Dictionary of the Christian Church*. Oxford.

Cursor Mundi. See under Morris, R.

Curtius, E. R. 1953. *European Literature and the Latin Middle Ages*. Trans. W. R. Trask. London.

Dahood, R., ed. 1984. *The Avowing of King Arthur*. New York.

D'Alverny, M. T., ed. 1965. *Alain de Lille: textes inédits*. Paris. Etudes de Philosophie Médiévale 52.

d'Arderne, S. R. T. O. 1959. ' "The green count" and *Sir Gawain and the Green Knight*'. *Review of English Studies* ns 10. 113–26.

Dante, *Convivio*. See under Busnelli, G. and Vandelli, G.

Davenport, W. A. 1978. *The Art of the* Gawain-Poet. London.

Davies, B. 1993. *The Thought of Thomas Aquinas*. New York.

Davies, C. S., ed. 1961. *A History of Macclesfield*. Manchester.

Davies, R. R. 1971. 'Richard II and the principality of Chester'. In *The Reign of Richard II: Essays in Honour of May McKisack*. Eds. F. R. H. Du Boulay and C. M. Barron. London. 256–79.

Davis, N. 1967, 1972. See list of editions.

———— 1970. 'A note on *Pearl*'. In Conley 1970. 325–34.

Davis, N. M. 1993. 'Gawain's rationalist pentangle'. *Arthurian Literature* 12. 37–62.

———— 1995. 'Recognition of worth in *Pearl* and *Sir Gawain and the Green Knight*'. In *The Middle Ages in the North West*. Eds. T. Scott and P. Starkey. Oxford. 177–202.

Day, M. 1940. 'Introduction'. In Gollancz 1940. ix–xxxix.

Death of King Arthur. See under Cable, J.

De Bruyne, F. 1946. *Etudes d'esthétique médiévale*. Bruges. Rijksuniversitat te Gent. Werken Uitgegeven door de Faculteit van de Wijsbegeerte en Letteren 97–9. 3 vols.

Delahaye, E. T., ed. 1989. *L'Orfèvrerie Gothique (XIIIe–debut XVe Siècle) au Musée de Cluny*. Paris.

Delany, P. 1965. 'The role of the guide in *Sir Gawain and the Green Knight*'. *Neophilologus* 49. 250–5.

De Looze, L. 1991. 'Signing off in the middle ages: medieval textuality and strategies of self-naming'. In Doane and Pasternack. 162–78.

Derolez, R. 1981. 'Authorship and statistics: the case of the *Pearl*-poet and the *Gawain*-poet'. *Occasional Papers in Linguistics and Language Learning* 8. 41–51.

Despres, D. L. 1989. *Ghostly Sights: Visual Meditation in Late-Medieval Literature*. Norman, Okla.

De Winter, P. M. 1983. 'Visions of the apocalypse in medieval England and France'. *Bulletin of the Cleveland Museum of Art*. December. 396–417.

Dickins, B. 1934. 'A Yorkshire chronicler'. *Transactions of the Yorkshire Dialect Society* 5. 15–26.

Diekstra, F. N. M. 1974. 'Jonah and *Patience*: the psychology of a saint'. *English Studies* 55. 205–17.

———— 1994. 'Symbolic narrative in *Patience*'. In Houwen and MacDonald. 187–206.

Dillon, H. A. 1890. 'On a manuscript collection of ordinances of chivalry of the fifteenth century, belonging to Lord Hastings'. *Archaeologia* 57. 29–70.

Dillon, H. A. and Hope, W. St. J. 1897. 'Inventory of the goods and chattels belonging to Thomas, Duke of Gloucester'. *Archaeological Journal* 54. 274–308.

Dinshaw, C. 1994. 'A kiss is just a kiss: heterosexuality and its consolations in *Sir Gawain and the Green Knight*'. *Diacritics* 24. 204–26.

Doane, A. N. and Pasternack, C. B., eds. 1991. *Vox Intexta: Orality and Textuality in the Middle Ages*. Madison, Wis.

Dobson, R. B., ed. 1983. *The Peasants' Revolt of 1381*. London. 2nd edn.

Dollimore, J. 1991. *Sexual Dissidence: Augustine to Wilde, Freud to Foucault*. Oxford.

Donatelli, J. 1993. 'The Percy folio manuscript: a seventeenth-century context for medieval poetry'. *English Manuscript Main Studies 1100–1700* 4. 114–33.

Dondaine, A. 1948. 'Guillaume Peyraut, vie et oeuvres'. *Archivum Fratrum Praedicatorum* 18. 162–236.

Donavan, M. J. *et al.* 1967. *Romances*. In Hartung and Severs. 1.

Doyle, A. I. 1982. 'The manuscripts'. In Lawton 1982a. 88–100.

———— 1983. 'English books in and out of court'. In Scattergood and Sherborne. 163–81.

Dronke, P. 1968. *Medieval Latin and the Rise of European Love Lyric*. Oxford. 2 vols. 2nd edn.

Duffy, E. 1992. *The Stripping of the Altars: Traditional Religion in England, c.1400–c.1500*. New Haven.

Duggan, H. N. 1976. 'The role of formulas in the dissemination of a Middle English alliterative romance'. *Studies in Bibliography* 29. 265–88.

———— 1986a. 'Alliterative patterning as a basis for emendation in Middle English alliterative poetry'. *Studies in the Age of Chaucer* 8. 73–105.

———— 1986b. 'The shape of the b-verse in Middle English alliterative poetry'. *Speculum* 61. 564–92.

———— 1987a. 'The authenticity of the Z text of *Piers Plowman*: further notes on metrical evidence'. *Medium Ævum* 56. 25–45.

———— 1987b. 'Notes toward a theory of Langland's meter'. *Yearbook of English Studies* 1. 41–70.

———— 1988. 'Final *-e* and the rhythmic structure of the b-verse in Middle English alliterative poetry'. *Modern Philology* 86. 119–45.

———— 1990a. 'Stress assignment in Middle English alliterative poetry'. *Journal of English and Germanic Philology* 89. 309–29.

———— 1990b. 'Langland's dialect and final *-e*'. *Studies in the Age of Chaucer* 12. 157–91.

———— 1994. 'The role and distribution of *-ly* adverbs in Middle English alliterative verse'. In Houwen and MacDonald. 131–54.

———— 1996. 'Some unrevolutionary aspects of computer editing'. In *The Literary Text in the Digital Age*. Ed. R. J. Finneran. Ann Arbor, MI. 77–98.

———— forthcoming. 'Libertine scribes and maidenly editors: meditations on textual criticism and metrics'. In Colley and Anderson.

Duggan, H. N. and Turville-Petre, T., eds. 1989. *The Wars of Alexander*. Oxford. EETS ss 10.

Dundes, A., ed. 1965. *The Study of Folklore*. New York.

Dyer, C. 1989. *Standards of Living in the Later Middle Ages: Social Change in England, c.1200–1500*. Cambridge.

Eadie, J. 1986. 'A new source for the green knight'. *Neuphilologische Mitteilungen* 87. 569–77.

———— 1987. 'Corrigendum'. *Neuphilologische Mitteilungen* 88. 108.

Easting, R., ed. 1991. *St. Patrick's Purgatory*. Oxford. EETS os 298.

Eckhardt, C. D., ed. 1980. *Essays in the Numerical Criticism of Medieval Literature*. Lewisburg.

Edge, D. and Paddock, J. M. 1988. *Arms and Armor of the Medieval Knight*. London.

Edward Plantagenet, *The Master of Game*. See under Baillie-Grohman, W. A.

Edwards, A. S. G. 1984. 'John Trevisa'. In *Middle English Prose: A Critical Guide to Major Authors and Genres*. Ed. A. S. G. Edwards. New Brunswick. 133–46.

Eldredge, L. 1979. 'Late medieval discussions of the continuum and the point of the Middle English *Patience*'. *Vivarium* 17. 90–115.

Eliade, M. 1955. *The Myth of the Eternal Return*. Trans. W. R. Traske. London.

Elliott, R. W. V. 1984. *The* Gawain *Country*. Leeds. Leeds Texts and Monographs ns 8.

Emerson, O. F. 1895. 'A parallel between the middle English poem *Patience* and an early Latin poem attributed to Tertullian'. *PMLA* 10. 242–8.

Emmerson, R. and Lewis, S. 1985. 'Census and bibliography of medieval manuscripts containing apocalypse illustrations, c.800–1500. II: Anglo-French apocalypses'. *Traditio* 41. 370–409.

Engelhardt, G. J. 1955. 'The predicament of Gawain'. *Modern Language Quarterly* 16. 218–25.

English Medieval Lapidaries. See under Evans, J. and Serjeantson, M. S.

Evans, J. and Serjeantson, M. S., eds. 1933. *English Medieval Lapidaries*. EETS os 190.

Everett, D. 1955. *Essays in Middle English Literature*. Ed. P. Kean. Oxford.

Excalibur 1981. Film. Dir. J. Boorman. USA.

Fáj, A. 1975–6. 'Poetic reminiscences and an ascetic principle in *Patience*'. *English Miscellany* 25. 9–26.

Faral, E., ed. 1924. Matthew of Vendôme, *Ars versificatoria*. In his *Les arts poétiques du XIIe et du XIII siècle: recherches et documents sur la technique littéraire du moyen age*. Paris. Repr. 1958. 106–93.

Farley-Hills, D. 1963. 'Gawain's Fault in *Sir Gawain and the Green Knight*'. *Review of English Studies* n.s. 14. 124–31. Repr. in Howard and Zacher 1968. 311–24
———Letter. *Review of English Studies* n.s. 26. 451.

Fasciculus Morum: A Fourteenth-Century Preacher's Handbook. See under Wenzel, S. 1989.

Ferrante, J. M. 1975. *Woman as Image in Medieval Literature from the Twelfth Century to Dante*. New York.

Ffoulkes, C. 1911. 'On Italian armour from Chalcis in the ethnological museum at Athens'. *Archeologia* 62. 381–90.
——— 1912. *The Armourer and his Craft, from the XIth to the XVIth Century*. London.
——— 1929. 'Some aspects of the craft of the armourer'. *Archeologia* 79. 13–28.

Field, R. 1986. 'The heavenly Jerusalem in *Pearl*'. *Modern Language Review* 81. 7–17.

Finlayson, J. 1974. '*Pearl*: landscape and vision'. *Studies in Philology* 71. 314–43.

First Knight 1995. Film. Dir. J. Zucker. USA: Columbia.

Fisher, S. 1989. 'Taken men and token women in *Sir Gawain and the Green Knight*'. In *Seeking the Woman in Late Medieval and Renaissance Writings: Essays in Feminist Contextual Criticism*. Eds. S. Fisher and J. E. Halley. Knoxville. 71–105.

Fled Bricrend: Bricriu's Feast. See under Henderson, G. 1899.

Fleming, J. V. 1981. 'The centuple structure of the *Pearl*'. In Levy and Szarmach. 81–98.

Fletcher, J. B. 1921. 'The allegory of *The Pearl*'. *Journal of English and Germanic Philology* 20. 1–21.

Floriz and Blauncheflur. See under McKnight, G. H., ed.

Fludernik, M. 1993. *The Fictions of Language and the Languages of Fiction: The Linguistic Representation of Speech and Consciousness*. London.

Foley, M. 1989. 'The *Gawain*-poet: an annotated bibliography, 1978–1985'. *Chaucer Review* 23. 251–82.

Foucault, M. 1981. *The History of Sexuality. 1: An Introduction*. Trans. R. Hurley. Harmondsworth.

Fowler, A., ed. 1970. *Silent Poetry: Essays in Numerological Analysis*. London.

Fowler, D. C. 1968. *A Literary History of the Popular Ballad*. Durham, NC.

——— 1984. *The Bible in Middle English Literature*. Seattle.

Fox, D., ed. 1968. *Twentieth Century Interpretations of* Sir Gawain and the Green Knight. Englewood Cliffs, NJ.

Francis, W. N., ed. 1942. *The Book of Vices and Virtues: A Fourteenth Century English Translation of the 'Somme le Roi' of Lorens d'Orléans*. London. EETS os 217.

Frank, R. W. 1957. Piers Plowman *and the Scheme of Salvation*. New Haven.

Frankl, P. 1960. *The Gothic: Literary Sources and Interpretion during Eight Centuries*. Princeton, NJ.

Frantzen, A. 1995. 'The disclosure of sodomy in the Middle English *Cleanness*'. Paper given at 1996 Kalamazoo International Congress on Medieval Studies.

——— 'The Disclosure of Sodomy in *Cleanness*'. *PMLA* 3. 451–64

Frappier, J., ed. 1936. *La Mort le Roi Artu*. Paris.

French, W. H. and Hale, C. B., eds. 1964. *Middle English Metrical Romances*. New York.

Friedman, A. B. and Harrington, N. T., eds. 1964. *Ywain and Gawain*. London. EETS os 254.

Friedman, J. B. 1981. 'Figural typology in the middle English *Patience*'. In Levy and Szarmach. 99–129.

Friedwagner, M., ed. 1909. *La Vengeance Raguidel*. Halle.

Fritz, D. W. 1980. '*The Pearl*: the sacredness of number'. *American Benedictine Review* 31. 314–34.

Froissart, J. *Chronicles*. See under Johnes, T.

Furnivall, F. J., ed. 1868. J. Russell, *The Book of Nurture*. In *The Babees Book*. Ed. F. J. Furnivall. London. Pt 1. 115–239. EETS os 32.

Fussell, P. 1979. 'The historical dimension'. In *The Structure of Verse: Modern Essays on Prosody*. Ed. H. Gross. New York. Rev. edn. 40–52.

Gage, J. 1993. *Colour and Culture: Practice and Meaning from Antiquity to Abstraction*. London.

Gallant, G. 1970. 'The three beasts: symbols of temptation in *Sir Gawain and the Green Knight*'. *Annuale Medievale* 11. 35–50.

Gallo, E. 1971. *The Poetria Nova and its Sources in Early Rhetorical Doctrine*. The Hague.

Ganim, J. M. 1983. *Style and Consciousness in Middle English Narrative*. Princeton.

Garbaty, T. J. 1962. 'Chaucer's summoner: an example of the assimilation lag in scholarship'. *Papers of the Michigan Academy of Science, Arts and Letters* 47. 605–11.

Gates, R. J., ed. 1969. *The Awntyrs off Arthure at the Terne Wathelyn*. Philadelphia.

Gauthier, M. M. 1972. *Emaux du Moyen Age Occidental*. Fribourg. 2nd edn.

Gawain and the Green Knight 1973. Film. Dir. S. Weeks. GB.

Gawain and the Green Knight 1991. Television film. Dir. J. M. Phillips. GB.

Gaylord, A. T. 1964. 'The promises in *The Franklin's Tale*'. *ELH* 31. 331–65.

Gellner, E. 1994. *Conditions of Liberty: Civil Society and its Rivals*. London.

Generydes. See under Wright, W. A.

Genette, G. 1980. *Narrative Discourse: An Essay in Method*. Trans. J. E. Lewin. Ithaca.

Geoffrey of Monmouth. *Historia Regum Britanniae*. See under Hammer, G. I.; Thorpe, L.

Gerbert de Montreuil. *La continuation de Perceval*. See under Williams, M. and Oswald, M.

Gest Hystoriale of the Destruction of Troy. See under Panton, J. A. and Donaldson, D.

Gillespie, J. L. 1975. 'Richard II's Cheshire archers'. *Transactions of the Historic Society of Lancashire and Cheshire* 125. 1–39.

Gillespie, V. 1984. ' "Lukynge in haly bukes": "lectio" in some late medieval English miscellanies'. *Analecta Cartusiana* 35. 90–119.

Gilligan, J. 1989. 'Numerical composition in the middle English *Patience*'. *Studia Neophilologica* 61. 7–11.

Ginsberg, W. 1988. 'Place and dialectic in *Pearl* and Dante's *Paradiso*'. *ELH* 55. 731–53.

Glasscoe, M., ed. 1978. *Julian of Norwich, A Revelation of Love*. Exeter.

Glenn, J. A. 1983–4. 'Dislocation of *kynde* in the Middle English *Cleanness*'. *Chaucer Review* 18. 77–91.

Goldberg, J., ed. 1994. *Reclaiming Sodom*. New York.

Gollancz, I. 1891, 1913, 1921, 1923, 1940. See list of editions.

——, ed. 1922. *St Erkenwald*. London. Gollancz's Select Early English Poems 4.

Goodman, A. 1981. *The Loyal Conspiracay: The Lords Appellant under Richard II*. London.

—— 1992. *John of Gaunt: The Exercise of Princely Power in Fourteenth-Century Europe*. London.

Goody, J. 1982. *Cooking, Cuisine and Class: A Study in Comparative Sociology*. Cambridge.

Goold, G. P., ed. 1968. M. T. Cicero, *De officiis*. London.

Gordon, D. 1993. *Making and Meaning: The Wilton Diptych*. London.

Gordon, E. V. 1953. See list of editions.

Gower, John. *Confessio amantis*. See under Peck, R. A.

Gradon, P. 1971. *Form and Style in Early English Literature*. Seattle.

Graesse, T., ed. 1890. J. de Voragine, *Legenda aurea*. Repr. 1969. Berlin.

Granscay, S. V. 1986a. *Arms and Armor: Essays from the Metropolitan Museum of Art Bulletin, 1920–1964*. New York.

—— 1986b. 'The interrelationship of costume and armour'. In Granscay 1986a.

—— 1986c. 'The armor of Don Alvaro de Calabria'. In Granscay 1986a.

Grant, E. 1982. 'The effect of the condemnation of 1277'. In *The Cambridge History of Later Medieval Philosophy: From the Rediscovery of Aristotle to the Disintegration of Scholasticism, 1100–1600*. Eds. N. Kretzmann, A. Kenny and J. Pinborg. Cambridge. 537–9.

Green, R. H. 1962. 'Gawain's shield and the quest for perfection'. *ELH* 29. 121–39. Repr. in Blanch 1966. 176–94. Repr. in Vasta. 1965. 71–92.

Greene, R. L. 1977. *The Early English Carols*. Oxford. 2nd edn.

Greenberg, D. F. 1988. *The Construction of Homosexuality*. Chicago.

Greenwood, O., trans. 1956. See list of editions.

Greer, G. 1971. *The Female Eunuch*. London.

Greg, W. W. 1924. Review of Gollancz 1923. *Modern Language Review* 19. 223–8.

Gregory, S. and Luttrell, C., eds. 1993. *Cligés*. Cambridge. Arthurian Studies 28.

Gross, C. 1991. 'Courtly language in *Pearl'*. In Blanch, Miller and Wasserman. 79–91.

Hahn, K. A., ed. 1845. U. von Zatzikhoven, *Lanzelet*. Berlin. Repr. 1965.

Hahn, T., ed. 1995. *Sir Gawain: Eleven Romances and Tales*. Kalamazoo, Michigan.

Hales, J. W. and Furnivall, F. J., eds. 1867–8. *Bishop Percy's Folio Manuscript: Ballads and Romances*. London. 3 vols.

Hali Meiðhad 1982. See under Millett, B. 1982.

Hali Meiðhad 1990. In Millett and Wogan-Browne. 1–43.

Hamel, M., ed. 1984. *Morte Arthure: A Critical Edition*. New York and London. Garland Medieval Texts 9.

Hammer, G. I., ed. 1951. Geoffrey of Monmouth, *Historia regum Britanniae*. Cambridge, Mass. Mediaeval Academy of America Publications 57.

Hanawalt, B. A., ed. 1992. *Chaucer's England: Literature in Historical Context*. Minneapolis. Medieval Studies at Minnesota 4.

Hanna, R., III, ed. 1974. *The Awntyrs off Arthure at the Terne Wathelyn*. Manchester.

———— 1978. 'Some commonplaces of late medieval patience discussions: an introduction'. In *The Triumph of Patience: Medieval and Renaissance Studies*. Ed. G. J. Schiffhorst. Orlando. 65–87.

———— 1983. 'Unlocking what's locked: Gawain's green girdle'. *Viator* 14. 289–302.

———— 1995. 'Defining middle English alliterative poetry'. In *The Endless Knot: Essays on Old and Middle English in Honor of Marie Borroff*. Ed. T. Tavormina. Cambridge. 43–64.

Hanna, R., III and Lawton, D., eds. forthcoming. *The Siege of Jerusalem*. East Lansing.

Hanning, R. W. 1977. *The Individual in Twelfth-Century Romance*. New Haven.

Harding, A. 1984. 'The revolt against the justices'. In *The English Rising of 1381*. Eds. R. H. Hilton and T. H. Aston. Cambridge. 165–93.

Harley, M. P., ed. and trans. 1985. *A Revelation of Purgatory by an Unknown Fifteenth-Century Woman Visionary*. Lewiston, NY. Studies in Women and Religion 18.

Harsent, D. 1991. *Gawain: A Libretto*. London.

———— 1994. 'Morgan le Fay'. In Royal Opera House. 36.

Harsent, D. and Porter, P. 1994. 'From page to stage: a conversation between David Harsent and Peter Porter'. In Royal Opera House. 28–35.

Hart, E. 1927. 'The heaven of virgins'. *Modern Language Notes* 42. 113–16.

Hartung, A. E. and Severs, J. B., gen. eds. 1967– . *A Manual of the Writings in Middle English, 1050–1500*. New Haven. 9 vols. published.

Harvey, J. 1995. *Men in Black*. London.

Harwood, B. J. 1991. 'Gawain and the gift'. *PMLA* 106. 483–99.

Hatcher, J. 1994. 'England in the aftermath of the Black Death'. *Past and Present* 144. 3–35.

Hausknecht, E., ed. 1881. *The Romances of the Sowdone of Babylone*. London. EETS es 38.

Heinrich von dem Türlin. *Diu Crône*. See under Scholl, G. H. F.

Henderson, G., ed. and trans. 1899. *Fled Bricrend: Bricriu's Feast*. London. Irish Texts Society 2.

Henderson, G. D. S. 1968. 'Studies in English Bible I llustration, I and II'. *Journal of the Warburg and Courtauld Institutesplain D 31.* 103–47.

Heng, G. 1991. 'Feminine knots and the other: *Sir Gawain and the Green Knight*'. *PMLA* 106. 500–14.

———— 1992. 'A woman wants: the lady, Gawain, and the forms of seduction'. *Yale Journal of Criticism* 5. 101–34.

Henisch, B. A. 1976. *Feast and Fast: Food in Medieval Society*. University Park, Pa.

Henry of Lancaster. 1940. *Livvre de Seyntz Medicines*. Ed. E. J. Arnould. Oxford.

Hewitt, H. J. 1966. *The Organization of War under Edward III, 1338–62*. Manchester.

Hewitt, J. 1860. *Ancient Armour and Weapons in Europe from the Iron Period of the Northern Nations to the End of the Seventeenth Century*. 2. Oxford.

Hieatt, A. K. 1968. '*Sir Gawain*: pentangle, *luf-lace*, numerical structure'. *Papers on Language and Literature* 4. 339–59. Repr. in Fowler 1970. 116–40.

———— 1976. 'Symbolic and narrative patterns in *Pearl, Cleanness, Patience* and *Sir Gawain*'. *English Studies in Canada* 2. 125–43.

———— 1980. 'Numerical structures in verse: second-generation studies needed (exemplified in *Sir Gawain* and the *Chanson de Roland*)'. In Eckhardt. 65–78.

Hieatt, C. 1974. 'The rhythm of the alliterative long line'. In Rowland. 119–30.

Highfield, J. R. L. 1953. 'The green squire'. *Medium Ævum* 22. 18–23.

Hill, L. L. 1946. 'Madden's divisions of *Sir Gawain and the Green Knight* and the "large initial capitals" of Cotton Nero A. X'. *Speculum* 21. 67–71.

Hill, O. G. 1967. 'The late-Latin *De Jona* as a source for *Patience*'. *Journal of English and Germanic Philology* 66. 21–5.

———— 1968. 'The audience of *Patience*'. *Modern Philology* 66. 103–9.

Hillman, M. V. 1945. 'Some debatable words in *Pearl* and its theme'. *Modern Language Notes* 60. 243.

Hinton, D. 1982. *Medieval Jewellery*. London.

Hinton, N. 1987. 'The language of the *Gawain*-poet'. *Arthurian Interpretations* 2. 83–94.

———— 1989. 'The language of the alliterative revival'. Unpublished paper. Session 175, International Congress on Medieval Studies, 5 May 1989. Kalamazoo, MI.

Historia vitae et regni Ricardi secundi. See under Stow, G. B.

History of the King's Works. See under Colvin, H. M.

Holland, B. 1917. *The Lancashire Hollands*. London.

Honorius of Autun 1844–64. *Elucidarium*. In *Patrologia Latina* 171. Ed. J. P. Migne. Paris.

Hopkins, A. 1990. *The Sinful Knights: A Study of Middle English Penitential Romance*. Oxford.

Horgan, A. D. 1981. 'Justice in *The Pearl*'. *Review of English Studies* ns 32. 173–80.

Horrall, S. M. 1985. '*Cleanness* and *Cursor mundi*'. *English Language Notes* 22.3. 6–11.

——— 1986. 'Notes on British Library MS Cotton Nero A x'. *Manuscripta* 30. 191–8.

Houwen, L. A. R. J. and MacDonald, A. A., eds. 1994. *Loyal Letters: Studies on Medieval Alliterative Poetry and Prose*. Groningen.

Howard, D. R. and Zacher, C., eds. 1968. *Critical Studies of* Sir Gawain and the Green Knight. Notre Dame, Ind.

Hudson, A. 1988. *The Premature Reformation: Wycliffite Texts and Lollard History*. Oxford.

———, ed. 1993. *Two Wycliffite Texts: The Sermon of William Taylor, 1406, and The Testimony of William Thorpe, 1407*. Oxford. EETS os 301.

Huizinga, J. 1924. *The Waning of the Middle Ages: A Study of the Forms of Life, Thought and Art in France and the Netherlands in the XIVth and XVth Centuries*. Trans. F. Hopman. London. Second edn, 1955. London.

Hulbert, J. R. 1931. 'A hypothesis concerning the alliterative revival'. *Modern Philology* 28. 405–22.

Hunbaut. See under Stürzinger, J. and Breuer, H.; Winters, M.

Huot, S. 1987. *From Song to Book: The Poetics of Writing in Old French Lyric and Lyrical Narrative Poetry*. Ithaca.

Ingham, M. and Barkley, L. 1979. 'Further animal parallels in *Sir Gawain and the Green Knight*'. *Chaucer Review* 13. 384–6.

Jacob de Voragine. *Legenda aurea*. See under Graesse, T.

Jacob, E. F. 1965. 'The giants, *Inferno* XXXI'. In *Medieval Miscellany Presented to Eugene Vinaver*. Ed. F. Whitehead, A. H. Diverres and F. E. Sutcliffe. Manchester. 167–85.

James, M. 1978. *English Politics and the Concept of Honour, 1485–1642*. Oxford. *Past and Present* Supplement 3. Repr. in his *Society, Politics and Culture: Studies in Early Modern England*. 1986. Cambridge. 308–415.

James, M. R. 1931. *The Apocalypse in Art*. London.

Jeanroy, A. and Vignaux, A., eds. 1903. *Voyage au Purgatoire de St. Patrice: visions de Tindal et de St. Paul*. Bibliothèque Méridionale publiée sous les auspices de la Faculté des Lettres de Toulouse. 1st ser. 8.

John of Gaunt's Register. See under Lodge, E. C. and Somerville, R.

John of Salisbury. *Policraticus*. See under Pike, J. B.

Johnes, T., ed. 1842. J. Froissart, *Chronicles*. London. 2 vols.

Johnson, L. S. 1984. *The Voice of the* Gawain-Poet. Madison, Wisc.

Jones, C. 1972. *An Introduction to Middle English*. New York.

Jones, R. T. 1972. See list of editions.

Jordan, R. 1974. *Handbook of Middle English Grammar: Phonology*. Trans. and revised E. J. Crook. The Hague and Paris. Janua Linguarum, Series Practica 218.

Jordan, R. M. 1987. *Chaucer's Poetics and the Modern Reader*. Berkeley.

Julian of Norwich. *Revelation of Love*. See under Glasscoe, M.

Justice, S. 1994. *Writing and Rebellion: England in 1381*. Berkeley.

Kaeuper, R. W. 1988. *War, Justice and Public Order: England and France in the Later Middle Ages*. Oxford.

Kaiser, R. 1937. *Zur Geographie des mittelenglischen Wortschatzes*. Leipzig.

Kaluza, M. 1892. 'Strophische gliederung in der mittelenglischen rein alliterier-enden Dichtung'. *Englische Studien* 16. 169–79.

Kamps, I. 1989. 'Magic, women and incest: the real challenges in *Sir Gawain and the Green Knight*'. *Exemplaria* 1. 313–36.

Kane, G. 1965. Piers Plowman: *The Evidence for Authorship*. London.

—— 1981. 'Music "neither unpleasant nor monotonous" '. In *Medieval Studies for J. A. W. Bennett aetatis suae LXX*. Ed. P. L. Heyworth. Oxford. 43–63.

Kane, G. and Donaldson, E. T., eds. 1988. *Piers Plowman: The B Version*. Rev. edn. London.

Kaske, R. E. 1970. 'Gawain's green chapel and the cave at Wetton Mill'. In *Medieval Literature and Folklore Studies: Essays in Honor of Francis Lee Utley*. Eds. J. Mandel and B. A. Rosenberg. New Brunswick, NJ. 111–21.

—— 1984. '*Sir Gawain and the Green Knight*'. In *Medieval and Renaissance Studies: Proceedings of the Southeastern Institute of Medieval and Renaissance Studies, Summer 1979*. Ed. G. M. Masters. Chapel Hill. 24–44. Medieval and Renais-sance Studies 10.

Kasmann, H. 1974. 'Numerical structure in fitt III of *Sir Gawain and the Green Knight*'. In Rowland. 131–9.

Kay, S. 1990. *Subjectivity in Troubadour Poetry*. Cambridge. Cambridge Studies in French 31.

Kean, P. M. 1965. 'Numerical composition in *Pearl*'. *Notes and Queries* 210. 49–51.

—— 1967. The Pearl: *An Interpretation*. London.

Keen, M. 1984. *Chivalry*. New Haven.

Kelly, E. M. 1967. 'Parallels between the Middle English *Patience* and *Hymnus ieiunantium* of Prudentius'. *English Language Notes* 4. 244–7.

Kelly, T. D. and Irwin, J. T. 1973. 'The meaning of *Cleanness*: parable as effective sign'. *Medieval Studies* 35. 232–60.

Kennedy, E., ed. 1980. *Lancelot do Lac*. 2 vols. Oxford.

Kennedy, E. D. 1989. *Chronicles and other historical writings*. Hartung and Severs 8.

Kerby-Fulton, K. 1990. *Reformist Apocalypticism and* Piers Plowman. Cambridge. Cambridge Studies in Medieval Literature 7.

Keyser, S. J. 1969. 'Old English prosody'. *College English* 30. 31–56.

—— 1969–70. 'Rebuttal'. *College English* 31. 77.

Kibler, W. W., trans. 1991. Chrétien de Troyes, *Arthurian Romances*. Har-mondsworth.

Kibler, W. W. and Wimsatt, J. I. 1987. 'Machaut's text and the question of his personal supervision'. *Studies in the Literary Imagination* 20. 41–53.

King Horn, Floriz and Blauncheflur, The Assumption of our Lady. See under McKnight, G. H.

Kittendorf, D. E. 1979. '*Cleanness* and the fourteenth-century *artes praedicandi*'. *Michigan Academician* 11. 319–30.

Kittredge, G. L. 1916. *A Study of* Gawain and the Green Knight. Cambridge, MA.

Kjellmer, G. 1975. *Did the 'Pearl'-poet write 'Pearl'?* Gothenburg. Gothenburg Studies in English 30.

Knights of the Round Table 1954. Film. Dir. R. Thorpe. USA.

Kooper, E. 1982. 'The case of the encoded author: John Massey in *Sir Gawain and the Green Knight*'. *Neuphilologische Mitteilungen* 83. 158–68.

Kottler, B. and Markman, A. M. 1966. *A Concordance to Five Middle English Poems*. Pittsburgh.

Kowalik, B. 1992. 'Traces of romance textual poetics in the non-romance works ascribed to the *Gawain*-Poet'. In *From Medieval to Medievalism*. Ed. J. Simons. New York. 41–53.

Krautheimer, R. 1982. *Lorenzo Ghiberti*. Princeton, NJ. Princeton Monographs in Art and Archaeology 3. Rev. edn.

Krishna, V. 1982. 'Parataxis, formulaic density, and thrift in the *Alliterative Morte Arthure*'. *Speculum* 1982. 63–83.

Kristensson, G. 1967. *A Survey of Middle English Dialects 1290–1350: The Six Northern Counties and Lincolnshire*. Lund. Lund Studies in English 35.

Kristeva, J. 1982. *Powers of Horror: An Essay on Abjection*. Trans. L. S. Roudiez. New York.

Kunz, G. F. and Stevenson, C. H. 1908. *The Book of the Pearl*. London.

Kyng Alisaunder. See under Smithers, G. V.

Lacy, N. J., ed. 1991. *The New Arthurian Encyclopaedia*. New York. Rev. edn.

Lafortune-Martel, A. 1984. *Fête noble en Bourgogne au XVe siècle: 'Le banquet de Faisan' (1454). Aspects politiques, sociaux et culturels*. Montreal. Cahiers d'etudes medievales 8.

Lagorio, V. and Sargent, M. G. 1993. 'English mystical writings'. In Hartung and Severs 9. 3049–137; 3405–71.

Lancelot. See under Micha, A.

Lancelot do Lac. See under Kennedy, E.

Lancelot du Lac 1974. Film. Dir. R. Bresson. France.

Langland, William. *Piers Plowman*. See under Kane, G. and Donaldson, E. T., eds.; Pearsall, D., ed. 1978; Schmidt, A. V. C., ed., 1978, 1987b; Skeat, W. W., ed.

Larking, L. B. 1858. 'Inventory of the effects of Roger De Mortimer at Wigmore Castle and Abbey, Herefordshire. Dated 15 Edward II, AD 1322'. *Archeological Journal* 15. 354–62.

Lawrence, R. F. 1966. 'The formulaic theory and its application to English alliterative poetry'. In *Essays on Style and Language: Linguistic and Critical Approaches to Style*. Ed. R. Fowler. London. 166–83.

——— 1970. 'Formula and rhythm in *The Wars of Alexander*'. *English Studies* 51. 97–112.

Lawton, D. A. 1979. 'Gaytryge's Sermon, *Dictamen*, and Middle English Alliterative Verse'. *Modern Philology* 76. 329–43.

———, ed. 1982a. *Middle English Alliterative Poetry and its Literary Background: Seven Essays*. Cambridge.

——— 1982b. 'Middle English alliterative poetry: an introduction'. In Lawton 1982a. 1–19.

——— 1983. 'The unity of alliterative poetry'. *Speculum* 58. 72–94.

——— 1988. 'Alliterative style'. In Alford. 223–49.

——— 1993. 'The idea of alliterative poetry: alliterative meter and *Piers Plowman*'. In *'Suche Werkis to Werche': Essays on Piers Plowman in Honor of David C. Fowler*. Ed. M. F. Vaughan. East Lansing. 147–68.

Lawton, L. 1983. 'The illustration of late medieval secular texts, with special reference to Lydgate's *Troy Book*'. In *Manuscripts and Readers in Fifteenth-Century England: The Literary Implications of Manuscript Study. Essays from the 1981 Conference at the University of York*. Ed. D. Pearsall. Cambridge. 41–70.

Leach, M., ed. 1937. *Amis and Amiloun*. London. EETS os 203.

Lecklider, J. K. 1994. 'An analysis of the structure and meaning of the Middle English poem *Cleanness* based upon a comprehensive examination of source materials'. Ph.D. Dissertation. University of London.

Lecoy, F., ed. 1975. Chrétien de Troyes, *Le conte du Graal*. Paris. 2 vols. *Les romans de Chrétien de Troyes* 5–6.

Lee, J. A. 1977. 'The illuminating critic: the illustrator of Cotton Nero A. x'. *Studies in Iconography* 3. 17–46.

Lee, S. L., ed. 1882–7. *The Boke of Huon of Burdeux*. Trans. Lord Berners. London. EETS es 40, 41, 43, 50. 4 vols.

Leff, G. 1967. *Heresy in the Later Middle Ages: The Relation of Heterodoxy to Dissent, c.1250–c.1450*. Manchester. 2 vols.

Levine, R. 1977. 'The pearl-child: topos and archetype in the middle English *Pearl*'. *Medievalia et Humanistica* 8. 243–51.

Levi-Strauss, C. 1969. *The Elementary Structures of Kinship*. Trans. J. H. Bell and J. R. von Sturmer. Ed. R. Needham. London. Rev. edn.

Levy, B. S. 1965. 'Gawain's spiritual journey: *imitatio Christi* in *Sir Gawain and the Green Knight*'. *Annuale Medievale* 6. 65–106.

Levy, B. S. and Szarmach, P. E., eds. 1981. *The Alliterative Tradition in the Fourteenth Century*. Kent, Ohio.

Lewis, C. S. 1962. 'The anthropological approach'. In *English and Medieval Studies Presented to J. R. R. Tolkien on the Occasion of his Seventieth Birthday*. Eds. N. Davis and C. L. Wrenn. Oxford. 219–30. Repr. in Howard and Zacher. 59–71.

Lightbown, R. W. 1978. *Secular Goldsmiths' Work in Medieval France: A History*. London.

——— 1992. *Medieval European Jewellery*. London.

Lindenbaum, S. 1990. 'The Smithfield tournament of 1390'. *Journal of Medieval and Renaissance Studies* 20. 1–20.

Lochrie, K. 1991. *Margery Kempe and Translations of the Flesh*. Philadelphia.

Lodge, E. C. and Somerville, R., eds. 1937. *John of Gaunt's Register, 1379–1383*. London. Camden Society 3rd ser. 42, 47. 2 vols.

Longman, J. and Cazelles, R., eds. 1967. *Les Très Riches Heures du Duc de Berry*. London. Repr. 1993.

Longo, J. A. 1967. '*Sir Gawain and the Green Knight*: the Christian quest for perfection'. *Nottingham Medieval Studies* 11. 57–85.

Loomis, L. H. 1958. 'Secular Dramatics in the Royal Palace, Paris, 1378, 1389 and Chaucer's "Tregetoures". *Speculum* 33. 242–55

Loomis, R. S. and L. H. 1938. *Arthurian Legends in Medieval Art*. London. Modern Language Association Monograph Series 9.

Lorenzo Ghiberti. *Commentaries*. See under Courtauld Institute; von Schlosser, J.

Love, Nicholas. *Mirror of the Blessed Life of Jesus Christ*. See under Sargent, M. G.

Luttrell, C. 1979. '*Sir Gawain and the Green Knight* and the versions of *Caradoc*'. *Forum for Modern Language Studies* 15. 347–60.

———— 1988. 'The folk-tale element in *Sir Gawain and the Green Knight*'. In Brewer 1988a. 92–112.

MacCannell, J. F. 1986. *Figuring Lacan*. Lincoln, Nebraska.

McClure, P. 1973. 'Gawain's *mesure* and the significance of the three hunts in *Sir Gawain and the Green Knight*'. *Neuphilologus* 57. 375–87.

McColly, W. B. 1987. 'Style and structure in the Middle English poem *Cleanness*'. *Computers and the Humanities* 21. 169–76.

McColly, W. B. and Weier, D. 1983. 'Literary attribution likelihood ratio tests: the case of the middle English *Pearl*-poems'. *Computers and the Humanities* 17. 65–75.

MacCracken, H. N. 1910. 'Concerning Huchown'. *PMLA* 25. 507–34.

McFarlane, K. B. 1972. *Lancastrian Kings and Lollard Knights*. Oxford.

McIntosh, A. 1963. 'A new approach to middle English dialectology'. *English Studies* 44. 1–11.

———— 1973. 'Word geography in the lexicography of medieval English'. *Annals of the New York Academy of Sciences* 211. 55–66.

———— 1982. 'Early middle English alliterative verse'. In Lawton 1982a. 20–33.

McIntosh, A., Samuels, M. L. and Benskin, M. 1986. *A Linguistic Atlas of Late Medieval English*. Aberdeen. 4 vols.

McKnight, G. H., rev. ed. 1901. *King Horn, Floriz and Blauncheflur, The Assumption of Our Lady*. London. Ed. J. R. Lumby 1866. EETS os 14.

McLaughlin, J. C. 1963. *A Graphemic-Phonemic Study of a Middle English Manuscript*. The Hague.

McNeill, G. P., ed. 1886. *Sir Tristrem*. Edinburgh. Scottish Texts Society 8.

MacQueen, J. 1985. *Numerology: Theory and Outline History of a Literary Mode*. Edinburgh.

Madden, F. 1839. See list of editions.

Malory, Sir Thomas, *Works*. See under Brewer, D. S. 1968; Vinaver, E.

Mandeville, John. *Travels*. See under Seymour, M. C. ed. 1963.

Mann, J. 1986. 'Price and value in *Sir Gawain and the Green Knight*'. *Essays in Criticism* 36. 294–318.

———— 1991. *The Narrative of Distance: The Distance of Narrative in Malory's* Morte Darthur. London.

———— 1994. 'Sir Gawain and the Romance Hero' in *Heroes and Heroines in Medieval English Literature*. Ed. L. Carruthers. Cambridge. 105–18.

Mann, J. G. 1932a. 'Notes on the armour worn in Spain from the tenth to the fifteenth century'. *Archaeologia* 83. 285–305.

———— 1932b. 'Notes on the evolution of plate armour in Germany in the fourteenth and fifteenth century'. *Archeologia* 84. 69–97.

Manzalaoui, M. A., ed. 1977. *Secretum secretorum: Nine English Versions*. London. EETS os 276.

Marie de France. *Guingamor, Lanval, Tyolet, Le Bisclaveret*. See under Weston, J. L.

Marti, K. 1993. 'Traditional characteristics of the resurrected body in *Pearl*'. *Viator* 24. 311–35.

Massera, A. F., ed. 1987. G. Boccaccio, *Eclogues*. Trans. J. L. Smarr. New York.

Matarasso, P. M., trans. 1969. *The Quest of the Holy Grail*. Harmondsworth.

Mathew, G. 1948. 'Ideals of knighthood in later fourteenth-century England'. In

Studies in Medieval History Presented to Frederick Maurice Powicke. Eds. R. W. Hunt, W. A. Pantin and R. W. Southern. Oxford. 354–62.

—— 1968. *The Court of Richard II*. London.

Matthew of Vendôme. *Ars versificatoria*. See under Faral, E.

Matsumoto, H. 1993. 'Alliteration of *wh* with *qu* in Middle English alliterative poetry'. In *Essays on English Language and Literature in Honour of Michio Kawai*. Ed. N. Yuasa. Tokyo. 61–1.

Mauss, M. 1954. *The Gift: Forms and Functions of Exchange in Archaic Societies*. Trans. I. Cunnison. London.

Mawer, A. and Stenton, F. M., eds. 1924. *Introduction to English Place Names*. Cambridge.

Mead, W. E. 1931. *The English Medieval Feast*. London.

Means, M. H. 1972. *The 'Consolatio' Genre in Medieval Literature*. Gainesville, Fl. University of Florida Humanities Monographs 36.

—— 1975. 'The homiletic structure of *Cleanness*'. *Studies in Medieval Culture* 5. 165–72.

Meech, S. B. and Allen, H. E., eds. 1940. *The Book of Margery Kempe*. London. EETS os 212.

Menner, R. J. 1920. See list of editions.

Merlin. See under Wheatley, H. B.

Metcalf, A. 1980. 'Gawain's number'. In Eckhardt. 141–56.

Metz, C. 1991. 'The impersonal enunciation, or the site of film'. *NLH* 22. 747–72.

Meyrick, S. R. 1821. 'Observations on the antient military garments formerly worn in England'. *Archaeologia* 19. 228–30.

Micha, A., ed. 1978–82. *Lancelot*. Geneva. 9 vols.

Middle English Metrical Romances. See under French, W. H. and Hale, C. B.

Middleton, A. 1990. 'William Langland's "kynde name": authorial signature and social identity in late fourteenth-century England'. In Patterson. 15–82.

Miller, E. and Hatcher, J. 1978. *Medieval England: Rural Society and Economic Change 1086–1348*. London.

Miller, M. Y. and Chance, J., eds. 1986. *Approaches to Teaching* Sir Gawain and the Green Knight. New York. Approaches to Teaching Masterpieces of World Literature 9.

Miller, W. I. 1993. *Humiliation and Other Essays on Honour, Social Discomfort and Violence*. Ithaca, NY.

Millett, B., ed. 1982. *Hali Meiðhad*. Oxford. EETS os 284.

Millett, B. and Wogan-Browne, J., eds. 1990. *Medieval English Prose for Women: Selections from the Katherine Group and Ancrene Wisse*. Oxford.

Mills, A. D. 1964. 'A comparative study of the vocabulary, versification and style of *Pearl, Patience, Purity* and *Sir Gawain and the Green Knight*'. Dissertation. University of Manchester.

Molland, A. G. 1983. 'Continuity and measure in medieval natural philosophy'. In *Mensura: Mass, Zahl, Zahlensymbolik im Mittelalter*. Ed. A. Zimmermann. Berlin. 132–44. Miscellanea Mediaevalia 16.

Moore, H. L. 1988. *Feminism and Anthropology*. Cambridge.

Moorman, C. 1955. 'The role of the narrator in *Pearl*'. *Modern Philology* 53. 73–81. Repr. in Conley 1970. 103–21.

——— 1963. 'The role of the narrator in *Patience*'. *Modern Philology* 61. 90–5.

——— 1968. *The* Pearl-*Poet*. New York. Twayne's English Authors Series 64.

——— 1977. See list of editions.

Morgan, G. 1979. 'The significance of the pentangle symbolism in *Sir Gawain and the Green Knight*'. *Modern Language Review* 74. 796–90.

——— 1985. 'The validity of Gawain's confession in *Sir Gawain and the Green Knight*'. *Review of English Studies* ns 36. 1–18.

——— 1986. 'Boccaccio's *Filocolo* and the moral argument of the *Franklin's Tale*'. *Chaucer Review* 20. 285–306.

——— 1987. 'The action of the hunting and bedroom scenes in *Gawain*'. *Medium Ævum* 56. 200–16.

——— 1991. Sir Gawain and the Green Knight *and the Idea of Righteousness*. Blackrock, co. Dublin.

Morgan, N. 1988. *A Survey of Manuscripts Illuminated in the British Isles IV: Early Gothic Manuscripts [II]*. London.

Morgan, P. 1987. *War and Society in Late Medieval Cheshire 1277–1403*. Manchester. Remains Historical and Literary Connected with the Palatine Counties of Lancaster and Cheshire 3rd ser. 34.

Morris, R. See list of editions.

———, ed. 1874–93. *Cursor mundi*. London. EETS os 57, 59, 62, 66, 68, 99, 101. 7 vols.

Morris, R. 1984. *Time's Arrows: Scientific Attitudes towards Time*. New York.

Morse, C. C. 1971. 'The image of the vessel in *Cleanness*'. *University of Toronto Quarterly* 40. 202–16.

——— 1978. *The Pattern of Judgment in the* Queste *and* Cleanness. Columbia, Mo.

Morse, R., ed. 1975. *St Erkenwald*. Cambridge.

Mort le Roi Artu. See under Frappier, J.

Morte Arthure. See under Hamel, M.

Murdoch, I. 1993. *The Green Knight*. London.

Muscatine, C. 1972. *Poetry and Crisis in the Age of Chaucer*. Notre Dame, Ind. Ward-Phillips Lectures in English Language and Literature 4.

Myers, A. R. 1959–60. 'The Jewels of Queen Margaret of Anjou'. *Bulletin of the John Rylands Library* 42. 113–31.

Neilson, G. 1900. 'Huchown of the Awle Ryale'. *Transactions of the Glasgow Archaeological Society* 4. 252–393.

——— 1902. '*Huchown of the Awle Ryale*': the Alliterative Poet: A Historical Criticism of Fourteenth-Century Poems Ascribed to Sir Hew of Eglinton. Glasgow.

Newhauser, R. 1989. 'Towards *modus in habendo*: transformations in the idea of avarice. The early penitentials through the Carolingian reforms'. *Zeitschrift der Savigny-Stiftung für Rechtsgeschichte* 106. Kanonistische Abteilung 75. 1–22.

——— 1990. 'The meaning of Gawain's greed'. *Studies in Philology* 87. 410–26.

——— 1993. *The Treatise on Vices and Virtues in Latin and the Vernacular*. Turnhout. Typologie des Sources du Moyen Age Occidental 68.

——— 1995. ' "Strong it is to flitt": a Middle English poem on death and its pastoral context'. In *Literature and Religion in the Later Middle Ages: Philological Studies in Honor of Siegfried Wenzel*. Eds. R. Newhauser and J. A. Alford. Binghamton, NY. 319–36. Medieval and Renaissance Texts and Studies 118.

Newman, B. 1987. *Sister of Wisdom: St. Hildegard's Theology of the Feminine*. Berkeley.

Newton, S. M. 1980. *Fashion in the Age of the Black Prince*. Woodbridge and New Jersey.

Nicholls, J. W. 1985. *The Matter of Courtesy: Medieval Courtesy Books and the Gawain-Poet*. Cambridge.

Nicholson, R. H. 1988. '*Patience*: reading the *Prophetia Jonae*'. *Medievalia et Humanistica* ns 16. 97–115.

Nicolas, N. H. 1832. *The Controversy between Sir R. Scrope and Sir Richard Grosvenor in the Court of Chivalry, A. D. MCCCLXXXV–MCCCXC*. London. 2 vols.

Nitze, W. A. and Jenkins, T. A., eds. 1932, 1937. *Le haut livre du graal: Perlesvaus*. Chicago. 2 vols.

Nolan, B. 1977. *The Gothic Visionary Perspective*. Princeton, NJ.

Nolan, B. and Farley-Hills, D. 1971. 'The authorship of *Pearl*: two notes'. *Review of English Studies* ns 22. 295–302.

Northup, C. 1897. 'A study of the metrical structure of the middle English poem *The Pearl*'. *PMLA* 12. 326–40.

Oakden, J. P. 1930, 1935. *Alliterative Poetry in Middle English*. Manchester. 2 vols.

Oakeshott, R. E. 1964. *A Knight and his Weapons*. London.

O'Bryan, D. W. 1985. 'Sodom and Gomorrah: the use of the vulgate in *Cleanness*'. *Journal of Narrative Technique* 12. 15–23.

Offord, M. Y., ed. 1959. *The Parlement of the Thre Ages*. London. EETS os 246.

Olrik, A. 1965. 'Epic laws of folk narrative'. In Dundes 1965. 129–41.

Olson, G. 1979. 'Making and poetry in the age of Chaucer'. *Comparative Literature* 31. 272–90.

O'Mara, P. F. 1992a. 'Robert Holcot's "ecumenism" and the green knight'. *Chaucer Review* 26. 329–42.

—— 1992b. 'Holcot and the *Pearl*-poet'. *Chaucer Review* 27. 97–106.

Original Chronicle of Andrew of Wyntoun. See under Amours, F. J.

Orme, N. 1992. 'Medieval hunting: fact and fancy'. In Hanawalt. 133–53.

Orton, H. 1962. *Survey of English Dialects, Volume I: The Six Northern Counties and the Isle of Man*. Leeds.

Osberg, R. forthcoming. 'The prosody of Middle English *Pearl* and the alliterative lyric tradition'. In Colley and Anderson.

Osgood, C. G. 1906. See list of editions.

Ott, A. G. 1899. *Étude sur les couleurs en vieux français*. Paris.

Ovitt, G. 1979. 'Numerical composition in the middle English *Pearl*'. *American Notes and Queries* 18. 34–5.

Owen, D. D. R. and Johnston, R. C., eds. 1972. *Two Old French Gauvain Romances*. Edinburgh.

Owst, G. R. 1926. *Preaching in Medieval England: An Introduction to Sermon Manuscripts of the Period c.1350–1450*. Cambridge.

—— 1961. *Literature and Pulpit in Medieval England: A Neglected Chapter in the History of English Letters and of the English People*. New York. 2nd rev. edn.

Palliser, D. M. 1976. *The Staffordshire Landscape*. London.

Panton, G. A. and Donaldson, D., eds. 1869, 1874. *The Gest Hystoriale of the Destruction of Troy*. London. EETS os 39, 56. 2 vols.

Paris, G. and Ulrich, J., eds. 1886. *Suite du Merlin: Merlin*. Paris. 2 vols.

Parlement of the Thre Ages. See under Offord, M. Y.

Parks, W. 1986. 'The oral-formulaic theory in Middle English studies'. *Oral Poetry* 1. 636–94.

Pastoureau, M. 1982. *L'hermine et le sinople: études d'héraldique Médiévale*. Paris.

—— 1983. *Armorial des chevaliers de la table ronde*. Paris.

—— 1990. *Couleurs, images, symboles: études d'histoire et d'anthropologie*. Paris.

Patch, H. R. 1950. *The Other World According to Descriptions in Medieval Literature*. Cambridge, Mass.

Patterson, L. 1989. ' "What man artow?": authorial self-definition in the *Tale of Sir Thopas* and the *Tale of Melibee'*. *Studies in the Age of Chaucer* 11. 117–75.

——, ed. 1990. *Literary Practice and Social Change in Britain, 1380–1530*. Berkeley. The New Historicism: Studies in Cultural Poetics 8.

—— 1991. *Chaucer and the Subject of History*. Madison.

Patton, C. 1994. 'Black bodies / white trails'. In Goldberg. 106–16.

Pauphilet, A., trans. 1923. *Queste del saint graal*. Paris.

Payer, P. J. 1984. *Sex and the Penitentials: The Development of a Sexual Code, 550–1150*. Toronto.

—— 1993. *The Bridling of Desire: Views of Sex in the Later Middle Ages*. Toronto.

Pearsall, D. A. 1955. 'Rhetorical "descriptio" in *Sir Gawain and the Green Knight'*. *Modern Language Review* 50. 129–34.

—— 1977. *Old English and Middle English Poetry*. London. Routledge History of English Poetry 1.

——, ed. 1978. W. Langland, *Piers Plowman: An Edition of the C-Text*. London.

—— 1981. 'The origins of the alliterative revival'. In Levy and Szarmach. 1–24.

—— 1982. 'The alliterative revival: origins and social backgrounds'. In Lawton 1982a. 34–53.

Pearsall, D. and Cunningham, I. F., intro. 1977. *The Auchinleck Manuscript: National Library of Scotland Advocates MS 19.2*. London.

Peck, R. A., ed. 1968. J. Gower, *Confessio amantis*. New York.

—— 1980. 'Number as cosmic language'. In Eckhardt. 15–64.

Peraldus, Guilielmus 1512. *Summa virtutum ac vitiorum*. Paris.

Perceval: The Story of the Grail. See under Bryant, N.

Perceval le Gallois 1978. Film. Dir. E. Rohmer. France.

Percy Manuscript. See under Hales, J. W. and Furnivall, F. J.

Perlesvaus: The High Book of the Grail. See under Bryant, N.; Nitze, W. A. and Jenkins, T. A.

Perry, A. J., ed. 1925. J. Trevisa, *Dialogus inter militem et clericum*. London. EETS os 167.

Peterson, C. J. 1974a. '*Pearl* and *St. Erkenwald*: some evidence for authorship'. *Review of English Studies* ns 25. 49–53.

—— 1974b. 'The *Pearl*-poet and John Massey of Cotton, Cheshire'. *Review of English Studies* ns 25. 257–66.

——, ed. 1977. *St. Erkenwald*. Philadelphia.

Peterson, C. J. and Wilson, E. 1977. 'Hoccleve, the Old Hall manuscript, Cotton Nero A. x and the *Pearl*-poet'. *Review of English Studies* ns 28. 49–56.

Phoebus, G. *Livre de chasse*. See under Tilander, G. 1971.

Pike, J. B. 1972. *Frivolities of Courtiers and Footprints of Philosophers*. Extracts translated from the *Policraticus* of John of Salisbury. New York.

Pilch, H. 1964. 'The middle English *Pearl*: its relation to the *Roman de la Rose*'. *Neuphilologische Mitteilungen* 65. 427–46. Repr. in Conley 1970. 163–84.

Pitt-Rivers, J. 1966. 'Honour and social status'. In *Honour and Shame: The Values of Mediterranean Society*. Ed. J. G. Peristiany. London. 19–78.

Plautus. *Three Comedies*. See under Smith, P. L.

Pohli, C. V. 1991. 'Containment of anger in the medieval poem *Patience*'. *English Language Notes* 29. 1–14.

Power, E. 1922. *Magical Jewels of the Middle Ages and the Renaissance, particularly in England*. Oxford.

Prince, G. 1988. *A Dictionary of Narratology*. Aldershot.

Prince Valiant 1954. Film. Dir. H. Hathaway. USA.

Prior, S. P. 1986. '*Patience*: beyond apocalypse'. *Modern Philology* 83. 337–48.

———— 1994. *The* Pearl *Poet Revisited*. New York. Twayne's English Authors Series 512.

Pritchard, V. 1967. *English Medieval Graffiti*. Cambridge.

Puttenham, G. 1589. *The Arte of Englishe Poesie*. Eds. G. D. Willcock and A. Walker. Cambridge. 1936.

Putter, A. 1995. Sir Gawain and the Green Knight *and French Arthurian Romance*. Oxford.

Quest of the Holy Grail. See under Matarasso, P. M.

Queste del saint graal. See under Pauphilet, A.

Rackham, O. 1989. *The Last Forest: The Story of Hatfield Forest*. London.

Radulphi de Coggeshall chronicon Anglicarum. See under Stevenson, J. 1875.

Raymo, R. R. 1986. 'Works of religious and philosophical instruction'. In Hartung and Severs 7. 2255–378.

Reddaway, T. and Walker, L. 1976. *A History of the Goldsmiths' Company, 1327–1509*. London.

Register of the Black Prince 1930–3. *Register of Edward the Black Prince*. London. 4 vols.

Reichardt, P. F. 1984. 'Gawain and the image of the wound'. *PMLA* 99. 154–61.

Reisner, T. A. 1973. *Pearl*, 44. *Explicator* 31. 55.

Renoir, A. 1958. 'Descriptive techniques in *Sir Gawain and the Green Knight*'. *Orbis Litterarum* 13. 126–32.

Revelation of Pergatory. See under Harley, M. P.

Rhodes, J. 1994. 'The dreamer redeemed: exile and the kingdom in the Middle English poem *Pearl*'. *Studies in the Age of Chaucer* 16. 119–42.

Ribard, J. 1984. *Le moyen âge: littérature et symbolisme*. Paris.

Ricks, C. 1974. *Keats and Embarrassment*. Oxford.

Rigby, M. 1983. '*Sir Gawain and the Green Knight* and the vulgate *Lancelot*'. *Modern Language Review* 78. 257–66.

Riley, H. T., ed. 1864. Thomas Walsingham, *Historia Anglicana* 2. London. Rolls Series.

———— 1868. *Memorials of London and London Life, 1276–1419*. London.

Roach, W., gen. ed. 1949–83. *Continuations of the Old French* Perceval *of Chrétien de Troyes*. Philadelphia. 5 vols: I. *The First Continuation: Redaction of MSS TVD*, ed. William Roach (1949). II. *The First Continuation: Redaction of MSS EMQU*, eds. William Roach and Robert H. Ivey (1950). III. *The First Continuation: Redaction of MSS ALPRS, with Glossary*, ed. William Roach and Lucien Fouley (1952–5). IV. *The Second Continuation*, ed. William Roach (1971). V. *The Third Continuation (by Manessier)*, ed. W. Roach (1983).

Robbins, R. H. 1943. 'A *Gawain* epigone'. *Modern Language Notes* 58. 361–6.

Robertson, D. W., jr. 1950a. 'The "heresy" of *The Pearl*'. *Modern Language Notes* 65. 152–5.

—— 1950b. 'The pearl as symbol'. *Modern Language Notes* 65. 155–61.

—— 1954. 'Why the devil wears green'. *Modern Language Notes* 69. 470–2.

Robertson, M. 1982. 'Stanzaic symmetry in *Sir Gawain and the Green Knight*'. *Speculum* 57. 779–85.

Robinson, N. P. 1986. 'The Middle English *Patience*: the preacher-poet, Jonah, and their common mission'. *American Benedictine Review* 37.2. 130–42.

Rogers, G. E. 1991. 'The Percy folio manuscript revisited'. In *Romance in Medieval England*. Eds. M. Mills, J. Fellows and M. Meale. Cambridge. 39–65.

Rohmer, E. 1979. 'Note sur la traduction et sur la mise en scène de *Perceval*'. *L'Avant Scène du Cinéma* 221. 1 February 1979. 6–7.

Roman de Brut de Wace. See under Arnold, I.

Romance of Yder. See under Adams, A.

Romances of the Sowdone of Babylon. See under Hausknecht, E.

Roney, L. 1994. '*Winner and Waster*'s "wyse wordes": teaching economics and Rationalism in fourteenth-century England'. *Speculum* 69. 1070–1100.

Rooney, A. 1993. *Hunting in Middle English Literature*. Cambridge.

Røstvig, M.-S. 1967. 'Numerical composition in *Pearl*: a theory'. *English Studies* 48. 326–32.

Rowland, B., ed. 1974. *Chaucer and Middle English Studies in Honour of Rossell Hope Robbins*. Kent, Oh.

Royal Opera House 1994. H. Birtwistle, *Gawain*. Opera programme. Royal Opera House, Covent Garden.

Rubin, G. 1992. 'Thinking sex: notes for a radical theory of the politics of sexuality'. In *Pleasure and Danger: Exploring Female Sexuality*. Ed. C. S. Vance. London. 2nd edn. 267–319.

Rubin, M. 1991. *Corpus Christi: The Eucharist in Late Medieval Culture*. Cambridge.

Ruck, E. H. 1991. *An Index of Themes and Motifs in Twelfth-Century French Arthurian Poetry*. Cambridge. Arthurian Studies 25.

Rudnytsky, P. L. 1983. '*Sir Gawain and the Green Knight*: oedipal temptation'. *American Imago* 40. 371–83.

Russell, J. *The Book of Nurture*. See under Furnivall, F. J.

Sacks, P. M. 1985. *The English Elegy: Studies in the Genre from Spenser to Yeats*. Baltimore.

St Clair-Kendall, S. 1988. 'Narrative form and mediaeval continuity in the Percy folio manuscript: a study of selected poems'. Dissertation. University of Sidney.

St Erkenwald. See under Gollancz, I., ed. 1922; Morse, R., ed. 1975; Peterson, C. J., ed. 1977; Savage, H. L., ed. 1926

St Patrick's Purgatory. See under Easting, R.

Salter, E. 1966–7. 'The alliterative revival'. *Modern Philology* 64. 146–50; 233–7.

———— 1983. *Fourteenth-Century English Poetry: Contexts and Readings*. Oxford.

Samuel, R. 1994. 'Gawain's musical journey'. In Royal Opera House. 21–5.

Samuels, M. L. 1988. 'Dialect and grammar'. In Alford 1988. 201–21.

Sapora, R. 1977. *A Theory of Middle English Alliterative Meter with Critical Applications*. Cambridge, MA. Speculum Anniversary Monographs 1. 24–5.

Sargent, M. G., ed. 1992. Nicholas Love, *Mirror of the Blessed Life of Jesus Christ*. New York.

Savage, H. L., ed. 1926. *St. Erkenwald*. New Haven. Yale Studies in English 72.

———— 1956. *The* Gawain-*Poet: Studies in his Personality and Background*. Chapel Hill, NC.

Scala, E. D. 1994. 'The wanting words of *Sir Gawain and the Green Knight*: narrative past, present and absent'. *Exemplaria* 6. 304–38.

Scase, W. 1989. Piers Plowman *and the New Anti-Clericalism*. Cambridge.

Scattergood, V. J., ed. 1975. *The Works of Sir John Clanvowe*. Cambridge.

———— 1981. '*Sir Gawain and the Green Knight* and the sins of the flesh'. *Traditio* 37. 347–71.

———— 1983. 'Literary culture at the court of Richard II'. In Scattergood and Sherborne. 29–43.

———— 1992. 'Alain de Lille and the prologue to *Patience*'. *Medium Ævum*. 61.1. 87–92.

Scattergood, V. J. and Sherborne, J. W., eds. 1983. *English Court Culture in the Later Middle Ages*. London.

Schiller, A. 1968. 'The *Gawain* rhythm'. *Language and Style* 1. 268–94.

Schleusner, J. 1971. 'History and action in *Patience*'. *PMLA* 86. 959–65.

Schmidt, A. V. C., ed. 1978. William Langland, *The Vision of Piers Plowman. A Complete Edition of the B-Text*. London.

———— 1984. 'The authenticity of the Z text of *Piers Plowman*: a metrical examination'. *Medium Ævum* 53. 295–300.

———— 1987a. *The Clerkly Maker: Langland's Poetic Art*. Cambridge.

————, ed. 1987b. William Langland, *The Vision of Piers Plowman. A Complete Edition of the B-Text*. Rev. edn.

Schofield, W. H. 1904. 'The nature and fabric of *The Pearl*'. *PMLA* 19. 154–215.

Scholl, G. H. F., ed. 1852. Heinrich von dem Türlin, *Diu Crône*. Stuttgart.

Schreiber, E. G. 1981. 'The structures of *Clannesse*'. In Levy and Szarmach. 131–52.

Secretum Secretorum. See under Manzalaoui, M. A.

Sedgwick, E. K. 1985. *Between Men: English Literature and Male Homosocial Desire*. New York.

Serjeantson, M. S. 1940. 'The dialect of Ms. Cotton Nero A. x'. In Gollancz 1940. xli-lxvi.

'Sermon of Dead Men'. See under Cigman, G.

Seymour, M. C., ed. 1963. J. Mandeville, *The Bodley Version of Mandeville's Travels*. London. EETS os 253.

Seymour, M. C. *et al.*, eds. 1975. *On the Properties of Things: John Trevisa's Translation of Bartolomaeus Anglicus*. London.

Shendan, R. and Ross, A. 1975. *Grotesques and Gargoyles: Paganism in the Medieval Church*. Newton Abbot.

Shepherd, G. T. 1970. 'The nature of alliterative poetry in late medieval England' Gollancz Memorial Lecture, 1970'. *Proceedings of the British Academy* 56. 57–76. Repr. in his *Poets and Prophets: Essays in Medieval Studies*. Eds. T. A. Shippey and J. Pickles. Cambridge, 1990. 173–92.

Sherborne, J. W. 1983. 'Aspects of English court culture in the later fourteenth century'. In Scattergood and Sherborne. 1–27.

Shoaf, R. A. 1984. *The Poem as Green Girdle: Commercium in* Sir Gawain and the Green Knight. Gainesville, Fl. University of Florida Monographs: Humanities 55.

—— 1990. '*Purgatorio* and *Pearl*: Transgression and Transcendence'. *Texas Studies in Literature and Language* 32. 152–68.

Sicille. *Couleurs en armes*. See under Cocheris.

Siege of Jerusalem. See under Hanna, R. III and Lawton, D.

Silverstein, T. 1977–8. 'Sir Gawain in a dilemma, or keeping faith with Marcus Tullius Cicero'. *Modern Philology* 75. 1–17.

——, ed. 1984. See list of editions.

Simek, R. 1993. *Dictionary of Northern Mythology*. Trans. A. Hall. Cambridge.

Simpson, J. 1991. Piers Plowman: *An Introduction to the B-Text*. London.

'Sir Amadace' and 'The Avowing of Arthur'. See under Brookhouse, C.

Sir Orfeo. See under Bliss, A. J., ed. 1966.

Sir Tristrem. See under McNeill, G. P.

Skeat, W. W., ed. 1869. *The Vision of William concerning Piers the Plowman*. London. EETS os 38.

Smith, A. H. 1956. *The Place-Name Elements*. Cambridge. English Place-Name Society 25.1. Repr. 1970.

Smith, P. L., trans. 1991. T. M. Plautus, *Three Comedies: Miles Gloriosus, Pseudolus, Rudens*. Ithaca.

Smithers, G. V., ed. 1952, 1957. *Kyng Alisaunder*. London. EETS os 227, 237.

The Spaceman and King Arthur 1979. Film. Dir. R. Mayberry. USA. Also called *The Unidentified Flying Oddball*.

Spearing, A. C. 1964. '*Sir Gawain and the Green Knight*'. In his *Criticism and Medieval Poetry*. London. 26–45.

—— 1970. *The Gawain-Poet: A Critical Study*. Cambridge.

—— 1972. *Criticism and Medieval Poetry*. London. 2nd edn.

—— 1976. *Medieval Dream-Poetry*. Cambridge.

—— 1980. '*Purity* and danger'. *Essays in Criticism* 30. 293–310. Repr. in his *Readings in Medieval Poetry*. Cambridge, 1987. 173–94.

—— 1987. See 1980.

—— 1994. 'Public and private spaces in *Sir Gawain and the Green Knight*'. *Arthuriana* 4. 138–45.

—— forthcoming n.d. 'A Ricardian "I": The Narrator of *Troilus and Criseyde*'.

Speed, D., ed. 1993. *Medieval English Romances*. Durham. 3rd edn. Durham Medieval Texts 8.

Speirs, J. 1949. '*Sir Gawain and the Green Knight*'. *Scrutiny* 16. 274–300. Repr. in his *Medieval English Poetry: The Non-Chaucerian Tradition*. London, 1957. 215–51. Repr. in Fox. 79–94.

Spendal, R. J. 1976. 'The manuscript capitals in *Cleanness*'. *Notes and Queries* ns 221. 340–1.

Stainsby, M. 1992. Sir Gawain and the Green Knight: *An Annotated Bibliography, 1978–1989*. New York. Garland Medieval Bibliographies 13.

Stanbury, S. 1988a. '*Pearl* and the idea of Jerusalem'. *Medievalia et Humanistica* ns 16. 117–31.

——— 1988b. 'Visions of space: acts of perception in *Pearl* and in some late medieval illustrated apocalypses'. *Mediaevalia* 10. 133–58.

——— 1991a. 'In God's sight: vision and sacred history in *Purity*'. In Blanch, Miller and Wasserman. 105–16.

——— 1991b. *Seeing the* Gawain-*Poet: Description and the Act of Perception*. Philadelphia.

——— 1993. 'Feminist masterplots: the gaze on the body of *Pearl's* dead girl'. In *Feminist Approaches to the Body in Medieval Literature*. Eds. L. Lomperis and S. Stanbury. Philadelphia. 96–115.

Statutes of the Realm. 1810–28. London.

Stephens, J. 1988. 'Paradigmatic and syntagmatic elaboration, and Middle English poetic style'. *Parergon* 6. 23–35.

Stern, M. R. 1955. 'An approach to *The Pearl*'. *Journal of English and Germanic Philology* 54. 684–92. Repr. in Conley 1970. 73–85.

Stevens, J. 1973. *Medieval Romance: Themes and Approaches*. London.

Stevenson, J., ed. 1875. *Radulphi de Coggeshall chronicon Anglicarum*. London. Rolls Series 66.

Stewart, F. H. 1994. *Honor*. Chicago.

Stewart-Brown, R. 1938. 'The Scrope and Grosvenor controversy, 1385–1391'. *Transactions of the Historic Society of Lancashire and Cheshire* 89.

Stock, L. K. 1991. 'The "poynt" of *Patience*'. In Blanch, Miller and Wasserman. 163–75.

Stokes, M. 1984. *Justice and Mercy in* Piers Plowman. London.

Stokes, M. and Scattergood, J. 1984. 'Travelling in November: Sir Gawain, Thomas Usk, Charles of Orleans and the *De re militari*'. *Medium Ævum* 53. 78–83.

Stow, G. B., ed. 1977. *Historia vitae et regni Ricardi secundi*. Philadelphia.

Stratford, J. 1993. *The Bedford Inventories: The Worldly Goods of John, Duke of Bedford, Regent of France (1389–1435)*. London. Reports of the Research Committee of the Society of Antiquaries of London 59.

Strohm, P. A. 1992. *Hochon's Arrow: The Social Imagination of Fourteenth-Century Texts*. Princeton, NJ.

Stürzinger, J. and Breuer, H., eds. 1914. *Hunbaut*. Dresden.

Suite du Merlin. See under Paris, G. and Ulrich, J.

Summa. See Peraldus.

The Sword of Lancelot 1963. Film. Dir. C. Wilde. GB.

Sword of the Valiant 1983. Film. Dir. S. Weeks. GB.

Szarmach, P. E. 1971. 'Two notes on *Patience*'. *Notes and Queries* 216. 125–7.

Tajima, M. 1978. 'Additional syntactic evidence against the common authorship of MS. Cotton Nero A.x'. *English Studies* 59. 193–8.

Talbert, E. W. and Thomson, S. H. 1970. 'Wyclyf and his followers'. In Hartung and Severs 2. ch 3. 354–80; 517–33.

Tasker, R. V. G., ed. 1945. Augustine, *The City of God*. Trans. J. Healey. London. 2 vols.

Tatlock, J. S. P. 1921. 'The epilog of Chaucer's *Troilus*'. *Modern Philology* 18. 625–59.

Tatlock, J. S. P. and Kennedy, A. J. 1927. *A Concordance to the Complete Works of Geoffrey Chaucer and to the* Romaunt of the Rose. Washington, DC.

Taylor, P. B. 1971. 'Commerce and Comedy in *Sir Gawain and the Green Knight*'. *Philological Quarterly* 50. 1–15.

ten Brink, B. 1871–83. *Early English Literature*. Trans. H. M. Kennedy, W. C. Robinson and P. Schmitz. London. 3 vols.

Tentler, T. N. 1977. *Sin and Confessions on the Eve of the Reformation*. Princeton.

Thiébaux, M. 1970. 'Sir Gawain, the fox hunt and Henry of Lancaster'. *Neuphilologische Mitteilungen* 71. 469–79.

—— 1974. *The Stag of Love: The Chase in Medieval Literature*. Ithaca.

Thomas, J. 1908. *Die alliterierende Langzeile des* Gawayn-*Dichters*. Coburg.

Thompson, M. W. 1988. *The Decline of the Castle*. Cambridge.

—— 1989. 'The green knight's castle'. In *Studies in Medieval History Presented to R. Allen Brown*. Eds. C. Harper-Bill, C. Holdsworth and J. L. Nelson. Woodbridge. 317–26.

—— 1991. *The Rise of the Castle*. Cambridge.

—— 1995. *The Medieval Hall: The Basis of Secular Society, 600–1600 AD*. Aldershot.

Thomson, W. M., ed. 1958. '*An Ureisun of God Almihti*'. In Þe Wohunge of Ure Lauerd *and other pieces*. Ed. W. M. Thomson. Oxford. EETS os 241.

Thordeman, B. 1939. *Armour from the Battle of Wisby, 1361*. Stockholm. 2 vols. Vitterhets Hist. och Antikbitets Akad. 27.

Thorpe, L., trans. 1968. Geoffrey of Monmouth, *History of the Kings of Britain*. Baltimore.

Tilander, G., ed. 1956. W. Twiti, *La venerie de Twiti*. Karlshamn. *Cynegetica* 2.

——, ed. 1971. G. Phoebus, *Livre de chasse*. Karlshamn. *Cynegetica* 18.

Tkacz, C. B. 1992. 'Aelfric and the green knight: hagiographic sources for the three-stroke beheading attempt'. *Geardagum* 13. 67–75.

Tolkien, J. R. R. 1929. '*Ancrene Wisse* and *Hali Meidhad*'. *Essays and Studies* 14. 104–26.

Tolkien, J. R. R. and Gordon, E. V. 1925, 1967. See list of editions.

Très Riches Heures du Duc de Berry. See under Longman, J. and Cazelles, R.

Trevisa, J. *Dialogus inter militem et clericum*. See under Perry, A. J.

Trigg, S., ed. 1990. *Wynnere and Wastoure*. Oxford. EETS os 297.

—— 1991. 'The romance of exchange: *Sir Gawain and the Green Knight*'. *Viator* 22. 251–66.

Tristram, P. 1976. *Figures of Life and Death in Medieval English Literature*. London.

Turner, V. W. 1969. *The Ritual Process: Structure and Anti-Structure*. London.

Turville-Petre, J. 1976. 'The metre of *Sir Gawain and the Green Knight*'. *English Studies* 57. 310–28.

Turville-Petre, T. 1977. *The Alliterative Revival*. Cambridge.

—— 1982. 'The lament for Sir John Berkeley'. *Speculum* 57. 332–9.

—————— 1987. 'Editing *The Wars of Alexander*'. In *Manuscripts and Texts: Editorial Problems in Later Middle English Literature*. Ed. D. Pearsall. Cambridge. 143–60.

—————— 1988. 'The author of *The Destruction of Troy*'. *Medium Ævum* 57. 264–9.

——————, ed. 1989. *Alliterative Poetry of the Later Middle Ages: An Anthology*. London.

Turville-Petre, T. and Wilson, E. 1975. 'Hoccleve, "Maister Massy" and the *Pearl*-poet: two notes'. *Review of English Studies* ns 26. 129–43.

Tuttleton, J. W. 1966. 'The manuscript divisions of *Sir Gawain and the Green Knight*'. *Speculum* 41. 304–10.

Twiti, W. *La venerie de Twiti*. See under Tilander, G. 1956.

Two Wycliffite Texts. See under Hudson, A. 1993.

Twomey, M. W. 1989. '*Cleanness*, Peter Comestor, and the *Revelationes Sancti Methodii*'. *Mediaevalia* 11. 203–17.

—————— 1991. 'The sin of *untrawþe* in *Cleanness*'. In Blanch, Miller and Wasserman. 117–45.

Ulrich von Zatzikhoven. *Lanzelet*. See under Hahn, K. A.; Webster, K. G.

Ureisun of God Almihti. See under Thomson, W. M.

Vance, E. 1991. '*Pearl*: love and the poetics of participation'. In *Poetics: Theory and Practice in Medieval English Literature*. Eds. P. Boitani and A. Torti. Cambridge. 131–49.

Vantuono, W. 1971. '*Patience, Cleanness, Pearl*, and *Gawain*: the case for common authorship'. *Annuale Mediaevale* 12. 393–405.

—————— 1972. 'The structure and the sources of *Patience*'. *Medieval Studies* 34. 401–21.

—————— 1975. 'A name in the Cotton MS. Nero A.x. Article 3'. *Medieval Studies* 37. 537–42.

—————— 1981. 'John de Mascy and the *Pearl* poems'. *Manuscripta* 25. 77–88.

—————— 1984. See list of editions.

Vasta, E., ed. 1965. *Middle English Survey*. Notre Dame, Ind.

Vengeance Raguidel. See under Friedwagner, M.

Vinaver, E., ed. 1971. *Works of Sir Thomas Malory*. London

——————, ed. 1990. *The Works of Sir Thomas Malory*. Oxford. 3 vols. 3rd edn. Rev. P. J. C. Field.

von Schlosser, J. 1912. *Lorenzo Ghibertis Denkwurdigkeiten*. (I Commentarii). Berlin. 2 vols.

Voyage au Purgatoire de St. Patrice. See under Jeanroy, A. and Vignaux, A.

Waldron, R. A. 1957. 'Oral-formulaic technique and middle English alliterative poetry'. *Speculum* 32. 792–804.

—————— 1970. See list of editions.

Wallace, D. 1991. '*Cleanness* and the terms of terror'. In Blanch, Miller and Wasserman. 93–104.

Walls, K. 1992. 'Saint Gregory's *Moralia* as a possible source for the middle English *Patience*'. *Notes and Queries* 273. 436–8.

Walsingham, Thomas. *Historia Anglicana*. See under Riley, H. T., ed. 1864.

Warner, G. 1912. *Queen Mary's Psalter*. Reproduced from Royal MS 2B vii in the British Library, with an introduction by Sir George Warner. London.

Wars of Alexander. See under Duggan, H. N. and Turville-Petre, T.

Watson, A. G. 1969. *The Manuscripts of Henry Savile of Banke*. London.

Watson, E. P. 1987. 'The arming of Gawain: *vrysoun* and *cercle*'. *Leeds Studies in English* 18. 31–45.

Watson, N. 1991. *Richard Rolle and the Invention of Authority*. Cambridge. Cambridge Studies in Medieval Literature 13.

—— 1995. 'Censorship and cultural change in late medieval England: vernacular theology, the Oxford translation debate, and Arundel's *Constitutions* of 1409'. *Speculum* 70. 822–64.

Way, A. 1862. 'The armour and arms belonging to Henry Bowet, archbishop of York, deceased in 1423, from the roll of his executors' accounts'. *Archaeological Journal* 19. 159–65.

Weber, R., ed. 1975. *Biblia sacra iuxta vulgatam versionem*. Stuttgart. 2 vols. 2nd rev. edn.

Webster, K. G., trans. 1951. U. von Zatzikhoven, *Lanzelet*. Rev. R. S. Loomis. New York.

Weeks, J. 1985. *Sexuality and its Discontents: Meanings, Myths and Modern Sexualities*. London.

Weiss, J. 1991. 'The wooing woman in Anglo-Norman romance'. In *Romance in Medieval England*. Eds. M. Mills, J. Fellows and C. M. Meale. Cambridge. 149–61.

Wenzel, S. 1986. *Preachers, Poets, and the Early English Lyric*. Princeton.

——, ed. and trans. 1989. *Fasciculus morum: A Fourteenth-Century Preacher's Handbook*. Philadelphia.

West, G. D. 1978. *An Index of Proper Names in French Arthurian Prose Romances*. Toronto.

Weston, J. L., trans. 1994. Marie de France, *Guingamor, Lanval, Tyolet, Le Bisclaveret*. Llanerch. Facs. repr. Originally published London 1900.

Wetherbee, W. 1972. *Platonism and Poetry in the Twelfth Century: The Literary Influence of the School of Chartres*. Princeton.

Wheatley, H. B., ed. 1899. *Merlin*. EETS os 10, 21, 36, 112.

Whitaker, M. 1981. '*Pearl* and some illustrated apocalypse manuscripts'. *Viator* 12. 183–201.

White, R. B., jr. 1965. 'A note on the green knight's red eyes'. *English Language Notes* 2. 250–2. Repr. in Howard and Zacher. 223–6.

Whitehall, H. 1930. 'A note on a north-west midland spelling'. *Philological Quarterly* 9. 1–6.

Whiting, B. J. 1947. 'Gawain: his reputation, his courtesy, and his appearance in Chaucer's *Squire's Tale*'. *Medieval Studies* 9. 189–234.

Whiting, E. K., ed. 1931. *John Audelay: The Poems*. London. EETS os 184.

Williams, A. R. 1991. 'Slag inclusions in armour'. *Historical Metallurgy* 24. 69–80.

Williams, B., ed. 1846. *Chronique de la Traison et Mort de Richart Deux Roy Dengleterre*. London. Repr. 1964.

Williams, D. J. 1970a. 'The point of *Patience*'. *Modern Philology* 68. 127–36.

—— 1970b. 'Alliterative poetry in the fourteenth and fifteenth centuries'. In *The Middle Ages*. Ed. W. F. Bolton. London. 107–58. History of Literature in the English Language I.

Williams, J. G. 1987. '*Proverbs* and *Ecclesiastes*'. In *The Literary Guide to the Bible*. Eds. R. Alter and F. Kermode. 263–82.

Williams, M. and Oswald, M., eds. 1922–5. Gerbert de Montreuil, *La continuation de Perceval*. Paris. 3 vols.

Wilson, A. 1976. *Traditional Romance and Tale: How Stories Mean*. Ipswich.

Wilson, E. 1968. 'The "gostly drem" in *Pearl*'. *Neuphilologische Mitteilungen* 69. 90–101.

———— 1976. *The* Gawain-*Poet*. Leiden.

———— 1979. '*Sir Gawain and the Green Knight* and the Stanley family of Stanley, Storeton and Hooton'. *Review of English Studies* ns 30. 308–16.

Wimsatt, J. I. 1970. *Allegory and Mirror: Tradition and Structure in Middle English Literature*. New York.

———— 1991. *Chaucer and his French Contemporaries: Natural Music in the Fourteenth Century*. Toronto.

Winters, M., ed. 1984. *The Romance of Hunbaut*. Leiden.

Withycombe, E. G. 1977. *Oxford Dictionary of Christian Names*. Oxford. 3rd edn.

Woolf, R. 1968. *The English Religious Lyric in the Middle Ages*. Oxford.

———— 1972. *The English Mystery Plays*. Berkeley.

Wright, C. E. 1960. *English Vernacular Hands from the Twelfth to the Fifteenth Centuries*. Oxford.

Wright, W. A., ed. 1878. *Generydes*. London. EETS os 55, 70.

Wrigley, C. 1988. '*Sir Gawain and the Green Knight*: the underlying myth'. In Brewer 1988a. 113–28.

Wynnere and Wastoure. See under Trigg, S. 1990.

Ywain and Gawain. See under Friedman, A. B. and Harrington, N. T.

Zimmer, H. 1956. 'Sir Gawain and the Green Knight'. In *The King and the Corpse: Tales of the Soul's Conquest of Evil*. Ed. J. Campbell. 2nd edn. New York. 67–95. Bollingen Series 11.

Subject Index

General Index

(Note: references to the names of characters in literary works are not included in the index.)

ARTHURIAN STUDIES